The
Encyclopedia
of Crafts

Q to Z
VOLUME 3

The Encyclopedia of Crafts

LAURA TORBET, Editor

Gary Tong, Illustrator

CHARLES SCRIBNER'S SONS • NEW YORK

Library of Congress Cataloging in Publication Data
Main entry under title:

The encyclopedia of crafts.

　　1.　Handicraft—Dictionaries.　I.　Torbet, Laura.
TT9.S37　　　　745'.03'21　　　　80-13431
ISBN 0-684-16409-4　　Set
ISBN 0-684-16661-5　　Volume 1
ISBN 0-684-16662-3　　Volume 2
ISBN 0-684-16663-1　　Volume 3

1 3 5 7 9 11 13 15 17 19 C/V 20 18 16 14 12 10 8 6 4 2

Printed in the United States of America

81-1740

q

qiviut. Spinning. The soft, fine wool underfleece of the Arctic musk ox. It compares in texture to **cashmere** and **vicuña,** but the yarn produced from the fleece is softer and stronger than cashmere. In addition, it is silky, warm, of very long **staple** and so gossamer light that one pound of cleaned qiviut can be spun into 10 miles of yarn. The musk oxen begin to shed the qiviut in warm weather and soon thereafter it can be pulled off in sheets from the outer guard hairs. There are musk ox in Alaska and the arctic reaches of Canada, but qiviut is still fairly rare, so whatever is found on the tundra is also picked up for use as well as taking it directly from the musk ox. Mature animals produce 5½ – 6 lbs annually. The raw wool does not shrink when boiled and takes dye easily.

quadruple treble crochet. Crochet. An extra-long **triple crochet** using four **overs** to create rows of very long vertical bars with narrow openings between them.

Work like the **triple triple crochet** stitch. *yo, work 2 loops off *, repeat * to * until one loop remains on hook (5 times).

quarries. Stained Glass. The term for diamond or rectangular shapes of glass. They are usually leaded together in a trellis or lattice design.

quarter binding. Bookbinding. A cloth-bound book with a **leather back.**

quarter-inch drill. Woodworking. See **drilling tools.**

quarter-round. Woodworking. See **molding.**

quartersawed. Woodworking. See **wood.**

quarto. Bookbinding. A book (abbr. 4to) made up of groups of four leaves, or eight pages. Also see **leaf, section.**

quartz. Gemcutting. Quartz is the most varied and available of gem materials. It is composed of silicon oxide without water and **crystal**lizes in the hexagonal system. Its **hardness** is 7, its **specific gravity** is 2.65 with some variance in the impure varieties. It is dissolved in hydrochloric acid and has a conchoidal **fracture** and vitreous **luster.**

Crystal quartz (also called rock crystal) is transparent with refractive indices of 1.544 and 1.553. It occurs in crystals from millimeters to meters in size and from a few **carat**s to several hundred pounds in weight.

Smoky quartz (also called cairngorm) is rock crystal with a brown to black (called morion) whiskey color. It is feebly dichroic and when it is heated to 450° C it becomes clear. The color can be restored by irradiating the crystal with X rays.

Rose quartz is colored in various tints of red due to inclusions of **rutile;** it is usually semitransparent or translucent and when the rutile is arranged in needles, exhibits a chatoyant six-pointed star.

Amethyst is one of the oldest known gemstones. It is violet to purple in color due to traces of iron; the color is densest at the tip of the crystal. When amethyst is heated to 450° C, it becomes colorless; if the temperature is raised to 550°, it becomes yellowish brown, resembling the color of citrine quartz (topaz quartz).

Most massive crystals of quartz are milky white or colorless. Some have inclusions of gas bubbles or drops of liquid. Inclusions of slender threads of **actinolite** or asbestos is characteristic of hair stone and needle stone quartz. Venus's hair quartz has strands of rutile enclosed in rock crystal. Gold quartz has inclusions of native gold.

Cat's eye quartz exhibits chatoyance due to inclusion of asbestos particles arranged parallel to the **C-axis;** the lustrous bands are white, gold, or brown against body colors green, red, or brown.

Tiger's eye has brighter chatoyance in alternating bands of yellow and brown; when viewed from different angles, the dark and light appear to change positions.

Hawk's eye is similar to tiger's eye but the bands are blue and gray due to inclusion of crocidolite.

Aventurine quartz has bright metallic flecks in reddish brown, yellow, white, blue, or green body color. The reflective points are caused by enclosed scales of mica. Green aventurine was called "imperial yu" by the Chinese and held in higher esteem than nephrite **jade.**

Crystal quartz is often **facet**ed with the densest color towards the bottom to add depth of color to the finished gem. Cerium oxide is the recommended **polishing** agent on felt for **cabochon**s, or on tin or plastic **lap**s for faceted stones.

Quartz also occurs as a fine, compact crystalline aggregate in both fibrous and granular varieties. Opaque, granular types are called jasper; translucent, fibrous quartz is called chalcedony; combinations of translucent and opaque material are called agates.

Petrified wood is caused by logs and whole trees covered by sand or ash and water. Over a long period of time, the silica substitutes for the wood cell by cell until it is completely replaced. The colors vary from brown, gray, and yellow to bright red and blue, green, and orange when cut transversely; when cut longitudinally, the fibers and cells of the wood are displayed.

Chrysoprase is a compact, granular apple-green variety of quartz due to inclusion of hydrated nickel; it is slightly translucent and has a splintery fracture. When it is heated its color becomes paler.

Jasper is opaque, granular compact quartz with conchoidal fracture. It occurs colored red, yellow, brown due to the inclusions of iron oxides and other impurities.

Flint and chert are similar to jasper but distinguished by dull and uninteresting color and markings. Flint is dark-gray to black; chert is light-gray to white.

Chalcedony is fibrous, compact, translucent quartz. It is slightly porous, resulting in a lower specific gravity and hardness than crystal quartz. The porosity of some varieties of chalcedony allows it to be artificially colored with dyes. It is polished with cerium or tin oxide on a felt buff.

Carnelian (also called cornelian) is a reddish chalcedony; sard is a brown colored variety. Their color is due to finely dispersed iron oxide inclusion.

Plasma is a dark green compact quartz. Bloodstone or heliotrope is a plasma with dark red spots scattered throughout. Prase is a translucent leek-green quartz often used as an imitation jade.

Agate is a banded variety of chalcedony which grows in layers as fine as 17,000 to the inch of uniform thickness and color. The bands are concentrically parallel to the surface of the stone. Colors vary from white, gray, black, to shades of red, brown, blue, green, and violet. Irregular markings often imitate patterns which give them their names. Spotted, landscape, dendritic (treelike), brecciated (resembling ruins) and moss agates are examples. Fortification agate describes prominent concentric bands of this stone. Fire agate is chalcedony with iridescent goethite inclusions.

Onyx is an agate with alternating plane and parallel bands of white and a contrasting color. It is a favorite for cameo and intaglio work. Sardonyx is white and brown. Also see **faceting, refraction** and **Gemcutting: Applications.**

quartz dust. Stained Glass. See **ballast.**

quartz glass. Glasswork. A naturally occurring glass composed of nearly pure **silica,** also known as quartz crystal. Vessels made of quartz crystal were highly prized in medieval times because the material is so hard it is difficult to carve, and because of its high index of refraction, which makes finished pieces exceptionally brilliant. **Lead-crystal glass** is the modern successor to quartz crystal for fine tableware.

Queen Charlotte's Crown. Quilts. A **pieced block** pattern named to honor the queen of George the Third. After 1770 it became known as Indian Meadow or Indian River. The block has zigzag patterns and is usually used as an **all-over** design. See ill.

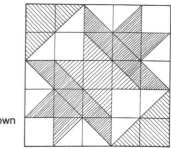

Queen Charlotte's Crown

queen conch. Shell Carving. (*Strombus gigus.* Also called fountain shell.) A shell used in cameo carving, fished from Florida to the West Indies. It is thicker than the helmet, permitting a higher relief. It has a yellow outer layer, a white **middle color,** and a pink **ground color.** It can be worked from either side to provide a pink or white ground. There is no distinct division between the colors. It is one of the least fragile of the cameo shells, but it tends to fade. A queen conch usually offers only one cameo. Also see **cowrie** and **Shell Carving: Shell, Tools and Materials, Cameo Carving.**

quench. Jewelry. The rapid cooling of metals from high temperatures, done by bringing them into contact with liquid, air, or solids, to soften and stabilize their working properties. After **forming,** and other techniques that put metal being worked under stress, causing it to become hard, **annealing** and then quenching are required. Often during working, metals need to be annealed and quenched several times.

Metals are usually quenched in liquid immediately after heating, although they are sometimes air-quenched, which means that they are allowed to cool in air at a normal rate. **Brass** should be **air-quench**ed, as the zinc in it may cause it to crack if it is cooled too fast.

A liquid quench can be water or **pickle.** The piece is dropped from above into water, but placed with pickling tongs into pickle so as not to splash the acid. Quenching in pickle cools the metal and removes **flux** and **firescale,** but also produces poisonous fumes. The liquid must be deep enough to cover the piece entirely, so as not to create uneven stresses on the metal. The metal must be immersed rapidly or fractures may result. Air-quenched metal may be pickled after it is cooled. Also see **Jewelry: Safety Precautions and First Aid.**

quenching. Metalworking. The process of cooling metal in liquid after it has been heated. Common quenching fluids are oil, water, **brine,** and **pickling** bath. Oil is recommended for some **steel**s because the rate of cooling is slower than water, and this reduces the chances of cracking or warping. A pickling bath removes surface **oxide** and cools the metal.

Quench the metal immediately after **heat treatment.** Pick up the hot metal with **tongs** and immerse it in the cooling liquid, moving it in a slow up-and-down or circular movement. Move it constantly to bring the metal in frequent contact with cool liquid and to avoid any concentrations of air bubbles, which cause an uneven **temper.** If one side cools faster than another, the object will warp. Do not drop hot metal into the solution, because a coating of vapor will form around it and prevent rapid cooling.

Quench thin objects, such as scissors, by dipping them along the cutting edges rather than from a point. Quench large pieces, such as an anvil, under a continuous stream of water.

quill. Beadwork. Porcupine quills, sometimes colored with vegetable dyes, were used by the American Indians to decorate clothing. The quills were collected, dyed, stored in bundles, and then moistened before using to make them pliable. They were stitched to tanned hide, generally with the **lazy stitch** or **overlay stitch,** in complicated geometric patterns. The dyed quills were also strung as long cylindrical beads. Gradually, with the introduction of imported **bead**s from Europe, quills were combined with, and later replaced by, **glass bead**s. Also see **Beadwork.**

quill. Featherwork. The hard, partially hollow stem of a **feather.** The term quill is also used for the large, stiff wing or tail feathers.

quill. Weaving. A small paper tube used to carry the **filling** yarn in a **boat shuttle.** The term stems from the time when goose feather quills were used for this purpose. Today the tubes can be bought at a weaving supply house or they can be homemade from drinking straws cut down to size, from brown wrapping paper, or even newspaper. To make a paper quill roll, cut an oval piece of paper the diameter and length needed. The quill can be taped together so that it will not unroll while the yarn is being wound around it. The quills are 4″ to 6″ long. Although a quill is not a **bobbin** the terms have become almost interchangeable and a quill is often called a bobbin. Also see **bobbin winder.**

quills. Stained Glass. See **brush.**

quillwork. Papercrafts. See **paper filigree.**

quillwork. Weaving. The use of porcupine quills, and sometimes bird quills, as an applied decoration on clothing, boxes, and other objects. It is a uniquely North American Indian craft, practiced in a manner of extreme excellence. Quillwork was a highly developed craft before the arrival of the Europeans in the New World. It is believed that the craft started with the Indians of the northeastern United States and Canada and then spread to the north central, northwest, and Great Lakes areas and south to the wooded southern areas. In fact, wherever porcupines roamed, the craft of quillwork existed. Where porcupines were scarcer, as in the Plains, the Indians obtained quills through trading.

Porcupine quills are at most 5″ long, are smooth and shiny and white in color with a brown tip; the natural coloration made quills effective in geometric patterns; the quills were also dyed using **natural dye**s and used on birch bark boxes; in **weaving;** in embroidery; and for wrapping, folding, and **plaiting** around sinew threads.

To prepare quills, soak them in water to render them pliable, then flatten them by drawing them through one's teeth, or by using implements of bone or metal. Hold the quills in one's mouth to keep them soft and flexible, and draw them through the teeth only when they are ready to be used.

Quillwork applied to birch bark boxes was a specialty of the Indians in the Northeast and Great Lakes areas. The Ojibwa (Chippewa) became the most noted for it. The boxes were made both for the Indians' own use as well as a tradeable item. Simple floral designs were worked on round and oval birch bark sewing boxes. Geometric patterns were put on vaulted boxes and naturalistic flora and fauna were put on larger boxes. Sewing boxes were sometimes covered with geometric patterns. Different tribes and different areas had their own designs but they all used the same technique, which was to push the dyed and wetted quill through holes in the bark box. The holes were made with an awl fashioned from an antler of elk or deer bone. The quills were bent on the inside of the box and left to dry bent and hooked on. A lining of thin bark was usually inserted to hide the quill ends and to keep them in place.

Woven quillwork, a technique perfected by the Cree and Canadian Chipewyan, demonstrates some of the finest work possible with quills. The softened and flattened quills were woven in and out over the **filling** of a simple woven band which gives the appearance of small cylindrical beads. The quills are pushed closely together and the filling behind them serves as padding. Geometric designs appear on white backgrounds on belts or pouches or as decoration attached to skins.

Embroidery using quills (and also moosehair) and attached with thread of sinew is thought to have been introduced to the Hurons and Iroquois by the French. Sinew is obtained from the tendon which runs down the back of a deer or other large animal. When cleaned and dried, it can be separated into fine threads. In quill embroidery, holes are first formed in the skin by piercing only the top surface of the skin with a pointed awl. For a stitch, the sinew would pass through two holes and secure the quills by going over them. The quills were folded around the sinew after being caught under it, and in good quill embroidery, the sinew stitches never showed on the surface since the quills were folded to conceal the sinew. The stitches used were the running stitch, the back stitch, and the buttonhole stitch. In the Northeast the quills were folded or wrapped around a single thread. In the Plains, Indians, such as the Sioux and Cheyenne, developed a method of wrapping, folding, and plaiting quills around two sinew threads. Working around a single thread was known, but not preferred. Designs were formed by wrapping, folding, or plaiting around the two threads, and these were incorporated into bold, geometric patterns and used as breast plates or on moccasins or around pipe stems. Larger areas of clothing were decorated than in the Northeast. In addition, quills were wrapped around fringes of buckskin and then sewn directly onto the clothes.

Although it is quite common to find small birch bark boxes offered for sale as a tourist commodity, other types of quillwork are no longer practiced. The use of beads and beadwork embroidery supplanted quillwork in the late seventeenth century when beads became easy to obtain from white traders.

quilt. Quilts. Stitchery. Any of a great variety of bedcovers that incorporate **quilting** in the construction. The term is sometimes very loosely used to refer to any soft, fluffy cover, even when tying or **tufting** has replaced the quilting. A quilt is usually made at home either by hand or by machine.

Also, to sew through several layers of material to give a **stitch**ed, puckery texture to the surface. A stitcher may quilt a banner or a garment using this step of the quiltmaking process. Also see **Quilts: Definition.**

quilt-as-you-go. Quilts. Any of various methods devised for **quilting** in small sections to avoid handling the entire quilt at one time. These prequilted sections can then be joined. This method eliminates the necessity of a **quilting frame** and makes it possible to quilt in even a limited space.

If sections are prequilted, these can range in size from 8–10″ squares or rectangles up to sections of about 30″. The sections are quilted in such a way that the quilting does not go all the way to the cut edge. The quilting should be contained within the section. Then the quilted sections can be sewn together by the **seam allowance** that joins the top layers, or the quilted sections may be joined by using strips of fabric between them, front and back. In this case the strips should also be **stuff**ed or padded like the quilt.

quilt back. Quilts. The lengths of fabric stitched together to make the reverse side of a quilt. The **backing** is always at least as large as the quilt top, and is preferably a few inches larger.

quilt block. Quilts. See **block.**

quilted clothing. Quilts. See **Quilts.**

quilted rug. Rugmaking. See **appliqué**d rug.

quilter's knot. Quilts. See **Quilts: Quilting, Hand Quilting.**

quilting. Quilts. Stitchery. The process of joining three layers of material (**backing, filler,** and decorative **quilt top**) by sewing with a series of small **running stitch**es. The quilting is the final process of making an **appliqué** or **pieced quilt** and it may be accomplished either by hand or machine quilting. Also see **quilting stitch** and **Quilts: Quilting, Machine Quilting, Hand Quilting.**

quilting. Weaving. See **quiltweave.**

quilting bee. Quilts. A social occasion planned for the purpose of **quilting** the **quilt top**s. Most often a woman did the **patchwork** or **appliqué block**s and **set** them together herself. At the quilting bee, a group of women **put in** the quilt and all shared in the quilting. In early American times, cold weather and impassable roads meant long winters devoted to **piecing** and making quilt tops. With spring came the quilting bees, festive occasions for pleasure and accomplishment.

Very skillful quilters were careful to invite only the finest of needleworkers to aid them. Or, if the situation could not be handled delicately, the quilt's owner might later discreetly remove the stitches left by someone less capable of sewing a fine line. Some neighbors and friends were invited to a quilting party specifically to tend to the children or help prepare the lavish supper that followed. The invitation was often clear regarding who had not been asked to join in the sewing. The get-togethers were occasions of merriment, however, with spouses, sweethearts, and families joining the quilters for the evening meal.

quilting foot. Quilts. An attachment made for sewing machines that aids the quilter in keeping rows of stitching evenly spaced. See ill.

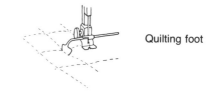

Quilting foot

quilting frame. Quilts. A device used to hold the three layers of a quilt during the **quilting** process. The frame consists of **rails** and **stretcher**s secured at the corners. The quilt parts are put in the quilting frame to facilitate the quilting process. Also see **Quilts: Quilting, Hand Quilting.**

quilting hoop. Quilts. A device to hold the layers of a quilt taut during the **quilting** process. It is similar to an embroidery hoop, but larger. Some quilting hoops have an adjustable stand or base so that it can be drawn up over the lap for ease in sewing. Many quilters prefer to use a **quilting frame** to a hoop, but the hoop has the advantage of being easily moved about and requiring little space. It is essential when using a quilting hoop that the layers be well **baste**d together. Also see **Quilts: Quilting, Hand Quilting.**

quilting motifs. Quilts. Various patterns were used so frequently in **quilting** that they became known by name, just as quilt patterns are known by name. Some of these were all-over quilting patterns, single designs used to cover an entire quilt. Others are **medallion** patterns that would fit into a plain or **pieced block.** Still others are medallion designs enlarged to fit over a cluster of blocks or the entire quilt. Following is a list of the best-known and most popularly used of these **all-over** and medallion designs:

basin	bellows
bee	birds
bell	Boozy Betty

broken plaid
cable
Catherine's Wheel
chain
church windows
circles
clamshell
clematis and grapes
comet
cornucopias
cowslip
coxcomb
crank
Cuddy's Lug
daisy
day lily
diagonal line
diamond
diamond scallop
difficult chain
dog's teeth
dog trail
donkey ear
double diamond
double line
English chain
fan
feather
feather circle
feather hammock
feather ring
feather star
ferns
flat iron
fleur-de-lis
flowers
gamboised
goose wing
hammock
hanging diamond
harps
heart
honeysuckle leaf
hourglass
interlaced diamonds

leaves
lost chain
lover's knot
meander
mother of thousands
oakleaves
ostrich feather
overlapping circles
peacock fans
pear
pennies
pineapple
plaid
plait
plate
Prince of Wales feather
princess feather
princess wreaths
rig
rope
rose
running feather
scissors
sheaf of corn
shell
shells
snail creep
spectacles
spider web
spiral
spiral shell
spray
square diamond
star
teacup quilting
trail
trellis
weeping willow
wheel
wheel of hope
wheels
whorl
wineglass quilting
wreath

quilting needle. Quilts. Usually a short, sharp **needle**, size 8 or 9, is used for **quilting**, but it is a matter of individual preference. Some quilters prefer a longer needle, and still others prefer the quilting needle after it is slightly bent. Whatever the length of the needle, it should always be sharp, and a thick shaft should be avoided, as it is harder to draw through the material.

quilting pattern. Quilts. The designs or linear patterns over which the **quilting stitch**es are sewn. The quilting patterns sometimes follow the design of the quilt. In other quilts, the patterns form grids of intersecting wavy or straight lines. In some, new shapes may be imposed over the **quilt top.** Also see **quilting motifs** and **Quilts: Quilting.**

quilting stitch. Quilts. The stitch that serves to securely join the three layers of a quilt—**quilt top, filler,** and **backing.** It looks the same as a **running stitch** and may be sewn in either of two ways: the stitches may be taken in and out, several at a time, as for a running stitch, or the quilt may be sewn by placing the point of the needle into the layers, then reaching under the quilt to pull it through. The point is then inserted from the back of the quilt so that it comes out on top. This one-stitch-at-a-time method is time consuming, but it is a traditional way of achieving extremely fine stitches. It is sometimes referred to as **push and punch.** Also see **Quilts: Quilting, Hand Quilting.**

quilting thread. Quilts. A thread made especially for **hand quilting.** It is strong and smooth, and it rarely knots or kinks as you sew with it. It is available in a limited range of colors. In lieu of quilting thread, or if a certain color is not available, you can substitute a heavy-duty **mercerized sewing thread.** Running **beeswax** over it will help to smooth it and ease the sewing. Any excess wax must be wiped off before sewing begins. The threads that work well are #50, #60, and #70 thread, used waxed; a regular quilting thread; or a heavy-duty thread. Also see **Quilts: Quilting, Hand Quilting.**

quilt patterns. Quilts. The **geometric** units or **appliqué block** designs from which quilts are made. Names came from the native flowers and trees, from political events, and from social affairs. They varied from one locale to another and from one period of time to another, reflecting changes in concerns and attitudes.

The older the pattern the more likely it is to have many names, because as it migrated from one community to another, different names were given to associate the quilt with incidents of home and national life. Almost the whole of this country's history can be read in the names of these traditional quilt patterns: **Algonquin Trail, Burgoyne's Surrender,** the **Log Cabin, Old Tippecanoe,** Texas Tears, and **Rocky Road to California.**

Identifying all quilts by their "correct" names is a formidable task, as several names may apply to one design and each name may refer to several different quilts. Sometimes the name of the block is changed depending upon the way the blocks are **set,** e.g., the Log Cabin block, in a certain arrangement, becomes **Barn Raising.** At other times, the color combinations affect the name, as a **hexagon quilt** put into a particular color arrangement becomes Grandmother's Flower Garden. But the complexities add to the interest because each change offers a new insight into the lives of the energetic and diligent quiltmakers. Also see **appliqué patterns, pieced patterns, quilt types.**

QUILTS

Quilting is an ancient art that is known throughout the world. **Patchwork** quilting is a folk art that developed in colonial America. While often used in combination, they are two distinct techniques.

Since antiquity, quilted clothes have served to protect the wearer. In the high mountain regions of China, inhabitants have been protected for centuries from the unrelenting icy winds by quilted garments. In Europe, the warrior whose greatest peril was the piercing arrow used quilted layers to make him less vulnerable. But the quilting with which most of us are familiar is that used on bedcovers. The word **quilt** has come to mean, in fact, a quilted bedcover.

Quiltmaking employs several techniques: **appliqué, piecing,** and quilting. Appliqué has a history as colorful, varied, and ancient as quilting. Remnants of Egyptian appliqué have been dated at several thousand years B.C. Medieval Europe was vibrant with flags and banners, using appliqué as the primary decorative method. Heraldic flags of the Middle Ages were dazzling in their use of textured fabrics and vivid colors; both piecing and appliqué were used in the intricate and brilliantly embellished standards.

In colonial America, quilting and patchwork grew out of a need for warm covers coupled with a need for beauty. The ingenious and inventive patterns that developed were a combination of the necessarily frugal approach to the use of materials and what was remembered of the colorful and elaborate use of **fabrics** in the countries from which these quiltmakers came. In the 1600s England was still resplendent in Shakespearean garb. The Puritans who came to America, in their religious fervor eschewing worldly pleasures, still had memories of the rich and ornate materials from France, the highly developed art of quilting in England and Ireland, the laces of Belgium, and the exciting, exotic designs coming into use on china and porcelain. Remembrances of all these tokens of a more genteel life remained with these early pioneers and must have prompted their keen zest for patterns and colors. They developed an incredibly complex and varied folk art, original and beautiful. It has remained, developing, and changing into what is today the most often practiced and collected of all the folk arts in America.

DEFINITION **Patchwork** is a process of **piecing** involving the joining of many small **patch**es or pieces of material. It is used primarily to make **quilt top**s, although it is often adapted for use on smaller articles—pillows, bags, and clothing.

The term "patchwork" is sometimes used to refer to the sewing on, or applying, of patches, as in **appliqué.** However, true patchwork is pieced work, used to make **pieced** quilt tops.

Patchwork developed because of a need, in colonial times, to utilize every scrap of material. Piecing was something of a **salvage art,** and **making do** was an everyday philosophy. Frosty winters in cabins that offered little more than a buffer against the frigid winds made the need for warm quilts a very basic one. That our pioneers developed the mathematically complex pieced patterns and sewed them with incredible skill attests not only to the capabilities but also to the unbounded spirit of the pioneers.

Simple **geometric** forms are the basis of most patchwork designs. They are usually planned so that they can be made up in squares or **blocks**. Each block is an arrangement of colored patches. When the blocks are **set,** or

join**ed**, new combinations and shapes appear, offering endless visual possibilities. Many examples of Op Art, an abstract painting form using optical illusions and effects, are based on the same principles as those used in patchwork design.

Appliqué quilts developed a little later than **pieced quilt**s because they required more specific control over the colors used. Often the appliqué blocks were alternated with blocks of solid color; thus, the fabrics used had to be chosen, not salvaged. The quilts required greater skill to sew, and were often made up for special use, as were **presentation quilt**s or wedding quilts. Appliqué designs were usually sewn on a block or square of fabric, and these blocks were then set in the same manner as the pieced quilt. Because of this method of joining blocks, or patches, appliqué quilts are sometimes included as patchwork quilts.

Quilting refers to the process of joining the three layers of a quilt—the quilt top, the **filler** or **padding,** and the **backing.** A series of small stitches, called **quilting stitch**es or **running stitch**es, is used to secure these layers and to add a pattern of stitches and relief work to the surface. The art of quilting has been so refined that many old **all-white quilt**s have no decorative surface at all other than the quilting. The result of the quilting process is a sturdy, thick, insulated bedcover with an overlay of rich surface texture and pattern.

Anyone can make a quilt at home, regardless of how little space is available. Patchwork blocks can be sewn with no more space than your lap, although of course table or floor space is important in cutting out the materials. There are various ways of prefinishing sections or portions of quilts so that the need for a **quilting frame** is eliminated entirely.

Pillow quilts, for example, are worked in small sections. It is only in the final assembly that more space is needed, and even then (if space is really a problem) you can always lay the portions out on the bed and sew there.

Other **quilt-as-you-go** methods will also simplify any space problem. If you are fortunate in having an extra room or a large house, a quilt can be set into a frame, adjusted to the correct height, and left up so that quilting can be sewn in any available time.

Quilts are frequently referred to as being either traditional or contemporary in design, although the somewhat generic reference has less to do with the era or year in which the quilt was made than with the style.

A traditional quilt is generally one made within the customary or prescribed boundaries of quilting. The methods and patterns are usually handed down from one generation to another along with certain customs, beliefs, and attitudes. Some pieced and appliquéd quilts gain an acceptance and popularity and are assimilated into what is acknowledged as traditional. Most quilts that have been repeated frequently enough to have names applied to them would be considered traditional quilts.

The contemporary quilt tends to step outside of the customary practices or limitations. A quilt made a hundred years ago may be considered contemporary if it disregards customary approaches for an emphasis on personal ones. In contemporary quilts there is less reliance on traditional patterns and a much more experimental use of fabrics. Many designers of contemporary quilts are more concerned with making a personal statement and are less in need of a serviceable bedcover. Stuffed and padded shapes in heavy relief, or even three-dimensional forms added to the surface, are not uncommon in innovative work. The quilt becomes a vehicle for a personal aesthetic statement.

The quilting process remains similar in these quilts, although generally the contemporary examples give less attention to the quilting stitches. Any free inventive, non-traditional, or unconventional use of piecing or appliqué combined with padding may be loosely defined as a contemporary quilt. Contemporary quilts are often designed as wall coverings and may never actually function as quilts in the common sense of the word.

The tremendous revival of quilting comprises both the contemporary and traditional approaches. Both have superb craftspeople, lively designers, inventive artists, and industrious workers, and the potentials seem unlimited.

PLANNING A QUILT   All **geometric pieced quilt**s are based on combinations of one or more basic geometric forms. Most **appliqué quilt**s use **appliqué** designs sewn to geometric forms such as square or rectangular **block**s or fabric. These are **pieced** together to form the **quilt top**; in this sense, an appliqué quilt is also pieced of geometric forms. The appliqué itself is a freer shape, but it is sewn to the blocks, making a geometric composition of the parts.

An **overall** design treats the quilt top as one large composition, and planning it is not unlike planning a drawing. Pieced quilts, however, involve the use of repeat units to make up the whole of the quilt design. Because appliqué designs themselves usually provide the primary decorative aspect, the repeat block is very simple. The same shape, the rectangle or square, is repeated. It may be varied in color, or all the blocks may be indentical in color. The basic plan for the appliqué quilt is often based on a **module,** or it may be a large **checkerboard** pattern, so the geometric shapes used when appliqués are applied to blocks are very simple.

In geometric quilts, the full splendor of the pieced patterns emerges. Almost all of the traditional quilts, as well as a large portion of the contemporary quilts, use geometric forms. The simplest and most basic are the circle, the square, and the rectangle. Among the other geometric forms that produce endless combinations and possibilities are the diamond, equilateral triangle, hexagon, isosceles triangle, octagon, parallelogram, right-triangle, and trapezoid. All the countless varieties and designs of traditional quilt patterns are based on various color arrangements of these few shapes.

DETERMINING QUILT SIZE   In quiltmaking, there are no ''standard'' **quilt** sizes. Many antique quilts seem unusual in size because bed sizes have changed over the years. At one time the master bed was nearly six feet wide, allowing room for the baby and perhaps a younger child. Later, the size decreased when **trundle bed**s for the babies were made to slide out from under the large bed. The pioneers' handmade beds were hardly made to any standard— except perhaps to the size of the people who used them!

Quilt sizes also vary depending on whether they are designed to go to the floor at the sides or if they cover just the mattress, touching the **dust ruffle** at the side.

To indicate the variety of sizes actually used, here are some measurements and the years in which the quilts were made:

$$76'' \times 86''—1785$$
$$100'' \times 101''—1785$$
$$74'' \times 93''—1800$$
$$98'' \times 104''—1850$$
$$84'' \times 84''—1850$$
$$80'' \times 80''—1890$$
$$76'' \times 82''—1910$$
$$86'' \times 104''—1965$$

Today, mattress sizes are standardized. Bed heights vary, but that can easily be accommodated for. Standard mattress sizes are:

$$27'' \times 52''—crib$$
$$33'' \times 66''—youth$$
$$38'' \times 72''—twin$$
$$54'' \times 75''—double$$
$$60'' \times 80''—queen$$
$$72'' \times 84''—king$$

A quilt is usually designed so that when finished it will cover the top of a bed and hang over the sides and foot. The amount of overhang may vary from just a few inches to enough to touch the floor.

It is essential to know the size of the area to be covered before it is possible to estimate the amount of material needed. To determine the area, first take the measurements of the top of the bed. Then if the quilt is to hang over 10″ at each side and at the foot, add 20″ to width and 10″ to length. The final measurements, standard mattress size plus 10″ at each side and at the foot, would be:

Width	Length	
53″	× 76″	—youth
58″	× 82″	—twin
74″	× 85″	—double
80″	× 90″	—queen
92″	× 94″	—king

If the quilt is to go to the floor, measure your bed height. Distance will vary with the type of mattress, casters, carpeting, etc. Usually about a 20″ drop will do. So, to have the quilt touch the floor you usually add 40″ in width and 20″ in length. The measurements would be as follows:

Width	Length	
73″	× 86″	—youth
78″	× 92″	—twin
94″	× 95″	—double
100″	× 100″	—queen
112″	× 104″	—king

Finally, if the quilt is to be pulled up over the pillows, an additional 6″ to 8″ must be added to the length. Again it would be essential to measure; pillow sizes vary greatly. In lieu of this, extra pillows could be made, or a pillow **sham** or **bolster** could be used.

Waterbeds usually have a wooden frame to support

them on all four sides. To measure a quilt for a waterbed, take the inside measurement of the frame. Then add 4" at each edge if the quilt is to be tucked in. If the quilt is to drop over the frame to the floor, measure carefully.

DETERMINING AMOUNT OF MATERIAL NEEDED   First determine the size of the finished quilt according to the directions given in the previous section. A **pieced quilt** 72" wide and 88" long would require two widths of 36" fabric for the top. Each of these would have to be 88" or nearly 7½ feet long. That makes a total of 15 feet, or 5 yards for the top. If your top is a two-color pieced pattern, you will need half that amount of each color. Then add a quarter to a third of the total amount of yardage needed in each color to allow for seams, **selvage,** and waste in cutting.

If the quilt is to be **appliqué**d, the material must be purchased for the **block**s as well as for the appliqué material. Figure the block material in the same way as for a pieced quilt, then place the appliqué **templates** on paper or fabric to determine the amount of fabric needed for each color for each block. Multiply by the number of blocks in the quilt.

The same method is used to determine the amount of **backing** material. Because the backing is usually used in full-width strips of fabric, little is lost in cutting, and the additional one-quarter to one-third is not needed. If you wish to have seams running the length of the quilt rather than crosswise (and lengthwise does look better), then you must figure for it. Remember that the back of a quilt can be pieced of several large areas of color. It is not essential that just one color be used.

Plan to allow yourself at least a few inches extra for seams or to straighten edges. It is always preferable to have too much material rather than too little, and it may be difficult to find your fabric again at a later date.

MARKING AND CUTTING   An important step in both **appliqué** and **pieced quilts** is the cutting. It must be done carefully and accurately or pieces will not fit properly, and the material will not lie flat. It is most important to take special care in cutting any **diamonds** or diagonals, such as a **two-patch, split four-patch,** or **split nine-patch.**

When a square is cut in half diagonally to make two triangles, the triangles cannot be sewn back together to produce a square because the seam would use up a half-inch slice of the fabric. The triangles obtained in bisecting the square would provide a pattern, and a ¼" **seam allowance** must be added to each edge. For example, if you want two triangles joined to make a 3" square, you would arrive at the pattern in this way: cut a 3" square, then cut it in half diagonally. Use one triangle as the pattern, adding ¼" on each of the three sides. When the triangles have been joined on the diagonal, the square will be 3½" × 3½", which allows for a ¼" seam around the outside. When it is joined to other squares it will finish at 3".

If all cutting is completed before sewing is begun, there will be no doubt about having ample material to finish the quilt.

Use good sharp scissors for all cutting. The scissors are the most essential tool for your quiltmaking (running a close second, of course, is your needle). If a poor or dull blade is used, your scissors will saw or chop the material.

If cutting is not done well, it will be impossible to sew accurately, whether in **piecing** or in appliqué. An irregular edge makes it very difficult to determine just where the joining line or seam is supposed to be.

All cut pieces must have the ¼" seam allowance on all edges. In appliqué, this edge is turned under and sewn down. In piecing it is the seam allowance.

After the design for a pieced **block** or for an appliqué block has been established, a template should be made for use in marking the pattern. There should be a template for each shape used, and it may be helpful at the start to make several of those that will be used the most. The template may be made in either of two ways: it may be the exact size of the finished piece, or it may have the ¼" seam allowance added to each outer edge. In marking the pattern for a **pieced quilt** it is generally recommended that the template be made the size of the finished block. That is, the ¼" seam allowance is not added.

Always place the templates on the fabric so that the long part of any one template is aligned with the **warp** (or lengthwise) thread or grain. A square would be placed straight on the grain. A triangle would have one edge on the straight. A diamond should be placed so that two edges run parallel with the grain and the other two edges are on the bias. With a circle, placement doesn't matter. A leaf shape would be placed so that the grain runs through the center, from tip to tip. All symmetrical shapes should be placed in this manner because it puts the bias portion in identical locations on the two sides and makes it easier to piece or appliqué and keep the shape symmetrical.

As cut pieces accumulate, some quilters run a single thread through an entire stack, skewering them or stringing them like beads. One **patch** or piece can easily be slid off the thread as it is needed.

It is important that the lines be drawn on the back or "wrong" side of the material. When the pieces are cut, an extra ¼" is allowed at each edge; when the pieces are joined, the pencil line will serve as a sewing guide (it is hidden in the reverse side when the block is turned face up).

If the template for the pieced quilt includes the ¼" seam allowance, which is the preference of some quiltmakers, a lead pencil or special tracing pencil for fabric can be used to draw around the perimeter. Cutting then follows the pencil line. No lines will ever show on the finished work, but the quilter must learn to accurately gauge the seams so that they are even. By measuring carefully on the first few, the ability to make a seam of exactly the right width is readily developed.

In cutting pieces for appliqué designs, one standard method is to draw around the template on the right side of the fabric. The material is then cut ¼" out from the pencil line. The primary disadvantage to this is that it leaves the lead or pencil lines on the outside. Even if the edges are accurately turned under, the lead sometimes rubs off on the **background** materials. The lead is not always removed by washing. It is disappointing to see a quilt to which someone has devoted hours of skillful stitching marred by lead smears. Many quiltmakers prefer to trace appliqué templates on the wrong side of the fabric with the ¼" added, as for a pieced quilt. Again, gauging the amount of fabric to turn under is relatively easy with a little attention and practice.

SEWING AND ASSEMBLING   When all materials are cut, the sewing can begin. If **appliqué** is being used on the **blocks,** the appliqué stitching should be completed first. Then the appliqué blocks are joined together following the same sewing procedures as those used for joining the **patches** or blocks of a **pieced quilt.**

Any of several **appliqué stitch**es may be used on the **quilt block**s. Both hand appliqué and machine appliqué are suitable, although handwork is preferable for lightweight materials. Machine appliqué works better on fabrics that are slightly stiffer, or that have some **body.**

To piece the quilt, either a hand or machine stitch may be used. If lines are cut on the straight or grain of the fabric, machine stitching will work well. If bias or diagonally cut pieces are used, they are sometimes more easily kept from stretching if sewn by hand. Because threads must be tied or carefully **backstitch**ed at each end, it does not necessarily save time to join small pieces by machine.

A strong thread is used for sewing, usually a #50 or #60. Whether hand or machine sewing is used, a **straight stitch** is sewn exactly at the inside of the ¼" **seam allowance.** Seams must be sewn evenly or the **quilt top** will not lie flat.

Sewing is accomplished by placing right sides of the material together and sewing on the wrong side. If lines were used to mark the patches, stitching can follow those lines.

In joining patches, they should, whenever possible, be sewn in straight lines. That is, the patches that make up the top row in a block are joined first; then the patches of a second row are joined. Then the two rows can be sewn together. This avoids having to sew corners, which are always difficult to do. Where lines of stitching cross, care must be taken to be sure that they meet precisely. They may be pinned or **baste**d at those intersections before sewing to assure perfect fit.

All seams are taken at exactly ¼". This applies to joining patches, joining blocks, or joining rows of blocks. When the pieces have been assembled, the quilt top is ready for the next step.

PRESSING   After the **patch**es are sewn they must be pressed. Traditionally quilters have insisted that the **seam allowance**s be pressed so that both fold over in the same direction. This makes a stronger seam. In many contemporary quilts, however, where heavier fabrics or materials with more **body** are used, corners may become too bulky. Also, when **quilting stitch**es are used to outline **pieced** patches, following the seams, the material of the seam allowance adds an extra thickness. In such cases, the seams are pressed open, and the thickness is evenly distributed and the quilted lines are equally padded.

Some of the pressing must actually be done as the quilt is **assemble**d. This will ensure that seams are pressed either open or facing the same direction, whichever method is used. When one row of patches (or **block**s) is sewn, those seams must be pressed before it is joined to the next row.

QUILTING   The **quilting stitch**es add the final touch to the **quilt top. Quilts** "come alive" as the relief pattern develops with the stitches.

Quilting may be accomplished in a number of ways. Machine quilting is a method that offers speed and ease, although it sacrifices the details of hand sewing. There are some instances when it may be preferable, and many contemporary quilters have made the sewing machine function like an extension of the hand.

Hand quilting is the other option, either by the traditional method of using a frame, or without a frame. Various **quilt-as-you-go** methods also do away with the **quilting frame.**

Finally, **quilting** may be accomplished by finishing small portions of a quilt and joining them later.

Quilting is the last stage in joining the three layers of a quilt. It provides a final pattern of stitching and at the same time secures the layers and makes a compact padded cover.

When the **quilt top** is completed, the **quilting pattern** is selected. Quilting has traditionally been done in a repeat pattern. More recently, quilters have adopted a freer approach, letting quilting grow out of and relate to the quilt-top design. The use of synthetic **filler**s has decreased the necessity for very close lines of quilting, making practical a greater variety in quilting patterns.

For traditional quilts there are many quilting patterns from which to choose. The **quilting stitch**es should relate in design to the quilt top. A **hexagon quilt** might, for example, have lines of quilting that follow the edges of the **piecing.** In an **appliqué quilt,** plain **block**s set between the **appliqué** blocks might be elaborately quilted. The appliqué designs could be outlined in quilting stitches.

In traditional quilts the quilting was necessarily in close rows. It held the **cotton** or **wool batting** in place and prevented it from shifting when it was washed. When **Dacron polyester batting** is used the problem of shifting is minimal, so there can be fewer lines of stitching.

Allover quilting patterns can be utilized in such forms as **diamond**s, wavy lines, or even simple crossing lines. It is simplest and often most interesting to just let the quilt grow out of the shape within the quilt top.

Quilting patterns are marked onto the finished quilt top as a guide for the quilting stitches. No matter how painstakingly perfect the piecing or the appliqué, the quality and value of the finished quilt is related to the intricacy of the quilting patterns, and the delicacy of the stitches. Quilting patterns are of two kinds, plain quilting and fancy quilting.

"Plain" quilting designs use straight crossing lines that hold the filler or **padding** in place with the grid pattern that results. The most common "plain" quilting designs are cross-bar, diagonal, diamond, double cross-bar, double diamond, and horizontal.

"Fancy" quilting designs include those that are linear and continuous, or "running," and those that are motif or "block" designs. The "fancy, running" quilting designs that are most often seen in traditional quilts are ocean wave, princess feather, rope, running vine, sausage or slave chain, serpentine, and teacup.

Of the "fancy, block" designs the most frequently used

are **acanthus, American eagle,** bell flower, bouquet, clamshell, daisy, day lily, dove of peace, fan, feather wreath, oak leaf, peacock fan, pineapple, spider web, star and crown, starfish, swirl, weeping willow, wheel of fortune, and widening circles.

These patterns appear over and over. There are many others, but most are variations of these basic ones. The "plain" quilting stitches are often combined with the "fancy." For example, if appliquéd **quilt block**s are **set** to alternate with solid-color blocks, a "fancy" design might be used to add detail to the solid block. Then, the "plain" quilting would fill in around it and over the appliqué blocks.

Although quilting patterns are sometimes marked in pencil, other markers are preferable, especially on the top of the quilt, because the lead lines show after the quilt is finished. **Tailor's chalk** or soap (sanded to a sharp flat edge) can be used to mark colored fabrics. Special fabric pencils in blue or white are available in notions departments or yardage shops. They will usually brush off. **Tracing paper**s have sometimes been used with the **tracing wheel** to mark patterns, but often with unsatisfactory results. Still other methods of transfer are available in fabric and needlework shops.

If your quilting pattern follows the lines of the piecing or **patchwork,** or if it outlines appliqué forms, it will be unnecessary to mark the pattern at all. The quilting will simply grow out of the quilt-top design.

Some traditional quilters **needle-mark** their quilt tops, which avoids any use of lines whatsoever. A needle is used to scratch or mark the surface of the cloth by pressing it onto the cloth and then drawing it across, maintaining pressure on the needle. This works especially well on **chintz** fabrics and on any with a satiny surface. Sized or starched fabrics will retain and show needle-marking, but it does not work at all on soft fabrics, such as **wool.**

If quilting patterns are printed on paper, a tracing may be made by first perforating the design. Use a tracing wheel or a large pin or needle, or machine-sew on the line of the design without threading the needle. The series of perforations left by any of these methods will be adequate for tracing and **pouncing.**

With the quilt top on a firm surface, such as a tabletop, pin the punctured pattern to the cloth, securing it at all edges. Then, using a **pouncer,** or a pad of soft cloth folded over **cotton,** dip the pad into cinnamon, cocoa, or a mixture of 1 teaspoon powdered **tempera** to 4 teaspoons cornstarch. (You may use 1 teaspoon of ultramarine, available at some drugstores, if you have no powdered tempera.) Pat the powder over the perforations and rub gently, taking care that neither fabric nor pattern moves. Then unpin and remove the paper and blow away any excess powder. Some parts of the quilting pattern may be marked in this way and quilted before the remaining areas are marked. If the entire quilt were marked at one time, some of the lines would blur before they could be sewn over.

MACHINE QUILTING   The **quilting** process may be accomplished with either machine or hand stitching. Common examples of machine variety may be seen today on ski jackets, pot holders, toddlers' clothes, and mattress pads. In these, the quilting serves primarily as a functional stitch to keep the layers together and prevent them from slipping. The stitching is usually done in closely spaced lines, crossed by more stitching lines running at right angles to those. Thus a grid pattern is formed that secures the **filler,** especially for when the article is washed. The lines of stitching often serve the dual function of being both utilitarian and decorative when they are sewn to form **diamond**s, **trapezoid**s, or wavy bands.

To quilt by machine, the layers of the quilt must first be stacked. The quilt **backing** is cut an inch or two larger than the **quilt top** and placed on a large flat surface. The filler is placed on top of the backing, and then the quilt top is placed on top of the filler. The three layers are **baste**d together, starting at the center and working out to the sides and the corners. The basting should cover all areas. No spaces larger than 6″ should be left without basting. Check the back of the quilt to be sure there are no folds or wrinkles. If the back is smooth, quilting may be started.

The machine is set so that the stitch length is about six to the inch, a large stitch. The tension on the machine should be loosened. Too much tension will pull the layers unevenly, resulting in puckers or folds on the back. Half the quilt is slipped under the needle and rolled tightly. Quilting then starts at the center and works out to the edges, row by row. Do not pull the quilt through the machine, but guide it gently. Be sure that the presser foot is not moving the top or bottom of the quilt out of position. Rows of quilting can be kept even with the use of a **quilting foot.**

If there is to be a combination of straight-line quilting with more decorative quilting, do all the straight lines first, and then go back to do the more elaborate patterns.

HAND QUILTING   **Quilting stitch**es are most often sewn by hand. In traditional quilts, the **quilting** is always done by hand. It is unquestionably more beautiful, although it is, of course, time-consuming. Hand sewing is more pleasant for quilting groups because it is quiet and allows for conversation.

Hand quilting has been developed to the point where some quilts may be made of a single piece of solid-colored or white material for the top, of which the only decorative element is the quilting. These are called **all-white quilt**s, and they show to best advantage the skills of an expert in quilting stitches and patterns.

Most quilts are worked, or quilted, on a frame or hoop, although many quilters prefer to work without either. A **quilting frame** is used to stretch the materials, and the quilting is worked while it is attached to the frame. Stitches are pulled so that there is no slack in the thread. This gives the characteristic puckering, creating a low-relief pattern on the **quilt top.**

A quilting frame, however simple, is essential for traditional quilting. Many varieties are available, and some can still be purchased through mail-order catalogs or shops that specialize in quilting supplies. A very simple one can be made with pieces of 1″ × 2″ or 2″ × 2″ pine boards. Two of the boards should be 6″ longer than the width of the quilt. These are the **rails,** or side boards, of the frame. The other two boards will act as **stretchers** between the rails, and they need be no more than 3' long. It is not easy to reach and sew across an area of more than about 18" from each side of the rail, and only a portion of the quilt is exposed at one time, the rest being rolled up on the rails (**a.**).

Stretchers cross the rails at right angles. They are held together with C-clamps (**b.**) or holes may be drilled and a peg or bolt slipped into place. A nut or key will hold it and keep the frame firmly in place. See ill.

Before the quilt can be **put in,** or attached to the frame, the rails must have fabric added to them. A wide twill tape or a strip of **muslin** or ticking will do, and it can be stapled or tacked to the rail. Place the rails parallel, then add the muslin at the top extending to the inside.

The top and bottom ends of the **quilt back** are then pinned to the muslin, with the **backing** lying smooth and flat. It is then **baste**d in place, using two or three rows of basting, if required, to make it smooth. Remove the pins. It is easiest to do this on a large surface, the floor being usually the most convenient. Place a sheet over the floor to avoid soiling the quilt.

The **filler** is then spread out over the backing to make an even layer of whatever thickness is desired. Most beginning quilters tend to use too thick a layer of filler, making it difficult to sew through and to keep stitches even. Both filler and backing should be 2–3" larger than the quilt top on each edge. The quilt top is then placed, face-up, on the filler. If a **quilting pattern** is to be marked on the quilt top, it is done before the top is put in.

These three layers must now be held together with basting stitches. The stitches should not be so large that the layers slip out of place between them. Basting stitches should start at the center, going to top, bottom, and corners. Additional lines of basting should be added until there are no large areas left open without basting. Check the backing to be sure there are no wrinkles or folds in the material. If there are, remove those basting stitches, smooth, and resew.

When basting is completed, the quilt is rolled onto the rails in such a way that the quilt top is what shows going over the rails to the outside and then under. **Roll** until about a 3' strip of the quilt is exposed.

The stretchers are then added and secured at the corners. This will hold the layers somewhat taut in the frame; however, it should not be so tight as to stretch any of the stitches in the pieced or appliquéd design.

The ends of the quilt exposed near the stretchers must be held in place. Long, heavy stitches may be used to secure the backing to the frame, or lengths of twill or bias tape can be used.

A support for the frame is now needed. Old quilting frames are usually built with legs attached, but they require more space to use and to store. The arms of chairs, or the backs of low chairs, will support the frame. This frame can be leaned against a wall when quilting is not under way.

Quilting can now begin. It is usually started at the center, and when an area is finished the quilt is rolled to one side or the other to expose any unquilted portions.

Some quilters prefer to use a very large frame that exposes the entire quilt at one time. Then as quilting is completed, the frame is rolled toward the center. This not only requires a large space, but it means that if any unevenness occurs in the fabric layers, it is trapped in the middle of the quilt and there is no way to ease it out.

The quilting is accomplished with the simple, in-and-out **running stitch.** With the left hand under the quilt and the right hand on top to manipulate the needle, the sizes of the stitches can be carefully controlled, even when several stitches are taken at one time.

Many quilters like to use a long needle, although **quilting needle**s are very short. Some quilters are not comfortable with a needle until it is slightly bent, or "broken in." Others throw the bent shaft away. So it is really a matter of personal preference, gained through trial and practice.

Quilting stitches should be small, and the consistency of stitch length is of vital importance. The number of stitches that can be taken at one time will vary according to the thickness of the layers, the weight of the fabric, and how tightly the quilt is held in the frame. Some quilters take several stitches at once, others insist that they must be taken individually, in an up-and-down movement. Two or three stitches at a time can easily be managed if the stack is not too thick (**c.**). See ill.

Quilting thread is smooth and strong and is preferred if it is available. Since it does not always come in a full range

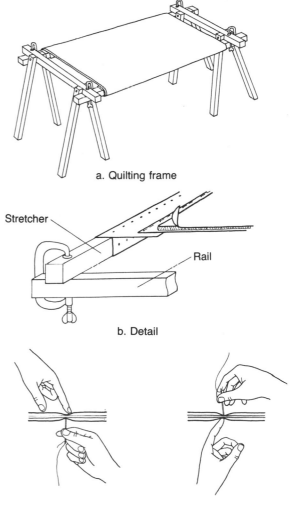

a. Quilting frame

b. Detail

c. Making hand quilting stitches

of colors, heavy-duty thread or a #50, #60, or #70 sewing thread may be used. Running the thread over **beeswax** will help smooth it.

The quilting thread may match or contrast with the quilt top, depending upon how much you want the stitches to show. White quilting thread is most commonly seen in old quilts, although any color can be used. It is helpful to quilt a sample piece to determine your preference.

In starting a line of quilting, traditional quilters insist that a knot is never used. The needle is slipped in near a seam, and several small running stitches are taken inside. They should not come out on the back. The needle is brought out on the top and only the shortest stitch is taken before the needle is reinserted, now heading in the opposite direction. The process is repeated once more, and then the needle emerges and the quilting is begun. The thread is ended in this same way. If the stitch can be started or ended near a seam, the double thickness makes it easier to lose these few stitches inside the quilt top.

When the quilting is finished, the quilt is **taken out** of its frame. All basting is removed. It is then ready for the final **binding.**

To quilt without a frame, the backing is laid out flat, probably on the floor, as few other work areas are large enough. The filler is spread out in an even layer over the backing. Then the quilt top is placed on top. The backing should extend beyond the top an inch or two. The filler should always come out to the edge of the quilt top or further. It must never end inside the edge of the quilt top.

Basting stitches are taken vertically and horizontally across the quilt, then diagonally. The back must be checked to be sure there are no puckers or folds in the material. If there are none, proceed with further basting. The larger the quilt, the greater the number of basting lines needed. Finally, a basting stitch is added at the outside edge.

The quilting can then proceed as described above. It is always easier to do quilting without a frame if a large table surface is available on which the quilt can be spread. This supports the quilt, making it easy to reach under the quilt with the free hand. Some quilters are able to quilt the well-basted layers by holding them in their lap. When all quilting stitches are completed, the edge is trimmed and the quilt is ready for binding.

This no-frame procedure works well on a quilt of crib size or perhaps on a single-bed size. It is difficult to use on a full-size quilt. An easier way to quilt a very large area is to keep it in small portions. Then, the quilted portions or sections can be joined and some final lines of quilting added over these lines so that the quilting pattern is continuous. Various **quilt-as-you-go** methods can be used. Some quilts may be finished without any true quilting, such as **tied quilts** or **comforter**s and preformed sections in **pillow quilts** or **biscuit quilts.**

BINDING   After removing it from the frame, the quilt is bound. This simply involves covering, in any of various ways, the raw edges of the three layers.

One of the simplest is a narrow **self-binding.** In this, the **filler** must be trimmed exactly to the edge of the **quilt top** and the **backing** is trimmed to extend evenly all around. If the binding is to be ½" wide, then the backing is cut to allow ½" plus ¼" **seam allowance.** The backing is then drawn up over the top of the quilt and is **slip-stitch**ed down at the edge.

If a wide self-binding is used, the excess filler may be used to pad it. For a 1" binding, trim the filler at 1" out from the quilt top. Trip the backing at 2" plus ¾" seam allowance. That allows ¼" to be turned under and ½" to overlap the quilt top. **Miter** the corner, and then slip-stitch the binding into place (**a.**).

Instead of a self-binding, a separate binding may be cut. If it is to be narrow, it can be cut on the bias. If it is to be wide, it will be easier to cut the binding on the straight of the material and **square the corners.** The binding is straight-stitched to one side of the quilt, right sides together, then brought around the layers to the other side and slip-stitched in place (**b.**). See ill.

There are prefinished bindings of many varieties available at fabric shops. **Blanket binding,** 2" wide, is not suitable for all quilts but works well on some. Woven binding and bias tape or bias binding are ready-folded and easy to use.

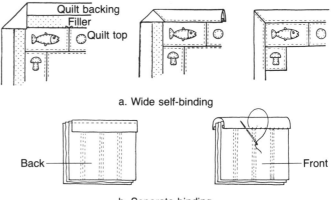

a. Wide self-binding

b. Separate binding

IDENTIFYING AND DATING OLD QUILTS   All quilts are identified by a pattern name, unless they are one-of-a-kind quilts. The name given to a quilt is usually taken from the name of the **block** design. This is true of most **appliqué** and **pieced quilt**s. Occasionally the **set** of blocks creates such a distinctive design that the quilt is known by the name of the set. For example, **Log Cabin** is the name of a pieced-block design, and **Streak of Lightning** is the name given to a particular arrangement of Log Cabin blocks.

If a pattern name is not known, determine first if the quilt is of any known type. If flowers appear, it may be one of the **flower designs;** if stars appear, it may fall under the category of **star patterns.** Determine if the quilt is pieced or appliquéd and if it falls into any category such as **patriotic quilts, storytelling quilts,** or **all-white quilts.** Sometimes the names are so descriptive that there is little trouble in identifying them, as with the **string quilt,** the **Tulip** quilt, and the **Pinwheel.** Other names are so imaginative that it would be impossible to find the name without being told.

Most block patterns have two or three names and some

as many as eight or nine. Each of these names, in turn, may refer to several different **quilt blocks.** This overlapping and repetition make it difficult to identify some quilts positively by just one name.

Quilt names have a way of changing, too. As patterns moved across the country from East to West, the names changed, reflecting the events and concerns of everyday life. **Job's Tears** is a superb example of this; it became Slave Chain, Texas Tears, and **Kansas Troubles,** to cite a few. Because of the manner in which they were sewn, appliqué quilts gave the quilter much more leeway with the design. Seldom are two appliqué quilts exactly alike—a flower was changed, leaves were added, and the pattern assumed a new name.

The study of quilt names offers an insight into the lives and the problems of Americans over the past several hundred years. Quilt names are still evolving. New quilts are being produced in abundance, and whereas some are repetitions of the traditional quilts, others are becoming a part of this folk art by adapting to and reflecting contemporary life. Also see **appliqué-border designs, appliqué-patterns, fancy quilting patterns, pieced-border designs, pieced-patterns, plain quilting patterns, quilting motifs.**

Because so few **quilts** are signed and dated, determining the age requires some research. The piece of fabric of most recent origin sets the earliest date at which the quilt could have been made. A knowledge of printed patterns and dye methods is valuable in this dating. Of course, even when dates can be established regarding the probable age of fabrics, that does not tell when the quilt was made. Often the material found its way into a quilt only after having served faithfully as a dress or shirt or apron for many years.

In the eighteenth century, wood-block printing and the copper-plate printing process were used to print fabrics. Vegetable or natural dyes were soft in color and can be distinguished from the later mineral dyes. Cylinder or roller printing, which came into use in the second quarter of the nineteenth century, has distinguishing features that make it possible to identify these fabrics. In the mid 1850s, aniline dyes brought new brilliance to printed and dyed fabrics.

Quilt colors and color combinations varied from one area to the next. Certain colors became more popular and are associated with specific areas; the **Amish quilt**s may sometimes be distinguished by their unique combinations of colors. **Trapunto** quilts were found in the South, heavier **padding** in the North. All in all, dating the quilts is difficult unless one studies textiles, dyes, and fabric printing methods thoroughly. The best information often comes with the quilt—a signature, or a bit of family history. Stories often accompany old quilts, so they should be pursued whenever possible. Sizes of quilts varied, sometimes offering a possible clue to age.

REPAIRING OLD QUILTS   Almost all old quilts are well worth the effort required to repair or renew them. Even if only portions are usable, retain those remnants to be made into pillows or baby quilts, or to be incorporated into clothes.

It is almost impossible to replace worn **patch**es on **pieced quilt**s that have been quilted because the removal of any one piece would cut into numerous lines of **quilting.** The best way to repair a frayed pieced shape would be to carefully **appliqué** a new piece of fabric over the top. In doing this, cut the patch to fit over the triangle or square of the quilt, allowing a ¼" **seam allowance.** This ¼" is turned under and **whip-stitch**ed or **blind-stitch**ed into place. If several patches in one area are to be replaced, apply them individually. If the patches are **pieced** together first they will never quite fit, because the quilt itself has already been stitched and is, therefore, somewhat compressed. After the individual frayed pieces have been covered, add appropriate lines of quilting, being careful not to go through to the **backing.** This will retain the appearance of quilting on the **quilt top.**

If new prints look too fresh and bright on an old quilt, try dipping them in coffee or tea to antique them. Coffee will add a warm beige cast; tea a greenish one. Test scraps of fabric first, remembering that repeated dippings will further darken the fabric. If fabrics need to be lightened or softened, they may require bleaching. Most **colorfast** fabrics will not fade readily in the sun, so a laundry bleach may be used sparingly. You may even be able to locate old **calico**es and prints, which would blend better with an old quilt.

If the worn piece is in a **tied quilt** or in a tied **coverlet** or **comforter,** the repair will be much easier. Provided that the material in general is still good and strong, a single stained or worn piece can be taken out, and a new one hand stitched in its place. However, if the threads of the quilt top fabric are weak, it is better to appliqué the repair on the top, as for a pieced quilt.

Some quilts are clearly tattered beyond repair. Unless they are of museum quality they are probably not worth saving intact, but sometimes their sentimental value makes them worth working with. If there are portions in a quilt that are still usable it might be possible to cut those out, saving as large a section as possible to be used, medallionlike, on another quilt of your own making. Or usable portions of a badly torn quilt could be cut out and bound at the edges and kept to be admired or used in some way in the home, perhaps as a baby quilt, doll's quilt, or pillow cover. Not every quiltmaker was an artist. Some used color combinations that you might find outlandish, and some simply did not sew well. A poorly made quilt may not be worth your time.

If an old quilt has some broken quilting threads, redo these one line at a time. Find a broken thread, undo enough of the stitches so that you have a few inches of the thread free. Thread that end into a needle and stitch it back into the quilt. Then do the same at the other end of the broken line. Use another new thread to retrace the stitches in between, proceeding with regular **quilting stitch**es. Each broken line of quilting must be done in this way if you wish to restore it to its original condition.

CARE OF QUILTS   **Quilt**s are made to be used. Stored away in boxes and chests, they yellow and age almost as much as when they are in use. Quilts need not be laundered often. It will be helpful to give them an occasional airing by hanging them on a clothesline in a breeze, or by running them through the "air" or "fluff" cycle of a clothes dryer. This fluffs up the **batting,** which sometimes mats with use.

If a quilt really must be washed, the way in which it is done depends somewhat on the quilt. An old **pieced quilt,** or a fragile or delicately stitched one, should be washed by hand. In a bathtub or large sink, immerse the quilt in warm sudsy water; mild detergent will not hurt it. Let it soak, then press it between flat hands, forcing the dirty water out and letting clean water in. Handle it gently. **Cotton** is one of the few fibers that actually gets stronger when it is wet, but you should avoid too much agitation, which might make the **filler** shift. Rinse well, drain, and hang outside to dry, or put in the dryer to fluff-dry. The freshly laundered quilt will not need ironing.

Wash an old quilt as you would a new one. If you are uncertain about the washability, consult an expert in a dry-cleaning establishment. Local art museums can be very helpful in locating reliable experts.

If there is uncertainty about the **colorfast**ness of the material in the quilt, again, see a dry-cleaning specialist. The cost of dry cleaning flat pieces such as quilts is not high. **Wool** quilts are difficult to hand-wash; dry-clean them.

Do not have any quilts, especially **appliqué quilt**s, pressed after cleaning. The **quilting** imparts an all-over texture and pressing flattens the quilting and fabric edges of **appliqué.** If some large areas of appliqué need touch-up pressing, do that yourself, using a heat setting appropriate to the fiber content of the material.

If quilts are made of sturdy new fabrics, if they are **machine-appliquéd,** and if you chose colorfast material for your quilts, there is no reason why they cannot be machine-washed. Use a cycle for delicate or fragile items. If that is not available, simply soak the quilt in the machine, then drain. Fill, rinse, drain, and spin. Use no agitation at all.

When a quilt is stored, it should be clean and fresh. It can be wrapped in **muslin** or other light fabric. It is best to roll quilts onto tubes so that folds will not be pressed in. This requires a large storage area, so if this is not possible, fold the quilt lengthwise and then roll it. Change the line of the fold occasionally to prevent the line from becoming permanent. If you must fold quilts on a shelf, be sure to re-fold them often. Stored fabrics need to breathe, so muslin between the layers is helpful. Avoid any airtight plastic bags or plastic sheeting. If dust is really a concern, an old sheet folded over the top will adequately protect the quilt.

quilt size. Quilts. See **Quilts: Determining Quilt Size.**

quilt storage. Quilts. See **Quilts: Care of Quilts.**

quilt top. Quilts. The decorative top layer of a quilt after the **block**s are finished and **set,** but before it is **put in** and quilted. The blocks may be **pieced, appliqué**d, embroidered, batiked, or decorated by any of a great variety of methods.

The term "quilt top" is always used to refer to the fabric blocks that have been joined to make a large piece of material, except in those cases where no **piecing** is used. For example, in an **overall** design, the quilt top is the single top layer that has been embellished in some way. In an **all-white quilt,** the top is the undecorated top layer of white fabric. The top is placed over the **filler** and **backing** material to **assemble** the quilt.

quilt types. Quilts. Many types, or kinds, of quilts are categorized and identified according to some specific characteristic. Rarely are any two of these quilts identical in terms of color or pattern, but they are similar in origin, function, structure, or use of materials. Following is a list of the best-known quilt types by name:

album quilt	**medallion quilt**
all-white quilt	**memory quilt**
Amish quilt	**modular quilt**
autograph quilt	**mosaic quilt**
baby quilt	nylon-stocking quilt
baptismal quilt	one-of-a-kind quilt
bar quilt	**patriotic quilt**
batik quilt	**Pennsylvania Dutch quilt**
bed rug	**pillow quilt**
beggar's blocks	**popcorn quilt**
best quilt	**postage-stamp quilt**
Bible quilt	**presentation quilt**
Bible-verse quilt	**presidents' quilts**
bicentennial quilt	**puff quilt**
biscuit quilt	**quilt-as-you-go**
blue-jeans quilt	**raised patchwork**
blue resist quilt	**remembrance quilt**
border quilt	**sampler quilt**
candlewick spread	**scrap-bag** quilt
cathedral-window quilt	scripture quilt
centennial quilt	signature quilt
checkerboard	**silk quilt**
chintz quilt	**slumber robe**
christening quilt	snowball quilt
cigar-band quilt	**state quilt**
commemorative quilt	**storytelling quilt**
cookie-cutter quilt	**string quilt**
cradle quilt	Suffolk puff
crazy quilt	**summer quilt**
crib quilt	Swiss patchwork
dark quilt	**throw**
diamond patchwork	**tithing quilt**
diamond quilt	**tobacco-bag quilt**
family-record quilt	**tufted quilt**
freedom quilt	**Victorian crazy quilt**
Friendship Medley	**white-on-white quilt**
friendship quilt	white quilt
Hawaiian quilt	whitework quilt
hexagon quilt	**"whole-cloth" quilt**
hit-or-miss	**wool-on-wool coverlet**
legacy quilt	**yo-yo quilt**

quiltweave. Weaving. A weave done on a **double cloth** construction that binds two fabrics together with a pattern of **stitching point**s. The stitching points are **warp** threads of the back fabric caught up by the **filling** of the face fabric. Between the two fabrics is a padding, or wadding of some substance, or yarn that is thick and soft. To do the stitching and have the right **shed** open up in order to insert the padding, at least five **harness**es must be used. Quiltweave, or quilting, may also be done on four harnesses by **"picking up"** the correct shed for the padding. In this case, more intricate quilting designs can be planned.

In either the **loom-controlled** or picked-up quilting, the padding is optional. Since padding gives a heavy fabric, it can be omitted in favor of having a lighter-weight fabric that has a subtle design. Also see **pick-up weaves.**

quiz. Toys. See **yo-yo.**

r

rabbet. Stained Glass. An L-shaped cut made in the edge of a wooden window frame, against which a finished stained-glass window is set.

rabbet. Woodworking. A rectangular groove cut on the edge or end of a board. Also see **joint** and **Woodworking: Jointing.**

rabbeting bit. Woodworking. See **router bit.**

rabbet joint. Woodworking. See **joint** and **Woodworking: Jointing.**

rabbet plane. Woodworking. See **plane.**

rabbit hair. Knitting. Two kinds of rabbit hair are spun into yarn: rabbit wool, which is soft, fine, and fluffy (and the kind most commonly used), and the beard hair, which is stiff, coarse, shiny, and sharp. Also see **angora** and **Knitting: Tools and Materials.**

rabbitskin glue. Découpage. See **hide glue.**

rabbitskin glue. Needlepoint. An inexpensive glue available at most art-supply stores. It is generally used to prime painting canvases but is also used in needlework. After a piece of needlework is completed, block it face down. When it is completely dry, a light coating of the glue on the back of the piece will prevent the needlework from distorting.

Since this glue comes in powder form, the right consistency is important: if too thick, it will form lumps on the back; if too thin, it will permeate the fibers. This glue is especially recommended for pillows and handbags, where there is no strong supportive backing. Also see **Needlepoint: Finishing.**

race. Weaving. See **beater, fly-shuttle loom.**

racing spool. Toys. (Also called spool racer, spool tractor.) A simple **action toy** made from a thread spool. A short nail is tacked into one end and a **rubber band** is hooked over it and drawn through the open center of the spool and out the other end. A metal washer is slipped over the rubber band and a stick is put partway through the remaining loop at the end of the band; a matchstick pencil, or small **dowel** will work. The spool is held and wound tightly. When released, the stick unwinds. It takes some experimenting to find the best length for the stick to make this simple tractor or spool toy. See ill.

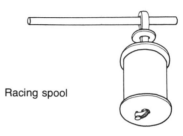

Racing spool

raddle. Weaving. An implement used to spread the **warp** uniformly as it is going toward the **warp beam** during **beaming.** It is a long, narrow wooden bar with short pegs of either wood or metal protruding from one side. They are usually spaced an inch apart. The length of the raddle usually conforms to the width of the **loom.** The warp passes through the pegs in small, even groups. Some raddles have a removable top that clamps over the pegs once the warp is spaced. This prevents the warp from slipping up and out as it is being wound onto the warp beam. In homemade raddles where nails are used as the pegs, a string can be wound over and between the nails to prevent this slippage. Although it is commonplace to tie the raddle on top or in front of the **back beam,** some weavers find it convenient to put it in some other position on the loom. There also are some raddles that can be set into the **beater.** Also see **beaming, dressing the loom.**

radial arm saw. Woodworking. See **power saw.**

Radiant Star. Quilts. A **pieced block** design that is identical to the **Feather Star** except for the center block. When the hexagon is used as the center block, the design becomes the Radiant Star.

Radical Rose. Quilts. An **appliqué block** design that dates from the Civil War period. It is one of many **flower designs** using overlapping areas of appliqué. See ill.

Radical Rose

raffia. Basketry. Weaving. A tough but pliable fiber stripped from the outer epidermis of the Madagascar palm. The individual strands are flat, generally ½" wide and 4–5' long. It is a versatile basketry material that may be braided, wound, or woven, and is adaptable to both large and small baskets. It is sold in loose twisted **hanks** of approximately 3–5 lbs each and graded Superior (AAAA) for the best, and Choice (AA) for good quality. Also see **Basketry: Tools and Materials, Coiled Basket Construction.**

raffia. Batik and Tie-dye. A fiber that comes from the raffia palm. It is thin, flat, and strong. Many tie-dye artists use it as a **binding material.** A natural color should be selected unless one particularly wants the added effect of bleeding from the colors. Synthetic raffias also are available, of which **Swiss straw** is one.

raffia needle. Basketry. See **tapestry needle.**

rafter square. Woodworking. See **squaring tools.**

rag book. Toys. See **fabric book.**

rag doll. Toys. A doll made of cloth and **stuff**ed with some flexible material. Rag dolls are among the oldest examples of folk toys. Usually made at home, they were soft and could be constructed of readily available materials. Because fabrics were precious, many of the dolls were patched, some having several layers of material. As one face wore out a new one could be sewn over the top. Some had stitching to raise an area to suggest a nose, with stitched or button eyes.

Rag dolls were extensively manufactured in England in the last half of the nineteenth century. They were cut and sewn from printed fabrics.

Some fabric dolls have smooth, flat faces covered with sizing or **gesso** and then painted. Some modern fabric dolls have faces painted with **latex paint**s.

The rag doll more often suggests a scrap doll, made at home from available materials; the **fabric doll** is most often printed and produced for sale. Also see **cutout painted doll, golliwog, making do.**

rag-doll puppet. Puppets. A **marionette** in which all the parts are made from **stuffed-fabric** sections. It is a simple beginning for a **string puppet.** The head may be **papier mâché** or stuffed fabric. The **stringing** for the rag-doll marionette is the same as for a marionette made of wood, though curtain rings may be substituted for **screw eye**s.

ragged. Basketry. See **willow.**

Ragged Robin. Quilts. A small circular **appliqué** design of six teardrop shapes. These shapes radiate from the center, suggesting a spiral form. This design is often used in the center of a **Feather Crown** appliqué.

Raggedy Andy. Toys. The twin of the popular **rag doll,** Raggedy Ann.

Raggedy Ann. Toys. A favorite **nursery character rag doll** made with orange hair, button eyes, and striped stockings. She was first made in 1915 by Johnny Gruelle, who copied her from an old rag doll that had belonged to his mother. He produced not only the doll and her twin, **Raggedy Andy,** but books and stories as well. The doll's name was inspired by James Whitcomb Riley's poems "The Raggedy Man" and "Little Orphan Annie." The stories, written by Gruelle for his daughter, were first published after her death at age fourteen.

Each homemade version of Raggedy Ann is individualized and unique, although all are soft, **stuff**ed dolls of an unpretentious character. Patterns and printed fabrics are often available for those who prefer a "genuine" doll, and the readymade dolls themselves are still being sold.

rag rug. Rugmaking. Weaving. Woven rugs using rag strips as the **filling.** These rugs go back to colonial times, when scraps of everything woven at home were saved. At rag sewing bees, the women would sew strips of scrap fabric together and wind them into balls, saving them for later use as rag-rug filling. At first, the rags were sewn together without color selection and these strips were used to produce an all-over pattern called "hit and miss" rugs. Certain designs were created within the hit and miss category, such as the filling stripes of the Betsy Ross pattern or the **plaid** of the Martha Washington design. After a time, women began to sort, sew, and ball the rags by color and, with this, they developed the "crossbarred" carpet, which largely replaced the hit and miss carpets. The **warp** was usually of neutral colors and the filling created the bright stripes of individual colors. Another technique using the single color balls was to weave an **inlay** of different colors in a background of hit and miss. Today, all of these rag-rug types are still woven. There is another type of rag rug in which the whole rug is inlaid and approaches a **tapestry** effect.

In weaving a rag rug, the filling is beaten down hard to create a compact, durable surface. The warp is not covered and its color is important in relationship to the filling colors. The warp can be **sett** so closely that the rug becomes **warp-faced** in a **rep** effect and the filling is seen only at the **selvage**s. In these cases, the color and design of the warp create the whole rug. The most popular yarn used for warp is inexpensive cotton yarn that has become known as **carpet warp.** The rag strips can be of used or new fabrics. Just about any material can be used, but if the rug is to be washable, the fabrics must be colorfast and of the same fiber so that any shrinkage will be equal. Stockings or panty hose with the toes and tops removed are also popular, as are **thrums.**

The advent of power loom weaving in the 1850s caused a temporary decline in the rag rug, especially in its use as the best floor covering in the house. However, it still was and is much used in the more private rooms of the household. In Canada it has not seemed to have suffered as much of a decline and is, today, still an esteemed product among the French-Canadian weavers of Quebec. Called "catalogne" by them, its workmanship is of the highest caliber and the colors are chosen and combined with great care. Also see **hoop loom, mill ends.**

rag shuttle. Rugmaking. Weaving. See **rug shuttle.**

rail. Puppets. (Also called perch bar.) A board with nails or hooks on which **marionette**s can be hung during a performance when they are not on stage. It is important that they be hung on the rail to prevent any tangling of the **string**s. If the **control** for the marionette has a hook on the end of it, it can be hung over a nail driven into the rail. If a **screw eye** has been used, either a hook or a nail tilted upward will do.

rail. Quilts. (Also called bar, side bar, side board.) A board or bar used at the side of a **quilting frame.** The rails are longer than the **stretcher**s. The ends of the **quilt top** and **backing** of the quilt are attached to the rails, so that while the full width of the quilt is exposed at one time, only a portion of its length is seen. The rails are **roll**ed as the **quilting** progresses.

railroad board. Toys. See **cardboard.**

Rainbow. Quilts. See **Joseph's Coat.**

raindrops. Weaving. See **Finnweave.**

raised. Weaving. See **shed.**

raised cup stitch. Embroidery. A looped stitch that is worked in a circle and gives the appearance of a cup, or can be extended as tubing. Suitable wherever a three-dimensional rounded effect is desired, such as for small flowers.

Make a triangle of 3 **back stitch**es, in the center of the area to be worked (**a.**). Using a blunt **tapestry needle,** slide under one back stitch. Do not go through the material. Take the thread over the needle, then under it (**b.**). Pull through gently to form a knot (**c.**). Repeat, making a second knot beside the first one on the same bar. Pull through, gently (**d.**). Continue, making 2 knots on each bar to make a complete ring of stitches by sliding the needle under the bar between each knot (at arrow) (**e.**). Work round and round, if necessary occasionally working two knots into the bars to increase the size of the cup (**f.**). See ill. Also see **stumpwork.**

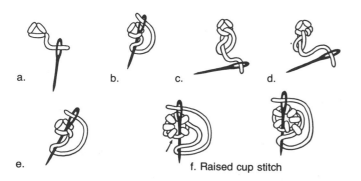

f. Raised cup stitch

raised embroidery. Embroidery. See **stump work.**

raised goldwork. China and Glass Painting. See **raised paste.**

raised honeycomb filling. Crewel. Embroidery. An **open filling stitch.** Lay basic squares as in **squared filling.** Do not tie them down. Starting at the top, using a blunt needle and contrasting color, whip over each thread from right to left, working down to the bottom. At the bottom of the line go down through the material to anchor the thread, come up again a fraction away, and whip up to the top on the same thread, again weaving the needle under from right to left (**a.**). Whip over all the vertical bars in this way, and then repeat exactly the same thing on the horizontal ones (**b.**). Because the thread crosses four times at the intersections, the cross effect shown in the diagram does not appear clearly. The bars simply become raised bumps where they cross (**c.**). The finished effect is like a honeycomb, and highly textured. See ill. Also see **honeycomb filling.**

a. Whipping stitch   b.   c. Raised honeycomb filling

raised increase. Knitting. See **Knitting: Increasing.**

raised paste. China and Glass Painting. (Also called relief color). A thick, pasty paint used to produce molded, raised areas of design that project from the surface of china. Raised-paste decorations can be modeled in high relief, or can be relatively flat. Very delicate, wirelike lines can be raised. The raised paste must be thoroughly dry before **firing.** After firing, raised areas are usually painted with **gold,** then refired. Use **Hancock's paste** for raised paste; apply it with a pointed watercolor sable **brush.** To fill in an area, drop small dots of paste from the brush, close together, so that they link up to form a smooth filling.

raised patchwork. Quilts. (Also called Swiss patchwork.) A process that combines the appearance of **patchwork** and **quilting** in one operation. It is similar to the **pillow-quilt** process, but has one further application: a **pieced quilt** pattern can be translated to this method. Instead of cutting one each of the pieces required for a **block,** two of each are cut. They are sewn and turned, as in the pillow quilt, then joined with a **slip stitch** or **whip stitch.** If the **prestuff**ed shapes are carefully joined, the finished work has the puffy, sculptured surface of true quilting.

raised patterns. Crochet. Any crochet **pattern** creating an uneven or "raised" surface. This term refers to various patterns, including overlay patterns, where a stitch is made over a stitch completed in a **previous row,** and designs made by the **cluster** stitch, the **loop stitch,** and the **around-the-post stitch.** Also see **Crochet: Patterns.**

raised seeding. Crewel. Embroidery. See **seed stitch.**

raised stem stitch. Crewel. Embroidery. The stem stitch worked over a foundation of **laidwork.** The raised stem stitch can be used as a banding stitch or as a **filling stitch.** In the case of the latter, the laidwork is tacked down invisibly. Slide the tapestry needle under the laidwork (**a.**). Do not piece the material. Work the stitch in rows beginning at the bottom and working upward (**b., c.**). When used to fill an uneven area, it usually needs an outline of **stem stitch.** A variation of the stitch is the raised stem stitch in a chevron pattern (**d.**). To reverse direction at the top foundation thread, slide the needle upward and under, keeping the thread to the left of the needle (**e.**). This stitch is effective when shaded or worked in several colors. See ill. Also see **chevron pattern.**

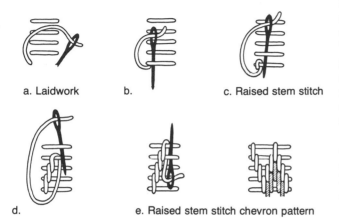

a. Laidwork

b.

c. Raised stem stitch

d.

e. Raised stem stitch chevron pattern

raised stem stitch in chevron pattern. Crewel. Embroidery. See **raised stem stitch.**

raised stitch. Needlepoint. See **pyramid stitch.**

raiser. Weaving. See **riser.**

raising. Jewelry. Metalworking. Raising is a generic term referring to all the hand-hammering processes used to make hollow, usually rounded shapes. **Silversmithing** has been referred to as "the art of raising." The term is often mentioned in connection with bowllike forms or containers, although combinations of raising techniques are used also to make sculpture and jewelry. Metals suitable for raising include **gold, silver, lead, copper,** and **brass** in sheet thicknesses of 14-, 16-, or 18-**gauge.** Also see **raising techniques** and **Metalworking: Raising.**

raising hammer. Metalworking. See **hammer.**

raising techniques. Metalworking. **Raising** techniques fall into two groups: in compressed metal forming, the metal is compressed by hammering it over a convex **anvil** or **stake,** and the walls of the finished object tend to be thicker than the original metal; in stretched forming, the metal is hammered into a concave anvil, stake, wooden mold, or sandbag, making the metal thinner.

COMPRESSED TECHNIQUES

A. *Angle raising.* In this basic operation, the metal is hammered against the stake into a series of relatively sharp angles, and the final form is reached when the an-

gles are gradually rounded out. The disk-shaped **blank** is hammered in spirals or concentric circles from the center to its outer edge. For instruction see **Metalworking: Raising.**

b. *Dutch raising.* A forming process developed in the Netherlands, used for shaping open pieces. Hammering progresses from the outer edge of the blank and spirals toward the center. Start by using a heavy **cross-peen hammer** and then progress with a heavy **rawhide mallet.** Do not make pronounced angles as in angle raising, but gradually form the rounded surface.

c. *Crimping.* A rapid raising process accomplished by hammering grooves into the metal in the long depression of a **valley stake,** which is designed to crimp metal. Use a **crimping hammer** and a rounded cross-peen hammer. The metal may be worked on a hardwood form with a groove, especially if the metal is **pewter.** Crimping is often used to start a form and then is followed by other methods. Its advantage is the possibility of rapid changes of angle, although the technique may be difficult for novices. For instruction see **Metalworking: Raising.**

d. *Edge thickening.* (Also called upsetting.) Hammering or compressing the edge of an object to thicken it. Tap the edge with a light hammer after each **course** with the hammer face, hitting exactly perpendicular to the edge to avoid bending the metal.

e. *Squaring a bottom.* (Also called bottoming.) Hammering to align the bottom to the sides, and to flatten the bottom so the object will stand. Shape the bottom on a vertical **bottoming stake** by hammering with a flat-faced **planishing hammer.** Use an extension arm if necessary for deep pieces.

Stretched techniques

f. *Blocking.* (Also called stretched metal forming, sinking, pressing.) Hammering metal into a concave mold to achieve the desired form. This is one of the oldest forms of raising, and may be started from an **ingot** or a thick piece of metal poured directly from the **crucible** into a mold. It is suitable for simple open shapes and is less difficult than compressing, but thicker metal is needed than for compressed techniques—blanks of ⅛" to ¼" thick, or sheet metal of 14 or 16 **gauge.** With a shaped concave mold, the process may be used to produce numerous identical pieces. For instruction see **Metalworking: Raising.**

g. *Sandbag method.* (Also called free-form shaping.) The process of stretching metal by hammering it over a sandbag. For instruction see **Metalworking: Raising.**

rake. Jewelry Metalworking. See **blacksmithing tools.**

raking. Jewelry. Metalworking. The process of cleaning a **buffing wheel** holding a wheel rake against a turning buff and moving it back and forth until the surface is clean and the buff has the desired shape. In **blacksmithing,** the term refers to raking the coals in the fire.

raku. Ceramics. Hand-built or quickly thrown groggy **earthenware** from Japan. It is associated with the tea ceremony. Raku uses a very rapid **glaze firing** cycle in which ware is placed into and removed from a red hot **kiln** with long **tongs.**

Glazes are traditionally shiny and fluid, and the pot, after being removed from the kiln, is placed directly into cold water, or it is carbonized by putting it into sawdust or leaves while it is still red hot.

Gloves are used in making raku to insert and remove pots from the kiln. The gloves must be fireproof, woven asbestos, insulated gloves.

raku. Enameling. A technique using flammable organic material to texture a molten enamel surface. The **enamel** is sometimes textured by contact with smoldering sawdust, pine needles, or leaves. Chemical solutions are also used for **fuming** to achieve the metallic **luster** of raku technique. A mixture of silver sulfide and copper carbonate added to liquid white enamel produces a brilliant luster, but is erratic and should be used with caution because of its toxicity. The work area should be well ventilated to prevent smoke inhalation. Also see **Enameling: Basic Operations.**

raku glaze. Ceramics. Any low firing temperature glaze, as well as any coloring oxide. Glazes are applied thickly, and unglazed areas give an attractive contrast. The **clay body** is usually **stoneware,** which is **bisque**d before glazing. Also see **wet firing.**

Rambling Road. Quilts. See **Kansas Troubles.**

ramie. Batik and Tie-dye. A strong, lustrous **fiber** obtained from the Malay ramie plant. The **natural fiber**s are used in weaving textiles.

ramie. Knitting. Spinning. Weaving. A fiber, also known as China grass, which is obtained from the stalk of a stingless nettle plant grown in Asia. The fiber is white with a silky luster; it is fine and extremely strong and elastic. Its drawback is the expense and difficulty of processing, since in raw ramie the fibers are cemented together by a natural gum.

rammer. Metalworking. See **sandcasting molding equipment.**

rampart gouge. Leather. An adjustable tool, similar to the V-gouge, that cuts U-grooves of an even depth in heavy leather, generally used in preparation for folding. See ill. Also see **Leatherwork: Creasing, Scoring and Folding Leather, Tools and Materials.**

Rampart gouge

rand. Basketry. To use a single **weaver** in **checked weave,** working it in front of one **stake** and behind the next. Also see **checked weave** and **Basketry: Woven Basket Construction.**

randing. Basketry. See **checked weave.**

Randolph Family Pattern. Quilts. An **appliqué block** that has been handed down through generations of the Randolph family, who brought it to Virginia in the 1800s. It is a pattern of four flowers and four buds radiating from a central flower.

random bargello stitch. Needlepoint. Long straight stitches worked over a varying number of mesh giving an uneven texture to the background of a needlepoint design. It can be worked in an even or uneven progression. Also see **Bargello.**

random stripes. Rugmaking. Weaving. See **stripe.**

Rapidograph pen. Crewel. Embroidery. An evenflow pen used for transferring a design onto almost any **background fabric,** except those highly textural fabrics such as **canvas,** which are too coarse for the fine point to write on.

The points of the pen are of various sizes. The pen must be filled with permanent ink when transferring designs. Care must also be taken to work in light lines to prevent the ink from bleeding into the fabric. Also see **Crewel: Transferring a Design.**

rapid rivet. Leather. See **rivet.**

rapping iron. Basketry. (Also called tapping iron.) A long, filelike tool with rounded edges used for tapping down the weaving so that the **round**s are tight and flat. See ill.

Rapping iron

rasp. Metalworking. See **file.**

rasp. Woodworking. A wood-shaping tool similar to a **file** but with coarser, individually cut teeth that will cut wood and similar materials without becoming clogged. Rasps come in a variety of shapes. Some of the most common are:

CABINET RASP Blunt-ended but slightly tapered, with one flat side and one rounded side. The tang may go into a handle (**a.**).

COMBINATION RASP Also half-round, but with no tang and with two degrees of coarseness on each face (**b.**).

RATTAIL (OR ROUND) RASP For smoothing or enlarging holes (**c.**).

RIFFLERS Smaller rasps with special shapes for reaching hollows, commonly used for finishing **woodcarving**s (**d.**).

Use a rasp as you would a normal file: Always start with the coarsest rasp you will need to smooth the major irregularities, and work toward the finest. Run the rasp diagonally to the direction of the **grain** to produce the best cutting action. When smoothing **end grain,** always work from the outer edge inward to avoid splitting the wood. See ill.

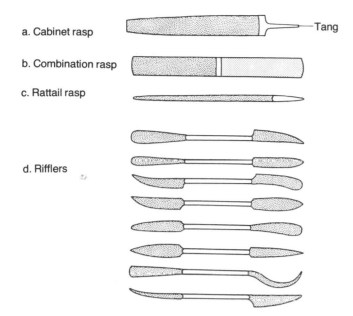

a. Cabinet rasp — Tang

b. Combination rasp

c. Rattail rasp

d. Rifflers

rasp-cut file. Metalworking. See **file.**

ratchet. Weaving. A toothed wooden or metal wheel found on both the **warp beam** in back and the **cloth beam** in front of a loom. The wheels are located at the right ends of the beams. The teeth of each wheel are inclined in one direction so that when a **pawl** falls into them, the wheel and beam are prevented from turning back, but can turn forward. The ratchets are used to release and tighten the **warp** as it is moved forward during weaving. The actual forward movement is usually manipulated by a handle attached to the cloth beam. The warp tension is then adjusted and held by ratchet and pawl. See ill. Also see **harness loom, loom, jack type loom, table loom, weaving.**

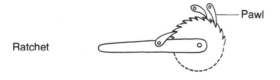

Ratchet — Pawl

ratchet screwdriver. Woodworking. See **screwdriver.**

ratchet spool. Toys. See **ticktack.**

ratiné yarn. Spinning. Weaving. See **novelty yarn.**

rattail. Macramé. See **satin cord.**

rattail rasp. Woodworking. See **rasp.**

rattan. Basketry. See **cane.**

rattle. Toys. Any toy that produces sound when it is shaken. Usually it has a short handle and a **ball**-like container that holds **bell**s, seeds, nuts, balls, etc. It is a common **cradle toy** and baby toy, made small enough to be easily grasped and lightweight enough for a baby to hold. Rattles are **universal toy**s and have been a part of reli-

gious and magical rites throughout history. Early rattles were sometimes known as **corals.** Also see **bell toy, emergent toy.**

rattletrap. Toys. (Also called clapper, horsefiddle.) A **sound toy** or **noisemaker** considered to be an **American folk toy.** It consists of a handle at the end of which is a star-shaped coin. A frame holding a thin wooden leaf spring is set over the coin and swings around it. When the handle is rotated, the frame swings around and the wood leaf raps or clacks sharply against the star coin. It is a favorite old-time Halloween toy. A similar **rattle** was known during the Middle Ages. There are other various kinds of rattles made from wood. See ill.

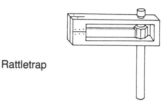

Rattletrap

ravel. Stitchery. To **fray** or fringe the **raw edge** of a **fabric** by drawing off the threads parallel to a cut line. Raveling for decorative effect requires that fabric be cut on either the **cross-grain** or **lengthwise grain** if the **fringe** is to form a parallel line.

Ravencroft, George. Glasswork. See **Worshipful Company of Glass Sellers.**

Ravenna. Mosaics. A city in northeast Italy, near the Adriatic Sea, that served as the imperial residence during the Byzantine Empire. The **mosaics** of this city are considered to be the finest in all of Europe. The oldest mosaics are in the mid-fifth century mausoleum of **Galla Placidia,** sister of Honorius, the emperor who chose Ravenna as the imperial seat. Also see **Mosaics.**

raw edge. Stitchery. The cut edge of a **fabric.** A raw edge is subject to **fray**ing or **ravel**ing. This may be undesirable, for example, in **appliqué** where edges have been turned under, as it disrupts the line to have threads of the raw edge pop out where they are not wanted. At other times there is a deliberate effort to fray or ravel a material for the textural effect. Much of the work in body coverings and denim art makes deliberate use of raw edges, since **denim** is woven with a white **weft** which gives a contrasting color to the **fringe.** The raw edges of **silk**s and **rayon**s tend to ravel and fray readily, and this characteristic is often capitalized on in **banners, wall hanging**s, and body coverings.

raw glaze. Ceramics. An unfritted glaze often applied to **once fired ware.**

rawhide. Leather. A term for cattle **hide** that has received some preparatory processing but has not been tanned. Rawhide is generally used for **lacing.**

rawhide hammer. Enameling. See **counter enamel, Enameling: Tools and Materials.**

rawhide mallet. Jewelry. A mallet with a wooden handle and a hammering head made of rolled rawhide used for flattening, **bending,** or **forming** metal. A rawhide mallet does not stretch or scratch metal, although it can dent it slightly. Rawhide mallets soften on the ends with use, and then work in a more pleasing and satisfactory way. They are available in several sizes. A medium-size mallet head, measuring approximately 1½″ × 3″, is the most useful. See ill. Also see **bracelet mandrel, horn hammer, ring mandrel, stake, steel block, support.**

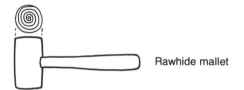
Rawhide mallet

rawhide mallet. Leather. See **mallet.**

rawhide mallet. Metalworking. See **hammer.**

rawhide maul. Leather. See **maul.**

rawstock. Leather. Skins or hides which are in a preserved state, ready for tanning.

Rayographs. See **photogram.**

rayon. Knitting. A man-made knitting fiber composed of cellulose. This relatively inexpensive yarn is available in many colors.

rayon. Spinning. Weaving. See **fiber.**

rayon. Stitchery. An absorbent, inexpensive **man-made fiber** which has a cellulose base, as well as the **fabric** woven from these **fibers.** The base raw material (wood pulp or cotton) is converted to a solution and then extruded through small nozzles and hardened to form fibers. Originally called artificial **silk,** rayon requires **dry cleaning** and is only moderately durable. It ranks second to cotton as the most widely used fiber. Stitchers occasionally use it in **wall hangings** because of the color range available and the smooth sheen of its surface.

Rayon is produced by any of three basic processes, and each type produced has different qualities. The specific type will affect the **dye** process. Viscose rayon is the most common and many dyes are made specifically for use on this fiber as well as **cotton** or **linen.** Cuprammonium rayon is similar to viscose rayon, but comprises a very small portion of the rayon on the market. Acetate rayon is the third and it has different characteristics. It is not usually recommended for home dyeing.

razor thinning. Découpage. The technique of shaving the back of a print with a razor blade to reduce the thickness or to remove the printing ink. Place the print face down on newspaper padding. Pull a single-edge razor blade gently from the center to the edges, taking care not to tear the print, until several layers of paper have been removed from the back. Also see **thinning prints.**

ream. Metalworking. See **reaming.**

reamer. Jewelry. (Also called broach.) A long, tapered tool with five sharp cutting edges used to enlarge drilled holes. It is inserted into the hole and twisted back and forth until the hole has reached the desired size. Also see **broaching.**

reamer. Jewelry. Metalworking. A tool for making holes more precise and for enlarging them. Also see **reaming.**

reaming. Metalworking. The process of enlarging or truing a hole with a **reamer.** To ream a hole, clamp the metal object so the reaming is done in a vertical position. Rotate the reamer in a clockwise direction, applying a little pressure on the **tap** wrench, which fits into the end of the reamer shank. Continue through the full length of the hole. Use a **lubricant** (except with **cast iron,** which should be reamed dry) for this process. Withdraw the reamer by turning it clockwise while you pull it out of the hole. Never reverse the direction of turning.

reamy glass. Stained Glass. An **antique glass** that is a light variant of **streaky glass.** It is produced in off-white, yellow, green, and light blue. It is much easier to cut than streaky glass, and is very susceptible to staining. Also see **glass.**

rear bridge. Puppets. (Also called back bridge.) In the **marionette stage** the rear bridge is behind the **bridge** and behind the **bench.** A **perch bar** is attached to the rear bridge.

rebate. Stained Glass. A grooved seating for a stained glass window. The window is set into the grooves and tied up to reinforcing rods. Also see **banding, fitting, reglet, saddle bar.**

Rebecca's Fan. Quilts. See **fan quilt.**

reciprocating flat lapping machine. Gemcutting. See **flat.**

reciprocating sander. Woodworking. See **sanding tools.**

reciprocating saw. Woodworking. See **power saw.**

reclaiming the screen. Silkscreen. Any one of the methods used to remove a **stencil** from the mesh stretched in a **screen frame** so that a new stencil can be wedded to the screen and the whole used again, rather than stretching a new piece of material in the frame. Removing photographic stencils from screens is so difficult that it is customary to stretch new material. Also see **cut film stencil, cut paper stencil, removing thinner.**

reclining twill. Weaving. See **twill weave.**

recto. Bookbinding. The right-hand page of facing pages, or the front side of a **leaf** of a book.

red brass. Jewelry. See **brass.**

red brass. Metalworking. See **brass.**

red brick clay. Ceramics. See **Ceramics: Clay.**

red bud. Basketry. See **dicky meadow.**

red colorant. Ceramics. See **pigment oxide.**

Red Cross. Quilts. Any of the great variety of **pieced blocks** that use the familiar symbol of the Red Cross. Sometimes a **four-patch** or **split four-patch** block is used in each corner, with the red cross dividing these blocks. One pattern called Red Cross is identical to **Maltese Cross.** See ill.

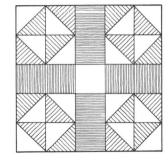

Red Cross

red gumwood. Woodworking. See **gumwood.**

red helmet. Shell Carving. See **bull-mouth helmet.**

red oak. Woodworking. See **oak.**

red rouge. Jewelry. See **buffing compound.**

red rouge cloth. Jewelry. (Also called rouge cloth.) A layered, soft flannel **polishing cloth** used for **hand polishing** small pieces. The dark layer (used first) is impregnated with red rouge and chemicals that act as a **polishing compound** to remove tarnish from the finished work. It can also be used to get a bright luster on metal when hand polishing. Residue from the rouge cloth can be removed with an old toothbrush and soapy household ammonia. The second layer of cloth is straw-colored and is impregnated with chemicals that prohibit the formation of tarnish. Metals should be thoroughly wiped with the cloth to impart a final luster and left unwashed. If metal filings should get into the cloth, they will scratch the work during final polishing.

redsmithing. Metalworking. See **blacksmithing.**

red tape. Dyeing. See **saffron.**

reducing designs. Rugmaking. See **transferring designs.**

reducing flame. Metalworking. See **flame.**

reducing patterns. Crewel. Embroidery. Needlepoint. See **enlarging and reducing a design.**

reduction. Ceramics. The process of **firing pottery** in a **kiln** using a reduced amount of oxygen. Also see **celadon, flashing, oxidation.**

reduction paste. Fabric Printing. See **extender.**

redwood. Woodworking. A light, aromatic, fine-grained, reddish brown **softwood** grown only in California. Although it dents and splinters easily and is not very strong, it is resistant to weather and therefore is used extensively for garden furniture, flowerboxes, shingles, and other outdoor items. There are two types: the common redwood, raised for lumber, and the sequoia, famous for its great size.

reed. Basketry. See **cane.**

reed. Weaving. A comblike removable part of the **beater** of a **harness loom.** It spreads and spaces the **warp ends** according to plan and pushes the **filling** down during **weaving.** Reeds come in all widths, heights and numbers—the latter is determined by how many dents per inch it has. Dents are the spaces between the blades or bars in a reed. They are all evenly spaced and the warp ends are pulled through them during **sleying.** For use in most handweaving, a fine reed would be a #20, which would have 20 spaces or dents per inch. A coarse reed would be a #6, which would have 6 dents per inch. The number of dents per inch is called dentage. Reeds can be made on special order to be of finer or coarser dentage than a #20 or #6. The number of reed used varies and depends on the size of the warp yarn used and the **sett.** When the sett is too high for a reed and there are too many ends crammed into a dent or dents, this is referred to as strong dents. Weak dents are those with too few warp ends for the fabric desired.

Today reeds are made of steel, but their name comes from early times when they were made of split bamboo or reed stalks which were kept at the proper spacing with cord wound around and between them. These handmade reeds could be made as fine as the commercially produced steel ones. Not too long ago, in out of the way places in the Mediterranean, one could still see a reed peddler with a pack of reeds on his back traveling from village to village selling them. Also see **jack-type loom, table loom.**

reed cutter. Basketry. See **shears.**

reed hook. Weaving. (Also called draw hook, entering hook, heddle hook, sley hook, threading hook, warp hook.) A hook used in threading the **warp** through the **heddle eyes** and in pulling it through the reed dents. In one version, it is a flat piece of steel with a notch or hook near the tip end and is mounted in a wooden handle. In some the hooked end is bent backward; others have a flat metal or wooden S-shaped piece with an indentation or hook at the ends under the curves of the "S." See ill. (p. 724).

Three types of reed hooks

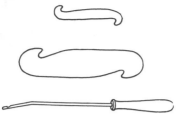

reeding. Weaving. See **sleying.**

reef knot. Lacemaking. Tatting. (Also called square knot.) A single knot, followed by another single knot, reversed. The reef knot is used when a lacer is finishing a section of **lace** or a lace piece; this finishing process is called **typing out.**

In tatting, it is used to **tie off end**s in finishing or when the **shuttle** needs more thread. To make a reef knot with the **bobbin**s, hold them so that you will be working with the butt or tail ends. Work the right-hand bobbin under and over the left, letting it drop through the loop, and tighten up. Then take the right-hand bobbin over and under the other bobbin, up through the loop, and tighten up. Cut off ends. Sometimes it is necessary to make another single knot to secure the ends well before cutting off. The knot is made the same way in tatting, except with the shuttle and thread. See ill.

Reef knot

reef knot. Weaving. See **square knot.**

reel. Kites. A simple stick with the line secured to it may serve as an adequate reel for your kite-flying needs, but you will probably find that a more sophisticated mechanism would make it easier. A simple bobbin cut from a 9–12″ piece of flat lattice and deeply grooved at each end is a big improvement over the stick; a double dowel-handled reel is better yet. The best kite reel, however (other than an elaborate meter-driven power reel), is a good, sturdy, deep-sea-fishing reel attached to a short fishing rod. It makes reeling much easier, and it makes your kite more sensitive to your directional commands. Also see **Kites: Flying.**

Reel, The. Quilts. (Also called Orange Peel, Orange Slices.) Either an **appliqué quilt** design or a **pieced-quilt**

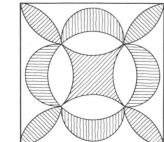

The Reel

design of **scallops** surrounding a circle. The reel design is representative of a once-universal domestic occupation—spinning. It is an old and popular design. See ill.

reel. Spinning. An implement around which spun yarn is wound and measured into a **skein** as it is removed from a **hand spindle** or **spinning wheel.** The first primitive reel was a stick with short arms going across each end. It was held in the hand as the yarn was wound around it. It is still used today and is considered efficient and compact (**a.**). The stick reel developed into the cross reel by turning one arm of the stick reel at right angles to the other. The skein wound around could now be twice the length, usually around two yards. This cross reel is called a niddy noddy, probably due to the characteristic nodding movement made by the spinner as the yarn is being wound around the reel (**b.**). The niddy noddy is also a hand reel with which the left hand grasps the center stick and swings and turns it, usually to the rhythm of a song. The yarn, guided by the right hand, winds over and under the arms at each end. Working with both hands in this manner was still slow, so the next improvement put the arms on a

a. Stick reel

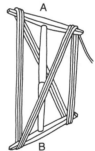

b. Cross reel with skein; arm A is at right angles to arm B

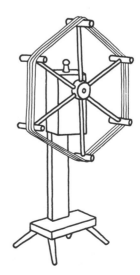

c. Warp reel

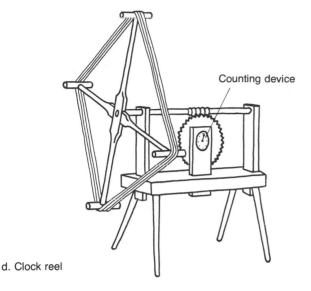

d. Clock reel

base with legs. The warp reel stands on the floor and is turned with one hand (**c.**). There are four or six arms. On the clock reel there is usually a device on the reel that counts the turns which are indicated on a clock. The turn around is 54″ or 72″. When forty turns are wound the wheel makes a loud click (**d.**). See ill. Also see **Spinning**.

reel. Tatting. See **shuttle**.

reel. Toys. A small grooved cylinder or spool for winding a line, cord, or wire. Reels are made of wood, metal, plastic, or cardboard and have many uses in toymaking.

reel. Weaving. See **warping reel**.

reeling. Spinning. See **Spinning**.

reelings. Weaving. Small amounts of yarn put around a piece of paper in order to plan the **warp arrangement**. Reelings can also be small amounts of yarn (used for either **warp** or filling) taken off the **cone** or **spool** for further reference. Also see **warp arrangement**.

refilling the mold. Candlemaking. See **Candlemaking: Refilling the Mold**.

refining. Jewelry. The process of removing impurities from crude metals.

reflection. Gemcutting. Reflection is the throwing back of light from a surface; the angle between the light striking the surface and a perpendicular to the point of contact is equal to the angle between the path of the reflected light and the perpendicular from the point of contact.

The quality of light reflected by a gem is called **luster**. A portion of the light on a transparent gem is absorbed into the stone and refracted. If this absorbed light strikes the back of the gem at a sufficiently oblique angle, it is totally reflected within the stone rather than passing out the back. See ill.

Facets are cuts on gems, particularly in the **brilliant** forms, at proper angles to maximize total reflection of light within the stone. Also see **faceting, refraction**.

Path of light reflected within a gem

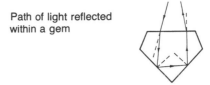

reflector. Stitchery. A small, circular faceted piece of glass set onto a metal base which has prongs extending out in back. By pressing the prongs through a fabric, then bending the prongs inward, the reflectors may be attached to **fabric**. Made originally as a safety device for bicyclists at night, they became popular first for decorating leather jackets, then for all kinds of clothes. They are especially popular, along with **rivet**s, in **funk**y costumes or **underground art**. Plastic and metal reflectors as well as glass reflectors are available in various sizes and in a variety of shapes.

refraction. Gemcutting. Divergence in the direction of light when entering and exiting transparent materials. The ratio between the angle of the light striking a transparent stone in air and the angle to which the light is bent through the stone is called the refractive index. This is a constant for each gem, independent of the angle of the incident light.

The angle the light is bent when passing out of a transparent stone is dependent on the angle at which it strikes the interior surface. If this angle is sufficiently close to perpendicular, the light will be refracted out of the stone. Otherwise, the light will be totally reflected back into the stone. The critical angle is the point of total **reflection**.

Gems with higher refractive indices have lower critical angles and thus less leakage of light. **Faceting** is an attempt to maximize reflection of light from a gem.

Refraction also produces dispersion of light. White light is constituted of the entire spectrum of colors, and each is refracted differently; violet light is refracted more than red light. This causes a widening of the spectrum, so that the colors are seen in narrow bands as in a rainbow. If light is refracted into, reflected within, and refracted out of a stone, this dispersion is increased; this is called the "fire" of a gem.

Some stones have double refraction (also called anisotropic); others have single refraction (also called isotropic). This is determined by the **crystal**line structure of the mineral. Images viewed through a doubly refracting gem are doubled, the separation of the images dependent on the difference in the gem's refractive indices. This is not pertinent to gemcutting, but it is used for identification of materials. Also see **facet**.

refractive index. Gemcutting. See **refraction**.

refractory. Ceramics. Resistant to heat.

refractory. Jewelry. A nonmetallic material that is heat retentive and heat resistant. Refractory materials are used in **kiln** linings or **crucible**s.

refractory material. Ceramics. Glasswork. Metalworking. Any of a number of substances that are resistant to chemical or mechanical change at high temperatures. Such materials include **firebrick, grog** (available commercially), and powdered alumina, magnisite, and silica, which can be added to **casting plaster** when making a mold for **investment casting.** These materials, either in brick form or as formable cement, are commonly used for the linings of furnaces.

register. Silkscreen. In the printing of two or more colors in any printing process, colors that accurately fit, or are positioned in exact relationship to every previous different color, are said to be "in register." Common evidence of bad registration are colors that hang out of the edges of illustrations in magazines. To register colors in silkscreen printing accurately, guides or marks for the positioning of paper stock on the **printing base,** and guide pins or blocks fastened to the base to make certain that the **screen frame** descends to exactly the same position for every print, must be used.

registration. Block Printing. The positioning of the blocks when printing multicolored prints so that the parts of the design are aligned exactly to form the total design. This is done by positioning the block in the same relationship to the edge of the paper for each printing. First, the paper must be cut to a constant size, with one corner, a right angle, to serve as the guide. A register board is made from a sheet of hardwood, with a raised strip called a lay ridge along two sides. The guiding corner of the printing paper will fit into this corner, and the block will be positioned accordingly, near the center of the register board. The position of the block is marked on the board with gummed paper tape, and the blocks are all lined up with this taped angle. The edge of the guiding corner of the paper is laid into the corner ridge of the board and lowered onto the inked block. Thus, the block is always constant in relation to the edge of the paper, and accurate registration is obtained. See ill.

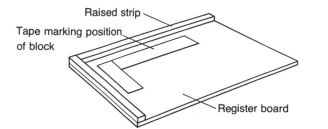

Raised strip

Tape marking position of block

Register board

registration. Fabric Printing. The correct placement or alignment of one **repeat** unit with another. The matching marks on a T-square, table, blocks, or screen frames are called registration marks or guides.

To mark the length of the fabric, make registration marks on a continuous strip of masking tape over the pins that hold the fabric in place along one side of the printing table. Mark the width of the fabric on another strip of masking tape placed along the edge of the T-square. Marks on the block or screen frame will match up with those on the tapes. Place the block or screen on one corner of the fabric, lined up with the tape on the table. Then place the T-square above the block or screen at right angles to the tape, with its head pulled tightly against the table. This marks the place where the first row of designs will be printed. Draw a registration mark with a pencil on the table tape where the edge of the T-square rests across the table to indicate placement of the T-square for the first row. This placement is a beginning for the two sets of guiding marks: the guides for the length of the fabric along the tape on the edge of the table, and the guides for printing across the width of the fabric on the block or screen frame to be lined up with those on the T-square.

To measure for the registration marks along the length of fabric, measure the length of the design unit plus any space to be left between units. This sum is the distance between the registration marks to be made on the tape along the table edge for placement of rows until the end of the fabric is reached. As you begin each new row, move the T-square to the new mark.

To determine placement of the registration marks across the width of the fabric, measure the width of the design plus any space to be left between units. This sum is the distance between the registration marks to be made on the T-square at regular intervals across the fabric width. Make a mark on a small piece of tape on the back of the block or screen frame touching the T-square; this mark will line up with those on the T-square.

Another method of registration, commonly used for silkscreen printing, is a guide rail with adjustable stops. For this method, the screen must be the width of the fabric. A metal guide rail is attached to the side of the printing table, with sliding stops along it. The space between

Registration

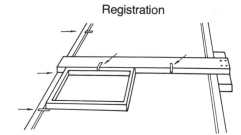

a. Registration guides

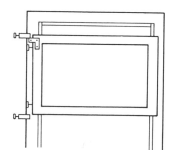

b. Top view of printing table and screen with adjustable stops for registration

the stops can be adjusted and locked to mark the length of the repeat. The screen has screws attached to the side against the guide rail for securing correct placement. See ill. Also see **Fabric Printing: Setting Up a Workshop.**

registration. Stenciling. When stenciling designs with two or more colors, or designs with interlocking shapes requiring more than one stencil, a method must be planned for lining up each stencil identically, so the final design will be exact. A simple method is to use one corner, a right angle, of each stencil as a guiding corner, which fits into an angle formed with masking tape or strips of cardboard on the surface to be decorated. Each stencil is then placed into this corner for printing, and the cut-out design is always in the center of the stencil, so the final design will line up or register.

Other methods may be devised according to the space on which the printing is to be done. Sometimes it is helpful to line up an outer edge of the stencil paper on either a vertical or a horizontal line taped to the surface to be printed. Some prefer to work out a system of pencil dots on the surface, which are lined up with holes punched in the stencil paper. In any case, as long as the cut-out design is placed in a constant relationship to the registration or guiding edge or corner, the designs on each stencil will line up in each step of the printing and result in an exactly coordinated final print. Also see **Stenciling: Designing and Cutting, Printing.**

reglet. Stained Glass. A U-shaped groove in wood or stone into which the finished stained-glass window is set. Also see **fitting, rebate.**

regular laid-in. Weaving. See **laid-in.**

regulator. Metalworking. See **oxyacetylene welding equipment.**

reifentière. Toys. See **turned-wood animal.**

reinforced lead came. Stained Glass. See **lead came.**

reinforcing mat. Plastics. See **glass fiber.**

reinforcing material. Plastics. Materials used to reinforce **laminating** and **casting resins** that not only increase the strength of the resin shell, but also reduce **brittleness,** shrinkage, and warping of the plastic during **curing.** They are usually natural or synthetic fibers, such as **glass fiber, jute, sisal, hemp, burlap, Dacron,** and nylon. The strength of the resin shell is directly influenced by the percentage and arrangement of these fibers throughout the whole. Parallel patterning of strands with each layer of resin and reinforcement alternating the direction of the fibers is the strongest. Right-angle arrangements and random patterns have less strength. Glass fiber has excellent strength and comes in several forms from loose fibers to woven cloth, but is also fairly expensive. Jute, burlap, and hemp have considerable bulk; Dacron and nylon have relatively little. When choosing your reinforcing material consider whether you want a bulky shell or an extremely smooth thin layer. Also see **Plastics: Laminating.**

reinforcing rods. Stained Glass. See **saddle bar.**

release agent. Plastics. See **mold release agent.**

releasing agent. Stained Glass. A mold release brushed onto the inner surface of a mold into which polyester or epoxy resin is to be poured. Its purpose is preventing the resin from sticking to the mold. Also see **dalle-de-verre, slab-glass lampshade.**

relief. Block Printing. A term used to describe shapes that project from the surface, with the background areas cut away.

relief. Stitchery. The projection of forms or shapes from a flat **background.** Some **panels** and **banners** have relief surfaces which result from heavily textured **fabrics** or from quilting or **gathering.** The use of decorative **moldings,** wood knobs, and cut wood shapes add relief to wood surfaces for toys and games. The use of high relief in **stuff**ed or padded work is identified with **soft sculpture.** Relief work falls into three ranges—**bas-relief, mezzo-relief,** and **alto-relief.**

relief carving. Woodworking. See **woodcarving.**

relief color. China and Glass Painting. See **raised paste.**

relief printing. Block Printing. Papercrafts. Any printing technique in which the design areas to be printed protrude from the background to receive the printing ink, and leave the background uninked. Printing blocks can be of various materials, such as wood, linoleum, vegetables, etc.

Although most designs are produced by cutting away parts of a block, relief printing blocks can also be built up. Shapes can be cut from cardboard or wood, and other materials such as **found objects** can be affixed to a background surface of plywood or similar thicknesses for an even print and to prevent the paper's being punctured during printing. Also see **Block Printing: Printing Techniques.**

relief soft art. Stitchery. A combination of **fabric collage** and **quilting, trapunto,** or **padding.** Most **relief** work is basically two dimensional and exploits light and shadow effects. The sculptured or relief surface results from the padding or **stuff**ing which may be added in layers or inserted in portions. Both hand stitching and machine stitching are suitable.

remembrance quilt. Quilts. Any quilt that incorporates the use of signatures, usually in India ink. Sometimes the quiltmakers fill a central **medallion** or **block** with their own names. At other times names are inked around **appliqué** or **pieced** designs. In this way, any quilt pattern can become a remembrance quilt. **Friendship quilt**s and **tithing quilt**s also sometimes have names added in ink.

removing fabric finish. Batik and Tie-dye. A cleansing process used in preparing **fabric** for **batik** and for **tie-dye.** Removing sizing or fabric **finish** makes the fibers receptive to dyes. All new fabrics must be washed in hot water with soap or detergent to remove **glazing,** starch, **sizing,** or those fabric finishes that will dissolve in water. If the fabric is densely woven or heavy, several washings may be required.

Other finishes, such as stain- or water-repellent finish, must be removed because they inhibit **dye penetration.** (**Permanent press** is a permanent resin coating and is not removable.) To remove the dye-resistant finish, soak the fabric for a half-hour in 190° F water to which has been added ½ ounce muriatic acid for every 2 gallons of water. Rinse and wash in detergent before proceeding.

Some water-repellent, wrinkle-resistant, and other finishes can be removed by a similar process of simmering the fabric for thirty minutes in a 190° F solution of ½ ounce hydrochloric acid to 2 gallons of water. Care must be exercised in the handling of the acid.

Because new finishes are continually coming on to the market, sample tests may be required on some fabrics before they are used. Also see **permanent finish, wash and wear** and **Batik and Tie-dye: Fabrics for Dyeing, Preparing the Fabric.**

removing thinner. Silkscreen. A solvent for removing **cut-film stencil**s from the silkscreen so that the **screen frame** and screen can be used for another subject.

removing wax. Batik and Tie-dye. The first step in removing **wax** from the finished **batik fabric** is to simply let any loose pieces fall away. Shaking the fabric will help. If the fabric is cooled by immersion in cold water, the thick areas of wax can be more easily brushed or rubbed off.

There are several possible methods for removing the remaining wax. **Boiling** is one of the simplest for those **dye**s that are **fast** to heat and boiling.

Ironing is especially good if the dye requires that it be **heat set,** as setting the dye and the removal of wax are accomplished at the same time.

Cleaning **solvent**s can also be used to remove wax. If a large container is used, the fabric can be immersed in it and the wax will sink to the bottom. The fluid at the top can be poured off and reused.

The easiest method of removing wax is to take the fabric to a commercial **dry cleaning** establishment. Also see **cleaning fluid.**

Renaissance stitch. Needlepoint. See **Gobelin stitch.**

repair heddle. Weaving. A **heddle** of strong string or cord made directly on the **harness loom** to correct a mistake in **threading.** Special steel heddles for the same purpose can be bought in handweaving supply stores. They snap onto the **harness** in the place where the error is to be corrected. Also see **string heddle.**

repairing the canvas. Needlepoint. To mend a tear, burn, or hole in the **canvas,** cover the canvas with stitches around the hole for a distance of about an inch. Unravel each thread of the damaged canvas and weave back under the worked stitches on the wrong side. Pull some long threads from the raw outside edge of the canvas. First weave under worked stitches on the reverse side using the worked stitches as a guide for the mesh size, and then across the hole, securing the threads on the opposite side of the hole. When this is done you will have a rebuilt area of canvas, and needlepoint can be done over it to repair the design.

For larger repairs, where weaving a new section of the canvas is impractical, cut a piece of the same mesh canvas slightly larger than the hole. Baste this small patch behind the hole and work the needlepoint stitch over the remaining damaged canvas edges. It is recommended that this type of repair be done on an **embroidery frame.**

repairs. Stained Glass. If **lead came**s loosen, the panel should be puttied or cemented again and the leads pressed back down onto the glass.

If a glass shape in a panel gets broken, the lead came should be cut with a **glazing knife** and bent back to remove the broken pieces. Make a **template** by taking stencil paper or cardboard and fitting it into the hole where the piece was. Cut the new piece of glass. Fit the lead back into place; solder, cement, or putty it, and press it back down onto the glass. Also see **cementing** and **Stained Glass: Care and Maintenance of Stained Glass Pieces, Glazing.**

repeat. Fabric Printing. A basic unit of design that recurs at regular intervals. There are various ways of repeating the basic unit to create continuous patterns on the **fabric.** The size of the repeat is determined by the size of the fabric. The repeat unit can be planned so that it is repeated continuously both horizontally and vertically to fill the entire surface. This is called a true repeat. A pattern that is continuous in one direction only can be used as a border or linear pattern. The rhythmic flow of the whole fabric is changed considerably by the arrangement of the repeat. See ill. Also see **Fabric Printing: Designing.**

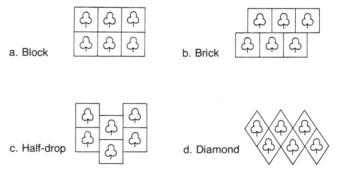

a. Block   b. Brick   c. Half-drop   d. Diamond

repeat. Knitting. (Abbr. rep.) A knitting term designated in a pattern by the phrase "repeat [or rep.] * to *." This indicates that every stitch between the two asterisks is to be repeated in sequence as many times as specified in the pattern. Also see **Knitting: Knitting Terms and Abbreviations.**

repeat. Weaving. A unit of a fabric pattern that is complete in terms of the **ends** and **picks** necessary to weave it. A pattern repeat can be as small as two warp ends or it can be the entire width of the cloth. This is also true of a filling repeat. Its smallest unit is two picks, but it can also be the entire length of what one is weaving. **Drawing-in drafts** and **treadling** patterns do not determine the repeat alone unless the same yarn in the same color is used throughout the **warp** and **filling**. The placement of different yarn colors, textures, and sizes affect the repeat, and placement must be established in conjunction with the drawing-in draft and treadling in order to find the true repeat.

repeat pattern. Batik and Tie-dye. A design in which a unit is used in sequence or repeated in a series or overall pattern. Such a pattern is sometimes designed so that the units interlock or overlap. In **tie-dye,** repeat patterns may result from tying in series or from various **binding methods.** The **batik tjap** is used in repeat prints to produce all-over patterns. Also see **tjap printing.**

repeat pattern. Papercrafts. A traditional papercraft technique of cutting shapes into folded paper to produce many repeated, identical shapes, such as the common paper-doll chain. A long piece of paper is folded in **accordion pleating** with both free ends on the same side (**a.**). The designs are cut into the folds, taking care to leave enough connecting pieces to hold the design together; it is then unfolded (**b.**). See ill.

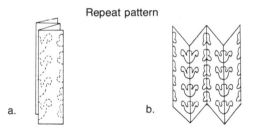

Repeat pattern

a.   b.

repeat * to *. Crochet. (Abbr. rep * to *.) A **pattern** direction indicating that all crochet instructions between two consecutive asterisks are to be repeated as many times as specified.

repetition throwing. Ceramics. The method by which most table and production ware is made. Pieces are checked with **calipers** and a **pot gauge** to make shapes of the same size but not of an absolute uniformity as in industrial work. A sameness in feeling and character is the objective. A whole group of pieces is usually done in one session to establish a rhythm of movement and work.

repoussé. Découpage. A term from the French, meaning "raised up," for a **paper sculpture** technique of pressing parts of a **print** from the back to make raised areas, which are stuffed with **bread-dough clay, French clay,** paper mash, or **silicone caulking** to create a three-dimensional effect. When the stuffed area has dried, the print with raised parts is glued to a flat surface.

Prints used for repoussé should be on sturdy paper. If two identical copies of the same print are available, cut out areas to be raised from one print. Dampen the print with water, place it right-side down on a soft surface, and gently shape the areas to be raised from the back with a modeling tool or spoon. Then fill the areas to be raised with mash or other material, allow to dry, and **glue** the areas to the second print, which has been glued to a flat background.

repoussé. Enameling. A style of enameling in which the **metal** is first worked to achieve the desired shape and then enameled. Ordinarily the metal is hammered from the back on a block of pitch or a sandbag; it may then be reversed and worked from the front, in a technique called chasing, for greater delineation. Also see **basse-taille** and **Enameling: Tools and Materials.**

repoussé. Jewelry. Metalworking. A process in which **sheet metal** is placed in **pitch** and worked from the back with **punch**es of different shapes and functions. The punches are struck repeatedly with a **repoussé hammer** to create low or high relief decoration in the metal. An asymmetrical design will be reversed in the finished work. The repoussé process is usually followed by **chasing,** which clarifies and defines the repoussé. Also see **annealing, bossing tool, embosser, modeling tool, repoussé tool, sealing wax, tracer.**

repoussé. Leather. See **embossing.**

repoussé hammer. Jewelry. (Also called chasing hammer.) Hammers with steel heads with polished faces in varying diameters up to 1¼″. The wooden handles are made in a specific shape—a thin taper ending in a larger oval, round, or pistol grip. The handle is designed to allow rapid repeated blows to the **chasing** and **repoussé tool**s. The light, bulbous end permits it to bounce off the tools. The face of the hammer is fairly broad, providing a large striking area so that vision is concentrated on the working of the tool on the metal, instead of on the hammer striking the tool. The head of the hammer is hardened so that it will not become dented during proper use. See ill.

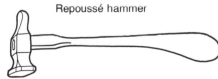

Repoussé hammer

repoussé tool. Jewelry. A variety of punch used to form a relief surface decoration on metal. The punch is hit with a **repoussé hammer.** Repoussé tools and chasing tools can be used interchangeably; however, there are slight differences in their shapes and in the angle in which they are held during working. Repoussé tools tend to have more rounded and blunt working ends and are held nearly upright while being used. Repoussé tools are used from the back, forming a relief surface decoration. Chasing tools have flat working ends with rounded-off edges and corners and are held at more of an angle to the metal being worked. Chasing tools are used to define and shade the front of the metal surface after repoussé. See ill. Also see **bossing tool, embosser, grounder, matting tools, modeling tools, planisher.**

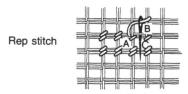

Repoussé (and chasing) tools

repp weave. Weaving. See **rep weave.**

representative. Basketry. See **handle liner.**

rep stitch. Needlepoint. (Also called **Aubusson stitch.**) This stitch is worked only on penelope canvas, which has doubled threads. The stitch itself is similar to the **tent stitch,** but it is worked diagonally over one horizontal mesh and crosses the two threads of one vertical mesh. The finished effect is that of double rows of small slanting stitches. See ill.

Rep stitch

reptile skin. Leather. See **alligator skin, lizard skin.**

rep weave. Weaving. (Also called repp weave.) A horizontal or **warp-faced** rib in a fabric that is based on a **plain weave** derivative construction. It has on occasion a large **rib** alternating with a small one. This formation is due to using a very heavy **filling** yarn followed by a fine one. The fabric can also be different colors on each side if the **warp** is planned as two alternating colors and if the **sett** is very close. See ill. Also see **rib weave.**

Rep weave draft

Resartglas. Plastics. See **acrylic.**

résau. Lacemaking. See **ground.**

resaw. Gemcutting. See **slabbing saw.**

residual clay. Ceramics. See **Ceramics: Clay.**

residual stress. Jewelry. Metalworking. Pressure formed in metal caused by rapid heating and cooling or by not working and hammering a cold piece of metal evenly. This may cause a metal object to come apart at the seams when **welding** or to distort or crack when **raising.** Avoid this by **tack welding** a seam before **running a bead** and by thoroughly preheating the general area to be welded before the molten welding **puddle** is formed. When raising a form, be sure to rotate the metal as you work and hammer all areas with the same thoroughness and intensity. Also see **cold forging.**

resin. Plastics. A liquid plastic used for laminating or **casting.** Resin is composed of giant molecules called **polymers. Catalysts** are added to resins to produce a chemical reaction called **wiring,** which changes the liquid into a solid form.

resin-metal casting. Plastics. (Also called cold-metal casting, epoxy-metal casting.) The process of casting with metal powder mixed into the surface coat of **resin.** It is used as a substitute for casting objects in **bronze** or other metals and may be used for outdoor sculpture. **Epoxy** resins are stronger, although **polyester** resins can also be used with specially prepared metal powders of **aluminum, brass, bronze, copper, tin, iron, lead,** or **silver.** The metal-resin mixture can also be made thicker (to the consistency of putty) by adding more **fillers, thixotropic** agents, and metal powder. It can then be shaped by hand or with modeling tools and knives, and left to harden on a sheet of **polyethylene,** which will not stick to it.

The following is an example of one epoxy-metal casting procedure. Other methods and plastic formulas may be evolved to suit varying requirements for strength and color, for example, using **lamination** techniques with **reinforcing material** between layers of resin under the **gel coat.** Try test mixtures before mixing a large batch.

Mix together equal parts by volume of epoxy resin and metal powder. (Six parts by weight of bronze powder to one part resin has also been recommended.) A thinner (also called a reactive dilutant) may be added to the resin. The thinner the resin, the more metal may be added, but the resin will weaken in strength.

Add a thixotropic agent, such as asbestos, to bring the mixture to a consistency which will not drip or run off the vertical sides of the mold.

Increase the normal amount of **catalyst** from 1% or 2% to between 2% and 4%, except when using **aluminum** powder, which needs just a little more than 1%. Measure the catalyst only according to the weight of the resin without metal and other fillers. Stir the mixture thoroughly.

Smear this resin-metal mixture into the mold. If the object to be cast is large you may have to build up the resin layers in each part of the mold by hand and then fit the pieces together after the plastic has cured. If the mold is small enough to be easily handled and rotated, you may put the pieces together and bind the mold closed with twine or rubber bands, before the gel coat of resin and metal has cured. Pour warm dry sand (about 100° F) into the mold to absorb excess resin and to help cure the resin more rapidly. Let the shell harden. Pour out loose sand and then pour catalyzed resin without metal into the still-closed mold. Rotate the mold so that the resin covers all the surfaces. Pour out the excess resin and repeat the warm-sand pouring. Let it cure. Repeat the resin and then the sand pouring a third time to build up a thick enough shell. Let the whole piece cure in the mold overnight at a temperature of about 125° F, or for several days if left at room temperature. Then remove from the mold.

FINISHING Do not try to chemically patina aluminum unless you have at least 10% **lead** in the metal mixture. Use organic acids such as **hydrochloric acid;** mineral acids will damage the surface. Brass powder can be colored by acid if there is copper or lead added to it.

resinous luster. Gemcutting. See **luster.**

resin removal. Depending on the specific nature of the material, resins and gums may be dissolved with one or more of the following solvents: turpentine, benzine, kerosene, carbon tetrachloride, 95% ethyl alcohol, ethyl ether, carbon disulfide.

resin resist. Batik and Tie-dye. See **cold resin resist.**

resist. Batik and Tie-dye. (Also called fabric resist.) A method of fabric design in which areas of the material are made resistant to **dye** before dyeing the fabric. **Tie-dye** and **batik** are two of the best-known resist techniques. In tie-dye the fabric is made to resist the dye by various **binding, knotting,** or tying techniques that prohibit the dye from penetrating the fabric completely. In batik, **wax** or **paste** is used to block off or close areas of the fabric and to inhibit **dye penetration.**

resist. Enameling. (Also called hard ground.) A protective coating painted on metal to protect areas from the erosive action of **etching.** When **electroplating** and **electroetching,** the resist is called stop-out.

Asphaltum is a black varnish composed of pitch from coal that is used as a resist with nitric and sulfuric acids. It is painted with a **camel's hair brush** onto the areas which are to be protected, for example, the raised areas in **champlevé.** The back and edges of the piece should also be coated. If lines are to be incised with a **scriber** or a knife, this should be done while the asphaltum is only partly dry, as it becomes brittle when thoroughly dry (about one hour). It is cleaned with petroleum solvents, such as benzine. The **metal** surface should be clean before applying resist.

One authority suggests compounding a hard ground for etching composed of one part yellow beeswax, one part asphaltum powder, and one-half part resin, diluted with benzine. Each is liquefied separately in a double boiler, and then they are mixed together.

Nail polish may also be used as a resist; lacquer thinner is its solvent. Beeswax is used as a resist when etching with hydrofluoric acid.

resist. Jewelry. A material that prevents acid from attacking metals, used in the **etching** process. There are a number of types of resists. Two are listed with their usages below.

ASPHALTUM VARNISH Probably the most traditional resist used. The metal to be coated with this must be absolutely grease-free. This can be achieved by **pickling** the metal. After it has been rinsed and dried, the asphaltum is painted on the back and edges of the metal and allowed to dry completely. This can take anywhere from six to twelve hours. Asphaltum drying can be hurried along by placing the work under an infrared heat lamp. However, as asphaltum is basically a form of tar, it may run or remain tacky if the work is placed too close to the lamp. Patience and air do the best job. If any brown areas appear—asphaltum is coal black—it means that the asphaltum layer is too thin and the acid will go through it. The piece must have another coat. When it has dried, coat the top surface and once again allow to dry. The design can then be scratched through the asphaltum with an **etching needle,** exposing the metal. As with all techniques, it is a good idea to make a small test the first time. Different thicknesses of asphaltum act differently when scratched through, and different ways of scratching make different lines. Asphaltum can chip; if it is applied too thickly, it can lift while in the acid solution, causing etching in undesirable areas. After the etching process is completed, remove the asphaltum with turpentine and a soft cloth.

BEESWAX Again the metal must be absolutely grease-free before applying beeswax. The beeswax is heated and melted in a pan. Do not overheat it, as it will first smoke and then catch fire. The liquid wax can be applied with a brush on warm metal. Warming the metal allows the beeswax to go on more evenly; otherwise it chills instantly and goes on too thickly. Warmed metal can also be dipped into the pan of wax, although this of course requires a lot of wax. After the wax has cooled, hold it above a candle to coat it with a film of carbon. In this way you can see the design better while engraving, because of the contrast between the black and the metal. After etching, beeswax can be removed with acetone, carbon tetrachloride, or a paste made with whiting and ammonia, after the larger amount of wax has first been removed by heating the work and wiping with a soft cloth.

If you heat beeswax—or any other wax—in a pan and it cools, before reheating, take a pencil or nail and make a number of holes that go all the way to the bottom of the pan. Wax melts first where it is the hottest, i.e., at the bottom. Pressure can build up while the top is still solid and the hotter wax can explode through the crust of cooler wax like a volcano.

Asphaltum is easier to work with than beeswax, although the drying period is long. It is also easier to clean off. Also see **intaglio, sandblasting, waterbreak.**

resist method. Ceramics. Techniques of decoration that involve blocking out areas of the design with something that will resist the **slip, glaze,** or colorant which is applied over it. Painted-on wax or latex, cut-out paper shapes, or leaves can be used as the resist. The completed object will show the natural **clay body** in the areas covered by the resist (which is burned away in firing, or peeled off before), and show the colorant or glaze on the other areas.

Paper resist works well with slip; cut-out paper shapes may be simply wetted and applied to the surface immediately before brushing on the slip. Obviously, a large cutout cannot be used on a tightly curved surface.

Wax resist is traditional—melted beeswax or paraffin is brushed on for the design; when it solidifies, the glaze is painted or sprayed over. Since wax is highly flammable, caution must be used in melting it. However, water-soluble wax emulsions are now available, and eliminate that hazard. The wax burns off safely in firing.

Latex resist is a special water-soluble preparation which is used cold and can be peeled off before firing or fired away. The technique and results are similar to wax resist; an advantage is that brushes used for latex resist can be cleaned in water.

resist patterns. Fabric Printing. Designs produced on **fabric** by protecting certain areas before dyeing with a substance such as wax so that those areas will resist the dye and remain the original color of the cloth. Various methods, such as direct painting, **block printing, stamping,** and so on, may be used for application of the resist substance.

resist process. Quilts. See **blue resist quilt.**

resorcinol. Woodworking. See **adhesives.**

respirator. Enameling. See **Enameling: Safety Precautions.**

ressort. Weaving. See **crapaud.**

retaining dam. Plastics. A surrounding wall to contain liquid **resin** before it **gels** when the resin is poured onto a flat surface and not into a **mold.** It may be made of weather stripping, **masking tape, modeling compound,** or other plastic.

retarding agent. Plastics. See **inhibitor.**

reticella. Lacemaking. An Italian lace that flourished from the end of the fifteenth century through the beginning of the seventeenth century. Apparently, it developed from the embroidery lace known as **cutwork.** The first mention of cutwork dates from the twelfth century. From the fifteenth to the seventeenth century, reticella was universally done, especially by ladies of high birth. The pattern books of that time, like the ones by Vinciolo published in 1587, show the geometric designs so characteristic of reticella.

Reticella is made in the same manner as other **needle lace**s. Place a double layer of cloth on a paper pattern; work a structure of threads back and forth in a geometric pattern. Work **buttonhole** and **overcast stitch**es on the thread structure, ornamenting with **picot**s, but solid, not open as in **bobbin** lace and **Carrickmacross.**

reticulation. Jewelry. A decorative method used to create a rippled effect on a specific **alloy** of **silver** and **copper,** 14K yellow gold, and sterling silver. The alloys are prepared and treated with a **torch,** causing ripples and undulations on the surface of the metal. This texture can be either shallow or deep. With practice, some extremely controlled patterning, although all with the same basic wavelike characteristics, can be accomplished. Since the technique of reticulation is being used more now than in past years, some metal supply houses are stocking reticulation silver, referred to by numbers that show the amounts of metal which make up the alloy (e.g., 830/1000 fine). This alloy will produce a superior reticulated surface. The method used for 14K yellow gold is different from the one described below.

Use a piece of sterling silver sheet metal at least 18-**gauge** and at least $1'' \times 2''$. To prepare the sterling, heat the metal without **flux** until it reaches **annealing** temperature, just prior to the beginning of a deep red color if done in a dimmed room. The metal will turn black from **firescale. Pickle** the metal in **Sparex #2** or sulfuric acid, 1 part acid to 2 parts water. The pickle will dissolve the copper and the silver oxides that have developed on the surface. Do not touch the surface of the metal with fingers or sharp tools from this point until the work is completed. After the piece is dried, heat again in the same way. This time the silver will remain white in color. Pickle. Repeat this a minimum of three times; five or six is even better. What is happening is precisely what happens when preparing for a **Swedish finish**—a thin layer of fine silver (pure silver) is being developed on the upper surface of the metal. The piece of metal is still sterling silver inside, but now it has a thin film of fine silver on its surface. Fine silver melts at 1751° F and sterling silver melts at 1640° F. When you later heat it with the torch, the temperature of the metal will be raised to the point where the sterling inside becomes molten, but the thin skin of fine silver will still be firm. The molten metal inside causes the fine silver skin to ripple, producing reticulation on the surface.

After the metal has been prepared in the above fashion, heat an **asbestos pad** so that there are no moisture or bonding agents left in it. While it is still warm, place the prepared metal on the asbestos. With the torch begin heating the metal with a **flame** that is slightly less sharp than a needle flame. Heat the metal in an area that is no larger than the flame. When the metal begins to show signs of collapse, adjust the torch so that there is more oxygen. This increases pressure and slightly pushes the metal. Once this has happened do not stop, but work back and forth across the metal from left to right. Move down the width of the flame and continue from right to left, and so on, back and forth down the full length of the metal. Be careful not to burn a hole through the metal, which is very hot.

The pattern of the reticulation can be varied considerably depending on how closely you use the flame, the different directions in which the flame is pointed, and how many times you work up and down the full length of the metal. Repeat the same pattern with the flame each time for maximum effect. When reticulation is completed, pickle the work. The reticulated metal is now ready for use. It can be worked in much the same fashion as sheet metal, although **soldering** is best accomplished along the sawn edge as opposed to the convoluted surface. Also see **Jewelry: Safety Precautions and First Aid.**

retractable steel tape. Woodworking. See **measuring tools.**

retting. Spinning. See **flax.**

reused wool. Spinning. Weaving. See **virgin wool.**

reverse appliqué. Stitchery. A kind of **appliqué** which is accomplished by a procedure that reverses the usual appliqué process. Areas are cut out from **fabric**s which are stacked. This process is more often referred to as **cut-through appliqué,** since the designs are cut through a top layer of fabric to reveal colors beneath.

reverse bezel. Jewelry. A **bezel** soldered to the back of a piece of work surrounding an area that has been cut out of the metal. A gemstone is placed in the bezel, showing through to the front of the work. The bezel is then pushed into position to hold the stone in place. A reverse bezel is used when a bezel on the front of the piece is undesirable for a particular design. Also see **prong setting.**

reverse Calabrian laid-in. Weaving. See **laid-in.**

reverse double half hitch. Macramé. (Also called reverse lark's head.) A basic **mounting knot** used to attach macramé **cord** to the **mounting cord,** or bar. It is like a **double half hitch** but is worked from the outside to the center.

Double the macramé cord and lay the loop end upward under the mounting cord or bar. Bring the loop over the top of the mounting cord and pull the loose cord ends through the loop so that the loop is under the cords. Tighten. See ill. Also see **Macramé: Basic Procedures.**

Reverse double half hitch

reversed tent stitch. Needlepoint. See **kalem stitch, knitting stitch.**

reversed twill. Weaving. See **twill weave.**

reverse flesh side. Leather. The side of a skin revealed by **splitting** away a layer from the flesh side of the **hide.**

reverse glass painting. China and Glass Painting. A technique, popular in the Victorian era, of applying oil paint and tinfoil to the back of a piece of glass, usually in a floral or still-life composition. Working in reverse, the details are applied first, then the larger areas, then the background, building up the composition on the back of the glass. The completed picture, which was viewed from the front of the glass, was then protected with a coat of varnish over the back.

reverse method. Mosaics. See **indirect method.**

reverse pairing. Basketry. A **round** of weaving often used to counteract the normal bending or twisting of **stake**s in the direction of the weave. It is similar to **pairing** except that the weaves are brought to the back of the work. The active **weaver,** coming from behind the first stake, passes (over the second weaver) in front of the second stake and returns to the back. In each **stroke** the active weaver must pass over the idle one. See ill.

Reverse pairing

reverse stitch. Knitting. Another name for the basic **purl** stitch. Also see **Knitting: Basic Procedures.**

reverse stocking stitch. Knitting. See **stocking stitch.**

reverse tracing. Rugmaking. See **transferring designs.**

reverse waling. Basketry. This **wicker weave** is made the same way as regular **waling,** except that each **weaver** in sequence passes under the others. It is used to balance or to give a mirror image to the regular waling as a part of **chain waling.**

reverse work. Tatting. (abbr. rw.) In tatting, the crest or rounded part of the **ring** or **chain** just completed faces upward. When going from a ring to a chain, or a chain to a ring, reverse the work before going on to the next **motif;** that is, turn the **lace** upside-down, do the next motif, and again reverse the work. See ill. Also see **insertion.**

Rings and chains with two shuttles

reversible doll. Toys. See **topsy-turvy doll.**

revolving punch. Leather. (Also called rotary punch.) A plierlike tool with a set of interchangeable sharp, hollow tubes (much like a paper punch) on a revolving barrel for punching six different sizes of round holes in lightweight leather in preparation for **lacing,** inserting **eyelet**s, **snap**s, **rivet**s, belt buckle tongues, etc. Place the leather flesh-side down with the center tooth, or tube, over the spot to be punched. Squeeze the handle while holding the leather steady. See ill. Also see **drive punch, punch, single tube**

Revolving punch

spring punch and Leatherwork: Tools and Materials, Care and Maintenance of Tools, Sewing Leather.

rheostat. Ceramics. Enameling. Stained Glass. A device that adjusts the flow of electricity to the **kiln** and controls the heat in the **firing chamber.** When the rheostat is turned up, less heat is transmitted to the kiln. Also see **glass drill.**

rheostat. Enameling. See **electroplating.**

rhodochrosite. Gemcutting. Magnesium carbonate with **hardness** of 3½–4½, **specific gravity** of 3.45–3.6, and refractive indices of 1.6 and 1.8. It is transparent and red-orange in color. Recommended treatment is **sanding** with 1,200 grit silicon carbide **abrasive** on leather or with 14,000 grit diamond powder on wood and **polishing** with cerium oxide on a felt buff. Also see **Gemcutting: Hand Grinding and Polishing, Rough Shaping.**

rhodolite. Gemcutting. See **garnet.**

rhodonite. Gemcutting. A manganese silicate of the **pyroxene** group **crystal**lized in the triclinic system. It has **hardness** of 5½, **specific gravity** of 3.53, refractive indices of 1.733 and 1.744, and black-veined pink or ruby-red **color.** It is carved by hand into novelty forms and polished with cerium oxide on leather. **Facet**ed gems are polished with tin oxide on a tin **lap.** Fowlerite is a variety of rhodonite found in New Jersey. Also see **faceting, polishing, refraction.**

rhodozite. Gemcutting. A gem **faceting** material with **hardness** of 8, **specific gravity** of 3.4, and refractive index of 1.69. Rhodozite is transparent and occurs in rose, green, or yellow varieties. The recommended angle for main crown and pavillion **facet**s is 40°. **Polishing** is done with Linde A on a tin-type **lap.** Also see **faceting, polishing, refraction.**

rhythm. Weaving. The sequence of movements made during **floor loom** weaving. Although it exists to some extent, or it can be built up, in weaving on other types of looms, it primarily is associated with stepping on the **treadles** to open the **shed,** throwing and catching the **shuttle,** and beating down with the **beater** on a floor **harness loom.** These functional actions make for a graceful body movement and, besides being one of the pleasures associated with weaving on this type of loom, allow for speed and result in a fabric that is of an even quality throughout. Each weaver develops his or her own rhythm. However, it is presupposed that the closing and opening of sheds is done in one movement without fumbling and the beat comes at the time the first shed is closing and the next one opening.

rib. Ceramics. A tool made of metal, plastic, or wood that is used for smoothing while **throwing** on a **potter's wheel.** The name derives from early potters using bones for this purpose. See ill.

Using a rib

rib. Weaving. (Also called **cord, rep.**) A straight, narrow, raised effect in a fabric running the total width of the **filling** or the total length of the **warp.** The rib effect is achieved through specific weaves, thick yarn or groupings of yarn in the filling or warp, cramming warp **ends** in the **reed,** or **stuffer thread**s. Also see **Bedford Cord, piqué, rep weave, rib weave.**

ribbed pattern. Knitting. See **Knitting: Construction.**

ribbed single crochet. Crochet. A stitch created in the same way as **single crochet,** except that the hook is only passed through either the front of the loop or the back of the loop of the previous **row** when working every row. This creates a strong horizontal rib in the crocheted fabric.

ribbing. Knitting. A vertical ribbed effect, created by alternating the **knit** and **purl** stitches in sequence. Each **stitch** must be kept vertically above its kind, and this is done by knitting—with an even number of stitches—in such a way that a stitch that is knit on the **front of knitting** side will be purled when worked from the **back of knitting** side. A narrow rib pattern (Row 1: * K 1, P 1 *; Row 2: * P 1, K 1 *) will make a thinly ribbed elastic (or stretchable) fabric. A broader ribbed pattern (K 3, P 3 in the above fashion) will have the look of definite vertical stripes. Also see **Knitting: Construction.**

ribbon. Embroidery. Work done on satin with fine narrow ribbons specially made for embroidery. The ribbons were stitched loosely to give an effect of relief, and the embroidery was sometimes enriched with gold metallic threads. Ribbon embroidery was extremely popular in the nineteenth century in Europe and America.

ribbon. Macrame. Ribbon may be used in place of more standard types of macramé **cord** and can be very effective when used as fringes on clothing or sashes. However, it is more decorative than durable and should be used appropriately. Also see **Macramé: Tools and Materials.**

ribbon. Stitchery. A narrow strip of **fabric** which is woven so that each edge is finished with a very narrow **selvage.** **Silk, rayon,** and **velveteen** are commonly used for ribbons made in a wide range of sizes and patterns.

ribbon doll. Toys. A **flat doll** made up from ribbons of various widths, patterns, and colors. Because ribbons have finished, or selvage, edges, only a top stitch or tack stitch is required to join them. Some ribbon dolls are partially stuffed; others are made in part from fabric-covered cotton cord, as are **string dolls**.

ribbon holes. Knitting. (Also called slots.) These are small openings in a piece of knit fabric through which a ribbon or a drawstring can be threaded. They are created by using the **over principle.** To make a row of ribbon holes:
Row 1: K 2, * yo, K 2 tog *, K 2. Repeat * to * to end of row.
Row 2: Purl, using each extra loop made in previous row by the yarn overs.

rib-rand. Basketry. (Also called Japanese weave.) A **weave** in **woven basketry** using one **weaver.** The **stroke** is made by coming in front of two **stake**s and in back of one. The total number of **spoke**s should not be divisible by three.

rib weave. Weaving. Simple weave construction producing a horizontal or vertical rib in a fabric. Horizontal rib effects are also known as **rep** (repp) **weave**s. Rib weaves are derivatives of **plain weave** using half-**basket weave**s as well as combinations of basket and plain weave. The fabrics can be used in apparel, but their bulk and weight make them more suitable for upholstery or rugs. These weave structures have been used in **wall hanging**s which give an op art look. See ill. Also see **group thread.**

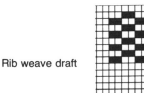
Rib weave draft

rice paper. Kites. A fine, delicate paper made from rice grass, often used in the Far East as a **covering** material for kites. Because of its fragile nature, it is recommended that a relatively heavy grade be used. Also see **Kites: Tools and Materials.**

rice stitch. Needlepoint. (Also called crossed corner stitch, William and Mary stitch.) A group of stitches in which one large cross is first worked over an even number (at least four) of mesh. Small **cross stitch**es are placed at the tops of each arm of the longer cross and meet at the corners. It is good as a **border stitch** background or **filling stitch.** See ill.

Richelieu. Embroidery. See **whitework.**

rickrack. Quilts. See **border.**

rick-rack. Stitchery. A ready-made decorative **edging** which has a zigzag or **sawtooth** pattern. The rick-rack has finished or **selvage** edges, like a braid or **ribbon,** so that it can be stitched directly on top of a **fabric.** Commercially manufactured rick-racks come in a variety of widths and colors, usually of **cotton.**

ricolite. Gemcutting. See **serpentine.**

riddle. Metalworking. See **sandcasting molding equipment.**

Riddles. Weaving. See **cross weave.**

riddling. Metalworking. The process of sifting **molding sand** into a **sandcasting flask.** Riddling rids the molding sand of any lumps and large particles that would prevent obtaining a sharply detailed cast of your **pattern** in the sand **mold.**

ridge stitch. Crochet. See **Crochet: Patterns.**

riding toy. Toys. A toy on which a child can sit and create movement. The stick horse, or **hobbyhorse, spring horse, rocking horse,** and **swing** are all riding toys. A coaster **wagon** or any similar large-wheeled toy is a riding toy. All require a certain force or impetus on the part of the child or other person.

riffle file. Jewelry. See **riffler.**

riffler. Jewelry. (Also called riffle file.) A **file** with specially shaped ends and blades that is able to reach into areas that are not accessible with ordinary straight or **needle files.** They are available in several sizes and from #0−#6 cut. See ill.

Rice stitch

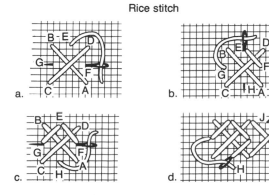

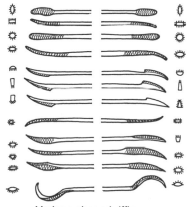
Various shaped rifflers

riffler. Woodworking. See **rasp.**

rigato. Jewelry. See **liner.**

rigger. Stained Glass. See **brush.**

right half-hitch. Tatting. The second part of the **double stitch** in tatting. A reversed forming of the first half of the double stitch. Also see **half-hitch, making the double stitch.**

right-hand twill. Weaving. See **twill weave.**

right-hand weaver. Basketry. The **weaver** the farthest to the right of all other weavers in weaving a given stitch. The term is therefore used primarily when giving directions on how to make a specific **weave.**

right side. Knitting. (Also called front of knitting side.) The side of the knitting designed to be on view.

right side of fabric. Stitchery. The top or outer part of the **fabric,** meant to be seen. In a **velvet, flannel, velveteen,** or **corduroy** this is very obviously the side that has the **pile** or **nap.** On **brocade**s or woven patterns it is the side on which the designs show clearly. In printed fabrics, the right side has a brighter, more clearly printed pattern. Some fabrics such as **muslin, broadcloth,** woven plaids or stripes, and **felt** can be used either way.

rigid heddle. Weaving. A frame constructed in one piece with a comb inside made of either metal or wood. The comb consists of slats each with a hole in the center and a space or slit between the slats. The **warp** is threaded alternately through a hole and then the adjacent slit. The rigid heddle is not hung as a **harness** is but is suspended on the **warp end**s, and manipulated by hand. By pulling the heddle frame up, the warp ends in the holes are lifted and one **shed** is produced. By pushing down, the ends in the slits rise up and the alternate shed is formed. The comb also functions as a **beater.** The rigid heddle makes weaving easier when it is used in place of a **heddle rod** or stick on a backstrap or similar type of loom without harnesses. The loom is easily collapsible and can be stored in a very small space with the work still in progress. Most rigid heddles come up to a width of 20″ so that only narrow fabrics can be woven. The rigid heddle can also be

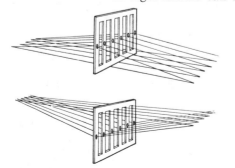

Rigid heddle weaving showing the two sheds possible; warp ends are attached to supports

mounted in a frame structure as a noncollapsible loom. It is also known as a heddle-reed or a slot and eye heddle. See ill. Also see **backstrap loom, band loom, box loom, harness loom.**

rim. Ceramics. See **Ceramics: Form.**

ring. Crochet. A **chain** that, when joined at the beginning and end with a **slip stitch,** forms a ring, and becomes the foundation for circular **motif**s or **medallion**s. A ring used in this manner would be found at the center of a motif or medallion, and the crochet would be worked from this center out toward the edges. Also see **Crochet: Basic Procedures, Basic Stitches.**

ring. Leather. See **belt finding.**

ring. Tatting. (Abbr. r.) A basic **motif** in tatting made on the **knot bearer** by the **loop thread** and consisting of a series of **double stitch**es. When the required number of stitches are on the loop thread, hold the stitches between the thumb and index finger on the left hand and pull the knot bearer to draw up the loop. When the first and last stitches on the loop thread meet, a ring is formed. This drawing-up procedure is known as closing a ring. When a ring is left open, forming an archlike motif, it is called a **chain.** See ill. Also see **corrections.**

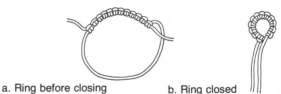

a. Ring before closing   b. Ring closed

ring-and-pin. Toys. An old folk toy that has appeared in many different forms and was a **game** known to the American Indians. It consists of a wood stick, the bottom part of which is a handle. The top is whittled down to make a more slender shaft. A heavy **string** or cord is tied to the handle. At the other end a series of rings is slipped over the string and the end of the string is tied to the last ring. The string with rings is tossed into the air and the pin is used to catch as many of the rings as possible.

It is also a variation of the **spear-the-fish** toy. See ill.

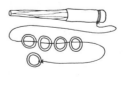

Ring and pin

ring animal. Toys. See **turned-wood animal.**

ring buff. Jewelry. A tapered **felt buff** with a wooden end that fits into the **tapered spindle** of the **buffing machine** and is charged with **buffing compound** and used to polish the inside of a ring. The wooden end is placed on the spindle while the buffing machine is running, otherwise it is difficult to center. Let go of the ring buff the instant it grabs the tapered spindle. If it wobbles after it is caught by the tapered spindle, a wide flat piece of wood, at least as wide as the felt portion is long, can be pressed against the lower third of the ring buff to help center it. To take off the spindle, turn the motor off and, when the rotation stops, unwind the **buff** by hand. Occasionally the ring buff gets so tightly threaded onto the spindle that it is hard to remove. When this happens, move it back and forth firmly toward and then away from you, and then unwind it by hand. If the buffing machine has two shafts, one on either side, you can hold on to the one opposite the ring buff so the shafts will not rotate while you are taking the buff off. If it has only one shaft and the ring buff is on it, take hold of the base of the tapered spindle and twist the ring buff off. See ill. Also see **buffing.**

Felt ring buff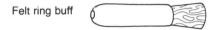

ring clamp. Jewelry. A round tool usually made of hardwood, such as maple, with a bend of metal around its center and a rivet running through its center that acts as a pivot point. There are leather safety pads on the jaws at either end. A wooden wedge is driven in at either end to hold the work at the opposite end of the ring clamp securely. The leather jaws prevent scratching of the work. The tool acts as an extension of the hand and is indispensable for holding small pieces securely while working on them, especially when **filing** and working with **abrasive**s. See ill. Also see **clamp.**

Ring clamp with wedge in position  Wedge

ring hoop. Crewel. Embroidery. See **embroidery frame.**

ring horse. Toys. See **turned-wood animal.**

ring mandrel. Jewelry. A tapered steel rod having sizes marked from 1 to 13 in quarter size steps corresponding to the sizes on a **ring sizer.** The last 3″ or 4″ of the shanks are unmarked and straight and are held in a **vise** while metal is bent around the **mandrel,** usually by striking it with a **rawhide mallet.** Ring mandrels are also manufactured without sizes. See ill.

Sized ring mandrel

ring marker. Knitting. A plastic ring used to separate areas in a pattern or to separate pattern repeats. See ill.

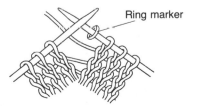

Ring marker

ring pad. Jewelry. A doughnut-shaped felt or leather pad used to support a **pitch bowl** or an **engraver's block.**

ring puzzle. Toys. See **prisoner's lock.**

ring shank. Jewelry. The band on a ring. A wedding ring, although called a band ring, could be considered a shank ring. Also see **carbon ring stick.**

ring-shank nail. Woodworking. See **nail.**

ring sizer. Jewelry. A series of metal rings, marked in half-sizes from 1, the smallest, to 13. The ring sizes are held together in order of progression on a larger circle of metal. They are used to measure the ring size of a finger. The sizes on the ring sizer correspond with the sizes on the **ring mandrel.** As there is more than one system of measurement used, it is wise to check the ring sizer against the **mandrel** to make sure that they use the same system.

Ring sizers come in two widths, one for narrow rings and one for wide rings. The size on the wide ring sizer is ½ size larger than on the narrow ring sizer, to allow for the comfortable bending of the finger in a wide ring. It is not necessary, however, to purchase one sizer for wide and one for narrow rings, as the narrow one will work for both with the following method.

After you have the correct size, determine its equivalent in length in preparation for sawing out the **sheet metal.** To do this, cut or tear a piece of paper the width of the ring you want to make and about 2½″ long. Place the paper's width half on one side and half on the other side of the line that shows the correct ring size. Remember this is for a wide ring, and you will be using the measurement on the mandrel that is one half size larger than the ring size. Wrap the paper tightly around the mandrel, making sure the paper overlaps the line that runs the length of the mandrel. Do not butt the paper against this groove, as it will surely slip, giving an incorrect measurement. When the paper is wrapped tightly around the mandrel, run your thumbnail along the lengthwise groove over the paper. This will produce two embossed lines on the paper. Remove the paper. The distance between the two lines corresponds to the circumference of the mandrel. The lines will be at a slight angle because the mandrel is tapered. Take the measurement in millimeters with a **steel** ruler at the widest part between the

Ring sizer

two lines. To this measurement, add 1 mm plus the measurement in millimeters of the **gauge** you are going to use.

For example, if the size of the ring using a narrow ring sizer is 8, make the ring ½ size larger, or 8½. Following the above formula the distance between the two lines on the piece of paper will be 57 mm plus 1 mm plus gauge. Let us say we are using 18-gauge metal, which is approximately 1 mm thick. The total formula reads: 57 mm plus 1 mm plus 1 mm, which equals 59 mm, or approximately 2⁵⁄₁₆″. See ill. on previous page.

ring stick. Jewelry. A stick of solid aluminum or wood covered with a thin metal sheath marked in size gradations and used to measure ring sizes. It is used for the **forming** process, and is excellent for working **wax** in preparation for **casting**, because of its light weight. Ring sticks that can accurately measure rings that have stones set in them are also available. Also see **ring mandrel, ring sizer.**

ring warp. Weaving. See **continuous warp.**

rinsing. Batik and Tie-dye. A procedure in **tie-dye** that follows each dyeing operation. Rinsing is usually continued until the rinse water remains clear. If several separate **binding**s and dyeings have occurred, a final rinsing may be necessary after the **binding material**s have been removed. The best rinsing is done by immersing the fabric in water. Faucet rinsing does not remove all the excess **dye.**

rip cut. Woodworking. A cut in the direction of the wood grain. It is best made using a ripsaw or a ripping or combination blade on a **power saw** and is usually used to split or divide a board along its length. Also see **Woodworking: Cutting and Sawing.**

ripper. Needlepoint. A sewing tool used in needlepoint for removing stitches. It has a sharp point and a cutting edge. Work should be done slowly in order not to rip the **canvas.**

ripping claw hammer. Woodworking. See **hammer.**

rippling. Plastics. Tiny ripples or waves in the cured **resin** surface caused by high **exotherm** or **curing** without an **air shield.** If maximum transparency without any **distortion** is required, as in the display of **embedment**s, polish the **casting** to remove the rippling.

rippling. Spinning. See **flax.**

ripsaw. Woodworking. See **handsaw.**

riser. Metalworking. A tube inside a metal-**casting** mold that allows the escape of gases and steam when pouring the molten metal. It is often joined to a cavity called a reservoir or shrinkage ball that supplies additional metal to the mold cavity as the metal shrinks. It is usually placed 2–3″ from the **sprue** in **sandcasting.** Its size de-

pends upon the shrinkage rate of the metal being cast—the greater the shrinkage, the larger the riser. Also see **gate** and **Metalworking: Sandcasting.**

riser. Weaving. (Also called raiser.) A **warp end** that rises when the **shed** is opened during weaving, as in the action of a **rising shed loom.** On a **weave draft**, a riser is indicated by a filled or "x"ed-in square and means that a warp end is over a **filling pick.** In reading a weave draft, a riser is called an up.

riser pin. Metalworking. See **sandcasting molding equipment.**

riser sequence. Weaving. See **chain draft.**

rising shed. Weaving. A V-shaped opening in front of the **reed** formed by the raising of some of the **warp** threads when the **harnesses** carrying these warp ends are pulled or pushed up. The raised threads form the top part of the opening with the threads of the bottom part remaining in place against the bottom of the reed. The **shuttle** carrying the **filling** goes through the **shed** opening. A rising shed is found in **jack type looms** and as part of the motion in **countermarch looms.**

Rising Star. Quilts. A **pieced quilt block** that is a **star pattern.** There are several variations of this name. See ill.

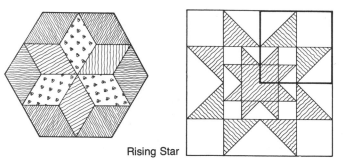

Rising Star

Rising Sun and Princess Feather. Quilts. See **Princess Feather.**

Rit. Batik and Tie-dye. See **household dye.**

rivet. Jewelry. A solid metal rod used to fasten parts together by hammering the ends into heads. Also see **bifurcated rivet, finding, riveting, rivet wire.**

rivet. Leather. (Also called cap rivet, rapid rivet.) A two-piece metal fastener available in several sizes for leather which is permanent (doesn't open and close) for decoration and joining. Rivets are available in different lengths for various thicknesses of leather. The rivet is set in a prepunched hole (punched through both layers of leather, if it is to be used for joining). Lay the rivet post on a pounding board, then put the leather over the post through the prepunched hole (or right sides facing out). Put the cap of the rivet on the post and push down. Strike the cap with a **mallet** or **rivet setter** to set it. See ill. Also see **finding, revolving punch, split rivet** and **Leatherwork: Gluing and Bonding Leather, Tools and Materials.**

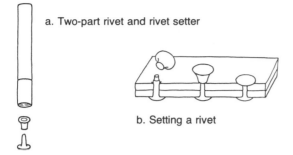

a. Two-part rivet and rivet setter

b. Setting a rivet

rivet. Metalworking. A metal fastener for permanently joining metal sheets or plates. It is a pin or bolt with a head on one end, which is passed through predrilled holes in the materials to be joined, and then hammered at the plain end to form another head.

Small general-purpose rivets are 1–8″ and 3–16″ in diameter. Common shapes are round head, oval head, flat head, and countersunk. They are made of soft **steel, copper** and **aluminum.**

Sheet metal rivets (or tinner's rivets) are commonly made of mild steel and coated with **zinc** or **galvanized**; of **copper**; or of black iron-oxide. Their size is classified by the weight per 1000 rivets and they all have flat heads. Use a **punch** to make the holes in the **sheet metal** to receive the rivet.

Large rivets must be preheated to red hot, but small ones are hammered in cold. Almost all rivets can be used with a rivet set or a riveting block or plate, which is a piece of metal with indentations into which the rivet head fits while the rivet is being hammered. See ill. Also see **riveting.**

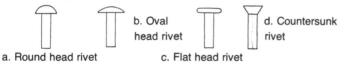

a. Round head rivet   b. Oval head rivet   c. Flat head rivet   d. Countersunk rivet

rivet. Stitchery. (Also called decorative rivet.) A flat, shiny decorative metal piece made in such a way that it can be applied to **fabric.** It has a narrow shaft on the back which is forced through a tiny hole in the fabric. By hammering or pounding the shaft, which has been slit, the metal is forced to spread so that the rivet is held in place.

Rivets are made in a great variety of shapes, sizes, and surfaces, and are used in much the same way as reflectors in decorating body **covering**s or clothes.

rivet hammer. Jewelry. A lightweight hammer with a slightly concave face used to round out the **rivet** heads. See ill. Also see **riveting.**

Rivet hammer

riveting. Jewelry. A procedure by which two or more pieces of metal are fastened together with the use of **rivet**s. A rivet can also be used as a decorative element, whether it is used to hold metal pieces together or just goes through one piece of metal, or to hold a pinstem in a **joint.**

To make a rivet to hold two pieces of metal together, place the two pieces of metal together and measure their combined thicknesses. This can be a visual measurement; a steel rule need not be used. Take a length of round wire and hold it securely in a **ring clamp** or a **pin vise,** or just support it securely against the **bench pin** or **bench.** File the end of the wire so that it is absolutely flat and square to the sides of the wire. Take the filed wire out of the holding device if you have used one and hold it up next to the two pieces of metal that you are going to rivet together. Allow the filed end of the wire to extend above the metal approximately 1 mm. Position your fingers so that you're holding the wire about 1 mm below the bottom of the metal and clip with cutting pliers; or, holding your fingernail at the spot on the wire as a marker, saw the wire off at this point. If you clip it the end will have to be straightened with a file. If you saw it, it will be straighter already. Carefully file the freshly cut end of the wire so that it is absolutely flat. It is extremely important that the drill bit you use to drill through the two pieces of metal be precisely the same diameter as the wire rivet. There are two ways to determine this: by using a **drill and wire gauge,** or by drilling a hole through a piece of wood, filing one end of the wire flat and inserting it through the hole from the bottom, bringing it to the top of the wood. In this way you can see if it is an exact fit. After you have determined the correct size bit, and prior to drilling the metal, make sure the metal is held securely together. One method is to tape the piece tightly with masking tape, making sure you don't cover the areas to be drilled. **Center punch** the metal, and drill. Insert the rivet.

It should be **anneal**ed, but **fluxing** and **quench**ing are not necessary. Position the rivet and metal over a **steel block,** with the rivet touching the block and extending an equal distance from both the top and bottom of the metal (**a.**). Using a **rivet hammer,** tap the top of the wire lightly until it begins to form the rivet head. Because the rivet is being supported on the steel block, it will also, although more slowly, be forming a rivet head on the bottom (**b.**). When the rivet is partially formed, turn the metal over and work from the other side, reversing several times until both rivet heads are formed. See ill. on next page.

When finishing the head of the rivet, take care not to mar the surrounding metal with the rivet hammer. If the wire is smaller than the hole, or if the rivet wire is too long, it will bend during the forming of the rivet heads and shear off. If the wire is too short, you will not have enough metal to form a rivet.

Another way of forming a rivet is to form one head of the rivet by holding the wire in a pin vise inserted through the hole. Place the rivet head against the steel block and form the other head of the rivet. Also see **beeswax, findings, rivet set.**

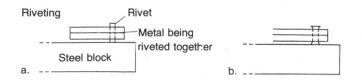

Riveting

Rivet

Metal being
riveted together

Steel block

a.

b.

riveting. Metalworking. The process of installing a **rivet.** To do so, mark the holes to be drilled on the metal and **center punch** these spots. Drill the hole using a **twist drill bit** with the same diameter as the rivet. **Countersink** the holes if you desire, the heads to be flush with the surface. Cut the rivet to size with a saw or clippers so that it is long enough to pass through both pieces and extend out a distance of 1½ times the diameter of the rivet. Press the rivet into the hole, head first. Back the rivet head with a rivet set that has a depression that corresponds to the rivet size. Hammer the headless end flat, to fill up the hole, and then round it if desired. See ill.

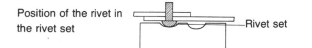

Position of the rivet in
the rivet set

Rivet set

rivet joint. Toys. A **joint** made by inserting a rivet through holes in each of the parts to be jointed and hammering the unflattened end to force it into a head. When used to add arms and legs to a **doll body** in **dollmaking,** a rivet joint allows for movement. Holes made in a **fabric doll** must be reinforced in some way before the metal rivet is inserted.

rivet set. Jewelry. A form of **punch** with a smooth, concave working end used to produce a rounded and polished rivet head. Place rivet set over a partially formed rivet head and strike lightly with a **ball peen hammer** while rotating the rivet set.

rivet set. Metalworking. See **rivet, riveting.**

rivet setter. Leather. A tool for inserting **rivet**s; it has a concave end to prevent the rivet from being scratched when set.

rivet wire. Jewelry. Nickel-silver wire used to hold **findings** for **joint**s or hinges. The procedure is the same as for all **riveting.** Do not hammer the rivet wire to a snug fit because this will hamper movement of the joint. Rivet wire is available in bundles and packages of assorted B & S wire **gauge** sizes. Also see **bifurcated rivet, rivet.**

Road to California. Quilts. See **Burgoyne Surrounded.**

Robbing Peter to Pay Paul. Quilts. An arrangement that occurs in some **block pattern**s in which each **block** design is completed by the design in the adjacent block. One block is "robbed" to "pay off," or finish, the design of another. **Lafayette Orange Peel** is a good example of Robbing Peter to Pay Paul, as is a variation called **Drunkard's Path.** See ill. Also see **Falling Timbers, Fans.**

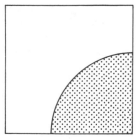

a. Basic patch

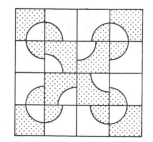

b. Fool's Puzzle

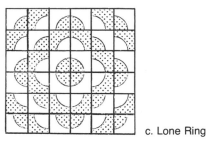

c. Lone Ring

rocaille beads. Beadwork. See **embroidery beads.**

rock crystal. Gemcutting. See **quartz.**

rocking. Puppets. A back-and-forth movement of the **control,** which rocks the **string puppet** in actions that alternate from side to side of the figures. Walking is suggested through a rocking movement of the **leg bar.**

rocking cut. Woodworking. See **whittling.**

rocking doll. Toys. See **Daruma doll, tumble doll.**

rocking horse. Toys. A traditional **toy** of a horse, usually wood, large and strong enough for a small child to ride. The horse is set so that both front and back legs rest on rockers, with the two left legs on one rocker and the right legs on the other. The rocking horse has been a favorite of children for generations; some antique examples were elaborately carved and painted.

Sometimes the name "rocking horse" is used to refer to any small toy animal that rocks. Recent rocking toys, or **bouncing horse**s, may be suspended from **springs** and are usually molded of plastic.

While this toy is sometimes called a **hobbyhorse,** that name also refers to a stick horse. See ill. Also see **chair rocking horse, riding toy.**

Rocking horse

rocking horse and rider. Toys. A simple **folk toy** that has been found in various parts of the world. It consists of two half-circles set side by side to make rockers, with a horse head at one end and a rider astride the horse. It is a favorite because when the balance is right, the horse and rider, once set in motion, will continue to rock back and forth for a long time.

rocking shoo-fly. Toys. See **chair rocking horse.**

rocking toy. Toys. See **balance toy, rocking horse.**

rock maple. Woodworking. See **maple.**

Rocky Glen. Quilts. (Also called Indian Meadow, Lend and Borrow, Little Sawtooth, Lost Ship.) A **pieced quilt block** made up of **split four-patch**es. Each **patch** has a **sawtooth,** or zigzag, pattern similar to Indian Trail and **Delectable Mountains,** but with a different arrangement of the patches. See ill. Also see **Sawtooth.**

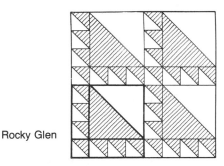

Rocky Glen

Rocky Mountain. Quilts. (Also called Great Divide, New York Beauty, Sunrise.) A very complex **pieced block** used in an **all-over** design. It combines a large circular **sawtooth** form with stars and diagonal bands of very sharp sawtooth.

Rocky Road to California. Quilts. See **Drunkard's Path.**

Rocky Road to Dublin. Quilts. See **Drunkard's Path.**

Rocky Road to Kansas. Quilts. See **Job's Tears.**

rococo stitch. Needlepoint. A beautiful eighteenth-century stitch used for small geometric designs, creating a pattern of small holes over the canvas and especially effective worked in silk or cotton thread. Begin the technique by forcing two holes in the **canvas** (A and B) six threads apart. Work long stitches between A and B and come up in the middle to work small **tacking stitch**es across each long stitch. Repeat six times for one rococo stitch. An entire piece can be effectively worked in this stitch with color changes to form a design.

rod. Basketry. Specifically, a year-old shoot of **willow,** generally the heavier pieces of **cane** or other material used in the framework of a basket.

rod. Metalworking. See **welding rod.**

rod. Puppets. (Also called center rod, central rod.) The main or central part of either the **vertical control** or the **horizontal control.** It is also called the **control bar,** and it is the piece to which **cross bar**s are attached. Also see **vertical rod** and **Puppets: Stringing the Marionette.**

rod. Stitchery. A long cylinder or pole used in hanging **panels** or **banners.** A brass rod offers good weight and, when also used at the bottom of a panel, helps hold the sides even. Wood rods or dowels may be also used and have the advantage of being easily sawed and colored, stained or painted. Various glass, acrylic, and other plastic rods are available in precolored lengths. In selecting a rod for hanging, consideration must be given to the width of the panel, since smaller diameter rods will sag or dip in the center when weight is added. Also see **Stitchery: Finishing.**

rod border. Basketry. See **border** and **Basketry: Woven Basket Construction, Border.**

Rodia, Simon (1879–1965). Mosaics. Simon was an Italian immigrant to the United States who, using only **mortar,** steel rods, an unbelievable assortment of **found-object mosaic** materials, and his own ingenuity, singlehandedly built an amazing complex of towers and walls in Watts, California. The Watts Tower, begun in 1921 as a personal statement of appreciation to America, took 33 years to complete. After much debate, the work of Simon Rodia was declared a cultural monument by the state of California. Also see **Mosaics.**

rod puppet. Puppets. Another name given to either the **stick puppet** or the **flat puppet.** Usually, however, it refers to a special form similar to a **hand puppet** but offering much greater control of the arm movements. The head must be attached to a **dowel** rod approximately 12″ long. It might be padded cloth, stuffed stocking, **Styrofoam, papier mâché,** or wood. Once head and dowel are firmly joined, shoulders are added.

A flat piece of thin **plywood** or heavy cardboard is cut for the shoulders, and a hole is drilled into the flat piece, just larger than the dowel. It is then slipped up over the dowel and held in place with a rubber stopper or a tightly wound rubber band just beneath it. This will make it possible to move the head from side to side without moving the shoulders. **Fabric** or **batting** is used to pad the shoulders. Arms hang loosely at the sides and a tape will attach the wood or stuffed hand to the shoulder. A weight is needed at the elbow.

Finally a means of controlling the figure must be added. For the hands it may consist of two wires, one from each hand, which go down to the base. Bicycle spokes are made of wire of just about the right weight. The stick for controlling the body may be short so that the hand holding the stick is concealed under the puppet's costume. The wires for the hands, however, should be kept long so that the hands of the **puppeteer** are out of sight. The rod puppet can be made with many variations. Animals can be controlled by either 1 or 2 dowel rods, with the wire controls going to other movable parts. Also see **shadow play, shadow puppet.**

rods. Weaving. See **lease sticks.**

rolag. Spinning. **Sliver** that has been rolled up from the **carder** after **carding.** It is literally "air rolled in wool." See ill.

Rolag

rölakan. Rugmaking. Weaving. A traditional Scandinavian weft-interlock **tapestry** technique that is used mainly for **flatweave rugs** and **wall hangings.** To a lesser extent it is found in pillows and upholstery. It is a **filling-face** weave with the various fillings that make up the pattern interlocking at points where there is a vertical color change. There are two types of weft-interlock: one is a single **interlocking** or Norwegian rölakan, and the other is a double interlocking or Swedish rölakan. Norwegian rölakan produces a reversible rug with no ridge or extra thickness where the two fillings join (**a.**). Each color section is woven over an even number of **warp end**s and all color sections start at the same side, i.e., the first **pick**s all go either left to right or right to left. Each color section weaves up pick by pick simultaneously and always moves in the same direction so that when the turns are made to return to the opposite side, the fillings lie over each other and as they are picked up in an order to insert in the **shed,** an interlock occurs. The vertical joinings can be moved by two warp ends either to the left or right. New colors can be introduced as long as they occupy an even number of ends. This allows for geometric patterns incorporating squares, diamonds, stepped verticals, horizontals, crosses, and stars. The joining is not as straight as in a **slit tapestry,** but rather resembles simple **dovetailing.** If care is taken that the interlocking is not pulled to one side or another, the joining becomes absolutely vertical and is flat and unnoticeable.

The double interlocking produces a joining that forms a definite ridge on the upper surface facing the weaver, but leaving the back side perfectly flat (**b.**). This ridge is a deterrent to its being used much, if at all, for rugs. How-

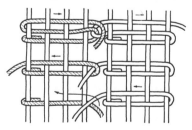

a. Single interlocking rölakan

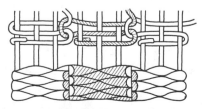

b. Double interlocking rölakan

ever, double interlocking does give a very sturdy joining that can be used to advantage in large and heavy wall hangings. The pattern areas in this type of interlocking span odd or even numbers of warp ends. At each turn of a filling yarn, it is interlocked so that interlocking occurs in every pick instead of every other pick as in the single interlocking. There can be several variations on both of these interlocking methods. See ill.

roll. Bookbinding. A wheel-like engraved finishing tool similar to the **fillet** but with a wider surface, used for ornamentation.

roll. Quilts. One turn of the **rail. Rolling** is done when a section of the **quilt** is finished. Therefore, if a quilter is on the third roll, that indicates how far the **quilting** has progressed. An average quilt requires 5 or 6 rolls, depending upon quilt size and how large an area is exposed for quilting.

roll-drawing spinning machine. Spinning. See **Spinning.**

rolled. Metalworking. See **metal.**

rolled candle. Candlemaking. (Also called swaddle.) A candle formed by **rolling,** such as a beeswax honeycomb candle. **Dipped** or **poured candle**s are rolled while malleable to smooth the outer surface. Also see **Candlemaking: Rolling.**

rolled glass. Stained Glass. A commercial or **machine-made glass** produced by rolling the **glass** out on a heavy metal table or marver with rollers that may be embossed with a texture which is pressed into the molten sheet as it is being rolled. The glass is produced in a constant thickness, usually ⅛". Also see **antique glass, cathedral glass, crossed slab glass, Flemish glass.**

rolled-paper work. Papercrafts. See **paper filigree.**

roller. Stained Glass. See **cathedral glass, crossed slab glass, machine-made glass, rolled glass.**

roller. Weaving. A long rodlike piece above the **harness**es in a **counterbalanced loom.** The harnesses are suspended from the roller by means of a cord wound around the roller at each end. It is the most common way of suspending harnesses in a counterbalanced loom. Alternate ways are through the use of either a **horse** or **pulley.**

roller shuttle. Weaving. See **boat shuttle.**

roller-type loom. Beadwork. See **loom.**

rolling. Batik and Tie-dye. A method of preparing fabric for **tie-dye.** The material can be rolled lengthwise over a rope or cord, or over itself to make a long tube. The tube can then be folded before **binding** is added. Endless patterns and variations are possible through rolling. A snake pattern is characteristic of this method. Also see **diagonal roll.**

rolling. Candlemaking. See **Candlemaking: Rolling.**

rolling. Quilts. Turning the **rails** over and over to wind up or **roll** the top and bottom portions of a quilt so that a newly exposed area can be quilted. When the center section is quilted, the rolling may go in one direction or the other to expose the unquilted portions.

rolling. Tincrafting. The technique of gradually bending **tinplate** into rolled surfaces with the use of round-nose **pliers.**

rolling mill. Jewelry. A hand-operated device composed of two polished hard steel rollers, used to reduce the **gauge** of **sheet metal.** A rolling mill can be used as a hammer substitute to flatten braided wire and ingots. A rolling mill increases the dimension of the metal depending on the direction it is fed into the machine. Rolling mills can be bolted to a steel stand that is bolted to the floor, or bolted to a sturdy workbench. A freestanding unit is more desirable. The rollers are available smooth, or with a series of grooves at one end in systematically smaller sizes used to reduce the gauge of wire. Some rolling mills have interchangeable rollers, smooth and grooved.

There are three gears on the top of the machine. The center gear, the smallest of the three, can be lifted out; the other two gears, which are considerably larger and mesh into the center gear, are then free to be adjusted independently. The gears are on a threaded shank that can be screwed up or down and that in turn adjusts the steel rollers. To be in the correct position for working, the rollers are adjusted so that they are absolutely parallel to one another. A space, however small, should be left between the rollers while making this adjustment; otherwise it will not be true. After the rollers are parallel, the center gear is replaced, interlocking all three gears, and is used from this point on to either increase or decrease the space between the rollers as required. This parallel position of the rollers is extremely important, as it is this adjustment that maintains the uniformity of thickness in the metal being rolled.

When rolling sheet metal down to a thinner gauge, adjust the rollers so that the metal just fits easily through the space between the rollers. Remove the metal from the mill and turn the center adjustment gear a maximum of one-quarter turn to lessen the opening. Insert the metal, and use a hand-over-hand motion when turning the rollers so that the metal will be rolled through in one continuous motion. If you stop before the metal goes through, the rollers will create an indentation in the surface of the metal. Continue with this procedure, reducing the opening by a quarter turn or less with each passing of the metal. Each time you roll the metal through, turn it over to help keep it flat. The metal will become harder each time you roll it through, due to **compression.** As it becomes harder it is more difficult to roll through; consequently, each turn that tightens the rollers should be-

come progressively less than a quarter of a turn. As the metal becomes harder it is being reduced; it may require **annealing** or it will **fracture.**

When you are rolling metal through the mill, the metal is being increased in length in the direction that it is being rolled through the mill. If you want to increase it in width, you will need to roll it through in the direction of its width. Most rolling mills are not very wide—about 5″ at the most—so this is not always possible.

If you are using a rolling mill to reduce wire, pass it through each groove at least twice, beginning with the largest space it fits into easily and working progressively down to the size you require. Do not skip a groove, or you can cause damage to the rollers.

To maintain the rolling mill, be sure that all metal going through the mill is absolutely clean and dry; before rolling, wipe the rollers clean with the palm of your hand to make sure they are free of dirt and dust, as even dust can be imprinted in the surface of the metal as it is rolled through the mill. When the mill is not in use, coat the rollers with a thin layer of light oil to protect them from corrosion. When rolling narrow metals through the mill, such as heavy round wire, keep the metal in the center of the rollers, thereby easing the wear on the machine and also keeping the pressure evenly distributed upon the metal.

A rolling mill is an expensive piece of equipment, but with a minimum amount of proper care it will last for many years. Also see **rolling mill techniques.**

rolling mill techniques. Jewelry. The **rolling mill** has uses beyond its normal functions of rolling metal into a thinner **gauge** and rolling down **wire.** The rolling mill can be used to create a form of inlay in metal. For example, the base piece of **sheet metal** will be silver and the inlays copper. The silver should be of at least 18-gauge, although a heavier gauge would be better because it becomes thinner as it is rolled. The copper should be of 18-gauge or thinner. The copper shapes are sweat-soldered to the silver sheet. After **soldering** and **pickling** are completed and the work is dried off, it is rolled through the mill, forcing the copper into the silver until it is level with the silver. The rollers in the mill must be tightened slowly each time after the work has passed through them. The pressure from the mill will stretch and malform the metal if it is passed through the rollers in the same direction each time; for example, a copper circle will become an elongated oval. If the copper inlay is to retain its original shape, it must be passed through the rollers in a different direction each time by a quarter turn. The inlaid shape will become considerably larger because as it is impressed, it also becomes thinner and stretched. After it has reached the same level as the silver, the rolling can stop or it can continue, stretching the form and the silver even more, in which case both will become thinner. If the work has been sweat-soldered together with a high melting **solder,** such as hard solder, it can be annealed if necessary and can then be cut apart and resoldered with a lower melting solder, riveted to other pieces, set in a **bezel,** or used in any other form of **fabrication.**

A rolling mill is used to press patterns into sheet metal.

Flat unsoldered round wire forms can be placed on top of the sheet metal, and the sheet metal and wire rolled through the mill together. The rollers must be adjusted to bear pressure on the wire, but not so tightly that it becomes impossible to roll the wire and sheet metal through. When the metal comes out of the mill, the wire will have impressed a design in the metal. This can be somewhat difficult to control, because when the wire is flattened by the rollers it changes, sometimes drastically, from its original shape. The wire will also become widened as it goes through the rollers, producing a wider impressed line. This should be taken into consideration when choosing the gauge of the wire.

A piece of textured fabric—even patterned lace—can be placed on sheet metal and rolled through to leave an imprint on the metal. Fabrics can usually only be put through the mill once, as the pressure from the rollers is so great that the fabrics almost always disintegrate. Forms can be cut out of heavy cardboard, placed on the sheet metal—no glue, or the patterns made from the glue will become imprinted as well—and rolled through.

To produce raised patterns, saw designs out of thin-gauge steel and roll the steel plate and another metal, such as silver, together. The cut-out sections of the steel will appear raised in the silver. The steel plate can be run through the mill numerous times on different pieces of metal. The designs should not be too small, as the steel plate becomes slightly misshapen and compressed, closing small forms, each time it goes through the mill. The number of times the steel plate can be used depends on how tightly the rollers are adjusted. To run a steel plate through the mill properly without its slipping, place the silver, which should be slightly larger than the plate of steel all the way around, on one side of the steel plate. On the other side of the steel place a piece of copper the same size and gauge as the silver and tape the edges all the way around, smoothly and tightly with masking tape. Roll the plate through the mill and remove the tape. In this manner, both the silver and the copper will be imprinted. More importantly, the metal on both sides of the steel plate acts as a cushion so the steel plate will last longer.

Virtually anything that is flat and that will not harm the rollers can be passed through them to make an imprint, but think twice about the materials before rolling. For example, coarse sandpaper would probably make a beautiful all-over texture, but the particles on the sandpaper would crumble as they were passed through the rollers and would severely scratch them. Test all materials first. Also see **annealing, riveting, sweat soldering.**

rolling of clay. Ceramics. See **Ceramics: Hand Building.**

rolling pin. Ceramics. A straight, wooden rolling pin is used for rolling out slabs of clay. It should not be left damp, as it tends to warp. Also see **Ceramics: Hand Building.**

Rolling Pinwheel. Quilts. A **pieced block** design that is a variation of **Pinwheel.** It uses a pinwheel in the center, then expands on it with **patches** that extend the pinwheel form.

Rolling Star. Quilts. See **Brunswick Star.**

Rolling Stone. Quilts. (Also called Block Circle, Johnny-round-the-Corner.) A **block** design for a **pieced quilt** sewn of diamonds, triangles, and squares in various ways to suggest a rounded form. The name probably came from the proverbial rolling stone that gathers no moss. See ill.

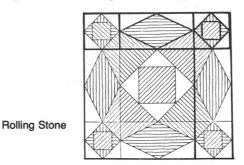

Rolling Stone

roll off. Batik and Tie-dye. The tendency of **dye** to run or roll away from the **resist** areas in **paper batik.** Heavy or thick paints do not roll off as readily as the more watery ones.

roll-over fold. Papercrafts. A paper folding variation in which a strip of paper is folded at regular intervals, with folds in one direction so that it folds over on itself.

roll stitch. Crewel. Embroidery. See **bullion knot.**

roll stitch. Crochet. See **bullion stitch bar.**

roly-poly. Toys. See **balance toy.**

roman. Basketry. The term given to **slewing** with five or more **rods.** It is the process employed for the quick **siding** of a basket.

Roman gold. China and Glass Painting. (Also called fluxed gold.) Powdered, matte **gold** colors containing **flux,** available in various shades of white, green, bronze, or yellow. After **firing,** the gold can be polished by **burnishing.**

Roman Squares. Quilts. Any of several old **pieced block** designs using short strips or oblongs of fabric. The best known is the **three-patch** block. In this, each block is made up of three different-colored rectangular blocks **set** together to form a larger rectangle. It was outlined by a solid-color strip, which separated the blocks. Later, in the late 1800s when **Victorian crazy quilt**s were being made as **throws,** primarily for show, the Roman Squares design was revived. It utilized bright colors, **silk**s, and **wool**s, and outlined the blocks with black.

A variation of the Roman Squares uses 3–6 strips of varying width sewn side by side to form a square. These squares are then set so that the direction of the strips alternates. No outlining **band**s are used between them.

Roman stitch. Crewel. Embroidery. See **Roumanian stitch.**

Roman Stripe. Quilts. A **one-patch** design for a **pieced quilt,** using rectangles. The rectangles were joined end to end, keeping all darks together in one strip, then lights, then alternating dark and light in joining the strips. The widths of the strips varied from one row to the next, making it possible to use even the tiniest scraps. The narrower the **patches,** the more choice the quilt was thought to be. A later variation alternated strips of colored pieces with solid black strips. Also see **Fence Rail.**

Roman stripe. Rugmaking. Weaving. See **stripe.**

rondel. Stained Glass. (Also called roundel.) An ornamental disk of glass such as **crown glass,** gathered in molten form and spun into a disk. The irregular center is known as a pontil mark. Rondels are also pressed by machine. They come in a wide variety of colors; hand-spun ones sometimes have several colors whirled through them. They are used for decorative effects in stained-glass work. Bottle bottoms are used as rondels and may have colors swirled through them.

roofing nail. Woodworking. See **nail.**

rope. Quilts. See **Quilts: Quilting.**

rope. Spinning. Weaving. Rope is a **cord** made of either **natural** or **synthetic fiber**s measuring ¼–5″ in diameter. To make rope, the spinner must do a lot of walking, which takes place during the spinning when the spinner walks backward to draw out the fibers as they turn on the hooks of a wheel. The backward pace must be consistent to insure uniformity. There are hand rope-making machines available that twist spun yarns into rope and which do not require walking backward.

rope handle. Basketry. A type of **basket handle,** either woven or wrapped around a **bow,** that gives the effect of rope. Also see **Basketry: Woven Basket Construction, Handles.**

rope stitch. Crewel. Embroidery. A stitch that gives a very three-dimensional ropelike effect. It is used as an outline stitch or as a solid filling when worked in rows. To make a narrow stitch, work the needle through the **background fabric** in a straight line (**a.**). It requires a bit of practice to keep the stitch smooth; a helpful hint is to keep the stitches long (**b.**). The raised variation is considered **stumpwork.** The stitches are worked loosely, forming a raised ridge (**c.**). For a wider stitch, work the needle through the background fabric at a 45° angle between parallel lines (**d.**). The wider stitch is raised on the loop side and resembles a slanting **satin stitch** (**e.**). See ill.

rope swing. Toys. The simplest form of a **swing,** consisting mainly or entirely of a long heavy rope tied securely to a tree or beam.

A single rope moves in a circle radiating out from the point directly below the branch from which the swing is suspended. The longer the rope, the larger the circle described by the swing. The **circle swing** and **bag swing** are examples of the single-rope variety. In a knotted-rope swing the rope is tied into a series of small-to-large knots which are spaced intermittently along the length of the rope to supply handles or footholds. The swinger can hang, stand, or (more or less) sit, using the knots to keep him/her from slipping.

A double-rope swing is suspended from two ropes. The ropes are tied to a tree or beam and attached to a seat of some sort. It moves in a straight plane, back and forth, and so requires an open lane or path for its movement. Both the **board swing** and the **tire swing** are double-rope swings. Also see **Toys: Rope and String Toys.**

rope tying. Batik and Tie-dye. A **binding** method used in **tie-dye** in which narrow strips of cloth are folded and bound with clothesline rope so that the **dye** cannot penetrate into the material. When the strips folded on the lengthwise or crosswise grain are bound they resemble ropes. The strips are first **accordion pleat**ed, then bound with **line, spiral,** or **crisscross binding.**

A diagonal stripe effect can be achieved by making the accordion pleats go diagonally across the fabric. A trellis effect results when one set of diagonal stripes is tied over a first set of diagonal stripes in such a way that the second row of accordion pleats goes to the corners diagonally opposite the first.

If the fabric is folded in half lengthwise before the diagonal stripe is tied, a zigzag stripe is achieved. By **folding** the fabric more times, multiple zigzags are formed. Also see **knotted tie-dye.**

rosa pallido. Coral Carving. See **coral.**

rosary. Beadwork. Since prehistory, man has counted knots, then **bead**s on a string, as a record of prayers. Beads became widely used and eventually part of church tradition, because they slipped through the fingers easily and could be counted in the dark. During the thirteenth century the use of strung beads was instituted by St. Dominic. These rosary beads contained 15 units of beads, with 10 small beads in each unit separated by larger ones. Because a prayer was recited at every bead, it became the custom to pay someone else to say these lengthy prayers.

In China, Japan, and India the rosary is traditionally used by Buddhists and Muslims to be sure that no prayer has been omitted.

Rosary beads have been made of everything from nuts

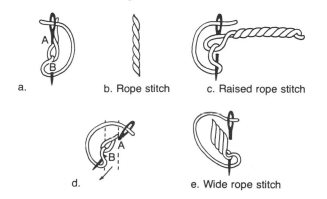

a. b. Rope stitch c. Raised rope stitch

d. e. Wide rope stitch

and **seed**s to scented beads of coffee beans, cloves, and tiny pomanders.

rosa vivo. Coral Carving. See **coral.**

Rose and Buds. Quilts. See **flower designs.**

rose countersink. Wookworking. See **drill bits.**

rose cut. Gemcutting. See **facet.**

rose fashion. Weaving. See **overshot, square-off.**

Rose in Bud. Quilts. See **flower designs.**

rosengang. Weaving. See **rose path.**

Rose of Sharon. Quilts. One of the all-time favorite **appliqué block** designs; it derived its name from a passage in "The Song of Songs," a book of the **Bible.** The poetic name and the charm of the design made it a popular favorite as a **bride's quilt.** A large flower is encircled by stems, leaves, and more flowers in almost all variations of this design. See ill.

Rose of Sharon

Rose of Tennessee. Quilts. See **flower designs.**

Rose of the Field. Quilts. See **presidents' quilts.**

rose path. Weaving. A name for patterns of countless varieties based on diamond and zigzag twills. The term is translated from the Swedish *rosengang,* which refers to the patterns' stylized floral look. The **threading** used is a **point draw,** but the **treadling** can be almost anything since a feature of rose path is its versatility and limitless possibilities. It can give either a small, repeated design, such as a floral effect with diamonds, crosses, and zigzags, or, with the right treadling, it can give texture effects. It has been used in Scandinavia for centuries, and today Scandinavian weavers are applying it to contemporary wall hangings. Also see **diamond twill, twill weave.**

rose quartz. Gemcutting. See **quartz.**

rose stitch. Crewel. Embroidery. See **bullion knot.**

rose stitch. Crochet. See **Crochet: Patterns.**

Rose Tree. Quilts. See **Prairie Rose.**

rosette. Beadwork. (Also called bull's eye or target.) A round disk of solid **bead embroidery** used as a decorative motif by American Indians on clothing, blanket borders, and horse trappings. The circle, varying in size from 1½–4″ in diameter, is made of rows of beads stitched on buckskin in a spiral design. The **overlay stitch** may be used to anchor the thread between each threaded bead, beginning at the center of the circle. After a few rows are secured, the overlay stitch can be done every two or three beads until the desired diameter is reached.

rosette chain stitch. Crewel. Embroidery. An interesting **border stitch** formed by two interlocking **chain stitch**es. It is best worked fairly small and closely; too large a stitch can easily become caught and pull when in use. It is most effective as a single line edging. Working on a line from right to left, using a blunt needle, come up at A, go down at B, a little to the left and below A, and come up at C, slightly to the right and below B. Hold the thread across and under the needle. Pull through, keeping the stitch lying flat on the material (**a.**). Now slide needle under the stitch at A. Do not pass through the material (**b.**). It is possible to achieve different effects by varying the distance between the rosettes (**c.**). See ill.

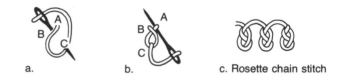

a.   b.   c. Rosette chain stitch

rosewood. Woodworking. A variety of tropical **hardwood** well known for its beautiful **figuring** and color. Its color ranges from reddish brown to purple with streaks of yellow and black. Rosewood takes a very high polish, is a good carving wood, and is excellent for interior paneling, cabinets, and furniture. It is quite expensive. The Brazilian variety is the most common.

Rose Wreath. Quilts. See **wreath patterns.**

rosin. A translucent yellow to dark brown resin obtained by distilling pine tree sap until its volatile oil is eliminated. Rosin is used in varnishes, soaps, cements, and driers for oils. Rosin dissolves in ethyl acetate, methyl alcohol, acetone, benzene, turpentine, and many petroleum distillates.

rosin. Metalworking. See **flux.**

rosin. Stained Glass. When using a gas **soldering iron,** keep a small amount of rosin nearby for **tinning** the iron bit. It is ready for use when the iron develops a green flame: dip it into the rosin and pick up a piece of solder on the tip.

rosin cement. Dust 4 parts plaster of Paris into 6 parts melted rosin; stir until completely blended. Stiffen the mixture by adding more plaster.

rosso. Coral Carving. See **coral.**

rosso scuro. Coral Carving. See **coral.**

rotary punch. Leather. See **revolving punch.**

rottenstone. Amber Carving. Ivory and Bone Carving. Jet Carving. Shell Carving. A soft, friable abrasive polishing agent composed of uniformly textured gray, brown, or olive-gray silica particles. It is named for its bad odor. It is used to polish plastics and soft organic materials.

rottenstone. Découpage. An abrasive powder, a little finer than **pumice,** used to smooth a **varnish**ed surface. Rottenstone is mixed into a light paste by mixing 1 part rottenstone to 4 parts lemon oil or linseed oil. It is rubbed over the surface with a cloth, then buffed to a high gloss. The surface is **wax**ed for a final polish.

rottenstone. Woodworking. See **abrasives.**

Rouault, Georges (1871–1958). Stained Glass. A French painter who designed stained-glass windows that were executed by **Paul Bony.** He is best appreciated from the stained-glass point of view for his use of black line and blending effects.

rouche. Batik and Tie-dye. See **ruche.**

rouge. Amber Carving. Coral Carving. Essentially, iron oxide (Fe_2O_3), a polishing agent used on metal, glass, soft gemstones, and other soft organic materials. It is obtained by calcining iron chlorides, sulfates, or oxalates in crucibles under controlled conditions. Black rouge is called "crocus," and the red is called "rouge."

rouge. Gemcutting. See **abrasive.**

rouge. Metalworking. See **abrasives.**

rouge cloth. Jewelry. See **red rouge cloth.**

rouge flambé. Ceramics. See **flambé.**

rough. Gemcutting. See **matrix.**

rough gilt. Bookbinding. A book is said to be rough gilt if the edges were gilded before the book was sewn.

roughing. Metalworking. See **blacksmithing techniques.**

roughing out. Woodworking. A term commonly used in **wood turning** or **woodcarving** to describe the rough shaping or cutting of a form into a generalized shape or size, before carving or turning the detailed shape.

roughing out tools. Woodworking. See **woodcarving tools.**

rough-sawn. Woodworking. See **wood.**

roulette. Ceramics. A tool used for producing a repeat decorative impressed pattern. This is a very old technique that consists of a carved wheel or cylinder, which when it is rolled over clay, produces a pattern. A roulette can be made of **bisque** clay or carved on a piece of blackboard chalk. Also see **impressing, mishima.**

Roumanian stitch. Crewel. Embroidery. (Also called American stitch, antique stitch, economy stitch, Indian filling stitch, New England laid stitch, Oriental stitch, overlaid stitch, Roman stitch, two short stitches.) This was one of the most important of the stitches used in early American embroidery, and many pieces were done exclusively in this stitch. The thrifty colonial workers found it easy to work up and it required little wool. Roumanian stitch is really a straight satin stitch tied down with a smaller slanting stitch in the center. If the small stitch maintains its slant well, the stitches will fit closely together with no separation between them, keeping the effect smooth. However, this small stitch may be worked on a greater slant if the area to be filled is wide. When several bands are worked side by side, the stitches should just overlap one another at the edge. If each row fits into the exact holes of the previous one, the stitches are apt to pull away a little and leave material showing in between. This is both an excellent **filling stitch** and **border stitch.** See ill. Also see **shading stitch.**

Roumanian stitch

a.   b.   c.   d.

round. Basketry. One complete circuit of **weaving** around the **basket,** e.g., one round of **slewing** followed by three rounds of **pairing,** and so on.

round. Bookbinding. To form the **back** of a book into a convex shape. Also see **rounding.**

round. Crochet. Knitting. A round is one complete row of stitches in **medallion crochet** or circular knitting. Also see **motif** and **Crochet: Motifs.**

roundabout. Toys. See **merry-go-round.**

round cape chisel. Metalworking. See **blacksmithing tools.**

round casting on. Knitting. See **Knitting: Casting On.**

roundel. Bookbinding. A motif used in cover decoration that consists of a double ring with a center dot.

roundel. Stained Glass. See **rondel.**

roundel. Weaving. See **Danish medallion.**

round drive punch. Leather. See **drive punch.**

round-eye needle. Stitchery. A **needle** that has a round opening for the thread. It is not as easy to thread as a **long-eye needle.**

round file. Metalworking. See **file.**

round-head knife. Leather. See **moon knife.**

round-head screw. Woodworking. See **screw.**

round-hole drive punch. Leather. See **drive punch.**

rounding. Bookbinding. The operation that gives a book its convex **back** and its concave **foredge.** Rounding prevents **starting** and takes up the swell that **knocking down** may have not removed.

After **trimming,** and before the glue has set hard, lay the book flat on the bench. Press the foredge with the ball of your thumb while the four fingers on top of the book pull the book toward you. At the same time, gently tap the back of the book with the backing hammer. Work on one side of the book, gradually shaping it, then turn it over and work on the other side. Keep turning the book and working it until the back has an evenly curved arc. If the glue dries while working, dampen it with a sponge and wait for a few minutes before continuing to round. Also see **backing.**

rounding. Leather. See **dressing.**

rounding up. Metalworking. See **blacksmithing techniques.**

round knitting. Knitting. See **circular knitting.**

round-nose chisel. Metalworking. See **chisel.**

round-nose chisel. Woodworking. See **wood-turning tool**s.

round-nose pliers. Basketry. A basic tool used for crimping or squeezing reed that is to be bent at an acute angle to prevent cracking. See ill.

Round-nose pliers

round-nose pliers. Jewelry. See **pliers.**

round petal. Beadwork. See **basic loop.**

round-point awl. Leather. See **awl and haft.**

round rasp. Woodworking. See **rasp.**

round reed. Basketry. See **cane** and **Basketry: Woven Basket Construction, Coiled Basket Construction.**

round rug. Rugmaking. A circular rug drawn on the **rug backing** with the aid of a pencil and string. The string is tacked to the center of the backing with the pencil attached at the other end. By stretching the string tautly and moving the pencil in a circular movement, the radius of the circle is established (**a.**). The perimeter is then drawn. This can be done directly on the backing, or on paper first and then cut out and traced. An oval is made by first drawing an arc between the two cross lines dissecting the center point. This gives one-quarter of the oval (**b.**). The other three-quarters are traced according to the first arc (**c.**). Round and oval rugs are more easily done on some backings than others because of the problem which arises in turning back the hem. Most techniques for **shaped rug**s are compatible for round or oval rugs. See ill. Also see **hemming.**

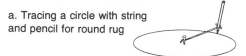

a. Tracing a circle with string
and pencil for round rug

b., c. Tracing for an oval rug

router. Jewelry. A type of **grinding** tool that fits into the handpiece of a **flexible shaft machine.** Also see **bur.**

router. Plastics. Woodworking. A portable electric tool used to cut **groove**s, **dado**s, and **rabbet**s; trim and shape edges; cut recesses; make **dovetail joint**s; and for innumerable other operations in wood, plastic, and related materials. It uses a wide selection of **router bit**s or cutters, which are easily interchangeable in the bottom of the tool. Because its motor runs up to speeds of 35,000 rpm, it is capable of precision work. In addition, it may be used for freehand cutting and with a **fence** attachment or **templates.**

A shaper is a permanently mounted shop machine that performs all the operations of a router except freehand work; it is used primarily for production work. It uses the same or similar types of router bits. See ill.

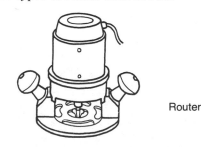

Router

router bit. Woodworking. A bit or cutter specifically designed for use in a **router** or shaper. The vast assortment of these cutters makes both tools very versatile. Shank sizes run from ¼" to ½". Most cutters are one-piece units that are locked to the router's shaft. Better router bits are made of high-speed steel or are **carbide**-tipped. The three basic router bits are: straight bit for cutting **groove**s, slots, and **rabbet**s; rabbeting bit for rabbets or step cutting; and corner-round bit for edge rounding. See ill.

Corner-round router bit and the shape it cuts

router plane. Woodworking. See **plane.**

routing. Plastics. Use a portable **router** for trimming edges and **grooving** surfaces. Use 6 to 10 blade cutters of 2″ to 3″ in diameter at speeds of 7,000 rpm. Increase the speed to 10,000 rpm if the cutters used are less than 1½″ in diameter and have only two or three cutting blades.

roving. Plastics. See **glass fiber.**

roving. Quilts. (Also called cording.) A slightly twisted **cotton** or **wool** cording. It is available by the yard at fabric shops. Also see **candlewicking.**

roving. Spinning. Weaving. A soft, continuous, ropelike form of fibers from which yarn is spun. Roving can pertain to **flax, silk,** or **wool.** Depending upon which spinning system was used, wool roving is made from either groups of carded **slivers** or from a combed top. Rolling out the sliver into a continuous length and holding it together with a light twist will give roving. Roving can also be made from the **tops** by drawing it through the hands under tension. This can be done two or three times in order to obtain a very narrow roving. Roving is finer in diameter than either sliver or tops, but it is greater in diameter than the yarn it will become. A finer and firmer yarn can be gotten from roving than by spinning from the raw material. When roving is used in spinning in ball form, it is generally placed in a round container to prevent its rolling around. A coil, or skein, of roving is usually placed on a **skein winder.** In former times, roving was wound directly around the **distaff.**

Roving is often used in weaving and is especially effective in nonutilitarian items like wall hangings. Also see **carding, combing, spinning.**

roving. Stained Glass. Fiberglass string set into **epoxy resin** as an **armature** to reinforce the resin. The use of rovings is not a necessary practice. The rovings are treated in a bath of pure resin, then in hardener mix, and then laid onto the epoxy from end to end between the **glass** when the mold has been half filled. Rubber gloves should be worn.

row. Crochet. Knitting. The worked crochet or knitting from one edge to the opposite edge one complete time. Each complete row adds to the length of the work.

royal water. Jewelry. See **aqua regia.**

rpm. Revolutions per minute.

rubber ball. Toys. See **beach toy, India rubber.**

rubber-band gun. Toys. A popular homemade **American folk toy.** It consists of a piece of wood that is more or less gun-shaped. It should have a handle and a "barrel" cut from a single piece of wood. A snap-type clothespin is securely attached to the end of the handle facing up, with the clamp or jaw part of the clothespin in line with the barrel. A rubber band is hooked over the muzzle end of the gun and then drawn back and inserted into the open jaw of the clothespin. It can also be loaded in reverse. To operate this shooting toy, the lower part of the clothespin, which functions as a trigger, is pressed, releasing the rubber band, which will fly several feet through the air. The amount of tension on the rubber band determines how far it will fly. The tension depends in turn on the tightness of the spring in the clothespin and the size of the rubber band.

rubber-band toy. Toys. Any toy that uses a rubber band to propel it. The band is usually attached and wound to put it under tension. When released, the rubber band assumes its original shape and the resultant action animates the toy. The **clothespin wrestlers** and **racing spool** are two common rubber-band toys. Some **paddle-wheel boats** operate under rubber-band power.

rubber block printing. Block Printing. Printing with an ordinary India-rubber eraser with simple designs cut into the surface, then inked and printed. Also see **Block Printing: Printing Techniques.**

rubber bowl. Jewelry. A bowl made of rubber used as a container for mixing **investment.** It facilitates the breaking out of dried investment because it can be squeezed out of shape, cracking the hardened plasterlike investment from its sides. Also see **centrifugal casting, lost-wax casting.**

rubber cement. Jewelry. A pressure-sensitive glue used to adhere a drawing to metal in preparation for **sawing.** Coat both the back of the drawing and the surface of the metal with rubber cement and allow it to dry. Use thin coats in both cases; otherwise globs of dried rubber cement will have to be sawed through, which will make for inaccurate sawing. When both paper and metal have dried, stick them together and rub lightly with your finger to secure the drawing. This is a good method to use for sawing out your design, but unless you have made a tracing you will lose your original drawing. Rubber cement is highly flammable. Also see **cement, transferring designs to metal.**

rubber cement. Leather. The basic glue used in leatherwork for hems, seams, etc. It is resistant to moisture, dyes, and finishes. Also see **ruffler** and **Leatherwork: Gluing and Bonding Leather, Tools and Materials.**

rubber cement. Plastics. See **adhesive.**

rubber cement. Toys. An **adhesive** that works especially well on paper. It is somewhat viscous and rubbery and makes its most permanent bond when both of the areas to be joined are coated and left to dry before joining. It is an extremely flammable material and care must be taken to avoid excessive inhalation of the fumes. It is fast-drying, nonwrinkling, and waterproof.

rubber-latex glue. Stained Glass. A latex-based **stopping-out agent** used in **aciding** and **lift ground**.

rubber mold. Candlemaking. (Also called latex mold.) Commercial rubber **mold**s are available through most hobby stores. They can also be made at home by coating objects that would make attractive candle shapes with liquid rubber, applying repeated coats on all but the flat bottom of the object. Allow each layer to set until tacky; after three or four coats, let the mold cure for several days, then peel the mold off and let it stand for 24 hours. Test the heat-resistance before pouring.

rubber toy. Toys. Any toy molded from rubber or made with rubber parts. It became common in toymaking after the middle of the 1800s, when it was used in **dollmaking** and for small animals and **ball**s. The development of elastic and later of rubber bands also affected toy production. The **India rubber** ball became tremendously popular, and has remained so for years. Rubber replaced the use of **gutta percha** and **gum arabic** for soft, nonresistant forms.

rubbing. Batik and Tie-dye. The transferring of a surface texture or textured design onto paper. A paper is placed over the textured surface and held or secured there. The area is then rubbed with **wax** (**paraffin** or crayons) to prepare it for a **batik** process. Papers with some rag content tend to be flexible enough to work well. Stiff papers do not pick up the patterns. When the waxed rubbing is completed, a wash of paint or **dye** is applied to the entire surface. Because the wax will **resist** the addition of paint or dye, the rubbed design will retain the original color. The untreated areas will absorb the paint or dye, as in **fabric** batik.

rubbing. Block Printing. A printing technique in which a print is made by rubbing a crayon over paper placed on top of textured material such as leaves, feathers, wood, lace, mesh screening, or crinkled paper or foil.

rubbing. Woodworking. The process of removing dust or brush or spray marks from a **finish** by rubbing, to produce a high gloss, starting with a coarse **abrasive** and ending with a fine one. Abrasives such as **steel wool, sand paper, rubbing compounds, pumice,** and **rottenstone** are used. Each finish has its own appropriate rubbing procedures. Also see **lacquer, shellac, varnish**.

rubbing compound. Woodworking. See **abrasives**.

rubbing down. Bookbinding. The operation performed with a **bone folder** to assure the firm adhesion of paper, **cloth,** or **leather** after pasting. It is also used to smooth a surface, remove creases, or to mold the shape of a book. When rubbing down, use a clean sheet of waste paper between the folder and the surface. Rubbing directly onto a surface can make it shiny or streaky.

rubbing varnish. Woodworking. See **varnish**.

rubellite. Gemcutting. See **tourmaline**.

rub-off batik. Batik and Tie-dye. A variation of **paper batik** that uses either a liquid adherent, such as rubber cement, or masking paper as the **resist** agent. The resist is applied to the paper, and when dry, covered with watercolor, ink, or thinned poster paint. After the paints or inks have dried, the resist agent can be removed. If rubber cement is used, it is rubbed off the surface of the paper, leaving clean white lines and areas. Masking papers that work well include Friskit paper, gummed paper, or masking tape. They are especially helpful in doing stenciled lettering. Hard-finish papers must be used if the adhesive materials are to be easily rubbed or peeled off.

rub stone. Jewelry. See **bench rub stone**.

ruby. Gemcutting. See **corundum**.

rubyfluid. Stained Glass. See **flux**.

ruby powder. Gemcutting. See **abrasive**.

ruche. Batik and Tie-dye. (Also called rouche.) Originally, a frilled or gathered lace used decoratively on women's clothes. The name is derived from the French *ruche*, meaning beehive, because the pattern is like honeycomb cells.

In **tie-dye**, **ruching** produces a pattern of adjacent cell-like shapes. "To ruche" means to **gather** fabric onto a stick. The **ruching stick** is inserted into a channel sewn for it.

ruching. Batik and Tie-dye. A method of forming **tie-dye** patterns in which the fabric is **gather**ed and drawn compactly around a piece of wood or similar object. Usually the fabric to be dyed is folded crosswise and a seam is made parallel to the folded edge (**a.**), just wide enough so that the wood **ruching stick** can be inserted into the channel (**b.**). The material is then gathered tightly by pulling or drawing the ends of the sewing thread and sliding the fabric together so that only a 2" or 3" area of the wood is covered (**c.**). Any of the **binding material**s can then be used to **bind** the fabric where it joins the wood, using a **crisscross binding** over the wood (**d.**). Many variations of ruching are possible using different wood objects and **clump tying** them, or the fabric may be ruched over wood sticks or dowels of different sizes, using a series of

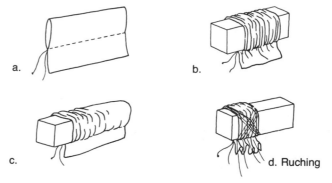

a.   b.

c.   d. Ruching

sewn lines and folds for the wood. See ill. Also see **diamond**.

ruching stick. Batik and Tie-dye. A smooth stick that is inserted into a stitched channel for the **ruching** in **tie-dye**. Wood dowels are commonly used; a square stick gives a different effect. A ruler, a length of broomstick, or any similar piece of wood can be used.

ruffler. Leather. A tool used on smooth leather to give a rough surface to facilitate proper penetration of glue.

rug adhesive. Rugmaking. See **backing the rug**.

rug backing. Rugmaking. The foundation of the rug in **embroidered, hooked,** and **latch-hooked rugs**. The stitches or pile that these techniques form are worked through the rug backing and cover it completely. Since the backing will be holding the stitches, knots, or loops together, it is important to buy one that is of durable quality. Durability, in the long run, is determined by wear, the surface the rug is lying on, and whether it is lined or not. Some backings are more expensive than others. **Burlap** is very reasonable, but even cheaper are feed and grain sacks which are split open and pieced together. It was with backings such as these that **rug hooking** became a popular art back in the 1850s. Backings are chosen with a mind to the technique that will be employed in making the rug, and according to the widths desired if **piecing** will be necessary. The average popular width is about 40", which would allow for a 3' wide rug with a **hem**. Backings are sold by the yard, so any length is obtainable. For embroidery, a stiffer backing, such as **rug warp cloth** or **canvas mesh,** is best. Canvas mesh is also used for latch hook. **Monk's cloth** was widely used for embroidery and hooking at one time, but its popularity has given way to the backings mentioned above. It is still a good backing to use for those who want a softer and more pliable fabric. For long, shaggy **pile,** the **Scandinavian rug backing** gives a perfect, firm background and has spaced rows so that there is no mistaking where to put each row of pile. Another European backing is **jute backing** that can be used for a variety of techniques either used by themselves or in combination with each other. A worn rug can become a backing for a new one, and in many instances, backings are crocheted or knit. A backing is usually totally covered, but an attractive, heavy fabric could be chosen, with the idea that its edges could be seen.

rug binding. Rugmaking. Weaving. A woven tape that can be sewn around the rug as a means of **finishing** the raw edges. The binding is of soft but strong cotton and comes in widths of 1¼–1½". It is available in neutral colors that can be dyed to match the rug if wished. There are also press-on bindings that are made to adhere to the back of the rug and to the edge by pressing with a warm iron. Also see **binding**.

rug braider. Rugmaking. See **braid-aids**.

rug comb. Rugmaking. Weaving. See **hand beater**.

rug filler. Rugmaking. Weaving. A variety of items that can be used as the **filling** in weaving a rug. When the term "filler" is used, it usually implies that the rug will be flat (without **pile**) and speedily woven with the filler providing almost all the interest and color. In speaking of yarn, it could actually refer to any **rug yarn,** but it usually refers to yarn of the thickest variety (from ½–1" or more in diameter), that comes in a multitude of colors and mottled mixtures. Wool is a high quality filler; most fillers are of thick, soft cotton, rayon, or acrylic, or a wool/synthetic blend. Other fillers include heavy **chenille** and other **novelty yarn**s, knit fabric strips, cut-up nylon stockings or panty hose, **thrums, mill ends,** remnants, and rag strips of all fiber varieties. Up to a few years ago, one of the above fillers could be woven up into a very reasonable rug. Fillers available in weaving supply stores today are much more expensive because of their extreme thickness and intricacy of yarn construction.

rug fork. Rugmaking. Weaving. A heavy **hand beater** usually with metal tines. It is used mainly on **upright rug loom**s, but it can also be used on a **harness loom** when the weaver wants the **filling** to be beaten in extra close, or when a **tapestry** rug is being woven and it is not possible to use the loom's **beater**.

rug frame. Rugmaking. See **hooking frame**.

rug hook. Rugmaking. See **hand hook**.

rug hoop. Rugmaking. See **hooking frame**.

rug knot. Rugmaking. Weaving. See **knotted pile**.

rug lacer. Rugmaking. See **braided rug, lacing**.

rug lining. Rugmaking. See **backing the rug**.

rug loom. Rugmaking. Weaving. An **upright loom** built especially for **rug weaving**. It resembles a **tapestry loom,** with **treadle**s to open two **shed**s and a **beater** the full width of the loom. There is a **warp beam** close to the top of the loom and a **cloth beam** near the bottom. The vertical **warp** runs between the two beams. Some models closer in authenticity to the looms of the Middle Eastern rug weavers use **string heddle**s and **shed stick**s to open the sheds and a **rug fork** to beat down with. Vertical rug looms are used for making **pile** and **flatweave** rugs. Rugs can also be woven on a **foot-power loom** or a simple **frame loom** such as the **Navajo loom**. There are also some two-shed **harness loom**s that are marketed as rug looms.

RUGMAKING

The making of a rug is the process of putting together various materials such as yarn, fabric, or leather in order to construct a heavy fabric for use as a floor covering. The actual techniques in the construction of rugs are varied and many and overlap into just about every known fiber craft field. There are, however, certain fiber craft areas that are specifically linked with rugmaking or that even originated with the construction of rugs. These areas include weaving, hooking, latch-hooking, braiding, knitting, crochet, and embroidery.

The term ''rug'' has come to denote a floor covering of limited size that covers only a portion of a room and is unattached to the floor, whereas a carpet, or carpeting, usually means a floor covering that covers the entire floor of a room (wall-to-wall), and comes on large rolls from which it is cut to fit the floor space; it is then tacked to the floor. However, though there have been many attempts to limit the definitions of the two words, they are still often used interchangeably.

The rug design, the colors, and the materials to be used are the choice of the rugmaker. Rug designs can be purchased, but the rugmaker often creates his or her own design and color scheme to blend with the specific interior in which the rug will be used. Ideas for rug designs can come from many sources, such as the motif in the upholstery or wallpaper in a room, impressions from nature, or patterns seen in travel or art books or in museums. If the designs are drawn to scale (small size), then through the process of **transferring the design** they are transposed to a larger or full size easier to follow when actually constructing the rug. There is a tendency to think of rugs as either rectangular or square, but there are many oval and **round rug**s being made and of late adventuresome rugmakers are trying their hands at freeform and **shaped rug**s. **Color blending** is another way rugmakers enhance the effects of their rugs.

The size of a rug depends on the need and desires of the rugmaker. The technique or the equipment may influence size—but limitations can often be overcome by piecing or **joining.** More often than not the design of the rug will have a border or a visual frame around a motif in the center or some other focal point. Often a rug is treated like a painting on canvas and the end result is a piece that will be hung on the wall rather than put on the floor. One of the predecessors of contemporary **wall hangings** were the **rya** rugs of Scandinavia that were designed as ''paintings in wool.'' In other eras and other countries rugs doubled as sofa, table, saddle, sleigh, and bed covers.

Although a rugmaker can use anything from fur or leather to yarn in the construction of a rug, the usual choices are yarn or fabric cut into strips. If the rugmaker opts to use yarn, then the **fiber** can be wool, cotton, or a synthetic. Wool is usually preferred and sometimes it is combined with such exotic yarns as those made from goat's hair, cowhair, camel's hair, alpaca, or silk. Wool fabrics are also preferred over other fabrics such as linen, cotton, or synthetics. All can be used, but combination of fibers is not always wise: wear might be uneven and the washability of the rug would be affected. The fabrics should be clean (washed if being recycled from some previous use) and dyed, if necessary, before cutting into strips.

In order to know what material and what technique will give the desired effect and also to be able to compute the cost of the overall rug a **rug sampler** should be made. Even if the rug will be made out of recycled fabric (and therefore the cost will be minimal), it is still a good idea to have a sampler to test the general technique and to see if there is enough material for the entire project. A sample will also indicate if the choice of **rug backing** (should one be used) is correct and if the rug will be of the appropriate thickness.

After the yarn or fabric is bought or prepared and the design idea is in a sketch, the methods of the desired technique are followed in making the rug. When the rug is completed it goes through **finishing** processes that are determined by the desires of the rugmaker and the technique used.

CLASSIFICATION   The most popular way to classify rugs is in two categories—those that are **flat** and those with **pile.** Flat rugs include **flatwoven** and **tapestry rugs, embroidered rugs, knitted rugs, crocheted rugs, braided rugs** and **appliqué**d **rugs.** Pile rugs include **hooked rugs, latch-hooked rugs,** rya rugs, and other **knotted pile** rugs obtained through **rugweaving** or embroidery. Pile can be inserted into almost any technique so that often rugs combine both flat and pile areas. Rugs like **shirred rug**s are neither flat nor pile, but have a unique texture that comes into being only through this particular technique. **Fur rugs** have a built-in pile if the fur used is long-haired.

Another way to classify rugs is to group them according to those rugs made by attaching the yarn to a backing or **ground cloth** (embroidered, hooked and latch-hooked rugs) and those in which the ground and top design and/or pile are constructed from scratch at one and the same time (woven, knitted, crochet and braided rugs). As can be noted, handcrafted rugs are also categorized according to the technique of their construction or, in the case of **rag rugs** and fur rugs, the mediums from which they are made.

HISTORY   Most people associate a pile fabric with the term ''rug.'' However, in ancient times rugs were often of a flat, or tapestry, weave akin to **Navajo weaving.** Early Egypt is known to have used tapestry rugs in temples and palaces, and there is a tapestry fabric dating from about 1480 B.C. in the museum at Cairo. Excavated wall reliefs show that these flat, tapestry rugs were also used in the kingdoms of Babylon and Assyria, and may have been imported from there to Egypt. The word for rug or carpet was ''tapis'' and the later word **tapestry** evolved from it.

The earliest pile rug that has survived to modern times is a 2400-year-old knotted and woven piece discovered in Pazyryk, Siberia, in burial mounds of the fifth century B.C. Scythian tribes. Almost totally intact, the rug measures 6 feet by 6 feet 6 inches and has roughly 350 knots to the square inch. It is a highly decorative work with bands of borders depicting lotus flowers, stags, and men on horseback. The survival of the rug from ancient times until today is due to the work of grave robbers who plundered the tomb not long after the burial. Taking the gold and jewels, they left behind the rug and similar objects. Water seeped into the tomb and permanently froze the tomb contents until the time of excavation.

As difficult as it is to pinpoint where rugs actually began, it is equally difficult to exactly trace their subsequent early development. However, since ancient times most of the creative activity seems to have centered around Persia, which became known as the rug leader of the world. The pinnacle of refinement in design and color was attained in the sixteenth and seventeenth centuries under the patronage of the shahs Tahmasp and Abbas I.

The Far East was also weaving rugs. The first recorded ones were made during the time of the T'ang dynasty in China in 618–906 A.D. Both the Near and Far Eastern rugs utilized highly symbolic motifs, with the Near Eastern ones being the more abstract. Colors were also symbolic, the meaning of a color varying from country to country. At the time only natural dyes were used and working with them developed into a fine art. The rich, glowing colors that resulted in **Oriental rug**s were in large part the reason that these rugs became a highly desired commodity as an item of trade with Europe. The advent of synthetic dyes was strongly resisted in Persia, where as late as the early 1900s there was a law decreeing that any importer or user of the "new" dyes would have his hand cut off.

The first country in Europe to actually make its own knotted rugs was Spain. By the twelfth century, there was a flourishing rug industry that owed its beginnings to the conquering Moors who brought over the rug weaving techniques of the Middle East. England began to produce her own rugs during the latter half of the sixteenth century, but they were largely adaptations of patterns from the Near East. Prior to learning the art of pile knotting, English rugs were needleworked. In France, Henry IV set up a carpet-weaving workshop in the Louvre in 1608 in order to free the French from having to depend on Near Eastern imported rugs. When this was soundly running, a second workshop called the Savonnerie was opened in an unused soap factory in the suburbs of Paris. Two centuries later, in 1825, the Savonnerie joined up with the Gobelins tapestry-weaving enterprise.

Early rugs, whether flatwoven or with a pile, were used for other reasons than simply as floor coverings. They were hung on walls or around pillars, used as partitions in tents, rooms, or open spaces, thrown over divans, chests, saddles, beds, carriage seats, tables, altars, and thrones—and in colder climes, used on sleds. It was not a common practice to have rugs on the floor, and up to the eighteenth century most ordinary European homes used hay or grasses, rushes, rush mats, homespun fabrics, or had bare floors.

In early times, the elaborate and beautiful creations of the East and Europe were mostly for kings, pashas, emperors, lords, and the priestly classes. However, weaving had been going on in the peasant cottages and simple rugs were made as home necessities. In Poland, the Balkans, and countries along the Mediterranean these rugs were mostly flatweave rugs, but in the cold northland, where additional warmth was always necessary, there developed the thick, shaggy rugs we have come to know as "rya." They are recorded as being made as early as 1450 in Sweden.

Perhaps the oldest rugs made in this country were the Navajo blankets—true representatives of American tapestry rugs. Originally these blankets were woven as apparel by the Navajos, who had learned the weaving craft from the Pueblo Indians sometime in the seventeenth century. However, traders and collectors put them on the floor and used them as rugs starting in the late 1800s.

In the new world of the colonists, a rug was considered a luxury. If there was any fabric on the floor, it was a large piece of floorcloth—a sturdy canvas painted on both sides (to lie flat and for durability), sometimes in tilelike patterns. Eventually rag rugs were made using discarded scraps of clothing. A variety of techniques were used from weaving to knitting, crochet, and later hooking. In the late eighteenth century came the handwoven colonial pattern rugs which were used interchangeably as coverlets and floor coverings. The manufacture of double cloth **ingrain rug**s followed along this trend of having flat, highly patterned rugs that were reversible. **Needleworked rug**s were done at first as imitations of Oriental rugs, but by the nineteenth century they had developed into a unique American style, depicting the homestead and the flora and fauna surrounding it.

However, the most famous of American rugs are the hooked rugs dating from the nineteenth century and sometimes known as "drawn-in" rugs because they were made by drawing-in first yarns and later rags with a hooked instrument through a piece of coarse **canvas.** Pile was both cut and uncut and design ranged from the simplest "hit and miss" patterns to the most detailed renderings of family, home, and historic scenes. Although this craft is known as "America's one indigenous folk art," it is held by some theorists that it did not originate in either the United States or Canada but rather in Norway, from where it made its way with sailors to Scotland, then to England, the settlers and later sailors bringing it to America. Hooked rugs were not held in especially high esteem in England—nor was the art widely developed there. But in America it proved to be a pioneer woman's chance for self-expression while making an object of utility out of something no longer usable.

With the coming of the power loom, hand production of rugs ceased in those countries involved in the Industrial Revolution. In the homes of the wealthy, having a power-made rug was a status symbol. Only in the areas where the peasant or Indian weaver could not afford the goods of industry was the craft of rugmaking kept up. In the United States the first carpet factory was set up in 1791 in Philadelphia by W. P. Sprague. Based on his successful and pleasing productions, the fledgling American rug industry was protected by a tariff levied against imported carpets.

The factory production of carpets brought a whole new set of names to the carpet world, all associated with pile rugs: Axminster, Wilton, Brussels, tufted are neither brand names nor various qualities of carpet, but refer rather to different types of weaving or the manner of attaching the pile to the background. Axminster and Wilton are woven on looms that fix the pile while simultaneously weaving the backing. Wilton, based on a Jacquard mechanism, is usually limited to a maximum of 6 colors in the pile design, while Axminster can use almost any design in any number or combination of colors. By individually inserting each tuft of pile the Axminster system most closely simulates a handwoven carpet. Brussels carpet is uncut Wilton; a loop pile results, giving a very high wearing quality. Whereas these three names and techniques have their origins in Europe, tufting is a unique American innovation by which the pile is mechanically punched through an already woven backing—a technique similar to the hooking of the early colonists. Knitted carpets are the most recent manufacturing method by which pile and backing are fabricated in one operation. It is a method somewhat close to woven carpets, although the pile and backing yarns are looped together rather than interwoven together.

The revival of hand rugmaking seems to have started in the 1920s in Scandinavia and Poland. Finland and Sweden took their traditional rya technique and used it to create "paintings in wool." In Poland the flatweave **kilim** held sway, but was so refined that it became more tapestry than rug. In the relatively short period since the revival began, rugmaking has become one of the most popular forms of hand workmanship in the sophisticated craft nations. Any number of techniques are used, with new tools for certain techniques being constantly invented or improved. The appeal of rugmaking no doubt lies in the fact that a unique, one-of-a-kind rug that fits a specific interior can result, while at the same time, if the rugmaker recycles old fabric, the craft can be quite inexpensive.

If one is not already involved in a specific craft, then the choice of techniques with which to make a rug is a purely individual one and is determined by the design and texture of the rug, the amount of money that can be spent on tools, the amount of space the individual has to work in, and the preference that the rugmaker has for the advantages and limitations of one technique versus another. The rugmaker has to find the technique that best suits his or her personality, pocketbook, and depth of involvement.

The rugmaking techniques most closely associated with the craft are embroidery, latch hooking, hooking, weaving, braiding, knitting, and crochet, or a combination of these techniques. Some methods lend themselves better to certain materials and to certain end results than others. Some craftsmen like to be mobile with their work, and their choice of technique would turn to one in which the tools are small and portable, such as embroidery, latch hooking, crochet, or knitting.

EMBROIDERED RUGS An **embroidered rug** probably requires the smallest tool of any rug—a needle that is large-eyed, thick, and somewhat blunt. Known as a **rug** or tapestry **needle,** these are the most common needles used, as their large eyes make it possible to thread through heavy rug yarns, a combination of lighter weight yarns, or cut fabric strips. Two other needles that are used are sacking or couching needles (curved with sharp points) and bag needles (a variation of the sacking needle) that have curved-up tips with which it is easier to pick up the backing threads in some stitches and with some closely woven backings.

Embroidered rugs are also known as needlework, needlepoint, or tapestry rugs—the latter name given because some stitches very much resemble a true woven tapestry. The wearability of this type of rug depends on the type of backing used to stitch on, as well as the type of stitch and yarn or fabric used. **Rug warp cloth** is one of the best backings to use, while **canvas mesh** is one of the most popular. Linen backings, **burlap,** and **monk's cloth** can also be used. For rya pile embroidered rugs there is a specific **Scandinavian rug backing** that indicates where the rows of pile are to go. On all backings a hem of at least 2″ should be left on every side. Narrow backings can be pieced together to form much larger rugs. Some rugmakers prefer to use a frame to which the backing is attached in a stretched and taut position for greater stability while working. However, this is a matter of choice and not absolute necessity.

Rug yarn of various weights in wool or synthetics or mixtures of the two is the most commonly used yarn. However, the more elegant **Persian rug yarn** can be used as well as fabric strips cut ½″ wide from a knit fabric, nylon stockings, or a soft woven fabric cut on the bias to prevent fraying. With fabric strips, the weave of the backing has to be coarse enough for the strip to go readily through.

A rug can be worked all in one **stitch,** or in a combination of stitches for greater textural variety. It also can be worked in flat stitches combined with pile stitches. Any flat stitch can be put into higher relief with strips of **padding** put under the stitch as it is being worked. Embroidered rugs often have an **edging stitch** to give the rug a more finished look. This is usually in either a **blanket stitch** or a **braid stitch.** Some of the stitches used for the body of the rug are **cross stitch, Hungarian stitch,** soumak or **knitting stitch,** Gobelin or **tapestry stitch, tent stitch** and the Turkey or Ghiordes knot that gives short or long pile. However, many other stitches can be used, as well as variations on the above. All stitches should be fairly short and compact in order to avoid catching and pulling up. Stitches should not be pulled too tightly. A slight looseness is better for wear as it is more resilient and it will insure that the backing material is well covered.

In doing an embroidered rug the design is either directly drawn or stamped on the backing, or a **graph paper** design is followed and the rugmaker counts threads or holes of the backing to equal squares on the graph paper. The **hemming** is done either beforehand or after the stitching of the design is completed. If an edging stitch is not used, a crocheted edging of heavy yarn can be made instead. To completely finish the rug, **rug binding** is used to cover the hem or a lining is put over the entire back of the rug. Often an interlining is put in to make a flat-stitch rug last longer and be softer to tread on. Interlinings can be of heavy flannel, terry cloth, or any soft woven fabric, whereas linings are of denim, serge, or some other tightly woven and durable fabric. A **fringe** can be added on to an embroidered rug if it enhances or complements the rug design.

LATCH-HOOKED RUGS Another technique that employs only one tool and is one of the simplest ways of making the ever popular rya or shag is the latch-hook method. A specific tool called a **latch hook** is used to pull **precut** yarn through a canvas mesh rug backing. The tool and the method of pulling the yarn through result in a Ghiordes knot, which can give short or long pile, depending on the length of the precut pieces.

If the yarn is not bought precut then either a yarn cutter is needed or a homemade **gauge** around which the yarn is wound from the skein and then cut into pieces the length of the gauge. The yarn cutter snips the yarn into uniform 2½″ pieces, while with a gauge the pieces can be any length desired.

The standard backing is canvas mesh, but other backings with open spaces can be investigated. For example, a knitted or crocheted rug can have latch-hook pile pulled through it—either in sections or over the entire rug. Rug yarn is commonly used, but some lovely texture or color effects can be achieved by mixing finer yarns with these thick yarns. The number of yarns in a mixture used as one knot should not be so thick that there is constant difficulty in pulling the group through the backing. Even finely cut strips of knit or tightly woven fabrics can be used.

Designs for a latch-hooked rug are usually fairly simple and bold—as they would be for any shag effect. However, if the **pile height** is around 1″, then there is leeway for a more intricate pattern. Although most latch-hooked rugs are of one pile height, it is quite possible to make a rug with a mixture of areas of two or three different pile heights, thereby giving a sculptured effect. The lowest pile height that can be easily handled with a latch hook is 1″ and the highest (determined by how it feels underfoot) would be 3–4″.

A very large rug can easily be made with the latch-hook method since the canvas mesh lends itself readily to joining and the pile hides the joining seam.

The rug design is either drawn or painted on the backing to be followed during the latch-hooking, or the backing is empty and the rugmaker reproduces the design on the canvas by counting squares of the mesh to coincide with the squares on a graph-paper design. The knots can be placed in every hole in straight rows, or in staggered positions alternating even-numbered holes in one row with odd-numbered ones in the next row.

The rug can be hemmed prior to latch-hooking or after the rug is finished. The depth of the hem is 1½–2″ and the corners of the stiff backing are mitered. If the hem is not made till the rug is finished, then masking tape or **overcasting** is put around the entire outside edge of the canvas to prevent fraying as the rug is being made. The masking tape is removed before hemming—the overcasting is not. When the rug is finished, either rug binding or a lining can be sewn on.

CROCHET RUGS The craft of crochet is popular for constructing apparel, trimmings, and three-dimensional masks and objets d'art. Its place in the rugmaking field is not as strong, even though it is one of the easiest and quickest ways to make a rug. As in embroidery, crochet employs only one simple tool—a crochet hook. The hook is large-sized and the yarn thick—a combination that makes for speed. No frame or any other structure is necessary to hold the rug as it is being made. When the last crochet stitch is finished, the rug is finished—hemming, binding, or **backing the rug** are unnecessary (though considered desirable by some rugmakers).

The best materials for crocheting a rug are heavyweight rug wool, cotton or cotton and rayon rug yarn, jute or sisal cord, or cut fabric strips. All of these should be of a thickness the diameter of fine rope, or slightly heavier. If knitting worsted or a medium-weight rug yarn is used, the yarn should be doubled to get the right thickness for a firm rug. Using multiple yarns as one yarn will provide texture and color interest, but such a combination is not easily handled with the hook. Cut fabric strips may be folded and pressed to conceal the raw edges. However, the strips can also be used as is; threads that fray in most fabrics will soon wear off when the rug is in use, and the crochet stitches are such that further fraying is prevented.

Crochet hooks differ in size according to the material used and the gauge desired. They are marked with either letters or numbers. The further the letter is from "A" or the higher the number, the larger the hook. Usually for rugs a large size like K (10½) or J (9) is used. Wooden hooks come in extra-large sizes with numbers 13–19 being most used for rugs. Crochet hooks can also be used for other rugmaking techniques—like hooking (through burlap) or knot-forming—in place of a latch hook.

To establish the gauge in the construction of a rug, crochet a small piece about 3 or 4 inches square. With heavy rug yarn about 3 stitches to an inch is the usual gauge. This trial piece will also show if the rug structure will be firm enough.

Although many tend to think of crochet rugs as small mats, the dimensions can be as large as a room. Crochet proceeds quickly and easily and, for even easier working, a large rug can be made of small sections joined together. Besides square or rectangular shapes, crochet lends itself to round, oval, or free-form rugs. The design involved in a crochet rug is very often concerned with texture—in the structure of the stitches or in the contrasts that occur with combinations of yarns or fabric strips. To finished areas of rugs of simple crochet stitches can be added other stitches that will corrugate, flute, or otherwise add more texture to the surface.

Intricate designs of a pictorial or abstract nature are also possible. These can be put in during the crocheting or embroidered on afterward. Cross stitch is a favorite embroidery stitch for this. Also popular is pile inserted into a crochet rug, usually with a latch hook or an embroidery needle.

Rugs of a geometric block design are popular. These blocks are crocheted separately in various colors as squares, rectangles, or long strips and then joined together to form the finished rug. In planning blocks or strips, size and color placement of the design can be figured out on a large piece of wrapping paper. However, working along with a full-size design is not usual in crochet. In most cases the stitch directions and the gauge are given, and if there is a pattern in the rug this is indicated by a chart on graph paper. A full-size drawing can be made based on the graph paper one, and this would serve as a guide to insure that the pattern was proceeding correctly.

Crochet stitches are based on loops through which other loops are drawn. The differences between stitches result from the manner in which these loops are picked up, the number of times the yarn is carried over the hook, and the way the yarn is drawn through the loop already made. A crochet rug begins with a chain stitch by which a chain of yarn is formed that determines the width of a rug or rug section. The ends of the yarn chain can be joined to the center for a round or oval rug. On this chain are constructed single crochet, double crochet, slip stitch, and other stitches or variations on the preceding ones. The construction of the stitches should be close so that the rug is firm and durable. Only when making something in the nature of **filet mesh** is an open construction desirable. Here a crochet network is interwoven with fabric strips, old stockings or panty hose, felt, leather or vinyl, fur, clothesline cord, or rope. This is a popular method of rugmaking since it utilizes old materials otherwise relegated to the scrap bin. For the filet mesh stitch it is possible to use a colored twine or cotton rug warp yarn as well as a thicker or better quality yarn. The interlacing material is what gives durability and thickness to the rug, and the filet mesh works as a grid holding it all together.

Crochet rugs should be blocked by **steam pressing.** It is rare to line one, but some rugmakers feel that a lining strengthens the rug. Others spray or coat the back with latex so that it will not skid.

KNITTED RUGS   **Knitted rug**s have just about the same advantages and limitations that the above-mentioned crochet rugs do. Their most obvious similarity is that they are both methods of construction employing a continuous strand of yarn from which the rug is totally constructed. No backing or lining is necessary. The yarn requirements are the same, and it is also true in knitting that using many yarns as one yarn can be somewhat difficult to handle. In addition, knitting has an elastic quality that should be taken into consideration when choosing yarns, needles, and gauge, and if making a rug in sections that will eventually have to fit together. One must work with a rather tight stitch as loose structures are impractical for rug use. The piece(s) must be blocked at completion.

The most commonly used needle sizes for rugs are #7, 8, 9, 10 in American sizes and #6, 5, 4, 3 in English sizes (which run small to large from #18 down). American large sizes go up to #15. Too small a size in needles and stitch makes a rug too fine and lightweight. Too large a size makes too loose a stitch for a good, firm rug texture. As with crochet, a gauge is established based on the relationship of needle size to thickness of yarn. The average gauge for rugs using heavy yarn and large needles is about 3–5 stitches per inch with about 4–7 rows per inch.

Patterns in knitting can be quite complex and are usually drawn out on a graph-paper guide. The basic knitting stitches have less texture than crochet ones, so interest

and design are dependent on good color choice and proportion and placement of colors. Most often used is the plain knitting or garter stitch. Care should be taken not to bind or finish off the rug too tightly. Binding off should be the same width as the beginning or casting-on, or the rug will be misshapen. A rug may be knit in blocks or as a complete unit. Embellishment of a knit background is often done with embroidery stitches or pile or latch-hooked knotted pile.

Very often a knit foundation is made to be completely covered with pile. This foundation is knit of a strong yarn with the pile either being inserted later or placed in position as the rug is being made. The latter or "laid-in" method was supposedly invented in colonial times as a poor man's attempt to copy Turkish work or knotted pile rugs. This pile is composed of small lengths of yarn or fabric strips that are laid-in across the foundation stitch and caught in place as the knitting proceeds. The exact method of laying-in varies, with some rugmakers inserting the pile strips so that one end protrudes on the right side and the other on the back side. This latter end is then pulled to the outer or right side. This folds the pile strip around the stitch just taken and brings both ends of the pile on the same side of the rug. Other rugmakers put the pile strip around the left needle and catch it in as they knit.

Knit rugs made in sections or blocks should be sewn together on the wrong side with carpet yarn or heavy sewing thread. The sewing stitches should have some slack so that the sections will lie flat when on the floor.

Very often a row or two of single crochet is made around all sides of the rug, both as a finishing touch and to provide a more stable edge. This would be worked with a crochet hook in a size compatible with the yarn being used. Due to the elastic nature of a knit rug, binding is also sometimes used to maintain the outer shape. It also serves as a protective edge against wear. A pad under the rug would increase the wearability of the rug.

BRAIDED RUGS   **Braided rug**s are done in the rhythmic technique of **braiding** to produce a sturdy, long-wearing rug out of cut fabric strips. The fingers are the only real tool employed, with a chair or table used to clamp the braids so as to hold them and maintain tension as one braids. The ease and speed of the technique depend much on the beforehand preparations, which involve cutting, **piecing** and folding the fabric strips. A **strip cutter** can be used to aid in the cutting and **braid-aid**s in the turning-in of the cut edges. Needles, **bodkin**s, or **lacer**s are used to sew or lace the braided strips together. Heavy carpet thread or **lacing** is used. It is important to use something durable for the sewing, since the braids themselves will have a long life and it is the thread holding them together that gives out first.

Materials used in braiding are usually rag-tag items or fabrics obtained from remnant counters or mill-end stores—which makes this one of the most economical methods of rugmaking. However, new fabrics can also be used, and other materials such as felt, yarn, cord, or grasses. Wool is considered by some as the best and only fiber for braided rugs. However, cotton and synthetics can also be used—especially for small kitchen and bathroom rugs. A variety of fibers should not be mixed too indiscriminately, since the wear will be uneven. Small, odd pieces of fabric strips can be sewn together for a completely random color and texture effect, or the color pattern can be planned first and then the cloth assembled that will fit into the color pattern.

The usual method of braiding is to use a three-strand braid. However, four- or five-strand braids can also be used. If the material used is very fine, then even a higher number than five can be used. Care should be taken when many strands are used for a braid that the resulting braid does not become too large and unwieldy for shaping into the rug. **Butting** is a technique used for sharp color changes. **Interbraiding** is a variation on the braiding process that can result in a self-fringe. Units or pieces can be braided individually and then laced together to form long runners or odd shapes. The design potential of braiding is just beginning to be tapped. Interesting free-form shapes are being constructed along with the traditional "colonial-type" oval or rectangular braided rugs.

When the last braid is sewn in place the rug is finished, with no rug binding or lining necessary. If there are any bumps in any areas, they should be steamed out. The only additional item is a **rug pad** that some rugmakers elect to put down for a softer rug.

HOOKED RUGS **Hooked rug**s are made with a hook that pulls yarn or finely cut cloth strips through a rug backing so that a continuous loop pile is formed on the right side of the backing. **Hand hook**s or crochet hooks (G or F size) are the traditional tools of hooking, while **speed hook**s and **punch needle**s are newer versions. A **hooking frame** to hold the backing taut is used with the latter two tools, while those using a hand hook can either put the backing on a frame or hold it in the hand. For those using fabric strips, a strip cutter will make the task of cutting strips easier. **Bent-handled scissors** or surgical shears with a bent handle are good to have on hand if the loops are to be cut and the pile trimmed down. This can be done with ordinary sharp scissors but the bent handle enables the blades to lie flat along the top of the pile so that a better and easier shearing job can be done.

The backing used should be strong, yet loosely woven so that it is easy to get the hook through the material. Durability of the backing is a factor in both the wear the rug will withstand and in the workout that the backing gets as the hook goes in and out of it. Burlap, cotton monk's cloth, and rug warp cloth are the fabrics most used as backing for hooked rugs.

Rug and other yarns, roving, jute, unraveled knit and woven fabrics, felt, stockings, neckties, and all sorts of fabric strips can be used for the pile loops. Yarn and fabric can be combined in one rug. Just about any yarn can be used, but textured yarns will often catch in a speed hook because of their unevenness. Fabric strips can range in width from $3/32-\frac{1}{4}''$. Wider strips than this can be hooked only with a hand hook. Quarter inch is the usual width for medium-weight woolen fabrics. The strips should not be cut too long or they will prove unwieldy. $1\frac{1}{2}-2$ yards would be the maximum for a speed hook or punch needle, and for a hand hook the length can be much shorter.

The design possibilities of hooked rugs are quite vast. They range from intricate to bold in pictorial, geometric, or abstract forms. There can be several different pile heights, cut pile mixed with the loop pile and texture effects produced by the direction of the hooking. In addition, the outside shape can range from simple squares, rectangles, circles, ovals, and half-circles to fancy curves and free-form ideas. Size is no problem since most backings are easily joined together and then overhooked in the joined area.

To execute it, the design must be stamped or drawn on the backing. For hand hooking the design is on the right side of the backing; for speed or punch hooking, the design is reversed and stamped or drawn on the back side of the backing.

A hem allowance of from $2-4''$ is made—the extra amount is often needed when attaching the backing to the frame. The edges of the backing should be overcast with cotton thread to prevent fraying. This is done prior to **transferring the design** to the backing. If using a hooking frame, the backing is attached to the frame with a staple gun, thumb tacks, or by **lacing** with a cord. For extra strength, double the backing at the point of attachment to the frame. Since pressure from hooking has a tendency to slightly stretch the backing and induce slackness, lacing is perhaps the best method to use. It is the quickest way to remedy the slackness.

With each different type of hook there is a different technique to hooking. In using the hand hook, the yarn or fabric is held between the index finger and thumb of the left hand, beneath the place where the hook will go through. The hook is held in the right hand and is pushed through the backing and pulls the material from the left hand up through to the front where, with a clockwise twist of the wrist, it is freed from this loop so it can move on to pull up the next. If there is difficulty in pulling the yarn or fabric through the backing, the hook can be pressed down to the handle and the hole will be widened.

With a punch needle the gauge is first set for the desired pile height and the needle tip inserted that corresponds to the size of yarn or fabric strip to be used. The punch needle is pushed through the back of the backing until the gauge touches the backing. When the needle is withdrawn the loop will remain the correct height. If the gauge is removed from the punch needle, it is possible to plunge the needle further down for longer pile. The needle works best when the loop is caught on the underside (right side) with the index finger and thumb and held in place as the needle is withdrawn.

With speed hooks both hands are used to work the hook so that it moves by itself across the taut backing. They are held perpendicular to the backing and their movement from one loop to the next is affected by different mechanical actions (according to the model of speed hook used). The pile height and density of loops are controlled by the speed hook.

Loops are not always a uniform height—an imperfection that adds to the handmade charm of the craft. The density of the loops depends on the thickness of the yarn or fabric strip and how high the loops are. Close density keeps the loops from pulling out easily and the backing from showing. However, if the loops are too dense, the fabric will buckle and not lie flat. The loops should have enough space to open up in. The higher the loops, the more space between rows and less stitches per inch. The shorter the loops, the closer the rows and more stitches per inch. For a ¼″ high loop the rows should be hooked so closely together that they will almost be touching. Two threads of the backing between the loops and two threads between rows of loops are usually sufficient to skip for higher loops of a medium-weight rug yarn or ¼″ fabric strips. More threads can be skipped to prevent crowding.

A design area or motif is outlined first by hooking and then filled in. It can also be outlined for greater emphasis once more after the filling in is completed. The smaller motifs are done first, then the larger ones, and finally the background. With a hand hook, in order to obtain interesting background texture, do not hook in straight lines except in the border of the rug. The loops can be placed in fan-shaped patterns or irregular ones following the contour of a motif. With a punch needle or speed hook it is easier to work in straight lines. When going from one motif to another, the yarn is cut and begun again. Ideally the back of the rug should look like a series of colored dots with no connecting strand between dots. Beginnings and ends of strands are pulled all the way through to the front and clipped to the height of the loops. When the rug is finished it should be inspected for spots where the backing may show, and filled in with random stitches of one or two loops. Hook the two outside rows close together, as this will form a thicker border on the edges, where the wear is heaviest.

After the rug is finished the loops can be sheared. If using a frame, **shearing rug**s is easier to do off the frame. The finished work is folded so a row of loops stands out. The blade of the scissors is inserted into the loops and they are cut through. Areas can be beveled or sculptured down to emphasize a design area or for shading. The **blooming** of cut yarn ends can be accomplished by steaming with an iron or pressing with a wet cloth and medium-hot iron.

As the last step, the rug edges are finished by hemming back or using rug binding. A lining can be put on if desired. A coating of liquid latex (many brand names) can be given the rug so as to prevent slipping and, in some cases, the loops or pile tufts from pulling out. Another method is to latex before hemming and then to press the hem into the latex so it is glued to the back. A secondary backing, or burlap lining, can also be pressed down over the latex. The latex should be able to bleed through so that the rug is skidproof.

RUGWEAVING Weaving entails making a rug through the interlacing of warp (vertical threads) and **filling** or weft (horizontal threads). The warp threads are held under tension on a loom to make the interlacing process easier. The filling is inserted between the warp threads with the aid of a shuttle or **butterfly.** Pile and certain surface textures are put in by knotting or wrapping around the warp threads.

Many woven rugs are **filling-faced,** i.e., the warp is totally covered and only the filling shows. They go by the name of flatweave, flatwoven, or simply flat rugs. The design is usually horizontal **stripe**s or narrow vertical ones running selvage to selvage. An elaboration on this would be tapestry rugs in which the filling is put in-between the warp threads according to a pictorial, geometric, or abstract pattern, and each filling color runs across the warp only as far as the pattern dictates. In the tapestry method various techniques such as interlocking, dovetailing, and slit tapestry play important roles. **Kilim** rugs are well-known examples of tapestry rugs using primarily the slit tapestry technique, while Scandinavian **rölakan** rugs show typical uses of interlocking.

Woven rugs appearing flat but actually having a slightly raised surface texture are made by a technique called **soumak.** There are highly-patterned examples of soumak rugs from the Middle East. Also associated with the Middle East are knotted pile rugs using the Ghiordes and Sehna knots. The Spanish knot is found in rugs originating mainly in Spain. These are all low-pile rugs. The Ghiordes knot in a high-pile version is a Scandinavian innovation and goes by the name of **rya.** The Scandinavians call the short pile **flossa.**

When soumak is used there is a plain-weave ground weave between every row of the soumak wrapping to hold the wrapping together. When knotted pile is put in, there is also a ground weave between every row of pile to hold the knots in place. The filling of the ground weave can be beaten down so closely together that it is identical to flatweave. **Looping** or **boutoné** is a short loop pile achieved not by knotting but by picking up loops of yarn to the surface. Since there is no knot, it depends completely on the ground weave to hold it in place.

Swedish knot is a variation of soumak and **weft chaining** can be used in place of soumak for the slightly raised knitted pattern effect. Weft chaining is not weaving but is somewhat akin to it as is **weft twining,** in that both need a warp element around which they are worked. In weft twining a soumak look can be produced through **countertwining** while **half turn**s and **full turn**s comprise simpler twining which can have elaborate patterns through color placement.

Rugs can be done totally in any of the above methods or be a combination of techniques and effects. In the weaving process, pile and soumak are put in by hand row-by-row, and after each row the ground weave is woven in before proceeding to the next row of pile or soumak. Selvage to selvage flatweave is loom-controlled, while the pile or soumak is **finger-manipulated.** The loom used can be very simple and involve only the two sheds or openings needed for flatweave. Examples of simple looms are upright looms such as frame looms, tapestry looms, **rug loom**s, Navajo looms, and warp-weighted looms. Simple **hoop loom**s can be used to make round rugs.

There are other woven rugs whose manner of interlacing produces the rug and the pattern. They are totally loom-controlled and therefore demand a more complex loom called a **harness loom.** Often a four-harness loom is all that is needed, but for some rug constructions **mul-**

tiharness looms are necessary. The majority of the rugs woven on harness looms are of a flatweave nature and depend on threading, treadling, sett, and color for the pattern differences. Boundweave and **Summer and Winter weave** are but two examples of weaves that lend themselves to rugs. Almost any weave with the right weight yarns could be adapted for rug use. Rugs like the Scandinavian **mattor** depend on a color change in the threading to make them work. Loom-controlled rugs woven with stuffer threads need enough harnesses to have a weave to cover the **stuffer thread**s, while to make **warp pile,** a second warp beam is needed. Warp pile is an example of a loom-controlled **pile weave,** as is **corduroy.** A lesser pile can be achieved through **chenille fabric**s or **twice-woven rug**s. **Double-faced rug**s can be made with or without pile on one or both sides.

There is also card weaving, which does not use a loom but rather a series of cards or tablets by which a type of warp twining is manipulated. Long bands are woven and these can be joined together to form a rug.

The major piece of equipment needed for weaving a rug is a loom. Other items that some rug weavers invest in are **rug fork**s or **hand beater**s, **rug shuttle,** or **ski stick shuttle**s and templates or stretchers. For precut pile, a homemade gauge is needed and a **flossa rod** for short pile.

The materials that a woven rug is made out of include a strong **carpet warp** or **rug warp** yarn for the lengthwise threads that will take the greatest strain during the interlacing process. Since they do not show in the flatweave rugs, their color is important only in that it may appear in the fringe. In loom-controlled rugs where the warp may show as part of the pattern, the yarn is chosen for its color and character as well as its durability. Warp yarns for a rug should not have too much give, be fairly smooth (i.e., without textured nubs or slubs), and not fray apart. Some commonly used warp yarns are 8/4 cotton rug warp, cotton **seine twine,** wrapping twine, linen rug warp yarn, and wool warp yarn.

The sett, or density, of the warp yarn on the loom depends on the type of rug being woven. For flatweave techniques it is essential that the warp be spaced so that it can be covered by the filling. The thicker a warp yarn, the further apart it is set.

Many types of **rug filler** are available to the weaver. The least expensive rugs to make are **rag rug**s using cut fabric strips as filler in a cotton carpet warp. The fabric strips should not be expected to cover the warp. The warp threads will be partially exposed and should be of a color that goes with the fabric being used. The fiber contents of the fabric strips can be mixed, but in some cases this will make the rug unwashable since a shrinkage problem will occur. It would be best to prewash and test the fabric—particularly if fiber content is unknown.

When using yarn, the choice should be for a softer yarn than the warp—but still sturdy enough to withstand the wear. The thickness of the filling yarn depends on the thickness of the warp yarn and how it is to interlace with it. In flatweave rugs, the heavier the warp yarn or more warp threads per inch, the finer the filling yarn. The finer the warp yarn or the less ends per inch, the thicker the filling yarn.

Finer filling yarns usually give a more flexible rug. Soft yarns compress more easily to cover the warp. Wool, because of its resilient nature, is a favorite as a filling yarn, but synthetics and other fibers such as Scandinavian **cowhair yarn** can be used. Since in a flat rug the filling and warp get the wear directly, without having pile to protect them, the choice should always be fibers and yarns that can take this wear.

Novelty items such as **horsehair** can also be used as filling. Leather and fur strips are usually combined with yarn to help hold the strips in place.

Yarns used in the pile are the most luxuriant in the rug. They should be resilient enough so that the pile stands up well to wear and is pleasant underfoot. Wool and silk were the pile fibers of the Oriental rug weavers. Today wool is the preferred fiber, but synthetics have become more readily available to the home craftsperson and are being tried more and more. Fine yarns can be mixed with thick ones, lustrous yarns with dull ones, and hard-twist ones with soft yarns. A pile yarn can be used alone in a knot or in a grouping of 3 or 4 strands. The determining factor in how many yarns to a group is how comfortably the pile knot fits around the warp threads that hold it in place. If the knot is too bulky and tends to undo itself, then the group is too thick to be used as a single knot. The top of the knot, or pile, should cover the ground weave filling. If it doesn't, then more yarns in a group or closer spacing should be tried.

Besides yarn, other materials like felt, leather, and bias-cut fabric strips can be used as pile. Combinations of fibers that might not work well as filling can be used in the pile without mishap.

A woven rug can be designed to show the beauty of its color, pattern, or material. A pile rug can be of one pile height and have an intricately patterned design, or the design interest can involve mixing various pile heights and cut and uncut pile. Short pile lends itself to extremely detailed designs, since a short pile calls for more knots per square inch. High pile or rya is best with large, bold patterns: the pile knots are sparser and the long pile tends to fall over and obliterate small details. **Color blending** can be used effectively to add interest to the large patterns.

In a simple flatweave rug, woven selvage to selvage, the horizontal stripes can be interspersed with vertical ones made by a **pick-and-pick** alternation of two colors. Combining the vertical and horizontal stripes can lead to other geometric forms.

The design in a loom-controlled rug is achieved through the threading and treadling. It is a structural design, since it comes about through the manner of interlacing. The plans for the design are charted on graph paper as the drawing-in draft and treadling or chain draft. Rugs woven according to the finger-manipulated techniques are usually constructed following a plan or drawing that is rendered to scale on graph paper with every square denoting a certain number of knots or a certain number of inches across or up the rug. A full-scale drawing or cartoon can also be used, but these are difficult to handle on a harness loom (the sketch should be placed under the work in progress to see if the pattern is going according to plan). On an upright loom the full-scale drawing can be taped to the back of the loom.

The size of the rug can be determined by the width of the loom, or the rug can be woven in sections that are later joined together. Most woven rugs are square or rectangular in shape, but it is possible to weave round rugs or free-form rugs.

The first procedure in weaving a rug is warping and dressing the loom, i.e., getting the warp threads measured out, in order, and strung or threaded according to plan under tension. The weaving process begins at the bottom of an upright loom or at the breast beam on a harness loom. A heading is woven first, and then the rug proper, according to the technique and pattern chosen. If the rug is to have a hem or fringe, this must be allowed for at the beginning and end of the rug. In getting the best coverage possible of the filling over warp, the filling should be in a loose diagonal in the shed. Further slack in the yarn for better coverage can be obtained by **bubbling.** If using a hand beater, the beating should begin at the point where the filling yarn entered the shed. Beating is done with sharp, fast strokes. The selvages on rugs with pile can have extra reinforcement in the filling since the pile does not usually extend to the selvage yarns. This bound edge or **argatch** can be done in several different ways. When the rug is taken off the loom, the beginning and end are hemmed, fringed, or given another type of **finishing edge.** The side edges are finished already by virtue of having the selvage.

MISCELLANEOUS RUGS   Rugs can also be produced by processes such as **felting,** quilting, shirring, and **appliqué.** With the exception of felting, these methods involve some degree of stitchery or, as in the case of **shirred rug**s, even crochet or knitting. Felting can also involve embroidery if the rugmaker feels that the felted rug texture is too plain and needs some color and design to make it more distinctive. Felted rugs are large thick sheets of matted wool or hair fibers usually of one color, but there is no reason that they could not be multicolored.

Of the above-mentioned techniques, probably appliqué is the most popular, since it often reuses old fabrics and thus becomes an economical craft as well as one that affords many design opportunities. The fabric used in the construction and the thread holding the materials together must be able to take the wear and tear given floor coverings.

In appliquéd rugs and quilted rugs, their close relatives, we have floor coverings in which a material or pieces of material are joined together and form a foundation that is embellished with or without concealing the background. The embellishment or decoration may be of other goods cut into ornamental motifs and appliquéd on top of the rug foundation fabric, or it may consist of embroidery. Quilted rugs are rugs ornamented with indented stitches (whether or not combined with appliqué or other embroidery) for it is the quilting that binds two or more materials together to supply sufficient body for a floor covering.

Fur rugs are popular and can be made by cut strips inserted into weaving or crochet or by arranging larger

pieces into a patchwork appliqué. A large fake-fur piece can be cut into a pelt shape the size of the entire rug and then sewn on to a felt backing that can also extend further than the pelt shape as a border.

There are many variations on appliqué. Button rugs, which are also offshoots of shirred rugs, are made of small pieces of fabric sewn on a backing in tufts. A simulated pile rug can be made by appliqué by sewing long folded strips of felt or jersey fabric to a burlap backing and then cutting the strips down to almost the stitching line. The strips are sewn on in rows that overlap each other. The color can be solid or a design can be formed by color placement in the rows.

FINISHING   The finishing a rug gets depends on the type of rug made, the materials used, and the process of construction followed. In some cases, the finishing is minimal, if any, while in others it is elaborate and involved. Finishing includes such things as **blocking,** pressing, **sponging, binding** or hemming, joining sections, **darning-in, hemstitching,** making a fringe or finishing edge, sewing on **tassel**s, or backing the rug with latex or a lining.

Steam pressing is perhaps the most minimal of finishing treatments given to a rug. It will improve the appearance of flat or low pile rugs—especially the latter, since steam will open up or bloom the cut ends of the yarn. With long pile, steam pressing is unnecessary except where a backing is buckled and the attempt is being made to steam out the excess buckling. Knit and crochet rugs need to be steamed or blocked to maintain their shapes. Corners that curl up on all types of rugs can sometimes be flattened out by repeated steam pressing.

Braided rugs that have edges that have "ruffled" or a center with bumps can be blocked in order to try to overcome this construction defect. Embroidered rugs that have been pulled out of shape during the work process should be blocked. While steam pressing alone is the application of water and heat without the rug's being fixed in position, blocking implies that the rug is stretched and tacked to its specified shape before steam or more excessive moisture, as in sponging, is applied.

Flat rugs and those having extremely low pile can be worked on from either side, with care taken that neither the stitches nor the pile is flattened out. Higher low pile and shag pile should be worked on right-side up. In either case, should the pile become flattened it is brushed up only after the rug is completely dry.

Rugs that are made in sections must be joined together. Very often this is done when the rug sections have been completed, since one of the principle reasons for joining is that the work proceeds in small, manageable portions rather than large, heavy, and cumbersome ones. However, when the reason for joining is the narrow width of a rug backing, this can be done beforehand or while the rug is in progress. This type of joining is permanent, since it involves overlapping the backing sections and then working through the doubled areas. The individual pieces of the backing should be of the same weight or mesh, and the warp and filling threads should be aligned correctly. The backing sections overlap each other from ⅜−2″ at the joining seam. This variance depends on the thickness of the backing and whether the overlap includes a selvage of the backing. A heavy backing would overlap less than a lighter weight one, and selvages need overlap only from ⅜–1″. If burlap sacks are used for hooked rugs (as they were in previous eras), they can be seamed together rather than overlapped. This can be done either by hand or machine stitching.

Swedish rug backings are not overlapped, but joined in the same manner as a woven rug. This is done by assembling the sections face down on the floor and sewing them together from the back. Large pieces or those with a design that must be matched at the joining should be temporarily pinned or tacked together with thread so as to prevent shifting during the final sewing, which is done with a **lacing stitch** (or one of its variations) using carpet thread, heavy duty cotton thread, or the yarn used in the rug if it is strong enough for this purpose.

Decorative stitches can be used at the joining on the right side of flat rugs such as embroidered, knit, or crochet rugs. It is best to steam press all joinings after sewing.

Binding or hemming is a necessary finishing for rugs on a backing: it turns back and covers the raw edges of the backing. Woven rugs have two selvages and two unfinished edges that can be bound, hemmed, or fringed. Crochet, knit, and braided rugs have finished edges produced by their respective techniques, but sometimes a binding is added for extra stability and strength at the edges. The binding is sewn to the hem in a position as close to the finished edge of the rug as possible, yet it should not show on the front of the rug. It can be hand-sewn or machine stitched if the rug is on a soft rug backing. In the latter case the binding is stitched on prior to the rug's being worked. When binding is sewn on all edges, the corners are mitered by folding the binding at the corner.

For a round or oval rug, a binding is made out of strong, firmly woven cotton fabric by cutting 2½″-wide bias strips and seaming them together in a length that will go around the rug. This bias binding is eased to fit around the curves and tucks are taken in as needed at the point of stitching to the backing.

All rugs on backings have a hem that is folded back at the rug edge, and this fold is attached to the rug and the raw edges of the hem hidden. A simple way to accomplish this in the case of soft backings or a rug that has not been too tightly woven at the hem edges is to fold the raw edges under the hem itself and sew this fold to the rug. Woven hems can also have finished edges manipulated out of the warp threads that secure the raw edge and that require no further folding back under the hem. In all cases when a hem is folded back, it should be done so as not to pull open the stitches or pile on the surface and force the background to show through. Strong yarn or thread to match the rug or backing is used to sew bindings or hem to the back. A large-eyed tapestry needle or a curved rug needle makes the sewing easier.

If a rug lining is used, then the binding can be omitted. Linings give a lightweight rug more body as well as lessening the wear on the rug. Linings are optional items in finishing and backing rugs, not necessary ones. If used, care should be taken that the lining is securely sewn at all edges and tacked down with stitches at random points throughout the rug center. Latexing the rug is another method of backing the rug and also assuring that the rug is skidproof.

Many rugs can also be completed by having fringes or finishing edges made out of the existing threads or added on to the rug. The existing threads would be the warp threads in a woven rug or the threads left on all sides of a rug backing when the crossing threads have been frayed out. It should be planned beforehand so there is an ample amount left at the rug edges for the subsequent fringe or finishing edge to be made. A fringe can be left loose or made into a braided, plied, or knotted **fringe**. Knotted fringes can be elaborate structures involving macramé or intricate knots, or simple adornments using just an **overhand knot**. Fringes when completed are anywhere from 2″ to 10″ in length. The original starting length of the yarn is longer, since a certain amount of yarn is taken up in the process chosen to complete the fringe.

Whipping and **wrapping** can add a decorative touch to fringes and to **tassels**. Tassels are larger groupings of yarn placed at the corners of a rug or at various selected points along the edge. In the case of tassels and a fringe that is added on, thought should be given to the color and type of yarn used so that it complements the rug.

If a fringe is not desired, various types of edgings can be made, such as **Damascus edge, looped edge, Philippine edge, Swedish braid, twined edge,** and **wrapped edge.**

rug needle. Rugmaking. A pointed steel tool with a large eye used in making **embroidered** or **needleworked rugs** and to lace braids together in **braided rugs.** Rug needles are also known as tapestry, rya, or canvas needles and are thicker than normal sewing needles. They are straight with a blunt tip. There is also a curved model called a sacking needle that is sharper and is especially useful for sewing on **rug binding,** or hemming, doing **edging stitch**es, and repairing frayed edges. Also see **finishing needle. needle.**

rug pad. Rugmaking. A thick cushion put underneath a rug to protect it, give it traction, and make it softer underfoot. Pads can be bought in standard rug sizes, or be cut to order, from a floor-covering store. They can also be homemade out of heavy felt padding, rubber lining, or foam rubber. The pad should be ½–1½″ smaller than the rug it goes under, and not so thick that the rug is visibly raised from the floor.

rug sampler. Rugmaking. A rug swatch of up to 1 foot square made to determine color, texture, and design effects; suitability of the technique and materials; and yarn and fabric amounts needed, thereby indicating the cost of the full rug. Based on the weight of the sampler and what proportion of the total final rug area it is, the weight of the total rug can be determined and the cost of the yarn or the amount of rag strips needed. For example, if one square foot weighed 10 ounces, a 5′ × 3′ rug, or 15 square feet, would weigh 150 ounces or almost 9½ pounds. The price per pound of the material is then multiplied by 9½. If there is a mixture of techniques, **pile height**s, and materials, the cost then would have to be averaged out based on what visual proportion each occupies in the rug.

Some general rules of thumb are: a **braided rug** of medium heavy wool will take approximately ¾ pound of fabric for each square foot, so, for example, a 4′ × 5′ rectangular braided rug would require about 15 pounds of fabric strips; a **hooked rug** of ¼″ **pile** would weigh about 8 ounces per square foot (depending on the weight of the backing used and how tightly or sparsely the individual hooks); a 2″ high pile **rya** rug will weigh in the vicinity of 11 ounces per square foot. Also see **yarn calculations.**

rug shuttle. Rugmaking. Weaving. (Also called rag shuttle.) A large **shuttle** designed to hold great quantities of yarn. It has a flat top and bottom, joined together by either two, three, or four 2″ dowels, or a solid, flat centerpiece, around which the **filling** yarn is wound. It is available in many sizes from 8″ to 20″ with the larger sizes being most preferred for **rug weaving.** Rug shuttles can be used to weave with rags or fur strips. See ill.

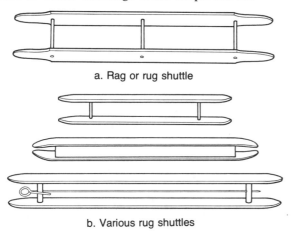

a. Rag or rug shuttle

b. Various rug shuttles

rug swatch. Rugmaking. See **rug sampler.**

rug warp. Rugmaking. Weaving. The yarns used as the lengthwise threads in a rug. In most cases, they are completely hidden so that they play no part in the design of the rug. A good, durable quality of rug yarn affects the weaving qualities of a rug, its feel, how it lies on the floor, and its wearability. The yarn should be strong and fairly smooth, and should not fray or have too much give. When the rug warp is visible, as in a **self-fringe** or in a **rag rug,** attention must be paid to its color and texture. **Cotton** and **linen** are the most commonly used, while **wool** is the traditional rug warp of **Oriental rug**s (although at times they are also made with a cotton warp). Navajo blanket rugs have a wool warp. In cotton yarns, **carpet warp** is the most popular. **Seine twine** or wrapping twine is even better in terms of body. The latter is the common twine which parcels are wrapped with in stores. It comes from 8- to 16-**ply,** is available in stationery or twine stores, and can be home dyed any color.

Specially prepared linen warp yarn can be used; its stiffness and inelasticity give a nice firmness to the rug. Its natural color makes it attractive as a fringe. However,

it is not as durable a fiber as either wool or cotton, and anything that is not labeled as warp yarn may fray.

If wool is used, it must be of a long-**staple**, coarse **fiber** that is tightly spun so that a hard yarn results that will be able to take the beating imposed on it while packing down the **filling.** Other yarns may be used if they have the above-mentioned qualities necessary for a warp yarn. These yarns include **hemp, jute, ramie** and many synthetics. If the rug is to be **warp-face,** or a combination of both warp and filling showing, many other yarns can be used with an emphasis on choosing their color and texture as well as their strength and durability.

rug warp cloth. Rugmaking. A somewhat stiff, quite heavy, and very strong cotton, available in two or three weights. They are all tightly woven in a **plain weave** and are of superior quality. Rug warp cloth is used as a backing for **embroidered** and **hooked rug**s. It is available in two or three widths measuring up to 200″. Also see **rug backing.**

rugweaving. Rugmaking. Weaving. The making of a floor covering by the process of **weaving** and related techniques. The best-known examples are **knotted pile, soumak,** and **flatweave rugs** which require only two **shed**s to weave. These are **finger-manipulated** techniques, whereas **loom-controlled** designs require more sheds. There are many designs that lend themselves to rugs—as long as the yarn used is durable and the **beat** and the **sett** are close enough to form a firm fabric. For **flat rug**s, **crackle, overshot,** or **Summer and Winter weave**s are often used. **Corduroy** is a popular **pile weave. Bound weave** gives almost the impression of a **tapestry weave** rug. Also see **boutonné, chenille fabric, flossa, hoop loom, ingrain rug, kilim, laid-in, log cabin pattern, looping, mattor, Navajo weaving, rag rug, rölakan, rug filler, rug fork, rug loom, rug warp, rug yarn, rya, stuffer thread, tapestry rug, twice-woven rug.**

rug wool. Crewel. Embroidery. Needlepoint. A sturdy three-ply yarn which can be used with canvas sizes 3, 4, 5, or 7 and wears well. In crewel, it can be used effectively on a fabric with a coarse weave, such as **Hessian cloth.**

rug yarn. Rugmaking. The name given to yarns sold primarily for use in **embroidered, latch-hooked,** and **hooked rug**s, and as the **pile** or **filling** in woven rugs. They can also be used in any other technique to make a rug or for any other purpose. Their common characteristics are durability and strength. Most are fairly inelastic, and some have a hard surface that accounts for their durability. Rug yarns are usually composed of two to six threads **plied** together. There are some that are made of all **wool fiber** of long **staple,** but more and more synthetics or blends of wool and synthetics are being used. Some rug yarn has been given a pronounced twist to emulate the Scandinavian rya rug yarns. Rug yarns can be divided into lightweight (or fine), medium, and heavyweight (or thick) categories. Heavyweight yarns can be about ¼″ in diameter and are most often of cotton or rayon or other synthetic. They have bulk built into them and are surprisingly light in proportion to their thickness. Also see **cowhair yarn, Persian rug yarn.**

rule. Woodworking. See **measuring tools.**

rule of thumb. A measure, based on the assumption that the distance from the end of the thumb to the first joint is about 1 inch.

runner. Lacemaking. See **worker.**

runner. Metalworking. A tube in a **mold** for metal **casting** through which molten metal enters the mold cavity. The main runner may branch into several smaller runners feeding various parts of the casting. Also see **gate.**

running. Batik and Tie-dye. See **bleeding.**

running a bead. Metalworking. The process in **welding** of making a molten **puddle** by heating the **base metal** and moving the puddle in a series of overlapping **bead**s along a seam to be joined, with or without a **welding rod.** Also see **Metalworking: Welding.**

running foot. Woodworking. See **wood.**

running pliers. Stained Glass. A glass-cutting tool used for long, thin, straight cuts. Place the pliers across the **score** line, perpendicular to it about an inch from the edge of the glass. Pressure applied to the handles will cause the score to run. Also see **Stained Glass: Cutting Glass.**

running stitch. Crewel. Embroidery. A simple **basting stitch** in which the needle is worked over and under the **background fabric.** Come up at A, go down at B and up at C, making a straight line of even stitches. The surface stitches are the same length as those on the back. Several stitches can be taken up on the needle at one time if the work is being done in the hand and not on a frame. It is recommended as a line stitch. See ill. Also see **overcast stitch, running stitch threaded.**

Running stitch

C B A

running stitch. Lacemaking. A stitch used in lacemaking to hold down the lace to the background netting, as in **appliqué** lace. This stitch is made with needle and thread in a straight line (different from the angle at which **overcast stitch**es are placed) or on an outline of a **motif** in a small continuous stitch.

running stitch. Leather. The commonly used stitch for sewing straight seams. The **needle** is run up through one hole, down through the next, and so on, until the seam is completed. For a stronger seam, stitch back over the seam, filling in the alternate holes. See ill. Also see **double needle stitch** and **Leatherwork: Sewing Leather.**

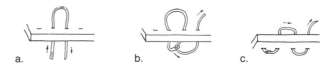

a.   b.   c.

running stitch. Quilts. Stitchery. A small, straight, in-and-out stitch, sewn two or three at a time, used for both **appliqué** and embroidery. In appliqué the running stitch is sewn so that the small part of each stitch shows on the top. The long part of the stitch is on the reverse side, making a fine pattern of short stitches or dots next to the hemmed edge. A single thread is usually used.

In embroidery, the running stitch is extremely versatile. It may be sewn with a single strand of sewing thread or with as many as six strands of floss. The length of the stitch can vary to give a nearly solid line or a lightly dotted line. The consistency of stitch length is of importance in this stitch, and has a greater effect on appearance than the length itself.

The **quilting stitch** is essentially the same as the running stitch if several stitches are taken at one time. On a thick quilt, or for especially fine quilting, the needle may take just one stitch at a time, going straight up, then almost straight down. Even when sewn in this more time-consuming way, the quilting and running stitches look identical. See ill.

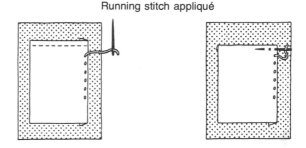

Running stitch appliqué

running-stitch embroidery. Stitchery. A way of drawing with thread on **fabric** by using just the **running stitch.** The **needle** becomes the drawing tool, making lines of thread, floss, or **yarn.** Running-stitch embroidery is often used to define areas or depict details in **banner**s, **soft sculpture, stitchery panel**s, and toys.

running stitch threaded. Crewel. Embroidery. (Also called interlaced running stitch.) A variation of the **running stitch** in which a **tapestry needle** threaded with a different colored yarn is laced back and forth as in **backstitch threaded.** Work interlacing in opposite directions creating an oval. It is very effective as a **border stitch.** See ill.

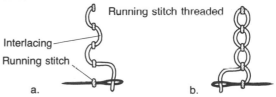

Running stitch threaded

Interlacing

Running stitch

a.   b.

running vine. Quilts. See **Quilts: Quilting.**

run system. Spinning. Weaving. See **yarn count.**

run wool. Spinning. Weaving. See **yarn count.**

Russian cross stitch. Crewel. Embroidery. See **herringbone stitch.**

Russian stitch. Crochet. The Russian stitch is made from rows of **double crochet** by passing the **crochet hook** through both loops of each stitch in the **previous row;** the entire **row** is worked. The yarn is then cut, and the crochet begun again from the other end. The Russian stitch makes a closely worked, smooth fabric and is often used to recreate tapestry designs.

rust retarder. Découpage. A liquid, usually available as a paint in various colors (also called rust-inhibiting paint), that is applied to metal surfaces to prevent rusting.

rutile. Ceramics. An impure form of **titanium dioxide** used as an **opacifier** and a **pigment oxide** to produce a brown or tan **glaze.**

rutile. Gemcutting. Titanium dioxide **crystal**lized in the tetragonal system with **hardness** of 6½, **specific gravity** of 4.25, refractive indices of 2.616 and 2.741, strong metallic to adamantine luster, uneven fracture, and brown **streak.** It occurs in red, brown, and black varieties. Main crown **facet**s are cut at 34° and main pavillion facets at 40−41°. Rutile is polished on a tin **lap** with Linde A. Titania is synthetic rutile. Also see **faceting, fracture, luster, polishing, quartz, refraction.**

rya. Rugmaking. Weaving. A Scandinavian term for long, knotted pile. The **pile height** is 1″ or over, the average height being 2−2½″. Because of its length, it is always cut pile which is **precut** or made over a **gauge.** Since rya rugs were supposed to have originated in Finland, the Finnish spelling, *ryijy,* is also used. Recently they have become known as shag rugs, a commercial term stemming from the shaggy, uneven appearance of the pile. The traditional rya knot which is used to make the pile in woven rya rugs is, in reality, the **Ghiordes** or Turkish **knot.** It can be formed also in **needleworked** or **latch-hooked rug**s. The rya effect can be obtained through **hooking,** but this is not the true rya, since no knot is involved. Because of its length, the pile is spaced much further apart than the short pile. Consequently, it falls over, which accounts for its shaggy effect. The fact that fine designs become blurred and details are lost also accounts for the shaggy effect. Most rya rugs are large and have bold patterns with emphasis on subtle **color blending.** Also see **pile rug.**

rya knot. Rugmaking. Weaving. See **knotted pile, rya.**

rya needle. Rugmaking. See **rug needle.**

ryijy. Rugmaking. Weaving. See **rya.**

S

saber saw. Metalworking. Plastics. Woodworking. See **power saw.**

sable brush. Enameling. A tool used for work with **metal luster, overglaze** shading and delicate **wet inlay.** Also see **Enameling: Tools and Materials.**

sacking. Stitchery. See **burlap.**

sacking needle. Weaving. See **needle, rug needle.**

sack swing. Toys. See **gunny sack swing.**

saddening. Dyeing. The process of dulling a color through the use of an iron salt **mordant.**

saddle. Ceramics. See **kiln furniture.**

saddleback. Bookbinding. A rounded **back.**

saddle bar. Stained Glass. (Also called support bar.) The name given to all bracing or reinforcing rods. Saddle bars go across the middle of the window, as distinguished from division bars, which are placed opposite the joint connecting two panels. Both types of bar are the same shape and length; saddle bars, however, can be bent to follow the contours of the lead so as not to interfere with the design of the window. See ill. Also see **copper tie, division tie, fitting, rebate, reglet, T-bar.**

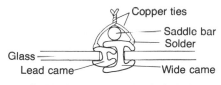

Saddle bar holding a leaded window

saddler's awl. Leather. See **awl and haft.**

saddler's haft and awl. Leather. A sharp wedge-pointed tool used to enlarge holes for hand sewing. See ill. Also see **Leatherwork: Sewing Leather.**

Saddler's haft and awl

saddler's needle. Leather. See **needle.**

saddle soap. Leather. A soap used for cleaning, softening, and finishing leather. Apply the saddle soap with a brush or sponge and work it into a lather. Remove excess lather with a cloth, then polish to a soft sheen. Also see **Leatherwork: Tools and Materials.**

saddle stamp. Leather. A variety of **stamp.**

saddle stitch. Leather. A **double needle stitch** commonly used for sewing heavyweight leather using two needles pushed through the same hole in opposite directions. See ill.

Saddle stitch

saddle stitched. Stitched or stapled down the center fold, so called because the fold is placed over an inverted V-shaped support, or saddle, to be stitched.

saddle wheel. Spinning. See **treadle wheel.**

safety beveler. Leather. (Also called skife.) A tool with a slightly curved frame into which are inserted replaceable single-edge razor blades used for **skiving** the edges of leather. A line should first be marked for the area to be skived. The safety beveler can be pushed ahead of you, like a regular knife, or carefully pulled toward you. See ill. Also see **bissonette edge tool, skiving knife,** and **Leatherwork: Creasing, Scoring and Folding Leather, Cutting and Edging Leather, Tools and Materials.**

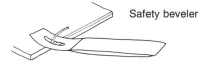

Safety beveler

safety edger. Leather. See **bissonette edge tool.**

safety precautions. Stained Glass. See **Stained Glass: Safety Precautions.**

safflower. Dyeing. See **saffron.**

saffron. Dyeing. An ancient, yellow dyestuff made from the dried pistils of the fall-flowering crocus. It was used by the Greeks, Romans, and Persians; the latter still use it in limited quantities for the dyeing of rug yarns. The fiber to be dyed is usually mordanted with alum before immersion in the dyebath. There is also false saffron, which is really safflower (an Old World thistlelike herb). This produces a **fugitive** yellow **dye,** and more important, a less fugitive red color. The term "red tape" comes from the fact that safflower dye was used to color the cotton cords used to bind legal documents.

Sage Bud. Quilts. A **pieced nine-patch block** design that has four pointed flowers in the outer four corners.

sagger. Ceramics. See **muffle.**

sagger clay. Ceramics. See **Ceramics: Clay.**

sagging. Glasswork. The tendency of glass to droop or sag in response to gravity when exposed to medium heat. Bottles deformed into ashtrays or other items are a pop use of sagging techniques.

sagging mold. Stained Glass. A concave surface into which glass can be slumped. Also see **lampshade molds.**

sago tree. Batik and Tie-dye. A tree found in Borneo, the bark of which provides a reddish-brown **dye.** The bark is chopped fine and mixed with a **mordant** to produce the dye. This brown and **indigo** blue comprise the traditional colors of **Javanese batik.**

Sagrada Familia. Mosaics. La Iglesia de la Sagrada Familia—the Church of the Holy Family—was designed by an early exponent of **Art Nouveau, Antonio Gaudí.** The church, located in Barcelona, embodies the ultimate in Art Nouveau construction, and its **mosaics** are among the most fanciful and inspired ever made. Gaudí's use of mosaics as an integral part of the structure did much to restore the art to the level of inventive originality from which it had fallen to a mere copyist role. The Sagrada Familia is considered by many to be one of the most important architectural structures of the late 1800s. For mosaicists it must stand as the most inspiring work since the mosaics of the Byzantine era. Also see **mosaics.**

Sailboat. Quilts. An asymmetrical **pieced block** design of triangles, that gives a **sawtooth** effect. The block can be **set** in a great variety of ways to produce startling and vigorous **geometric** patterns.

sailcloth. Kites. See **Kites: Tools and Materials.**

sailcloth. Quilts. Stitchery. A strong, **plain-weave fabric** originally made of **cotton, linen** or **jute.** It is now primarily a cotton and **synthetic blend.** It is a heavy fabric, actually a lightweight **canvas.** It comes in different weights and qualities and is suitable wherever strength of fabric and **body** are important. It is excellent for some **stuff**ed work, and is often used as the **background** material for **machine appliqué.**

sailor's knot. Weaving. See **weaver's knot.**

sailor's palm. Stitchery. (Also called marine thummel.) A modern version of the **thummel,** consisting of a leather band that fits around the palm and in which there is a hole for the thumb. The **thimble** itself is a flat metal disk, crossbarred and pitted to catch and force the needle for very heavy stitching.

sailor's thummel. Stitchery. A **thimble**like finger guard worn on the thumb. It is usually a ring rather than a cap, with depressed areas of crosshatched lines to catch the end of the needle. Originally, the ring was made from bone.

St. Louis Star. Quilts. See **star patterns.**

St. Valentine's Patch. Quilts. See **Double Hearts.**

sal ammoniac. Metalworking. See **flux.**

Salish loom. Weaving. See **Salish weaving.**

Salish weaving. Weaving. Weaving done by the Salish Indians living on the northwest coast of the United States and inland on both sides of the Canadian border. Although they twined many items, the Salish are noted for their **twill weave** and twined blankets that are made on a **frame loom** called the Salish loom. In the early days, the yarn used for **warp** and **filling** was spun of mountain goat's wool or the hair of white dogs which were kept for the purpose of wool production. The dogs are thought to have been of a Pomeranian type. If the blankets were solely of goat's wool or dog's hair, they were woven as large bed covers or as cold-weather cloaks for the Indian aristocracy. Commoners wore blankets woven of the inner bark of the cedar tree or cattail fluff. The thick blankets were usually limited to white. However, the ceremonial blankets were of white ornamented with brown and black stripes in both warp and filling so that a **plaid** resulted. With the coming of the white man, the Salish obtained commercial yarn that they used mainly for filling and that gave a more decorative (because of more colors available) and finer weight blanket. Current work is done of sheep's wool.

The Salish loom that is currently having a renaissance among non-Indian weavers is a two-bar frame loom, consisting of two wooden, horizontal rollers fitted into slots in two vertical posts. Wedges hold the rollers in place and are removed to lessen tension as the weaving progresses. The rollers are of various lengths to be used according to the fabric width desired. The rollers can be turned to keep the weaving in a position convenient to the weaver. Weaving, or **twining,** on a two-bar loom commenced by using a **continuous warp** which either went around both rollers and then was cut to remove the blanket when finished, or went around both rollers but began and ended around a heavy cord that was in a horizontal position across the back of the loom and served as the **warp end bar** does in an ordinary frame loom. It was possible to pull this cord out at the completion of weaving and have a four-**selvage**d blanket that required no cutting or fringing. In either case, the twining or weaving was done as the warp was moved around the rollers so that a piece twice the length between rollers could be woven.

An alternative method was to have a continuous warp going just around the roller bars with no end cord and to weave the two layers as one. When weaving was finished the rollers were withdrawn and the blanket had a fringe of long loops at each end.

Simple **weft twining** was done or the twill weave was **finger woven** by opening the **shed**s with the fingers. Work proceeded downward. Whether the blanket was twined or woven, twining was always used first to secure the warp ends in place.

There are theories that in early times the Salish tribes migrated from the Southwest, the heart of **Indian weaving** in North America, and brought the frame loom with them. This would make them an offshoot of the early Pueblo weavers who developed a frame loom between 1100 and 1300. There is evidence that the Salish were early users of the two-bar loom. However, some believe that another type of Salish loom—a one-bar **warp-weighted loom**—was in use prior to the two-bar loom, and that the two-bar loom developed from this one-bar. In the one-bar loom, the warp was attached over a narrow rod which was then laced tightly to a thicker horizontal bar inserted into two vertical posts. The warp was weighted at the bottom in small groups. Frequently, the bar was hung from the ceiling and raised up as the work proceeded down. Small items such as the smaller cloaks, sashes, tump lines (headstraps for carrying packs), dancing aprons, and mats were made on the one-bar loom, while the larger twill weave blankets, and both twill weave and twined ceremonial blankets, were woven on the two-bar loom.

Salish twined designs are symbolic representations of nature such as birds, butterflies, trees, mountains, and lightning rendered in geometric shapes such as diamonds, zigzags, squares, etc. See ill.

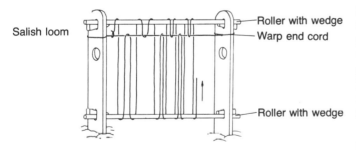

Salish loom — Roller with wedge — Warp end cord — Roller with wedge

Salix. Basketry. See **willow**.

sal soda. Batik and Tie-dye. See **washing soda**.

salt. Batik and Tie-dye. The **assistant** used in **dyeing** with **fiber-reactive dyes**, **direct dyes**, **household dye**s, and some **acid dyes**. It is common uniodized table salt. Also see **paste resist**.

salt clay. Toys. An **inedible dough** that can be shaped for use in dough sculpture. The salt clay recipe uses ingredients found in any kitchen and is safe for children to use.

The salt clay is cooked, but not baked, and should not be considered a permanent material. Small objects and ornaments can be fashioned from this clay. It is difficult to seal completely and tends to absorb moisture on rainy days. **Salt dough** is a similar but more permanent material.

In a saucepan place 2 cups coarse salt (ice cream or kosher salt, or table salt if the coarse is not available) and 1 cup boiling water. Boil together. In another bowl place 1 cup cornstarch. Add cold water until it can be poured. Pour the cornstarch mixture into the boiling salt water, stirring constantly until very thick and transparent. Pour onto wax paper to cool.

Shape small objects from the clay and allow them to dry. If cracks appear, try to press them out. Several days may be required for the drying, depending on the humidity. Extra clay can be stored in wax paper or flexible plastic wrap and kept in the refrigerator. Finished pieces can be colored with **acrylic paint**s, being sure that all the salt is covered. **Marking pen**s can be used to add color. **Shellac**, clear nail polish, or any **sealer** should be used as a **finish** over the pen drawing.

salt dough. Toys. An **inedible dough** used in the **baker's art**. The kneaded dough is often used in making lattice baskets, figures, mirrors, and other decorative pieces. It is similar to **salt clay**, but it requires baking.

Mix together 4 cups flour, 1 cup salt, and 1½ cups hot water. Stir until all ingredients are mixed. Knead on a floured board until the dough is smooth (10 to 15 minutes). A very sticky dough may require additional flour; a stiff dough may need a small amount of water. Bake the pieces at 300° F for 1−2 hours, depending upon the thickness of the dough.

salt garden. Toys. See **crystal garden**.

salt glaze. Ceramics. A textured **glaze** produced by throwing coarse rock salt into the kiln firebox or through ports entering the kiln chamber. The sodium combines with the silicate in the **clay body** to form a hard, glossy glaze that is acid resistant. Keep the studio well ventilated, because chlorine gas is released during salt glazing. Salt glaze is applied to once-fired stoneware. Also see **firecord, once fired ware**.

Saltonstall Quilt. Quilts. One of the earliest known surviving quilts from colonial times. It is an exquisite **split two-patch pieced** quilt of beautiful workmanship and color. It is a simple design in which the triangles combine to form patterns of **diamond**s, hourglasses, squares, and stars. It was made in 1704, and is still in the possession of the Saltonstall family.

salvage art. Quilts. A designation sometimes given to **pieced quilt**s, or **patchwork**, because it involves a process of utilizing scraps. Fabrics of all sizes, colors, and type are salvaged for pieces as well as for **stuffing**. Also see **making do**.

sampler. Crewel. Embroidery. Needlepoint. A piece of needlework with a collection of stitches or patterns that can serve as a learning exercise for a beginner as well as be a permanent reference. Also see **Needlepoint: Background and History.**

sample rack. Stained Glass. (Also called glass rack.) Samples of glass kept in the studio. They can be mounted between strips of **zinc came** for glass storage and should be labeled for quick identification.

sampler blanket. Weaving. A **warp** woven to experiment with new ideas and techniques and to see how patterns will look with a variety of colors, **treadling**s, yarn weights, and yarn textures. It can be of any length and any width. Usually a wide warp will be composed of many different sections, each having a change of **drawing-in draft** and/or **warp arrangement.** The sections are all made and put on the **loom** as one warp. The usual method followed in weaving the blanket is to have the first sample contain **filling** yarn the same as the yarn in the first warp section on the left. This will be the only sample where warp and filling match. In the other samples that are made as the filling weaves **selvage** to selvage, the crossings of filling with warp will give unexpected effects. The second section of samples is then woven with the filling matching the yarn of the second warp section from the left. The weaving continues in this manner with the filling choice determined by each succeeding warp section. Changes are often made in the filling yarn or in the treadling when it is seen that an unplanned or accidental sample looks good but needs a little improvement. Often the accidental sections prove to be better looking than the planned sample. In commercial weaving mills, there are often sample looms set aside for these blanket warps. They are also done in handweaving studios prior to choosing samples for commercial power-loom reproduction. Handweavers do them for their own satisfaction and to obtain a large number of experiments from just one warp.

Small sample blankets of just one **threading** are made when the weaver wants to determine for just one idea the **sett** and **beat,** quality and amount of yarn used, color relationships, size and effect of the pattern, suitability for end use, and the reaction of fibers and colors to various **finishing** methods. The samples, if not kept for the **weaver's records,** can be used for small items like pin cushions, covers for booklets, and ornamentation on greeting cards and on clothes.

sampler book. Quilts. Stitchery. See **fabric book.**

sampler quilt. Quilts. (Also called legacy quilt.) A quilt made up of a great variety of **block** designs, both **pieced** and **appliqué**d. It served as a sampler of patterns. In early American villages, an outstanding quilter made a final quilt, leaving for friends and other quilters a sampler collection of favorite blocks and variations of well-known patterns.

Any quilt that is a collection of favorite blocks is a sampler quilt. It provides a **portfolio** from which a pattern might be chosen to be repeated as the block design for another quilt.

San Blas appliqué. Stitchery. A method of **appliqué** developed by the Cuna Indians of the San Blas Islands that resembles **reverse appliqué** or **cut-through appliqué.** The women apply the appliqué to their **mola**s, or pullover blouses.

sand. Ceramics. Granular particles of disintegrated rock, generally impure silica, used in throwing clays to decrease shrinkage. Sand is also used in **ovenware** and refractories.

sand. Stained Glass. Decomposed granite rock with a high silica content, used to texture **epoxy resin** and concrete surfaces. Also see **dalle-de-verre, sandblasting.**

sandalwood. Candlemaking. A widely used scent. Also see **Candlemaking: Adding the Additives.**

sandbag. Jewelry. A canvas pillow filled with sand, used as a supportive device when **forming** metal into shapes that would be difficult or impossible to achieve on a nonyielding support. It is also sometimes used for simple **chasing, repoussé,** or **embossing** techniques because it is firm but pliable. Also see **edge thickening.**

sandbag method. Metalworking. See **raising technique** and **Metalworking: Raising.**

sandblasting. Jewelry. A process used to produce a frosted finish on metal, plastic, or glass. Fine **abrasive** materials such as sand, quartz, and **carborundum** are blown by compressed air through a hose inside a sealed box that has a glass window to allow viewing of the work. The equipment is fairly expensive, and it is a technique not often used, although it has great possibilities. To sandblast involves patterns on jewelry, block out areas to remain highly polished with **beeswax** or masking tape. It is possible to hand hold work for a light sandblasting. Remove the **resist** to reveal the contrast between the original polished surface and the frosted sandblasted surface. An entire piece can be sandblasted.

sandblasting. Metalworking. (Also called abrasive blasting.) A cleaning and finishing process usually associated with industry, but now also used for sculpture, in which **abrasive** particles are propelled against a metal surface. Sandblasting removes **scale,** dirt, and rust and creates a soft, lustrous surface finish. It also is used in preparation for coating some outdoor sculptures with sealants. The work is dry-blasted at high speed with particles of silica sand, **steel, aluminum oxide,** or, in cases where it is necessary that surface removal be minimal, nut shell or glass beads. This produces microscopic rough areas that facilitate the adherence of lubricants, paints, or other applied liquid coverings.

sandblasting. Stained Glass. The method in which a thin layer of color is etched off the surface of **flashed glass,** allowing the base color to show through. Portions of the glass that will not be etched are masked off with two layers of masking tape. The glass is then treated with a pressurized spray of fine **sand,** which scrapes away the unmasked flash. **Aciding** is an alternate method of etching flashed glass. Also see **masking.**

sand candle. Candlemaking. A candle formed by pouring hot melted wax into hollowed-out sand or into a mold packed with sand. An attractive crust of sand coats the candle surface. If mold is used, the sand should be mixed with **bentonite** and **polymer emulsion**s to produce a more durable shell. The dampness of the sand and the **temperature** of the hot wax determine how thick the sand crust will be. The hotter the wax and the drier the sand, the thicker the crust.

For a thick sand coating, melt the wax to at least 220° F; this may require heating the wax over a direct flame, which is not very safe; make sure the melting pot is dry and be extra careful. Pour the hot wax slowly or spoon it out to avoid disturbing the sand. **Wick** and candle with a weighted wick, a manganese core **wire wick,** or a wick attached to a metal **wick holder.** Fill any depressions by **refilling the mold.** Also see **Candlemaking: Molding.**

sandcasting. Ceramics. The process of shaping wet sand to form a **mold** for building textured **pot**s and **form**s. It is especially fun to do outdoors, at a beach—although fresh water must be used for the plaster, since salt speeds up the plaster's drying time.

A convex form in the shape of the finished piece is made in the wet sand, then a layer of plaster is carefully poured over the sand. If the mold is large, it should be reinforced with strips of cloth and thickened with additional layers. Once the plaster has hardened, a **slab** of clay can be pressed into the hollow of the plaster shell; the sand caught in the plaster will texture the clay surface. If the resultant clay form is roughly hemispherical, two such forms can be joined by **luting** to form a pot.

sandcasting. Metalworking. A casting process in which a **pattern** of the desired object is used to make an impression in special **casting sand,** the pattern is removed, and molten metal is poured into the empty sand **mold.** Although it is the most important casting method for industry, it is also used by craftspeople because it is low in cost, requires little expensive or complicated equipment, and design or pattern changes may be made easily without great expense or damage to molds. This process is best used on patterns that are nearly symmetrical or relatively simple in shape. Also see **Metalworking: Sandcasting.**

sandcasting. Mosaics. The making of a **mosaic** by embedding mosaic material in a sand setting bed that has been poured into a simply constructed wooden form. The sand should be flattened with a board before the material is set, and in setting, gaps should be left between the individual pieces of material to allow the **bond** to get a better grip. The sandcasting technique has some similarity to the **indirect method,** except that it offers considerably more opportunity to vary the elevations of the final surface.

Once all the material has been embedded, a bond such as **cement** or plaster should be poured into the form and over the material. **Metal mesh** embedded in the bond will give strength to the **backing.** Allow the bond to set until it is hard before you remove the wooden form. Brush away any sand that clings to the mosaic surface and trim the raw edges of the bond to complete the casting. Also see **indirect method.**

sandcasting flask. Metalworking. See **flask, sandcasting molding equipment.**

sandcasting molding equipment. Metalworking. Tools and accessories needed to make a sand mold for **sand casting.**

FLASK   A wood or metal box frame which surrounds the sand mold. It has two detachable sections which fit together: the cope is the upper half, and the drag is the lower half (**a.**).

MOLDING BOARD   A flat wood or metal surface to put the pattern on. Make sure that the board is thick enough not to bend or sag under the weight of the sand-filled flask.

BOTTOM BOARD   A board like the molding board but placed on top of the cope just before the flask is turned over.

RIDDLE   A wire-mesh sieve used to sift lumps out of the **molding sand** (**b.**).

RAMMER   (also called tamp) A wooden tool used to tamp or pack the molding sand into the flask. Use the flat end of the rounded part to tamp the sand on the surface and the wedge-shaped end to work sand beneath the surface (**c.**).

SLICK AND OVAL   (Also called slick, spoon and slick) A metal tool used to repair and smooth surfaces of the sand mold. Use it as you would a spatula or flat knife and pat the sand in place (**d.**). The rounded oval and the rectangular slick may be together at opposite ends of one tool or they may be two separate tools.

BELLOWS   Use a bellows to blow loose sand off the sand mold.

STRIKE-OFF BAR   A straight piece of metal or wood used to scrape sand off the top of the flask.

SWAB   A brush made of camel hair or flax used to moisten the molding sand. If it has a rubber bulb on the other end which can be filled with water to wet the brush, it is called a molder's bulb. The swab and molding bulb may be joined together into one tool, but are often made into two separate tools (**e.**).

RISER PIN   (Also called gate pin, sprue cutter, and gate cutter.) A hollow tube with thin walls from 8 to 15 inches long, used to cut a **sprue** or **gate** hole in the sand mold. They come in varying diameters, with sprue cutters generally tapered. To use: press the tube into the molding sand in the flask until it touches the pattern. Then carefully withdraw it, bringing the sand out inside the tube.

DRAW SPIKE Draw spikes are inserted into the **pattern** while it is in the sand mold and used to carefully withdraw it without disturbing the sand around the pattern. Holes should be previously made in the pattern so that you can easily screw or hook the spikes into it (**f.**).

TROWEL AND LIFTER Any flat, sharp-edged piece of metal or large knife can be used to cut, lift, and smooth the sand in the mold, but these two tools are designed specifically for that job. They are especially useful for making repairs in the sand walls after the pattern has been lifted out with draw spikes (**g., h.**). See ill. Also see **Metalworking: Sand Casting.**

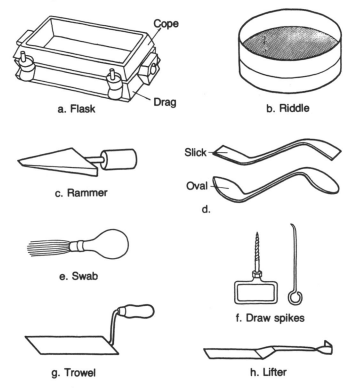

a. Flask   Cope   Drag   b. Riddle

c. Rammer   Slick   Oval   d.

e. Swab   f. Draw spikes

g. Trowel   h. Lifter

sanded glass. Stained Glass. Sheets of **antique glass** can be annealed on iron tables that have **sand** spread on them. The sand leaves small indentations on one side of the glass giving it an overall random texture. Also see **annealing.**

sander. Woodworking. See **sanding tools.**

sanding. Gemcutting. An operation between grinding and polishing in which the stone is given its final shape and all surface defects are removed. Sanding is an important step because no visible scratches are removed by polishing.

Loose silicon carbide or aluminum oxide **abrasive** in grits from 400–1200 or sanding cloths of the same grit are used.

Sanding is done wet with water to prevent overheating of the stone and to flush away the cuttings. Sanding cloths should be broken in before using by rubbing with a flat

rock to dislodge loose and oversize grains. Well-worn cloths are saved for the finest sanding.

Drum sanders are devices which clamp abrasive strips to the outside of a wheel by means of a split screw or expansion and attach to a horizontal arbor in a manner similar to a **grinding wheel.**

Disk sanders operate both horizontally and vertically. The abrasive cloth is cemented to a leather backing over a wooden disk. For sanding **cabochon**s, the disk should be concave; for sanding flats, it should be slightly convex to prevent overcutting the edges.

Belt sanders consist of an abrasive cloth belt running between a drive wheel and an idler wheel. They offer a firm sanding surface on the wheels and a very flexible surface between the wheels.

Recommended speeds for sanding are between 2,000 and 3,000 surface feet per minute. For example, an 8″ sanding drum or disk should be operated at 1,000–1,400 rpm. Also see **cabochon, flat, polishing** and **Gemcutting: Hand Grinding and Polishing, Tools and Materials.**

sanding. Plastics. Power tools used to sand wood, such as the belt sander, disk sander, or orbital sander, can also be used to power sand plastic. Use fine grade sandpaper and do not overheat the surface. To sand plastic by hand, wrap a piece of sandpaper around a wooden block to avoid making fingerprints on flat surfaces while sanding. Also see **Plastics: Finishing.**

sanding. Woodworking. The process of smoothing a wood surface with the aid of **sandpaper.** Sanding may be done by hand with the sandpaper used by itself, over a sanding block, or with the aid of a power **sanding tool** such as an orbital or belt sander. Sanding is one of the first steps in preparing a wood surface for a finish. Also see **Abrasive** and **Woodworking: Finishing.**

sanding belt. Woodworking. See **abrasives, sanding tools.**

sanding block. Woodworking. See **sanding tools.**

sanding drum. Jewelry. A short abrasive-coated tube that fits into the handpiece of a **flexible shaft machine.** Also see **abrasive.**

sanding tools. Plastics. Woodworking. Tools using **abrasives** (such as sandpaper or sanding cloth) used to smooth wood or other surfaces. The tools vary in complexity. Hand sanding is best for smoothing surfaces other than very flat planes, especially for final finishing.

A sanding block is a block of scrap wood around which the sandpaper is wrapped and held by the fingers at the sides. Commercial sanding blocks of padded wood or metal, with built-in clamping features to hold the sandpaper, are available.

An orbital sander is an electrically powered hand pad sander (**a.**) in which sandpaper is clamped over a padded sole; the motor moves the sole through a tiny circular orbit 5,000–10,000 times a minute. The circular orbit permits use across as well as with the grain; it is used primarily for light and finishing sanding.

The reciprocating sander is virtually identical to the orbital sander, except that the motion is back-and-forth rather than circular; some pad sanders permit both sanding actions. The reciprocating action should be used mainly with the grain.

The portable belt sander uses a continuous flat sanding belt that revolves around two drums (d.). The cloth-reinforced belt may be of any of a number of abrasive materials in a variety of grades. Belt sanders are generally used for heavier sanding, but may be used with fine-**grit** belts for finished work. The stationary belt sander generally uses larger belts, and the sanding surface faces up rather than down.

In a disk sander, a specially cut disk of sandpaper or sanding cloth is attached to a flexible flat rubber disk. Such a disk is a common accessory of a **portable electric drill.**

A combination sander is a stationary tool that combines both a belt sander and a sanding disk. It is equipped with an adjustable table for sanding **bevels** and for other operations. It is a production tool used for cabinet work and modelmaking. See ill.

a. Pad sander (orbital or reciprocating)   b. Portable belt sander

sand mold. Metalworking. See **mold.**

sandpaper. Découpage. Various grades of sandpaper are available for use in smoothing the découpage **finish.** Fine sanding is done with wet or dry sandpaper that has a black abrasive side. The back side is marked with gauge numbers for degree of abrasiveness, with higher numbers for the finest, or smoothest, papers. Grades #400 and #600 are commonly used for smoothing the découpage finish.

sandpaper. Woodworking. See **abrasives.**

sand toy. Toys. Any of several toys that incorporate sand or are used in the sand. One kind of sand toy is an enclosed box in which sand trickles through openings to mechanically move parts of a scene or a setting. When all the sand has run through and the motion stops, the box is tilted or turned upside-down to move the sand and reactivate the toy. The sand sometimes strikes paddles to move a **paddle wheel,** or it may drop onto a balanced blade that tilts with the weight of the sand. In others, the moving sand simply suggests a moving landscape, as when the running sand resembles a waterfall in a painted setting.

Any scoops or containers used by children when playing in the sand are also sand toys. Shovels and sand pails are the most common. They are sometimes used to gather and mold damp sand for making sand castles. Also see **beach toy.**

Sanforized. Stitchery. A trademark term or label which indicates that **fabrics** will not **shrink** more than 1%. A Sanforized-Plus label indicates a **finish** which imparts qualities similar to those of **wash-and-wear.** Sanforized-Plus 2 refers to a fabric which has passed tests for **durable press.**

Sanforized-Plus. Stitchery. See **Sanforized.**

Sanforized-Plus 2. Stitchery. See **Sanforized.**

sanguine. Découpage. A term, derived from the French word for blood, used to describe a color scheme of dark reds and including terra-cotta, dark brown, madder red, scarlet lake, and white. This palette is often used in tinting traditional **prints** for découpage.

sapphire. Gemcutting. See **corundum.**

sapphire powder. Gemcutting. See **abrasive.**

sapwood. Woodworking. The sapwood is the large living, but not growing, area of a tree between the outer growth rings of cambium and the inner core of heartwood. Because the sapwood carries water and nutritional elements up the tree in the sap, it is most prone to disease. It is usually lighter in color than the **heartwood** and generally softer. Also see **wood.**

Sarah Furman Warner Coverlet. Quilts. A bedspread of extraordinary beauty and charm, made around 1800. Its central area depicts life in a small New England town. Houses, trees, and the church line up along a main street along which men, women, and children promenade. The large outer area, or the **border,** of the **coverlet** is resplendent with vines, urns, birds, fruits, and flowers in trailing lines of pattern. This quilt belongs to the Henry Ford Museum in Dearborn, Michigan.

An example of a similarly exquisite **appliqué** is the **Phoebe Warner Coverlet.** It is uncertain who actually made these coverlets; perhaps the cousins Sarah and Phoebe, although family history suggests that Ann Walgrave Warner—Phoebe's mother—made the Phoebe Warner Coverlet.

Saran Wrap. Plastics. See **polyvinyl chloride.**

sarcosoma. Coral Carving. The brittle, pink, horny outer covering of coral. This flaky material is removed before carving. Also see **Coral Carving: Working the Material.**

sard. Gemcutting. See **quartz.**

sardonyx. Gemcutting. See **quartz.**

sardonyx helmet. Shell Carving. See **king helmet.**

sarrasinois. Weaving. See **tapestry.**

sateen. Stitchery. A **cotton** or **rayon fabric** that has a **satin**like **finish.** The smooth surface results from the particular weave which places more **filling** or **weft** threads on the surface than a **plain weave,** where **warp** and weft threads appear in even amounts. Sateens are plain or printed and were at one time used for bedspreads, robes, and draperies, though now their **sheen** makes them particularly desirable in **stuffed fabric** hangings and **soft sculpture.**

satin. Quilts. Stitchery. A **fabric** produced by satin weave which gives a smooth, lustrous, rich-looking surface. The hand slides smoothly over the **lengthwise grain** of satin since more **warp**s than **filling** threads are exposed. When more filling threads than warp threads are exposed, the material has a **crosswise sheen** and is known as **sateen.** The exposed threads, called floats, are longer than in most fabric weaves and they give the characteristic smooth appearance and feel to both fabrics. Satin is usually made of **silk** or **rayon** though sometimes of **cotton** or **nylon.** Satin comes in a variety of weights and its unusually soft texture makes it especially appealing to designers of **stuff**ed **stitchery** and body coverings.

Satin cord. Macramé. (Also called rattail.) A round, braided **cord** made of satin-finish rayon over an inner core end. It is sometimes called nylon tubular cording. Also see **Macramé: Tools and Materials.**

satin finish. Jewelry. A soft finish on metal, composed of small scratches going in one or many directions. This type of finish can be accomplished with both wire and **bristle brush**es, used on the **buffing machine,** or by hand using an **emery paper finish.** It is a type of **matte** finish. Also see **buffing compound, liner, Swedish finish, wire brush.**

satin luster. Gemcutting. See **luster.**

satin spar. Gemcutting. See **gypsum.**

satin stitch. Crewel. Embroidery. (Also called cushion stitch, embroidery stitch.) A series of long, closely laid

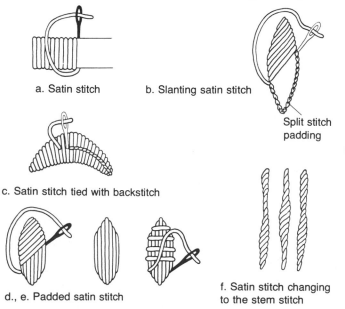

a. Satin stitch   b. Slanting satin stitch

Split stitch padding

c. Satin stitch tied with backstitch

d., e. Padded satin stitch

f. Satin stitch changing to the stem stitch

parallel stitches that have a smooth satin effect (**a.**). A slant helps to keep the stitch together. **Split stitch** padding insures neat and even edges. Make the longest stitch first in the area being filled; this establishes the direction of the stitch in the entire area. The slanting variation and larger shapes are worked over split stitch padding (**b.**). Longer satin stitches are secured in the center with **backstitch**es (**c.**). Work three layers of the satin stitch in three different directions for a padded effect (**d.**). The middle layer does not have to be completely filled (**e.**). The satin stitch alternated with the **stem stitch** produces an unusual line that varies in width (**f.**). See ill. Also see **flat stitch, Roumanian stitch, sheaf stitch filling.**

satin weave. Weaving. The third basic weave in the three basic constructions. The weave's distinguishing characteristic is that it presents an all-over appearance without any noticeable interlacing points. In reality, there is a faint **twill** line of interlacing points, but the way they are located makes them barely visible to the human eye. Satin is usually woven with a fine silk or synthetic yarn. If it is made of fine cotton yarn, it is known as sateen. Because of the fine yarn that is usually associated with satin, it is not that popular with handweavers. However, another characteristic of satin is that it exposes either all **filling** or all **warp** on the surface of the fabric. This makes it a good weave to use in order to have maximum exposure of an especially interesting warp or filling yarn. Another detriment to the weave's appeal to handweavers is that it takes at least five **harness**es to make what is known as a true satin. Since many weavers work on only four harnesses, they can only use what is known as a mock satin—a weave that is nothing more than a broken **warp-faced** or **filling-faced** twill. This weave goes by the name of crowfoot.

Satins are identified by the number of harnesses it takes to weave a particular satin. This number is also the number of **end**s and **pick**s in one repeat. The method of **drafting** satin weave on **graph paper** is rather unique and involves the use of a "counter." Taking the number of harnesses, one divides this into two numbers not divisible into each other. For example, an 8-harness satin would be divided into the numbers 3 and 5. One of these numbers is used as the **counter.** "Move number" and "base number" are synonyms for "counter." It is implied in speaking of satins that every end and every pick interlaces only once and for the rest of the repeat **float**s either on the surface or back of the fabric. Using this fact, one starts in the lower left-hand corner of the drafting repeat and this becomes

Mock satin (crowfoot)

8-Harness satin

Filling faced   Warp faced

the first **raiser** or interlacing point. From here, using the counter number, one counts and moves upward and across to locate the positions of the other raisers. When the repeat is completed, there should be only one interlacing point indicated on every end and every pick. This will give a filling-faced satin. For a warp-faced satin, the interlacing point becomes a **sinker** and all other ends are raisers.

Satin fabrics are not noted for their strength or durability due to the very few interlacing points and the long floats caused by so little interlacing. However, the sparse interlacing does make for a soft, pliable, and smooth fabric. See ill.

saturation. One of the three qualities of color, it is also known as purity, chroma, or intensity. Highly saturated colors are those that are not mixed with white or black pigments. Colors of very low saturation are those that differ from neutral gray by only a suggestion of the basic color. Thus an orange **hue** would be described as having high saturation to the extent that it approximated the color of the setting sun, whereas an orange of low saturation would approach the color light brown.

The quality of saturation is easy to demonstrate with the use of pigments. Paint a swatch of any **primary color,** and then paint a swatch of the same primary color mixed with a gray of the same **value** as the primary color. The difference between the two swatches is a difference of saturation.

Color schemes in any medium—weaving, batik, stained glass, needlepoint, etc.—are likely to be more pleasing if the relative saturations of the colors used are approximately the same. Primary and secondary colors at maximum saturation, used together, create a lot of **tension** and are harder to handle in a pleasing way than colors that are all grayed by an equal amount.

saturation. Batik and Tie-dye. Complete penetration or soaking of a **dye** into **fabric. Wetting out** aids in dye saturation, helping to ensure that the fabric has absorbed the maximum dye level.

sausage. Quilts. See **Quilts: Quilting.**

Savannah Beautiful Star. Quilts. See **star patterns.**

saw. Beadwork. With hard materials such as plastic tubing, wood stripping, or doweling, a saw can be used to cut the piece into the desired bead lengths. A back saw, tenon saw, or miter saw with a rigid back brace is the best tool for this purpose. The stiff spine is there to ensure the straightest possible cut. The material to be cut should be held steady in a miter box or bench stop during the sawing operation.

saw. Woodworking. See **hand saw, power saw.**

saw blade. Jewelry. Cutting edges available are made in graduated sizes from #8/0 to #14; #8/0 being the finest, #14 the coarsest. #2/0, 3/0, and 4/0 generally cover most situations. The difference between sizes is slight; test each blade to select the one that handles the best. The finer the

blade, the narrower it is in width and depth. Heavier blades do not necessarily make sawing heavier-**gauge** metals easier. See ill. Also see **beeswax, chisel cutting, sawing.**

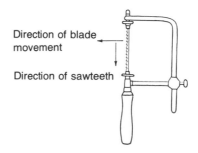

Direction of blade movement

Direction of sawteeth

saw cut. Woodworking. A term in whittling. Also see **crosscut, kerf, rip cut** and **Woodworking: Cutting and Sawing.**

sawdust. Puppets. Toys. The powdery soft fragments of wood made by the action of the saw blade as it eats into the wood. It was, for many years, a standard **filler** used for **stuff**ed animals and **dolls.** When long curls of the wood are used it is known as **wood wool.** Both have now been almost entirely replaced by foam or **synthetic** fillers.

This fluffy sawdust pulp may be mixed with an **adhesive** and various other materials to make a **composition** which can be modeled. Home craftspeople often use it mixed with a glue to form **sawdust mâché** which is used for **puppet heads** or **doll heads.** Also see **Puppets: Making the Puppet Head.**

sawdust head. Toys. See **composition.**

sawdust mâché. Puppets. Toys. A **modeling material** made up from a mixture of **sawdust** and **wheat paste.** The degree of fineness of the sawdust determines the texture of the modeling material. Also see **plastic wood** and **Puppets: Making the Puppet Head.**

saw frame. Enameling. See **jeweler's saw.**

sawframe. Jewelry. (Also called jeweler's saw.) An adjustable steel frame with a wood handle, available in varying depths from 2½″ to 8″. The most commonly used depth is 3″, although a frame of 4″ depth covers more uses and has a good balance to it. The deep, 8″ sawframe facilitates making turns without having the sawframe hit the edges of the metal when sawing large pieces of sheet metal. A new sawframe has usually been covered with grease or oil to prevent its rusting during warehouse storage. Remove this grease as completely as possible by wiping the frame with paper towels. There are three **thumbscrews** on a sawframe. The two opposite each other on the top and bottom of the frame are for holding and tightening the **saw blade** in position (**a.**). The third thumbscrew on the back of the sawframe is for adjusting the space between the top and bottom of the frame to fit the blade (**b.**). This is a one-time adjustment. See ill., next page. Also see **chisel cutting.**

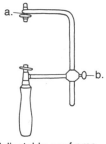

Adjustable sawframe

sawhorse. Woodworking. (Also called carpenter's horse.) A bridgelike support, usually made of wood, with a horizontal plane about waist-high. It is used as a support for sawing and assembly operations in carpentry, cabinetmaking, and general wood construction work.

sawing. Amber Carving. See **Amber Carving: Cutting.**

sawing. Jewelry. There are four basic sawing lines. Once you can saw these correctly, you can saw anything, no matter how complicated. They are: straight, curved, right angle, and obtuse angle. Use copper sheets to practice on—a sheet about 2″ × 2″ of 20-gauge is best.

All cutting from the saw blade is done on the downstroke. Although a very small amount is removed on the upstroke, it is actually scraped away.

Draw the lines you are going to saw directly on the copper with a sharpened pencil. Begin the lines at the top and draw toward the edge of the copper, in one clean line. When sawing, look at the line directly in front of the blade, not at the blade. As you are sawing, blow away the metal fragments that will come up with the saw blade and cover the line: you should always be able to see where you are sawing. The piece of copper being sawed must be supported against the **bench pin.**

To begin sawing, put your thumbnail directly against the line. With the saw blade make one or two upstrokes, holding the **sawframe** tipped at a slight angle toward the top of the bench. Remember, the cutting is done on the downstroke; the upstrokes will make a slight slot in which sawing can begin. Without this slot the blade will tend to grab and skid along the edge of the metal, chewing it up. On a real piece of work this chewed edge would have to be removed. Saw with smooth, even strokes. Be prepared to break lots of blades when you first begin, and don't be discouraged. Some of the most common reasons why blades break are: not supporting the metal well enough; turning the metal at a different speed than the saw blade; turning the saw blade without sawing a place for it to go; and having the blade too tight in the sawframe, which produces a very high pitched ping when testing it. Another common error is removing a blade from the work to saw in another area without supporting the work solidly against the bench pin. Laying the work down with the saw blade through it and still in tension, and putting the sawframe away after you have finished sawing without releasing the tension are two other common mistakes.

When sawing a piece which has a long, complex sawed line, and a blade breaks, it is not necessary to saw all the way back in. Instead, place the new blade in the lower thumbscrew and tighten and insert the top end of the blade—without bending it sharply or it will snap—into the place where the old saw blade broke. Make sure the teeth of the new blade are facing in the correct position to saw. Tighten the top thumbscrew in the usual manner, but keep holding on to the work you are sawing in order to support it. Turn the sawframe and the work simultaneously in the correct position to support it on the bench pin to continue sawing.

If it is necessary to set the work down without removing the saw blade, pull the work down to the bottom of the blade, and carefully lay the work on its side, sawframe and all. If no strain is put upon the blade, it will not snap.

Sometimes when a saw blade breaks, a small section of the blade remains in the line you were sawing. When you insert a new blade and it just won't saw, check the area, as this may be the cause. Usually the bit of blade that you were sawing is thick and can be got out with the edge of a fingernail. If stuck tighter, a pair of tweezers, and if still tighter, the point of a scribe, can pull it toward the sawed part of the line, from where it can be pulled out or poked through. Occasionally when a blade breaks, a very small piece of it will remain trapped between the rectangular nut and the sawframe. Usually it goes undetected. If when inserting a new blade you tighten it in the usual fashion, test it, and begin sawing, and the blade slips out of tension, check for that little piece of blade. Take good care of your sawframe and it will be a faithful tool for years.

Try to get a sawframe with an all-steel frame. If you cannot get a blade to stay in tension and if it keeps slipping, completely unscrew the thumbscrew and check the inside of the rectangular nut. It may or may not be serrated, but it may have a burr somewhere around the rim. Formerly, these were always removed at the factory. If not, the burr must be removed so that the nut will come in direct contact with the frame. This burr can be removed with a flat file. Make sure when doing so to keep the inside surface of the nut flat; don't let it become rounded from the filing process. The direct contact between the frame and nut under pressure from the thumbscrew is what holds the saw blade in position.

sawing. Shell Carving. See **Shell Carving: Sawing.**

sawing-in. Bookbinding. Cutting sawcuts across the back of the **sections** for **kettlestitch**ing or **cords.** After the sections have been repaired or collated they are placed between boards, inserted into the **lying press,** and, with a pencil and **try square,** marked for kettlestitches, **tapes,** or cords. When sawing, pinch the sections together near the cut you are making to prevent them from tearing. If you saw too deeply it will leave a visible gap inside the book after it is bound. The kerf should be sufficiently deep to accept the binding material and no deeper. For kettlestitching it should just reach the inside fold of each section. The kerfs for cords are sometimes made wider at the bottom by tilting the saw. Sawing-in is usually executed before the application of **endpaper**s, as they tend to tear during the operation.

sawtooth. Quilts. Any pattern of **zigzag**s. Sawtooth pattern is made up of a series of triangles sewn into a very active and attractive design; it is often used in **borders**, and may be **appliqué**d or **pieced**. Also see **pineapple quilt**, **sawtooth edging**.

Sawtooth. Quilts. Stitchery. (Also called Lend and Borrow, Rocky Glen.) A **block** design for pieced quilts that features a zigzag line as the dominant decorative element. Variations of both **Delectable Mountains** and **Kansas Trouble**s are **sawtooth** quilts. The Sawtooth block is similar to Indian Meadow, a name by which it is also known. **Winged Square** is also a sawtooth block.

Sawtooth is also a name sometimes used for the **Feather Star**, a completely different design that incorporates a sawtooth edge. See ill.

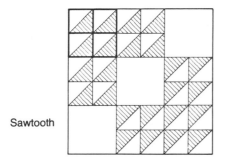

Sawtooth

sawtooth edging. Quilts. A zigzag pattern set into the edge of a quilt, serving as a decorative **border**. It is accomplished by setting fabric triangles between the outer edges of a quilt. Triangles may be made in either of two ways. In the first, two triangular pieces of fabric are seamed on two edges, then turned right-side out to form finished triangles. In a second and easier method, squares of fabric are first cut, then folded in any of several ways to make a triangle of which the raw edges are folded under. In one, the square is folded diagonally twice, and the triangle thus formed is pinned and set into the edges. In a variation, the square is folded diagonally once, then the two opposing points are folded in to touch the third point. The exposed folds may face up or down to be stitched. The edges of the **quilt top** and quilt **backing** cover the raw open edges of the triangles. Also see **sawtooth**.

sawtooth wheel. Crewel. Embroidery. (Also called pounce wheel.) A revolving cogwheel with a wooden handle which, when drawn across a design on **perforating paper**, punches small evenly spaced holes in the paper. Also see **Crewel: Transferring a Design.**

Saxony wheel. Spinning. See **treadle wheel**.

Saxony yarn. Weaving. See **Navajo weaving**.

scaffolding. Weaving. See **scaffold weft**.

scaffolding nail. Woodworking. See **nail**.

scaffold weft. Weaving. (Also called patchwork weaving, scaffolding, scaffold wefting, warp interlock.) An unusual **interlocking** technique in which both **warp** yarns interlock with warp yarns, and **weft** yarns with weft yarns, so that clear-cut areas of specific color effects can be produced. It somewhat resembles the color effect of **block pattern**ed **double cloth,** but the scaffolding technique is done within the single thickness of the cloth. Because of the interlocking process, it is often found listed under **tapestry** techniques. However, it does not usually appear as **filling-faced** as is tapestry, but as solid color pattern areas of a **balanced** or open **plain weave**. The technique is rather obscure. About the only such textiles that exist are from pre-Columbian Peru where there was considerable variety and complete mastery. These textiles have become the best and only source of reference for this technique.

A **frame loom** can be used to do scaffolding. It is set up with an extra, temporary skeleton, or scaffold filling cord that is stretched crosswise or horizontally on the loom. This filling serves as a framework to secure the warp. Small discontinuous warps are stretched around and between these temporary filling cords and are connected **end** to end. The discontinuous warps are warps of limited length which depend on the size of the specific color pattern area being worked on. Neighboring warps are interlocked, **dovetailed,** or even knotted together. These small, connected warps are then filled with discontinuous **weft**s that are likewise interlocked, dovetailed, or knotted together. When the warps are completely interlaced with their fillings, the scaffolding weft cord is removed. See ill.

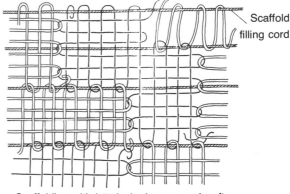

Scaffold filling cord

Scaffolding with interlocked warps and wefts

scaffold wefting. Weaving. See **scaffold weft**.

scale. Glasswork. Metalworking. (Also called firescale.) An **oxide** film that forms as a result of heating or oxidation on the surface of **ferrous** metals or metals containing **copper alloy**s. It is caused on **castings** by the heat of the molten metal touching the silica in the plaster mold and may be removed by pickling the casting in a solution of 1 part sulfuric acid to 60 parts water overnight. Prevent scale from forming during **soldering** by coating the surface with **flux** before soldering or by quickly dipping the object in a solution of 50% **nitric acid** and 50% water after soldering and then rinsing in water.

scale drawing. Rugmaking. Weaving. See **transferring designs**.

scale model. Toys. A small copy, reduced according to a fixed ratio. Many scale models are not actually toys, but **miniature**s.

Scalex. Enameling. See **firescale.**

scallom. Basketry. A type of **stake-up** accomplished by securing a **hoop** around the ends of the **stake**s.

scallop. Quilts. Stitchery. A series of curves, or portions of a circle, used in rows or **bands**. Scalloped edges are sometimes found on quilts, made by piecing and turning two half-circles or elongated half circles. Scallops are also used in **appliqué block**s and **border**s and are a commonly used **quilting pattern** in traditional quilts.

scalloped border. Basketry. See **border.**

scalloping. Stitchery. A **seam finish** of **scallop**s produced through the use of a **scalloping shears**. Also, any decorative edge in the shape of scallops. **Banner**s sometimes are bordered or edged in large scallops.

scalloping shears. Stitchery. **Shears** made similar to **pinking shears**, but having a **scallop**ed edge on the blades. The scalloped pattern imparted to the **fabric** during cutting may be used as a **seam finish** or the scallops may be incorporated into the design. **Panel**s, **banner**s or toys made from **felt** or other **nonwoven material**s often employ this kind of edge finish.

Scandinavian knitting. Knitting. The knitting of Sweden was strongly influenced by **Norwegian knitting**; however, the Swedish designs are more sophisticated, colorful, and varied. It is among the best examples of **color knitting**. Variations of Dutch and German knitting are found in the colored work.

Scandinavian pile rug. Rugmaking. See **flossa, knotted pile, needleworked rug, pile rug, rya.**

Scandinavian rug backing. Rugmaking. A very firmly woven backing of linen **warp** which is completely covered by the woolen **filling** and is used for making **knotted pile rya** rugs with a needle. At certain intervals (usually about ⅝″ apart) there is a row of exposed warp without any filling. In this row of unwoven warp go the knots that form the pile. The backing is an excellent **ground cloth,** but its use is limited to the rya pile and the pile can only be placed in the indicated rows and not where the rugmaker wishes. A lighter weight quality of the same backing is used for rya pillows.

scapolite. Gemcutting. A white, pink, or yellow gem faceting material with **hardness** of 6, **specific gravity** of 2.6–2.7, and refractive indices of 1.545 and 1.555. It is polished on a tin **lap** with tin oxide. Also see **cabochon, faceting, polishing, refraction.**

scarfing. Metalworking. See **blacksmithing techniques.**

scenery. Puppets. See **set.**

scent. Candlemaking. Any oil-base perfume or special candle scent used to add fragrance to the candle. **Patchouli** and **sandalwood** are among the more popular of the fragrances used in candlemaking.

scented beads. Beadwork. See **perfumed beads.**

schablonenscheren. Stained Glass. See **pattern shears.**

schiller. Gemcutting. See **luster.**

Schoolhouse. Quilts. See **Log Cabin.**

scientific toy. Toys. A **learning toy** designed to encourage study and activity in the area of science, such as microscopes, weather laboratories, star finders, and toy planetariums. Ant houses, seed-sprouting jars, and barometers can be made at home to provide the same kind of scientific study.

scissors. Découpage. Small, sharp, curved scissors such as cuticle or embroidery scissors are usually used for découpage. The cutting blades should be 2½–3″ long. Also see **Découpage: Setting Up a Workshop.**

scissors. Leather. Sturdy scissors or **shears** with a serrated edge are used for cutting leather and suede. See ill. Also see **bezel shears, fringe** and **Leatherwork: Cutting and Edging Leather, Tools and Materials.**

Heavy-duty leather scissors with serrated blade edge

scissors. Stitchery. Toys. A steel-bladed tool for cutting **fabric** or other thin materials. It is smaller than **shears**. Two opposing blades slide against each other in cutting and the fingers slip into loops at the ends opposite the cutting points.

Scissors are available in cutlery shops or fabric shops in numerous different sizes. All may be referred to as sewing scissors, though sometimes that term refers specifically to the largest of **cutting scissors**. Next in size is the **trimming scissors**, and **embroidery scissors** are the smallest. Other commonly used cutting tools are **pinking shears, scalloping shears** and **seam ripper**s.

Paper scissors are essentially the same as sewing scissors. Many people reserve old, dull, or unsharpened scissors for paper, but for much craft work involving paper it is essential to have a good, sharp pair. Paper does not wear out the blades. Children's paper scissors have rounded, blunt-pointed blades to prevent injury. They are sometimes called children's scissors or school scissors.

A heavy-duty utility scissors should be kept for cutting twine, cardboard, or cord. Also see **Stitchery: Tools.**

scissors toy. Toys. A movable **folk toy** that works similar to a pair of scissors. Two crossed sticks are **join**ed at the point of intersection, then a second crossed pair is attached to the first, and so on. When the end pieces are opened and closed, the entire line of crossed sticks moves in and out. Usually animals and figures are attached in various places on the sticks so that they appear to dash back and forth when the toy is moved.

sclerometer. Gemcutting. An instrument for determining exact **hardness.** It consists of a **diamond** point exerting a uniform pressure on the test material; the width of the scratch produced is microscopically examined and compared to that of known materials. Also see **Mohs scale of hardness.**

scorching. Leather. A decorating technique in which designs of a darker tone are impressed in leather with a **stamp** or other tool which has been lightly heated, actually burning the leather. A hobbyist's woodburning tool can also be used on leather.

score. Plastics. To make an incised line in a **plastic** sheet with a sharp tool, such as a **burin** or mat knife, preparatory to cutting. Also see **Plastics: Cutting.**

score. Stained Glass. A line drawn with a **glass-cutter** on a piece of glass where the glass is to be broken. Before stained glass can be broken or cut, it must first be scored. A score-line is drawn once; repeating the score in the same place dulls the cutter and generally prevents the glass from breaking properly.

The correct pressure on the glass-cutter leaves a thin line on the glass; too much pressure causes small slivers of glass to bounce up during scoring. Also see **circle cutter, copper foiling, running pliers, tapper** and **Stained Glass: Cutting Glass.**

scorer. Jewelry. A wood-handled steel tool designed to cut a V-shaped groove in metal to facilitate bending angles. The groove is then used for the line on which the metal is folded, as in the forming of a box or **hollow construction.** Also see **box construction.**

scoring. Ceramics. The process of roughing up the edge of a **leather hard** piece of clay where it is to be joined by **luting** to another piece of clay. Scoring is unnecessary on plastic clay. Clay may be scored by scratching it with a **needle awl** or stylus, or by cutting short notches with a knife. This roughed-up surface gives the clay "**tooth**" and gives the binding material (usually **slip**) more surface to grip.

scoring. Papercrafts. The technique, used in making paper projects, of pulling a dull blade along a pencil line to make an indentation to facilitate folding. A rounded knife blade or the tip of scissors or a compass point is pulled along a penciled fold line, using a metal rule as a guide. The pressure on the knife must be very light. The indentation should not be more than half the thickness of the

paper. To fold along the scored line, hold the paper with fingers on each side of the line and fold away from the scored groove.

Curved lines are scored with a compass point, with a French curve, or freehand. For very heavy cardboard, scoring is sometimes done with a single-edge razor blade, cutting no more than halfway through the board. See ill. Also see **diagonal scoring.**

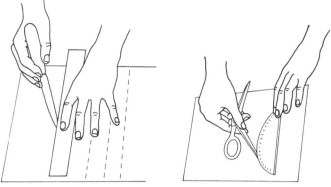

a. Straight scoring   b. Curved scoring

scoring. Plastics. See **Plastics: Cutting.**

scoring. Stained Glass. See **score** and **Stained Glass: Cutting Glass.**

scoring. Tincrafting. The technique for inscribing a fine line on tinplate with an **awl** or scribe to facilitate bending along a predetermined fold line. Scoring is particularly helpful in constructing right-angled boxes or fold-over joints. Also see **Tincrafting: Folding the Tin.**

scoring leather. Leather. See **Leatherwork: Creasing, Scoring and Folding Leather.**

scorper. Jewelry. See **graver.**

Scotchgard. Stitchery. Toys. The brand name of a stain-repellent **finish** that can be applied to any **fabric** to make it oil and water repellent. Many **upholstery materials** can be purchased Scotchgarded; other materials may be treated with this finish professionally or sprayed at home from a pressurized spray can of a Scotchgard solution. The treatment makes fabric resist dye, so the finish should be avoided in any fabrics selected for batik or tie-dye.

Scotch plaid. Weaving. See **plaid.**

Scotch rug. Rugmaking. Weaving. See **ingrain rug.**

Scotch stone. Jewelry. An extremely fine-grained stone mined in Scotland, available in numerous sizes from ¼" to 1" square and in varying lengths. It is used as a fine abrasive on metals to remove pits, scratches, small areas of unwanted **solder,** or other imperfections or blemishes when further buffing or filing is undesirable, especially when a piece of work is nearly finished and **files** or **rifflers** might scratch adjoining areas.

Dip the Scotch stone in water. Rub back and forth on the blemish to remove it. This can take a little time and some elbow grease. As you use the Scotch stone, the water will turn a dark gray; part of the stone is being removed and mixing with the water. When this gray becomes light in color, the residue should be rinsed from the work, as it means the abrasive action is diminishing. Fresh water and more rubbing with the stone can then continue if necessary. The Scotch stone will quickly wear down to fit the shape of the area being smoothed.

Scotch stone. Metalworking. See **abrasives.**

Scotch stone. Woodworking. See **sharpening stone.**

Scottish stitch. Needlepoint. See **flat stitch.**

scouring. Spinning. See **spinning, wool.**

Scrap Bag. Quilts. See **Joseph's Coat.**

scrap doll. Toys. See **rag doll.**

scrape-off batik. Batik and Tie-dye. A variation of **paper batik** in which crayon or **wax** is applied to the paper in a thick coat. Both waxed and unwaxed areas are then covered with India ink or poster paints and left to dry. When dry, the waxed areas are scraped to reveal the colored or clear area beneath.

scraper. Ceramics. A plastic scraper or a triangular metal paint scraper with the corners filed away that is used for cleaning tables.

scraper. Woodworking. A tool with a **burred** edge used to scrape the surface of wood. It may be a paint scraper, for removing unwanted **finish**es; it may be a **chisel**like **wood-turning tool;** or it may be a simple blade for removing blemishes or small gouges left in wood after **planing.**

A hand scraper is a thin, flat blade, usually a rectangle about 4″ × 8″ but sometimes of a curved shape (**a.**). A cabinet scraper is a smaller blade attached to a double handle (**b.**).

To sharpen a scraper, place the scraper in a **vise;** with a flat **file,** file the edge perfectly square and flat. Remove it to an **oilstone** for a finer squared edge, being certain there are no low dips or concavities across the edge. Return the scraper to the vise and rub a **burnisher** along the squared edge at a 15° angle to press out or roll over the edge to create the needed **burr.**

To use a hand scraper, hold the tool in front of you with both hands, with your thumbs up and the burred edge down. Tilt the top of the scraper at a 45° angle away from you and scrape by pushing, or tilt it toward you and pull over the surface of the wood (**c.**). Adjust the angle and cutting pressure as necessary to obtain the smooth surface desired. Finish by sanding with fine sandpaper. See ill.

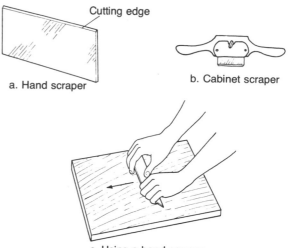

Cutting edge

a. Hand scraper

b. Cabinet scraper

c. Using a hand scraper

scrap glass. Stained Glass. It is a good idea to save all but the tiniest pieces of glass left over when a large sheet of glass is cut to make pieces for a project. Scraps are best kept in boxes separated by color and type. The scraps can be used for projects like jewelry, lampshades, or **mosaics,** in a **lamination,** and in the fused glass technique. Also see **lampshade construction, polyester resin technique.**

scraping. Plastics. See **Plastics: Finishing.**

scraping cut. Woodworking. See **whittling.**

scrap metal. Jewelry. Leftover metal. Some possible uses for this metal when it is in good condition, however small the piece, are for making **shot,** for use in **fusing,** or for melting in the **centrifugal casting** process. When it is unsuitable or unusable under any conditions, it can be sold to a refiner. This is mostly true for gold, silver, and platinum, where the saved scrap can add up to fairly large sums of money. Refiners will not purchase scrap such as copper, brass, or bronze except in quantities greater than a jeweler would use. Also see **sweeps.**

scrap puppet. Puppets. (Also called instant puppet.) A **hand puppet** made from scrap material, or **found material.** Any ready-made form remotely suggesting a human or animal head is a potential puppet, particularly for an imaginative child. An ice-cream cup, a paper cup, or a Styrofoam cup can suggest head shapes. A few lines drawn with **marking pen,** and a handkerchief or bandana for a costume, and a puppet is created almost instantly. Various kinds of boxes can be used, including small milk cartons, salt boxes, or even cottage-cheese boxes. Some will need **felt** for covering the face and a good-sized wad of **batting** for hair. Blown-out eggshells make somewhat fragile **puppet head**s, but are easily replaced after the next scrambled-egg breakfast. Small matchboxes, with the inside tray slipped out and discarded, fit easily around one or two fingers. Disks cut from cardboard or flat disk caps can be glued on for faces. There are endless puppet possibilities in **making do** with everyday throwaways. Once children are introduced to the delights of **puppetry,** they will invent numerous new puppets.

scratch awl. Leather. See **awl and haft.**

scratch batik. Batik and Tie-dye. See **incised batik.**

scratch brushing. Jewelry. See **bristle brush.**

scratch carving. Shell Carving. Low-relief carving in mother-of-pearl, traditionally seen in small plaques depicting Chinese life scenes and landscapes, often with **fretwork** edges.

If a border of fretwork is planned, it should be done before graving the design. Map out the design on thin paper, paste it to the shell plate, and cut the lines with a graver. Or give the plate a wash of Chinese white, draw the design directly upon the shell, and then grave the lines. Remove the paper by soaking it in water and scraping it off, and the Chinese white by scrubbing it with water. Use a brush to scrub out graved lines. A light sanding will bring the lines into relief, and the cleanness of the cuts will reveal whether the tools were sharpened often enough while working. Polish. The lines may be darkened to heighten the contrast with India ink, indigo, or jeweler's tripoli. Also see **grubby, nacre, nautilus, porosity** and **Shell Carving: Shell, Tools and Materials.**

scratch compass. Leather. A tool used to scratch a line along the sewing path, providing a recessed groove in which stitches can be made below the surface of the leather, thus protecting them from rubbing. Also see **patent leather compass.**

scratch drawing. Toys. A drawing method used in **cookie art** or **edible toy**s. The scratch method is accomplished by painting frosting or marshmallow coating over a chocolate, gingerbread, or other dark dough cookie. A line is then scratched through the frosting to make an incised pattern.

scratch removal. Plastics. See **Plastics: Care, Cleaning, and Maintenance.**

screen. Ceramics. A wire mesh for sieving materials. Also see **sieve.**

screen. Puppets. The sheet of material on which a **shadow puppet** performance is given. If the shadow puppets are small, a piece of window-shade material will do. Other partially transparent fabrics also work well and may be stretched over an empty picture frame. For full-size **shadow play**s, a screen may be made by stretching a sheet across an open double doorway. A large frame is required for a stage-sized screen to accommodate adult figures. The screen must always be stretched smooth and flat, since it is usually **backlight**ed. Also see **marionette stage, silhouette, silhouette puppet** and **Puppets: The Puppet Stage.**

screen. Silkscreen. See **Silkscreen.**

screen. Stitchery. See **hardware cloth.**

screen frame. Silkscreen. A rigid wood or metal support to which the screen for silkscreen printing is attached. Wood screen frames are best made from kiln-dried spruce or white pine that is free of warping. The corner joints must be strong enough to withstand the considerable stress placed upon the members when the screen is stretched. Wood sections from 1″ × 2″ to 2″ × 3″ are used, depending on the size of screen to be stretched.

The screen material must be tacked or stapled to the bottom of the frame or to the outside edges, much in the manner of stretching artist's canvas on stretchers. Care must be taken to ensure that the screen is tympan-tight and free of creases or ripples. Tacks or staples must be driven in hard enough and at close enough intervals so that the material does not tear away at the shank of the fastener. Some screen builders use a piece of ½″ cloth tape to reinforce the screen fabric at the line of attachment.

It is customary to apply gummed tape to the inside of the frame across the edges where the wood meets the screen to keep ink and solvents from running under and between the cloth and wood. See ill.

Screen frame

screen hinge. Silkscreen. A combination clamp and hinge used to secure the **screen frame** to the **printing base** for silkscreen printing. See ill.

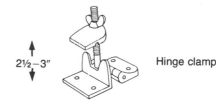

2½–3″   Hinge clamp

screw. Metalworking. Screws used for metal are of four basic types.

SHEET-METAL SCREW

A straight metal fastener with a large head and a tapered shank threaded its entire length. It is used to join thin sheet metal to other pieces of sheet metal. The heads may be flat, oval, or round, and are often slotted to receive a Phillips-head screwdriver. They come in a variety of sizes up to 2″ in length ⅜″ in diameter (**a.**).

MACHINE SCREW

A metal fastener with a straight, finely threaded shank. It is used to hold sheet metal and thin plate to heavier stock. Machine screws are available in a variety of heads, including flat, round, oval, fillister, and Phillips. They range in sizes from #0 (.06″) to ⅜″ in diameter and up to 3″

in length, with varying numbers of threads per inch. These screws are also used to join two parts where one has a **tapped** hole (**b.**).

CAP SCREW

A larger machine screw with a heavier head and a partially threaded shank for larger stock. The heads may be square, hexagonal, fillister, or stocketed (for an allen **wrench**). The sizes range from ¼″ to 1¼″ in diameter and from ½″ to 6″ long. They are most commonly made of steel (**c.**).

SET SCREW

A straight headless screw threaded the entire length of the shaft. Instead of a head, one end is slotted to accept a screwdriver or socketed for an allen wrench. Set screws are commonly used to fasten pulleys to collars or shafts, or as fine adjustment screws. They come in standard sizes similar to machine screws (**d.**). See ill.

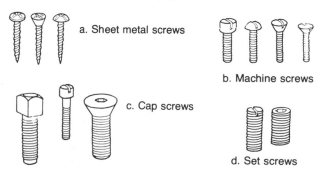

a. Sheet metal screws

b. Machine screws

c. Cap screws

d. Set screws

screw. Woodworking. A wood screw is a straight metal fastener with a large head, a straight shank, and a threaded portion about ⅔ of its length that tapers to a pointed tip. It has more holding power than a nail and can be removed without damage to the wood surface. Screws are made in a variety of metals, such as brass, copper, steel, aluminum, and nickel; steel screws may be bright (uncoated), blue (see **bluing**), or **galvanized.**

Screw sizes are given by length and a number representing the diameter. The length is measured from the widest portion of the head to the tip. Screw diameters, measured at the shank, range from #0 (0.06″, about ¹/₁₆″) to #24 (0.372″, about ⅜″); the most common are numbers 6 (0.138″) and 8 (0.164″). Lengths range from ³/₁₆″ to 6″, with several size numbers in each length; number 6 screws are available from ⅜″ to 1½″, and number 8 from ½″ to 2″.

Most screws are slotted to receive a common **screwdriver** of the appropriate size; some have a cross-shaped indentation for a Phillips-head screwdriver. There are a number of head shapes. Flat-head screws is the most common screw. Use it where you will **countersink** the screw flush with or below the wood surface (**a.**). A round-head screw is used where it will be visible and accessible for easy removal (**b.**). The oval-head screw is halfway between the previous two in shape; use it where it may be partially countersunk, where it may have to be removed, and where a finished appearance is necessary—to hold on a removable panel in a piece of furniture, for instance (**c.**). In a Phillips screw, the cross-shaped slot offers more gripping power for the special screwdriver, so use it for screw-

ing into hardwoods and in cases where accidental damage to the wood surface is to be avoided. Heads may be flat, round, or oval (**d.**). The lag screw (or lag bolt) is a hybrid; it does not take a nut and the body is tapered, so it is a screw; but the head is square and unslotted, more like a **bolt.** It is larger and coarser than normal screws, and is most commonly available in black iron; use a wrench to drive it into heavy timbers and to fasten machinery to floors. Diameters are given in direct measurement, from ¼–1″, rather than in numbers, and lengths range from 1–16″ (**e.**). See ill. Also see **Woodworking: Screwing.**

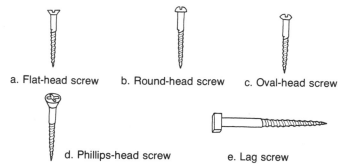

a. Flat-head screw   b. Round-head screw   c. Oval-head screw

d. Phillips-head screw   e. Lag screw

screwblock. Basketry. (Also called screwbox.) A tool consisting of two blocks of wood fastened together with bolts and thumbscrews. It is used to hold **rods** and **stakes** upright and in a straight line for **squarework.** See ill.

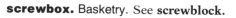

Screwblock

screwbox. Basketry. See **screwblock.**

screwdriver. Woodworking. One of the most frequently used craft tools, used for inserting **screws.** Keep several types and sizes in your tool collection. If the screwdriver is too small or too large for the screw slot, it can distort the screw head or gouge the surrounding wood. When purchasing screwdrivers, choose one ordinary screwdriver with a square shank so that if you have a difficult screw to loosen, you can fit a wrench on the square shank for extra leverage. Long screwdrivers allow more leverage and are less likely to tilt in the screw slot. Use short ones only for places where there is little working space. Phillips-head screwdrivers are for Phillips screws. Magnetized Phillips-head screwdrivers work well, but ordinary magnetized screwdrivers sometimes drop the ordinary slotted screws.

When installing very long screws you may put a screwdriver bit into a carpenter's **brace,** or when driving many screws, a screwdriver attachment may be attached to a power drill.

Phillips-head screwdriver and Phillips screw

An automatic (or ratchet) screwdriver is a hand-operated, spring-loaded tool; by simply pushing on the handle, you can either drive or remove screws. It comes with standard and Phillips-head tips and is ideal for multiple screwing. See ill. Also see **Woodworking: Screwing.**

screw eye. Puppets. A short screw that has a ring at the end in place of the flat head. The shaft of the screw extends to form this loop. Also see **arm string, back string, base, control point, free joint, marionette head, puppet head, rag-doll puppet, screw-eye joint, swivel joint** and **Puppets: Making the Marionette Skeleton.**

screw-eye connection. Puppets. See **screw-eye joint.**

screw-eye joint. Puppets. (Also called screw-eye connection.) The screw-eye is used to join parts of a **marionette** in such a way as to allow for free movement at the **joint.** When two screw eyes are to be joined, as in connecting the arm to the shoulder, one screw eye is opened with pliers so that the two can be linked, and then the open end is closed or tightened. Or the two screw eyes may be bound together with a short wire. A **screw hook** can be used to slip into a screw eye. The hook is then tightened with pliers, making it into a screw eye. The disadvantage of screw-eye joints is that there may be too much freedom of movement. To control this, a **leather hinge** may be used to limit the movement in at least one direction. Also see **swivel joint.**

screw hook. Puppets. Similar to a **screw eye** but with an open loop. It is sometimes used in the construction of a **marionette.** Also see **screw-eye joint** and **Puppets: Making the Marionette Skeleton.**

screwing. Woodworking. See **screw** and **Woodworking: Screwing.**

screw nail. Woodworking. See **nail.**

screw plate. Jewelry. A flat plate with numerous holes, either single or double notched, for threading wire to form screws. They are usually sold with corresponding taps for threading the wire into the hole. Entire pieces of jewelry can be put together with screws. They may be planned as part of a piece of work that may eventually someday need repair, such as an enameled piece that has a tendency to chip, or a piece that contains a material that would be destroyed by exposure to the intense heat of a torch or a kiln. Screws can either be concealed in the construction or used as a decorative element.

scribe. Stained Glass. A term used for a **glass-cutter.** The scratched line made with it on the glass is called scribing.

scribe. Tincrafting. See **awl, scoring.**

scribe. Woodworking. See **marking tools.**

scriber. Enameling. A utensil with a pointed, hardened steel tip used for incising a line in metal. It is used to mark areas, for engraving, for opening pits and bubbles, and for sgraffito. See ill. Also see **color testing, resist** and **Enameling: Tools and Materials.**

Scriber

scriber. Jewelry. A cutting tool with a hardened steel point used for cutting light lines into metal surfaces. These lines can then be used as guidelines for **sawing** or **soldering.** Lines should be scribed very lightly, as a deep cut is difficult to remove should you slip or scribe something incorrectly. Scribers can be used in conjunction with a steel rule. With some control the scriber can be used to cut deeper, almost like a **graver.** Some scribers have extra points in the handle to replace the original point when it wears out. These can also be used as **soldering point**s, although this will ruin the hardened point. Also see **machinists's scriber.**

scriber. Metalworking. A narrow, rod-shaped tool with a sharp pointed end, used to scribe or mark lines on metal. Scribe a straight line by holding the scriber like a pencil with the point against a straightedge or **square** and draw it along the edge, tilting it in the direction you are moving.

scribing. Tincrafting. See **scoring.**

scrim. Rugmaking. See **canvas mesh.**

scrim. Stitchery. See **cheesecloth.**

scrimshaw. Ivory and Bone Carving. Scrimshaw is most commonly associated with the estimated 3,000,000 whale bone and tooth carvings of the 20,000 Yankees who manned the whaling vessels from the mid-nineteenth to the early twentieth century. The derivation of the term is obscure, perhaps from the Dutch word *skrimshander,* meaning "lazy fellow."

Some experts consider a piece of scrimshaw genuine only if it has been carved at sea; of course, this was not the only place that whale bone and tooth were carved. The origins of the craft have been disputed; its beginnings are sometimes attributed to seventeenth-century whalers from Hull, England. The French are credited with a great deal of influence on American and English ivory carving due to the simultaneous imprisonment of Dieppe ivory workers and American captives in the War of 1812. Under the tutelage of **les laboureurs,** the American prisoners were taught the carving trade and supported themselves (often in grand style) while still prisoners of war. It is assumed that these prisoners returned to America and continued to practice this new craft. In the 1840s, the New England whaler began hunting in the Bering Straits, obtaining walrus tusk and **narwhal ivory,** as well as Eskimo carving techniques.

Most scrimshaw depicts whaling episodes and historical scenes. Common design motifs were often found, although magazine pictures such as *Godey's Lady's Book* prints were also used. Implements such as pie crimpers, tool handles, spinning wheels, sewing tools, toilet articles, boxes, canes, and parasol handles were carved for the women at home. Whole teeth and bone also replaced metal and wood fittings aboard ship which were destroyed by the sea air. Scrimshaw was also used as an item of barter. Very few pieces are signed, and many of the scenes are unidentifiable. Today, scrimshaw is held in very high regard.

Whale teeth, panbone, and **baleen** were brine-cured and left to dry in the sun. The ribs on the teeth were abraded with sharkskin. The most common tool employed was the jackknife, although sail needles, **Eskimo style**s, and all manner of improvised tools were used. The workshop aboard ship afforded saws and many other tools for cutting and engraving. Shipboard dyes were tobacco juice, ink, soot, and berry juice. But many carvings were colored after the ship returned home. Polishing the finished piece was achieved using ash and the palm of the hand.

scripture quilt. Quilts. See **Bible quilt.**

scrivelloes. Ivory and Bone Carving. See **elephant ivory.**

scroll saw. Woodworking. See **power saw.**

scroll snips. Metalworking. See **snips.**

scroll stitch. Crewel. Embroidery. See **coral knot.**

scrub brush. Stained Glass. Used in cleaning finished stained-glass **panel**s and lampshades. The type recommended is a long, modified figure-eight brush with close bristles at least 1″ long. Also see **lampshade construction** and **Stained Glass: Tools and Materials.**

scrubs. Stained Glass. See **brushes.**

sculpturing wax. Candlemaking. Sculpturing wax can be used by candlemakers to form a wide variety of hand-shaped candles or ornamental decorations for candles. It can be purchased in most hobby shops or art-supply stores, or made by combining equal portions of low-**melting-point** wax, medium wax, and **beeswax** with a small amount of **stearic acid,** and melting it at 200° F. The melted wax can then be poured out in a thin layer onto a glass plate with clay retaining barriers or onto a thin metal sheet with sides. Flowers or other decorative shapes can be cut from the cooled layer of wax and shaped into three-dimensional forms. A heating lamp above the work area will keep the wax malleable. Entire flowers with a **wick** center can be constructed using the same technique. Dipping in cold water will set the final design.

scumming. Ceramics. A white **efflorescence** that can show up and mar the surface of fired clay and **terra cotta.** It is caused by soluble basic salts and is brought to the surface of the clay during handling.

scutching. Spinning. See **flax.**

sea amber. Amber Carving. See **amber.**

sea island cotton. Quilts. Stitchery. **Cotton fabric** woven from extra-long **fibers** of cotton from Central America and Mexico. It is the one **cotton fiber** considered to be of higher quality than **pima cotton.**

sealant. Plastics. Coating used to seal the surface of a material. Shellac, lacquer, varnish, **polymer emulsion** or other sealants are necessary to seal a mold before **casting,** embedding, or laminating plastic, and to close the pores on **foam** before **resin** is applied to its surface; polyester resin will dissolve **polystyrene** (also called Styrofoam, Dy-lite) foam if it comes in contact with it. Also see **casting plaster, embedment** and **Plastics: Casting.**

sealant. Woodworking. A substance that seals wood and prevents wood stain, filler, or natural resin from **bleeding** through to the final surface finish. **Shellac, lacquer,** or **varnish** may be used as a sealant depending on what it is to be applied over and how it is applied. Always ensure that the sealant does not contain the **solvent** of the material that it is supposed to seal.

sealer. Découpage. A coating, usually diluted **shellac** or clear plastic spray, used to seal and protect a surface and to keep subsequent coats of finish, such as **varnish,** from sinking in. In découpage techniques, most surfaces requiring a sealer, such as paper **prints** and wood, should be coated with a shellac solution of 1 part white shellac to 1 part denatured alcohol, applied with a **brush** in a thin, even coat.

sealer. Toys. A thin, colorless liquid applied to wood to prepare it for painting. It prevents paint from soaking into the wood. Wood sealers are usually applied by brush and must be thoroughly dry before paint is added. Shellac and vinyl sealer are commonly used. If an undercoat is used a sealer is not necessary. Many craftspeople prefer to use a wood sealer followed by an undercoat before painting. Also see **acrylic spray.**

sealing wax. Jewelry. A hard, brittle wax used as a supportive material to fill in depressions in the back of thin **repoussé** work and in hollow metal beads.

sealskin. Bookbinding. See **leather.**

seam. Jewelry. The terms "seam" and "**joint**" are sometimes synonymous, although "joint" has more than one meaning. They refer to any edges that have been joined by **soldering** or to any piece of metal, such as a wire end, that has been soldered to a piece of flat metal. The first is more likely to be referred to as a seam, and the second more likely to be called a joint, but either term would be correct.

seam. Knitting. A seam is the union formed by joining two pieces of knitted fabric together. Seams are usually found at the sides and shoulders of a knit garment (joining front to back and body to sleeves). Seams can be made by **backstitch,** by **weaving together,** or by **oversewing.** See ill.

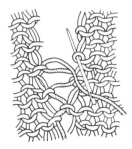

Vertical seaming

seam. Stitchery. A line of **stitch**ing used to **join** two pieces of **fabric,** usually by sewing them together near the cut or **raw edge.** A **plain seam** uses only a single line of stitches, the **French seam** and **flat fell seam** use two, and a **bound seam** uses three.

seam allowance. Quilts. The amount of material allowed at the edge of a fabric to be taken up by a seam. In any **patchwork** it is essential to add the seam allowance to the **finished size.** Sizes or dimensions in directions should always indicate whether or not seam allowances are included. Also see **modular quilt** and **Quilts: Marking and Cutting.**

seam allowance. Stitchery. The amount of material allowed at the edge of a **fabric** to be taken up by a **seam.** In any sewing, either by hand or by machine, it is essential to add the seam allowance to finished measurements. Sizes or dimensions in directions should always indicate whether or not seam allowances are included.

seam binding. Stitchery. (Also called iron-on seam binding.) A narrow **ribbon**like piece of **fabric,** woven with **selvage**s, used to **finish** a **seam** or **hem.** Seam binding is thin or lightweight with very little **bulk,** usually made of **rayon.** Some seam bindings have an **adhesive** backing so that they can be **set** by ironing.

seam finish. Stitchery. Any of various ways of **finishing** or **binding** the **raw edge**s of a **plain seam.** Among the most often used seam finishes are the **overcast seam, bound seam, stitched-edge seam,** French seam, flat fell seam and **topstitched seam.** Also see **false French seam.**

seam ripper. Stitchery. A small hand tool that has a tiny curved blade opposite the handle end which can be slipped between the **stitch**es of a **seam** to cut the threads quickly and easily. Care must be taken not to cut the **fabric.**

seasoned ivory. Ivory and Bone Carving. See **elephant ivory.**

seasoning. Woodworking. See **wood.**

Secession Quilt. Quilts. An **all-white quilt** finished in 1860 by the wife of General P. D. Cook of South Carolina. An ardent secessionist, she recorded her views in intricate stitching using a **trapunto** technique. This **patriotic quilt** includes the names of General Cook, George Washington, and several governors of South Carolina, along with an eagle, garlands, shields, and the figure of Liberty.

secondary color. See **primary color.**

second-cut file. Metalworking. See **file.**

secondo coloro. Coral Carving. See **coral.**

section. Bookbinding. The basic unit that composes a book. It is formed by **folding** and cutting a printed or plain sheet one or more times. Sections are numbered or lettered at the inside bottom of each first page with a **signature.**

Folding a standard sheet once produces a folio (fol). Folding a folio once produces a quarto (4to), consisting of four **leaves.** Folding a quarto once produces an octavo (8to), consisting of eight leaves. Folding the octavo once produces the sexto-decimo (16mo), consisting of sixteen leaves. These four terms refer to the number of times a sheet has been folded and not to size. The size is determined by the measurements of the original sheet. A section is commonly referred to as a signature among most commercial printers. See ill.

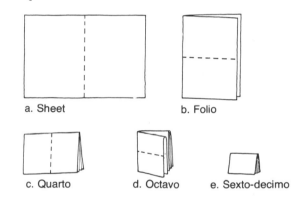

a. Sheet   b. Folio

c. Quarto   d. Octavo   e. Sexto-decimo

sectional warp beam. Weaving. A **warp beam** with wooden pegs, steel rods, or wire loops spaced at 2″ intervals across the width of a beam. Around the circumference, the beam is divided by the pegs into at least 4 sections—and sometimes more if it is very wide in diameter. Ideally, the beam should be a yard around the circumference. A sectional warp beam is used specifically for **sectional warping,** where the warp is beamed and lies between the pegs in sections rather than being spread out evenly across the entire beam. Some sectional warp beams are combination beams in that the outside planks with the pegs can be reversed so that the pegs are on the inside of the beam and the weaver can use either sectional or **chain warping.** Also see **sectional warping.**

sectional warping. Weaving. **Warping** in sections directly from spools onto the **sectional warp beam** on a **harness loom.** The warping and **beaming** operations that are used with conventional **warp beam**s are combined. This can be done because the **warp** is not wound beforehand on either a **warping reel** or **warping board** but is beamed in 2″ sections from a **spool rack** onto the warp beam. Each section is beamed separately, and within each section all **ends**

are wound simultaneously. Any section can be wound first, but most weavers prefer to start in the center and then fill in the alternate side sections. One section is completely wound to the total number of yards desired, cut off from the yarns in the spool rack, and the next section is then wound in similar fashion. This procedure is followed until all the sections are wound.

Necessary additional equipment for sectional warping is a large spool rack, since each end in a section must feed off an individual spool. There must be as many spaces in the rack as there are ends in a section of 2″. The spools are arranged on a rack in the order in which they are to appear in the warp, starting at the upper right or left and working down the spool rack before returning to the top space again. In this same sequence, the yarns travel through a **tension box,** another highly advisable piece of adjunct equipment. The tension box takes the place of **lease stick**s and **raddle.** After coming from the spool rack, the yarns go through the tension box and are attached either to a back **apron bar** or collected as a group and tied around the center starting peg.

Prior to arranging the spools on the rack, the width and the total number of ends to be used must be determined. The total number is then divided by the number of sections lying within the width—keeping in mind that each section accommodates 2″ of ends.

The sections are wound by turning the warp beam in the correct direction so it can unwind properly for weaving. The weaver must keep track of how many revolutions are made in each section so that the entire warp is the same length. A tension box has an optional attachment called a **counter** that counts every turn of the warp beam and thereby insures that each section is the same length. If for some reason there is no counter, guide strings can be cut to the exact yardage needed and attached to each starting peg in a section; or the starting peg can be marked and every revolution can be counted and noted down.

After a section is completed, the **cross** can be maintained with a cord. When all sections are beamed, lease sticks can be passed through all the crosses. This is optional but desirable. An alternate method is to spread the section when it is completed and paste a piece of masking tape across the warp ends so that they stay in the order that they were wound. Cut the ends in front of the tape, or far enough from the cord so that it won't slip out. To make sure that the cut ends don't flop around when the next sections are being wound, tape them with another piece of tape to the warp beam. When all sections are completed, the taped ends are lifted off the warp beam and brought over the **back beam** by slowly unwinding the warp. At this point lease sticks can be inserted if this is desired. If not, unwind enough warp until the sections reach the **beater** so that the ends are long enough for **threading.**

Sectional warping is a practical method of warping for long and wide warps. There is minimal handling of the warp yarns and order and tension can be easily maintained. See ill.

sedge. Basketry. A basketry material from a coarse, grasslike plant that grows in tufts or clumps in wet ground. It is most commonly used for **coiled basketry.**

sedimentary clay. Ceramics. See **Ceramics: Clay.**

seed bead. Beadwork. Small, round **glass bead**s, sometimes called chalk beads, of various sizes from $^1/_{16}$″ in diameter. Seed beads are graded #10−13 according to size, the largest number being the smallest. Seed beads, sold in small tubes or by the pound, are available in transparent or opaque colors. Beads smaller than $^1/_{16}$″ diameter, called petite beads, are sometimes available.

Seed beads, which are widely used today for all types of beadwork, are the characteristic bead of **American Indian beadwork.** The seed bead became popular around 1840; it was preferred by Indian women because of the wide range of colors available. Also see **embroidery bead.**

seeder. Leather. A **stamp** available in many sizes. When struck with a **mallet** it leaves dotlike impressions in **tooling** designs. Seeding is usually done after all beveling and **shading** is completed.

seed pearls. Beadwork. Small **pearl**s in soft, iridescent colors, obtained from fresh water. When fresh, they are not too difficult to pierce, and are called "nature's most perfect bead."

seeds. Beadwork. Seeds, collected from nature or from the grocery store, are a readily available material that can be drilled or pierced for **beadmaking.** Some seeds, such as rose hips, beechnuts, sunflower and melon seeds, peas, and acorns should be pierced while fresh and soft; if dry, they can be pierced with a red-hot knitting needle or a metal skewer. Some dried seeds must be boiled in water to soften for piercing. Seeds can be colored by immersing them in **dye** and then varnishing them when dry.

seeds. Glasswork. Small bubbles of air trapped in molten glass. Also see **fining.**

seeds. Stained Glass. Textures like seeds, **bubble**s and other movement within **antique glass** are characteristic of the irregularities created by the individual glass blowers at their art. These irregularities have the effect of trapped sunlight. They are created by throwing into the pot of molten glass mixture a few raw potatoes, which give off oxygen bubbles as they are burned up.

seed stitch. Crewel. Embroidery. (Also called crumb stitch, dot stitch, speckling stitch.) A small double stitch with one stitch laid directly over the first. Work the second stitch diagonally across the first (**a.**). The made stitch forms a firm, round, slightly raised "bump" on the fabric (**b.**). The finished effect appears as one raised stitch instead of two. When worked with thread which matches the background fabric in color, seeding gives an attractive tex-

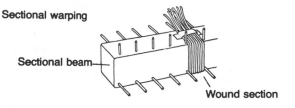

Sectional warping

Sectional beam

Wound section

tured effect. The density of the "seeds" renders various shadings from light to dark. An area can be filled in with an even density or scattered for a shaded effect.

A variation used in **stumpwork** is raised seeding, which is worked in the same way except the stitch is left loose to create a bump on the **background fabric.** The thickness of the thread will hold the stitch in place (**c.**). See ill. Also see **shading stitch.**

a.   b. Seed stitch   c. Raised seed stitch

seed stitch. Knitting. See **moss stitch** and **Knitting: Construction.**

seed yarn. Spinning. Weaving. See **novelty yarn.**

seersucker. Weaving. See **plain weave.**

segmented doll. Toys. Any doll made from a number of **join**ed segments or parts. **Ball joint**ed dolls, **peg-joint dolls,** and **jumping jacks** are segmented.

segma snap. Leather. See **snap.**

segma snap tool. Leather. See **snap.**

segrinato. Jewelry. See **liner.**

Sehna knot. Rugmaking. Weaving. See **knotted pile.**

seine twine. Rugmaking. Weaving. (Also known as cable cord, cable twine.) A strong, tightly twisted cotton yarn suited for **warp** in weaving rugs or tapestries or other projects calling for above average beating to cover the warp. It has excellent **tensile strength** with just enough elasticity to permit complete recovery after stretching. However, **twists** vary, and an overtwist should be avoided, as it is too elastic. Seine twine is made up of several plies of long **staple,** high-grade cotton and comes in various sizes depending on the number of plies. A size 6 or 9 is most preferred by weavers. Also see **ply.**

select wood. Woodworking. See **wood.**

selenite. Gemcutting. See **gypsum.**

selenium. Stained Glass. See **antique glass colorants.**

self-binding. Quilts. Stitchery. **Binding** a piece of material by using some of the same material brought over a **raw edge** to finish it. In a **wall hanging,** either the front material can be turned over the edge onto the **backing,** or the backing material can be turned over the raw edge and onto the front fabric. In **quilting,** it is usually the backing material that is used in the self-binding.

Sometimes self-binding is used to simply mean a binding of the same material, though not necessarily part of the same piece. A certain color or print used in a **panel** or a **quilt top** can be repeated as the binding.

self color. Crewel. Embroidery. A term that refers to work in which the thread matches the color of the background fabric. Also see **whitework.**

self-extinguishing. Plastics. Said of plastics that stop burning immediately upon removal of a flame.

self-fringe. Rugmaking. Weaving. See **fringe.**

self-hardening clay. Puppets. Toys. See **craft clay.**

self-righting doll. Toys. See **Daruma doll, tumble doll.**

selvage. Knitting. Selvage edges are the edge made by **casting on,** the side edges created as the knitting proceeds, and the edge formed by **casting off** at the finish of the knitting. Also see **edge.**

selvage. Quilts. Stitchery. The self-finished edge on a woven material that prevents the **warp,** or lengthwise threads, from **ravel**ing. Because the threads at the selvage are closer together and more tightly woven than that of the rest, the edges tend to **shrink** more in washing than the rest of the material. Selvages are therefore usually cut off before sewing.

selvage. Weaving. (Also spelled "selvedge.") The two lengthwise or warpwise edges of a woven fabric. This is the point where the **filling** yarns go around the **warp** to return back to the other side of the cloth in a subsequent **shed.** Unless the selvage is being done as a decorative feature, it should be woven as straight as possible. There should be no loose loops hanging out at the edge, which is the mark of not pulling the filling in firmly enough at the edges, and neither should there be any indentation at the selvage, which shows the weaver pulling or drawing in too tightly and then loosening up to compensate for it. If the weaver continually pulls in too tightly, the fabric will get narrower and narrower, and the selvage threads will be cut by the **beater.** The selvage gives a firm edge against this cutting action by being made stronger than the rest of the warp. This is done by doubling the edge threads either just in the **reed,** or, in the case of rugs or other heavy pieces, in both the **heddle**s and the reed. A minimum selvage is made by doubling the first two and last two ends at the fabric edge. On wide fabrics the selvage can extend from ¼–1". Selvages can also be made of a stronger yarn than the rest of the warp, or they can be threaded on special **harness**es so that their weave is handled separately from the weave of the fabric. Usually the weave is **plain weave,** but it can be something more patterned for a specific effect.

In weaving with many different filling colors, the weaver has a problem of what to do with the different yarns so that long floats of yarn do not appear at the selvage between blocks of color. The floats or loops can be left if the fabric is to be cut for sewing or the selvage is hidden, as in a hem. If the selvage remains intact and will be seen, then the various colors are always picked up by the thread entering the shed so that they are held next to the selvage. The entering thread can also twist around these other colors, in which case an almost braided effect results.

A floating selvage is one that is not threaded through any heddle but is sleyed through the reed. Since it is not attached to any harness when a shed is made, it neither rises nor sinks, but lies in a neutral horizontal position. Usually on **floor loom**s, it can be seen midway in the angle of the shed. A floating selvage assures the weaver that the end threads will always be caught by the filling, whereas if they are threaded in the pattern of the rest of the warp, it sometimes happens that they are left uncaught. On a **Navajo loom**, a floating selvage is used, but is twisted after every row of filling to give a tighter, firmer edge to the blankets and rugs. It gives a distinctive twined look to the edges.

Pieces woven on a **backstrap** or **frame loom** can also have horizontal selvages and are known as four-selvaged weavings. Also see **bubbling**.

selvedge. Weaving. See **selvage**.

semee. Bookbinding. See **semis**.

semidry tripoli. Metalworking. See **abrasives**.

Seminole patchwork. Quilts. A colorful, highly decorative, complex method of **piecing** developed by the Seminole Indians. Basically, Seminole **patchwork** is made by first sewing together several very long and narrow strips of fabric, side to side. They are then cut crosswise into short strips and sewn back together again. In resewing they may be angled or reversed, or new sections may be inserted. The possibilities for new combinations and new patterns in the assembly seem limitless. The Seminole Indians wear costumes incorporating their traditional patchwork; such clothing may be seen on the Dania Reservation in Hollywood, Florida.

semis. Bookbinding. (Also called semee.) A term borrowed from heraldry by the bookbinder, meaning "sprinkled"; it refers to a type of design using small tool forms placed at regular intervals over a surface.

Senna knot. Rugmaking. Weaving. See **knotted pile**.

sennit. Macramé. (Also called braid.) A sennit is a (sometimes twisted) rope made by repeating a particular knot over and over for the length of knotting cords. A sennit is often a series of **square knot**s or **half knot**s, but can also be made with **half hitch**es, **alternating reverse double half hitch**es, and **chain knot**s. Also see **alternating half hitch, knot, single chain**.

separated. Tatting. (Abbr. sep.) See **Tatting: Abbreviations**.

separating disks. Jewelry. Cutting disks ⅞" across. Some have both sides coated with **carborundum**, a **cutting compound**. They are extremely brittle and break easily but are excellent for cutting through sprues for their removal after casting. They are used with a **flexible shaft machine**. Wear safety goggles when using the disks.

separator. Plastics. See **mold release agent**.

sequins. Beadwork. Thin, flat, shiny, bright, round or oval disks pierced with a small hole. A sequin is also known as a paillette or, if slightly concave, a couvette. The hole is either in the center, to one side, or at the edge, depending on the way the sequin is to be strung or attached. Sequins are available in a wide variety of colors and sizes.

sequoia. Woodworking. See **redwood**.

sericin. Spinning. Weaving. See **silk**.

series fabric joint. Toys. Multiple **hinge joint**s, usually made with fabric to **join** wooden parts. For example, a series of wood blocks set end-to-end with little or no space between them can be joined to a long strip of cloth or wide twill tape. Glued together, the fabric joins the wood pieces and allows for articulated movement. Toy snake and trains are sometimes made in this way.

serigraphy. Silkscreen. Silkscreen printing used as a fine arts medium, as distinguished from commercial copying processes. Originally serigraphy referred to images produced by painting or drawing with various mediums directly onto the screen, but now any of the methods available for making the **stencil** are in use by serigraphers. The one most in use is the **tusche stencil** method because it is the method best adaptable to improvisation and experiment. **Tusche** is available as crayon, pencil, or liquid, and it is possible to use two mediums concurrently to achieve different textures and brush effects. Textured material, such as screening, sandpaper, or rough-textured wood, can be placed under the silkscreen while the screen is rubbed over with a tusche crayon, thereby creating textures and tones in the stencil that are otherwise difficult to achieve in the process without introducing **photographic stencil** methods and a half-tone screen.

Liquid tusche can be spattered, poured, or impressed onto the screen with a sponge, or with leaves or any other experimental material. Sometimes tusche is used in combination with **cut-paper stencil** methods because blocking out of large areas sharply is easier with this paper technique.

serpentine. Gemcutting. (Also called bowenite, verdantique, and williamsite.) Magnesium silicate and water **crystal**lized in the monoclinic system with **hardness** of 2½−3, **specific gravity** of 2.2, green color, and white **streak**. It has a granular **fracture,** a greasy, nonmetallic **luster,** and is polished with chrome oxide on leather or wood. Chrysotile is a variety which is a source of asbestos. Ricolite has green bands throughout. Also see **cabochon** and **Gemcutting: Hand Grinding and Polishing, Rough Shaping**.

serpentine. Quilts. A winding, turning, twisting form. An **appliqué**d serpentine might make an appropriate **border**

or **band** design. It is also used as a **fancy quilting** pattern because the serpentine form can fit into a border, offering a variety in shapes. Also see **Quilts: Making a Quilt, Quilting Patterns.**

serrated edge. Découpage. See **Découpage: Cutting.**

serrated snips. Tincrafting. A variety of tincutting **snips** in which the cutting blades are notched to produce a slightly irregular cutting line. Several types of serrated snips can be purchased at most hardware shops. They vary primarily from an extremely fine serrated blade to a relatively coarse-toothed cutting edge. The more pronounced the serrations or toothings, the more pronounced the beaded effect on the finished cut line. Each variation has its place in the tincrafter's shop.

servitor. Glasswork. See **gaffer.**

Sesame Street puppet. Puppets. Any of a series of very popular **hand puppets** that resemble the well-known characters of the "Sesame Street" television show. They are usually made of **felt** and feature a large, wide mouth, which can be opened and closed with the **puppeteer**'s fingers. Also see **felt puppet.**

set. Batik and Tie-dye. Stitchery. To fix permanently. Sometimes heat may be used to set a **dye** or to set an **iron-on tape.** An incorrect solvent may set a stain.

set. Gemcutting. See **slabbing saw, tube drill.**

set. Metalworking. See **blacksmithing tools.**

set. Plastics. See **curing.**

set. Puppets. (Also called scenery, stage set.) Stage decor, consisting of **wings** or **flats**, **backdrop**, and **props**, which makes up the setting of a play. Also see **silhouette** and **Puppets: The Puppet Stage.**

set. Quilts. The special way in which a collection of finished **blocks** is **join**ed, or sewn, together. For a series of **appliqué** blocks, the set may alternate a solid block with the decorative ones, or the appliqué blocks may be separated with strips or **band**s of color. Blocks may be outlined, trellislike, in solids or prints. When **geometric** designs or **pieced** blocks are set, the block designs may combine to produce new **block patterns.** Pieced blocks are often set to make an **all-over quilt top** design; the possibilities of varying combinations are almost limitless.

Some block patterns are visually altered so completely by the way in which they are set that it is the set that identifies them. **Log Cabin,** for example, can be set in such a way as to suggest zigzag rows, and it is then identified as **Streak of Lightning.** If the Log Cabin blocks are set into diagonal bands, the finished quilt is called **Straight Furrow;** kept in continually enlarging squares, it is called **Barn Raising.** This multiple naming has led to many disagreements among quilters as to the "correct" name for a pattern, because one is the name of the block design (the

usual name for a quilt) and the other is the name of a specific set for that block. Sometimes both names are used, which may either clarify or complicate the identification. In **Pineapple Log Cabin,** for instance, the "pineapple" refers to the set and "log cabin" identifies the block design used.

The set of the blocks is a vital aspect of quilt design. It allows for the tremendous variety of quilt tops produced from just one block design.

set. Weaving. See **sett.**

set. Woodworking. The outward angle or bend of the teeth of a saw blade. The outward set makes a cut slightly wider than the width of the blade itself to ease the sliding of the blade through the wood. Teeth are set differently in various saws. Although the crosscut saw and ripsaw blades both have alternating teeth set to one side, the ripsaw teeth are set at a slightly smaller angle, thus producing a narrower **kerf.**

set hammer. Metalworking. See **hammer.**

setoff. Bookbinding. See **offset.**

set of the blocks. Quilts. See **set.**

set screw. Metalworking. See **screw.**

set stamping. Leather. See **stamping.**

sett. Weaving. The number of **warp ends** per inch that are put into the **reed** on a **harness loom.** It can also be used when referring to the ends in a cloth already off the loom. Sett is determined by the warp yarns used and the desired effect in the cloth. It, in turn, determines the **density** of the cloth and can be very loose or open when a gauzy look is desired, or very full and tight when a **warp-faced** effect is needed. However, the sett should not be so full that there is difficulty in opening the **shed.** Sett can be changed with every dent or in sections of the reed. This is called a spaced warp. If many warp ends are put into a few dents, this is called cramming. When dents are left empty (sometimes an inch or more) this is known as skip denting. To determine what the sett should be in order to obtain a **balanced cloth** with a yarn of unknown size, wind it around a ruler with each yarn barely touching the one next to it. Count the number of yarns that lie within one inch and divide by two for a tightly interlaced weave, like plain weave. If weaving a looser weave, like a twill, divide by 1½. The result is the number of ends per inch that should be sleyed. This rule is only approximate if warp and **filling** are not to be of the same yarn.

Sett is also spelled "set" and is sometimes called the sley or denting. Often in **warp specifications** and **weaver's records,** it is noted "epi," ends per inch. The term is also used for **frame loom** and other nonharness loom weaving. Also see **sleying.**

setter. Ceramics. See **kiln furniture.**

setting. Woodworking. See **nailset** and **Woodworking: Nailing.**

setting down. Metalworking. See **blacksmithing techniques.**

setting the quilt. Quilts. After the individual **block**s of a quilt have been completed, they are sewn together into a **quilt top.** The **join**ing, or sewing, of these blocks is known as "setting the quilt." Also see **Quilts: Sewing and Assembling.**

setting up. Basketry. See **upsetting.**

setting up. Plastics. See **curing.**

settling. Ceramics. A solid material in **slip**s and **glaze**s that settles when not used. To reclaim a settled glaze, pour off the liquid, and cut and grind the solid part. Rework the reground glaze into the same liquid.

set tool. Metalworking. See **blacksmithing tools.**

7-K. Batik and Tie-dye. See **acid dye, direct dye.**

sewing. Lacemaking. A sewing in **bobbin lace** is made when two areas need to be joined together or otherwise attached to another part of the lace.

Bring the **worker**s through to the point where you will begin the sewing, **twist** once and remove the **pin** from the pinhole. Insert a fine **crochet hook** into the pinhole, pick up one of the worker threads, and make a **loop.** Through this loop pass the other worker **bobbin,** butt end first; pull both threads up snugly. Twist the workers and continue to do the lacework with the same workers.

When making a sewing with a **half stitch** pair, use the thread from the **leader** bobbin to form the loop. See ill. Also see **joining.**

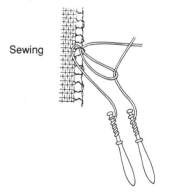

Sewing

sewing. Stitchery. See **Stitchery.**

sewing a single-section book. Bookbinding. Mark the spine for **sawing-in.** The first mark is made 1″ from the **head** and the last is made 1″ from the **tail.** Divide the remaining space into equal spaces of 1–1½″. Pierce holes with the **awl** at these marks, making sure that the awl penetrates exactly through the **back** fold.

Using a medium-weight single linen **thread,** begin sew-ing from the inside of the book. Push the needle from the inside to the outside, leaving a 3″ tail on the inside, and proceed until the last penetration brings you to the inside of the book again. At this point check that the original tail and the needle are on opposite sides of the long center stitch. Draw the thread to tighten the stitches and tie the ends across the long center stitch. Trim the end to a ⅜″ tail and fray it with a needle so it will not groove the paper when pressed. Press the book between **pressing board**s for a short while to shape.

A thin single-section book can be trimmed with a sharp knife and a straightedge. Be sure the blade is sharp. If it is too thick for hand **trimming,** clamp it in the **lying press** and trim it with the **plow.** See ill.

a. Sewing for three holes   b. Sewing for more than three holes

sewing basket. Stitchery. A box or basket in which all the tools essential to sewing or mending are kept. Often, work in progress is also kept in the sewing basket so that when a few free minutes present themselves, everything necessary is readily available. Sewing baskets and boxes have been handmade in a tremendous variety of design and styles of workmanship. They may be nothing more than a shirt box into which the essentials are placed, or they may be carefully compartmentalized containers with drawers, boxes, cases, and monograms or names.

"sewing bird." Rugmaking. See **braided rug.**

sewing bird. Stitchery. (Also called hemming bird, hemming press, sewing press.) An unusual and delightful sewing tool, seldom seen or used now, which holds **fabric** tightly in a clamp. It is especially helpful in **hemming** and some kinds of stitching to have the material held taut. The sewing bird consists of a table vise or C-clamp that holds the tool securely to the table. Perched above the vise is a bird, wings spread, made in such a way that when the tail is pressed, the beak opens. Pressure from a spring under the tail then forces the beak to close on the fabric. Older birds are made of cast bronze, though the Victorian ones are pressed tin. Some have **velveteen** cushions on the top for pins. A few contemporary wood craftspeople have again started making similar clamps, although usually without the birds. Any clamping device of this general description is called a sewing bird.

sewing frame. Bookbinding. A simple construction, consisting of a platform or table upon which the **section**s rest while being sewn and a frame of two uprights and a crossbar to which the **cord**s or **tape**s are attached with tacks or tied around the bar. In the more sophisticated models available commercially, the cords or tapes pass through a slot in the table to the underside where they are attached to small metal keys; the height of the crossbar is adjustable to control their tautness. See ill.

Simple sewing frame

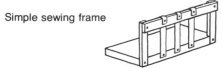

sewing haft. Leather. See **awl and haft.**

sewing leather. Leather. See **Leatherwork: Sewing Leather.**

sewing machine needle. Stitchery. A slender shaft of steel that has a sharp pointed end and a hole very near that same end through which the sewing thread is drawn. The opposite end is set into the sewing machine. Needle sizes vary with the machine and the material. Directions should be followed for each machine. Among the special needles available are the **ball-point needle** and the leather needle, which is slender and has a three-sided shaft so that it can readily pierce thick material.

sewing on cords. Bookbinding. Hand sewing books on **cord**s was the common method employed in binding before the advent of binding machines. The sections are sewn together over unbleached linen cords drawn across the **back.** It provides a strong back yet allows flexibility.

Mark the back of the book for **sawing-in,** leaving ¾″ at the **head** and **tail.** Divide the space between these marks into unequal distances, making no more than five sawcuts for a standard-size book. Do not include **endpaper**s in the book until after sawing, as they are apt to tear. Saw the marks across the back and tilt the saw a little to make the kerf a bit wider at the bottom. String the cords in the **sewing press** and tighten until they are tight enough to sing when plucked. Lay the endpapers on the book and mark them at the positions of the sawcuts; make needle holes in them at the marks with an **awl.** Place the first **section** on the sewing table and sew all along. Sew the sections for **sewing on tapes,** but do not make ties. Press down the sections between the cords with your fingers as you sew. Finish the sewing as you would with tapes and cut the cords, leaving 1¼″ ends. Fray the ends so they will not create lumps under the **board paper. Knock down swell.** See ill.

Sewing on cords

sewing on tapes. Bookbinding. **Section**s can be stitched together over cotton or linen **tape**s that lie across the **back**s of the sections. This method of binding is usually employed when it is desirable for a book to lie flat when open, such as music scores or books with a narrow inner **margin.** Sewing on tapes is a looser binding than other styles, but this does not effect its strength. Its use on heavy books will prolong the life of the volumes.

Average-size books are generally sewn on three tapes, and larger books on more. Many of the operations are identical to the ones used in the **lockstitching** method of binding.

Mark the book back for **sawing-in,** making double marks

the width of the tape at unequal distances along the back. Place the first section on the **sewing frame** with the fold touching the tapes. Tighten the tapes and sew the first section (**a.**). Sew the second section and tie it to the first section (**b.**). When pulling the thread, always draw it along in the direction of the back fold of the section; if you pull it at right angles to the fold it may tear the paper (**c.**). Sew the third section and make a **kettlestitch** at the tail (**d.**). At the fourth section, make a tie at each tape (**e.**).

The first four and last four sections are sewn all along; the sections between are sewn off and on, or alternately, to minimize bulk from too much thread (**f.**). Finish with two or three kettlestitches down the back and cut the thread, leaving a tail of 1″. Cut off the tapes, leaving a 1¼″ tape tail on each side. If there is excessive **swell** because of the stitching, **knock down** the swell, leaving the tape outside the boards when hammering. Knocking down will cause the tapes to **cockle** between the threads; hold each tape by both ends and pull to straighten. If you pull a tape out there is no remedy but to resew the whole book.

While sewing, **rub down** the stitches every so often with a **bone folder,** to keep them firm and smooth. A **French groove** is often used on the **case** of a book sewn on tapes to accommodate the extra bulk at the hinge. See ill.

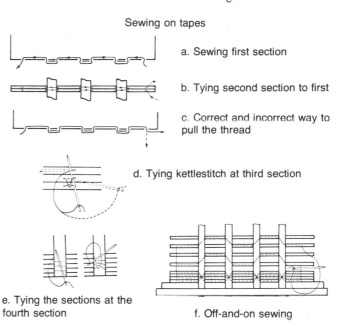

Sewing on tapes

a. Sewing first section

b. Tying second section to first

c. Correct and incorrect way to pull the thread

d. Tying kettlestitch at third section

e. Tying the sections at the fourth section

f. Off-and-on sewing

sewing press. Stitchery. See **sewing bird.**

sewing scissors. Stitchery. See **scissors.**

sewing thread. Quilts. Stitchery. A fine cord made up of strands of spun **silk,** flax, or **cotton,** or of **synthetic fiber**s. It is used in sewing either by hand or by machine.

Mercerized sewing thread has been the most available thread for many years. A **heavy-duty thread** also of cotton is similar, though the cord is heavier. For **satin stitch appliqué,** the heavier duty thread gives a smoother, fuller coverage. **Polyester thread**s, those most commonly available today, are much stronger but not as satisfactory for many kinds of sewing: they often tend to twist and knot while being used.

Various combinations, such as **synthetic** coatings on cottons, keep appearing on the market.

A #50 mercerized cotton thread has been available in over 150 colors, although it is now being discontinued by many shops in favor of **synthetic thread**s.

White thread comes in a range of sizes, from 8 (coarse) to 100 (fine). Black is available from size 8 to 70. Also see **buttonhole twist** and **Stitchery: Materials.**

sewn joint. Toys. See **stitched joint.**

sewn spiral. Batik and Tie-dye. A **tritik** method for **tie-dye** in which a running stitch is taken with single thread for a small spiral, or double thread for a large spiral. A pencil can be used to draw the spiral, starting with a central dot and winding around and around. The stitches then follow the pencil line and are pulled very tight, either from one end or both. The fabric will resemble a spiral shell. If both ends are pulled, the excess length is wrapped along the groove formed in the packaged fabric and the ends are **tied** together. If one end is pulled it is wrapped around the spiral to the other end, where it can be tied to the knot. The tying-off should be done so that the excess thread always follows the pulled thread of the stitches. The method used to sew the spiral can be used to sew a square, a rectangle, or a triangle.

sewn strip rug. Rugmaking. See **joining.**

sewn tuck. Batik and Tie-dye. A **tritik** method of making lines or stripes for **tie-dye.** The material is folded, then a line of **running stitch**es is taken near the fold. The tucks can be sewn in rows, curves or **zigzag** lines.

sexto-decimo. Bookbinding. (Abbr. 16mo) A book made up of groups of 16 leaves, or 32 **page**s. Also see **leaf, section.**

sgraffito. Ceramics. A method of decoration that is done by scratching through the clay **slip** on **leather-hard** clay to expose the **clay body** underneath. See ill.

Sgraffito

sgraffito. China and Glass Painting. A technique of scratching a design through unfired **enamel** or **glaze** to expose the contrasting fired enamel or unglazed surface. This technique, used in decorating glass, produces a two-

color linear relief surface. The tool used can be an awl or a needle mounted in a cork. Also see **China and Glass Painting: Glass Painting.**

sgraffito. Enameling. A technique in which the design is scratched through an unfired coat of **enamel** to expose the **metal** or a prefired enamel base. A **scriber,** toothpick, sharpened chicken bone, or the pointed end of a brush is used to incise the lines. Enamel may be dusted onto a coat of **binder** and the design scratched through when dry, or liquid enamel may be sgraffitoed. Also see **underglaze.**

shade. A variant of a **hue** made by adding black. Also see **monochromatic color triangle.**

shader. Leather. A kind of **stamp.**

shader brushes. China and Glass Painting. See **brushes.**

shading. Beadwork. A technique used in **bead flowermaking** to vary the colors of **glass bead**s in petals or leaves. After the petal is completed, leave enough bare wire to add another row of contrasting colored beads around the outer edge (**a.**). For additional gradations of color, a row of second-color beads can be fed onto the wire end and wrapped around the petal again. To tip a petal with contrasting color, change the color of beads on the top half of the last two rows (**b.**). See ill.

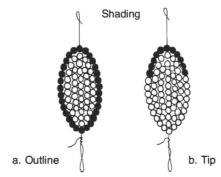

Shading

a. Outline   b. Tip

shading. Leather. The use of shading **stamp**s to give the effect of dimension and shaded areas to tooled designs. Also see **tooling.**

shading. Stenciling. A technique used in stenciling to apply color within the design areas in graduated tones and highlights, giving the area a more realistic effect than the flat, crisp, two-dimensional shape characteristic of stenciling. Shading can be done by **stippling** darker or lighter tones with a **stencil brush.** The background color of the surface to be decorated, usually a pale tone, also can be left in areas as a highlight. Also see **Stenciling: Painting.**

shading stitches. Crewel. Embroidery. Shading stitches can bring life and realism to any design by using yarns with slight color variations. They make it possible for the skilled needleworker to truly "paint in wool." Perhaps the most important and most difficult of the shading stitches is **long and short stitch.** Also see **block shading, brick**

stitch, burden stitch, chain stitch, Roumanian stitch, seed stitch, split stitch.

shading yarn. Crewel. Embroidery. Needlepoint. See **ombré yarn.**

shadow appliqué. Stitchery. See **shadow work.**

shadow box. Découpage. A three-dimensional composition, combining techniques such as découpage, **paper sculpture,** or **repoussé,** that is mounted inside a box with a glass front and a frame or edging. For a heightened illusion of dimension, architectural details of scenes are often depicted in accentuated perspective. Cutout details are mounted in a free-standing position, propped up with **ladders.** Shadows are often painted in to heighten the dimensional effect. Parts of the picture also can be molded and then padded with **bread-dough mixture,** cotton, or **papier mâché,** as in repoussé.

shadow play. Puppets. A performance of shadows projected onto a **screen.** The shadows may be those of full-size human figures shown onto a large sheet for a screen, or they may be of intricately cut **shadow puppet**s. In contemporary **puppetry** various new materials are used, including **acetate sheet**s, Plexiglas, colored gels, plastic, fabrics, and papers. The shadow play may occur within a stage of specific shape by covering a part of the screen area. For example, a large cardboard with a hole in it will isolate a circular area to suggest a well or a tunnel. Any shape can be used in this way to define an area for action.

Flexible materials such as kitchen or dry-cleaning plastic bags and fabrics may be used over a cutout of cardboard or over a wire frame. The materials can be moved to suggest actions. Some shadow plays are performed with **silhouette** figures attached to rods. They are operated in a manner similar to **rod puppet**s, except that they perform behind a screen by projecting shadows. Other figures are suspended by **nylon leader** or nylon thread from **control bar**s held above the screen. Also see **backlight.**

shadow printing. Fabric Printing. See **partial overprinting.**

shadow puppet. Puppets. A figure whose shadow is cast onto a **screen** or wall. Anybody who holds his hands in front of a strong light to cast black shadows on a wall produces a rudimentary shadow puppet. Some additional folding of the hands, and a wiggle of the thumbs or extended fingers, and wolves or rabbits leap magically across the wall. All children are fascinated by such **shadow-play** wizardry, as are most adults. It is this play of animated shadows that is the basis of the shadow-puppet theater.

Shadow puppets are **silhouette**s or **cut-out figure**s used to cast shadows on a screen in a theatrical performance. Ancient Chinese shadow puppets took advantage of the luminous color that could be achieved when animal hide, cut to shape, was stained or dyed and **backlight**ed. As the light came through the puppet, varying amounts of color

also showed. Some Egyptian shadow figures, or silhouette puppets, made of leather had stiff black outlines, and the cutouts were transparent color areas, giving an effect similar to that of stained glass.

Filigree patterns in shadow puppets project onto the screen, enriching the silhouettes with minute, precise details. Some Javanese shadow figures were brilliantly painted, even when they were opaque. Since the screen was actually viewed from both sides (women and children sat in front of it, men behind it), the painted surfaces could be enjoyed by the men.

The screen for a shadow play is an important aspect of the production. The area of black, or shadow, that surrounds the white or viewing area adds dramatic impact. The screen is most commonly square or rectangular, but it could also be circular or any form that fits the scenic effect of the play. That is, a cave, a dungeon, the interior of a house or castle, or even the dreamlike story or fantasy within a head all make likely settings for a shadow-puppet performance.

The shadow-puppet theater offers a very sophisticated medium for serious performance. Along with paper, cardboard, and wood, drawings can be made in ink on **transparent material,** such as an **acetate sheet** or Plexiglas, so that finely drawn lines suggest figures. Wire constructions can be used and **manipulate**d in a manner similar to **rod puppet**s, and wire drawings will project a clear sharp shadow. **Nylon leader** can be attached to **flat puppet**s, which may then be controlled from above somewhat in the way a **marionette** is handled. A **puppeteer**'s hands may have paper cutouts added so that they become the shadow figures. Even the human figure can be used on a very large screen, using masks to exaggerate and emphasize features. Also see **animated figure, articulated puppet, silhouette puppet.**

shadow-puppet stage. Puppets. See **Puppets: The Puppet Stage.**

shadow quilting. Quilts. When transparent fabric is used as the top layer in **quilting** it produces an effect of shadow and light known as shadow quilting. It is effectively used in **English trapunto** and **Italian trapunto,** or **stuffed quilting,** as well as in the usual three-layer quilting. When this method is used employing only a transparent white fabric as the top layer, it may be called an **all-white quilt.**

A variation of shadow quilting is achieved when a colored material is used as the **padding** or **filler.** A woven material can be used for this, either yardage or blanketing. A synthetic blanket works very well, as it is fluffy and resilient and can be washed. With the blanket or colored filler between, transparent fabric can be used for both the **quilt top** and the back, or the sheer material can be used for the top only, with a regular fabric for the **backing.**

Another method of shadow quilting uses a layer of transparent fabric over a simple **pieced** or **appliquéd** top. The result is a soft, delicately colored quilt top, and the **quilting stitches** are then used to go through the transparent layer as well as through the usual three layers of the quilt.

The most common fabric for shadow quilting is **cotton**

organdy; other usable sheer fabrics are lawn, **muslin, organza,** fine **silk,** and voile. Any transparent fabric will work, but thought must be given to choice if washability is required.

shadow series. A group of surface colors related to a single **hue** and ranging from a **tint** of that color with white to a dark mixture of the color with black. Intermediate steps in the series are compounded of the hue with stepped shades of gray. The shadow series colors are all of equal **saturation** but of varying brightness or **value.** The shadow series mixed as paints is used in illustration to give the effect of greater or less light falling on a uniformly colored object. For example, a painting of an orange would use several colors of a shadow series in orange to indicate highlights and shade. Members of a shadow series of colors are very harmonious when used together for any kind of color scheme, especially when the unmixed hue is part of the composition. Harmonies of this kind are called monochromatic harmonies and often include **broken colors** as well as **tint**s, **shade**s, and grayed variants of the basic hue. Also see **color, color harmony, monochromatic color triangle.**

shadow stitch. Embroidery. One of the most important stitches in **whitework.** It is simply a **herringbone** stitch that is worked on the back of the fabric. On the front side it appears as a double row of **backstitch**es with a solid or lacy shadow, depending on the closeness of the stitches. When worked on sheer material, the effect on the right side is an opaque band bordered by a row of back stitches. The closer the stitches, the more opaque and distinct this band will be. See ill.

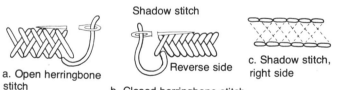

a. Open herringbone stitch

Shadow stitch

Reverse side

b. Closed herringbone stitch

c. Shadow stitch, right side

shadow stitching. Stitchery. Embroidery done on semi-transparent or **transparent material** in which the threads crisscross on the back or reverse side of the **fabric** to let the color of the threads show through on the front. The threads usually cross in a regular pattern, such as variations of cross stitches, to form areas of stitches that are so close together and heavy that shadow shapes of color show through. The thread showing on the front of the fabric is minimal, just tiny stitches outlining shapes. The total effect of this work is very delicate, giving soft, shadowy pastel colors. This is sometimes referred to as **shadow work.** When a similar technique is used employing fabric instead of thread for the color areas it is called **transparent appliqué.**

shadow work. Embroidery. See **whitework.**

shadow work. Stitchery. (Also called shadow appliqué.) A general term for any **stitchery** in which a semi**transparent fabric** is used over colored thread or fabric. The color ef-

fect is softened or shadowlike, as in **transparent appliqué,** shadow quilting, or **shadow stitching.**

shaft. Jewelry. The bar extending from one or both sides of a **buffing machine,** onto which the **tapered spindle** and the **buffing wheel** fit.

shaft. Weaving. See **harness.**

shaft and whorl spindle. Spinning. See **spindle.**

shag. Rugmaking. Weaving. See **pile, rya.**

shake. Woodworking. See **wood.**

shale. Ceramics. A rock that is formed from sedimentary clay or mud. It is used as an ingredient of bricks.

shank. Jewelry. See **ring shank.**

shaped rug. Rugmaking. A rug that is an unusual shape and something other than a square, rectangle, oval, or circle. It can be an abstract free form, a stylized geometric shape, or any form decided upon by the designer. A shaped rug can be made in just about any rug technique employed, but it is easier to use some techniques rather than others. **Hooking** is perhaps the freest medium in which to attempt an odd-shaped rug. The technique permits the hooker to wander all over the **rug backing** in any direction desired. The pliable backing that most hookers use allows for easily turning back the **rug hem** even on irregular edges. Latex backing provides the most stable shape. Weaving can also be used to make free-form rugs. Embroidery, appliqué and latch hooking lend themselves to shaped rugs. In latch hooking, however, the stiffness of the backing can present problems to a worker inexperienced in manipulating this backing. Crochet and knitting can also be tried in forming a shape, and to a lesser extent, braiding, where the technique allows for only limited shaping. See ill. Also see **backing the rug, shaped weaving.**

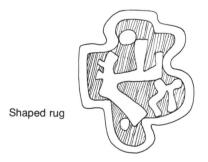

Shaped rug

shaped weaving. Weaving. A **fabric** where the selvages are curved or indented according to a desired shape rather than in the usual weaving format of a rectangle or square with the **selvage**s parallel. There are several ways of achieving these shapes. One way is through the use of a shaped **cardboard loom,** where the form is already established in the shape of the loom and no further manipulation is necessary during or after weaving the piece. The finished piece and the loom are one and the same shape.

Another method involves the first, relaxing the **warp tension,** and then pulling in on the **filling** yarns to achieve gradual curves. The reverse method of pulling on certain **warp** threads to shorten them, thereby obtaining a curve, can also be used. The **warp end**s can also be cut as the weaving progresses and darned or woven back into the body of the fabric. They would be cut according to a pattern that would diminish the shape of the fabric. To increase a shape, weave into the fabric inserts that can spread the warp or filling for a better fit or to curve a wall hanging. The shape can also be indicated only through the filling while the areas of warp are left empty. The filling is kept from sliding about with **hemstitching, twining** or an **embroidery stitch** such as the **blanket stitch.** When the piece is removed from the loom, the **exposed warp** is left as a **fringe,** is finger- or needle-woven, or subtly darned into the weaving. **Loom-controlled** shapes can be achieved through tubular **double cloth** that can later be constructed into **fiber sculpture, three-dimensional wall hanging**s, or garments without side seams. When doing shaped weaving without the use of a shaped loom as a guide, a definite form can be followed by marking its outline on the warp, or having a paper pattern behind or underneath the warp to use as a guide. Shaped weaving need not necessarily be weaving, but can be another technique, such as twining.

Although shaped weaving can be done for any purpose, it is primarily associated with the weaving of **wall hanging**s or garments. In the latter case, either a section of the garment, such as the armhole or neckline, is woven to shape while the sides remain parallel; or the whole garment is woven to a specific form. In either case, little or no cutting or sewing is required to obtain the final shape. Also see **finger weaving, loom-shaped, needleweaving.**

shaper. Woodworking. See **router.**

shard. Glasswork. Pottery. A chip or fragment, especially of earthenware.

sharkskin. Leather. Skin from the sharks, used mostly commercially.

sharpening. Woodworking. The most important safety measure in woodworking is keeping all cutting tools and blades sharp. Each cutting tool, whether **saw, plane, drill bit, scraper,** or **chisel,** must be maintained by sharpening its edge.

Grinding is done on a **grinding wheel;** it is necessary only when the blade is chipped or to restore the proper bevel. Honing (or **whetting**) is performed first on an oilstone and then on a slipstone for a finer edge. Stropping produces an extra-sharp edge. It is done on a piece of fine wood or cowhide rubbed with jeweler's rouge. Also see **Woodworking: Grinding and Sharpening.**

sharpening stone. Block Printing. Stenciling. (Also called Arkansas stone.) A stone against which **cutting tool**s are rubbed to sharpen the cutting edge. Sharpening is especially important for woodcutting tools, which must be kept razor sharp. Plenty of salad oil or thin machine oil should be put on the stone when sharpening.

Various shapes of stones are available. A universal-shaped sharpener may be used for all gouges and curved cutting edges. The wedge-shaped sharpening stone is sharp on one side for the V-tools and rounded on the other for the gouges. This is used for sharpening gouges with the bevel on the inside of the curve. The gouge is rubbed up and down with a little oil inside the curve, moving the stone from side to side to avoid wearing grooves in the bevel. If the bevel is on the outside of the curve of a gouge it can be sharpened on an ordinary flat sharpening stone. The bevel is placed against the stone and the tool is rotated back and forth on its axis so the bevel is sharpened at a constant angle. See ill.

Sharpening stone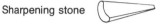

sharpening stone. Stained Glass. See **oil stone.**

sharpening stone. Woodworking. (Also called oilstone, whetstone.) There are two general types of sharpening stones: natural and manufactured.

The manufactured oilstones, such as an India stone, consist of an abrasive material like carborundum and a binder. They are rectangular in shape and available in a variety of grades or grits, often in a combination stone with a coarse side and a fine side. The synthetic stone is best used for the initial sharpening because it is relatively coarse and removes the steel quickly.

Natural sharpening stones are sometimes called slipstones. They are of a very hard stone. Examples are the Arkansas, Washita, and Scotch stones. These are used for fine sharpening and may also come in flat wedge shapes with rounded edges (gouge stones) to aid in sharpening a V or U gouge as well as regular chisels and blades. Other shapes may also be obtained for specialty blades.

To prevent steel particles from clogging the pores of a sharpening stone, rub oil or water into it as a lubricant. Also see **Woodworking: Grinding and Sharpening.**

sharps. Leather. See **needle.**

sharps. Stitchery. See **needle.**

shave. Basketry. See **cleave.**

shaving. Leather. See **skiving.**

sheaf stitch filling. Crewel. Embroidery. (Also called faggot stitch filling.) This **filling stitch** consists of three upright **satin stitches** tied together in the middle with two **overcasting stitches** that do not pierce the fabric until the second stitch is completed. The sheaves may be put in horizontal, vertical, or diagonal rows.

shear. Jewelry. To cut metal with **shears** or with the use of a **foot-operated shear.**

shear cutter. Jewelry. Metalworking. See **bench shears.**

shearing. Metalworking. The process of cutting or separating metal with scissorlike blades. Metal shearing is done with tin **snips** or **bench shears.**

shearing rug. Rugmaking. Cutting the loop **pile** on hooked or woven rugs. Besides giving a different texture to the rug other than that of the loops, shearing deepens or heightens a color—particularly those of a medium value range. On **hooked rug**s, this is easier to do when the rug is off the hooking **frame**. Shearing can also create different pile heights or a shade higher in the center than at the edges. The latter is done by bevel cutting of the pile; it leaves the shape with shading around the edges. Also see **bent-handled scissors**.

shearing scissors. Rugmaking. See **bent-handled scissors**.

shearling. Leather. (Also called woolskin.) A term for wooled sheep and lamb skins that have been tanned with the wool intact. Shearling scraps are commonly used for applying dyes and antique finishes and for polishing leather.

shears. Basketry. (Also called reed cutter.) A tool used primarily to prune or shear large **reed** or **willow rod**s, or to cut a group of smaller rods at one time. See ill.

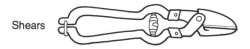

shears. Glasswork. The scissorlike implement used in the handling of molten glass. Special shears for the purpose have steps in the cutting edge of the jaws that make the shears useful for holding and shaping molten pieces such as handles. It is one of the more surprising operations of a rather dramatic craft to see a glassmaker cut the rim of a molten vessel much as one would cut leather. Ordinary tinsnips work almost as well as the shears designed for the purpose, and tinsnips are a lot cheaper.

shears. Jewelry. Shears are heavy-duty scissors of various sizes and shapes used to cut **sheet metal** and **wire**. Some are designed to cut straight lines and others to cut curves. When purchasing, check to see the heaviest **gauge** metal they can handle; it will probably be 16 or 14 gauge. To use shears properly, the blades should be opened and the metal placed far back into the jaws. This will provide good leverage for the best cutting. After the shears have cut the metal to about three-quarters of the length of their blades, they are pushed forward and cutting continues along the same line to provide a smooth, continuous cut. For added leverage the bottom part of the handle can be placed against the bench, and the cutting section provided with the top handle. See ill. Also see **bench shear, foot-operated shear, nippers, plate shears, snips, universal shears**.

shears. Leather. See **scissors**.

shears. Stitchery. (Also called cutting shears.) Cutting tools, usually larger than **scissors**. Some may be straight-handled, but most shears have a bent handle. The advantage to this is that it allows the lower blade to remain flat on a table surface during cutting. The bend accommodates the hand. A convenient-sized shears for most household sewing is 7–8″ long. Most shears have one half-rounded blade tip and one pointed one.

shears. Tincrafting. See **snips**.

shed. Weaving. The V-shaped opening or separation formed by raising and/or lowering the **warp end**s so that the **filling** can pass through them in order to interlace and form **cloth**. When there is no opening, i.e., when all ends are at rest and at a level, the shed is referred to as closed. When some ends are up and others are down, the shed is referred to as open. A clear shed indicates an opening that does not have a stray end running through the middle of the shed and impeding the passage of the filling. Sheds that are not clear usually indicate uneven **warp tension** or a mistake in the **threading** or **sleying**. The shed appears between the **fell** and the **reed** on a **harness loom** and between the fell and the **shed stick** on a **frame** or **primitive loom**. On these looms, when the shed is not opened with the shed stick but with leashes or picked up by hand, an extra stick is often inserted to maintain the opening for ease in weaving. This is called a **shedding device** and, on primitive looms, it is a simple arrangement, although the procedure of obtaining the sheds is quite slow. The shedding device on harness looms is much faster, though more complex. The opening of the shed is called the **shedding motion**. The lower part of a harness loom shed is referred to as sunk, and the upper, raised. How this is achieved classifies the loom as being either **rising shed** or **sinking shed**. Looms such as the **countermarch** have both rising and sinking sheds. The number of different sheds possible on a **floor loom** depend on the number of **treadles** available and the kind of **tie-up** that is used. On most **table loom**s the number of sheds is limitless, as is true on a primitive loom. Also see **string heddle**.

shedding device. Weaving. A means (other than picking up with one's fingers) of obtaining a **shed**. On **primitive loom**s, this is done with a **shed stick** or **string heddle**s or leashes. On **floor** or **table loom**s, the **harness**es open up the shed by being activated by **treadle**s or finger **lever**s. A shedding device enables the weaver to pass the **filling** across the entire width of the **warp** instead of just working across warp **end** by warp end, which is necessary when picking the shed up by hand. See ill.

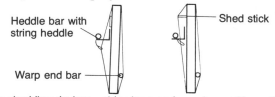

Two shedding devices—side views on frame loom with continuous warp

shedding motion. Weaving. A term used in reference to a **harness loom**. It describes the action of the **harness**es in obtaining a **shed** in order to pass the **filling shuttle** between the **warp** threads so that they can interlace to form **cloth.** A loom must have at least two harnesses to have a shedding motion. This motion involves the raising and/or lowering of the warp **ends** by means of the **heddles** and harnesses. The loose **pick** is laid between these raised and lowered ends. **Beating** follows and then the next shed is formed. The shedding motion is activated differently on different types of looms. Also see **counterbalanced loom, countermarch loom, floor loom, jack loom, table loom.**

shed regulator. Weaving. A device that is an optional part of the **harness** in a **counterbalanced loom.** It regulates the height at which the **shed** opens so that all threads are on the same level and there is room for the **shuttle** to pass through with ease. See **balanced tie-up.**

shed roll. Weaving. See **shed stick.**

shed stick. Weaving. A flat, long, smooth stick used on **frame, Navajo, ground, backstrap** and **warp-weighted loom**s to separate the **warp** threads in an over and under arrangement. When turned on its side at right angles to the warp, the shed stick will open up one **shed** of the **plain weave.** The second shed for plain weave is formed by a **heddle bar.** To maintain this shed, a stick is sometimes put in. It is then called a shed sword. At times, on ground and backstrap looms, in place of a flat piece of wood, a thick round stick is used. Then the shed stick is called a shed roll and the shed is obtained by pulling the roll toward the weaver. Although a **batten** is normally used, on some occasions, the shed stick is used to push down the **filling** after inserting it into the shed. Also see **backstrap loom, frame loom, Navajo loom, shedding device.**

shed sword. Weaving. See **shed stick.**

sheen. Gemcutting. See **luster.**

sheen. Stitchery. A luster or shine that some **fabric**s are given through the way in which they are woven. Extra threads float on the surface of the weave to give the sheen, as with **satin** and **sateen.**

sheepskin. Bookbinding. See **leather.**

sheepskin. Leather. The skin from mature sheep, available in various shades. Sheepskin is soft and pliable; it is generally used for garments and linings. Also see **skiver.**

sheer fabric. Batik and Tie-dye. Quilts. Stitchery. Lightweight or semi**transparent fabric,** including **chiffon, organdy,** lawn, **batiste,** and voile. These are sometimes used in **shadow quilting** and **transparent appliqué.** All accept dye readily and are therefore suitable in batik and tie-dye. They have a special affinity for vat and fiber-reactive dyes.

sheet. Bookbinding. The full size of **paper.** When folded it becomes a **section.** Paper is always sold by the sheet size, even if it is cut before delivery.

sheeting. Plastics. Sheeting is used as a protective covering for work area surfaces, as an **air shield,** or as a **mold release agent.** Examples of plastics sold in sheeting form are **cellophane, polyethylene, polypropylene, Mylar, vinyl, polyvinyl chloride,** and **polystyrene.**

sheeting. Puppets. Quilts. Stitchery. Any **cotton fabric,** such as **muslin** or **percale,** woven in widths that will fit standard-size mattresses. It is used to make sheets, to line blankets and **quilts,** or for any large-scale **stitchery** projects. As it is relatively inexpensive, it is used for **puppet theater curtain**s and is excellent for use in batik and tie-dye.

sheet lead. Puppets. **Lead,** rolled flat, which can be cut with scissors. It has long been used for **marionette hand**s and feet because of its weight and flexibility. It is so soft that a hole can be forced through the lead to attach hands to arms or feet to legs.

Sheet lead may be difficult to locate. If so, it is possible to make your own sheet without too much difficulty. Lead can be purchased from a plumbers' supply in small quantities. It melts at a very low temperature, so any steel ladle or steel tool that will adequately hold the lead will do. An ideal way is to melt the lead outside over a barbecue, eliminating most of the danger of a spill. An old plate, smooth concrete, or any similar smooth surface can be used to receive the lead. Fill the plate with water, then pour the melted lead in a puddle onto the plate. A little experimentation may be needed to get the desired thickness, but the lead can be remelted, so nothing is lost in practicing.

This method of making marionette hands and feet is a project in itself and, of course, should not be attempted by a child without constant supervision and assistance. It is certainly an adventure and a process which will enthrall most children. Also see **glove-type hand.**

sheet metal. Jewelry. Metal in sheet form, available in various **gauge**s. Its cost is determined by weight. When purchasing sheet metals, check for scratches. Surface scratches are unimportant and almost all metals will have them. If, however, you can run your fingernail over the scratch and it catches, it is more than a surface scratch, so do not hesitate to ask for another piece of metal. Also see **brake, cast iron, mokumé.**

sheet metal. Metalworking. See **metal.**

sheet metal gauge. Metalworking. (Also called metal wire and sheet gauge, American Standard Wire gauge, Brown and Sharp gauge.) A device to measure the thickness of wire and sheet metal by inserting the metal into one of the slots in the edge of the gauge. When the metal fits snugly, read the number on the disk surface. Check the size in several locations on the sheet metal to be sure you are not measuring a **burr** on the edge.

sheet-metal rivet. Metalworking. See **rivet.**

sheet-metal screw. Metalworking. See **screw.**

sheet-metal shield. Jewelry. (Also called centrifugal casting shield.) A large tub made of sheet metal. The shield is used as a safety guard with the **centrifugal casting machine.** The casting machine is placed inside the shield and the machine and the shield bolted down permanently to a sturdy work table. Sheet-metal shields are manufactured, but one could be made of a steel oil drum cut down with a welder's cutting torch. There should be ample space for easy access to the casting machine. The side walls should be at least 4−6″ higher than the centrifugal casting machine to catch spillage of molten metal which can fly from the machine during casting. The shield will stop most of the molten metal but not necessarily all. Also see **centrifugal casting.**

sheet moss. Beadwork. A natural, dried moss available in sheets from the florist or dime store in a dull, natural green or dyed bright green. The sheet moss is cut or pulled apart to fill flower pot or container tops to make a decorative covering for the base of **bead flowers.**

sheetrock. Woodworking. See **gypsum board.**

sheet tin. Tincrafting. See **tinplate.**

shelf life. Plastics. The period of time a **resin** will remain usable when stored in the original, closed container at a certain temperature. **Polyester resin** generally has a shelf life of three months at 70° F, or six months at 40° F. Every resin has its own shelf life.

shell. Beadwork. Sea shells have been used to make beads from earliest times by breaking, grinding, and boring them. Shell walls were often cut into flat disks and holes bored through the center. Shell beads range in color from white to silver gray and tan to dark brown.

Besides use as adornment, shell was probably the most commonly used material for barter and currency. The North American Indians strung shell cylinders for use as coinage, called **wampum.** Various species were used: clams, conus, abalone, olivella, and spiny oysters. Shell currency was also used in prehistoric Europe, in the South Seas, and in Africa. The **cowrie** shell beads were used not only as currency in Africa, but also as a magic symbol and a treasured decoration. In areas where sea or freshwater shells were not available, egg shells (usually ostrich) were used.

Disk-shaped shell beads are made by first breaking the shell into small, irregular pieces. Each piece is then drilled; thick shell is drilled halfway through from each side. Finally the drilled pieces are strung on a cord and smoothed by rolling on a fine-grained sandstone slab until they are disk shapes of the desired diameter. The shell beads made by the Santo Domingo Pueblo in New Mexico, called *heishi* or *heshe,* are fine examples of discoidal beads.

shell. Shell Carving. The rigid external covering of various marine creatures. Also see **cowrie, helmet, nacre, nautilus** and **Shell Carving: Shell.**

shellac. Amber Carving. See **Amber Carving: Finishing.**

shellac. Découpage. Papercrafts. A common **sealer** for wood prepared from purified lac resin. Shellac is available at the hardware store in two colors—orange or bleached white—as is its **solvent,** denatured alcohol. It is used to seal paper **prints,** wood, and painted surfaces.

shellac. Gemcutting. See **dop.**

shellac. Plastics. Woodworking. One of the oldest types of wood finishes, used as a protective coating and **sealant** on wood and other porous materials. Like **lacquer,** it was originally made from a natural resin formed by a variety of scale insect on sumac trees in the Far East. Now it is synthetically made and thinned with denatured alcohol.

There are two basic types of shellac: orange and white. Orange shellac is unbleached; because of its orange color, it is generally used on darker wood or on wood where the color is desired. White shellac contains bleaching agents to produce a clear finish or eggshell-white color. It is recommended on surfaces where the natural color of the wood is desired. Its disadvantages are that it turns milky when subject to moisture and does not keep as long in storage as the orange shellac.

Shellac is bought by the pound or cut; this term indicates the weight of pure lac per gallon of alcohol—five-pound cut is recommended.

Shellac's most important use is as a sealant undercoat on raw or stained wood surfaces to prevent **bleeding.** It is also used as the base for alcohol sealer stain—**pigment** dissolved in shellac—that seals and stains the wood in one operation.

Shellac is rubbed with pumice stone and oil for fine finishing. Place a small amount of powdered FF **pumice** stone in a shallow bowl. On a flat felt rubbing pad, place a few drops of light machine oil and then use it to pick up a bit of the pumice. Begin rubbing the pad lightly in the direction of the grain, going evenly over the entire surface. Continue rubbing until imperfections disappear. Then clean the grime from the surface with a clean rag. Polish with a **wax** or oil polish for a high gloss.

shellac stick. Jewelry. A shellac stick is used to hold small pieces of metal while **engraving.** Shellac sticks have a wooden handle with a circular piece of wood centered on top of the handle. This piece of wood is covered with about ¼″ of a hard, brittle, opaque shellac. Place the metal on top of the shellac stick and heat lightly until the metal sinks a little bit. When it cools, it will be cemented to the shellac. After work on the metal is completed, remove it from the shellac by supporting the shellac stick against a work bench and striking it sharply with a mallet. Any shellac that remains on the metal can be removed by dissolving it in alcohol.

shell amber. Amber Carving. See **amber.**

shell beads. Beadwork. See **shell.**

shell candle. Candlemaking. A candle molded by dipping a balloon filled with tepid water into a 160° F **wax bath** as many times as is required to build up a solid wax shell. A water filling for the balloon is better than air in that water will not expand and cause the balloon to burst when dipped in hot wax. Once the wax solidifies, pour out the water and remove the balloon; smooth and even the rim of the shell with a sharp knife. **Wick** the candle, using the **container candle** wicking technique; fill the shell with a different colored **low-melting-point** wax, preferably not above 130° F. See ill.

Wax surrounding balloon mold

SHELL CARVING

Sea and freshwater shells have been used and worn throughout history. Museums the world over display numerous examples of shell that have been worked and utilized by man. Beautiful in its natural state, it is often found already polished by the sea, with holes bored by marine parasites, ready to be strung and worn as a pendant or necklace. Its softness contributed to its widespread use before the advent of metal tools.

One of the most frequent uses of shell was for buttons. These small items often received fine, delicate carving. The most commonly used material was mother-of-pearl. The thickest shell carvings known were the buttons worn on the hats of mandarins of the sixth rank. The Chinese have been among the most active in the use of shell; in the thirteenth century they invented the first abrasive paper by cementing crushed shell to parchment with resins, and over the ages have produced volumes of exquisitely carved **fretwork,** shell engravings, and inlaid and veneered articles.

It was during the Renaissance that the discovery of tropical shells with multicolored layers provided the material for the first shell cameos. Cameo carving is now the most popular and respected form of shell carving.

In seventeenth-century Amsterdam the Belequins family achieved renown for their black-line engravings on the shell of the **nautilus.** Originally ivory carvers, they abandoned this difficult and more expensive material in favor of shell, coral, ostrich eggshell, and various other more quickly worked substances.

In Torres del Greco, Naples, The School of Coral still provides instruction in cameo carving and tortoiseshell, mother-of-pearl (**nacre**), ivory, and of course coral work. It was a cameo carver, Benedetto Pistrucci, who was Chief Engraver to the mint during the reign of George III of England.

The American Indians have traditionally decorated their clothes and headdresses with shell. And, at one time, they also used it for currency.

Shell has been of use as a vessel in its natural form, and its application extended to furniture, weapon, and musical instrument decoration, fans, canes, jewelry, parasols, boxes, game pieces, and religious articles.

SHELL A project in shell will of necessity be of limited size and thickness. Generally, iridescent **nacre** is worked; some of the most common sources are **abalone,** meleagrina, and the **nautilus.** Many shells picked up on the beach will reveal an iridescent inside when scratched. **Helmet, conch,** and **cowrie** shells are used for **cameos** because they have different-colored layers. Abalone has a **middle color** that is very thin; it is somewhat less effective for cameos unless a shallow relief is desired.

Shells fall prey to various conditions rendering them less worthy of any great investment of labor or time. Sometimes a flaw only limits a shell's application. For **fretwork** it is possible to use shell with some imperfections as they may be removed with unwanted portions of the design. If the shell is to be engraved, it is necessary to have a flawless surface so the lines will be eminently visible. When cutting blanks from a piece of shell, the projected use of the material dictates whether it is more economical to cut it into many blanks or only one large one. The thickest part of the shell is best utilized for the cameo.

The helmet shell is the material of the professional cameo cutter. It is harder to work and more expensive than cowrie. But it offers more color variety, is flatter, and, because of its thickness, a higher relief carving may be achieved. The shells commonly used for **cameo carving** are: **black helmet, king helmet, queen helmet, bull mouth helmet, horned helmet, queen conch, tiger cowrie, panther cowrie, gold ringer cowrie, snake's head cowrie, money cowrie, poached egg.**

Keep shell soaking in water when not working on it until the piece is finished. Save leftover scraps and thinner edge pieces of shell for smaller objects such as buttons, beads, jewelry, and mosaic and inlay work. Apart from the exotic and magnificent specimens obtainable from mineral shops and hobby supply houses for cameo carving and other serious carving projects, shell material for carving can be provided by local beaches and lakes. Many shells that may look plain at first glance may reveal an iridescent inside when scratched, or may be used to dramatize other materials when combined with them. Also see **blind, grubby, scratch carving.**

TOOLS AND PREPARATION If the shell retains any remains of the animal, boil it briefly to dislodge them. Remove the **conchyolin,** the horny crust of the shell, if it is not to be utilized. Some of it may be pried off with a knife, loosening it with light glancing blows from a plastic hammer. Other tools that might be employed are an electric drill with an abrasive head, rotating files and the flexible drive shaft, and hand files and sandpaper. Dental drill bits can be used to remove the first layer of shell for a cameo.

Because shells are thin, power tools must be used with care to avoid removing too much carving material. A power-driven tool should only be employed in the beginning stages and only for short duration. The heat created by the long application of power tools can cause a shell to separate.

To facilitate workability, soak the shell in water prior to working (3–21 days) and store it in water until the project is finished. Chinese white, India ink, pen, colored china marking pencils, and enamels are used to outline designs and color-code sections to be removed.

At various stages it is convenient to hold the shell in a stationary position; this may be accomplished in a variety of ways suitable for the stage of the work. The shell may be filled with **beeswax** and when solid dopped with more beeswax to a board or the bench. This helps prevent the shell from breaking while drilling. It can also be clamped in a **leather-lined vise** for sawing. A piece of **carpet underlay** provides a grabbing cushion for underneath the shell when it cannot be clamped. It may also be used folded over the shell with a wood clamp to hold it gently in place. Small pieces can be held on a dopstick and held in a vise; a **wood vise wedge** may help with odd shapes. Shell is drilled with a twist drill to permit the entry of a saw blade for cutting out the center of a shell. Rough cutting of shell can be done with a handsaw, hacksaw, jeweler's saw with a fairly coarse blade, electric hacksaw, or diamond lapidary trim saw well lubricated with water.

Shell is made of extremely compact overlapping plates; it lends itself to sawing, drilling, and abrading rather than carving. It dulls tools very quickly; they will need constant sharpening. With the smaller carving tools a jeweler's loupe is of use. Assorted needle files, a **needle drill**, chisels, gouges, veiners, **Eskimo style**s, and gravers can be used for carving shell. Constant lubrication speeds up operations, reduces wear on tools, minimizes dust, and enables you to wash away the dust to view the progress. The abrasives commonly used to polish shell are emery, **pumice**, white tripoli, and **putty powder**. Smooth surfaces on shells with a hardness of 3–4 on the Mohs hardness scale can be polished on a muslin lap with rouge and tin oxide. Carved and faceted surfaces are polished with **Linde A** and tin oxide with a wax and wood lap. Most of the shell is polished by hand. Also see **fretwork, scratch work.**

SAWING   Sawing shell is most quickly accomplished using short downward strokes, with a liberal amount of water used to lubricate and cool the blade. Saws used in cutting shell are hacksaws, jeweler's saws, a diamond lapidary trim saw, and fretsaws, all equipped with medium-coarse blades. Whenever possible, cuts should be made toward the thinner edge of the shell, starting from a predrilled hole in the thicker center of the shell. To start a cut on the edge of shell begin the kerf with a triangular file. Also see **porosity.**

POLISHING   Most shell work is polished by hand. There is the danger of too much heat from a power buffer, causing a shell to separate. Some pieces are too fragile to subject to a machine, and there also exists the possibility of removing delicate details.

Pieces with a hardness of 3–4, if smooth-surfaced, may be polished on a muslin lap with rouge and tin oxide. If carved or faceted, polish with **Linde A** and tin oxide with a wax and wood lap.

For hand polishing, begin with flour sandpaper, progress to emery or **pumice powder** applied with a wet rag, rinse the piece, and apply lapidary's white tripoli powder or putty powder with a wet rag and rinse. Next apply a medium solution of copper sulfate dissolved in water; this solution, when combined with the calcium carbonate of **nacre**, produces a calcium sulfate salt that is a fine abrasive. After this application the shell is ready for its final rubdown, which may be by hand with a clean rag, or gently with a dry buffing wheel. **Pumice pencil**s cut to the shapes required are helpful in polishing cameos. Finely powdered pumice mixed with olive oil and applied with a Q-tip, rag, or soft piece of wood facilitates the second stage of polishing a carved piece. Too much polishing can cause loss of definition of your carving, so exercise restraint. The final polishing is accomplished with a soft, clean, dry rag.

Most polishing should be executed with a circular motion. You may find it easier to polish on a lap board, moving the piece on a stationary abrasive surface.

CAMEO CARVING   A **cameo** carving is a relief carving in polychrome shell. During the Renaissance, long after the Greeks and Romans had begun the original cameo carving in precious stones of contrasting colors, shell cameos appeared with the discovery of tropical shells of varying hues. Cameo carving is the most highly respected form of shell carving and the most dearly paid for. Although time-consuming, it is not difficult.

The shell has three colors: the thin outer layer is generally removed completely, although it can be incorporated into the design as a third color; the white or cream **middle color** is carved in the figure or design that will stand in relief against the **ground color** of the third layer.

Cameos are sometimes carved into the intact shell, or into a blank cut from a shell. Perla refers to round cameos and garbo to oval ones. Cut the blank from the thickest part of the shell, or, if working with scrap, determine where the best color is and cut with this in mind. Misjudgment can result in uneven strength of color in the background, undermining the effectiveness of contrast. Use a light behind the shell to help determine where to cut the blank. Saw out the blank, dop it to a dopstick, and clamp it in a vise. If working a whole shell, hold it down on a piece of carpet nailed to a board or the bench. Sandpaper or file the exterior layer away to expose the white inner layer.

Outline the design with India ink; file away the unwanted portions of white shell using a medium flat file. Some of this may be removed with dental points in a flexible-shaft machine, but the amount of work that may be safely removed with a power tool is minimal.

High-grade carbon steel carving tools (chisels, rifflers, gouges, and gravers) are used to remove shell from the outer edges first, working in toward the design. Working close to the figure, define its edges with a V-shaped graver or a veiner, carefully pecking away at the material. Twist gouging tools as you move forward, and do not attempt to make deep cuts in one stroke.

Details are cut into the figure or landscape with chisels and gravers; a darning needle ground down on an abrasive stone can be formed into any required shape for minuscule detail work.

Smooth down the background and polish. Shaped pieces of pumice will help in polishing crevices. Work slowly so as not to remove details.

TORTOISESHELL Tortoiseshell is the mottled gold-and-brown horny substance that provides body armor for the tortoise. It is an elastic material that is easy to work with, with a warm visual appeal, pleasant touch, and a hardness of 2½. Its lambent nature has made it a favored material for articles that receive intimate handling—musical instruments, toilet articles, ornamental combs, snuffboxes, and jewelry. Because of its workability it is employed as an inlaying and veneering material in frames, furniture, and other objects.

The shell from only three species of tortoise is commonly used. The loggerhead tortoise (*Thalassochelys caretta*) supplies carvers of the Far East with a shell of dark and blond mottlings that is used in the cabinet inlay known as **boulle work.** The green turtle (*Chelone mydas*), commonly known as the soup turtle, is the second-favored shell. It resembles horn, has a green reflection, and is widely used in veneering. The welding capabilities of this shell are inferior. The hawksbill (*Chelone imbricata*) is the most commonly used shell and the easiest to obtain in the Western world. It is culled from the Antilles Islands in the Caribbean, usually when the turtle comes ashore to lay its eggs. It is the smallest of the sea turtles and rarely exceeds three feet in length. Its shell is made of 13 translucent amber plates marbled with umber and red in the carapace, or back, and blond plates in the plastron, or belly. The thickest and best plates for large carvings are the main plates which are generally 13″ × 18″ and ¼″ thick in the middle. Other back plates measure 7–8″ across the diagonal. Although there are many imitations, verify tortoiseshell material under an ultraviolet light, where it will fluoresce yellow-brown. Also, sawed tortoiseshell gives off an acrid odor. See ill.

Tortoiseshell is sold by the plate. When purchasing shell avoid ones with limpet marks (as these go right through) and flaking edges. Ridged plates can be flattened under pressure. Small pieces may be welded together. The thicker the plate, the more depth there will be to its polish, and the greater will be the reflective quality.

The tools used to carve tortoiseshell are the same as for amber. When working on thin pieces they should be glued to a thin piece of wood backing for both sawing and carv-

ing. To saw out pieces of the center of a piece, first drill a hole to permit entry of a saw blade. The absence of grain in this material simplifies all the techniques used.

Objects may be forced into tortoiseshell while it is in a softened state from boiling, either to embed them or just to leave a decorative impression.

For inlay boil the tortoiseshell for half an hour. Push the inlay into the shell surface and place the shell between two boards, or attach metal stamps or other objects to one of the inner faces of the boards and clamp until dry. It is also possible to press heated metal objects into tortoiseshell.

For veneering, the shell must be flattened before sawing. Boil the plate for one hour in water to which has been added approximately one handful of salt for each quart of water. This is not a steadfast recipe, as the age of the turtle dictates the amount of salt and boiling time. You may want to test-boil strips of the shell to find the best recipe for your piece. A younger shell is boiled for less time; an older shell requires less salt. Too much salt can replace the protein in the plate and diminish its bonding properties. After boiling, place the plate between two boards and clamp the four corners until the shell is dry and flat.

Remove the shell from the press and trim the thin edges as far back as necessary to provide a face that is thick enough to be sawed into layers. Trim the edges using a piercing saw with a medium-fine blade. Measure the thickness of the plate with calipers and mark the cutting lines with a white china marking pencil.

Before sawing, make a starter cut for the sawblade with a triangular file. Clamp the plate in a **leather-lined vise.** Saw the plate with a backsaw, using slow, measured strokes; use water to lubricate the blade.

After sawing, polish both sides to produce the greatest transparency. Tortoiseshell is sometimes foiled with silver foil before applying as a veneer. The addition of colors to the glue can produce interesting effects. Small pictures are also sometimes painted with enamel paint under light-colored shell. Bond the tortoiseshell to other materials with cold, flexible bookbinder's glue. Flat veneers are weighted after gluing. Bend curved pieces to shape over the base you are using it on, wrap a thick card around it, and tie together with bookbinder's tape. Using string or cord can leave an impression on the shell.

Tortoiseshell welds to itself—far better than cementing, as it leaves no telltale joint—and it is possible to combine small pieces to make a larger piece with more possibilities.

The pieces to be joined must be grease-free, and the edges to be welded together **skive**d to produce an even joint. The traditional process is to envelope the joint in wet linen or paper, and then crimp it between hot pincers. Today, the overlapping edges are skived as thin as possible, the pieces are washed in mild detergent to remove any grease, and boiled for an hour. The edges are overlapped and pressed between thin wood blocks using as many clamps as are necessary to keep the blocks together. The blocks, clamps, and shell are returned to the boiling water for half an hour more. The apparatus is removed from the boiling water to tighten the clamp a few times during this boiling until the clamp is tightened as far as it can go, then the piece is removed and allowed to cool.

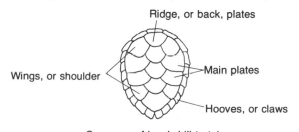

Carapace of hawksbill tortoise

If the weld fails, it should not be reheated: too much heating will cause brittleness. It will have to be glued.

When sawing a welded piece, it should be attached to a ⅛" wood backing to prevent it from breaking.

Tortoiseshell can be formed into a variety of shapes. Boil it as for inlaying or veneering, then curve it to shape. It must be held by padded clamps or a holding jig until it dries. Thin strips of shell can be tied into ornamental knots or woven.

Polishing transforms tortoiseshell from an inert, dull brown material to a lustrous, warm golden, highly reflective surface. From its rough state it is scraped (traditionally with a piece of glass, but a razor in a holder or any sharp scraping tool will serve) to a uniform surface. Both sides of the plate are polished equally or it will not become transparent. After scraping, begin sanding the surface with a medium-grade sandpaper, then a fine grade, until you feel the plate can become no smoother. Dip a soft cotton rag in olive oil and spread the plate with **rottenstone**. Work this fine abrasive over the surface until a polish begins to appear. With a clean rag, also dipped in olive oil, apply putty powder and rub the shell until all marks of the previous abrasive have disappeared and there are no surface imperfections left. With yet another fresh rag, polish the shell vigorously with olive oil and buff the shell with a soft clean cloth. If you have exercised enough vigor in your polishing, the shell should reflect nearby objects.

If you have an old piece of tortoiseshell that could stand a touch of rejuvenation, use olive oil alone or with a fine abrasive, depending on the condition of the surface, to restore its sheen.

shell knot. Macramé. See **bobble.**

shell stitch. Crochet. Shell patterns are formed when a group of three or more **yarn-over** stitches are worked into one common stitch in a manner that forms a fluted, fan-shaped surface. The **chain stitch** can be used between stitches to place some background space between the shell motifs. Also see **Crochet: Patterns.**

shell tool. Leather. A kind of **stamp.**

shelter cape. Leather. See **capeskin.**

shepherd's hook. Lacemaking. See **tambour hook.**

Sherman's March. Quilts. See **Shoo-fly.**

Shetland knitting. Knitting. Shetland knitting is the style of knitting traditionally practiced by natives of the Shetland Islands, located off the northern coast of Scotland. Although certain Shetland knitters copy Fair Isle patterns, the traditional Shetland patterns are Norwegian in origin. The wools used have been scoured and spun, and the patterns are knit in white, cream, fawn, brown, gray, and black on very fine needles known as **wires.** On the northernmost island of Unst, the gossamerlike Shetland lace is knit; shawls made of this lace are highly prized throughout the world. The lace patterns vary according to the individual knitter, but all are variations on a few truly native patterns. Also see **Fair Isle knitting, Faroe Island knitting.**

Shetland lace pattern. Knitting. See **Knitting: Construction.**

shibori. Batik and Tie-dye. The Japanese name for the **spot technique** in their traditional tie-dye, used on cottons and silks **dyed** with **indigo.**

shielded metal-arc welding. Metalworking. See **welding.**

shingle nail. Woodworking. See **nail.**

Shining Star. Quilts. See **Missouri Star.**

Shinkolite. Plastics. See **acrylic.**

Ship's Wheel. Quilts. See **Harvest Sun.**

shirred rug. Rugmaking. A rug made of cut fabric strips that have been gathered or shirred together with thread. It requires much material, as all the fabric strips stand on end like ribbon candy and form a luxuriously thick rug with a hard-wearing, nubby surface. This surface is formed by the closely compacted edges of the strips. The rugs are reversible.

The fabric is first cut into strips ¾–1" wide and as long as possible or desired, depending on the color planning and design. The width of the strip determines the thickness of the rug. The strips need not be joined beforehand. The shirring can be done with a needle and thread or a crochet hook. If hand sewn with a needle and thread, the strips are gathered through the center of the strip with running stitches and then sewn together in rows. For additional strength a **carpet warp** thread should be used for the shirring. The gathered edges should be about ⅝" deep.

If done with a crochet hook there are various methods. Perhaps the simplest is to use a steel crochet hook and poke it through the material to catch the fabric into a chain stitch made with crochet thread. The crocheting of the chain stitch and the shirring of the strip take place at one and the same time. After a long enough piece has been shirred, a new strip is shirred and attached to the original strip using single crochet through the two chain stitches.

Hand-gathered or crochet shirred rugs should have tight and even folds to ensure a firm rug. Shirring can also be done with knitting needles, but the rug is much softer and fluffier, since the strips are picked up into a knitted base as the knitting proceeds and do not stand as upright as the sewn or crocheted strips.

In the past, shirred rugs were sometimes called "chenille" rugs because the gathered strip resembled a fabric caterpillar. The shirring technique in early times differed in that the "caterpillar" was applied or stitched to a linen or **canvas rug backing.** The gathering of the strip was not centered, but at one edge, and it was the gathered edge that was sewn onto the backing. The caterpillar thus became a **pile** on a rug that was nonreversible. On the back side of the rug only the thread stitches attaching the caterpillar to the backing showed.

Another technique called shirring was to fold the cloth strips in half and then sew the folded edge to the backing. By sewing the folds closely together, one raw edge of a cloth strip held up the next raw edge and the pile was formed. Since no actual shirring or gathering took place, this method could also be used in making **appliquéd rugs**.

Yet another variation on shirring to come down from the past is called button rug. In this technique small circular or square pieces of fabric were folded in four and the apex of the folded piece sewn to the backing. The whole surface of the rug was formed of these small pieces or buttons.

Although shirred rugs are not often made today, they were popular in a period ranging from about 1820 to 1850. It is thought that they were an outgrowth of **yarn-sewn rugs**. When fabric mills appeared all over New England and cloth became an easily available commodity, the switch from yarn to cloth strips was made. But since the strips could not be sewn through the backing, they were sewn to it. The sewing thread used was not as strong as is available today. Consequently the threads broke and the rug disintegrated. It is thought that this weakness prompted early rugmakers to move from shirred rugs to **hooked rugs** using cloth strips.

shisha work. Embroidery. (Also called mirror work.) Originally done in India with mica or mirror disks. The Indian word *shisha* means a glass or crystal and perfectly describes this glittering embroidery.

Because it would be difficult to cut mirrors, Mylar is a good substitute. Mylar is mirror-like aluminum backed with linen or cotton and easy to cut. A network of cotton threads are laid first over the circle of Mylar or mirror. These are stitches that hold the Mylar firmly in place. Work **buttonhole stitch**es around the holding stitches to form a decorative ring. These rings can be worked in a geometric pattern or scattered in a freeform design. See ill.

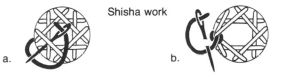

Shisha work

Shiva Acrylic. Plastics. See **acrylic paint.**

shivering. Ceramics. **Cracking** and buckling caused by the **glaze** contracting slower than the body while cooling. Also see **crazing, dunting.**

shoddy. Quilts. See **linsey-woolsey.**

shoe doll. Toys. A doll made from an old shoe, considered to be a **slum toy.** The heel becomes the face, with tacks or paint for the eyes and mouth, and the rest is "dressed," or wrapped, in a blanket. It is a **poor child's doll,** one example of which is in the **Museum of Childhood** in Edinburgh. Such a doll attests to the imaginative powers of a child. It is an example of a **making do** approach to the use of found materials.

shoelacing stitch. Leather. See **cross stitch.**

Shoo-fly. Quilts. A **geometric block** design **pieced** in a variety of ways. It is usually a **nine-patch,** although in some versions the central square is enlarged, leaving four small squares in the corners with rectangles between them.

Some variations are Corn and Beans, Double Monkey Wrench, Handy Andy, Hen and Chickens, Hole-in-the-Barn-Door, Kitty Corner, Lincoln's Platform, Love Knot, Monkey Wrench, Puss-in-the-Corner, Sherman's March, Tic-Tac-Toe, and Wrench Quilt. See ill.

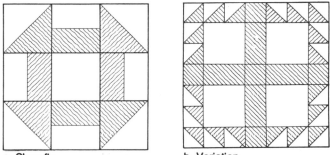

a. Shoo-fly   b. Variation

shoo-fly rocking horse. Toys. See **chair rocking horse.**

shooting toy. Toys. See **peashooter, popgun, rubber-band gun, slingshot.**

shop. Glasswork. The five-man commercial **glassworking** team, also called a **chair.** Also see **gaffer.**

short clay. Ceramics. See **Ceramics: Clay.**

short draft. Weaving. See **draft, profile draft.**

shortness. Jewelry. Brittleness in metal.

shortness. Metalworking. See **brittleness.**

short oblique stitch. Needlepoint. See **fishbone stitch.**

short pile. Rugmaking. Weaving. See **flossa, pile.**

short-small. Basketry. (Also called luke.) A 4″ length of willow rod.

short staple. Spinning. See **staple.**

shot. Jewelry. Small balls of metal, generally larger than those used in **granulation,** taking their name from balls of a similar size used for ammunition. They can be used singly or in groups as decoration. They can be soldered on in groups or groups can be soldered together first and then soldered to the work, which makes them easier to handle. Use as little **solder** as possible, or it will flow all over the work, all over the shot, or both.

To keep shot in place for soldering, a mixture of **Klyr-fyre** and **flux,** or **gum tragacanth** and flux, can be applied and allowed to dry completely.

To make shot, cut lengths of wire or pieces of sheet

metal into pieces of equal size. Flux; paste flux is excellent for this.

To make shot with a slightly flat bottom, place lengths of wire or sheet metal on a **charcoal block**. Several can be done at the same time, but place them about ½" apart, as they tend to roll from the pressure of the torch when being heated. Turn the torch on to a hot flame and melt one ball at a time. As it becomes molten, the metal will pull in on itself and become nearly spherical, due to **surface tension** and **capillary action**. After the ball has formed, slowly turn off the air in the torch, producing a reduction **flame** that will leave the ball free of oxides.

To make shot that is completely spherical, prepare a charcoal block with a series of small, half-round depressions in it. This can be done by rotating a tool such as a **dapping punch, repoussé tool,** or ball **bur** on the surface of the charcoal block. Follow directions for slightly flat shot, above. Also see **casting grains, shotting.**

shot. Stitchery. See **filling.**

shot. Weaving. A common reference to one passage of the **filling** carrier through the **shed**. See **pick.**

shotting. Jewelry. A method of preparing metal pellets of an irregular shape for **casting**. Metal is melted in a **crucible** and drops of the molten metal are poured from a height of several feet into a pail containing water. As the metal falls it forms irregular pellets that **freeze** (become hard) into shape before hitting the water. Although these can be made, they are more easily purchased ready for use, and are referred to as **casting grains**. The same method was used for making ammunition during the Civil War, except that the molten metal was poured through a metal screen from a great height, producing round pellets all of roughly the same size. Also see **centrifugal casting, granulation, shot.**

shoulder. Ceramics. See **Ceramics: Form.**

shoulder. Leather. See **side.**

shoulder. Woodworking. In a mortise-and-tenon joint, the shoulder is that part of the tenon on which the mortise rests. Also see **joint** and **Woodworking: Jointing.**

shoulder bar. Puppets. A **cross bar** on the **control** which is connected by **string**s to the shoulders of a **marionette** and by which the figure is made to move up and down. Also see **shoulder string** and **Puppets: Stringing the Marionette.**

shoulder blanket. Weaving. See **Navajo weaving.**

shoulder string. Puppets. The connecting **string** or line between the **shoulder bar** and the shoulder of a marionette. Also see **Puppets: Stringing the Marionette.**

shovel. Metalworking. See **blacksmithing tools.**

shredded foam rubber. Stitchery. Toys. Crumbs or small broken pieces of **foam rubber** used for **stuffing** three-

dimensional forms. It is lightweight and easy to use but does not pack as firmly as some other stuffing or **filler** materials.

shrink. Stitchery. To compact **fiber**s through the addition of heat and moisture, as in washing, **press**ing or steaming. In **preshrink**ing, the **fabric** is deliberately contracted or drawn together so that it will not shrink later.

shrinkage. Ceramics. The progressive decrease of clay in weight and size in both firing and drying due to loss of liquid. Clay shrinks 5—10% while drying and an additional 8—12% during firing. Total shrinkage for plastic throwing clay from wet to glazed ware is between 13% and 24%. **Grog** and perlite, a fine lava rock, are added to ceramic sculpture to control shrinkage and drying problems. Also see **volcanic ash, wollastonite.**

shrinking. Metalworking. See **blacksmithing techniques.**

shrinkage. Weaving. The contraction of fibers and yarns and a subsequent increase in their density causing a change in the size and the shape of the fabric. Shrinkage is due to moisture or some agitating action such as that associated with **fulling** and **felting**. It can be done in an ordinary water bath or under special conditions, as in **London shrinkage**. Shrinkage is affected by **fiber** content, type of yarn, weave, and the number of **end**s and **picks-per-inch**. The only true way to determine the amount of shrinkage a fabric will have is to test a small sample of the fabric and keep accurate measurements at each stage of the shrinkage. Shrinkage gives a thicker and firmer cloth and a fuller texture. It can be used to create unique sections in the cloth when different yarns with different percentages of shrinkage are used in various sections. Mixing these yarns would cause an irregular or pebbly surface effect after shrinkage. Also see **finishing.**

shrinking. Plastics. See **distortion.**

shrink rule. Metalworking. See **distortion.**

shrip up. Basketry. To remove the side shoots or branches from a coarse **rod**. Use a knife to cut the side shoots off as close to the main stem as possible.

shut-eye doll. Toys. A doll with eyes that open and close by a counterbalance system of lead weights. This type of closing eye was first used around 1870.

shuttering. Stained Glass. A term used to refer to pieces of lath wood that are used in making forms to cast concrete or epoxy molds. Also see **dalle-de-verre, dalle-de-verre mold, epoxy resin, lamination, lampshade construction, polyester resin technique.**

shuttle. Tatting. The primary implement in making tatted lace. It serves the function shared by all shuttles used in the fiber arts—that of holding **thread**. The shuttle is composed of two bladelike sides, elliptical in shape, tapering to equal tips at each end. These sides are held apart by a centerpiece upon which the thread is wound.

Historically the first tatting shuttles were used for a knotting technique that later developed into the art of **tatting** as we know it. These first shuttles were much larger, to accommodate the cordlike thread used in making the knots. During the eighteenth and nineteenth centuries, shuttles were made of bone, horn, wood, German silver, and sterling silver. They were about 6″ long and the tips did not touch, to allow the cordlike thread to wind off better. Today, traditional tatting is done with fine thread, so the shuttles are smaller, about 3″ long, ¾″ wide, and ⅜″ thick at the center.

There are three variations of shuttle used today. One is made of metal, with fixed, closed tips and a removable reel in the center. The reel may be wound by hand or by using the bobbin-winding attachment on a sewing machine. This shuttle has an extending **pick**, shaped like a small hook, used to facilitate picking up the **loop thread** through a **picot** to **attach** or for making **correction**s. After the thread is wound on the reel, place it back into the shuttle in this manner: Hold the shuttle in the right hand, with the pick toward the left; place the reel into the shuttle with the thread hanging down on the right side of the reel to indicate that the reel was wound clockwise.

The second and third types are similar to each other. They both have a bridgelike separation in the center that is not removable. There is a tiny hole in this bridge to tie the end of the thread to, facilitating the securing of the thread in **winding the shuttle**. The one difference is that one has the tip of one blade end extending into a tapered point, a pick, and the other has tips of uniform length and shape.

Wind the thread clockwise, and do not wind beyond the shuttle blades, as this extra thread is likely to become soiled before it is engaged in the tatted work. The blade tips touch with just sufficient pressure to keep the thread from slipping out too easily, but at the same time not so tightly as to make the reeling off of the thread difficult. See ill.

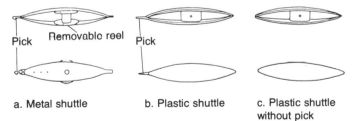

a. Metal shuttle   b. Plastic shuttle   c. Plastic shuttle without pick

shuttle. Weaving. An implement designed to carry the **filling** yarn through the **shed** during **weaving**. In most cases, it travels from one side of the **web** to the other, being either passed or thrown. Shuttles are made of wood and come in various sizes and forms—the choice depending on the weight of the yarn used, the width of the shed opening, the type and width of the item being woven, and the type of **loom** being used. With **boat shuttle**s the yarn unwinds automatically, while with other shuttles it has to be unwound by hand. Also see **belt shuttle, fly shuttle, netting shuttle, rug shuttle, ski shuttle, stick shuttle.**

shuttle hook. Rugmaking. See **speed hook.**

shuttle race. Weaving. See **beater, box loom (#2), fly shuttle loom.**

siah qalem. Jewelry. A form of decoration used in India: depressed areas forming intricate designs in metal are filled with black lac (lac is combined with black pigment to form black lac).

siccative. Ceramics. A medium that dries the oils used in **overglaze** and **underglaze** decoration.

side. Leather. Half of a full **skin** or **hide**. In processing, hides (with heads and shanks cut off) are cut in half lengthwise along the back, making two pieces—called sides, or side leather—for easier handling during **tanning**. The side is divided into sections: the **back**, which is the most desirable leather, and the **belly**. The back is divided into two sections: the shoulder and the **bend**. See ill. Also see **latigo** and **Leatherwork**.

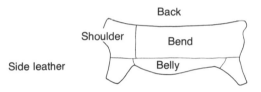

side bar. Quilts. See **rail.**

side board. Quilts. See **rail.**

side cutter. Basketry. (Also called diagonal cutter.) A tool used to cut and to **pick off** pieces of **cane**. It is not used on **willow** or **hedgerow** because it tends to crush the structure before it cuts, leaving a rough end. See ill.

Side cutter

side-cutting pliers. Stained Glass. Pliers with serrated noses that aid in **stretching lead** came and for cutting copper wire. Also see **lead came.**

side kick. Silkscreen. A prop or jack to hold the **screen frame** in the open position while inserting or removing stock. In its simplest form, the side kick is a short length of wood strip, about 3″ in length, that is screwed into the side of the frame near the hinged end and swung down to brace against the **printing base** when the frame is to be kept open. Commercial silkscreen equipment often uses counterweights or springs for the same purpose.

sidestitched. Bookbinding. Stitched or stapled down the side along the back edge. This procedure is often used with single **sheet**s, or leaves.

siding. Basketry. The term given to the weaving or building up of the side of a basket. It can also refer to the side of the basket itself.

siding. Bookbinding. Siding is the application of **cloth** or paper sides to a quarter-bound or half-bound book.

With **quarter-binding,** paper sides are applied after the cloth back has been attached. Paper should overlap the cloth by ⅛″, with an allowance of ⅝″ for the turn-in. With **half-binding** the corners are put on before the paper.

Cloth sides are generally used with a **leather** back and corners. Cut the cloth so that it just overlaps the **head, tail,** and **foredge** by ⅝″. Trim the leather corners and back about ⅛″ with a sloping cut along the edge where it will meet the cloth. The cloth should also overlap the edges of the leather as far as you have sloped them, approximately ⅛″. Paste the cloth and place it in position on the board and press down. Trim the cloth on the inside of the cover, if necessary, to make it even. Paste **endpapers** down, **nip** in the press, inspect to be sure everything is in its correct position, and place under a light weight to dry. See ill.

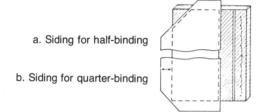

a. Siding for half-binding

b. Siding for quarter-binding

sienna. Ceramics. An earthy substance containing iron and **manganese oxide** that is brownish yellow when raw and brick red or orange-red when burnt. Also see **ochre.**

sieve. Ceramics. Regular mesh or perforations made of metal, nylon, or wire that control the grain size of the material which is passed through it. The screen of a sieve, called lawn, must be mounted on a frame, usually circular, and made of wood, metal, or plastic.

Glazes and **slip**s are run through a sieve to remove lumps and assure an even mixture. More than one sieve is used in this process—working from coarse mesh to fine in the process.

sieve. Enameling. See **Enameling: Tools and Materials, Basic Operations.**

sieve size. Gemcutting. See **abrasive, grinding wheel.**

signature. Bookbinding. An identifying mark at the bottom of the first page of each **section.** Both alphabetical and numerical sequences are employed. If it is the alphabetical sequence that is used, J, V, and W are traditionally omitted. "Aa" or "2A" is generally the way a book is marked when there are more than 23 sections. Because titling identifies the first section, the sequence of numbers or letters usually begins on the second section. Binders have individual methods or systems of using signatures, and this absence of standardization makes it necessary to carefully note each individual's system in the book you are working on before haphazardly tearing it apart. The signatures help in **folding** and **collating.**

"Signature" also means section; the term is widely used by printers.

signature quilt. Quilts. See **tithing quilt.**

Silastic RTV. Plastics. See **silicone plastic.**

silhouette. Découpage. Papercrafts. A traditional papercraft technique of cutting the outline shapes of a form from a piece of paper, generally all black, with no internal detail. The **cutout** is then mounted on a piece of paper of contrasting color. To make a portrait silhouette, cast a shadow of the subject on paper through a projector or a reducing apparatus. The paper should be smooth and thin. Draw the outline, fill in the profile with black ink, and then cut it out. Cutting with small, sharp scissors is done with the cutting hand held in one position while the hand holding the paper moves it according to the outline, feeding it to the scissors. This style of cutout is also called a closed silhouette because there are no internal cuts.

silhouette. Puppets. An outline, usually a profile, of a figure or shape. It is utilized in **puppetry** in various ways: among the most common are the **shadow puppet** and **silhouette puppet.** The silhouette is black, or dark, and is shown either by **backlight**ing or by placing it in front of a light **screen.**

Props or stage **set**s for **shadow play**s are often designed by using silhouettes of the objects to be suggested.

silhouette puppet. Puppets. A **cut-out figure** used in front of a lighted **screen** or shown from behind a **back-light**ed screen. A character is depicted by means of its **silhouette.** It is similar to the **shadow puppet.** The **flat puppet** also has a silhouette or outline form, but details are usually shown on the figure itself.

silica. Ceramics. (Also called flint.) Silica is the essential glaze ingredient, but its melting point is too high for silica alone to suffice as a glaze. For this reason, it cannot be used on **earthenware clay, stoneware clay,** or **porcelain clay** bodies.

silica. Glasswork. Stained Glass. Silica is the most abundant material on earth, silicon dioxide (SiO_2). It provides about 60% of the weight of the planet. It is the principal constituent of glass, and indeed **silica glass** is nearly pure silica sand. Silica is the material that appears naturally not only as sand, but as quartz, cristabolite, flint, agate, opal, and sandstone.

silica gel. Plastics. A desiccant for removing moisture in objects before **embedment.**

silica glass. Glasswork. A variety of glass composed of nearly pure silica (SiO_2), and not mixed with soda, lime, potash, or other **flux** that lowers the fusion point. Silica glass is difficult to manufacture because it requires a specially constructed furnace, capable of attaining temperatures above 1700° C, and because the molten glass is quite viscous even at that temperature, which makes **fining** very slow. Silica glass can be successfully fined under a vacuum, a costly procedure; however, the glass obtained makes exceptionally hard, temperature-resistant, transparent pieces that have the property of transmitting the visible spectrum of light as well as the infrared and ultraviolet with very little energy loss.

siliceous chalk. Ivory and Bone Carving. See **chalk.**

silicon. Metalworking. See **steel.**

silicon. Woodworking. See **wax.**

silicon carbide. Gemcutting. See **abrasive.**

silicon carbide. Jewelry. A man-made material invented while trying to produce synthetic diamonds. **Carborundum** is a trade name of this material, but the word has become synonymous with silicon carbide.

silicon carbide. Metalworking. Woodworking. See **abrasives.**

silicone caulking. Découpage. A clear plastic **filler,** available from the hardware store, that can be used as a shortcut stuffing material for **repoussé.**

silicone plastic. Plastics. (Also called silicone rubber, cold-cure silicone rubber.) A plastic based on silicone and carbon. It is used for flexible mold release agents, sealants (e.g. Silicon Seal), lubricants, and protective waxes. Cold-cure silicone rubber (e.g., Silastic RTV) is ideal for use in molds when accurate reproduction of delicate details and multiple castings are desired.

silicone rubber. Plastics. See **silicone plastic.**

Silicon Seal. Plastics. See **silicone plastic.**

silicon spray. Candlemaking. A spray used on the inside of **molds** before pouring the wax to facilitate the release of the hardened candle. Also see **Candlemaking: Preparing the Mold.**

silk. Kites. Once the finest kite **covering** material, it is almost never used today because of its cost, scarcity, and relative difficulty in handling as compared with the cotton and synthetic sailcloths now available. Also see **Kites: Tools and Materials.**

silk. Knitting. A strong, natural, knitting filament with good tensile strength, available in rich colors. Silk is not used extensively today, primarily because of its cost, but it was traditionally used in the knitting of stockings, fine coats, vests, and some kinds of knit lace. Also see **silk knitting.**

silk. Quilts. Stitchery. A natural **animal fiber** from the cocoon of the silkworm. It also refers to any **fabric** made from silk fibers.

Since many **colorfast** dyes work only on natural fabrics, silk has advantages in batik or tie-dye. It is more expensive than most other fabrics, and extreme heat must be avoided. **Satin**s (made from silk) lend themselves beautifully to tie-dye and batik.

Since **dry cleaning** is the preferred method of cleaning silk, its uses are limited in **quilting.** Occasionally, however, special **quilts** are made from it. The **Victorian crazy quilt** was one type of quilt which often utilized silks, and these were made more for show than use.

Silk fabrics have a beautiful luster and the fibers are exceptionally strong. Because of its smooth texture and lustrous **sheen,** it is often used in **appliqué.** While silk is difficult to **hand-appliqué** if edges are turned under, it can readily be **machine appliqué**d. The tendency of the material to **fray** at the edges may be capitalized upon in **stitchery.**

silk. Spinning. Weaving. One of the oldest **fibers** known to man, and the only natural one to come in **filament** form. According to Chinese tradition, it was used in China as long ago as the twenty-seventh century B.C. However, silk raising, or sericulture, was a closely guarded secret of the Chinese until the sixth century A.D., when it spread to the West by way of the Middle East. Silk fiber is obtained from the cocoons made by the caterpillar of the silkworm. Amounts of silk anywhere from 300 to 1,600 yards come from one cocoon. Usually the silkworms are cultivated and continuously fed mulberry leaves, thereby producing the finest silk. In some cases the silkworms are undomesticated and feed on the leaves of other trees. These produce a light brown filament known as wild, or tussah, silk. The silkworm spins the cocoon by emitting two filaments from "silk ducts" below its mouth. They are covered by silk gum, or sericin, before they come out. As this liquid is emitted, it solidifies on contact with the air, so that the cocoon becomes a hard object cemented together. To unwind the silk, the cocoon is put through a delicate process, started by first heating the cocoon in boiling water to dissolve the sericin. After heating, the filament ends of four to ten cocoons are caught, unwound, twisted slightly, and combined with a number of other similarly prepared filaments to make a raw silk thread which is then wound on a reel. It consists of about 48 individual filaments. Thrown silk is a **ply** yarn made of several strands of raw silk. Douppioni is made from two cocoons which have nested together. Since they are not separated in unwinding the filaments, the raw silk thread is uneven and has a large diameter. Silk does not have to be spun, since the filaments are long enough to be used directly as yarn. However, there is spun silk which is **carded** and spun like wool or cotton. It is a lower quality of silk thread and is made of short pieces or broken filaments which come from pierced cocoons, the coarse outer portion of the cocoon which has been removed by brushing, and the inner portion which remains after the raw silk has been reeled off.

Silk yarn is extremely strong—a filament of silk is stronger than a steel wire of the same diameter. It is also extremely fine, smooth, has a beautiful natural gloss, and is very expensive; it is outpriced only by **vicuña.** Also see **degumming, yarn count.**

silk canvas. Needlepoint. **Canvas** made of evenly woven silk available in size 28 and smaller. This type of canvas is recommended for **petit point** using **silk yarn.**

silk embroidery. Embroidery. Silk manufacture is said to have started in China as early as 2000 B.C. Whether or not the date is accurate, it is certainly true that the secret of silk cultivation was carefully guarded by the Chinese; by the sixth century A.D. the secret reached the Western world by way of Constantinople. The legend goes that it was smuggled into the city by two monks who concealed the silkworms in a hollow cane.

By the twelfth century, silk was produced in Greece; it was worked in **cross stitch** and **counted-thread embroidery.** Silk remained a rare and expensive luxury in Europe until the fifteenth century. Silk was combined with **metallic thread**s and worked on ecclesiastical vestments and Elizabethan clothing.

In America, silk was used for costumes in colonial times, but it was hard to come by, and really did not have as much impact as wool on the American scene. In the 1930s, Mrs. Theodore Roosevelt, Jr., produced some unique silk embroideries to be used for panels and folding screens. One of her major works, a large hanging illustrating the story of the Golden Cockerel, was mounted into the paneled wall of the dining room at Sagamore Hill. A concealed spotlight in the opposite wall picked up the sheen of the silk and metal threads, so that the whole embroidery seemed to gleam with a light of its own. The faces were worked all in one color in **split stitch,** in the medieval manner. Starting in the center of each cheek, the stitches are worked round and round in widening circles. This is repeated in the forehead and chin, then all the stitches are brought together invisibly with flowing lines as the areas join. The embroidery was done in stout floss, an untwisted flat silk similar to that used on Chinese robes, which has a beautiful matte sheen. The panel is now in the Smithsonian Institute.

Today, silk thread for embroidery is still hard to obtain, although small groups of dedicated craftspeople are working with it. Embroidery in cotton floss, which is similar in effect and much more readily available, is being carried out with great exuberance. Also see **metallic thread embroidery** and **Needlepoint.**

silk embroidery floss. Embroidery. See **silk yarn.**

silk knitting. Knitting. An often highly patterned, brightly colored form of knitting done with silk thread. **Arabian knitting** from the seventh to the ninth centuries is among the oldest existing examples of silk knitting. Silk knitting was further developed and extensively practiced in Florence during the Renaissance. There are also some fine examples of Spanish ecclesiastical knitting in silk, made in the sixteenth century. **Viennese lace** is also knit silk. Also see **Florentine knitting.**

silk pad. China and Glass Painting. (Also called pounce.) A pouncing pad, made of soft wool or cotton batting covered with a piece of Japanese or China silk tied with a rubber band, used to blend the painted surface to flatten and even out the brushstrokes for a smooth surface. If the silk fabric is new, wash it before using. Keep the silk soft and clean by washing after each use. Always iron the fabric to remove wrinkles after it has been washed. If the fluff from the batting works through the fine silk, use two layers of silk. The padding is done with a deft, pouncing motion over the entire surface.

silk pin. Stitchery. Similar to a **dressmaker's pin,** used to temporarily fasten layers of material together. Silk pins are rustproof and thin and leave no marks on fabric. A sewing machine can sew right over these pins when they are placed at right angles to the line of stitching.

silk quilt. Quilts. Those quilts that combine the more elegant fabrics into an **all-over pattern** are called **silk** quilts, although they actually use many fabrics other than silk. **Brocade, satin,** and **velvet** are used, joined by dozens of different embroidery stitches. Silk, being more fragile, requires a **muslin** lining.

SILKSCREEN

Silkscreening is a printing process in which the image is transferred to the material or object to be printed by forcing ink through a fine mesh cloth or screen, the nonprinting area of which is blocked by adhering or painting onto the screen a substance that will harden and fill the holes in the mesh. Basically, silkscreen printing is a kind of **stencil** printing technique. Stencil printing, such as children's spatter-painted greeting cards or identification markings on packing crates, has the problem of requiring supports for an isolated nonprinting area, such as the center of a circle. Silkscreen printing obviates the problem by supporting all parts of the stencil on cloth or wire mesh through which ink or paint can pass freely.

The historical forerunners of silkscreen printers are the Japanese, who first glued human hairs to their intricate stencils as supports for unattached parts of the design. Eventually the hair bridges evolved into a grid work of threads to which were attached the stencil parts. Evidence of the supporting fibers was minimal in the completed prints, the ink being sprayed or brushed across the stencil in such a way that some filling-in under the supports occurred. Woven silk as a support for the stencil was used experimentally around 1870, but the process did not yet use a **squeegee** to force the ink through the mesh. Americans working around 1910 developed the use of a squeegee and a large number of other techniques that have resulted in making silkscreen printing an important commercial process as well as one well suited to the craft studio.

The ability of the screen process to print on any material, of any size and thickness, with any coloring material, and in any quantity has made screen printing the method of choice for jobs as varied as textile decoration, wallpaper manufacture, electronic printed circuit manufacture, book cover printing, posters, glass decorating, plastic container identification, and display panel printing. No other printing process is capable of laying down as thick a layer of ink as is the screen process, and the variety of inks or paints available for use is prodigious.

At its simplest, silkscreen printing consists of seven steps. The screen is stretched onto a **screen frame** in a manner very similar to stretching artist's canvas onto stretchers. The stencil is prepared by one of several methods. The **cut-paper stencil, block out stencil, Tusche stencil, cut film stencil,** and **photographic stencil** methods are all in common use, and each has its own virtues and drawbacks. In the making of stencils, there is still room for experimentation. The screen frame is mounted directly to a table or to a separate printing base with **screen hinges** or ordinary door hinges. It is customary to fit the frame with a locating pin or to fix blocks on the printing base so that the screen is always lowered into the exact same position, i.e., in register, and without any tendency to twist from side to side. This is especially important when prints require more than one color and the colors have to fit together exactly. Paper, cardboard, cloth, or whatever material is to be printed is positioned to the register marks or guides on the printing base and the screen is lowered into contact with the material. Silkscreen ink is poured in a line along one side, inside the screen frame and clear of the printing area.

A squeegee is grasped in one hand and the paint is scraped across the screen from side to side, using uniform pressure and speed. The screen is raised on its hinges, and the print removed and hung up to dry. For subsequent prints in the same color the process is repeated as many times as necessary, one print being laid down right to left and the next from left to right. For additional colors, the screen is replaced with the screen stencil for the next color and the work proceeds, always being sure that earlier colors are completely dry.

The traditional mesh material for silkscreen printing is, of course, silk. For many specialized kinds of screen work, silk has been supplanted by Dacron, nylon, stainless steel, and bronze cloths, but for much studio work silk is still the chosen material. Multifilament Dacron has most of the advantages of silk and has higher strength and resistance to solvents and abrasion than silk. It is considerably cheaper than the previously prized Swiss silk, and it is also more uniform.

Supplies for silkscreen printing are available from a number of distributors, and a comprehensive catalogue from one of them can be a useful instructional tool as well. A very complete catalogue, which also includes machines and supplies for industrial applications, is available by writing to the Educational Department, Advance Process Supply Co., 400 N. Noble St., Chicago, Illinois 60622.

It is recommended that the beginner start with an educational kit that includes a professionally made screen frame that will serve as a model for constructing one's own.

SETTING UP A WORKSHOP Craftspeople who do silkscreen work on a regular basis will eventually require a work area and facilities that make the production of print editions fairly efficient. Space must be provided for the basic equipment: the printing unit, consisting of the **screen frame** mounted to its **printing base;** the **squeegee;** inks; an ink-mixing palette; a sink; racks or hangers for drying prints; and (if photographic stencils are made) a darkroom including a sink, lights for making exposures, trays for solutions, and perhaps an enlarger.

silkscreen. Ceramics. In ceramics, the silkscreen technique is sometimes used in decorating **tiles. Glaze**s and color pigments are squeezed through the screen directly onto the tiles, which are then fired.

silk-screened doll. Toys. A doll to which features or details are added by the use of the silkscreen process. The fabric or **felt** is screened while it is flat and then the doll is assembled. Many craftspeople find this a practical way to produce a quantity of dolls.

silkscreen ink. Silkscreen. Any of the paintlike coloring materials used for silkscreen printing. Most silkscreen inks contain chemical driers that help speed drying of the print, but this presents the problem that the inks tend to dry in the **screen** and block the **mesh** unless the printing process proceeds without long stops. Inks most commonly used are oil-base, requiring turpentine or turpentine-substitute solvents and thinners, although some inks for school use or special applications are water-base. Water-base inks cannot be used with **Tusche stencils** that use glue as the stencil material, because the inks would tend to dissolve the **stencil.**

The viscosity of silkscreen inks must be carefully controlled to produce a good print. In general, the ink should be thinned, if necessary, to the consistency of heavy cream, or so that the ink runs quickly off a raised squeegee full of ink. The hardness of the squeegee and the consistency of the ink work together to produce the specific quality of image. Soft, dull squeegees with a thick ink will lay down heavier, less distinct images, and hard, sharp squeegees used with thinner inks will produce images that reflect more detail in the stencil. Such sharpness, however, may be at the price of opacity of color.

Silkscreen process suppliers customarily carry a number of lines of inks, some highly specialized and of limited interest to the studio craftsperson. A sampling of the wide variety available includes gloss and flat poster ink, fluorescent ink, cellulose ink, quick setting ink, enamels, lacquers, ink for printing on plastics, metallic ink, ink for printing on all types of woven fabrics, adhesives, compounds for etching glass, and acid-resistant compounds for copper electronic circuit board manufacture. This list suggests the wide applications of the silkscreen process in industry.

silkscreen printing. Fabric Printing. Standard silkscreen techniques can be applied to fabric printing, using **dye paste** or **textile color** and varying the technique according to the fabric. Before printing, make preliminary tests on scrap fabric for desired color and consistency. Thin silk, for example, requires a thin paint and a rapid stroke of the squeegee with light pressure. Heavier fabrics require thicker paint and a firmer stroke. Dye paste prints better when the squeegee is held at about a 45° angle. Textile colors require that the squeegee be held in a nearly upright position. Since the screen itself is larger than the design being printed, take care to avoid picking up wet color on the underside of the screen frame. The order of printing can be varied so that **repeat** units are printed alternately rather than continuously, giving each unit time to dry before the adjacent areas are printed. This scheme should be worked out when planning the **registration** method.

After each print, lift the screen by raising one corner gently and peeling the screen away from the fabric; do not lift it straight up. The fabric must dry thoroughly before another color can be printed; a fan may be used for drying. The silkscreen should be cleaned thoroughly after each color is printed. If the printing process must be interrupted for a short time, leave the screen where it was last printed to keep the mesh damp and unclogged. Also see **Fabric Printing: Setting Up a Workshop, Preparing Fabric, Finishing.**

silk stems. Beadwork. A technique in **bead flowermaking** of finishing wire stems by tying, then wrapping, embroidery floss around the **stem wire.** The floss is cut at the end and secured with a small piece of masking tape.

silk yarn. Embroidery. Needlepoint. This yarn is available in three varieties: a heavy yarn similar in weight to **tapestry yarn;** silk embroidery floss, a two-ply six-stranded thread with a high sheen; and twisted silk, a two-ply tightly twisted thread also having a high sheen. Both the silk embroidery floss and twisted silk are excellent for **petit point** and fine embroidery. Due to the high cost of silk, cotton thread is an excellent substitute.

silky luster. Gemcutting. See **luster.**

silver. China and Glass Painting. Dry, powdered silver is called matte silver because it has a dull surface after **firing.** It is mixed with **lavender oil** and brushed on the china in a thin, even coat. Two or three coats of matte silver, with firing after each, gives a rich surface. After firing, **burnishing** with sand polishes the silver to a shiny luster. If silver becomes dull, restore the luster with silver polish.

Liquid bright silver is available in jars for painting on china. Before application, be sure the china is absolutely clean. Use cloth moistened with alcohol for cleaning, then wipe the surface with a few drops of **lavender oil** on a soft, lintless cloth. After firing, the silver has a high, opaque, silver glaze. Two coats are generally applied for a solid, lustrous coat, with firing after each application. For a soft, satiny gloss, called silver **luster,** mix together matte and liquid silver. Also see **white gold.**

silver. Enameling. See **metal, metal foil, metallic luster.**

silver. Jewelry. (Ag) **Specific gravity** 10.50; melting point 1063° C, 1971° F; boiling point 2970° C, 5431° F; **hardness** 2.7. Silver is found naturally in flake and mass form and recovered from other metals through various refining processes; it is usually found with gold, **copper,** lead, and zinc ores. Annealed pure silver is the best conductor of heat and electricity known. Pure silver is the whitest of metals, can be polished to a **luster** of high reflectivity, is second only to

gold in its malleability and ductility, and is half the weight of gold. The term **fine silver** refers to silver that is 999.0 parts silver per 1000 parts. High fine silver refers to 999.5 parts-per-1000 silver.

Pure silver is too soft for use and is alloyed with various other metals, such as gold, copper, nickel, tin, and manganese. Sterling silver is the most common **alloy,** consisting of 925 parts silver to 25 parts copper. It has a melting point of 893° C, 1665° F. Its **annealing** temperature is 593–649° C, or approximately 1100–1220° F. Through the various fabricating methods employed to form silver, it becomes work hardened and needs annealing to return it to a malleable state. It can be quenched in air, water, or a dilute acid solution and will remain softened. Overheating silver can scar the surface and cause a thick **firescale** which produces a darkened or freckled section when polished. Firescale can be prevented by using **Prip's flux** or by immersing the silver in a **pickle** solution.

Liver of sulfur is used to **patina** silver. High silver content alloys formed by the addition of gold, palladium, and other **noble metal**s produce good-looking, tarnish-resistant materials. The reaction of silver to nitric acid reveals its composition: A drop of nitric acid applied to a filed notch in pure silver will bubble creamy-white; in sterling it will be a cloudy cream; in **coin silver** it will turn dark to blackish in color; and in silver plate on copper it will turn green, as it also will in nickel silver.

Coin silver is an alloy of sometimes less than 800 parts silver used for coins. Old coins are almost pure silver, some with traces of gold, copper, or nickel. **Silver solder** is another important alloy. Also see **buffing compound, fabrication, work hardening.**

silvering. Plastics. The effect of reflected light in a vacuum created inside a plastic by the incomplete bonding of adjacent materials during **casting.**

silver luster. Ceramics. A metallic **luster overglaze** produced by silver chloride. Add bismuth and **fat oil** as a **binder** to produce a metallic luster with green or yellow tints.

silver nitrate. Enameling. See **fuming.**

silver nitrate. Stained Glass. See **staining.**

silver resist. China and Glass Painting. A china-decorating technique in which a paste mixture of **French chalk** and **gum arabic** is painted in fine lines and, when dry, covered with **silver** luster. After **firing,** thin, sharp lines are left where the paste was. Dissolve the gum arabic in water, add the chalk, and mix on a clean saucer or tile. Add a few drops of **medium,** using just enough to bind it together. If necessary, thin the mixture with water. Apply the paste mixture with a fine sable **outlining** brush.

silversheen. Gemcutting. See **obsidian.**

silversmith. Jewelry. An artisan that makes objects of silver by using any of the **forming** techniques.

silversmithing. Jewelry. Metalworking. (Also called metalsmithing.) The art of shaping silver and other **malleable** metals into three-dimensional forms with hammers, anvils, stakes, and other tools. **Compression** of the metal is one of the two basic methods for shaping. This process is employed in the **raising techniques** of crimping, raising, and Dutch raising. The other method involves stretching the metal to achieve the desired form; this method requires a thicker-gauge sheet metal. The techniques of **sandbag** shaping, **blocking in a mold, pressing,** and **sinking** are stretching processes.

Cycles of **hammering, annealing** the work-hardened metal, **edge thickening, bouging,** and **planishing** bring a sheet of metal to the desired shape.

Before the metal is cut to disk form for traditional conical or cylindric hollowware shapes, the mathematical center of the square of the metal is determined and marked with a **center punch** and hammer. This punch mark is useful as a reference point for future measurements. Leaving the center punch mark on the outside and bottom of the finished piece is a tradition among hollow ware craftspeople.

silver solder. Jewelry. A **solder** consisting of silver that has been **alloy**ed with one or more metals, such as **brass, copper,** zinc, nickel, manganese. The purpose of the alloying is to control the melting and flowing points of the solders, which are all below the melting point of sterling silver (over 1600° F). Solder is available in many forms—sheet, strip, wire, **pallion**s, and powder. Sheet solder is best for the beginner. There are a number of silver solders available that melt at different temperatures, the highest-melting of which is **IT solder.** Their names in descending order of flow points are as follows: IT, 1490° F; hard solder, 1435° F; medium solder, 1390° F; easy solder, 1325° F; extra easy solder, 1145° F. Differences in the hardness of these solders is so slight as to be negligible.

Solder is available at different flow points to help in the construction of a piece of work. If you have a piece that will require three solder **joint**s, the first joint could be done with hard solder, the second with medium, and the third with easy. Because each flows at a lower temperature than the one before, the previous joints will not melt. It is also possible to solder many joints with the same solder at the same or different times; although it will flow again, the flow can be contained by using **yellow ochre.**

Silver solders can be used to solder not only silver, but copper, brass, bronze, **nonferrous** alloys, and steel and iron. That is to say, it can be used on all metals with which silver can be alloyed. The ideal situation is to use those solders that come as close as possible to the color of the metal being used. For example, there are solders for all of the colors of gold, for platinum, and for alloys that approximate the colors of brass, bronze, and copper (these are referred to as **spelter solder**s).

During soldering it is important to heat the metal so that the solder will flow as quickly as possible. Solder may melt and pull itself up into a ball. This means that the metal is not as hot as the solder. Change the angle of the flame on your torch so that it heats the metal. When the metal reaches the correct temperature, the solder will

flow. If you allow the flame to play on the balled-up solder too long, it may lose its flowing capabilities either because of building up an oxide on its surface or burning out of metals in the solder alloy. It may also mean that your solder has a lower melting point and a higher flow point than is required. The temperature difference between these two points is usually less than 100° F, which is a matter of seconds when **soldering.**

Some solders are marked when purchased, others are not. It is important to identify them in some way. The easiest is to mark them on one end "E" for Easy, "M" for Medium, "S" for Soft, and so on. Also see **flux.**

silver solder. Metalworking. See **solder.**

silver soldering. Metalworking. See **soldering.**

silver stain. Stained Glass. A mixture of silver salts which when fired over the surface of a piece of glass results in various shades of yellow stain in the glass. The action of this silver stain was not discovered until the fourteenth century. Also see **staining.**

silver sulfide. Enameling. See **raku.**

simple knot. Macramé. See **half knot.**

simple laid-in. Weaving. See **laid-in.**

simple weaves. Weaving. Those structures composed of only one set each of **warp** and **filling** threads. There is infinite variety here due to the manner of interlacing, color patterns, type of yarn used, the **sett,** and the **beat.** They are usually grouped together according to certain basic characteristics of interlacing. The term "simple" merely serves to differentiate these weaves from the **compound** ones. Also see **basic weave, plain weave, tabby, twill weave.**

simplified horizontal control. Puppets. A **control bar** for the **marionette** that is a simplified version of the **horizontal control.** Because it has fewer **string**s or control bars, it is easier for children to manage. Also see **Puppets: Stringing the Marionette.**

Simpson-type mixer. Ceramics. See **wet pan mixer.**

simulacrum. An image or representation of a human figure. This definition includes dolls, but the term is more often used to refer to a large figure. Some common forms of simulacrum are store window **mannequin**s, scarecrows, snowmen, wax-work figures, and ventriloquist's dummies.

simultaneous dyeing. Dyeing. A method of dyeing used with natural **dyeplant**s that suffer too much in the process of cooking. The dyeplant is put in a cheesecloth bag, immersed in a cold bath with the fiber to be dyed, and both are brought to a simmer. In this way there is only the heating process and the immersed fiber can pick up the **dye** instantly.

Sinclair's lock. Toys. See **prisoner's lock.**

sindanyo. Ceramics. A durable, very hard asbestos used for making throwing **bat**s. They are expensive, but last forever.

singeing lamp. Basketry. An exposed-wick lamp used for burning whiskers or fine hairs off a completed basket. With the basket continuously moving, it is rotated an inch or so above the lighted wick.

singerie. Découpage. See **chinoiserie.**

singing top. Toys. See **humming top.**

single. Spinning. Weaving. See **sungle.**

single buttonhole stitch. Leather. (Also called buttonhole stitch, single loop stitch.) A **lacing** stitch that completely covers the edge of the leather. Lacing six times the length of the seam will be needed. The stitch is done much the same as the **whipstitch,** except that you loop back through each stitch before you pull it tight. See ill. Also see **double buttonhole stitch, edge stitch** and **Leatherwork: Sewing Leather.**

   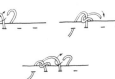

a. Single buttonhole stitch   b. Single loop stitch

single casting on. Knitting. See **Knitting: Casting On.**

single chain. Macramé. A single chain forms a narrow, tightly worked **sennit.** It is knotted with two or more **cord**s by working the **half hitch** continuously one cord over the other, either right over left or left over right. Also see **alternating half hitch.**

single corduroy. Rugmaking. Weaving. See **corduroy.**

single crochet. Crochet. (Abbr. sc, scr.) See **Crochet: Basic Stitches, Decreasing.**

single-cut file. Metalworking. Woodworking. See **file.**

single decrease. Knitting. See **Knitting: Decreasing.**

single decrease cast off. Knitting. See **Knitting: Casting Off.**

single dovetailing. Weaving. See **dovetailing.**

single drive punch. Leather. See **drive punch, punch.**

single-fold cutting. Papercrafts. See **symmetrical cutting.**

single interlocking. Weaving. See **interlocking.**

Single Irish Chain. Quilts. See **Irish Chain.**

single loop stitch. Leather. See **single buttonhole stitch.**

single Mexican lace. Weaving. See **Mexican lace.**

single-rod roped handle. Basketry. See **Basketry: Woven Basket Construction.**

single-shape doll. Stitchery. Toys. (Also called one-piece doll.) A stuffed, un**joint**ed doll. The single shape usually includes head, arms, body, and legs. Front and back are placed with right sides of the fabric together and stitched at the edge, leaving a small opening so that the material can be turned right-side out and **stuff**ed. The hair, features, and clothes are then added to the stuffed doll form. The advantage of making a doll in this manner is that the various body parts are prejoined, and no final assembly is needed. See ill.

Single-shape doll

single sleying. Weaving. See **sleying.**

single soumak. Rugmaking. Weaving. See **soumak.**

single thread. Tatting. When working with one **shuttle,** the **ring**s and **chain**s are connected by a single thread. To **attach** rings with one shuttle, make a ring, **close,** allow enough thread from the shuttle to compensate for the size of the ring, and work another ring. The single thread within the chain is created by the **loop thread,** which is pulled up enough to shape the chain. Also see **edging.**

single-thread canvas. Needlepoint. See **canvas.**

single tube spring punch. Leather. A punching tool, much like a paper punch, which has interchangeable tubes of various diameters for punching holes in leather. Also see **combination punch, revolving punch.**

single warp knot. Rugmaking. Weaving. See **knotted pile.**

Single Wedding Ring. Quilts. Either of two **pieced quilt** designs. In one, a series of tapered **rectangles** is joined to form circles; when the circles overlap it is called the **Double Wedding Ring.** The other Single Wedding Ring is identical to the **Crown of Thorns block.**

sink a print. Découpage. (Also called bury a print.) A term for covering a print with many layers of **finish** until the print is embedded in the glossy coating and the paper edges of the print cannot be felt with the fingers.

sinker. Weaving. A **warp end** that does not rise when a **shed** is opened during weaving or that is pulled down (sinks) when a **treadle** is stepped on. The latter is the action of a **sinking shed loom.** On a **weave draft** a sinker is indicated by an empty square and it means that a **filling pick** is over a warp end. If the weave draft is for a sinking shed, the sinkers are indicated by being filled or "x"ed in. They still refer, however, to the filling going over the warp. In reading a weave draft, a sinker is called a "down."

sinking. Metalworking. See **raising technique.**

sinking shed. Weaving. A V-shaped opening in front of the **reed** which is formed by the lowering of some of the **warp** threads when the **harnesses** which carry these warp ends are pulled down. The lowered threads form the bottom of the opening, while the threads of the top part move up. The **shuttle** carrying the **filling** goes through the **shed** opening. A sinking shed is the main action of the harnesses in a **counterbalanced loom** and forms half of the motion in a **countermarch loom.**

sintering. Ceramics. An intermediate stage in firing a **glaze** or **clay body:** the liquid stage has not yet begun, but the solid stage (reactions between two solids) has produced fusion, causing an increase in strength and a decrease in **porosity.** Also see **Tammann temperature.**

sintering. Gemcutting. The process of fusing a mixture of powdered metal and **diamond** with heat. The resulting material is soldered to saw blades, **drilling jigs** and carving tools.

sisal. Macramé. Sisal is a natural fiber available as macramé **cord** that is excellent for use in decorative knotting. Also see **Macramé: Tools and Materials.**

sisal. Plastics. See **reinforcing material.**

sisal. Weaving. A fiber obtained from the leaves of the agave plant, which is cultivated in tropical America and East Africa. It is primarily used to make rough-textured **rope** and **twine.**

sister. Spinning. See **maiden.**

Sister's Choice. Quilts. See **Four-X Star.**

size. Batik and Tie-dye. A chalk-starch filler in which some manufactured **fabrics** are soaked before **calendering.** It is a fabric **finish** which adds **body** to the material. The **sizing** prevents **wax** from penetrating the fabric and must therefore be removed before the **batik** or **tie-dye** process is used. Also see **removing fabric finish.**

size. Fabric Printing. (Also called **dressing.**) The substance applied to new fabric to give it body or strength.

size marking. Leather. See **Leatherwork: Weight Designations and Grading.**

sizing. Batik and Tie-dye. Quilts. Stitchery. A nonpermanent **finish** given to most **cotton fabrics** to increase weight, crispness, and luster. The sizing adds **body** or stiffness that often makes the material easier to handle, especially for **appliqué.** Because of the starchy surface, the material will take and hold a **crease** made by the fingers as it is sewn. Occasionally, **linen** and **rayons** are sized. A few sizings are made to be permanent, including some used on **organdy** or glazed **chintz.** A starchless quality returns when the fabric is ironed. Substances such as glue, wax, casein, or clay are used in nonpermanent sizing.

Because the sizing interferes with the fabric's absorption of **dye** and its receptivity to wax, it must be removed before **batik** or **tie-dye** processes are used. Also see **removing fabric finish.**

sizing canvas. Needlepoint. A process by which the **mesh** of the **canvas** is treated with a preparation made from glue or starch to keep the canvas stiff while working. Most canvases today are presized.

sizing the warp. Weaving. Coating the **warp** yarns with a solution so that they will not fray apart and break or stick together while the **shed**s are being opened during weaving. **Linen** is most commonly associated with sizing, and the size used is a solution of flaxseed which is made by soaking one part flaxseed to about twenty parts water and then boiling and straining it. The chained warp is soaked in this solution or, more often, the solution is sponged on as it is being wound on the **warp beam** or as it rolls forward toward the **harness**es. Some weavers wet the linen with water, which works temporarily. A better size is starch. For the clingy synthetics, a nonstatic spray may be used or a fabric softener solution.

skein. Basketry. Thin strips cut from the outer part of **willow** rod or other material with the aid of a **shave,** used for the **wrapping** or weaving of a basket.

skein. Knitting. A quantity of yarn wound into a coil for the purpose of being dyed or sold. Skeins are sold by weight; an average skein weighs several ounces. Also see **ball winding.**

skein. Spinning. Weaving. (Also called **hank.**) A specified amount of yarn wound in a loose, long coil or a circle on a **reel, swift,** or niddy noddy. Skeins are made commercially by commercial spinners for sale to handweavers, and they are made by handspinners at home from their **handspun** yarn. The commercial product usually weighs 8 oz and has a circumference of 44–54". Handspinners measure off the yarn into knots of 80 yards. A knot is 40 turns on a reel or a niddy noddy that measures two yards around. The skeins are seven knots or 560 yards. There is a knot tied in the yarn to indicate each 80-yard length. Due to the differences in the sizes of reels, amounts are not always kept at the above. Skeins may be made any desired length for a definite purpose. After the skein has been wound, it is twisted into a compact loop to be stored or sold. Also see **spinning.**

skein dyeing. Dyeing. Dyeing yarn after spinning. It is wound into skeins or packages weighing from one to two pounds. Home dyers wind the yarn into skeins, tie it loosely to prevent tangling, and submerge the skein in the **dyebath.** The skeins may be totally immersed, or only partially. The latter is called **dip dyeing** and allows for different colors in one skein by dipping sections of the skein in different dye baths. Commercially the yarn is wound around perforated spools or tubes, put into the dyeing machine, and the dye circulated around the packages in a two-way motion and forced under pressure through the perforated spools to insure dye penetration to all parts of the yarn on the spools. Yarn dyeing is less costly than **stock dyeing** but more expensive than **piece dyeing.** Also see **warp dyeing.**

skeining. Spinning. See **spinning.**

skein winder. Spinning. Weaving. See **reel, swift.**

skeinwork. Basketry. Skeinwork refers to weaving with **skeins,** i.e., the outer part of **rod**s of **willow** or other material.

skeleton. Puppets. (Also called body.) The wood **framework** of a **marionette.** The head is attached to the skeleton, which is composed of body, arms, and legs joined with **swivel joint**s and **hinge joint**s. The skeleton may be carved, or it may be made up of lengths of **dowel** or shaped sticks. Shoulders and hips are horizontal pieces from which arms, legs, and a central dowel for the body are hung. **String**s attached to the skeleton are run up to the **control bar** so that the figures can be **manipulate**d by the **controller.** Also see **Puppets: Making the Marionette Skeleton.**

skeleton harness. Weaving. See **doup.**

skew chisel. Woodworking. See **chisel, wood-turning tools.**

skewer. Candlemaking. See **ice pick.**

skife. Leather. See **safety beveler** and **Leatherwork: Cutting and Edging Leather.**

skillet cloth. Stitchery. See **kettle cloth.**

skimmer. Toys. The T-shaped stick of wood used to push and steer the **hoop** in the traditional **hoop-roll** game. Also see **cleek.**

skin. Leather. A term for the pelt of small animals, such as sheep, goats, small calves, pigs, lambs, and rabbits. The pelt of larger animals is classified as a hide. See ill. Also see **side** and **Leatherwork.**

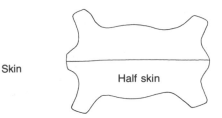

Skin   Half skin

skin animal. Toys. Any toy animal made from the hide or natural skin of the animal being represented. Rabbits, sheep, and cows are among the most common.

skip. Crochet. (Abbr. sk; also called miss in **pattern** directions.) Skipping stitches produces an open design, one with spaces or holes formed in a particular pattern. When a crochet pattern instructs you to skip a certain **stitch** or stitches, you simply count off the number of stitches specified from the hook and work your next stitch into whatever stitch you come to. For example, if instructions are to skip 3 ch., you must count off 3 chain stitches from the stitch you have just worked, and then work the next stitch into the 4th chain from the hook.

skip. Weaving. See **float.**

skip denting. Weaving. See **sett.**

skip-lacing. Beadwork. See **lacing.**

skipping rope. Toys. See **jump rope.**

skirting. Spinning. The removal with shears of dirty and low-grade wool from the outer edges of the shorn **fleece.** Also see **sorting.**

ski shuttle. Rugmaking. Weaving. A **shuttle** used most often for rug weaving because of its capacity to hold heavy, thick yarns. It is long and gracefully shaped with two ends pointing upward, like the tips of skis. There are two hooks built into the top side of the shuttle, and around these the yarn is wound in a circular manner. The shuttle is quite low in height, so that even if fully wound with heavy yarn it glides easily through the **shed.** See ill.

Ski shuttle

skittle. Toys. A wooden pin used in the **game** of **nine pins.** Also, any of various small homemade games in which wood **peg**s are knocked over with **marble**s or small **ball**s.

skittle doll. Toys. A **doll** made from a piece of **turned wood** that is shaped like the pin used in the game of **skittle**s, or **nine pins.** Skittle dolls are also made from the pins themselves, which suggest the head and legless body of a doll. The skittle doll is a form of a **poor child's doll,** although sometimes skittles were made especially for use as doll forms.

skiver. Leather. A term for the thin **grain** layer that is split from a **sheepskin,** generally used for linings.

skiving. Bookbinding. See **paring.**

skiving. Leather. (Also called shaving.) The technique of paring away layers of leather on the underside of the hide to reduce bulk where the piece will be folded, overlapped, or hemmed. A **skiving knife** or a **safety beveler** is used for skiving. Also see **French skiver, head knife, spoke shave, square point knife** and **Leatherwork: Creasing, Scoring and Folding Leather, Cutting and Edging Leather, Sewing Leather.**

skiving knife. Leather. A knife used for paring or **skiving** leather on the underside until it is thin enough to fold over or hem. See ill. Also see **bevel point knife, safety beveler, splice** and **Leatherwork: Creasing, Scoring and Folding Leather, Cutting and Edging Leather, Tools and Materials.**

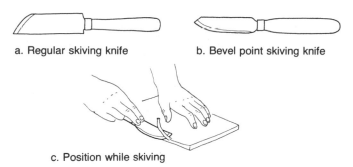

a. Regular skiving knife   b. Bevel point skiving knife

c. Position while skiving

skull. Jewelry. See **ghost.**

slab. Ceramics. Clay that has been rolled or cut into sheets of nearly uniform thickness. It is used for making **tiles** and **mosaics** and is the basic material in making **slab pot**s.

slab. Leather. The flesh side of a skin, closest to the body of the animal. The slab is generally processed with a **suede** finish on one side.

slab beam. Weaving. See **back beam.**

slabbing saw. Gemcutting. A saw used to cut flat slabs of rough stone. Prior to 1934, the mud saw was the only tool available to gemcutters for sectioning large pieces of stone. This saw consisted of a steel disk on a horizontal spindle rotating through a sump tank filled with water and silicon carbide **abrasive.** The rotating disk picked up enough grit to slice through a stone clamped in a vise and weighted to bear against the edge of the blade. This process was dirty, noisy, and slow.

Modern slabbing saws run in a basin of oil, or water, for coolant and have a hood for protection from noise and possible shattering of material. They use a blade 12″ and up in diameter. They are designed to slab material held rigidly in a vise with automatic feeds to control the speed of the cut, and a cross-feed on the vise, so that several sections may be cut in series. Coolant for slabbing saws is a half-and-half mixture of motor oil and kerosene, or a

specially formulated water-soluble "wetting" agent available at lapidary suppliers. The coolant must be occasionally cleaned of accumulated sludge to maintain its effectiveness (**a.**).

In the last forty years gemcutters have been using bronze or mild steel blades charged with **diamond.** Blades are made either by notching the edge, inserting diamond powder and hammering the edge closed, or by **sintering.** The diamond blade does not have teeth, but it does have a set (the cutting edge is slightly larger than the blade thickness) to provide clearance for the blade to enter the work without binding.

Care should be exercised not to start a cut with the blade at an angle other than 90° to the surface of the work. If another direction is desired, first notch the point of entry with the blade perpendicular, then reposition the rough so the blade enters the opening in the desired position.

If the diamond saw blade seems dull when it is first used, it is because the diamond grains are still sealed in their metal bond. Make several cuts in a brick or a discarded silicon carbide **grinding wheel** to expose the cutting surfaces.

Be sure that the material to be sawed is solid, because if it breaks while sawing, it could damage the blade. Clamp the rough in the vise, advance it until it almost touches the blade, and start the saw. After cutting in about ½″, feeding by hand, back the work off the blade and examine the cut to see if the feed and speed are correct. Close the hood, and restart the saw. When the cut is completed, do not allow the rough stone to move past the blade, as a small sliver where the slab breaks off can cause damage to the blade. This can be avoided by hand-feeding the last of the cut or installing a stop. If the blade is dished or bent out of square with the vise, it will wear out the diamond on one side and make the blade useless.

Slabs are generally cut ¼″ in thickness.

Most gemcutters do not own a slabbing saw. Cut slabs are available at rock shops where one can also have a slab custom cut.

The trim saw (also called cut-off saw and resaw) is a smaller sawing machinery with a vise for small slabbing (or without one for hand-held cutting). It has a splash guard over the blade and a hand rest in front for holding the work. It uses a diamond blade of smaller diameter than the slabbing saw, spinning at a faster speed in thinner thicknesses for slitting gem material. The trim saw may be used for removing unwanted material quickly, roughing out concave material, and rough-shaping a blank for a **cabochon** cut (**b.**). In the last case, notches on the trim saw are made up to the outline on the base of the blank (**c.**). The cut extends farther on the underside due to the curvature of the blade. A number of cuts perpendicular to each other are made, leaving a patch of teeth which can be trimmed off, or nibbled away with pliers (**d.**).

The slab grabber is a device for holding the heel ends of rocks which have had slabs cut off. The material is held in the slab grabber which in turn is held in the vise of the slabbing saw for further slabbing (**e.**).

Shafting for diamond saws and bearings must be extremely rigid and sealed to protect against abrasive and water. The minimum arbor diameter is ⅝″ for blades up to

10″. Saw-blade collars or flanges should be at least one-fourth to three-fourths of the blade diameter to avoid sideplay or wobble. The optimum speed for operation is 3,150 to 4,000 surface feet per minute. A 4″ blade should spin at 3,000 to 4,000 rpm; an 8″ blade at 2,000 rpm; a 12″ blade at 1,200 rpm.

Moderate, firm—but never forced—pressure is recommended. See ill. Also see **machinery** and **Gemcutting: Rough Shaping, Tools and Materials.**

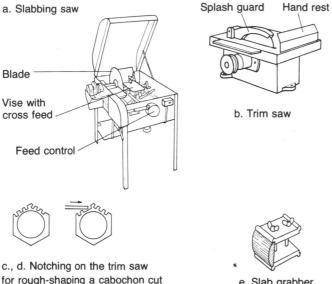

a. Slabbing saw

Blade

Vise with cross feed

Feed control

Splash guard   Hand rest

b. Trim saw

c., d. Notching on the trim saw for rough-shaping a cabochon cut

e. Slab grabber

slab glass. Stained Glass. Slab glass is made by pouring molten **glass** into a mold and allowing it to harden without pressure. It is a thick glass—8″ × 12″ × ¾″. It differs from pressed glass, which hardens in a mold under pressure so that a design is imprinted into the glass. Pressed glass is usually made in small, geometric pieces used in lamps, borders, and windows. Also see **cement, crossed slab glass, dalle-de-verre, Norman slab glass.**

slab-glass lampshade. Stained Glass. A lampshade made of scraps and pieces of **slab glass** held together with **Kwik solder** rather than standard **solder.** Any of the molds used in regular **lampshade construction** will serve here. After wax or petroleum jelly has been applied to the mold as a **releasing agent,** apply the slab glass pieces at random and hold them in place with pins or nails. Starting at the bottom and working upward, spread the Kwik solder between the slab pieces with a **spatula.** When the piece has dried, remove the mold. Also see **liquid solder.**

slab grabber. Gemcutting. See **slabbing saw.**

slab pot. Ceramics. An object made by slab building, a method of making pottery by hand. Pieces of clay are pressed by hand, cut to the desired shape, and assembled when **leather hard.** The pieces are scored where they are joined and covered with **slip.** Also see **coiled pot, pinch pot, pressing** and **Ceramics: Hand Building.**

slabstock. Weaving. See **back beam.**

slack. Stained Glass. See **full and slack.**

slack tub. Metalworking. (Also called slake.) A container or tub filled with water and used for temporary baths and **quenching** when **forging.** Sometimes a slack tub is built into the end of a **forge,** and may have a small tub inside the larger one filled with **brine** or oil.

slag. Metalworking. Dirt, acids, **oxide**s, and other impurities that come to the surface when welding metal. One to 4 percent silaceous slag consisting of acid, basic, and neutral oxides is added to **wrought iron** to increase the fusibility, toughness, malleability, and **ductility** of the metal.

slake. Ceramics. To moisten clay with water, usually by sifting dry clay into water without stirring.

slake tub. Metalworking. See **slack tub.**

slanting Gobelin stitch. Needlepoint. A variation of **Gobelin stitch** in which the stitches are worked diagonally.

slate. Mosaics. A hard rock that has formed naturally into smooth, slablike layers. Slate is found in nature in a wide range of colors, from subtle grays and bluish tints to greenish tones. It is usually found in thinner slabs than **marble** and is far easier to cut. Its natural matte finish, when combined in a **mosaic** with glossier materials, can create exciting contrasts in a work. Slate is available through most building-supply outlets.

slath. Basketry. The structure made by the bottom **stake**s of a base. This structure is most visible at a stage after the stakes have been **tied in** and **opened out.** Also see **Basketry: Woven Basket Construction.**

Slave Chain. Quilts. See **Job's Tears** and **Quilts: Quilting.**

sledgehammer. Metalworking. See **hammer.**

sleeve board. Stitchery. A tapered board, slightly smaller than an average sleeve, which is padded and **fabric**-covered for use in **press**ing. Because materials can be pulled over the board for pressing, it is especially helpful on nonflat pieces. It is commonly used in clothing, and like the **tailor's cushion** is very helpful when making toys or **three-dimensional stitchery.**

slew. Basketry. A weave made by working two or more willow **weaver**s together as one. The **stroke** simply goes in front of one **stake** and behind the next. It is visually distinct from **double randing** because of the tapered effect of the **willow rod**s, which blend together to look more like just one weaving element. Also see **Basketry: Woven Basket Construction.**

slewing. Basketry. The process or use of the **slew** weave in **willow** work. Also see **Basketry: Woven Basket Construction.**

sley. Weaving. See **sett.**

sley hook. Weaving. See **reed hook.**

sleying. Weaving. (Also called reeding.) The action of drawing the **warp end**s through the **dents** in a **reed**. This is usually done with a **reed hook** according to a planned **sett**. It can be done from the front of the **loom** with the reed in the **beater**. **Slip knot**s are tied to keep the warp ends from slipping out of the reed once they are pulled through, and to keep the beater movable. The reed can also be removed from the beater and attached to **lary stick**s in front of the beater. The warp is then sleyed from underneath the reed and the ends are pulled from the top of the reed down through the dents. These methods are done in the direction of back to front sleying of the warp. When **dressing the loom** from front to back, both the warp **chain** and the weaver are in front of the beater, and the warp ends are pulled from the front to the back of the beater and secured there in slip knots. In all cases, the center of the reed should be found and marked first so that the warp is properly centered. To draw two ends through each dent is known as double sleying, and drawing one thread through each dent is called single sleying. See ill.

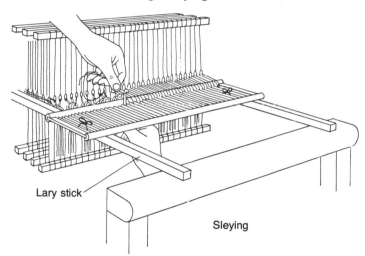

Lary stick

Sleying

slicing. Metalworking. See **blacksmithing techniques.**

slick. Metalworking. See **sandcasting molding equipment.**

slick and oval. Metalworking. See **sandcasting molding equipment.**

slick chisel. Woodworking. See **chisel.**

sliding T bevel. Woodworking. See **squaring tools.**

slingshot. Toys. A **folk toy** that can easily be made at home but that is potentially dangerous and may be lethal. For this reason, the sale of slingshots is now limited by law. The slingshot at one time was used for hunting, as a pebble can be hurled with great velocity and accuracy by a skillful operator. It consists of a forked piece of wood in the shape of the letter Y, usually cut from a sturdy tree branch. A heavy strip of **rubber** is tied between the two forks; the length of the rubber is about three times the distance between the forks. A leather pad is sometimes threaded onto the rubber and positioned halfway between. The stick is held in one hand. A pebble or similar missile is placed in a fold of the leather, or in a fold of the rubber band, and drawn tautly back toward the operator. When released, the rubber snaps forward propelling the pebble. Any slingshot, even a small one made with a rubber band, is a shooting toy and must be used with great care and discretion.

slink. Leather. (Also called half calf.) The skin of a prematurely born calf, with the hair left on it, used for small projects and clothing. These skins range from 6–10 square feet in size and are usually brown and white or black and white.

Slinky. Toys. See **balance toy.**

slip. Ceramics. The suspension of clay or **glaze** particles in water. To make slip, soak small pieces of clay in water to form **slurry** and brush the slurry through a sieve when saturated. Add **pigment oxide**s to color slips. A slip must be aged a few days before use.

slipcase. Bookbinding. (Also called slipcover.) A sturdy, separate case for slipping the book into for protection.

slipcasting. Ceramics. The process of making ceramic forms in molds of plaster, using liquid clay bodies or **slip**. Slip is poured into the mold to fill it; the plaster begins to absorb the water from the slip, so a crust of solid clay forms on the inside surface of the mold. Once enough clay has been deposited in this way, the rest of the slip is poured off. As the clay dries, it shrinks away from the mold; the form is removed when it is **leather hard**. Also see **coiled pot, jigging, pinch pot, slab pot,** and **Ceramics: Throwing.**

slip clay. Ceramics. See **Ceramics: Clay.**

slipcover. Bookbinding. See **slipcase.**

slip decoration. Ceramics. **Slip,** applied by brushing or **trailing,** may be used as a partial or complete covering on a ceramic form. See ill.

Slip decoration

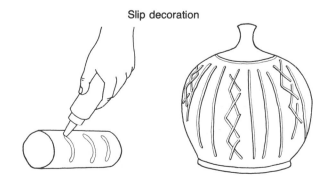

slip gauge. Ceramics. An instrument used to measure the thickness or consistency of a **slip** or a **glaze.**

slip glaze. Ceramics. A **glaze** made from slip clay that contains sufficient **flux** to adhere to the **clay body.** Albany slip clay is the commonly used variety. It fires brown-black at cone 8–10. The addition of 2 percent cobalt to Albany slip produces a semigloss jet black glaze. Wrenshall slip clay fires to a pale yellow at cones 6–10 with the streaked characteristics of rutile. Test slip clay before using it in quantity as a glaze because the slip composition can vary slightly. Albany slip lacking the brown colorant produces a pale, semitransparent tan glaze. Slip glaze is easy to apply and fires with few, if any, defects. Also see **engobe.**

slip knot. Crochet. See **Crochet: Basic Stitches.**

slip knot. Lacemaking. The first part of a **weaver's knot.** Form a **loop** and hold the crossing of threads forming the loop between the thumb and index finger. With the index finger of the other hand, reach through the loop, place that finger over the thread on the top of the cross of the loop being held, and lift that thread through the loop. Pull thread through just enough to make a soft, loose knot, and retain the loop thus formed.

slip knot. Weaving. A knot that forms a loop similar to a crochet loop. It is used temporarily to hold together groups of **warp end**s that have been threaded through the **heddle**s or through the **reed,** so that they will not be pulled out. It can be untied, or slipped out, with a tug of one hand. Slip knots made at spaced intervals can be used instead of **chaining** when taking a warp of a **warping board** or **reel.** See ill. Also see **threading.**

Slip knot

slippage. Weaving. A fault in finished, woven fabrics where the **warp ends** slip or slide over the **filling picks** and vice versa. It is caused by either too open a **sett** or not enough **picks per inch.** Rough or hairy yarn retards slippage to some extent, as does **shrinkage** or **fulling.**

slips. Bookbinding. The **tapes** and **super** that extend beyond the **back** of the book and are glued to the waste leaf. Also see **cloth jointed endpaper.**

slip stitch. Crochet. (Abbr. sl st.) See **plain crochet** and **Crochet: Basic Stitches.**

slip stitch. Knitting. (Abbr. sl st.) A stitch that is simply passed from the first needle to the second needle without knitting the stitch. Also see **slip stitch principle.**

slip stitch. Quilts. Stitchery. Similar to a **blind stitch,** but the **needle** picks up just one or two threads of the backing, then one or two threads of the upper fabric. It should be invisible from either side. This stitch is used in **appliqué** and in **hemming.** See ill.

Slip stitch

slip stitch principle. Knitting. When a slipped stitch is used as part of a **decrease,** it must be slipped knitwise (as if to knit). If slipped purlwise (as if to purl) the stitches will be crossed in the decrease. There are exceptions, such as when a **slip stitch** knitwise is used as a pattern principle. Also see **Tunisian knitting.**

slipstone. Block Printing. See **sharpening stone.**

slipstone. Woodworking. See **sharpening stone.**

slip trailer. Ceramics. (Also called tracer.) A stiff, rubber bulb with a nozzle that is used to direct a controlled stream of **slip** or **glaze** onto a surface. It is similar to a cake icing decorator that is used in cooking.

slit tapestry. Weaving. A **tapestry** technique or method of changing the **filling** colors in adjacent areas that produces vertical openings or slits. The weaving does not proceed **selvage** to selvage, but rather back and forth in small areas determined by the design. Each filling weaves to the point where the color changes and then turns back. The slits are created at the juncture of the colors. A clean-cut, straight-line opening between the color change is produced. If this same meeting and turning point is used for many filling repeats, the height of the slit increases, and a vertical line, known as a straight slit, develops. A **diagonal** color change may be woven with a series of short slits developing whose height is determined by the angle of the diagonal, as well as by the size of the yarn used. Such a diagonal slit may move very gradually to the right or to the left over one or more **warp end**s and hardly be seen. If the diagonal is steep, a stepped effect is produced known as a stepped slit. The process of making these short slits, while following the line of a diagonal, is known as stepping or diagonal in pairs since the filling interlaces with the same warp ends twice or more before moving on to the next step of the diagonal. In weaving a diagonal, the area that decreases the number of warp ends is woven first, and the area that increases its number of warp ends is put in after the decreasing area. Curves and circles are managed in the same way.

In order to weave a vertical slit, two filling yarns are started at opposite edges of their respective color areas. In the same **shed** of **plain weave,** they are drawn toward each other to the meeting point of the areas and there they surface. The shed is changed and the two fillings are inserted again and return to their original starting point. In the return movement, they turn back over the adjacent warp ends. This forms the edges of the slit. More than one slit may be worked at a time across the width of a tapestry. Many weavers prefer to weave each area independently before going on to the next area. They then weave that area completely. Between each slit, the weaving can go over as many, or as few, warp ends as is practical or necessary to the design. When making a turn in the weaving, the filling should not be pulled tightly or else the warp end around which the turn is being made will be pulled out of line, leaving a gap instead of a slit. Contemporary artists have used this idea of pulling on the filling to create shaped openings in their **wall hanging**s. The early Peruvians also used this same concept. They made openwork fabrics that were elaborately planned and patterned so that almost half the fabric was composed of open spaces. If used as an **openwork** technique, the warp need not be completely covered as in traditional tapestry. In fact, it can be completely **warp-faced**; there do not have to be color changes. One color can be used for all the woven areas. Individual butterflies or **bobbin**s must still be used for each woven area.

Slits may or may not be sewn up after weaving. They may be sewn up while the work is still in progress on the **loom,** or when it is finished and off the loom. To sew or not to sew depends on the design consideration, the length of the slit, and the weight of the tapestry. In especially large tapestries, the weight of the piece could force a long slit open. Slits do detract from the overall strength of a finished tapestry. This consideration has to be weighed against the textural and design effects obtained through the use of slits. Coptic, Gothic, Gobelin, Aubusson and Peruvian tapestries make use of slits, as do the blanket-rugs found in **Navajo Weaving.** They are also an integral part of **kilim** weaving. The Gobelin tapestries have a distinctive look due to stepping in small amounts to produce tiny slits, and to the stitching together of any slit longer than ¼" or ⅜". Most sewing of slits is done on the wrong side, making sure there are no stitches visible on the right side. The French Gobelin method sews on the right side with stitches placed very close and parallel to the filling threads. The stitch can be compared to a simple **lacing stitch** in that the manner of insertion into the edges and then going from side to side draws the edges together, but it is much denser than a lacing stitch. In this way it would resemble a buttonhole stitch. The same kind of stitch can be used also on the back of the tapestry with a blunt-tipped tapestry **needle** and strong, fine thread such as silk thread.

A slit may be just a necessary adjunct to a color change or it may be very much a part of the design. Decorative and textural contrast and shading effects are created by slits. Slits are used to break up an uninteresting plain surface and their placement can help to delineate a form. In a practical vein, slits are used as neck openings in ponchos or as holes or openings for use as buttonholes, lacing eyelets, pockets (with the pocket interior sewn on the back), to hold the cord or string in a drawstring bag, or the rod in a wall hanging. In **Peruvian weaving** the slit is repeatedly used to make a woven **fringe.** This is slit weaving that is open at one end. Contemporary weaver-artists, such as the Colombian Olga de Amaral, have used long slits ingeniously to form wall hangings where two warp layers are interwoven through the slits and the slit becomes a structural concept. Moik Schiele of Switzerland has used the slit so that it has depth as well as length and width. She has worked with different **warp tension**s on a double

beam loom, so that woven areas bellow in and out in between stable, straight woven areas. In the United States, Lenore Tawney uses the slit to shape her hangings. Showing tremendous control over the openings and the weaving of long, thin areas she staggers the slits or diminishes the woven areas while enlarging the spaces so that the surface is enlivened and moving. Her manipulation of space and solid area is closely akin to **Peruvian lattice** work. See ill. Also see **Gobelin bobbin, Spanish lace, teething.**

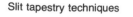

Slit tapestry techniques

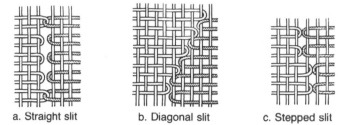

a. Straight slit   b. Diagonal slit   c. Stepped slit

slit weaving. Weaving. See **slit tapestry.**

sliver. Spinning. A strand or rope of **carded wool** or cotton that is ready for spinning. There is no twist; the fibers are straight and parallel, and the strand is fairly continuous. Also see **carding, rolag, roving, spinning.**

slot and eye heddle. Weaving. See **rigid heddle.**

slots. Knitting. See **ribbon holes.**

slub yarn. Spinning. Weaving. See **novelty yarn.**

slumber robe. Quilts. (Also called throw.) Quilts considered too fancy or too elegant for the bed were often kept in the parlor. They were made up from **silk**s and **velvet,** and were usually smaller than a regular quilt, although there was no standard size. Also see **best quilt, Victorian crazy quilt.**

slum toy. Toys. A toy devised from discarded, cast-off, or found material. It exemplifies a **making do** approach. There is a famous collection of slum toys in the **Museum of Childhood** in Edinburgh, collected by Edward Lovett. In it are the **poor child's doll,** a **shoe doll,** and other dolls made from bones or rolled fabrics. Also see **Toys: Dolls.**

slurry. Ceramics. A **slip** mixture that is rough, wet, sandy, thick, and is half-mixed.

slurry. Glasswork. Metalwork. Gemcutting. A suspension of abrasive particles in a liquid medium. Slurries are applied or flowed onto wheels of smooth surfaces to accomplish very fine polishing or cutting of hard materials.

slush. Enameling. See **enamel.**

slush casting. Plastics. Metalworking. A **casting** process in which fluid plastic **resin** or molten metal is swished around in a **mold** by turning or rotating the mold until the fluid starts to become rigid, forming a thin shell on the mold surface. Any excess is poured out.

In plastics, a **promotor** or **accelerator** may be used with the resin to reduce the time you must spend rotating the mold.

In metalworking, **lead** is recommended as a slush-casting metal for the home craftsperson because of its low melting point. Plaster molds should be prepared with **investment** refractory material and dried in a **burn-out kiln.** Permanent molds made of **bronze** are used for slush casting large numbers of copies in **pewter;** the molds are chilled before the molten metal is poured in.

slype. Basketry. A point or tapered cut at the end of a **rod** to permit its easy insertion in the weaving of **borders, siding,** and the like. See ill. Also see **Basketry: Woven Basket Construction.**

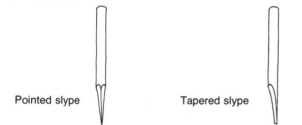

Pointed slype   Tapered slype

small ball. Macramé. See **bobble.**

small handle. Basketry. A handle made separately and attached to the completed basket, generally used on small baskets that will not hold much weight. Common types are the wrapped handle, single-rod roped handle, and simple ring handle. Also see **Basketry: Woven Basket Construction, Handles.**

smalti. Mosaics. (Also called smalti tipo antico, Byzantine enamel, and Byzantine glass.) The material that is considered the ne plus ultra among professional mosaicists. Smalti are glass **tesserae** of irregular, slightly rectangular shapes that have been chipped from slabs or pancakes of the finest (usually Venetian) glass. They are most noted for their reflective brilliance and their intensity of color, which has been achieved not with dyes but by combining the molten glass with mineral oxides that completely permeate the material. Approximately 5,000 colors are available commercially, and the Vatican is said to have more than 25,000 different hues of smalti in its workshops. Art supply outlets sell smalti by the pound with the more exotic colors, such as gold, being the most expensive, and the earthy tones the cheapest. Gold smalti, unlike the colored variety in which the pigment goes all through the glass, is produced by sandwiching gold leaf between two layers of glass. Gold hues range from a light yellow shade to an almost copper tint. As a rule of thumb, roughly three pounds of smalti will cover one square foot of backing. Also see **pressed glass** and **Mosaics: Tools and Materials.**

smalti tipo antico. Mosaics. See **smalti.**

smalto. Mosaics. The singular form of **smalti.**

SMA welding. Metalworking. See **welding.**

smelting. Jewelry. The process of separating metals from nonmetallic materials, or separating metals from metals, either in their natural state (ore) or in reprocessing and reclaiming metals.

smithing. Metalworking. See **blacksmithing, forging.**

smocking. Embroidery. Smocking is a method of stitching folds of cloth in place so that the gathered area of a garment will be firmly and decoratively secured. The folds are first gathered evenly side by side, and the stitching is then worked across their surface. When the gathering threads are withdrawn the smocked folds can be stretched apart but will spring back into place because of the nature of the stitching.

The only traditional needlework of England, this type has been done since early times to secure the gathers of peasant smocks. Farmers working at manual tasks needed warm garments: quilted coats and jackets were too restraining to their movements, so smocks were found to be ideal, as the gathers—held close to the body by the honeycomb stitching—were still able to stretch like elastic.

The stitches most commonly used are **honeycomb filling** and **stem stitch.**

smocking. Knitting. A method of decorating a **ribbed** knit fabric with hand sewing, done in such a way that it pulls the ribs of the knitting into symmetrical patterns. Smocking is usually done with one or more colors other than the color used in the knitting. Also see **honeycombing.**

smoked ware. Ceramics. The discoloring of a **glaze** or **clay body** by a smoky reduction-fire that stains pots with carbon which will not burn out. **Raku** and sawdust firing are a mixture of smoking, or carbonization, and reduction.

smoke grinder. Toys. See **do-nothing machine.**

smoking. Candlemaking. A candle will smoke when it burns if it is made from a wax of poor quality or if it has too large a wick. Also see **Candlemaking: Possible Problems with Molded Candles.**

smoky quartz. Gemcutting. See **quartz.**

smoothing. Metalworking. See **blacksmithing techniques.**

smoothing plane. Woodworking. See **plane.**

Smyrna cross stitch. Needlepoint. (Also called double cross stitch.) A **cross stitch** with an intersecting **upright cross stitch,** most effective when worked over four mesh. Work the top cross stitches in the same direction. It gives a solid backing and is often used on rugs. See ill.

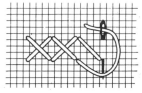

a. Cross stitch

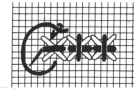

b. Smyrna cross stitch

Smyrna knot. Rugmaking. Weaving. See **knotted pile.**

Smyrna stitch. Rugmaking. See **cross stitch.**

SNAG. Jewelry. See **Society of North American Goldsmiths.**

snail trail. Crewel. Embroidery. See **coral knot.**

snake's-head cowrie. Shell Carving. (*Cypraea caput serpentis.*) A shell with a dark and light brown and white exterior layer, a white **middle color,** and a violet **ground color,** used in cameo carving. A shell will yield one ring-size cameo. Also see **cowrie, helmet** and **Shell Carving: Shell, Tools and Preparation, Cameo Carving.**

snakeskin. Leather. Any skin from various species of snake, such as **cobra skin.**

snap. Leather. A metal fastening, available in many sizes, used to join two pieces of leather, which can be fastened and unfastened frequently. Snaps come in four parts: the snap button and socket, the eyelet and stud. There are various types of snaps (segma snap, birdcage snaps). All are set with the same basic method, using a snap setter

Parts of a segma snap

a. Button   b. Socket   c. Eyelet   d. Stud

e. Segma snap tool

f. Snap button

Cap   Eyelet   Spring   Post

g. Snap button fastener

Anvil

h. Four-post snap setter

(made especially for setting each type of snap). Mark and punch the hole for the socket to go through; put the socket over the matching anvil on the snap setter plate; place the leather over the socket, right side up; place the button over the socket and push down in place. Put the large concave punch of the setting kit over the button and strike with a **mallet** to set the button and socket. Punch a hole for the eyelet to go through and place the eyelet over the small anvil on the setting plate. Place leather over the eyelet, right side up. Place the stud on the eyelet, then place the correct punch over the stud. Strike with mallet to set stud and eyelet. See ill. Also see **finding, revolving punch** and **Leatherwork: Tools and Materials.**

snap a string. Quilts. See **chalk line.**

snap button. Leather. See **snap.**

snap button fastener. Leather. See **snap.**

snap line. Woodworking. See **marking tools.**

snap setter. Leather. See **snap.**

snip. Stitchery. To **clip** or cut with a short, quick stroke.

snips. Jewelry. Tools used for cutting thin **gauge sheet metal, wire,** and **solder.** Also see **aviation snips, nippers, shears.**

snips. Metalworking. (Also called tin snips, hand snips.) Scissorlike tools used for cutting **solder, wire,** and thin sheet metal (14-**gauge** or lighter). They are not as heavy as metal-cutting **shears.**

STRAIGHT SNIPS These have straight blades for cutting straight lines or large curves in metal 22-gauge or thinner. The blades are 2—4½″ long (**a.**). See ill.

CURVED SNIPS These are also called hawk-billed, pattern, or scroll snips. These have curved blades and are used for cutting small circles, scroll patterns, and abrupt turns without bending the metal (**b.**). See ill.

AVIATION SNIPS These are used for smaller work (up to 20-gauge) and will cut straight or circular cuts. They may be purchased with blades curved left (which cut to the left) or right (which cut to the right), or with straight universal blades.

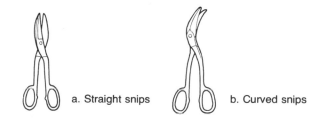

a. Straight snips   b. Curved snips

snips. Tincrafting. A tool used to cut sheet metal, such as **tinplate.** A wide variety of snips are available, varying in length and sturdiness of the tool, and in the kind of cut delivered by the cutting edge. It is desirable to have available both a smooth cutting pair and at least one grade of **serrated snips.** Also see **Tincrafting: Tools and Materials, Preparing the Tincan.**

snitch knot. Weaving. An adjustable knot that is used universally in attaching a **treadle** to a **lam** on a **floor loom.** The attaching is done according to the **tie-up** pattern. Two pieces of strong cotton or nylon cord are used. One piece goes through a drilled hole or screw eye of the treadle, and the second piece goes through a drilled hole or screw eye of the lam. One piece is shorter and is made into a loop by doubling the piece and tying the two free ends in an overhand knot. If screw eyes are used, the shorter piece goes through the eye found on the upper side of the treadle and is looped through itself in order to be held in place. If there are drilled holes instead of screw eyes, the overhand knot that forms the loops must be of a size that will not go through the hole when the treadle is pressed and the cord is pulled taut. After the loop is attached, the loose end is folded back over itself to form a smaller loop. Through this smaller loop, pass the untied ends of the larger piece of cord coming from the lam. This larger piece has been attached to the lam by doubling the piece, going through the screw eye found on the under side of the lam, and looping over itself to be held in place. With a drilled hole, two separate pieces of cord are used. They are equal in length and are tied with an overhand knot at one end. This knot then goes through the drilled hole. After the free ends have passed through the treadle cord loop, the loop is pulled tight and the free ends are tied into an overhand knot, or a single plain knot. Before this final knot is made, the treadles are checked to see that they are all at the same level with each other and that the harnesses are at the correct height. If they are not, then the loop of the treadle cord is moved up or down to shorten or lengthen the lam cord. A snitch knot is a very secure and tight knot that does not come apart unless the final knot is undone. See ill.

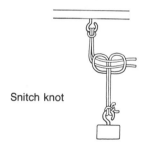

Snitch knot

snowball quilt. Quilts. See **popcorn quilt.**

snowflake. Papercrafts. A papercraft design in which a thin paper circle is folded several times and intricate shapes are cut into the folded edges. There are endless variations of patterns possible. Fold the circle in half, then in half again, then fold this section in thirds, creasing folds sharply (**a.**). Cut designs into the folded sides so that these folds are the centers of the points, making one point long and one short for a 6-pointed snowflake (**b.**), or making equal points for a 12-pointed medallion. Unfold (**c.**). See ill.

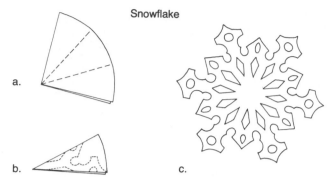

Snowflake

snuffed. Leather. Snuffed leather is **grain** leather that has had the hair removed and the outer surface lightly pared away by buffing.

soak. Glasswork. The period of time in the **annealing** of **glasswork** that glass pieces are allowed to remain at the **annealing point** so that intenal stresses are relieved.

soak cementing. Plastics. See **cementing** and **Plastics: Cementing.**

soaking fire. Stained Glass. See **firing stain.**

soak temperature. Ceramics. See **heat soaking.**

soap bubble blowing. Toys. The blowing of iridescent bubbles from soapy water. For good bubbles, make the following solution: 2½ cups hot water (rain or distilled water, preferably); 1 heaping tablespoon of soap (Castile or palm-oil flakes). Dissolve, then add: 4 tablespoons glycerin. Stir or shake vigorously. Siphon off the clear liquid or strain it through a cloth. Cool. Add food coloring if desired.

Various kinds of **bubble blowers** can be devised to aid in the production of soap bubbles.

The addition of glycerin to the water makes the soap film more durable, thus making it possible to blow a bubble within a bubble. Also see **Toys: Ephemeral Toys.**

soap carving. Toys. The carving or **whittling** of a bar of soap. Because soap is soft, a paring knife is sufficiently sharp. Bars of laundry soap are large enough for carving. Hand soaps are somewhat small, but can be used. Homemade soaps can be cut into chunks of any specified size to accommodate the carver's needs. The soap carving is fairly durable but can dent or break. **Soap toys,** made of nonpermanent material, are considered **ephemeral toys.** The carved chips can be saved for use in washing. Also see **bath toys, floating toys** and **Toys: Ephemeral Toys.**

soapstone. Gemcutting. See **talc.**

soap toy. Toys. See **soap carving.**

Sobo. Plastics. See **polyvinyl alcohol.**

Society of North American Goldsmiths. Jewelry. A nonprofit organization formed to bring together goldsmiths and silversmiths for the purpose of encouraging the art of goldsmithing through education in both the United States and Canada. SNAG became officially recognized in March 1970, at its first conference and exhibition, Goldsmith 70, held in St. Paul, Minnesota. The exhibition was sponsored by the Minnesota Museum of Art in cooperation with SNAG. Some of the purposes and aims of the organization are to recognize excellence in design and craftsmanship; to establish professional standards for exhibitions, competitions, and private workshops; to set guidelines for the education and training of goldsmiths and silversmiths; to establish a national intern-apprentice program and slide archive; to expand the conference, discussion programs, and symposia; and to continue professional and student exhibitions.

sock doll. Toys. A soft **fabric doll** made by **stuffing** a sock.

If a baby sock is used, cut the sock just above the ankle (**a.**). The toe becomes the doll's head and the heel makes the seat. Stuff the sock with **Dacron polyester batting,** then tie it about halfway between the toe and heel to suggest a neck or division between the head and body. Cut the bottom of the sock to make legs (**b.**). Stuff the body section and stitch leg seam together (**c.**). Cut the top of the sock in three parts (**d.**). Stitch the stuffed arms to the doll body (**e.**). The decorative edge at the top of the sock is used for a cap (**f.**).

If an adult sock is used, the stuffing and tying are finished in the same way and then the ribbed portion of the sock is slit to make the two long legs. An additional sock is cut off at the end of the ribbing, and the ribbed portion is slit in half to make the two arms. Hair and features are added with yarn, felt, or floss, utilizing appliqué or embroidery.

The sock doll is excellent for the beginning dollmaker because the sock provides a structure for the body. It makes a safe, durable, washable doll for a baby or small child, and is a much-loved version of the **rag doll.** Sock dolls are a **making do** type of doll. See ill. Also see **nylon stocking doll.**

Sock doll

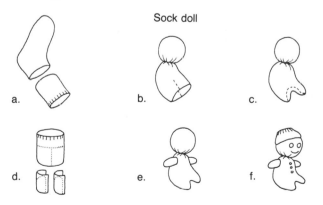

socket chisel. Woodworking. See **chisel.**

sock puppet. Puppets. (Also called stocking puppet.) A **hand puppet** made using a stuffed gym sock or work sock as the **puppet head.** Usually, a small cardboard tube, made by rolling and taping lightweight cardboard, is wrapped or padded with **stuffing** to suggest the head. Then a sock is

pulled over the stuffing, working it into the desired shape. The sock is then tied around the tube at the base of the head. Features and hair are added, and clothes may be attached to the sock material. Also see **nylon stocking puppet, soft head.**

soda ash. Batik and Tie-dye. See **washing soda.**

soda ash. Ceramics. A very active alkaline **flux** used in **glazes** as a **frit** ingredient. Small quantities of soda ash increase the workability and strength of a **clay body** and reduce **shrinkage** while drying. Also see **casting slip, deflocculent.**

soda glass. Glasswork. See **soda-lime glass.**

soda-lime glass. Glasswork. A type of glass composed of approximately 15% sodium oxide (Na_2O), 9% calcium oxide (CaO), 3% manganese oxide (MgO), 1% aluminum oxide (Al_2O_3), and 72% silica (SiO_2). This is the oldest class of glass; simple forms were fabricated as early as 1500 B.C. in Egypt.

Soda-lime glass is the most common form used today and is the material for windows, bottles, containers, lightbulbs, glass fiber, and building blocks. It tends to have a greenish tinge, which is due to traces of iron oxide, a common impurity and one that is difficult to keep out of the mixture. The greenish cast is often cloaked by adding traces of manganese oxide, which adds complementary color, or by adding arsenious oxide, potassium nitrate, or sodium nitrate. These other materials tend to keep the iron oxides in a clearer chemical state. Also see **Murano.**

sodium bicarbonate. Batik and Tie-dye. A powdered substance used in **fixing** colors for some **dye** methods using **fiber-reactive dye**s. It is the common household baking soda, available in grocery stores.

sodium bicarbonate. Stained Glass. **Bicarbonate of soda.** Also see **hydrofluoric acid** and **Stained Glass: Safety Precautions.**

sodium silicate. Ceramics. See **casting slip, deflocculent.**

soft enamel. Enameling. See **enamel.**

soft figure. Stitchery. Toys. (Also called soft figure sculpture.) A three-dimensional **stuffed figure** of any size that has human form. Usually made of **fabric,** like stuffed **nylon stocking dolls,** the **soft figure** can be cloth, **papiermâché, sawdust mâché,** or any **soft sculpture** material.

soft form. Stitchery. See **soft sculpture.**

soft glaze. Ceramics. Any **glaze** containing **white lead** or **boric acid** as a **flux** that can be scratched with a steel knife after firing. Also see **earthenware glaze.**

soft head. Puppets. (Also called fabric head.) A **puppet head** that is made by putting **stuffing** into a **fabric** form. Soft heads are used in **sock puppets, nylon-stocking pup-**

pets, and **felt puppets**. Also see **Puppets: Making the Puppet Head**.

soft jet. Jet Carving. Soft jet is mined from the upper layer of lias rock and has a hardness of 2½ – 3 on the Mohs scale. The nature of this variety of **jet** makes it difficult to work. It is brittle and flakes and chips and loses its polish quickly. It cannot be sawed into slices or carved with fine detail as can **hard jet**. It can be used for beads and objects with little detail.

soft marionette. Puppets. See **stuffed marionette**.

soft sculpture. Stitchery. (Also called soft form, soft stitchery.) An art form in which three-dimensional shapes are built up through the **piecing** and **stuff**ing of various soft materials. The work is sculptural in nature, though flexible or soft and stuffed. This sculpture is formed outside of the traditional use of the word which is reserved for bronze, wood, and stone. It is sculpture as an expression of concepts, regardless of technique.

While it actually began much earlier, soft sculpture really emerged in the 1950s. Three-dimensional weaving, stuffed fiber and fabric forms, plastics and molded forms, sculptured soft materials, and combinations of hard and soft were all being explored. Claes Oldenburg's works were among the first to expand the traditional concept of sculpture with soft work. He was joined by well-known weavers, stitchers, and quilters who have moved from two-dimensional work into the more unlimited ranges of three-dimensional work, with their new ideas and approaches springing up simultaneously all over the country.

Fabric collage started as flat pieces, began to move into three-dimensional forms with shirred, **fold**ed, and stuffed materials. Pieces became environmental—the viewer was invited to touch, to move parts. Soft sculptures, created from **fiber** and **fabric**s, are now both woven and nonwoven, of every variety, treated with paint, embroidery, printing and dyeing methods of all kinds, and **appliqué**. Among the common stuffings are **cotton** and **Dacron polyester batting**, Styrofoam blocks and pellets, straw, rags, nylon stockings, **foam rubber**, plastic bubble packing material, and **kapok**.

Soft stitchery includes not only the more traditionally used fabrics and fiber techniques of weaving and sewing but braiding, crochet, knotting, knitting, and **stitchery** as well. Along with fibers, fur, feathers, plastic, metal, rubber, paper, polyethylene, and any other material which suits the purpose may be used.

Soft sculptures are created with as wide a range of expression as that found in other sculptural media—as abstract or as literal as the sculptor chooses. Some are serious, others are humorous spoofs on the overseriousness of sculpture. Many are **funk**y, lighthearted, decorative, and beautiful comments on the world today. Also see **Stitchery: Stitchery Forms**.

soft soap. Ceramics. See **master mold**.

soft solder. Metalworking. See **solder**.

soft soldering. Metalworking. See **soldering** and **Metalworking: Soldering**.

soft soldering flux. Metalworking. See **flux**.

soft stitchery. Stitchery. See **soft sculpture**.

soft twist yarn. Spinning. Weaving. See **twist**.

soft water. Batik and Tie-dye. Water that has few mineral salts and is therefore preferred for **dyeing**. If rain water, unpolluted by the atmosphere, is available, it can be used. When only hard water is available, it can be softened by the addition of a water softener, such as **Calgon**. About ¼ teaspoonful to one pint water is sufficient.

softwood. Puppets. Toys. A porous, sometimes opengrained, nonresistant wood that can be easily carved or worked. The softest of these is **balsa wood**. Other softwoods are basswood, sugar pine, buckeye, butternut, poplar, **redwood**, and white pine. These are suitable for simple **woodcarving** and for **puppet head**s. In general, the softwoods are **light wood**s in color, whereas the **hardwood**s are dark; although there are exceptions to each. The term "softwood" does not relate to durability. Redwood, for example, is a soft wood to carve, but is an extremely durable wood. Resins, tannin, and aromatic oil function as preservatives in wood, making some softwoods very long-lasting. Softwoods cannot be polished to a high finish.

softwood. Woodworking. With **hardwood**, one of the two main classifications of wood. Softwoods come from conifer or evergreen trees (such as **cedar, fir, pine, redwood,** and **spruce**), which have narrow, resinous leaves. They are generally (but not always) soft, and light in weight and color. Because they are soft, they are easy to cut or carve and are commonly used for general carpentry, building construction, wood pulp, **woodcarving, whittling,** and furniture that is not destined for heavy use or that will be painted. Also see **wood**.

softwood plywood. Woodworking. See **plywood**.

solander case. Bookbinding. A closed bookcase with a removable top into which a book is placed from **tail** to **head**.

solder. Jewelry. Metalworking. An **alloy** used to join pieces of metal together in the process of **soldering**. Solder melts at a lower temperature than the **base metal**s being joined. It flows into the joint by the capillary action of the liquid being drawn to heated areas, and it bonds to the surface of the base metal. Solders are divided into two main groups: hard solder and soft solder. Individual solders are named according to the metal that is predominant in their composition or are given the name of the metal they are designed to join. Most metals may be soldered with solder made of the metal with which they are alloyed. Metals requiring solders mainly constituted of their own material are: platinum, gold, silver, **copper, brass, nickel, aluminum,** and **lead.**

Hard solder or **silver solder** is solder that melts at temperature above 1000° F and is used for joining iron and precious metals.

SOFT SOLDER (COMMON SOLDER)   **Tin** and **lead** alloys available in bars, solid wire, or **flux**-core wire with acid or rosin in the center, or soldering paste with flux in it. Soft solder is used for joining metals where high strength is not important, for repair work, and for joining metals with low melting points, such as **pewter,** tin, or lead. It is never used on precious metals such as gold and silver. The following are examples of the varieties of soft solder alloys: 70% tin with 30% lead, 63% tin with 37% lead, 60% tin with 40% lead, 50% tin with 50% lead (also called half-and-half, plumber's solder), Belmont 300 solder (which contains cadmium and melts at 300° F), and bismuth solder (which contains the element bismuth and melts at 241° F). The greater the amount of lead, the lower the melting point and the less strength the joint will have. When soldering joints right next to each other, choose a solder for the first seam with the highest melting point, then ones with lower melting points so as not to melt previously joined seams.

ANTIMONIAL TIN SOLDER   A high-tin solder made of 95% tin and 5% **antimony,** used for soldering objects where lead (in soft solder) would create a health hazard. It melts at 452° F and requires a corrosive flux made of zinc-ammonium chloride, stannous chloride, and free **hydrochloric acid.** Use this flux when soldering copper, copper alloys, low-alloy **steel,** and cast **iron.** Remove this flux when soldering is completed or it will corrode the metal.

SPELTER SOLDER   (Also called spelter, brazing solder, brazing alloy): A brass alloy in rod, lump, or powder form used as a solder when **braze welding.** It contains equal amounts of copper and **zinc** and small amounts of other metals according to the color and melting temperature desired. Nickel, lead, phosphorus, or tin may be added. Tin gives the compound a white color. Varieties used for braze welding include spelter bronze, white spelter solder, phoscopper, white brazing rod, yellow bronze, and copper. Each has a different color and melting point. An all-purpose alloy is yellow bronze spelter (it melts at between 1595° and 1625° F) for use on copper, brass, and **bronze.** Also see **soldering, Metalworking: Soldering, Welding.**

solder. Stained Glass. A bonding agent used in fixing or welding joints, used in soldering metals, including lead, tin, sheet metal, bronze, and copper. Solder is a mixture of metals known as an alloy. The solder mixture used in stained glass is 60% tin and 40% lead. The melting temperature of lead is 621° F, that of tin is 450°; in the 60 : 40 combination, the melting temperature is 390° F. The best form of solder is ⅛" solid wire solder. Do not use resin core solder. Also see **acid brush, copper foiling, fitting, floated solder seam, liquid solder, tinning** and **Stained Glass: Glazing, Tools and Materials.**

solder. Tincrafting. A metal alloy that, when melted, can be used to bond or join separate pieces of **tinplate.** It is sold as both hard and soft solder, but only soft solder is used in bonding tin, as it is a tin and lead alloy. By varying the proportions of tin to lead, the melting point of soft solder can be significantly varied. A 50/50 mixture has a melting point of 450° F, and a 60% tin alloy melts at 390° F. The 50/50 variety is the most common type, and can be purchased at almost any hardware store. An alloy of this type is known as a eutectic alloy because its melting point is lower than that of either of its components. Also see **Tincrafting: Joining the Tin.**

solder filing. Jewelry. When a fine solder is needed for a specialized technique, the **solder** can be filed. Make sure the solder has been cleaned first. Mix the fine solder filings with **flux** and deposit as the work is fluxed. This technique can be used with **mokumé, filigree,** and any other technique that may require subtle or delicate amounts of **soldering.**

soldering. Jewelry. Metalworking. The process of joining pieces of metal together by fusing **solder** to the **base metal.** The base metal itself is not melted or fused; instead, the melted solder **alloy** bonds to its surface and is held there by the attraction of the electrons in the atoms of each metal for the other.

There are two basic types of soldering: silver soldering, which uses **silver solder** or **hard solder;** and soft soldering, which uses soft solder or common solder. A third type of soldering, called sweat soldering, may be used with either hard or soft solder, and is used for making joints where the solder is invisible.

Soft soldering is a soldering process requiring relatively low heating temperatures, usually between 240° and 500° F, which is used where no mechanical strains will be put on the object; it is used for low-melting metals such as **pewter,** and for all alloys containing **tin** or **lead** in sizable quantities.

Sweat soldering is used to join broad, flat surfaces along the entire surface. The resulting **joint** is nearly invisible. Sweat soldering can be used on small pieces as in jewelrymaking. Also see **brazing, cotter pin, heating frame** and **Metalworking: Soldering.**

soldering. Tincrafting. The flowing in the presence of heat of a **solder** alloy between two separate pieces of **tinplate** to join the two pieces together. Also see **Tincrafting: Joining the Tin.**

soldering copper. Metalworking. An iron rod with a piece of **copper** on one end and a wooden handle on the other. The copper end is heated by a charcoal fire torch or by putting it into an oven, then used for **soldering.** The tools are usually sold in two pairs of coppers. One copper pair is lightweight for soldering light-**gauge** metals and the other is heavy for thicker-gauge metals. While one member of a pair is being used, the other is heating: in this way the soldering can be accomplished without interruption. The size is designated by the weight of the pair. For example, a two-pound copper is a pair, each one weighing one pound. See ill.

Soldering copper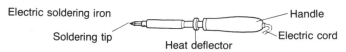

soldering copper foil. Stained Glass. See **copper foiling.**

soldering gun. Metalworking. See **soldering iron.**

soldering iron. Metalworking. An electrically heated metal tip mounted on a handle, used for **soldering.** It ranges in size from 25–550 watts and maintains a uniform heat. A variation on the soldering iron is the soldering pencil, which has removable and interchangeable tips. The soldering gun is also electrically heated but has a handle on a gunlike grip and a wire at its tip instead of a rod. It is often used in soldering smaller-**gauge** wires and sheets. When any of these soldering tools is used extensively, the point becomes covered with an **oxide** coating that keeps the heat from flowing to the metal to be soldered, and keeps the tool from picking up **solder** efficiently. The point must be cleaned with a file, and then tinned. See ill. Also see **tinning.**

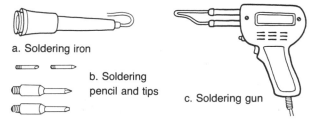

a. Soldering iron

b. Soldering pencil and tips

c. Soldering gun

soldering iron. Stained Glass. An essential tool for stained glass, available in good hardware stores. An electric 200-watt iron will give maximum efficiency, although a 100-watt iron will do. Soldering irons operate on 110 volts.

A soldering iron should be chosen with care. A cheap iron does not heat evenly, and soldering guns do not always work. Choose a soldering iron with a medium-sized tip, such as ⅜″, for good flexibility. The soldering iron should have a metal rest, iron mesh, or an **asbestos** pad it can lean on during **glazing** so that the table will not be burned. In England, gas soldering irons are often used because the heat is more easily controlled.

If the iron bit is badly pitted or very dirty and untinned, it can be filed smooth, first with a rough file and then with a fine one, and the end tinned. See ill. Also see **floated solder seam, lampshade construction, rosin, tinning** and **Stained Glass: Glazing, Tools and Materials.**

Electric soldering iron — Handle

Soldering tip — Electric cord

Heat deflector

soldering iron. Tincrafting. A copper-headed, long-shafted tool used in **soldering** to heat the joints to be soldered and to melt the **solder** to the point where it will easily flow between the two pieces of **tinplate.** A mechanical soldering iron must either be heated with a **propane torch** or over an open gas flame; an electric soldering iron heats up when it is plugged in. If a considerable amount of soldering is to be done with the nonelectric type, it helps to have several irons in the fire so that a hot one is always ready. Whatever the type, the tip of the iron must be filed or scraped down to the clean copper surface, coated with **flux,** and tinned with an even coating of solder before using. Also see **Tincrafting: Joining the Tin.**

soldering pad. Jewelry. See **asbestos pad.**

soldering pan. Jewelry. See **carborundum pan.**

soldering pencil. Metalworking. See **soldering iron.**

soldering point. Jewelry. A long, pointed tool used to pull **solder** along a **joint** or **seam** after the solder has begun to flow. Heat the soldering point and the metal in the flame of the **torch** at the same time to enhance **capillarity** and prevent freezing. A soldering point can also be used to press slightly warped sheet metal together during **sweat soldering.** Hold the soldering point as nearly parallel to the work as possible when pressing the metal together. If you use the sharp point and push down on the metal with it, it will cause a bad pit. Pressure from the soldering point should be used just prior to and during the actual flowing of the solder. Care must be taken not to press too far, too hard, or too quickly, or the metal will fracture.

File the soldering point to remove old solder which will adhere to the new surface. A **machinist's scriber,** a piece of iron coat wire about 12″ long that has had the paint removed with emery paper, or a piece of stainless steel rod of the same size can be sharpened for use as soldering points. Stainless steel soldering points can be purchased, but they are somewhat hard to find. They work best of all, because they are poor conductors of heat and even when the tip is red hot, the section you are holding remains a comfortable temperature. Also see **pick soldering.**

solder joint. Jewelry. See **joint.**

solder seam. Jewelry. See **joint.**

solder snippet. Jewelry. See **pallion.**

solid dye. Candlemaking. See **coloring.**

solid mesh. Crochet. See **space.**

sol lace. Lacemaking. (Also called sun lace.) The various types of sol laces are classified as **needle lace** and are similarly started and worked. Brazilian sol, Danish hedebo, Nanduti, and Spanish sol have their **motif**s sketched onto heavy linen or some sturdy fabric first. Then a **running stitch** is put through the cloth over the motif lines. (When the lace is finished, these running stitches are cut, releasing the **medallion.**) A structure of thread is then worked back and forth through the running stitch pattern in a spiral with a small **netting needle** or **shuttle,** and it is on this structure of threads that the lace is worked.

Brazilian sol lace is worked in knotted and **darning stitch**es. Danish hedebo lace is worked in **buttonhole stitch**es, in patterns of circles and pyramids. Nanduti is native to Paraguay, Mexico, and Central America. It uses darning stitches. Polka Spiderweb lace is very similar to Nanduti. Spanish sol lace is worked in knotted and darned stitches and **wheels**.

Estonian sun lace motifs are drawn on transparent paper and taped to cardboard. A row of back stitches is put through the outside line of the motif. On the thread structure that is then worked through these back stitches, decorative stitches are worked.

Tenerife lace motifs are worked over molds of metal, wood, or rubber. In this it differs from the other sol laces. Molds come in all sizes and shapes, such as round, square, and rectangular. The edges are scalloped or notched to hold a structure of threads. The lace is worked in knotted and buttonhole stitches. This lace was originally made on Tenerife Island, one of the Canary Islands. See ill.

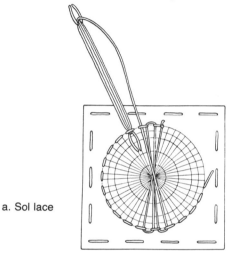

a. Sol lace

Solomon's knot. Macramé. See **square knot.**

solution dyeing. Dyeing. Dyeing the liquid that becomes a man-made fiber before this liquid is extruded through the spinnerettes. A commercial process, it gives man-made fibers colors that are bright, clear, and fast. Also see **fiber.**

solvent. Batik and Tie-dye. A fluid used to dissolve **wax** in the **batik** process. The most commonly used solvents for **removing wax** are **mineral spirits,** carbon tetrachloride, commercial **cleaning fluid,** benzine, gasoline, white gasoline, and **kerosene.** Care must always be taken in using any solvent; most are flammable and some are toxic.

solvent. Candlemaking. Benzene, carbon disulfide, chloroform, and turpentine all serve as wax solvents. Trichloroethane (vinyl trichloride) and Triasol (trichlorethylene and ethylene dichloride), are available through most hardware outlets and are recommended for removing any wax that has stuck to your candle molds.

solvent. Découpage. Papercrafts. A liquid used to dissolve another material. In découpage, turpentine is used to thin **varnish** as well as to clean varnish brushes; denatured alcohol is used to thin **shellac** and to clean shellac brushes. These are the standard solvents. When using other **sealers** or **finish**es, follow the directions on the can.

solvent. Metalworking. Woodworking. (Also called thinner.) Any of a variety of chemical agents used to thin finishes like **shellac, paints, lacquer,** or **varnish** so as to ease their application, or as a cleaning agent in removing dirt, grease, wax, or oil from wood surfaces or equipment.

Several solvents are commonly used in woodworking. Denatured alcohol is composed of hydroxides of organic radicals; it is used to reduce or thin shellac, liquid spirit **wood stains,** alcohol stains, and powdered aniline dye stains. Turpentine is a resinous substance that exudes from several varieties of coniferous trees and is distilled. It is used in woodworking to thin or reduce oil or enamel paints, linseed oil, varnish, varnish stains, oil stains, penetrating wood **sealers,** and most waxes. Lacquer thinner is a blended solvent composed of xylene, toluene, and other **hydrocarbons.** It is used in woodworking to thin or reduce brushed or sprayed lacquers, powdered stains, shellac, and liquid spirit stains. Benzene is a colorless, volatile, and very flammable liquid obtained from coal tar. It is used as a solvent for varnishes, paints, and enamels as well as to remove grease. Mineral spirits is a petroleum distillate used as a solvent for many paints. It is often called paint thinner.

solvent. Plastics. (Also called thinner.) A chemical that dissolves another substance. It is used for **cementing** certain kinds of plastics together and for cleaning tools soaked in **resin** or paint. Sometimes blended solvents such as methyl alcohol and **acetone** are more efficient than one solvent alone. Lacquer thinner is an example of a blended solvent used to thin **epoxy** and **urethane** resins. It is made of xylene, toluene, **methyl ethyl ketone** (MEK), **methyl isobutyl ketone** (MIBK), and **cellulose.**

Many solvents are highly flammable, cause skin irritations, or give off toxic fumes, as in the use of chlorinated **hydrocarbons** (benzene, toluene, **ethylene dichloride, methylene dichloride**). Less harmful solvents are ethyl alcohol, ether, and **acetone.** Do not clean plastics with a solvent unless you are sure it will not **craze** the surface.

solvent bonding. Plastics. See **cementing** and **Plastics: Cementing.**

solvent cementing. Plastics. See **Plastics: Cementing.**

sorting. Spinning. The process of dividing the **fleece** according to the quality or grade of the **wool.** This is determined by **crimp,** length, fineness, elasticity, strength, and luster. The best wool is found on the shoulders and sides of the sheep. It is medium long, soft, and strong. Wool from the hollow of the back, and slightly beyond, is rather coarse and long. Right around this area is wool of relatively good quality—long, strong, though coarse. Britch wool, which is found on the hind legs and tail, is stiff, straight, and very coarse. In the thigh area, the wool is short and weak. The amount of "best wool" depends on the breeding, feeding, and general living conditions of the sheep. When wool is sorted by an experienced hand, a quick touch can determine as many as twenty distinct grades in a fleece. A handspinner does not divide the wool so finely, but it is still essential to know where the grade division comes, since the coarse wool must be separated from the best wool. See ill.

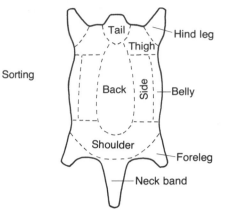

Sorting

soumak. Rugmaking. Weaving. A rug and **tapestry** technique in which **filling** threads are wrapped around **warp** threads in an over and back under manner and always going over more than they go under. It produces a raised, diagonal **herringbone** or **twill** effect. The appearance depends on the direction and the technique of **wrapping.** Herringbone is the one predominantly worked and is also referred to as an arrow, knitted, or chained effect. Besides these two pattern possibilities, there are pronounced or subtle surface textures depending on the thickness of the yarn or yarns involved in the **butterfly** used to make soumak and the number of **warp end**s gone over and under. A difference in the latter results in longer or shorter skips or **floats** left on the surface. This raised texture arises from the **plain weave** that is usually put after every row of soumak. It is firmly beaten so that it packs under the soumak and pushes it up from the background. There can be two or many rows of plain weave in-between every soumak row. At least one row is needed to bind down the soumak and prevent it from slipping around. When used solely for tapestry, this row is sometimes omitted. The plain weave is usually completely hidden by the soumak since it is woven in a finer yarn than the soumak.

Soumak is a very flexible technique—it can go across entire rows and cover the surface completely, as in traditional **Oriental rug**s; it can be in specific design areas or scattered at random; it can be put in around curves or contours and one version places it vertically. In traditional rugs, it changes color as often as a tapestry and the color changes, if done on a vertical, must be locked together or the filling ends darned in if they are left hanging on the back side of the piece. The complexity of design of the traditional rugs is, no doubt, the reason why soumak is often included under **tapestry weave**s. However, it has nothing to do with the structure of either a tapestry or **flatweave rug** (even though it is classified as part of the latter group) since the design is superimposed on the surface and could exist without the plain weave structure. Its inclusion in the flatweave groups is undoubtedly because it is closer in effect to this than to **pile rug**s.

The name "soumak" (for which there are many other spellings: soumakh, sumak, sumakh, summak, sumaq) originates from the name of a town, Shemakha, a Caucasian site, west of the Caspian Sea, which was once the capital of a region noted as a weaving center for soumak rugs, saddle covers, saddle and other bags, belts, and animal trappings. Although this is where the technique came to prominence in the nineteenth and twentieth centuries, it goes back much earlier to 2000 B.C.—a date attributed to its use by the Swiss lake dwellers.

Soumak can be done over and back under any number of warp ends. Traditionally, in the Caucasian work, the wrapping count was over four warp ends and back under two. However, with contemporary weavers, it is an arbitrary decision depending on the **sett** and how long a float is desired. The soumak pattern yarn can be the same as the plain weave background. In this case, a **stick shuttle** is used instead of a butterfly. If the soumak is a new pattern filling on a butterfly, it must be secured at the edge by looping around the **selvage** threads and later involving it into the next plain weave **shed,** or by darning it in once it is off the loom. If the **ground weave** and the pattern are the same yarn, weave the plain weave row from right to left. On a closed shed, take the pattern filling and count from the left four warp ends. Between the 4th and 5th ends, insert the filling front to back. Bring the filling back to the surface by inserting back to front two ends to the left between ends 2 and 3, holding the previous yarn up so that the yarn surfaces under the previous float. If the yarns were held down, the filling yarn coming up from the back would surface over the previous one. Surfacing over or under the previous float is what sets the direction of the diagonal slant. To go on with the soumak, count from where the filling surfaced another four warp ends, so that you will insert front to back between ends 6 and 7 and come back to the surface between ends 4 and 5. This counting and manner of insertion continues across the warp or design area (**a., b.**).

In traditional soumak, each float is pulled so that it is not lying loose, but not so tightly that the warp is distorted. However, many craftspeople today pull down on the floats so that they are hanging as a decorative feature of their **wall hanging**s.

Beat down on the row of soumak and weave a **pick** of plain weave going from right to left. Beat again, close the shed, and start the next row either on the right (if you have a separate pattern butterfly) or on the left (if the pattern and ground are the same). If it is started on the right because of the change in direction, the diagonal will slant in a different direction even though pulled under the previous float as in the row just completed. However, if the second row is started at the left and a different slant is desired (for example, to achieve the herringbone effect), then the filling yarn must go over the previous float.

The above version is also sometimes called Oriental soumak, no doubt because of its association with Oriental rugs. A characteristic is that it includes several warp ends in each wrapping. Single soumak is wrapped around one warp end and is more commonly known as **Swedish knot.** Greek soumak is also worked on one warp end but uses three wrappings before going on to the next end (**c.**). While the Oriental soumak forms a float and the Swedish knot a tight knot, the Greek soumak forms a knot cluster that gives a raised texture and spaces between the warp ends. With all of these three, there are variation possibilities.

They are all worked from the right, or top side, with the exception of the Swedish knot, which is worked from the wrong side. They all can be worked right to left, or left to right.

There is also a vertical soumak which can cover the entire surface of a fabric vertically, or form diagonal or straight lines running in a pattern up the fabric (**d.**). This is not exactly the same sort of wrapping as the traditional soumak, since under every float there are a certain number of picks of plain weave. The amount of the plain weave determines the length of the float. The pattern yarn wraps around two warp ends at every skip over the plain weave. This wrapping gives it the same diagonal slant as the filling-wise soumak and it can slant in either direction.

In embroidered rugs, the same effect is achieved by a stitch known as **knitting stitch,** stem stitch, or soumak stitch. See ill.

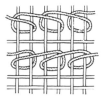

a. Open traditional soumak

b. Closed traditional soumak

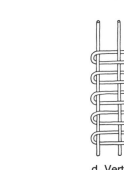

c. Greek soumak

d. Vertical soumak

soumak stitch. Rugmaking. Weaving. See **knitting stitch, soumak.**

sound toy. Toys. Any plaything designed primarily to produce noise or sound. The **rattle** is the most obvious example of a sound or noise toy. Among other common ones are the **whistle, bull-roarer, rattletrap, kazoo, ticktack, straw horn, crickets, buzz buttons, pipes,** and **drums.** Sometimes the term "sound toy" refers to any box, doll, or animal that contains a mechanical device to create sound; **musical toys** such as music boxes, **baby dolls** that cry, and "talking" animals may also be called sound toys. Also see **crow call.**

souring. Ceramics. Aging of clay to improve its **plasticity** and other qualities.

soutache. Macramé. A thin, ridged **cord** suitable for macramé knotting. Also see **Macramé: Tools and Materials.**

space. Crochet. The opening or hole that is an integral part of the crocheted mesh worked in a piece of **filet crochet.** Filet crochet is made up of two parts, usually called **solid mesh** and **open mesh.** Spaces are, obviously, found in the open mesh areas of the work.

space. Tatting. (Abbr. sp.) The distance between two **double stitch**es left by the **loop thread** on the **knot bearer,** which when pushed up becomes a **loop** forming a **picot.**

spaced warp. Weaving. See **sett.**

space marker. Leather. (Also called pounce wheel.) A tool with interchangeable revolving wheels of various sizes, with teeth to mark even, uniformly spaced marks (5, 6, or 7 stitches per inch), in preparation for hand sewing leather. Except with very lightweight leather, the holes may have to be further enlarged with an **awl and haft.** See ill. Also see **Leatherwork: Sewing Leather.**

Space marker

spackle. Papercrafts. Dry, powdered spackle, normally used for patching plaster and available from the hardware store, is mixed with water to the consistency of thick cream, then brushed over the completed, dry papier mâché surface to smooth out any roughness. When completely dry, the spackle is then sanded lightly with fine sandpaper.

spackle drawing. Toys. A process for decorating wood surfaces in which a spackle is used to make a linear pattern. A cake-decorating tube, pastry tube, or similar squeeze tube is filled with a vinyl spackle that is forced out in a thin line onto unpainted, painted, or paper-covered wood. Stains and paints can be added when the spackle has set.

spade bit. Woodworking. See **drill bit.**

spale. Basketry. A thin rib or strips of wood integrated into the weaving for strength. Also see **bye-stake.**

spall. Stained Glass. A term used to refer to a chip on the edge of a piece of **glass.** Also see **dalle-de-verre.**

spalling. Ceramics. **Thermal shock** that causes deterioration of corners and faces of **refractory** bricks in the **kiln** due to sudden heating and cooling.

spalling. Jewelry. The breaking off of fragments of **investment** on the inner surfaces of the mold during casting. These fragments can ruin the work by becoming included in the metal. Some causes of spalling are: incomplete sealing of **seams** and **joints** in the **wax model;** extremely thin areas in the wax model or thin undercuts; and heating the investment too quickly during **burnouts.** Also see **centrifugal casting.**

spangle. Beadwork. See **sequins.**

spangle. Ceramics. See **specking.**

spangle. Lacemaking. The **bead**s attached to some kinds of **bobbin**s in **bobbin lace** are sometimes called spangles. They serve to give weight to the bobbin, to help pull the more delicate threads in place, to keep the bobbins from rolling on the **pillow** (which would tend to untwist the thread), and for decoration. Such a bobbin is referred to as "spangled."

Spanish eyelet. Weaving. See **Spanish lace.**

Spanish knot. Rugmaking. Weaving. See **knotted pile.**

Spanish lace. Weaving. (Also called Spanish eyelet, Spanish openwork.) An **openwork technique** that creates spaces or eyelets by weaving over a fixed number of **warp ends** and having the **filling** pull these warp ends together into groups. The number of warp ends in a group is determined by the size and the shape of the pattern and the size of the yarn used. The width of the openings between groups is determined by how tightly the filling yarn is pulled. Spanish lace is similar to **slit tapestry,** with the exception that in Spanish lace, the filling yarn is continuous from **selvage** to selvage and appears in the openings as a diagonal line. There are no openings without this diagonal filling such as there are in a slit weave. Spanish lace can also be woven so that the filling does not pull in the groups; then a faint slit occurs with just a trace of the diagonal filling. The weaving directions can be changed within each group; the diagonals then run in opposite directions. Groups can be woven on top of each other or staggered in successive rows so that the eyelets are staggered. Variations in Spanish lace are more pronounced if the filling yarn is much thicker and softer than the warp. The course of the filling yarn through the warp groups then appears as a raised effect.

To weave Spanish lace, weave the last **pick** of a selvage-to-selvage **plain-weave shot** going from left to right. Open the next **shed** and pass the filling through right to left going under half the number of ends in a group (six are illustrated here). Bring the filling out and beat down with a **hand beater** or comb. Change sheds and return the filling left to right going under the other three warp ends in the group. Pull the filling so that the ends are drawn gently, but firmly, into a compressed group. Beat down. Change sheds and go under the original three warp ends and, if you do not want to make the eyelet higher before going on to the next group, then go under the next three ends. Pull the first group together as you come to the surface with the filling. Beat down. This procedure is repeated for all the groups; the filling runs from right, from left, and again from right before moving on to the next group. After finishing a row, the lace is then worked from the left with the filling going from left, from right, and from left before

Spanish lace with groups arranged directly above each other

going on to the next group. A **butterfly** of yarn is usually used, since it is easier to manipulate than a **shuttle,** between the small groups of warp ends. See ill. Also see **Peruvian weaving.**

Spanish mahogany. Woodworking. See **mahogany.**

Spanish openwork. Weaving. See **Spanish lace.**

Spanish sol lace. Lacemaking. See **sol lace.**

spar. Jet carving. **Inclusion**s of quartz between the layers of **jet.**

spar. Kites. The horizontal or transverse sticks on a kite **framework** (as in the **diamond kite**) or the cross-stick that supports the wings (as in the **Coyne kite**). Because kites depend on the same forces that propel sailing ships, nautical terms are often used by kitemakers. Also see **Kites: Construction.**

Sparex #2. Enameling. See **cleaning metal.**

Sparex #2. Jewelry. A dry, partially neutralized granular acid compound used to **pickle** metals. It does the work of sulfuric acid but is less caustic. Follow the directions on the can for mixing. It will not burn holes immediately in clothing if splashed, but holes will develop after several washings. Even though Sparex is less dangerous than sulfuric, nitric, or other acid pickles, it should be handled with the same care. Also see **electric pickler** and **Jewelry: Safety Precautions and First Aid.**

spar varnish. Candlemaking. A liquid that can be painted on a semiporous surface, such as a **ceramic mold,** to keep it from absorbing hot liquid wax.

spatula. Enameling. A tool used for applying **enamels** moistened with **binder** in the **wet inlay** technique. See ill. Also see **firing** and **Enameling: Basic Operations, Tools and Materials.**

Spatula

spatula. Mosaics. A flat, flexible-bladed implement of thin metal or rubber, somewhat similar in appearance to a wide but short-bladed **palette knife.** It is used in **mosaics** for **buttering** or spreading **bond** or **grout** onto the back of the **tessera** or the **backing** or between the individual bits of mosaic material. Also see **Mosaics: Tools and Materials, Setting the Material.**

spatula. Stained Glass. A flexible mixing tool with a flat metal blade, or a flat rubber paddle attached to a wooden stick. Also see **dalle-de-verre, lamination, staining** and **Stained Glass: Tools and Materials.**

spear blade. Woodworking. See **whittling tools.**

spear point chisel. Woodworking. See **wood-turning tools.**

spear-the-fish. Toys. A **game** made up in endless varia-tions, all of which involve a pin and a series of rings. A **string** attached to one end of the pin runs through the rings and is attached to the final one. The rings are tossed into the air and the object of the game is to spear or catch the rings on the pin.

This game was a popular **folk toy** throughout North and South America, and was known to Eskimos and Indians of pre-Columbian times. The skill involved in the manipula-tion of this toy was such that it not only intrigued children as a test of their skills, but was used for gambling among adults of various Indian tribes.

The Eskimos made this game of walrus ivory and used an ivory pin in a variation called "gazinta." It was "zimba" to the Iroquois, and "toss-and-catch" to the chil-dren of Ecuador, who used a version made of wood. The game is also known as hoop-and-pole, **ring-and-pin,** lover's game, pommawonga, and probably other names as well. See ill.

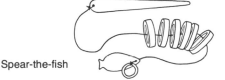

Spear-the-fish

special millwork. Woodworking. See **millwork.**

specific gravity. Gemcutting. The ratio of a material's weight to the weight of an equal volume of water—a mea-sure of relative density. Water at 4° C is the standard, with specific gravity of 1; heavier materials have higher specific gravities. This property is used for identification of gems.

A pycnometer is a small flask used with a scale to deter-mine a stone's specific gravity. Fill the pycnometer to the top with water, dry the outside, and weigh the filled flask. Then place the stone in the flask, which will displace its volume of water; remove any air bubbles clinging to the stone with a wire. Then reweigh the flask. The difference between the two weighings is the difference between the weight of the stone and an equal volume of water. Next dry the stone and weigh it. The weight of the stone divided by the difference between the previous two weighings pro-duces the specific gravity.

Another method of finding the specific gravity is to use indicators—chips of identified materials of known specific gravities, or especially weighted glass beads—along with dense solutions, liquids that are heavier than water, such as methylene iodine which has specific gravity of 3.31. The stone and indicators are floated on the dense solution, which is then gradually diluted with benzene. One by one, the indicators will sink as the solution becomes less dense; an indicator that sinks at the same time as the stone will have the same specific gravity.

specking. Ceramics. (Also called spangle.) Dark specks caused by coarse **iron oxide** particles in clay bodies and **glazes.**

speckling. Bookbinding. See **edge coloring, jaspering.**

speckling stitch. Crewel. Embroidery. See **seed stitch.**

spectrum. An arrangement of the **hues** of visible light in order of wavelength. A prism can disperse light and dis-play the color spectrum on a screen. The order of refracted colors displayed as a bar of colors from shortest wavelength to longest is: violet, indigo, blue, blue-green, green, yellow, gold, orange, red. Of course there are a great many more distinguishable spectral colors than those named. Diffraction gratings, very fine parallel lines scribed on a reflective surface, are also capable of produc-ing the dispersion of hues characteristic of prisms.

speed drill. Woodworking. See **drill bit.**

speed hook. Rugmaking. An implement used in making **hooked rug**s that is faster than either a **hand hook** or a **punch needle.** There are several varieties of speed hook, of which the shuttle hook is the most common and the most enduring, since other models come and go with the sea-sons. All models operate on the same principle: that of working from the back of the **rug backing** and pushing the yarn through to the front. It takes two hands to operate most models: one hand is used to steady and to guide, and the other is used to act as the pushing force in getting the yarn through. Only the shuttle hook has interchangeable gauges and needles. The speed comes from the action of the speed hook, in that the tool "walks" across the back-ing. Speed hooks take some skill to operate well and to get the benefit of the speed, whereas the hand hook and punch needle require more time and patience than actual skill. The shuttle hook is operated by shifting its wooden sec-tions up and down. As the right section goes down, the needle in it plunges through the backing carrying the yarn through. The section is raised and the left section is low-ered to secure the yarn loop on the right side. The hook then gives a little skip to the next position and the motions are repeated. There is also an eggbeater type of hook with a handle that is turned to activate the needle. A frame is required with speed hooks in order to steady and hold the fabric taut. See ill.

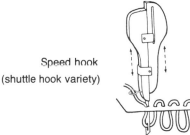

Speed hook
(shuttle hook variety)

speed wheel. Spinning. See **spinning head.**

spelter. Metalworking. See **solder.**

spelter solder. Jewelry. (Also called brazing solder, bronze solder.) **Solder** that has melting points of 1300–2050° F. It is basically a form of brass in that it is copper and zinc in varying proportions, producing a range of colors. Spelters are used in much the same way as **silver solder,** but the advantage is their range of color when sol-dering copper, brass, or bronze. When purchasing a spelter solder, check to see which **flux** to use with it. Care must be taken not to overheat the spelter, as the zinc burns out and leaves pitting along the **seam.** Also see **soldering.**

spelter solder. Metalworking. See **solder.**

spermaceti. Candlemaking. While advocates of **beeswax** will deny it, spermaceti is considered by many to be the finest candle material ever discovered. Unlike a candle of beeswax, a spermaceti candle burns brighter and never drips. A spermaceti candle was used to set the standard to define **candlepower.** Spermaceti is a fatty substance found only in the heads of whales; today, because of the protection and scarcity of whales, its supply is extremely limited.

spessartite. Gemcutting. See **garnet.**

spey blade. Woodworking. See **whittling tools.**

sphalerite. Gemcutting. A gem **faceting** material with **hardness** of 3¾, **specific gravity** of 4 to 4.1, refractive index of 2.369, and marked **cleavage.** Sphalerite is soft; it occurs in yellow-brown or red varieties. It is cut on a 320 grit silicon carbide **grinding wheel** or a stationary 200 grit diamond **lap. Polishing** is done with red rouge and tripoli and 10% graphite on a tin lap. Also see **faceting, polishing, refraction.**

sphene. Gemcutting. Calcium and titanium silicate **crystallized** in the monoclinic system with **hardness** of 5½, **specific gravity** of 3.4, and refractive indices of 1.90−2.02. It occurs opaque to transparent brown, yellow, red, and green varieties with some dichroism. Recommended **faceting** angles for crown and pavillion are 30 and 40°, respectively. Facets are polished on a tin **lap** with tin oxide. Also see **polishing, refraction.**

sphere. Gemcutting. Gem material has long been cut into perfectly round shapes. Chinese lapidaries cut small **quartz** spheres to be carried in the hand to cool the palms. Crystal quartz spheres were used as burning lenses as well as for foretelling the future.

The material is cut to a cube on the **slabbing saw.** Then the corners are rounded by grinding. The rough sphere is made circular on the sphere-cutting tool.

The sphere-cutting tool is made from a piece of iron pipe mounted on the shaft of either a vertical or horizontal running motor; a second piece of iron pipe is used to hold the sphere in position by hand while it is rotated. Silicon carbide **abrasive** is put onto rags or paper in the ends of the pipes progressing from 100−600 grits. The sphere is turned as it rotates until the smooth shape is formed and all scratches are removed.

The sphere may be polished on a buffing wheel, or a piece of canvas or felt is tied over the ends of the pipes and the conventional slurry of tin or cerium oxide is used for **polishing.**

Before the grinding operation is completed, the sphere should be painted with a colored lacquer or varnish so that high spots and scratches show up easily.

The pipes used as sphere cups should be about ¾ of the diameter of the finished sphere. As the grinding wears down the pipes too, a sharp edge will develop which could cause injury; round it off with a file. Motor speeds are 750 rpm for a 2″ sphere and up to 1,725 rpm for smaller sizes. See ill. Also see **drilling jig, machinery.**

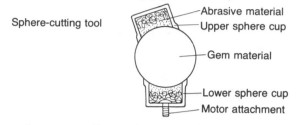

Sphere-cutting tool
— Abrasive material
— Upper sphere cup
— Gem material
— Lower sphere cup
— Motor attachment

sphere cup. Gemcutting. See **sphere.**

sphere jig. Gemcutting. See **drilling jig.**

Spice Pink. Quilts. See **flower designs.**

spider's web. Crewel. Embroidery. A circular **detached** stitch that can be worked in a variety of ways. Lay an uneven number of foundation spokes (**a.**). To secure the center threads, slide the neddle under all the threads, loop the thread over the needle, draw through, and pull upward (**b.**). To fill in the web, begin in the center and work outward, using a **tapestry needle.** Slide the needle under 2 spokes, back over the last spoke, and then under the next 2 spokes, including the wrapped spoke. Continue working under 2 and back over 1 until all the spokes are covered (**c.**). For a woven effect, weave thread under and over each spoke around the circle until it is filled (**d.**). To make the raised variation, thread another blunt tapestry needle with a short thread of another color and pass it under the spokes of the web after the securing knot is formed. Lift the center of the web by the short thread (**e.**). Weave under and over the spokes with the original thread as in the woven variation. The completed web will be raised in the center. The finished web can be outlined with the **stem stitch** or left plain. See ill.

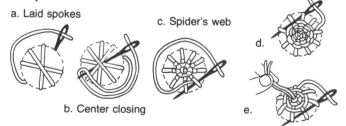

a. Laid spokes
c. Spider's web
d.
b. Center closing
e.

Spider Web. Quilts. An **all-over geometric** pattern based on the **Maltese Cross block,** as are **Kaleidoscope** and **Arkansas Traveler,** which it closely resembles. The arms of the Maltese Cross are made up of narrow crosswise bands of color. When the pieces are joined, these bands form a circular, spider web pattern.

The Spider Web is a name also applied to any **pieced block** that uses crosswise bands in the same manner, as in a star or flower form. Also see **Quilts: Quilting.**

spike. Woodworking. See **nail.**

spindle. Spinning. A device for twisting **fibers** together in order to make them into a continuous strand of **spun yarn.** Generally, it consists of a stick or shaft snugly fitted into a **whorl** or weight and can be made from just about anything. There is a notch at the top of the shaft to catch the spun yarn. The first spindle to be used by early man was no doubt a simple stick which he rotated along his thigh in order to twist the fibers. The yarn he spun, he wound around this stick. Later on, the whorl was added so that the spindle could be suspended and rotated quicker. This became known as the drop spindle. The earliest verified date of the use of the drop spindle was the nineteenth century B.C. (based on tomb paintings in Egypt). Other methods of spinning were also employed, such as twirling the spindle in a cup or gourd or on the ground where the spinner sat.

The hand spindle became mechanized in India and by the fourteenth century, the **spinning wheel** had supplanted the spindle in Europe. The spindle still exists on a spinning wheel, but it is now held by various attachments in a horizontal position and turned by a **driving band** running from the whorl, or pulley, to the large wheel. The spindle is now made of iron and, when improvements were made on the wheel so that spinning could be faster and easier, it was made hollow at one end in order to function in conjunction with the new improvements. In the faster spinning wheel, called a **treadle wheel,** the yarn only passes through the hollow passage on its way to the flyer and the bobbin where the yarn is wound. Both the flyer and the bobbin are supported by the **spindle shaft.**

There are many types and sizes of hand spindles in use today. The length of the shaft varies from a few inches to more than two feet with 9–12″ being the average length. They are all light and portable, and the yarn spun on a hand spindle can be as fine as any spun on a spinning wheel. See ill.

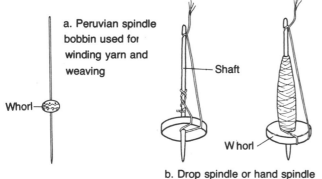

a. Peruvian spindle bobbin used for winding yarn and weaving

Whorl

Shaft

Whorl

b. Drop spindle or hand spindle

spindle. Weaving. The stationary shaft in a boat or **fly shuttle** on which the **bobbin** or **pirn** is placed. It is also another name for an early type of bobbin used as a **shuttle.** Also see **boat shuttle, flyer assembly.**

spindle pulley. Spinning. A small, round, grooved piece called a **whorl** on the **spindle shaft** of a **spinning wheel.** The **driving band** goes around it as well as around the **bobbin pulley.** A spindle pulley is found on both the **wool wheel** and the **treadle wheel,** while a bobbin pulley is found only on the treadle wheel. When the wheel is acti-

vated, the spindle pulley will turn the **flyer** on a treadle wheel or the **spindle** on a wool wheel. Also see **flyer assembly.**

spindle shaft. Spinning. A short stick upon which yarn is spun and wound. The term refers mainly to the **treadle wheel** where this stick, or shaft, is inserted through the **flyer, bobbin,** and **pulleys.** It has an **orifice,** or eye, at one end for the spun yarn to pass through. Also see **flyer assembly.**

spindle top. Toys. (Also called mountain top.) A type of **whip top** in which the string or whip is held in place by a handle. The handle is set temporarily into the top. The cord is pulled or whipped through an opening in the handle that is directly over the top. The **top,** sent into a spinning motion, drops away from the handle. An early museum example of this kind of top is one made of ivory in about 1850. The spindle top is usually made of wood and is **lathe-turned.**

spindle turning. Woodworking. See **wood turning** and **Woodworking: Wood Turning.**

spine. Bookbinding. (Also called backbone.) The part of the cover of a book which protects the **back** and on which the **titling** is done. The bound edge of the book.

spine. Kites. The rigid rod, **mast,** or center **spar** that constitutes the central axis of the kite. Also see **Kites: Construction.**

spine. Weaving. See **netting shuttle.**

spinel. Gemcutting. A mineral composed of magnesium aluminum oxides **crystal**lized in the isometric system with **hardness** of 8, **specific gravity** of 3.6, single refracting (isotropic) with a refractive index of 1.7. It is transparent with a vitreous **luster** and conchoidal **fracture.** It occurs clear and colored red (in several tints and shades), blue, yellow, and black due to inclusions of chrome and iron oxides. Crown **facets** are cut at 37°; pavillion mains at 42°. Spinel is polished with Linde A, chrome oxide or tripoli on lead or tin **laps.**

Synthetic spinel is available in a spectrum of colors; it is hard, brittle, and has a higher refractive index than natural spinel. A blue synthetic spinel closely resembles aquamarine, but it has a greater specific gravity; clear synthetic spinels are called synthetic **zircons** although they are different because they are isotropic. Also see **faceting, polishing, refraction.**

spines. Weaving. See **herringbone.**

spinner. Spinning. A person who spins yarn. It can refer to either a male or female, while a spinster is definitely a woman who spins yarn.

SPINNING

Spinning is an ancient craft of necessity—necessary to do if one was to have yarn or thread with which to weave, knit, crochet, sew, or do any number of other fiber crafts. When machines took over the spinning process, handspinning went into a state of decline, with only the odd **spinner** here and there still practicing the craft. Not until the 1960s did a revival on a great scale take place. Then began a renaissance that is still growing.

Today some people still spin out of necessity—because the type and quality of yarn they want is not commercially available—while others prefer to spin their own yarns so that the finished craft item is already being designed in the type of yarn that is spun. With some handspinners, it is a counteraction against machine-spun yarns with their sameness and sleek perfection. Most handspinners prefer a rough, irregular quality to their **handspun** yarns, although it is still the mark of a good craftsperson to be able to spin a fine, even yarn.

The origins of spinning are lost in the passing of time. However, it is assumed that people first spun with the hands alone, twisting the fiber strands between the fingers of one hand while the other drew out the fibers. Another method was to roll the fibers between thigh and palm with the other hand drawing out the strands. Both techniques are still used today in primitive cultures.

Yarn that is spun must be maintained that way and stored, and it was perhaps originally wound around a stick or stone. At some point, a long, thin stick was used for the twisting as well as to hold the finished yarn. When it was made to rotate, the hand spindle was born. The rotating was aided by the addition of a clay or stone **whorl** and it is the whorl that provides a clue as to the age of spinning. The spindles, being wood, disintegrated with time, but the whorls did not. There is some evidence that spinning was going on in Mesopotamia as early as 5000 B.C. More conclusive proof was obtained as a result of an unusual drought in Switzerland in 1853–54 when the water level of a lake in Zurich fell much below normal: A stone age civilization came to light that used spindle whorls and deer horn weaving tools that were used by the Swiss lake dwellers of about 3000 B.C. At later lake excavations, a spindle whorl with spindle was found with linen thread still attached to the spindle.

Spinning was not only developed among the Swiss lake dwellers, but appeared simultaneously in many parts of the ancient world. In cases where there is evidence, the yarn was always of incredible fineness, showing the extreme prowess of the ancient spinners. One example from the time of the Middle Kingdom in Egypt (2133–1991 B.C.) is a picture of women managing two drop spindles at the same time. To do this, they were obliged to balance themselves on stools and take off most of their clothes so that the fine threads would not get caught up on their garments. It seemed to be common to spin yarn so fine that cloth having 160 **warp** threads to the inch could be woven.

In all the areas where spinning developed it was through the use of the spindle, either with or without the whorl. In time another tool appeared that aided the spinning process and made it a mobile occupation: a stick or staff to which a bundle of the fiber to be spun was loosely bound. Called a **distaff,** it was either held in the left hand or stuck in the belt. Its origins are likewise shrouded in mystery. There is one portrayed on an ancient Greek vase of 560 B.C., and it was most likely known much before that time—perhaps even in an earlier Egyptian era.

In many parts of the world today the spindle and distaff are the accepted and only tools for handspinning. Often, a traveler in Greece, the Balkans, or Peru comes upon a spinster seated at some distance from her home or walking along a road using a spindle and distaff.

The spindle was for many ages the only apparatus for converting fiber into usable thread. It was, and still is, used with or without the whorl, although the whorl is accepted as a necessary part of the spindle as it gives uniformity and momentum to the rotation of the spindle while at the same time prolonging the rotation. In an effort to increase the speed and ease of spinning yarn, the spindle was taken out of the hand and mounted horizontally between two supports so that it could be rotated by a large wheel connected to the spindle by a **driving band.** The driving band rests on a pulley which takes the place of the whorl. The large difference in diameter between the pulley and the wheel makes for a fast rotating spindle produced by a slow, steady turning of the wheel. The spindle could thus be better controlled and turned at a faster and more uniform rate.

There can be no doubt that the **spinning wheel** evolved along the lines described above, but it is difficult to state the location of its first development, although many textile experts agree that this could have been India at some undetermined date. The Indian spinning wheel rests on the ground with the spinner sitting, crouching, or kneeling on the ground and driving the wheel by hand. With some modifications, this wheel is still used in India today. When this wheel was adopted by European spinners in the Middle Ages, it was raised upon leg supports so that the spinner could walk back and forth during the spinning process. This wheel became known as the "great wheel" or "walking wheel," and in time acquired many other names. One of its popular names today is **wool wheel.**

The hand-turned or hand-driven wheel had a feature that was time consuming and that broke the momentum of spinning—the stoppage of the spinning process so that the spun yarn could be wound onto the spindle. Improvements were made to eliminate this and a new wheel was developed with a **flyer assembly** that took care of the yarn winding and a **treadle** with which to steadily drive the wheel by foot. The flyer assembly was an idea of Leonardo da Vinci in the fifteenth century, but as far as is known no models or trials were made. This was left to Johann Jürgen, a German wood carver, who independently arrived at practically the same version of a flyer assembly as da Vinci's and put it to use in 1530. A foot treadle was added and the **treadle wheel** was completed. There are many variations and many different names. One notable version is the German wheel in which the flyer assembly is situated directly above the **driving wheel.**

Handspinning on either the treadle or wool wheel persisted for centuries as an important home industry. It was dealt a death blow during the last half of the eighteenth century when three inventions were perfected that completely revolutionized the craft of spinning. These inventions were James Hargreaves's spinning jenny (1764), Richard Arkwright's throstle machine (1769), and Samuel Crompton's mule spinner (1779). The spinning jenny enabled the spinning of a number of threads at once by having a belt turn multiple spindles. The throstle, or roll-drawing spinning machine, used a system of rollers to draw out the **sliver** into **roving** prior to spinning. In the mule spinner the spindles were set in a traveling frame to reduce the strain on the yarn produced by the roller spinning method. Arkwright's idea for even winding has a parallel in the flyer assembly that da Vinci devised 250 years earlier. Da Vinci had the **flyer** moving back and forth so that the thread was evenly wound onto the **bobbin** or spindle which remained horizontally stationary. Arkwright used a moving bobbin rather than the moving flyer and so produced a machine which spun hundreds of spools of yarn simultaneously. After that, many improvements were made in the details of spinning machinery but the general principles are those mentioned above. Modern machinery has made for a more rapid conversion from raw fiber to yarn. However, it has not surpassed the character and quality of the fine yarn produced by the early hand spinners using a drop spindle.

Handspinning, as a profession, died with the advent of modern spinning machinery. However, it was kept alive in mountain and rural areas the world over. In the United States, it persisted in varying degrees in the southern Appalachian Mountains, among the Indian tribes, and in isolated pockets here and there. When the current revival came about, there were spinners around who could pass their knowledge on and act as teachers. Today, spinning is popular on all types of equipment that fall under the general categories of spindle, wool wheel, and treadle wheel. Spinners have become ingenious at adapting or repairing foreign, relatively unknown, equipment. They spin for the craft for its own sake, or as a means of producing yarns for other fiber crafts.

PROCESSES   Spinning is the final process in a series of steps necessary to convert the raw fiber into thread. This process is a three-part operation involving: the drawing out or **drafting** of the fibers; the twisting of the fibers to form a continuous strand called **yarn** or **thread;** and the winding of the finished spun strand into a **yarn package.** However, prior to this, there are preparatory steps that have as their object the removal of small impurities and the alignment of the fibers so that the final product—the spun yarn—will be of the desired character and quality. With fibers that are comparatively short, alignment is necessary so that they lie in a position parallel and overlapping one another before adding the **twist** that will hold them together. The differences between various fibers have necessitated the development of special preparatory processes particular to specific fibers, and slightly different methods of handling them during spinning. The favorite fibers used for handspinning are the natural ones, with **wool** being the leading favorite, followed by **flax.** The unavailability of **cotton** and **silk** make them trail far behind.

Wool preparation

Of all the fibers wool, due to its rough nature and **crimp,** tends to cling together and is the easiest to spin. It is possible to buy **fleece** that is totally ready for spinning. However, there are a number of spinners who prefer to buy fleece at various untreated stages. For these spinners the following preparatory steps must be gone through: **teasing** or picking to clean the fibers; **carding** to further clean them, align them and prepare them into **rolag**s; **combing** to align long fibers as used in the spinning of **worsted.** For many spinners, these preparatory steps have yet an earlier stage—that of choosing the right fleece from a good breed of sheep. Some spinners raise their own sheep and are involved in even more preliminary steps such as breeding and shearing.

Among sheep breeders the **Merino sheep** stands out as producing the finest wool. This does not mean that only **merino wool** is spun, but that a grading system exists for all wool that puts merino at the top of the scale. As all sheep do not produce the same quality of wool, neither is the wool the same on all parts of a fleece from a given sheep.

Grading or **sorting** must follow the purchase of the fleece. The spinner goes over the fleece to separate the best wool from the not so desirable fibers, such as those found in britch wool. If the sorting is not done accurately, weak and short fibers will be mixed with strong and long ones, resulting in unevenness in spinning and difficulty in handling the finished yarn. Such yarn will have weak spots, will break under tension, and will have uneven tension in the yarn itself producing fabric and garments that will be distorted after washing. Dyeing will result in uneven and variegated colors if gray and black fibers are not separated from white ones.

The quality of a fiber is determined by the **staple** length, strength, diameter, texture, luster, and crimp. Besides being able to recognize these qualities, a spinner should be able to evaluate the conditions of the natural oil or **yolk** in a fleece—a mixture of **suint** and **lanolin,** the last being an important ingredient in spinning. If a fleece has passed a period of time since shearing in unventilated storage, the natural oil will have hardened and the fleece must be scoured. The natural oil facilitates wool spinning so that spinners prefer to spin "in the grease" with the original oil of the fiber still intact. If it has been removed by washing or scouring, then it should be replaced before spinning by sprinkling olive or mineral oil over it. The natural oil accounts for a considerable proportion of the weight of a fleece, and spinners will find the fleece noticeably lighter after scouring. Many knitters and weavers prefer to use the yarn in the grease when making the finished product as this gives them a built-in water repellent. A good example is the wool yarn used for the Irish Fisherman and Aran Isle sweaters. For any dyeing the yarn must be washed or the dyestuff will not penetrate the grease properly to adhere to the fiber.

The scouring, which can take place at any time from the purchase of the fleece to the completion of the item, should be done in soft water (or rainwater, if possible). The fiber, yarn, or cloth is immersed in a warm to mildly hot soapy bath. Either a commercial wool scouring agent or a mild detergent is used. The bath should be large enough so the wool can move freely and not be compressed. No rubbing or excessive agitation should take place as this will lead to **felting.** Only a gentle squeezing is needed to be sure the soapy water penetrates deeply to get all the dirt and grease out. Various procedures can follow, with some spinners preferring a second or even third soapy bath. However, with each successive bath or rinse, the water temperature must stay the same. When the water runs clear, the wool is lifted out and squeezed gently (or it can be run through the spin cycle of an automatic washer). After the excessive moisture is removed, the wool is air-dried.

After scouring and teasing, either carding or combing takes place, and wool fiber is in rolag or roving form, ready to spin. Only long wool fibers are combed, but just about all wool fibers are carded. Using either the rolags or the fiber arranged around a distaff, the spinner is now ready to use either the spindle or the wheel.

Flax preparation

Like wool, flax may be bought from a commercial supplier. Usually it is imported from a country where flax and **linen** are still important industries. When bought from a supplier the flax is sold either in prepared bundles called stricks or in **flax top**s—long, ribbonlike strips. If the tops have been cut into smaller pieces it is called cut flax.

If a spinner were to grow his or her own flax, it would require an attempt to raise tall plants in order to get the longest fiber possible. When the base of the stem begins to turn yellow, the flax is ready to be pulled up by the roots—a method of harvesting which preserves the full length of the fiber. It is tied up in bunches and set in the fields to dry. After drying, the flax undergoes rippling (during which the seeds are retained for the next year's planting), retting, breaking or grassing, scutching or swingling, and, hackling or heckling (also called hetcheling). It is now in two forms, line (long) and tow (short) and ready for spinning. How well all these preparations are carried out results in a good or bad quality of flax fiber. Today, all these steps are done by manufacturers.

The preparation of flax for spinning is long and arduous. **Dressing the distaff** calls for care and attention or the spinning will go badly, and the linen yarn will not be of a good quality. For the spinning of line fibers, the arrangement on the distaff is such that the long fibers can be pulled out of the flax bundle during spinning without tangling the remaining fibers on the distaff. A fan-shaped web of the flax from a strick is made on a cloth or apron in one's lap. The fibers are crisscrossed so that there is no fiber running straight down (as it was in the original strick bundle). The web is then taken from the lap, placed on a flat surface and transferred to the distaff. The distaff is placed with its point at the apex of the fan and then gently rolled from right to left with the web being wound around it—tighter at the top than at the bottom. A ribbon is crisscrossed around this cone of flax on the distaff to hold it in place. As the flax is used, the cone becomes smaller and the ribbon is adjusted and retied.

If the fiber has been bought as tops then it can be spun without the distaff by keeping the coil in one's lap, drawing it out much longer, and then spinning. Tow, or the short flax fibers, are first combed smooth, drawn out to a

length and then twisted into a narrow strand of roving to be laced in and out around the prongs of a **tow fork.** The roving is unlaced as needed. It can also be rolled up into a ball to hold in the lap while spinning.

Whether using a drop spindle or a flax wheel, the fiber is more easily handled when slightly damp, since then the fibers stick to each other. The necessary dampness can be attained by dipping the thumb and forefinger of the hand doing the drawing out into a small cup of water. On old wheels, there was a place for a container on the wheel or where a gourd could be hung. Another old-time practice was wiping the thumb on the lower lip to collect moisture. Today, the cup is usually placed on the bench where the spinner sits, or as an alternative to a cup, a wet sponge in a dish can be used. Wet spinning can result in either a fine or heavy yarn, but one that is—in either case—smooth and glossy. A dry spun yarn is rough and uneven.

Other fibers

Many spinners like to go on to challenges with other fibers after having been successful with wool and linen spinning. Usually this is in the realm of other animal fibers such as **alpaca, Angora, camel hair, cashmere,** and **llama.** However, cotton and silk can be experimented with as well as synthetic fibers, the hair of one's own dog, human hair or a mixture of fibers. **Vicuña** comes from an endangered species and is unobtainable. **Qiviut** and the musk ox are on the rise and in time may be purchasable but, at the moment, in the United States it is reserved for the use of the Eskimo.

The animal fibers other than wool from sheep are known as novelty fibers and can be bought from many wool suppliers cleaned, carded, and ready for spinning. If obtained in their natural state the cleaning and carding procedures follow as for wool. In spinning the shorter fibers follow wool methods and for the longer ones, worsted methods.

Angora is more easily obtainable as the rabbit fur than as the goat's hair. There are spinners who grow their own rabbits for the fur. The staple length varies from ½" in very young rabbits to 7−8". Plucking the fur is the best procedure to preserve fiber length, the best length and quality is obtained from 5−18 month-old rabbits. **Sorting** is necessary since the fur varies, as wool does in a fleece. It should be laid flat as it is neatly plucked and sorted, and if stored it should be put in airtight containers with tissue paper separating the layers and keeping them flat. Once treated this way it is spun uncarded following worsted methods. Since it is a light and delicate fur it requires careful handling in order to get the right amount of twist so that it remains strong while its softness is retained. With a spindle, the spindle is better rotated in a bowl rather than used as a drop spindle, since the fibers slide past so quickly. A finer thread can be spun if the angora is lightly teased and carded.

Long hair from dogs like the Samoyed are easy to spin into a lovely yarn, but even poodle clippings can be spun up. Fibers can be used alone or carded with wool. All qualities of yarn can be obtained, depending on the dog's hair used. The procedure follows the scouring, carding, and oiling as in the preparation of sheep's wool. If a long time elapses between combings or clippings, the hair should be stored in an airtight container in a cool place, and with a moth repellent added.

Cotton, when obtainable, is usually found in sliver form ready for machine spinning. This can be used by hand-spinners but, due to the "ginning" treatment to get the seeds out, the fibers are short and the springiness and life is reduced. The alternative is to separate the cotton hair from the seed by hand and then whip it up or "willow" it by beating the fiber mass with a flexible stick until it becomes a bundle of fluff. It can be carded also, but very fine cards are necessary. Spinning it takes quite a bit of practice and follows the method used for other short fibers in that drop spindles are best not used and the spindle should be rotated in a shallow bowl. On a wheel, the treadling and winding on are done slowly in order to accommodate a short drawing out and a firm twist. Synthetic fibers are usually spun in the same way.

Silk prepared for spinning is also a rarity. When it can be obtained, it is not in the **filament** state but in shorter lengths. These lengths, which should go through a **de-gumming** process, can be about 2 yards long. They are cut into shorter lengths of about 3½–4", carded or combed, and spun like worsted or wool on either a wheel or spindle.

Using a drop spindle

Spinning can range from being a simple operation in which only the fingers—without any other tools—twist the fibers, to the complexities of a **spinning stick,** a drop spindle, or a **spinning wheel.** One of the most popular tools today is a drop spindle, which can be homemade or bought at reasonable cost from a supplier. There are many suppliers as well as many different models, but all have the same basic design: a stick with a notch in one end and a removable whorl at the opposite end.

To begin spinning on a drop spindle, a piece of already spun, somewhat fuzzy yarn, about 3 feet long, is first tied to the spindle shaft just above the whorl. After tying it is then wrapped around the shaft, brought down and wrapped around the bottom knob of the whorl or the tip of the spindle sticking out below the whorl, and then taken up to the notch at the top of the shaft where it is hitched around the notch. This piece of yarn, called the **leader,** will serve as a starting strand. The spindle hangs down from it. At the other end the teased fibers or the tip of the rolag are spread out in a fanshape and wrapped over the leader. This is held in place with the left hand while the spinner reaches down with the right hand and gives the whorl a clockwise spin. The rotating action of the spindle twists the end of the leader and at the same time draws on and twists the unspun fibers held against it.

The fingers in drafting are held in such a way that only as many fibers are pulled and allowed to slip between the thumb and forefinger as are required for the thickness of the yarn to be spun. This is the work of the left hand while the right controls the twist in the following way: As soon as the right hand starts the spindle, it moves to a position just below the left hand, with the thumb and finger preventing the twist from running up into the unspun wool. The left hand moves upward and draws out more fibers and holds them, while the right hand releases the twist so it moves upward. This action, between the left hand drawing out and the right hand controlling the twist, is carried

on while the spindle is kept turning by the right hand periodically reaching down and giving the whorl another spin.

As spinning goes on the spun yarn gets longer and the spindle glides down away from the hands. When it just about reaches the floor, the spindle is picked up, the hitch at the notch removed, and the yarn wound around the shaft. The hitch is then restored and spinning resumes.

Drop spindle spinning can be done while sitting, standing, or walking. The unspun fibers are either in rolags, tied to a distaff, or held together as a loose mass in the left hand. There are of course many personal variations in spinning styles that develop as the spinner gains expertise.

There are also other methods of spinning with a spindle and whorl arrangement. One of these involves spinning in a shallow bowl or saucer. This method is used by some of the Indians of Central and South America, who rest the tip of their small spindles in bowls or gourds while twirling them within the bowl or gourd. The yarns spun are quite fine and the technique works well with yarns that cannot support the weight of a falling spindle and whorl. **Navajo spinning** sometimes uses a small cup to rest the bottom point of the spindle which is rotated against the right thigh.

Using a wool wheel

Spinning on a spinning wheel is practically identical to the spindle process except that now the spindle is held by supports in a horizontal position, and the turning of the spindle is achieved by a driving band running from a large or drive wheel to the spindle. On a wool wheel the supports are called **maiden**s and are part of larger structures called **spinning head**s, which can accelerate the speed and make for smoother spinning. The whorl has become a pulley for the driving band to rest on, and the drive wheel is revolved by the right hand pushing on the wheel's spokes. The wheel can also be revolved by a **wheel finger,** which allows the spinner to step away further from the wheel and still propel it comfortably.

The drafting (left) hand performs all the actions which are to draw out the rolag, control the twist, and keep the wool twisting over the spindle tip while moving away from the tip (straight out to the side) with the rolag.

For spinning, a leader is used that is wound around the spindle in a spiral coil. The rolag fibers are attached to the leader with a slight twist and held together with the left hand while the right hand revolves the wheel clockwise. As the drafting hand moves gradually away from the spindle, the length of spun yarn gets longer. When it is about 20–22" long, the wheel-turning is reversed just enough to unwind the spiral and is then turned clockwise again to wind the spun yarn onto the spindle. The spun yarn is now held in front of the spindle and is wound on from the pulley outward in a cone shape. Enough leader is left to repeat the operation. In order to maintain an even twist throughout the yarn, the length of yarn spun each time and the number of turns of the drive wheel during the spinning of one length should remain constant.

Using a treadle wheel

On a treadle wheel the spindle has become a **spindle shaft** and part of the flyer assembly. The drive wheel is turned by the spinner's right foot operating a **treadle.** The tension of the driving band regulated by the **tension screw** becomes quite important, as this affects the amount of twist in the spun yarn as well as the speed with which the yarn is drawn through the **orifice** and onto the **bobbin**. The driving band is continuous and doubled so it simultaneously works the **spindle pulley** and the **bobbin pulley.** The latter is of smaller diameter than the former so that it revolves faster, enabling the yarn to be wound upon the bobbin at the same time as it is twisted and drawn.

During spinning the fibers are in both hands with the right hand controlling the drafting and the left the twist—although these hand positions may be reversed if the spinner desires.

A leader is attached to the back of the bobbin, passed over the first **guide hook** on the tip of the **flyer,** then over all the other guide hooks and through the orifice of the spindle. A rolag is spread out at one end and joined by twisting to the leader. This connecting point is held with the left hand and treadling begins slowly. The yarn will move at once toward the orifice so that the right hand must immediately begin drawing out more fibers from the rolag. The left hand releases the twist and moves backward toward the right hand. The hold is re-established and the left hand acts as a brake on the new length of fibers until the twist reaches the fingers, at which time the left hand moves again toward the orifice. The procedure is repeated while the treadling goes on continuously until the rolag is finished. At that time, the yarn is moved to the next guide hook, a new rolag picked up, and spinning resumed.

WOOLEN AND WORSTED SPINNING   The drop spindle was and is used to spin both wool and flax. The wool wheel was closely associated with wool spinning in colonial times, but if a distaff was added it could be used for flax. On the treadle wheel, wool, flax, and other fibers can be spun. Although the type of spinning equipment can make spinning faster, it is the length of the fiber that determines how it is done.

In woolen spinning, the fibers (whether they be sheep's wool or otherwise) are short and must first be carded into a rolag construction (a roll of evenly spaced fibers with air at the hollow center). The rolag is attenuated and twisted but the tubelike construction is kept so that at the point of inserting twist, the fibers are at right angles to the length of the rolag. The draw is short to avoid pulling apart the short-fibered rolag. A yarn spun on the woolen system is soft and hairy, since the fibers are not lying smoothly and parallel to each other within the twisted strand. If a treadle wheel is used that has two grooves on the spindle pulley, the warp or deeper groove is used to give the shorter fibers a firmer twist.

Worsted spinning and its related process, combing, are designed to insure that long fibers lie parallel as the twist runs in. This gives a smooth yarn, firmer and not as hairy as a woolen spun yarn. A long draft is used, and only enough twist is put in to hold the fibers together. The right hand does most of the drawing out with a slightly sidewise motion while the left does the rest by drawing away from the right so that the fibers are spread out, fanlike, across the left forefinger. The right strokes upward smoothing the fibers as the twist runs in. This means that in worsted spinning on a treadle wheel, the hands change positions so that the right hand is closest to the orifice and the left is in a back position holding the fibers. For a long, loose twist the tension is tightened to wind the yarn onto the bobbin faster. The weft or shallower groove on a spindle pulley is used to form the least twist.

FLAX SPINNING   The degree of success attained in spinning flax is measured by how well the distaff or roving has been prepared. The spinner should be able to easily draw out just enough fibers to make the yarn. Only the twist necessary to hold the fibers together is allowed to run into them. As this twist is about to run into the fibers they are smoothed toward the distaff or roving.

In using a drop spindle, the left hand remains stationary holding the fibers and opening and closing the forefinger and thumb to release or restrain the flow of fibers, and preventing the twist from running into the fiber mass. At the same time the right hand moves up and down—down when drawing the fibers, up when smoothing the yarn. The finger and thumb of the right hand are kept moist. This hand must also keep the spindle rotating.

On a treadle wheel with a distaff, the distaff is placed to the left and slightly in front of the orifice. The water source for keeping the fingers moist should be near the orifice. The left hand starts and with wet finger and thumb draws down with a slight twist of a few fibers from those hanging lowest on the distaff. These are twisted around the leader and treadling begins very slowly. The left hand controls the drawing out while the right smooths toward the distaff. The right hand takes over from the left to draw out when the left has to be dampened. The distaff is revolved so that the fibers are drawn down evenly around the whole cone of flax. A perfect linen yarn spun from line is very smooth and very even with only enough twist to give the necessary strength. Line is spun for use as warp or weft and tow for weft.

In spinning tow on a treadle wheel, the procedure followed is like that for worsted spinning. The right hand does the drawing out from the tow roving, which is held in the lap as a wound ball, or interlaced around a tow fork. The twist is a loose one as the right hand draws out and smooths the fibers back toward the roving.

SKEINING   After a period of spinning the spindle or **bobbin** reaches its full load of yarn and must be emptied for spinning to continue. When this stage is reached a process called skeining or reeling takes place. This empties the spindle or bobbin of its yarn, leaving only enough for a leader, and at the same time measures it. The emptying is from spindle or bobbin onto a **reel** or **swift** and the yarn is now in **skein** or hank form ready for scouring, **dyeing** or winding into balls of yarn, bobbins for **shuttle**s, etc.

The early stick reels measured one yard with each turn around the reel. Improvements for ease and speed resulted in the cross reel or niddy noddy that reeled off 2-yard lengths in each turn. After 80 yards, a knot was made and after 80 knots a skein of 560 yards was taken off. Clock reels or click reels made the counting easier as well as the skeining. Simple reeling tools such as a stick reel or niddy noddy can be made at home or bought from a yarn supplier. The more elaborate equipment usually is obtained at antique shops or auctions. Swifts are easier to find than standing reels but are not as easily used for reeling as true reels. The normal route is to make the skein of a determined length as accurately as possible on a reel and then put it on a swift or skein winder to be wound off into smaller or more compact forms.

When the reeling of a skein is completed the beginning and end of the yarn are tied together with a firm knot and the skein is tied here as well as in two or more other places with a contrasting yarn. These ties are all loose ones and the skein is now ready for scouring or dyeing. If it is to be stored, it is twisted into a compact bundle by slipping the hands inside it, stretching the skein, twisting it, and then slipping one loop from the right hand through the other loop on the left.

YARNS AND THEIR DESIGN   Yarns can be spun in a variety of textures and thicknesses on either the spindle or wheel. One of the most common practices is **plying,** which makes a yarn heavier, either for strength or texture. Plying entails taking two strands of a singles yarn and twisting them into one. This can be extended so that three, four, or more strands can be combined into one. They are known as 2-**ply,** 3-ply, 4-ply, etc., yarns.

Usually a single yarn is spun in a Z-twist. The most common plying is to take two Z-twists and spin them into an S-twist or the opposite direction from which they were originally spun. However, two Z-twists can also be plied in a Z-twist to make a very hard yarn, or a Z-twist and S-twist can be combined together in a Z-twist. Plying can be done with a loose or tight twist. A thin yarn can be plied with a thick one, different colors can be plied together, or the plying can be done unevenly in order to obtain interesting texture effects.

On a drop spindle, plying is done by taking two **cone**s or **spool**s of the previously spun singles and tying the two ends of the singles to a leader of an S-twist. The two singles pass through the fingers of the left hand with each one located on either side of the middle finger. The spindle is rotated counterclockwise and spinning proceeds as normal.

On a treadle wheel either spools or extra bobbins are used and the singles from these are tied to the leader and passed between the fingers of the left hand. Plying commences by treadling very regularly and quickly. For an S-twist the wheel is turned opposite to what it was during spinning.

Using either the spindle or wheel the yarn should be passing through the fingers freely and at the same rate. To do this the spools, cones, or bobbins must be on a **spool rack** or something approximating one so that the yarns feed off their source easily and without tangling.

Novelty yarns that are handspun fall most commonly into the slub and flake category. A slub yarn is controlled in the drafting so that thick unspun areas alternate with finer, tightly twisted spaces. Slub yarns can be plied for

even greater variety and interest in texture. Flake yarns have a small amount of unspun fiber—usually in a contrasting color—inserted into the yarn as it is being drawn out, having the twist hold them in place.

Other types of novelty yarns obtainable through handspinning are a spiral, controlled in the plying; bouclé, controlled in both the amount of twist given initially to the singles, and in the manner of plying; and nub yarns, in which small bits of contrasting color or fiber are inserted as the yarn is being plied.

Yarn design can be planned and begun as early as the teasing, carding, or combing. The key is to control the process in order to obtain the desired yarn, although the reverse system works too, in that through experimentation and accident a handspinner discovers a unique type of yarn design.

Although there are many fiber craftspeople who are handspinners, there are also those who prefer to buy machine-spun yarns. Through the years there have been many developments in spinning machinery in order to approximate a number of the yarn effects achieved by handspinners. There are other novelty yarns that are best left to the machine since their construction depends on intricate equipment. Whether machine or handspun, there are some yarn characteristics basic to both processes but more identifiable with machine-spun yarns. One of these characteristics is **yarn count,** which is a system of measuring the thickness of a yarn and the relative number of yards per pound. This is much more uniform and precise with machine-spun yarn by virtue of the spinning being done with a hundred or more spindles in operation at the same time and controlled by a single apparatus, as opposed to a handspinner doing one spindleful at a time and perhaps being affected by moods, time of day, and other variables. As much as the handspinner may opt for perfection, he or she is much more open to disturbances than a machine. When craftspeople buy machine-spun yarn they have every reason to believe that they will get the right thickness of yarn when a certain count or size is specified, and that they will then be able to calculate costs based on the yards-per-pound of a given size.

The fiber components of a yarn are known to a handspinner since he or she has spun that yarn from its fiber source. However, machine-spun yarns are often composed of many blends that blend natural fibers together, man-made fibers together, or a combination of both. If the blend is not stated on the yarn package, then **burning test**s can be performed by the craftsperson to help identify the fibers.

Often the fiber may be known to a purchaser, but its quality remains unknown. Names such as **virgin wool, rug yarn,** and **mercerize**d cotton help to identify particular qualities. There are others that pertain to specific natural or man-made fibers.

spinning. Metalworking. See **metal spinning.**

spinning head. Spinning. A device for holding the **spindle** in a horizontal position on a **wool wheel.** There are many of these devices. One simple method consists of two upright posts which hold the spindle by rawhide, string loops, or braided corn husk loops. This is an early type of support that was common in the Midwest, where it can still be found on antique wheels (**a.**). A flat piece of wood in the shape of a paddle, where the loops holding the spindle are pulled through the paddle, is called a bat head (**b.**). This was found mainly in eastern Canada as well as the eastern United States. In 1802, Amos Miner of Marcellus, New York, patented a head composed of two wheels—a small, or Miner's, wheel mounted over a yet smaller wheel into which the spindle was set (**c.**). The **driving band** is connected from the **driving wheel** to the Miner's wheel. Another short driving band connected the two small wheels. The driving band turns the Miner's wheel, which turns the small wheel and spindle. The added speed given by the extra wheel and belt prompted this to be called a speed wheel. They were common in the New England area, but they did not seem to have penetrated into the Midwestern states. See ill.

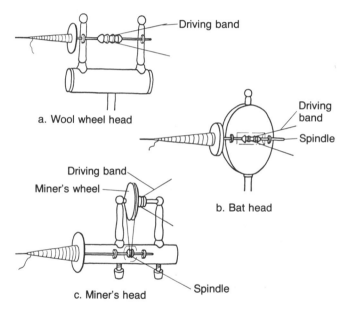

a. Wool wheel head

b. Bat head

Driving band
Miner's wheel
c. Miner's head
Spindle

spinning jenny. Spinning. See **Spinning.**

spinning-star wheel. Toys. See **pinwheel.**

spinning top. Toys. See **spin top.**

spinning wheel. Spinning. A stand with a large wheel and other attachments used to spin **fiber** into **yarn** speedily. The spinning wheel developed when a **hand spindle,** a much slower spinning implement, was mechanized. It is thought this occurred during the Middle Ages in India to benefit the huge cotton complex. The spindle, which was rotated by hand in a vertical position, was placed horizontally between two supports and rotated by a large wheel with a continuous cord going around it which connected the wheel and the spindle. The **whorl** of the hand spindle became the pulley for the cord to go over. All this was put on a stand with the spindle at one end and the wheel at the other. If the first spinning wheel was of the type now found in India, the stand was just barely off the ground and the

spinner had to kneel or sit on the ground. When the spinning wheel reached Europe, it was raised off the ground and put on legs, so that the spinner could sit in what to Westerners was a more comfortable position. The Indian spinning wheel may have entered Europe through Holland, a great textile center in medieval times. From there it could have conceivably gone to England, where the first authentic record of the use of spinning wheels dates from the fourteenth century. This first wheel became known as the "great" wheel, among other names. Today, it still is known by many names; **wool wheel** is one of the more popular ones. It is operated by turning the large **drive wheel** with the right hand, while the left hand draws out the loose fiber to be spun. Although control over the spindle was greater than a hand spindle, and it could be turned at a more uniform rate, the momentum was broken every time a length of yarn was spun, for at that point spinning had to stop and the yarn had to be wound on to the spindle. During the sixteenth century, improvements were made on the great wheel. A foot **treadle** was attached to the wheel by means of a connecting rod. This revolved the spindle at great speed and left both hands free to draw out the fibers. An automatic winding bobbin, called a **flyer assembly,** was another addition. Now a spinner could draw out, twist, and wind in one operation and without interruption. The next improvements on the spinning wheel occurred in the mid-eighteenth century, when it was converted to a machine capable of turning multiple spindles at a very fast speed, and was powered by a source other than a spinner. Handspinning died as a profession and only in isolated cases, as among the Navajos and the mountain folk in the Appalachians, was it still practiced. Not until the 1960s did it begin to emerge as a popular craft and both types of wheels, as well as the hand spindle, found acceptance.

As well as having many names, there are also many styles of spinning wheels. Both names and styles often reflect the country of origin. The styles usually fall into either the wool wheel group (those operated by hand turning the wheel), or the **treadle wheel** group (those having a foot treadle and a flyer assembly). The main part of the wheel is still the spindle with the rest of the parts serving only to rotate the spindle or guide the fibers. Sometimes a **distaff** is attached to the treadle wheel so that the fiber source is close at hand. Also see **Spinning.**

spinster. Spinning. See **spinner.**

spin top. Toys. (Also called spinning top.) A top spun by hand as contrasted to a **spring top** or **whip top,** which are activated by a string action or string. The spin top may have been derived from the primitive spindle whorl used in spinning. Both the Greeks and Romans had spin tops and spin tops were familiar to children in medieval times. See ill.

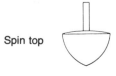

Spin top

spin turning. Woodworking. See **wood turning.**

spiral banding. China and Glass Painting. See **banding.**

spiral binding. Batik and Tie-dye. A fabric **binding** method that produces a partial **resist** in **tie-dye.** The strings are **tied** on in a spiral pattern, either single or double. Spiral binding is sometimes called open binding. See ill. Also see **crisscross binding** and **Batik and Tie-dye: Basic Procedures for Tie-dye.**

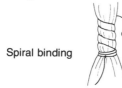

Spiral binding

spiral folding. Batik and Tie-dye. A **folding** method in which **fabric** is wrapped onto a stick or similar object in such a way that the edge of the material makes a spiral pattern. When the spirally wrapped fabric is tied with **line binding** or **band tying, chevron** or **zigzag pattern**s emerge in the tie-dyed fabric. See ill.

Spiral folding

spiral ribbing. Knitting. A **ribbed pattern,** worked on three or more **double pointed needles** or on **circular needle**s. A spiral rib is achieved by moving one stitch to the right every sixth row. There are many variations of this pattern. Also see **Knitting: Construction.**

spiral yarn. Spinning. Weaving. See **novelty yarn.**

spirit level. Woodworking. See **squaring tools.**

spitball. Toys. A chewed piece of paper that is rolled while moist into the form of a small **ball.** Spitballs or spitwads are the delight of many children and are sometimes used in **peashooter**s and **blowpipes.** Also see **pith ball.**

splash pan. Jewelry. A low metal pan placed in the base of a **polishing hood** and filled with water to catch the dust and debris created during **buffing.**

splice. Leather. When **lacing,** it is often necessary to splice two pieces of lace together as it runs out, to avoid using cumbersome lengths. Split the ends of the two pieces of lace to be joined with a **skiving knife**—one on the grain side, and the other on the flesh side, from about ¾″ from each end. Coat both skived ends with rubber cement. Let dry, overlap the ends so they form one length of a thickness equal to the rest of the lace. Press the ends together and tap with a **mallet.**

splicing. Knitting. A method of joining the initial end of a new ball of yarn to the yarn at the end of the ball or skein

of knitting in use. In a plied yarn, cut away about 5″ from half the plies in both the old and new yarns. Overlap the 5″ ends of both yarns and continue the knitting, knitting the joined ends into the fabric. Also see **joining, ply.**

splicing. Macramé. (Also called joining.) A method of adding new **cord**s to the work. Insert the new cord as a **holding cord** when working a row of **double half hitch**es. Work several double half hitches over both holding cords, pull the short end to the back of the work and continue working (**a.**). To splice within a **square knot,** overlap the new cord in the center of the knot. Tie several square knots over the three cords, pull the old cord to the back of the work and continue working (**b.**). See ill.

a. Splicing with double half hitches

b. Splicing within square knot

splicing. Rugmaking. Weaving. See **piecing.**

splicing threads. See **tie off ends.**

spline joint. Woodworking. See **joint.**

splint. Basketry. (Also called split.) A long thin strip of wood skillfully split or cut from white **oak** or a similar sapling, used for laundry or hunting baskets and for chair seating. Also see **Basketry: Plaited Basket Construction.**

splintery fracture. Gemcutting. See **fracture.**

split. Basketry. See **splint.**

split. Leather. (Also called deep buff.) A layer from the flesh side of leather which is split off from the hair side, or **top grain,** for **tanning.** The split, which has a nap but no grain and is not as strong as top grain, is usually processed to make **suede,** is embossed, or lacquered. Also see **crocking, doeskin, splitting** and **Leatherwork.**

split. Woodworking. See **wood.**

split board. Bookbinding. A cover **board** constructed of two sheets of binder's or other board glued together except for a 2″ space that runs the length of the board along the edge. Into this slit the **slips** (or **tapes** and **super**) overlapping from the back edge of the binding are inserted and glued, attaching the boards to the body of the book. After they are attached they may be covered with **cloth** or quarter-, half-, or fully bound in **leather.**

split four-patch. Quilts. The basic **four-patch** in which any of the squares have been split diagonally into triangles. This block is the basis of endless **geometric** quilt designs. When any square is split into triangles, a **seam allowance** must be made. Also see **Quilts: Marking and Cutting.**

split nine-patch. Quilts. The basic **nine-patch** in which any of the squares have been split diagonally into triangles. The split nine-patch is the basis for literally hundreds of **geometric** quilt designs. When any square is split into triangles, a **seam allowance** must be made. Also see **Quilts: Marking and Cutting.**

split punch. Leather. See **nailhead punch, punch.**

split reed. Basketry. See **cane.**

split rivet. Leather. A type of **rivet** with two prongs at a slight angle. Holes are prepunched for the rivet to go through. When hammered, the rivet prongs spread across the back of the leather to hold it in place. See ill.

Split rivet

split stitch. Crewel. Embroidery. (Also called Kensington outline stitch.) The name describes this stitch precisely. A small straight stitch is taken and the needle comes up in the center of the existing stitch, splitting the thread. It is used as an outline stitch, or as padding over which another stitch is worked as in the padded satin stitch. It can be worked in rows all worked in the same direction and is useful for shading. See ill. Also see **line stitch, long and short stitch, shading stitch.**

Split stitch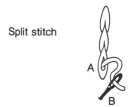

splitting. Jewelry. Dividing or splitting metal with chisels from the edge without loss of any metal. Metal can be split either hot or cold. Also see **chisel cutting.**

splitting. Leather. A finishing process in which leather hides are separated into layers. Any layer from the underside is called a **split;** the outside layer is called the **grain** side. The numbers of layers into which a **hide** is split depends on its thickness and the use for which the leather is intended.

splitting. Metalworking. See **blacksmithing techniques.**

splitting chisel. Metalworking. See **blacksmithing tools.**

split two-patch. Quilts. A **two-patch,** divided diagonally to form four triangles. When any square is split into triangles, a **seam allowance** must be made. Also see **Quilts: Marking and Cutting.**

spodumene. Gemcutting. A silicate of lithium and aluminum of the **pyroxene** group **crystal**lized in the monoclinic system. It has a **hardness** of 6¾, **specific gravity** of 3.17, and refractive indices of 1.651 and 1.677 with a vitreous **luster.** Spodumene has perfect **cleavage** in two directions parallel to the **C-axis.**

Spodumene usually occurs as opaque ash-gray crystals; however, when transparent, it is cut into gems. Colored green it is called hiddenite; the white variety is called triphane; a lilac colored spodumene is called kunzite. It is **facet**ed with crown mains at 43° and pavillion facets at 39°, and is polished with tin oxide on a tin **lap.** Also see **cabochon, faceting, polishing, refraction.**

spoke. Basketry. The radiating **warp** made of **rod**s used to form the framework of the **base** of a **woven basket.** Upon them the flexible elements, or **weft,** are woven. The arrangement of these spokes will determine the shape and weave of the basket. See ill. Also see **Basketry: Woven Basket Construction.**

Spokes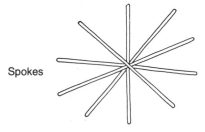

spokeshave. Leather. A pull tool like a carpenter's plane for **skiving** very heavy leather. As the tool requires both hands to use, the leather must be securely fixed to the table with tape or clamps.

spokeshave. Woodworking. See **plane.**

sponge acid etching. China and Glass Painting. See **acid etching.**

sponge printing. Block Printing. See **found object printing.**

sponge stick. Ceramics. A tool consisting of a sponge fastened to the end of a stick or dowel for absorbing excess water from inside pots during throwing; it is especially helpful while making small-necked forms.

sponging. Rugmaking. Weaving. A partial **shrinkage** obtained by dampening the piece with a sponge, by rolling it in a wet cloth, or by **steam pressing** it. **London shrinkage** is one type of sponging. Sponging is often done as part of blocking tapestries or small **flat rug**s. Also see **finishing.**

spool. Weaving. A cardboard, wooden, or metal cylinder with flanged edges around which yarn or thread is wound. A cardboard cylinder without the flanged edges can be called either a spool or tube. Also, small plastic spools that are used in **boat shuttles** are usually referred to as **bobbins.** Spools are one way of packaging yarn or thread for sale. They are placed on **spool racks** for **bobbin winding** or **warping**.

spool chain. Toys. (Also called spool rattle.) A baby toy made by stringing a series of colorful spools onto a continuous elastic cord. Care must be taken in selection of paints and the way they are applied, to be sure they will not be harmful if the paint is chewed.

spool doll. Toys. A figure with plastic or wooden thread spools for its basic form. It may be made in any of several ways.

One kind of spool doll is strung onto two elastic cords. One cord is knotted, then threaded through several spools to make a leg. The other leg is made the same way. Then the two cords go through 3 or 4 spools for a body, separating again for the arms. One large spool or several small ones are used for the head, which is tied on separately. A spool from fishing line or something similar will work.

A second kind of doll uses a single spool for the body. A wooden bead, either strung or glued to the spool, makes the head. Sometimes two or three spools are used for the body, with spool sizes and shapes determining the specific arrangement.

Other spool dolls are made by gluing spools together to suggest a figure. Spools are treated as any wood in terms of paint or color.

spool knitting. Knitting. An early method of producing knitted fabrics using a spool with a hole through the center and pegs around the rim, or a circular knitting frame. There are many variations of this special way of knitting. The wooden thread spool or ends from rolls of paper are the most common contemporary spool knitting frames. Four nails are evenly spaced around the rim. See ill. Also see **peg knitting**, **rake knitting**.

Spool knitting

spool loom. Toys. See **weaving spool**.

spool racer. Toys. See **racing spool**.

spool rack. Weaving. A wooden vertical frame on a stand with removable horizontal steel rods on which are placed **spools** for **bobbin winding** or **warping**. In the latter case, the spools are placed on the rack in the same order in which they fall in the warp repeat; and a **warping paddle** is used in winding the warp. Although with solid color warps a spool rack is not essential and some makeshift arrangement can be devised to hold the spools, it is a necessity if the method used is **sectional warping**. Most floor-standing spool racks can hold from 20 spools up to as many as 70. These very large spool racks are called creels.

There are also smaller, hanging spool racks that carry only 10 spools. Another small type of spool rack rests on the floor and can hold from 2 to 8 spools or **cones**. See ill. Also see **warping reel**.

Spool rack

spool rattle. Toys. See **spool chain**.

spool top. Toys. See **finger top**.

spool tractor. Toys. See **racing spool**.

spool wire. Beadwork. Fine **wire** used in **bead flowermaking** comes on a spool. It is available in graded gauges: the higher the number, the finer the wire. For general work, 28-gauge galvanized, annealed steel wire is used; for larger sections requiring more body, 26-gauge wire is used. For assembling completed pieces and for lacing, 32–36-gauge wire is recommended. Brass spool wire is also available.

spoon and slick. Metalworking. See **sandcasting molding equipment**.

spoon gouge. Woodworking. See **gouge**, **woodcarving tools**.

spot. Leather. See **nailhead**.

Spot Bronson. Weaving. See **Bronson weave**.

spot dyeing. Dyeing. The spotting of fabric or yarn with a dye to obtain a variegated color. The dye can be of paste consistency or a water solution, depending on how strong the mottling is to be. If the fabric or yarn is wet, the dye will spread; if the fabric or yarn is dry, it will be contained in the area it touches. Bleach is used in the same manner to obtain lighter effects on fabric or yarn that is already dyed. Also see **warp dyeing**.

spot setter. Leather. See **nailhead punch**.

spot stitch. Beadwork. See **overlay stitch**.

spot stitch. Lacemaking. See **leaf stitch.**

spot technique. Batik and Tie-dye. A method used in tie-dye to produce spots or dots of **resist** on a dyed fabric. The traditional Japanese spot technique is called **shibori.** In India, a similar use of tiny dots in patterns is referred to as **bandhana work.**

When very small dots are to be made, a fine fabric must be used and the **binding** should be a very fine thread.

In one method of spot tying, a needle is used to prick the fabric and draw up a small point of the material. The binding is used directly under the needle, wrapped once or twice, and tied. The more binding used, the bigger the spot.

Spots may be picked up between thumb and forefinger, then thoroughly bound so that almost the entire spot resists color. There is always a bit of color in the center of the dyed fabric spot.

Several spots may be tied at once, joining them to produce spots within another shape. By **folding** or **gather**ing the material in various ways a great variety of spot tie-dye shapes can be produced.

spotting. Gemcutting. See **drilling jig.**

spot weave. Weaving. A classification of weaves whose similarity is a **plain weave** background with spots, or small areas, of **floats.** These floats can be varied as to size, distribution, and placement, so that either a textured all-over effect, or a pattern, can be achieved. The threads that float tend to be deflected from their vertical or horizontal alignment. In some cases, because of the **threading** and/or **treadling,** this deflection is more extreme and open areas occur. These spot weaves are then considered a variety of **lace weave,** like **mock leno.** Also see **Bronson weave, huck, huckaback weave, mock leno weave, Swedish lace.**

spot welder. Metalworking. An electric welding machine used for **spot welding** sheet metals together at specific spots or locations. The spot welder comes in small portable models useful in home craftwork for sheet metals up to 18-**gauge,** and in larger models up to stationary industrial machines capable of joining thick **mild steel** bars and rods. On small models, the heat and current are so localized to the area between the tips that the sheets of metal may be handled with bare hands even when the current is on. However, do not put your fingers between the tips when the current is on. To maintain peak performance of the portable spot welder, clean the **copper** tips or points with a small **mill file** and the arms or jaws with **steel wool.** Make sure the electric cord and plug are secure and not damaged before plugging it in. Test-weld pieces of metal scrap of different gauges to determine in advance the time and pressure needed for proper fusion of each. The heavier the sheet, the longer the current should remain on.

To use a spot welder, clean rusty, dirty, or heavily **scaled** metal surfaces at the weld points. Place the metal between the welder arm tips so that the pieces overlap ¼ – ½". The metals should touch each other at the point being welded so that the arms of the welder do not have to act as clamps.

Without turning the current on, squeeze the lever handle (also called tong level), which closes the jaws, and apply moderate pressure to see if the distance between the tips is adequate. Adjust the switch screw up or down only if the thickness of the metals is greatly different from the previously adjusted distances between the tips, or to compensate for the file cleaning, which may have taken off too much metal from the points or jaw tips.

Turn on the current. Squeeze the lever handle and keep it down until a sizzling sound is heard and a blue flash is seen. The weld is then complete. **Galvanize**d coatings are poor electrical conductors and do not weld as easily as uncoated metal. When spot-welding galvanized sheets, tilt the sheet between the jaws as soon as the current is on so that the tips can penetrate the coating to start the weld. See ill.

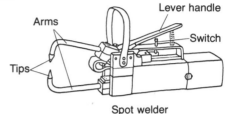

Spot welder

spot welding. Metalworking. A type of electric welding in which the welding heat results from the electrical resistance of the metals being joined. When the **spot welder** is turned on and the tips of the arms are pressed together with sheet metal between them, the electricity attempts to pass from one tip to the other but is partially blocked by the metal that resists it. Heat accumulates at that point on the metal and a single weld the size of a small **rivet** results. Although this weld is stronger than a rivet, the outstanding feature of spot welding is the ease and speed with which a weld can be made on sheet metals of 18-**gauge** or thinner. Operating a portable spot welder can be as fast and easy as operating a stapler or staple gun.

spot yarn. Spinning. Weaving. See **novelty yarn.**

spout. Ceramics. See **Ceramics: Form.**

sprang. Lacemaking. A Nordic word for a fabric made on a frame with the hands by intertwining the warp threads. It is a very sturdy fabric structure, and can be made to have a lacy look by leaving open spaces in the work. Sprang is primarily used for wearing apparel such as stockings, caps, gloves, and other garments made with cotton or wool yarns. During the eighteenth and nineteenth centuries, military sashes of very fine silk yarn were made with dates, regimental numbers, and the officer's initials worked into the spranging. These sashes were often up to 12" long and 30" wide.

Excavation has unearthed sprang works such as a woman's hairnet near Aarhus, Denmark, dated about 1400 B.C. (the Danish Bronze Age); cylindrical bags and fabrics from Asia and the central coast of Peru, dated about 1100 B.C. (the late preceramic age); and a shirt from Tonto Monument, Arizona, dated possibly as early as A.D. 1300. Coptic sprang fabrics discovered in Upper Egypt at Achmin, dating from a period of A.D. 1800 onward, were skillfully executed and in a good state of preservation because of the dry climate. These pieces from Egypt are the best examples ancient sprang yet unearthed.

Because of the openness of the multiended structure, it is thought that sprang is the ancient forerunner of **bobbin lace.**

sprang. Weaving. A method of **fabric** construction in which vertical, parallel elements, or **warp** threads, which are securely attached at top and bottom and stretched taut, are twisted around each other to form a netlike textile. The method is **plaiting** by interlocking the yarns. By using the fingers and a stick, the interlocking or twisting takes place in the center of the warp length. Because the warp threads are firmly anchored at both ends, a twist at one end forms a mirror image twist of itself at the other end; i.e., the pattern is symmetrical on both sides of a center point. No **filling** is used. Only at the end, when there is not enough room to twist any more, can a yarn be passed through the center of the fabric to secure the twists.

Also called Egyptian plaitwork, **frame plaiting,** twined plaiting, or knotless **netting,** the word "sprang" is of Scandinavian origin. The technique is very ancient and fragments of it have been found all over the world and from all ages; in Denmark from Bronze Age sites, in the excavations of the Swiss Lake Dwellers, in ancient Egyptian tombs as well as in Coptic ones and in pre-Inca Peru burial grounds where especially exquisite and complex examples have been found. Present day aborigines in New Zealand use sprang to make hammocks, as do the Indians of Mexico, who are also known for their sprang market bags. Sprang is a new technique among contemporary fiber artists. It has become popular through the pioneering efforts of Peter Collingwood of England, who has used it extensively in **wall hanging**s.

Any nonelastic yarn or cord can be used as the warp. It is strung around two cross bars (as in a metal or wooden frame), or as in a **backstrap loom,** or it can be tensioned as in a **warp-weighted loom.** If the cord is strung around two cross bars, the warp is either wrapped in a continuous manner so that a **figure-8 warp** results, or each warp yarn is cut twice its length, doubled, and attached to one bar with a **lark's head knot.** The latter method results in a **self-fringe** at one end. One of the cross bars must be movable to allow for the contraction of the warp due to the twisting. The side bars of a frame are also useful for keeping the sprang structure stretched out across the width. Sprang is elastic in all directions, and if it is not held out taut, the structure and pattern of the piece will not be seen. Small ties to the sides can be made at intervals to achieve this tautness. In addition to the frame or bar supports, dowels or **shed stick**s are needed to make and keep the twists.

To begin, wind an even number of warp threads around the two cross bars (**a.**). A dowel or shed stick is woven across the warp ends going from right to left, over one and under one in a **plain-weave** fashion. To do single-twist sprang, in which one warp thread twists around an adjacent one, the first of two twisting steps is begun on the right side. With the warp threads numbered from right to left, take another dowel or stick and start lower than the

first dowel by pulling thread #1 under #2 and #4 then place it on the dowel. Warp thread #3 is pulled under #6 and placed on the dowel next to #1. This is repeated across the width of the warp with the right hand working the dowel or stick as in **leno,** and the left hand maneuvering the threads. When completed, there will be two warp threads over the dowel on the left and two under on the right (**b.**). The first dowel is removed, and the second, with the twisted warp, is pushed to the top bar. Another dowel is inserted into the shed created by the interlinking warp threads, and is pushed to the bottom bar.

The first dowel will now work step two in the twisting of this simple sprang. This begins on the right, where warp thread #2 is now on the outside. This is picked up and taken under #1 and over onto the dowel. #4 is next and this is taken under #3 and on the dowel. This is continued across to the left side (**c.**). The first and second steps are repeated alternately until the center is reached. The twists are always pushed to the top and bottom with the dowels. Extra dowels should only be removed when there is no danger of losing a twist.

In the center, the sprang is held together by a variety of means. It can be a dowel permanently inserted, if this fits the design plan, or a filling yarn can be inserted and by **twining, chaining, weaving,** or knotting it across, hold the sprang together. The locking of the twists can also be managed by not inserting anything, but by overlapping or interlooping one warp thread over the next thread and by pulling the second warp thread under and over the first. This chainlike effect is repeated across the warp width and at the end, the last loop is tied with an extra piece of yarn to the edge warp yarn or to the side support.

By using two or more warp threads as a unit in the twisting, a more complicated sprang is formed. Openings can also be formed by omitting a twist between the two thread units that would normally twist around each other,

Sprang

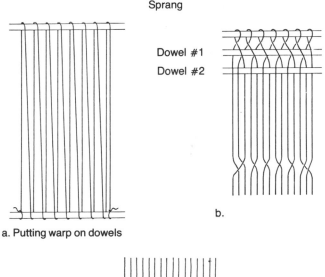

a. Putting warp on dowels

Dowel #1
Dowel #2

b.

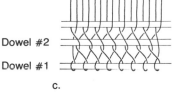

Dowel #2
Dowel #1

c.

or by working individual sections and later connecting them together. New colors can be introduced into the warp by using a **weaver's knot** or a **square knot** for attaching the new color. See ill.

spraying glaze. Ceramics. See **Ceramics: Glazing.**

spray paint. Toys. Any paint packaged in an aerosol spray can. Spray enamel is the most common; it is available in glossy or matte finish. **Lacquer, epoxy paint, urethane liquid plastic,** clear plastic, **fixative,** undercoat, and various oil base paints are all available as sprays.

spread. Gemcutting. See **cabochon.**

spreader. Enameling. A tool used for applying enamels in the **wet inlay** technique. See ill. Also see **Enameling: Basic Operations, Tools and Materials.**

Spreader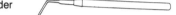

spreader. Weaving. See **raddle.**

spreading the warp. Weaving. That part of **dressing the loom** that takes place prior to **beaming** in order to insure that the **warp** threads do not fall in bunches as they revolve around the **warp beam.** The warp is spread to approximately its full width with the aid of either a **raddle,** or the **reed** in the **beater,** or by eye. The warp **ends** are straightened out so that they will lie in as straight a line as possible from the beginning to the end of the warp. As the warp is being beamed, the raddle or reed will ensure that the spreading and the straightening will remain intact until beaming is completed. If no raddle or reed has been used, then it is up to the weaver to constantly keep the warp spread out evenly and straight as it goes over the **back beam.**

sprig. Ceramics. A small bas-relief decoration made in a small **press mold** that is stuck to a **leather hard** clay surface. A sprig mold can be carved in **bisque** or plastic.

sprig mold. Ceramics. See **sprig.**

spring. Basketry. The angle of the sides of a basket. It is made at the upsetting of the basket and helps determine the final shape. Also see **flow.**

spring. Toys. A coiled spring wire used in various toys to animate or move them. A **jack-in-the-box** is operated by a coiled wire spring that is compressed and held in place by a lid. When released, the spring quickly returns to its original shape, forcing the jack to pop out of the box. Key **windup toys** utilize springs made from tightly wound flat strips of metal. As the tension is gradually released, the **stored energy** moves the toy. Also see **Toys: Mechanical Toys and Moving Toys.**

spring clamp. Woodworking. See **clamping tools.**

spring dividers. Bookbinding. A 6″ spring divider is used as an aid to the correct placement of letters and decorative **tools** when **titling.**

spring dividers. Metalworking. See **measuring tools.**

spring dividers. Woodworking. See **measuring tools.**

springerle. Toys. A traditional **cookie art** of southern Germany and Switzerland. It is made with a **carved wood cookie mold** and is unique in that the carving is done on a cylindrical rolling pin. The carved wooden form is rolled over the **edible dough,** impressing designs in it. The designs are cut apart before baking. The springerle cookies are made from a light dough and, because the dough is stiff, retain detailed relief patterns.

spring horse. Toys. A toy similar to the **hobbyhorse,** but that moves on springs instead of rockers. In early spring horses of the late nineteenth century the hind legs of the animal were attached to a solid wood base. A long leaf-spring supported the front and the movement of the rider brought on a galloping bounce. Recent ones suspend the horse from coil springs attached to a wooden frame.

spring ring. Jewelry. A commercially made, circular, tubelike finding, made of a spring and a piece of metal that moves back and forth. This piece is kept closed by the pressure of the spring inside and when closed around a plain ring, holds work, such as a string of beads, together. Also see **finding.**

spring temper. Jewelry. A characteristic of work-hardened metal. For example, wire that has been drawn through the **drawplate** becomes springy due to its rearranged, compressed molecular structure. Also see **work hardening.**

Springtime Blossoms. Quilts. See **Hearts and Gizzards.**

spring top. Toys. A **top** that is set in motion by a spring device. The spring is set into the top and operated by a handle. The coil wire spring is compressed by a movement of the handle; when it is released the spring flies back to its original shape, turning the base of the top.

spruce. Kites. A white, relatively soft, coniferous wood used for kite **framing,** most frequently cut into flat ⅜″ × ⅛″ strips. Spruce is very strong for its weight, and in flat stick form it is probably the best material to use for constructing flat kite frameworks. Also see **Kites: Tools and Materials.**

spruce. Woodworking. A family of evergreen trees with needle-shaped leaves, drooping cones or berrylike fruit, and a wood that is soft, fairly strong, and generally free of knots. It is grown mainly in the western United States and Canada and is used for timbers in heavy construction work and as pulpwood for newsprint and other papers. Because it has good resonating qualities, the red spruce has been adopted for making the sounding boards of some musical instruments. The Sitka spruce grows up to 300 feet tall, and the Engleman spruce up to 150 feet.

sprue. Jewelry. Metalworking. A round channel through which molten metal flows into the **flask** during **centrifugal casting.** Also, prior to the **burnout,** a round cylindrical shape branching off the **sprue cone,** and sometimes off other sprues. See ill. Also see **centrifugal casting machine, separating disks, sprue cutter, sprue former, vent.**

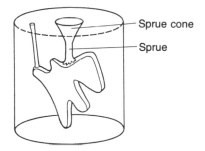

Sprue cone
Sprue

sprue button. Jewelry. (Also called button.) Extra metal that fills a portion of the **sprue cone** area after **centrifugal casting.** Also see **flask, sprue, sprue cutter.**

sprue cone. Jewelry. A cone-shaped form made of metal or wax. This form is in the positive and acts as the base for the **sprue**s, and when removed (metal) or melted (wax) forms a negative, or concave, cone shape into which molten metal flows during **centrifugal casting.** There is also a form of flattened sprue cone that works extremely well. Also see **centrifugal casting machine, flux, investing, separating disks, sprue button, sprue cutter.**

sprue cutter. Jewelry. A pair of heavy-duty pliers with sharpened parallel jaws at right angles to the handles, used to clip **sprue**s from a **casting.** The sprues should not be clipped too closely or the casting may be damaged. The remaining portion of the sprues can be filed or ground off. Also see **centrifugal casting, flexible shaft machine, separating disks.**

sprue cutter. Metalworking. See **sandcasting molding equipment.**

sprue former. Jewelry. A manufactured form available both in rubber and aluminum. The rubber type has an area in the center that is filled with wax to form a flat **sprue cone,** and an outer flange into which a **flask** fits tightly (**a.**). After pouring and setting of the **investment,** the form is twisted off. With the aluminum type the same basics apply, but the form of the sprue cone is conical, some having several low rims in the base to allow for the fitting of different-size flasks (**b.**). Both types of form can be used over and over, making forming the sprue cone in wax for each new casting unnecessary. See ill. Also see **centrifugal casting.**

a. Rubber sprue former   b. Aluminum sprue former

spun-glass work. Glasswork. A technique used in **flamework** to make small objects of unusual appeal. Heat a glass rod in the **glass fire** until molten and then attach it to another piece of solid glass. Pull the end of the melted rod to reduce the molten material in diameter. Loop and stretch it for attachment onto a previous loop or to another part of the cooler glass piece. See ill.

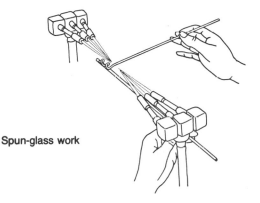

Spun-glass work

spun roving. Plastics. See **glass fiber.**

spun yarn. Spinning. Any yarn that has gone through the process of **spinning. Fiber**s of short **staple** must be spun, but fibers of a long staple, silk, and synthetic **filament**s may be loosely twisted in a process called *throwing,* or not twisted at all. In order to spin filaments, they must first be cut into short, staple lengths. Spun yarn can be tightly or loosely spun, and it can be a single element as well as a **plied** structure. Also see **spinning.**

spur. Ceramics. See **kiln furniture.**

square. Bookbinding. The projection or overhang of a cover over the leaves of a book. The square is generally about ⅛″ and is designed to protect the edges of the leaves. Also see **leaf.**

square. Leather. A metal ruler with a square side used for general measuring and as a guide for cutting leather with a **utility knife.** See ill. Also see **Leatherwork: Tools and Materials.**

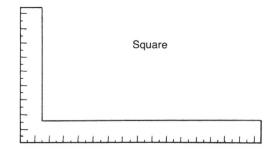

Square

square. Metalworking. Plastics. Woodworking. Squaring is the process of working all the surfaces of a piece of **wood, plastic, metal,** or other material until they have been made smooth and true, at right angles (90°) to the adjoining surfaces, and opposite surfaces are parallel. The process of squaring stock is fundamental in all these crafts. To perform the squaring operations, accurate **squaring tools** are needed. Also see **Woodworking: Marking Out and Squaring.**

square. Papercrafts. A square shape can easily be cut by folding a rectangle of paper diagonally, matching up sides, and cutting away the excess paper. See ill.

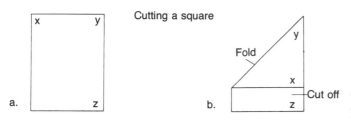

Cutting a square

a.

b.

squared filling. Crewel. Embroidery. A **filling stitch** that is worked over vertical, horizontal, and diagonal **laidwork.** The variations in color and filling stitches are limited only by the imagination. Make small slanting stitches at the intersections of the laidwork (**a.**). Diagonal laidwork is secured with small vertical stitches (**b.**). To make diagonal slanting stitches over laidwork, slide needle under the intersection (**c.**). Skip one intersection between rows and al-

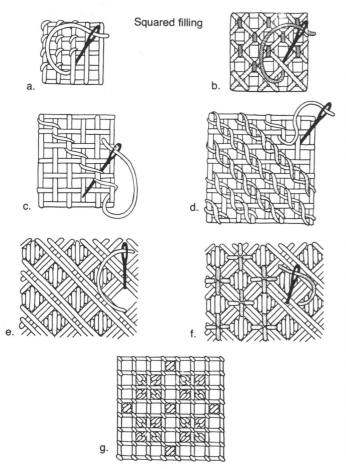

Squared filling

a.

c.

e.

b.

d.

f.

g.

ternate colors (**d.**). Make **satin stitch**es in the large diamonds formed by diagonal laidwork (**e.**). Secure the intersections with four short stitches (**f.**). The **detached chain stitch** can be used as a filling (**g.**). See ill.

squared paper. Weaving. See **graph paper.**

square file. Metalworking. See **file.**

square frame. Crewel. Embroidery. Needlepoint. See **embroidery frame.**

square knot. Lacemaking. See **reef knot.**

square knot. Macramé. (Also called double knot, flat double knot, Solomon knot.) One of the basic macramé knots. The square knot is formed with four **cord**s from two **half knot**s.

Place the #1 cord over cords #2 and #3, place cord #4 over #1, bring it behind #3 and #2, and pull it to the front over #1 (**a.**). Pull tight. Knotted in this fashion, the square knot is formed with a ridge on the left-hand side. If the sequence is reversed (i.e., cord #4 over cords #3 and #2; place cord #1 over #4, bring it behind #2 and #3, and pull it to the front over #4; pull tight), the knot is formed with a right-hand ridge (**b.**). See ill.

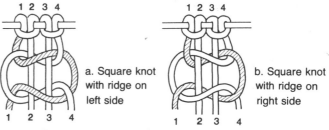

a. Square knot with ridge on left side

b. Square knot with ridge on right side

square knot. Weaving. (Also called reef knot.) An easily opened knot used to temporarily attach two **warp end**s or pieces of **filling** on a **shuttle.** By pulling apart the two ends that are close together, the knot is quickly untied. It will not slip or untie by itself unless the yarns are of unequal size. See ill.

Square knot

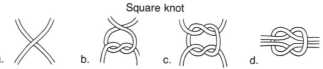

a.   b.   c.   d.

square knotting. Macramé. Square knotting is an early term for macramé work and the one still used by many sailors who practice the craft.

square knot with picot. Macramé. (Also called centipede knot, flat knot with picot.) Two **square knot**s with a **picot** (loop) formed between the two knots on either side. It forms a loopy two-edged fringe when worked in series, and is often worked directly beneath the **mounting cord** or bar.

Using four cords, make one square knot. Make a second square knot, pulling the outer left- and right-hand cords out to the desired length to form small picot loops as you push the knot up the center cords until it is directly below the first knot. The tightened knots above and below will hold the loops in place. See ill.

Square knot with picots

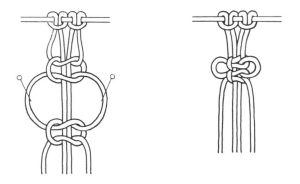

square medallion on five needles. Knitting. See **Knitting: Construction.**

square-off. Weaving. To weave a pattern so that it looks the same from all directions. This is done in **overshot** by **treadling-as-drawn-in.** Diagonal twill blocks run through the center of the pattern. To eliminate this, and yet square-off the design, a treadling on reverse twill blocks, called "rose fashion," is used. The term "square-off" is also used with other weave patterns and with color patterns like **plaids.**

square point knife. Leather. A knife used for trimming, cutting, and **skiving** leather. See ill.

Square point leather knife

square the corners. Quilts. Stitchery. To **bind** the edges in such a way as to produce a perfectly square corner. Unlike **miter**ing, which gives a diagonal line at the corner, squaring leaves a line parallel to one edge.

To square a corner, as on a **quilt, banner,** or **wall hanging,** a **band** or strip of **fabric** is cut on the **straight.** It must be double the width needed plus the **seam allowance** on each edge. Take for example a **panel** 20″ × 30″. It is 20″ across the top and if a 1″ **binding** is desired, the band is cut 20″ long and 2½″ wide. That allows a 1″ binding on the front, 1″ **fold**ed over for the back, and a ¼″ seam at both front and back. One length of the band can be machine-sewn, though the second side must be sewn by hand if the seam is to be concealed. When the 20″ band has been sewn in place, the opposite 20″ edge is also finished. Then bands are cut for the 30″ edges. These edges will now be 32″ in length (less the ¼″ seam allowance) because of the binding already added at each end. Another ½″ should be allowed at the ends, since these bands must cover the **raw edge**s of the 20″ bands. The second pair of bands or strips would be cut 33″ long by 2½″ wide. The last two bands are sewn in the same way as the first two, being sure that the raw ends are covered. In hand stitching, the second edge of the band, the material allowance at the corner, is turned under. This makes an easily sewn square corner, suitable for edging any rectangular-shaped piece of work.

squarework. Basketry. Flat weaving for square forms or boxes. A **screwblock** is often used to hold the work in place while doing squarework.

squaring a bottom. Metalworking. See **raising technique.**

squaring tools. Metalworking. Plastics. Woodworking. Tools used to **square** or lay out lines on pieces of material that are to be cut or assembled. These tools are sometimes calibrated for use as **measuring tools.**

A framing (or carpenter's or rafter) square is an L-shaped steel tool with two flat legs meeting at a 90° angle. The longer leg (the tongue) is commonly 24″ × 2″; the shorter (the blade), 16″ × 1½″. Larger and smaller sizes are available; it is commonly used for squaring and laying out lines on larger stock.

A try square has a tongue typically 8″ long, with the blade often ½″-thick wood; it is useful for smaller boards and for laying out joints (**a.**).

A combination square has a grooved 12″ tongue that is adjustable, sliding in and out of the blade; the metal blade has one right angle and one 45° angle and often has a small spirit level.

A bevel square (or miter gauge or sliding-T bevel) consists of a smooth 12″ steel tongue that slides and pivots in the handle. It has a wing nut to lock the blade at any desired angle, and is thus very useful for transferring irregular angles and checking bevels (**b.**).

A level (or spirit level) is a tool for checking the level of a surface; all levels are designed for checking horizontal planes, most also for vertical, and some for 45°, angles (**c.**). A bubble within a slightly curved glass tube hits the center mark when the surface on which the level is placed is at the desired angle. See ill. Also see **Woodworking: Marking Out and Squaring.**

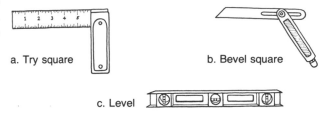

a. Try square   b. Bevel square

c. Level

squaring up. Stained Glass. One of the methods for enlarging a drawing to a **cartoon.** It is done by dividing the drawing into squares or grids. The full-size frame for the cartoon is divided into the same number of squares. The design is then reproduced square by square, using proportionately larger measurements.

squeak toy. Toys. A **sound toy.** Some squeak toys are made from rubber and have a small opening through which air can pass to the hollow inside. As the air moves through rapidly, as when squeezed, a squeaking sound is made.

squeaky. Basketry. A term describing **reed** or **willow** that has become dry in the working and needs to be wetted.

squeegee. Glasswork. Silkscreen. A strip of rubber, neoprene, or soft plastic material about ³⁄₁₆″ thick and 2″ wide that is fixed into a wood holder so that the rubber projects an inch or so beyond the holder. It forces **silkscreen ink**

through the screen **stencil**, with a scraping or wiping action, in the making of silkscreen prints.

Squeegees are manufactured in three grades of flexibility, the softer squeegees being capable of laying down a heavier layer of ink, and the harder ones capable of printing sharper detail. This is mainly a rule of thumb, because the consistency of the ink itself also contributes to printing clarity. Beginners are advised to start with a squeegee of medium hardness.

Because the squeegee is drawn across the screen at an angle of about 45°, the corners of the working edge become blunt in time, with an accompanying loss of sharpness in the image produced. At this point, the blade can be reversed in the holder or resharpened by running it along a long piece of sandpaper, being careful to keep the strip of rubber perpendicular to the paper. A jig or guide should be devised to ensure that the squeegee stands straight. See ill.

Squeegee

squeegee oil. Enameling. See **binder, overglaze.**

squirrel cage swift. Spinning. Weaving. See **swift.**

Squirrel Nutkin. Toys. See **Peter Rabbit.**

stabbed binding. Bookbinding. A binding that is joined by cords laced through holes pierced along the **back edge.**

stabbing clamp. Bookbinding. A device used to hold a binding while piercing or stabbing holes along the **back edge** that will receive the **cord**s to join the **section**s to each other or the **boards** to the text.

stabilizer. Glasswork. A chemical compound added to glass in glassmaking to make the resultant product insoluble in water. Also see **water glass.**

stabilizer. Plastics. See **inhibitor.**

stable. Ceramics. A **glaze** that has a well-balanced formula and is acid resistant when properly fired. Excess **pigment oxides**, for example, may render a glaze unstable. Also see **acid resistance.**

stacked felt. Stitchery. A method of **felt appliqué** in which a small design is applied to a larger piece. A shape is then cut from the **background** piece so that it enlarges on the design. This process is repeated, and as the layers of **felt** are stacked, the design becomes increasingly larger and more complex. The felt is stacked in this way using up to 10 or 12 layers of felt.

Each shape usually echoes or exaggerates the one sewn to it. The effect is one of **relief** pattern. It is used primarily in **banner**s, **wall hanging**s and simple felt **garment**s. The approach is also particularly suited to the use of lettering.

stacked Y-stitch. Stitchery. A **Y-stitch** used in such a way that one stitch touches the next, making a line that looks continuous. Its appearance is identical to fly stitch.

stacking. Basketry. The undesirable effect of having one **round** of **weaving** exactly repeat the previous round, going over the same **rod**s the previous round went over, and under the others.

There are several ways to prevent stacking. Where a weave uses an even number of stakes in the pattern (most simply, over-one, under-one), use an odd number of stakes. Where the pattern uses an odd number of stakes (e.g., over two, under one), make sure the total number of stakes is not divisible by that number. **Chasing** or **pairing** can also prevent stacking. Also see **stagger.**

stacking figure. Toys. See **acrobat.**

stack throwing. Ceramics. See **throwing off the mound.**

staff. Stitchery. A pole, either horizontal or vertical, used to support a **banner**. The staff for a **flag** is usually vertical and the flag is attached at one side so that the wind can unfurl it by blowing the flag out away from the staff. The staff for a banner is often a crosspiece attached at the top of a long pole or **standard**. It is the staff from which the banner is hung. Sometimes the staff is also called the standard, though when a crosspiece is used the vertical pole is the standard and the cross-piece is the staff.

stage floor. Puppets. The area on which the **marionette**s perform in a theater. The figures are suspended from above so that the feet touch the stage floor. In the **puppet theater**, there is no actual stage floor, only the **playboard.** Also see **Puppets: Marionette Stage.**

stage set. Puppets. See **set.**

stagger. Basketry. The act of insetting the second row of a **round** or course of weaving so that the **active element** produces an alternating weaving pattern, i.e., the element goes under the rods or stakes that it went over in the previous row and vice versa.

stain. Ceramics. Any **oxide** or prepared pigment that is used for coloring **glaze**s, **slip**s, or clay bodies; it is also used as an **overglaze** and **underglaze** decoration.

stain. Découpage. A paint that is applied and then partially wiped away with a cloth to give the appearance of texture to the surface. A stain can be given to wood before the application of a **sealer**. This wash of color over the wood, which brings out the grain and lightly colors it, is then used as a background on which to apply the **cutout**s. Also see **antiquing.**

stain. Stained Glass. See **staining.**

stain. Woodworking. See **wood stain.**

STAINED GLASS

Traditionally, stained glass has been glass constructed in patterns or **mosaic**s and held together in a **panel** with **lead came.** Polyester and **epoxy resin**s and **copper foiling** are modern materials and methods that have expanded the craft to include stained-glass lampshades, **mobile**s, free-standing forms, leaded-glass lanterns, terrariums, and light boxes. In addition to being cut and assembled into forms, glass can be treated with special paint, acid, stain, and enamel, and can be fused, laminated, and fired in a **kiln.**

The basic ingredients of stained glass are high-**silica sand** with 1% iron, soda ash, limestone, and borax or potash. Firing these materials to temperatures of 3000° F produces a high-quality glass. Too much iron in the sand produces a glass with a greenish cast like that of a Coke bottle and changes subsequent coloration. The addition of pigments (metallic oxides), due to their varying coefficients of expansion within the glass, causes stained glass to respond differently than **plate glass** during cutting.

It is believed that glassmaking began around 3000 B.C. in the Middle East. Alexandria, Egypt, was the first major glass-producing center. The Greeks and Romans learned glassmaking techniques from the Egyptians and introduced new colors and forms. Under Constantine and the later Byzantine emperors, great emphasis was placed on the use of stained glass to enhance churches and palaces. During the fourth and fifth centuries, mosaics of glass were made for churches, and new furnaces and blowing equipment were introduced to expedite the work.

The craft of stained glass entered Europe through Germany and Austria in the north, and Spain and France in the south. Charlemagne first saw stained glass accomplishments in A.D. 800. Deeply impressed, he reproduced what he had seen in his own palace at Aix-la-Chapelle. He and his successors, by commissioning the work of many artists, laid the foundation for Gothic art and architecture and the development of the stained glass window.

During the Middle Ages stained glass windows were used to communicate religious stories to an illiterate population. At that time, the cost of producing these could be supported only by the Church; thus, as the patron for this craft, the Church set the standards for artistic expression. In this era of the great cathedrals, stained glass windows reached an apex of artistry. The windows of the cathedral at Chartres represents one of the greatest triumphs in the art of stained glass.

By the fifteenth century the role of the individual craftsperson was emerging; religious subjects were still depicted, but in a more personal manner. During the Renaissance stained glass was superseded by **painting on glass;** gone was the simplicity of the Romanesque and Gothic church windows with their direct use of glass as the dominant design element. Instead, scenes were painted on white or clear glass.

A few centuries later, stained glass was to be relegated to a craft category. However, during the nineteenth century, the construction of many new churches and the renovation of older structures created a need for stained glass. Ancient formulas and techniques were rediscovered and new ones invented. **Antique glass** was one result of this. By 1835, **opaque glass** was being manufactured in the United States, and by the turn of the century, colors such as "apple-green," "opaque turquoise," "sunburst," and "peachblow" were initiating the **art glass** decades. The nineteenth-century interest in medieval art also contributed to the revival of stained glass as an art form. In England, the Pre-Raphaelite painters also designed stained glass windows.

The Art Nouveau period, at its height between 1890 and 1910, witnessed more radical changes in the decorative arts than had occurred in the past one hundred years. The period rejected romanticism and the overembellishment of the Victorian period; instead, there was a great emphasis on Oriental art and textiles, medieval art, and the architectural forms and motifs of the Egyptians, Byzantines, Moors, and Romans. The foremost exponent of Art Nouveau stained glass was **Louis Comfort Tiffany;** others included Victor Durand and John La Farge who, like Tiffany, worked in the United States. Tiffany's experiments with pigmentation and metallic oxides created luminescences and colors never before seen. With this glass he created stained glass panels and lamps, as well as blown-glass pieces that have never been duplicated. In addition to his unique **favrile glass,** he was also known to incorporate sea shells, rocks, pebbles, and other found objects into his works to achieve the effects he desired. He seems to have pioneered the use of copper foiling to hold together small pieces of glass and other objects. Tiffany's glass manufacturing works closed in 1928; by the early 1930s, the Art Nouveau period had ended.

Contemporary stained glass has been influenced by the Bauhaus in Germany, which renewed and revitalized the use of stained glass in architecture. During the 1950s, many leading European painters such as **Matisse,** Léger, **Rouault,** and **Chagall** were given commissions to do stained glass pieces. Stained glass as an art form has been expanded by new materials such as epoxies, resins, and silicone, but its use of light and color remains its fundamental property. Also see **aciding, antique glass colorants, cutting glass, enameling, firing, fused glass technique, lamination, lampshade construction, polyester resin technique, staining.**

SETTING UP A WORKSHOP   The ideal work area for the professional is a large, well-lighted studio with good ventilation, high ceilings to allow for large panels, plenty of electrical outlets, and storage space. Ideally there should also be separate rooms for **glazing, aciding,** drawing, and **firing.** But most people do not have this type of work space.

To get started, you will need a well-lighted, dry room that has several electrical outlets and space for a worktable and glass storage. Fluorescent lighting is better than incandescent, and sunlight is the most desirable. It is also useful to have a **portable light box** (18″ × 24″ is good). Shelves and glass **sample rack**s are needed for storing materials. A peg-board is suitable to hang tools on. **Lead bin**s are useful for keeping **lead came** from getting tangled and twisted. A garbage pail on wheels that fits under the **cutting bench** is very helpful.

Because of the many different activities that take place in this one room, the area should be kept as organized, uncluttered, attractive, and comfortable as possible. See ill.

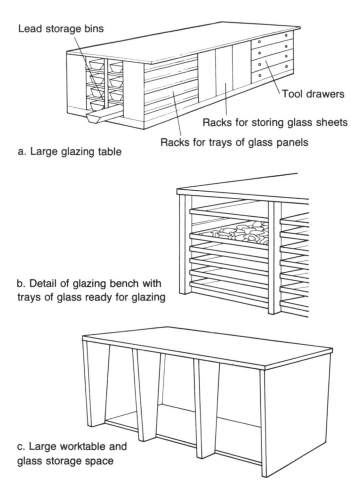

a. Large glazing table

b. Detail of glazing bench with trays of glass ready for glazing

c. Large worktable and glass storage space

TOOLS AND MATERIALS The following is a basic list of tools for working in stained glass: **soldering iron, glass-cutter, glazing knife, grozing pliers, plate pliers, needlenose pliers, lead vise** or other vise, **stopping knife** or oyster knife, **lathkin, mat knife** or single-edge razor blades, brush and dustpan, **scrub brush,** T-square, right angle, straightedge at least 18″ long, compass, pushpins, **masking** tape, 4-H pencil, grease pencil, black felt-tip pen, drawing board at least 30″ × 30″, large board such as plywood for **glazing** (referred to as workboard), and a sharpening stone, such as an **oilstone.**

Either **antique glass** (imported handblown glass available in many colors) or **machine-made glass** (less expensive but also less subtle in color and texture) is used. Both can be purchased from glass supply houses or from a local stained-glass studio. Outside of large cities, glass can be acquired from mail-order suppliers. Packages of glass samples are available from which realistic selections of colors and textures can be made. Suppliers will ship small orders as well as packages of scrap glass.

Lead came is available in a variety of sizes and textures. To begin, select either ⅜″ or ¼″ flat lead; buy more than needed to compensate for mistakes and getting used to handling it.

Solder is available from supply houses. Do not use core solder, no matter what a hardware dealer might say; 60% tin, 40% lead solder is good.

For **flux,** use **oleic acid** with lead came, zinc chloride or rubyfluid with **copper foil** and a past flux for general soldering with both. Copper foil is available in rolls of precut strips with adhesive backing or in sheets with or without adhesive. **Glazing putty** can be purchased in a hardware store. **Whitening** and **plaster of Paris** can be purchased in hardware stores or from building suppliers. **Farrier's nails** or **glazing nails** (1″ blued nails) and almost 12′ of **glazing strip**s made of wooden lath or 1″ × 2″ should be purchased. Lightweight drawing paper, 30-lb kraft paper, 80 or 90-lb kraft paper or stencil paper, and carbon paper are all available in art supply stores and are needed in various operations.

The care and maintenance of tools involves keeping the pliers oiled to prevent rust. Place glass-cutters in a jar with oil-soaked cotton at the bottom to keep the wheels lubricated and functioning properly. Glass should be stored so that jagged edges do not stick out of the racks to be tripped over. Brushes should not be left in the flux or the bristles will fall out. Build platforms of wooden strips with spaces between them for small pieces of glass to fall through; this enables the worker to stand above and not in the glass scraps when cutting glass or **grozing.**

BASIC PROCEDURES In learning stained-glass techniques it is best to begin by making a small, uniform **panel** assembled either by **glazing** or by **copper foiling.** Glazing produces a stronger bond and is used for large panels. Copper foiling is used for intricate, delicate, smaller pieces and for lamps such as those made by Tiffany. Glazing is the traditional method for glass work; copper foiling is the easier technique with more applications.

In either technique, start with a drawing or sketch; water colors provide the closest feeling in color to glass. Lead aids the structure of large panels; balanced lateral and horizontal support should be planned for, although it is not critical in small pieces. It will take time to understand the limitations glass imposes, and at first you may design panels with weak joints or hard cuts. For instance, sharp inside curves are very difficult and right angles are almost impossible. Joints where the leads converge are weak.

After the sketch has been decided on, a **cartoon** or full-size drawing is made from it. Then patterns or **template**s are cut out using **pattern shears** for **lead came** and regular scissors for **copper foil.** The cartoon is pinned to the workboard. Cutting the glass is the next stage. Make sure the workbench or cutting table does not wobble and is free of glass chips so that the glass can be placed flat for scoring.

After all pieces of glass have been cut and placed in their designated spot on the drawing to match them up to the cartoon, put away scraps of glass and clear a spot for glazing or copper foiling.

Solder one side of the panel and turn it over carefully to prevent it from snapping, especially if it is a large one. Keep the center of the panel supported on the edge of the table while pulling the panel toward you. Then, lifting the panel, support it in the center with your hands and then slowly slide it back over to the other side.

Glazing or puttying the panel follows soldering. The stained-glass piece is then cleaned and polished and ready to be hung or fixed into place. Also see **fixing, score, turning large panels.**

CUTTING   Hold the **glass-cutter** with the handle resting between the base of the index and middle fingers, with the index finger resting on the back of the grozing section of the cutter (**a.**). It should always be held at right angles to the glass, and is usually drawn toward the cutter. In cutting a curve, use the whole arm. Think of the cutter as an extension of the index finger. A good uniform cut is practically invisible, and is heard during the cut-line (**b.**). If the cutter is pressed too hard, small splinters of glass will scatter on either side of the line (**c.**). Practice on window glass by scoring it and breaking it several times.

In stained glass there is a right and wrong side for cutting. One usually cuts on the smoother side, but if there is doubt, a small **score** made on either side of glass will help determine which side accepts the score better. With **flashed glass,** the white side, or side without the flash, is the side to cut. The red side is too hard to cut.

Place the glass flat on the cutting table and select a **template** from the **cartoon.** Position it on the edge of a sheet of glass for the most economical use of the glass, leaving a ½″ margin; then cut around the template. Make a cut that will separate the piece of glass with the pattern from the whole sheet of glass.

To help in breaking the glass, tap the underside of the glass along the score line with the back of the glass-cutter head (never tap with the cutting wheel). This should be done sharply but not too heavily, starting at one end and working to the other. An internal fracture will begin to develop along the line; it is then ready to break. Holding the glass on both sides of the cut line is helpful, since glass can break during tapping and, if not supported, fall to the floor. Don't try to catch falling glass; let it fall. To break the glass, hold the edge, placing your hands on either side of the cut-line. Press up with your fingers and pull the glass apart at the same time. The glass should break evenly along the line. In breaking straight cuts, the cut-line can be laid on a table edge and held with one hand while the other hand, using sharp downward pressure, breaks the glass (**d., e.**). Now that it has been separated from the sheet, the glass piece remains to be cut to the shape of the template. Hold the template firmly in place and draw the cutter along the edge of the paper, starting ⅛″ from the edge of the glass farthest away from you. (Glass chips if it is cut right at its edge.) Draw the cutter toward yourself; glass cannot be scored more than once.

Glass shapes are cut in sequence, starting with the more difficult curves, so that there will be enough glass to support the break. Also, if the curve does not break correctly and the glass has to be cut again, time hasn't been wasted on the easier cuts, which are usually successful (**f.**). In cutting circles, remove the pieces in segments with several straight cuts and then remove the sharp corners with the grozing teeth (**g.**).

When cutting difficult shapes such as tight inside curves, score the glass with ever deepening secondary lines and sometimes crisscrosses (**h.**). Then tap the glass and remove successive pieces at a time with the **plate pliers.** To tap these curves, start at the apex of the curve and work outward. To tap shallow curves, start at each end and gradually meet in the middle. Always cut concave curves first to preserve the points.

Right angles are difficult to cut and should be avoided (**j.**).

Use plate or glass pliers to break off small pieces of glass or thin pieces that are impossible to break with the fingers. Hold the pliers with the index finger between the handles and a firm but not pinching grip on the glass (**k.**). The movement is a simultaneous breaking and pulling action.

Thick glass that is uneven can be cut by placing newspaper under the thinner sections to make the piece level. If the glass doesn't part through tapping, take a firm grip of the glass with the plate pliers and twist.

Some **antique glass** reds and yellows are hard to cut. There is practically no cutting noise or visible line after scoring. Pressing very hard, firmly guide the cutter along the template and then tap the glass to break it. See ill. below and next page. Also see **dulling, full and slack.**

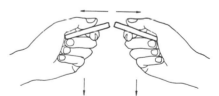

a. Holding glass cutter correctly   b. Good score   c. Poor score

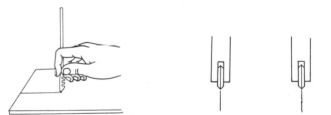

d. Breaking a straight cut by hand

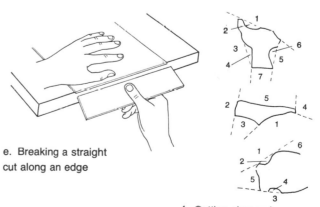

e. Breaking a straight
cut along an edge

f. Cutting shapes in sequence
(Continued)

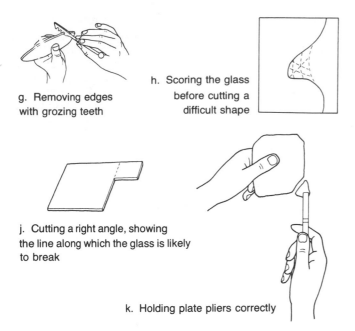

g. Removing edges with grozing teeth

h. Scoring the glass before cutting a difficult shape

j. Cutting a right angle, showing the line along which the glass is likely to break

k. Holding plate pliers correctly

GLAZING Glazing is the process of putting precut pieces of stained glass together with **lead came**s.

Choose a workboard that is large enough for the piece and accepts nails easily, such as wall board. Fasten the **cartoon** to the board with a double-faced masking tape.

Nail two **glazing strip**s a little longer than the piece at right angles to each other over the drawing in either the lower left- or right-hand corner. Use a right angle to make them square. Leave the border of the drawing showing. Leave extra space for the outer channel of the border lead if using H-lead.

Cut two pieces of border lead about an inch longer than the finished piece and open the ends that were flattened by the knife—do this by drawing the **lathkin** through the channels. Lay them along the inside edges of the wood strips with the open side facing the panel. The corners are formed by slipping one piece of lead into the other at right angles.

Start building from this corner by inserting the corner piece of glass into both strips. Tap the glass into place with the handle of the **glazing knife** if it is solid wood or by using a small wood block and hammer. Metal will shatter the glass. Make sure the position of the glass and the drawing underneath match up.

The first piece of glass can be removed from the second piece of lead added to it. Trim the lead right to the edge of the glass and flatten the ends by tapping them gently with the handle of the glazing knife. Open the lead into which this piece fits and, once they are interlocked, tap the lead down, securing the joint.

The next piece should support the first and be built on by the following piece. It should help lock the first piece into the border leads. Each following piece will be built out on a diagonal working back and forth between the border leads (**a.**). Try to avoid creating holes of missing glass (**b.**).

When kinks develop around curves in the lead, put the glazing-knife blade under the lead to support it and tap the lead with a small hammer (**c.**).

Use the **stopping knife** to help leads melt squarely and to lift corners of leads that have been knocked out of shape (**d.**).

While building out with glass and lead, hammer **farrier's nails** (1″ blued nails) in critical spots to hold the glass in place. Hammer the nails in just far enough to hold the glass and to be pulled out easily. In nailing next to lead use a small block of wood between the nail and the lead (**e.**). When fitting the next piece, remove the nails. When all the pieces have been put in place with lead, trim the ends that stick out beyond the drawing.

Instead of interlocking the corners of the border leads, you may join by mitering leads. To miter leads, place one end at right angles to the other, overlapping it and cutting the miter through both pieces (**f.**, **g.**). Add the remaining border strips, interlocking the corners or mitering them as done originally, and tack two more glazing strips along the remaining finished edges to lock the panel in place (**h.**). Go over all the joints and make sure they are flattened securely.

The next step is soldering the **joint**s. First make sure the joints fit tightly. If they are dirty, clean them with a small wire brush or steel wool. If the **soldering iron** has a copper tip, it must be tinned before soldering.

Using a stiff brush, **flux** each joint. Then, holding a strip of solder so that it touches the joint, take the soldering iron and touch the tip of the **solder.** A small, smooth drop of solder is instantly produced on the joint. Do not keep the iron in place longer than is necessary to melt the solder because it will quickly melt right through the lead came. Solder all the joints on one side of the panel. Then remove the glazing strips, turn the panel over, and repeat the same process on the other side.

When all joints on both sides are soldered, the next step is puttying. This is a method of caulking and waterproofing the piece. It is best done right after soldering; otherwise, the oleic acid residue should be removed with cleaning powder and a rag or brush. Use white, black, or gray putty with a linseed-oil base. It comes in cans and should be a hardening type. Use a protective glove-coating cream to cover the hands. Gather a ball of putty and push it under the lead leaf where it overlaps the glass, covering all the leaded areas. Then, with a lathkin or a putty knife, press the leads down to force out extra putty and make the seam tight. With a razor, nail, or ice pick trim away excess putty.

Turn the panel and do the other side. Wash the glove cream off your hands.

The final process is cleaning and polishing the panel. Sprinkle **whitening** on the piece, wipe off the excess, and brush the piece energetically to remove grease and dirt.

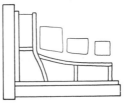

a. Building from corner into a diagonal (correct)

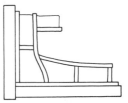

b. Leaving a hole (incorrect)

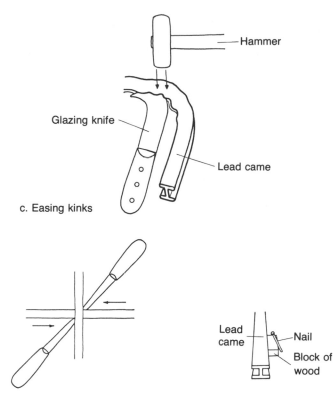

c. Easing kinks

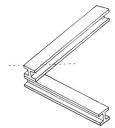

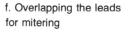

d. Squaring lead with the stopping knife

e. Holding lead in place

f. Overlapping the leads for mitering

g. After cutting the miter

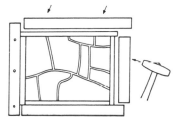

h. Adding remaining glazing strips

j. Joining concentric circles of lead came

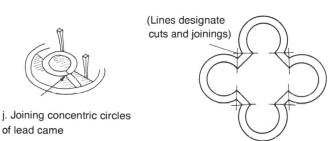

(Lines designate cuts and joinings)

k. Leading a complex shape

Then take a soft terry-cloth towel and polish the glass. See ill. Also see **double glazing, tinning, turning large panels, warp and buckle.**

SAFETY PRECAUTIONS   When using **hydrofluoric acid,** keep a bucket of cold water handy. Dip your hands into the bucket after each contact with the acid solution. When you have finished, wash your hands with soap and water. Wear protective clothing that adequately covers the body. Do not work with acid if your hands are cut. Do not wear plastic gloves. If you do get an acid burn, apply **bicarbonate of soda** and see a doctor.

Breathing the dust of artificial resins while polishing, grinding, or sawing them, and direct contact of the hands and other parts of the body with such resins are dangerous to health. Use proper ventilation, such as a fan that draws the air out from the studio. The fumes given off by some hardeners increase when the resin heats up. They are attracted to water, and thus the more watery parts of the body are particularly vulnerable to external and internal dermatitis. A mask and goggles can be worn for polishing or grinding resins. Also, use resin cleansing creams on the skin, not crude solvents. Use disposable containers for mixing resins to eliminate use of solvents for cleaning them. Polyester resins are combustible with turpentine, **alcohol, acetone,** and other organic substances. They should be kept away from each other. Cloths that have been used with resin should not be kept around the studio; wet them down before disposing of them.

Some ingredients in stained-glass cement are very poisonous and should be stored properly. An alternative is to use premixed glazing putty.

Lead is poisonous when ingested. Do not eat while working with lead; wash hands thoroughly after glazing to avoid lead poisoning. The danger from escaping lead fumes during soldering is said to be negligible.

Cutting **dalle-de-verre** or **slab glass** sends large, dangerous chips of glass through the air. Goggles are essential; gloves are optional. Rugged clothes and shoes are also recommended because flying slab glass can cut right through thin shoes or clothing.

Limited contact with **asbestos** is advised, as asbestos has been found to be a carcinogenic material.

To avoid cutting yourself on the sharp edges of glass, dull each piece of glass as it is cut. Clean and bandage all cuts. Also see **dulling.**

Stained Glass Association of America. Stained Glass. An organization that publishes a quarterly magazine, "Stained Glass," which lists member studios and suppliers as well as other stained-glass craft information. Their address is 1125 Wilmington Avenue, St. Louis, Missouri 63111.

stained glass batik. Batik and Tie-dye. Any lightweight **batik** fabric in which some of the residual **wax** is ironed into the material, giving it a translucence. The effect is apparent when the light source comes behind the fabric, as in a window or on a lampshade.

stained-glass cookie. Toys. See **translucent cookie.**

staining. Stained Glass. The stain used in stained glass is a mixture of silver nitrate and **gamboge**, with **gum arabic** added. The result obtained is comparable to a yellow wash applied over a section of a painting. The silver nitrate causes a molecular change in the glass—a fact that explains why the stain in medieval glass has survived, whereas the paint has worn off. Penetration of the glass molecules by the silver nitrate causes an ionization that produces a yellow light where previously there was a white light.

The harder the glass, the less receptive it is to stain. Some English glass is made exclusively for staining; all French glass is sensitive to stain, and German glass is mixed. Before staining is done on a large scale, small samples of stains should be made on glass, since individual colors of glass take stain differently. For each glass, a record should be kept of the time and the **firing** temperature of the **kiln** for future reference. There is a wide range of stains on the market; the lightest is **silver stain**, which becomes a light yellow. Small sample packages of colors can be obtained. The stains are corrosive and should be stored in glass or ceramic jars.

The stain comes in a granular form that has to be ground with a **mortar and pestle** or with a **muller** on a slab made of glass or marble. Water is added, and a **spatula** or palette knife is used to move the stain around during grinding—a very tedious job. It is helpful to wet the surface of the glass slightly to preserve fluidity when the stain is applied. Hard-bristled **brushes** and a badger can be used to apply the stain to the glass, which is painted on in the desired pattern. Because the stain combines with the molecular structure of the glass and is not an added layer, it is applied to the side opposite the one being painted. During firing, the stain develops color, or darkens. It does not lighten and is easily overfired. Stain is fired at a different temperature from that required for paint; therefore, firings of paint are completed before staining. Stain can be matted and whipped, worked in **lift ground** or **oil and water technique,** and masked, as in **painting on glass.** See ill. Also see **aciding, firing stain, kelp, masking, matting, metaling, overfiring, reamy glass, whipping.**

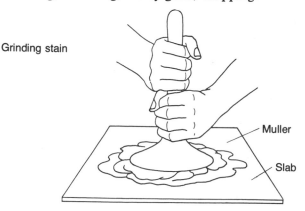

Grinding stain

Muller

Slab

staining flashed glass. Stained Glass. **Flashed glass** takes staining on both sides. Often the white side takes the stain better. The instructions for staining **antique glass** also apply to flashed glass. When the glass has been etched through the process of **aciding,** the edge of the acid bite takes the stain well, often providing a yellow halo around the original color. Strongly tinted flashed reds are not affected by stain, whereas light red or salmon flashes seem to lose their red ions and turn yellow and bronze colored. This is the only color that displays this phenomenon.

stainless compound. Jewelry. See **buffing compound.**

stainless-steel flux. Stained Glass. See **lampshade construction.**

stain repellent. Batik and Tie-dye. Stitchery. Toys. See **Scotchgard.**

Stairsteps. Quilts. See **Box Quilt.**

stake. Basketry. A heavy **reed** or **willow rod** that forms the structure of the basket sides and upon which the **siding** is woven.

stake. Jewelry. A piece of hardened steel with an extremely smooth surface, available in many shapes and sizes. Stakes can be held in a **vise, extension arm,** or **bench hole** and are used in **forming.** Metals are hammered against the stake's surface. In a sense, the stake is a type of **anvil.** The surface of the stake must not be marred as any defect would transfer to the surface of the work. Make sure metal is always absolutely clean and dry before using a stake. It is a good idea to wipe the palm of your hand across the surface of the stake to remove any dust or metal filings that may have settled on its surface. To form the metal, rest the metal against the stake with a space between the metal and the stake, toward which the metal is then hammered. Also see **doming, forging, mallet, planishing hammer, rawhide mallet.**

stake. Metalworking. See **anvil.**

stake up. Basketry. (Also called staking up.) To insert the **stake**s alongside the **spokes** of the base before beginning the **upsetting.** If an odd number of stakes is needed, only one stake is placed beside one of the spokes, instead of the normal two. See ill.

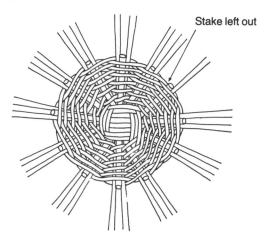

Stake left out

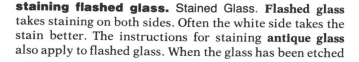

Staking up from the bottom of a basket

stalk stitch. Crewel. Embroidery. See **stem stitch.**

stamp. Ceramics. An embossed or intaglio form used to work a pattern on clay. Stamps are carved in plaster and are used to sign ware as well as for decoration. Remember to carve design in reverse. Test the stamp on a **slab** of clay to avoid error. See ill.

Stamps

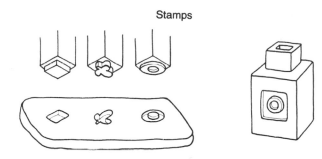

stamp. Leather. A drive tool available in various raised designs for **stamping** and **tooling.** Stamps are placed on damp leather prepared by **casing** with a **mallet** or a **maul** to leave an impression of the design on the leather. The various stamps available have been designed to give specific effects and can be used to create set stamping patterns or to achieve textural effects in tooled designs. Some of the commonly used stamps are shown here. A wide range of sizes are available in most stamp variations. See ill. Also see **embossing, matting, scorching, shading** and **Leatherwork: Tools and Materials.**

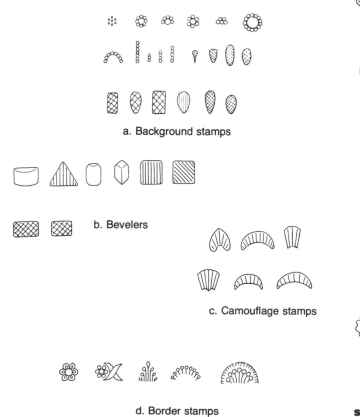

a. Background stamps

b. Bevelers

c. Camouflage stamps

d. Border stamps

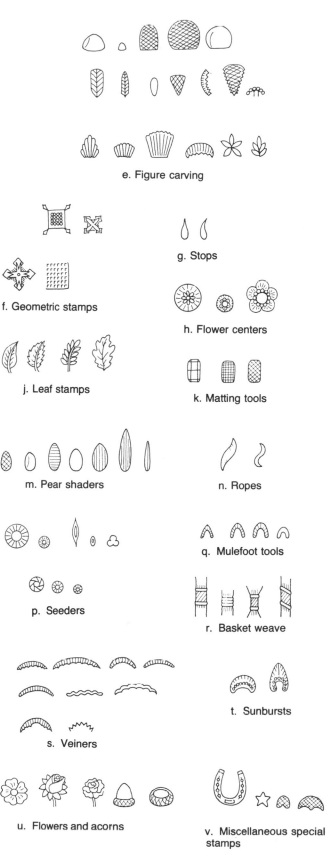

e. Figure carving

f. Geometric stamps

g. Stops

h. Flower centers

j. Leaf stamps

k. Matting tools

m. Pear shaders

n. Ropes

p. Seeders

q. Mulefoot tools

r. Basket weave

s. Veiners

t. Sunbursts

u. Flowers and acorns

v. Miscellaneous special stamps

stamp batik. Batik and Tie-dye. See **printed batik, tjap printing.**

stamping. Block Printing. A printing technique in which a **printing block** is cut with a simple shape, then inked and pressed down on paper or fabric. Stamped prints are generally repeated for all-over patterning or borders.

stamping. Bookbinding. See **tooling.**

stamping. Fabric Printing. The process of transferring a design to **fabric** by pressing a color-coated object, such as a cork or a potato block, onto its surface.

stamping. Jewelry. A procedure in which patterns are made on smooth metal surfaces with the use of different types of punches. Also see **embossing, grounder punch, matting tools, United States Stamping Law.**

stamping. Leather. The process of using a stamping die or **stamp** to embed decorative patterns and borders on moistened, **top grain** leather which has been vegetable tanned. The project must first be cut out, then moistened from the flesh side for lightweight leather with a sponge and cold water until the **grain** side darkens. Leave the grain side up on the work surface (a marble slab or pounding board) until it begins to show signs of drying. It is then ready to be decorated. Heavyweight leather is prepared by **casing.** To stamp the pattern, hold the stamp vertically over the moistened leather and strike with a **mallet.** When the design is completed, let the leather dry thoroughly before proceeding with the work. Stamping, when done by itself or with an **embossing wheel** to produce decorative patterns, is called set stamping. When the **swivel knife** is used to outline a design and the stamps used for detail and texture, it is called **tooling.** See ill. Also see **chrome tanning, pear shader** and **Leatherwork: Setting Up a Workshop, Tools and Materials.**

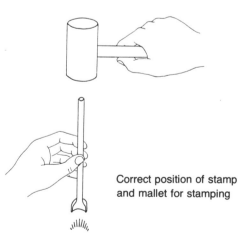

Correct position of stamp and mallet for stamping

stamp printing. Batik and Tie-dye. (Also called batik printing.) A method of printing **wax** designs onto **fabric** for **batik.** In traditional stamp printing, the **tjap** is used. This is also known as **tjap printing** or wood-block batik.

Any object, tool, carved wood piece, cork, or spool can be used in this stamp batik process.

standard. Stitchery. The vertical pole by which a **flag** or **banner** is carried. Sometimes the standard and the **staff** are the same, as when the standard is long enough so that the flag may be hung from the same pole. Usually the standard is long enough to allow the flag to hang free.

Also, the emblem or insignia sewn onto fabric used to identify a nation, a military group, a city, etc.

standard harness. Weaving. See **doup.**

standard tie-up. Weaving. See **tie-up.**

standing frame. Crewel. Embroidery. Needlepoint. See **embroidery frame.**

standing press. Bookbinding. A heavy, fixed piece of equipment used to hold a book flat while it dries. See ill.

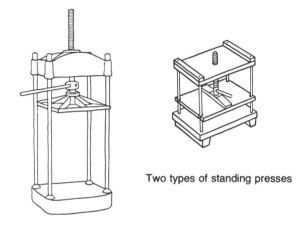

Two types of standing presses

standing reel. Spinning. See **Spinning.**

standup toy. Toys. Any toy that can stand up by itself. It may be a **wood cutout** sawed from wood thick enough to let the figure stand. Paper **cutouts** often have a tab on the reverse side, a triangular shape that folds out to add support. Sometimes notched cards are slipped into matching notches on the cutouts to make the toys stand up.

stannic chloride. Enameling. See **fuming.**

stannic oxide. Amber Carving. See **tin oxide.**

staple. Spinning. Any **fiber** whose length is expressed in inches. This includes all natural fibers except silk. Silk and synthetics can be made into staple fibers by cutting the **filament**s into pieces. These pieces are made into yarn by spinning them into a continuous strand. Staple fibers, whether natural or man-made, measure from ¾" to 15" in length. Because of this variance, fibers are graded as to long staple and short staple. Long staple, natural fibers are much desired because of their superior luster, strength, and fineness. A length suitable for **combing wool** would be a long staple. In combing **cotton,** the fibers would be 1⅛–2½" in length. Also see **flax, linen.**

Star and Cross. Quilts. See **star patterns.**

star and crown. Quilts. See **Quilts: Quilting.**

Star and Planets. Quilts. A **pieced block** pattern of a six-pointed star set into a circle. A triangle is pieced at each of the star points, and the whole block is made into a square.

Star and Plumes. Quilts. See **Princess Feather.**

starch. Papercrafts. Bottled liquid starch from the grocery store is used as a **papier mâché paste** for the **paper-strip method** or for making **paper mash.**

starch. Stitchery. A thickening agent available in powder, liquid, or spray form. A **fabric** can be dipped in the liquid or in a solution made with powder. The spray starch is applied from an aerosol can. When the starched material is ironed, it takes on a smooth surface which is colorless in thin layers and odorless. Starch is sometimes used to stiffen fabric to give it more **body** and to make it easier to machine appliqué. The stiffened material is more easily handled in **soft sculpture** and toymaking.

star crack. Stained Glass. See **firecrack.**

star facet. Gemcutting. See **facet.**

starfish. Quilts. See **Quilts: Quiltmaking.**

Star Flower. Quilts. (Also called Golden Glow.) An **appliqué block** design that uses four petals offset and overlapped by four more petals. A circular shape is set into the center of the flowers. This is a common design seen in many variations; it does not usually require a pattern.

Star of Bethlehem. Quilts. A name given to a variety of **pieced block** designs, all of which have eight-pointed stars. This name most commonly refers to the single large star, composed entirely of diamond shapes, that forms an **overall** design of a **quilt top.** Other patterns that are also designated by this title are pieced blocks to be **set** into an **allover** quilt top. See ill. Also see **diamond patchwork, Eight-pointed Star, star patterns.**

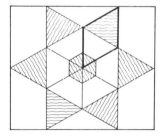

Star of Bethlehem

Star of the East. Quilts. See **star patterns.**

Star of the Four Winds. Quilts. See **Star of the West.**

Star of the West. Quilts. A simple **geometric four-patch,** four-pointed star **block** pattern. It was originally called Clay's Choice, in honor of Henry Clay of Kentucky, who had lost the presidential campaign to dark-horse candidate James K. Polk. This **pieced quilt** design was also known as Harry's Star and Henry of the West. Eventually, Clay was forgotten entirely, and the quilt became known as Star of the West.

The name "Star of the West," however, also refers to at least a dozen other **star pattern**s that developed from the original Clay's Choice. Among these is Star of the Four Winds. See ill.

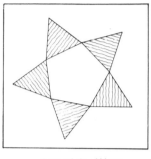

Star of the West

star patterns. Quilts. **Geometric** patterns, usually **pieced,** of triangles and squares. The **piecing** method lends itself especially well to sharp points and exact repeats, so it is not surprising that there are literally hundreds of star patterns. The names vary from one locality to another and are often associated with a specific place. Others assume the name of a quilter (such as Aunt Eliza's Star) or a famous person (such as **Dolley Madison Star**).

The star designs are among the most difficult patterns of the **pieced quilts;** they are also among the most varied and popular. It is an exacting process to stitch the bias-cut edges so that they remain flat and unstretched, and to retain the sharp points of the stars.

Some star patterns join to form additional stars when the **block**s are **set.** Among these are **Hunter's Star** and **New Star.** Others, as **Star of Bethlehem,** form one great central star that covers the **quilt top.** A third variation uses star blocks set so that the stars alternate with blocks of solid color or printed fabric that are not pieced.

Among the four-pointed star patterns are Arrowhead Star, Chicago Star, **Geometric Star,** Iowa Star, Jackson Star or Four Stars, **King David's Crown,** Odd Star, and Star and Cross. Some of the five-pointed star patterns are Five-point Star, Savannah Beautiful Star, **Star of the West,** and **Union Star.** Six-pointed star patterns include Hexagonal Star, Old Colony Star, **Rising Star,** Star of the East, Texas Star. Eight-pointed star patterns include **Blaz-**

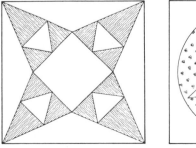

Iowa Star

Union Star

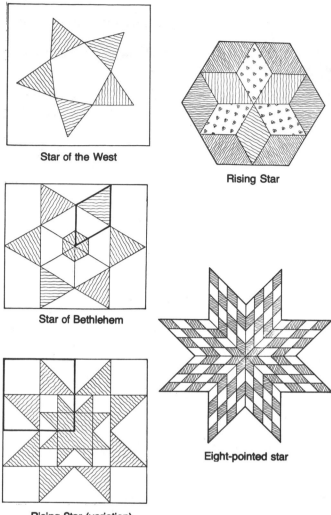

Star of the West

Rising Star

Star of Bethlehem

Eight-pointed star

Rising Star (variation)

ing Star, Christmas Star, **Falling Star, French Star,** North Carolina Star, **Octagonal Star,** Odd Fellow's Star, **Pieced Star, Rising Star** (variation), St. Louis Star, Tennessee Star, and Virginia Star (also called Star-upon Star). See ill.

Star Spangled Banner Quilt. Quilts. A quilt made in 1840 consisting of five large and very intricately **pieced** stars. The **quilting** itself is exceptional, incorporating **cotton-stuff**ed spread eagles in high relief spaced between the star **blocks**. The words of the "Star Spangled Banner" were stitched into the quilt almost 100 years before it officially became the national anthem. This one-of-a-kind quilt is in the Shelburne Museum in Shelburne, Vermont.

star stitch. Stitchery. A simple **stitch** often used with **appliqué** made by crossing three or four straight stitches. The final stitch then catches and holds them all at the center.

Three stitches cross one another to form a six-pointed star (**a.**). After taking the third stitch, the needle is drawn through at the center, over the three stitches, and back to the reverse side (**b.**). This final small tacking stitch holds the longer stitches securely in place (**c.**). See ill.

Star stitch

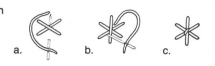

a.   b.   c.

starting. Bookbinding. A condition that occurs in books when the **back** loses its roundness and becomes concave and the **foredge** (normally concave) loses its shape and begins to jut forward.

starting yarn. Spinning. See **leader.**

Star-upon-Star. Quilts. See **star patterns.**

starving the tip. Metalworking. See **backfire.**

Star-within-Star. Quilts. (Also called Broken Star, Carpenter's Wheel, Double Star.) Any of several **star patterns** beginning with a central **pieced** star that by use of succeeding rows of diamond or square pieces builds up to double and triple star shapes. It is similar to **Dutch Rose.**

state quilt. Quilts. A quilt made to point out historical or geographical features of a particular state. These quilts can be one person's creative efforts or those of many.

static electricity. Plastics. See **electrostatic charge.**

stationary belt sander. Woodworking. See **sanding tools.**

staurolite. Gemcutting. (Also called fairy cross.) Iron, magnesium, and aluminum silicate **crystal**lized in the orthorhombic system with **hardness** of 7½ and **specific gravity** of 3.7−3.8. It is reddish-brown or yellow-brown and occurs in opaque to translucent varieties. Crown and pavilion **facet**s are twinned at 60° or 90°.

stay. Papercrafts. Stenciling. (Also called tie.) A term for the strips of background paper that are not cut, serving the function of holding the cutout design together. Stays are particularly necessary in intricate cuttings and in folding paper several times and cutting for **repeat pattern**s.

stays. Découpage. See **bridges.**

steam casting. Jewelry. A type of **casting** in which steam is used to force metal into the cavity produced by the **burnout** of a wax model. The preparation of the model, including **sprue**s, **sprue cone,** and burnout, is nearly identical to that of **centrifugal casting,** except that a **centrifugal casting machine** is not required. The main sprue coming from the **wax model** to the sprue cone area should be 14-**gauge,** and the sprue cone area should be large enough to hold sufficient metal for the casting as the metal is melted directly in the cavity provided by the sprue cone. The distance from the base of the sprue cone to the wax model should be not more than ¼". A metal jar lid large enough so that its sides will extend down over the outside edge of the **flask** can have a handle screwed to the center top of it. The inside of the lid should be packed with 4–6 layers of wet asbestos and left submerged in warm water just prior to casting. Metal can be melted directly in the sprue cone; when it has become molten, the lid is placed on top of the flask and held down tightly. The water in the asbestos immediately becomes heated from the molten metal, producing steam pressure that forces the metal into the cavity of the burned-out wax. The flask itself should be placed on a porous substance such as an asbestos block to allow for the escape of gases through the bottom of the investment flask.

steamer. Batik and Tie-dye. Any large container used for **steaming** or to **heat set dye**s. While commercial steam cabinets and **autoclave**s offer many conveniences, any large kettle can be used to make an improvised steamer or steam kettle. A pressure cooker or home canner is adequate for this use. The capacity of the container sets the limits as to the amount of fabric that can be steamed at one time. An average home canner can hold about three yards, although the amount will vary according to the weight of the fabric. Before placing it over the heat source the steamer should have about 2″ of water in the bottom. A rack should sit about 6″ above bottom, or 3–4″ above the water. Coffee cans with both ends removed can be used with a cake rack or plate set on top. The rack should be covered with a pad of papers, cloth, or paper towels, as no water condensing on any surface should come in direct contact with the dyed fabric.

steamer. Fabric Printing. A vessel in which printed **fabric** can be exposed to steam heat in a **fixation** process to give the colors **fastness**. A steamer must provide boiling water in the bottom, a rack for the fabric, and padding to protect the fabric completely from splashing.

An enamel canning pan or preserving kettle can be used as a steamer. Turn the jar rack upside down to serve as a shelf for the fabric. Place newspapers and padding around the fabric to protect it from splatters of the boiling water. For padding, use thick carpet underfelt, or Fiberglas insulating material (**a.**).

A larger steamer to accommodate larger yardages of fabric can be made from a galvanized iron garbage can. Prop the can up on bricks over an outdoor fire or over a gas ring or burner, or use electric immersion heaters. Line the shelf or basket (of galvanized wire or stainless steel) and the interior of the steamer with padding. No metal should touch the fabric bundle—only padding. To accommodate more fabric, hang several baskets one above the other, with the fabric protected by padding above as well as below; or, if you wish, simply hang the fabric bundle from a stick resting across the mouth of the can. Because the lid is a source of dripping, pad it densely and tie it with sacking material, or replace the lid with several thick layers of padding on a simple supporting frame (**b.**).

The fixation process is basically the same for any type of steamer. The steamer should not be hermetically sealed but should provide a free escape for steam and the volatile by-products given off during the steaming process. See ill. Also see **steaming.**

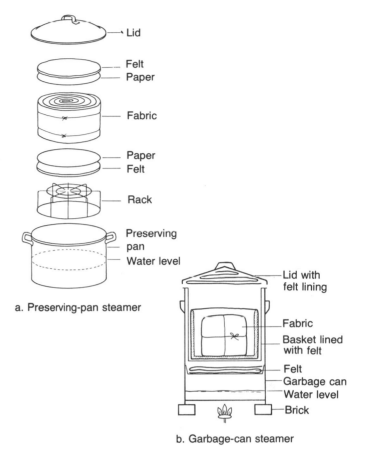

a. Preserving-pan steamer

b. Garbage-can steamer

steam fixation. Fabric Printing. See **steaming.**

steaming. Batik and Tie-dye. The process of applying moist heat for **fixing dye** colors in **direct-dye painting, tie-dye,** or **batik.** If the batik process has been used, **wax** must first be removed by **ironing.** The dyed material is then rolled with paper or cloth between the rolls so that the fabric does not touch itself. A heavy fabric may have to be rolled and steamed, then removed from the steam bath and rerolled in the opposite direction to give thorough steaming at both ends. The dyed fabric should make a bundle compact enough so that it does not touch the sides of the **steamer.** The roll of fabric is coiled so that it will fit onto the padded rack. Another pad is placed over the coil. Finally, a heavy pad of newspapers or other padding is placed over the top of the kettle so that it extends over the edge all the way around. A lid can be pressed down over this and weighted. Some pressure can develop but the padding allows enough steam to escape to avoid dangerous pressure. Steaming time may vary from 5–30 minutes, depending upon the amount and weight of the material being steamed. Fabric must be thoroughly rinsed according to dye instructions after the steaming is finished.

steaming. Fabric Printing. A **fixation** process in which the dry, printed **fabric** is exposed to the action of steam long enough for colors to become permanently affixed to the fibers. Various types of **steamer** arrangements can be used, depending on the amount of fabric to be steamed. The steamer should be large enough to hold the fabric—bundled and tied, with padding around it—so that it can be reached by steam but be protected against water. There will be splashes rising from the boiling water, drips falling from above, and steaming condensation on the inside walls of the steamer. If the printed fabric gets wet before the fixation process is completed, the colors will run. However, if the material is too well protected and the steam does not penetrate, the fixation will be incomplete and the colors will run when they are washed.

The fabric bundle must be carefully packed. If the fabric is folded just as it is, the printed patterns may transfer on to the part of the fabric against which they are folded. To prepare the fabric for steaming, place a layer of newspaper or, preferably, a thin cloth on a table; then place the printed fabric over it. Roll the two layers together from end to end. The roll will be as long as the width of the fabric and several inches in diameter. Flatten the roll with your hands, then roll it up from one end. Tie the bundle with string, finishing with a bow to make the bundle easy to open when it comes out of the steamer. The bundle must be small enough to fit inside the steamer shelf with layers of padding around it. Place the fabric in the steamer after the water is boiling vigorously. Replace the lid quickly so that steam won't be lost. The steaming is usually done for about an hour. Because the fabric is so tightly packed, there is danger that the steam penetration will be uneven. For this reason many craftspeople automatically double the time, taking care that the steamer doesn't boil dry. After one hour the parcel can be opened and rerolled from the other end. The steamer can be refilled with water, if necessary, and the parcel steamed for an additional hour. Always unroll the bundle immediately after removing it from the steamer. After fabrics printed with **dye paste** have been steamed, the excess **dye** and **thickener** must be washed away in detergent, and the fabric rinsed and dried.

steaming. Woodworking. A technique in which wood is subjected to steam to make it pliable and easy to bend. It is commonly used on furniture forms with rounded curves.

steam pressing. Rugmaking. Weaving. The quickest and easiest method of **finishing** a **fabric, tapestry,** or **rug.** A steam iron is used or an ordinary iron is placed over a damp pressing cloth. The least amount of shrinkage occurs with steam pressing, since the amount of moisture is usually limited. However, this depends on the fiber involved and repeated steam pressings may result in much more shrinkage. For just a very light pressing, or to get creases and wrinkles out, place a piece of brown wrapping paper over the pressing cloth. The moderately hot iron is smoothed over the paper with a series of short pats. Also see **blocking.**

steam set. Batik and Tie-dye. To **fix** a **dye** or make it permanent by **steaming.** This can be accomplished with a home canner or **steamer** or with an **autoclave.**

stearic acid. Candlemaking. (Also called stearin.) A soft, opaque, white, odorless, waxlike fatty acid derived from natural animal and vegetable fats used as an additive to **paraffin** to make candles harder, more opaque, and better burning. It was first discovered in the early nineteenth century by Michel Chevreul. It is normally added in quantities of 5–30%—the higher the percentage, the greater the opacity or the whiteness of the candle. In glass **container candle**s or in dipped candles where translucence is desired, stearic acid is not used.

stearin. Candlemaking. See **stearic acid.**

steel. Metalworking. Steel is an iron **alloy.** Pure **iron** is not strong enough for many uses, so it is mixed with other elements to enhance its qualities.

Carbon steel is an iron alloy with carbon as the principal supplementary element. The hardness, strength, and **ductility** of this steel are determined by the amount of carbon contained; the more carbon, the greater the hardness and **brittleness.** (Cast iron may have 2–4% carbon, more than the maximum of 1.7% in carbon steel.) Other alloys may be added for specific properties.

There are three types of carbon steel: Low-carbon (or mild) steel contains up to 0.30% (or 30 points) carbon. It is tough, ductile, easily **weld**ed, machined, or formed, and is a good benchwork metal. It is available in sheets, bars, rods, and angle **stock.** Medium-carbon steel contains 0.30–0.60% carbon and is strong and hard, but not as easily worked or welded as mild steel. It can be heat-treated for greater strength, and is used for tools and machine parts. High-carbon (or high-speed) steel contains 0.60–0.70% carbon. It is very hard and strong, and is often used for cutting other metals in **drill bit**s, machine tools, **dies,** and fixtures. It can be **temper**ed, but if it is heated to yellow or white it may burn and crack.

Alloy steel is named according to the prominent metal added to the steel to increase its **toughness,** strength, and resistance to corrosion or wear. For example, nickel and chromium increase toughness, and silicon increases resiliency. If only one other metal is added to the steel, it is a binary alloy; if two metals are added, it is a ternary alloy.

Cor-Ten steel is a recently developed alloy popular for outdoor sculpture, bridges, and other external structural work. It is about 40% stronger than ordinary structural steel and costs approximately 50% more than mild steel. It rusts to a certain point and no further because the rust forms a self-sealing protective covering. A disadvantage of this metal is that the rust coating bleeds and runs during weathering and will stain any light-colored base. Outdoor sculpture should be **sandblast**ed when fabrication is complete so the surface will rust uniformly to a final earthy color.

Stainless (or nickel-chromium) steel is the name for a group of alloy steels that resist corrosion (although they will rust if exposed to moisture long enough) and are extremely hard. Chromium (more than 10%) is added to the iron to improve toughness and hardness; nickel is added to improve strength, toughness, and resistance to wear and corrosion; molybdenum may be added to increase strength at high temperatures and resistance to corrosion and abrasion; and silicon may be added to increase resistance to high-temperature oxidation. Stainless steel has a

50% greater rate of expansion than mild steel, so in **welding,** only small areas should be heated at a time to prevent warping. The precise heat control necessary is best provided by an **arc** or **heliarc** welder.

Nickel steel is an alloy of iron and nickel noted for its excellent **tensile strength,** durability, corrosion resistance, elasticity, and machinability. It is used for structural steel, casting, gun metal, and boiler plates.

Tool (or tool-and-dye) steel is a group of alloy steels used for tools with cutting edges that will be subjected to high temperatures, or when **heat treatment** is needed. Tungsten is added to iron to produce high-speed steel for tools that cut metals even after becoming red hot, and for **heliarc welding electrode**s. Tungsten carbide (tungsten with carbon) is **braze**d onto the cutting tips of plain carbon steel tools. Manganese may be added to decrease brittleness from sulfur, to increase hardness and tensile strength, and to reduce brittleness at high temperatures (allowing the metal to be worked hot). Vanadium may be added to improve the **grain** and to increase both hardness and resistance to wear at high and low temperatures. Molybdenum may also be added to increase strength at high temperatures.

steel block. Jewelry. (Also called bench block, surface plate.) A block of steel, one surface of which is always either ground to a fairly smooth finish or polished. Smaller blocks can be polished on all six faces. It is used when a solid, unresisting surface is needed for processes such as **rivet**ing, **stamping, bending** corners, flattening **sheet metal** with a **rawhide mallet,** truing up a straight edge, and **forging** small sections. Also see **joint.**

steel-core came. Stained Glass. See **lead came.**

steel pin. Jewelry. Heavyweight steel straight **pin**s of the type used in sewing can be used to hold work in position during **soldering.** They can be pushed into an **asbestos pad** or a **magnesium block.** The pins used in jewelrymaking must be of a heavy **gauge** to avoid melting during soldering.

Steel T-pins—the "T" is their shape as well as their name—can also be used to hold work in position for soldering. Steel T-pins are usually not available at a jewelry supply house. They are, however, nearly always available at a shop that carries women's wigs or at hair salons, as heavyweight steel T-pins are used to hold wigs on styrofoam head forms. Also see **cotter pin, iron binding wire.**

steel wheel glass-cutter. Stained Glass. See **glasscutter.**

steel wool. Découpage. Massed hairlike steel shavings used for smoothing and polishing. Steel wool is available at hardware stores. The grade numbers increase as the steel wool becomes finer. For general use in découpage, #400 is used for smoothing rough surfaces, #600 for smooth surfaces, and #0000 for final polishing after the **finish** has been sanded.

steel wool. Jewelry. An abrasive material composed of long, fine, steel shavings, available in a variety of grades ranging from #0000 (4/0), the finest, to #3, the coarsest. Each grade produces a different quality of semi-**matte** finish. It is important that the steel wool be rubbed in one direction to produce a uniform quality. Steel wool will not remove scratches from metal, but if a piece of work is finished and for some reason there is a scratch that cannot be removed without causing damage or destruction of the piece, a coarser steel wool used in the direction of the scratch will not only blend in the scratch, but save the piece. Also see **hand polishing, Swedish finish.**

steel wool. Metalworking. Plastics. Woodworking. See **abrasives.**

steel wool. Stained Glass. See **Stained Glass: Glazing.**

Steeplechase. Quilts. (Also called Bows and Arrows.) A **pieced block** design that is a slight variation of the **Drunkard's Path.** In this design, the quarter circle is sewn into two diagonally opposed corners. When **set,** a pattern of circles overlays alternating corners.

steep twill. Weaving. See **weave twill.**

steerhide. Leather. A term for the **hide** from mature cattle that have been raised for beef.

stem. Beadwork. See **basic row.**

stem beads. Beadwork. Large green beads used for stringing on **stem wire** to finish **bead flowers.** The most commonly used size is 8/0 mm. Also see **beaded stems.**

stem fiber. Knitting. See **bast fiber.**

stem stitch. Crewel. Embroidery. Needlepoint. (Also called crewel stitch, outline stitch, stalk stitch.) An excellent outline stitch or filling stitch when worked in rows. The thread may be held either to the left or right of the needle,

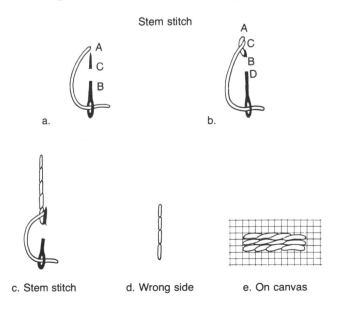

Stem stitch

a.

b.

c. Stem stitch   d. Wrong side   e. On canvas

but the same side should be used consistently. When used for outlining, hold the thread away from the shape. This stitch can be worked on linen and **canvas.** See ill. Also see **line stitch, looped stem stitch, raised stem stitch, smocking.**

stem stitch. Rugmaking. Weaving. See **soumak.**

stem wire. Beadwork. Several weights of **wire** available in 18″ lengths are used for mounting flowers on stems in **bead flowermaking.** Stem wire is available in two forms: galvanized, and bright basic (which is firmer and stronger). The gauge numbers increase as the wire becomes finer; for heavy flowers, use 12-gauge wire; for medium-size flowers, use 14-gauge; and for small ones, use 16-gauge.

stencil. Batik and Tie-dye. Toys. A form or shape cut from metal, oiled paper, parchment, or similar material and used as a guide in transferring or arranging a design. In **batik,** the stencil may be used as a guide in painting waxed areas. The shape to be drawn or reproduced is usually cut as a negative area. For example, if a drawing of a bird was used, the bird shape would be cut out and removed from the center of the stencil sheet. In painting, the area around the bird would be protected from the **wax. Contact paper**s can be used for simple self-adhesive stencils in batik.

Stencils are commonly used in lettering, and the letters always retain a characteristic appearance that results from the connecting lines of the stencil. In the letter "B" the large shape would be removed, but the two half-circle centers would have to remain. The parts of the stencil that hold them in place leave lines that become part of the finished letter. Stencils are also used in air brush or **direct-dye painting.**

In **toy**making, stencils provide a pattern for painting on wood with enamel or acrylic. The self-adhesive stencils are easily made and used, and may be peeled off when paint is dry.

stencil. Enameling. Material used to prevent the application of **enamel** to an area. A sheet of paper, for example, may be used to screen an area for a second dusting. Stencils may be selected for design motif, repetition, or form.

stencil. Silkscreen. Any of several kinds of material that block the openings of the **mesh** used in silkscreen printing. When the **squeegee** is scraped across the screen with a load of ink, the stencil prevents the passage of ink onto the nonprinting areas of the material being printed.

Stencils range from the simplest **cut-paper stencil** and **block out stencil** to the versatile **tusche stencil, cut-film stencil,** and varieties of the **photographic stencil.**

stencil. Stenciling. A design cut out of **stencil paper** or cardboard through which paint or other medium can be directly applied to produce an impression on paper or **fabric** in the cut-out areas only.

stencil board. Stenciling. See **stencil paper.**

stencil brush. China and Glass Painting. Stenciling. A brush especially for stenciling, available from art supply stores, although any brush can be used as long as the bristles are short, stiff, and flat across the ends, for easy **stippling** of the color. See ill. Also see **Stenciling: Painting.**

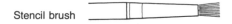
Stencil brush

stencil cutting. Découpage. See **Découpage: Cutting.**

stencil-cutting tool. Silkscreen. Specialized knives used to cut the lacquer layer of **cut-film stencil** materials or to cut paper for a **cut-paper stencil.**

The Ulano swivel knife is a precision tool that has a very small triangular blade set in a chuck that rotates freely on ball-bearings so that the blade cutting edge remains pointed into the work even through very tightly drawn curves in a way that is hard to match with fixed blade tools. Twisting the knurled knob at the other end of the tool while holding the chuck will lock the blade, making it more suitable for cutting straight lines. The replaceable blades are made of a very hard steel and require little sharpening. The tool is widely available in graphic arts supply stores, or from the manufacturer: Ulano Graphic Arts Supplies, Inc., 610 Dean Street, Brooklyn, N.Y. 11238. Ulano also carries a wide variety of supplies for silkscreen work.

Standard fixed-blade film stencil knives are, of course, much cheaper than the swivel knife, and are adequate for most work. Double-line cutters have two parallel blades fixed to a handle with either screw-adjustable space between the blades or double-edge interchangeable heads. These cutters make it easy to cut straight lines of even thickness. Bow compasses are also available with small blades set into the leg of the compass opposite the center point.

It is important, especially in the cutting of film stencils, to use a blade that is very sharp. Too dull a tool, pressed too hard, will dent the backing sheet and may interfere with good adhesion when the stencil is fixed to the screen. See ill.

Ulano swivel knife

stenciled quilt. Quilts. A rare kind of bedcover from the 1800s that utilizes a stencil for the decorative pattern. The **stenciling** was done on large pieces of fabric that were sometimes **quilted** and sometimes used simply as bedspreads, with no layering or **quilting.** Some stenciled quilts were made up from **block**s decorated by stenciling. The blocks were often **set** with **band**s of color.

STENCILING

Stenciling is a printing technique in which **paint** is applied directly through design areas cut out on **stencil paper** to produce a painted impression on the surface to be decorated. The uncut parts of the stencil paper mask the area that is to remain unprinted. Because the boundaries of the design areas are cut, stenciling is generally characterized by simple, unconnected shapes, often repeated in patterning.

Stenciling has traditionally been a popular method for household decoration of walls, furniture, and linens. It was popular in nineteenth-century America and was considered a suitable accomplishment for ladies to master, along with needlework. Kits for painting were available with instructions, stencils, tracings of pictures, drawing paper, oiled paper for cutting one's own stencils, tracing paper, and so on. Still-life paintings and floral arrangements, which were well suited to stenciling, were common. Such stenciled compositions were called **theorem work**.

Itinerant decorators, who traveled the countryside combining a little portrait painting with house decorating, decorated house after house with stenciled walls and floors. The patterns for walls were inspired by more costly wallpaper, but because of the nature of stenciling, the motifs were more simple. Walls were decorated with stenciled patterns accented by horizontal borders, or friezes, along the edges of ceilings and floors. Generally, a more elaborate pattern was done above the fireplace. The patterning was based on simple repeat motifs of stylized foliage, leaves, ribbon swags, or geometric shapes. Favorite symbols were also popular, such as the pineapple for hospitality, the willow for immortality, or the eagle for American liberty. The colors were flat, without **shading**, and bold—red, yellow, green, and black on pale backgrounds.

The fireplace, the focal point of the living room, usually received additional decoration. The space over the mantel often was painted with a landscape or still life, combining stencil and freehand painting. A fireboard, used to close off the fireplace during the summer, was usually decorated in similar patterning.

As early as 1775 stenciled designs on furniture were produced in England and Wales using metallic powders. When the Empire style of furniture, with gilt and inlaid decorations, became popular in America, country artisans developed adaptations of the style, sometimes using stencils and gold leaf or gold powder but more often less expensive bronze powder. Chairs were popularly decorated in this way. The wood was first coated with varnish slightly thinned with turpentine. The stencil was pressed onto the surface when the varnish became tacky. The powder was applied with a velvet pad, or **"pounce,"** through the stencil openings. When the varnish was slightly drier, **shading** was added freehand or with a **bob**. After the design dried it was protected with another coat of varnish. As the demand for stenciled furniture increased, methods were developed for manufacturing them with simplified techniques, using fewer stencils for each pattern and flatter color application. In the 1820s Lambert Hitchcock developed a method for mass producing stenciled chairs at his factory in Connecticut.

French wallpaper murals that covered an entire room were popular in the early nineteenth century. Around 1825 **Rufus Porter** developed a rapid technique combining stenciling and painting to produce such murals directly on plaster walls. The backgrounds were rapidly painted, and then details of architecture, boats, and so on, were added with stencils; foliage was stippled on with a cork or a brush.

Stenciled decorations eventually were replaced by even less expensive ways of decorating. Nevertheless, the technique of stenciling was skillfully developed, and fine works of art were produced.

TOOLS AND MATERIALS   The basic tools required for stenciling are **stencil paper**, a **stencil knife**, a **stencil brush**, **paint**, and a surface to be decorated. For designing you'll need tempera paint, pencils, brushes, tracing paper, masking tape, and paper for trail prints. Stencil paper can be purchased, or prepared from paper or cardboard by coating it with melted paraffin. Various knives may be used to cut the stencil, such as a utility knife. A single-edge razor blade or embroidery or cuticle scissors may also be used. Knives must be very sharp. Have a **sharpening stone** on hand. A punch can be used to make small holes. A cutting board on which to cut stencils may be needed to protect the worktable. The type of paint will depend on the surface to be decorated. In general, any thick paint can be used for stenciling. A sponge or a stencil brush may be used to apply the paint.

Cleaning materials will also be needed: a solvent, such as turpentine or paint thinner for oil paints; water for tempera paints; and paper toweling, newspaper, and cloths.

SETTING UP A WORKSHOP   Stenciling is a portable craft: the **stencil**s, **brush**es, and **paint** are lightweight and can easily be moved to decorate walls, floors, and so on. For stenciling smaller areas, a well-lighted worktable and a water source for cleaning up are useful.

DESIGNING AND CUTTING   In designing for stenciling it is essential to keep the cutting process in mind. The problem in cutting is to keep the details in place on the **stencil** by leaving just enough background **stencil paper** to hold them together.

These supporting strips, or **stay**s, do not allow any **paint** to print; the paint is printed only through the cut-out areas of the stencil. This way of cutting stencils with detail is what gives stencil work its characteristic appearance of flat, unconnected shapes and what makes stenciling good for repeated all-over patterning. The designs best suited to this technique are therefore clear, definite shapes, without very small details. Designs can be planned by cutting folded paper cutouts for symmetrical or repeated patterns.

Designs for stenciling have traditionally been simple, although various methods have been developed for adding detail. Multicolor prints can be made, with a stencil cut for each color to be used and then printed one at a time, allowing each color to dry before applying the next. In designing for prints with two or more colors the design should be placed in the center of the stencil paper, always in the same relationship to the corner that will be used for **registration** so that all stencils will line up properly to form a completed design. Multicolored designs can also be printed without registration by **overprinting** designs on a shape already printed.

In designing for multicolor stenciling, the completed design should first be painted on paper in colors matching the colors to be used. Generally, darker colors are printed over lighter tones. Using tracing paper, a pattern is cut for each color, tracing only the areas of that color. This is transferred to the stencil paper by rubbing the back of the tracing paper with a soft pencil. The outlines of the areas to receive color are traced on the stencil paper with a border of at least 3" all around the design to protect the background from accidental splashes during printing. Cut the stencil over a heavy board, cardboard, or a piece of glass. The **stencil knife** must be very sharp for easy cutting. The knife is held like a pencil so that the tip does the cutting. The stencil should cut without exerting too much pressure. Cut all the way through in one stroke for clean edges, turning the paper so that you always cut toward you. Begin cutting the smallest areas first, continuing until all areas that are to receive color are removed. Be careful not to cut into the stays. These strips must not be too narrow or paint will spread underneath them. When all areas to be colored are cut away and removed, the stencil is ready for printing. A stencil for each color is prepared in this way, with the design always in the same relationship to the guiding edge or corner that has been selected for registration.

Another way to add richness and lifelike detail to stenciled designs is by **shading.** Darker tones are stippled onto parts of the stencil to add depth. This is a traditional technique used for stenciling still-life and floral arrangements called **theorem work.** And, of course, freehand brushwork is often used in stenciled pictures, especially for fine lines, such as stems. See ill.

PRINTING   Place the **stencil** on the surface to be decorated. It may be helpful to tape it in place. Be careful to observe **registration** marks if two or more colors are to be printed. Stencil the lightest color first and allow it to dry before printing the second color. Use **paint** that is fairly thick. Dip the **stencil brush** in the paint, then brush it on paper until almost dry. Holding the brush vertically, apply paint to the cut-out areas of the stencil with a gentle dabbing or **stippling** movement, working from the edges toward the center of each opening. If the paint is brushed from side to side it will spread under the **stays** and spoil the crisp edges of the design. If the paint is too thin, **bleeding** may occur. The backs of the stencils must be kept clean to avoid spotting the background.

The way in which the color is applied will affect the appearance of the design. For the solid, flat areas that are usually associated with stenciling, the paint is applied

Stencil stay

with equal pressure over all the cut-out areas. Unequal pressure may be used for **shading,** and various tonal effects can be added by changing the color. The edges of areas may be accented by applying color to the edges only, leaving the center of the areas the background color.

CARE AND MAINTENANCE OF TOOLS   **Stencil**s should be wiped clean after each printing with the appropriate solvent and a soft cloth. Clean stencils often: Wipe off oil paint with a rag dampened with turpentine; clean off acrylic paint by scrubbing the stencil with a stiff brush under running water. Any rips in the stencil can be repaired with tape. Brushes should be wiped with rags or toweling, cleaned in solvent, and then washed in warm water and mild soap. Allow brushes to dry bristle-end up in a jar or can.

stenciling. China and Glass Painting. Stenciling is used in decorating china to reproduce designs many times. If a number of pieces are to be decorated, use metal stencil sheeting. It is similar to lead foil and will readily wrap around curved surfaces. Use ordinary **stencil paper** for general work. Hold the stencil in position with tape, and apply the color with a **stencil brush** or **silk pad.** Stenciled designs can be superimposed one over another to build up intricate designs.

stenciling. Fabric Printing. Standard stenciling techniques can be applied to fabric printing, using **textile color.** Before printing on **fabric,** make preliminary tests on scrap fabric for desired color and consistency. The paint should not need much thinning because it is used rather dry and in small quantities. Mix the paint on a glass slab and apply it with a stencil brush. Dab the brush through the stencil. When the stencil is removed, the pattern should have clear, sharp outlines. To avoid blurring the edges of the design, be sure to hold the brush in an upright position and to keep the stencil firmly pressed down on the fabric during printing. If the design is blurry, the paint may be too thin. Avoid paint that is too thick, however, because it gives the fabic an unpleasantly thick surface. Allow the color to dry before **overprinting** with additional colors. Also see **Fabric Printing: Preparing Fabrics, Finishing.**

stenciling. Quilts. A decorative painting process in which colors are applied to a fabric through openings cut in parchment, paper, or metal. The design is drawn onto the stencil material and the areas to be painted are cut away. The surrounding material shields the cloth from the color. Small ties or lines of the stencil material must be left to connect parts of the stencil to hold it together. This gives an identifying characteristic of spaces to the stenciled design. A separate stencil is required for each color. Either dye or paint is used.

Early American **stenciled quilt**s are rare. Few were made, and these were usually done at home.

stenciling. Tincrafting. See **Tincrafting: Finishing the Tin.**

stenciling ceramics. Stenciling. Stencils can be used to apply decorations to any clean, dry, ceramic form by using a fast-drying spray enamel paint or by applying enamel paint with a **stencil brush.** Simple, cylindrical shapes are best so that the stencil can be securely taped in place: the stencil may not lie flat on more complicated shapes. If the inner edges of the stencil pop up, place double-faced masking tape under them and press down. For spray painting, the areas not to be sprayed must be masked by taping newspaper over them; only the cut-out design areas of the stencil should be exposed. Place the ceramic piece on the floor and spray over it, holding the spray at a right angle to it, about 15″ away. Spray thin coats in short spurts to avoid overspraying and running. Let the paint dry thoroughly before removing the stencil. Any uneven edges can be cleaned up by scraping with a utility or **stencil knife.** Always keep the back of the stencil clean. Masking tape may also be used as a stencil for straight lines. After the paint is dry, the piece may be given a protective coating of clear acrylic spray. Also see **stenciling with spray paint** and **Stenciling: Designing and Cutting, Printing.**

stenciling fabric. Stenciling. Stenciled designs can be applied with **textile color** on fabric that has first been washed to remove any sizing. **Stenciling with spray paint** can be done on lightweight, delicate fabrics. Also see **Stenciling: Designing and Cutting, Printing.**

stenciling floors. Stenciling. Standard stenciling methods can be used for decorating floors. The floor must first be cleaned to remove dust and old wax. Then give it two coats of floor-and-deck enamel, letting it dry between coats. When the background color is thoroughly dry, the stenciling can begin. Work in one area at a time so there is always some place to walk. For the stenciled colors, use a quick-drying floor-and-deck enamel. When the stenciled design is completely dry, the floor may be given a protective coating of polyurethane varnish. Also see **Stenciling: Designing and Cutting, Printing.**

stenciling furniture. Stenciling. Stenciling is a traditional method for decorating furniture and household objects. General stenciling procedures are followed after freeing the surface to be decorated of varnish or wax. Traditionally, furniture was stenciled with **bronze powder,** producing classic designs such as those on Hitchcock chairs. Today, various types of **paint** are used on furniture. After the design is applied, a protective coating may be used, such as polyurethane or regular varnish.

stenciling walls. Stenciling. For stenciling walls, general procedures for stenciling are followed, using a **paint** that is appropriate for the surface to be decorated. A plumb line can be made by tying a weight onto a string and tacking it near the ceiling as a guide for straight, vertical lines on the wall. General guidelines can be drawn with chalk, using the plumb line and a yardstick. Printing may be facilitated by taping each stencil in place on the wall before applying paint. Also see **Stenciling: Designing and Cutting, Printing.**

stenciling with spray paint. Stenciling. Spray paint can be used instead of a **stencil brush** or a **bob** to apply **paint** through a **stencil** onto the surface to be decorated. Spray-painting produces a unique effect that can be varied from a misty quality to a solid color. The technique requires elaborate preparatory work, consisting of carefully covering or **masking** all areas except for the stenciled cut-out area to be sprayed. To produce thin, even coats and to avoid **bleeding,** the applicator or spray can should be held about 15″ from the surface to be sprayed. Spray-paint stenciling is particularly successful for large, simple designs or designs with colors blended in one area. Also see **Stenciling: Designing and Cutting.**

stencil knife. Stenciling. (Also called chip knife.) An all-purpose stencil knife is available from art-supply stores for cutting stencils and for general utility. Stencil and frisket knives have interchangeable blades that can be set into a plastic handle. Aluminum stencil knives, similar to the X-Acto knife, have a chuck to hold retractable and replaceable steel blades. See ill. Also see **Stenciling: Designing and Cutting.**

Stencil knife

stencil paper. China and Glass Painting. Stenciling. (Also called stencil board.) Stencil paper is available from art-supply stores ready to be cut for stenciling. Various substitutes can be made from paper or cardboard, with the application of a moisture-resistant coating such as melted wax or paraffin, brushed on after the design is cut. Adequate substitutes can also be made with waxed paper, oiled paper, vinyl, or paper coated with varnish. **Frisket paper** can be useful for detail work. Also see **Stenciling: Designing and Cutting.**

step cut. Gemcutting. See **facet, preforming.**

stepped slit. Weaving. See **slit tapestry.**

stepping. Weaving. A **tapestry** technique in which curves or very steep **diagonals** are manipulated. The technique consists of moving and weaving from **warp end** to warp end according to the design so that a stepped series of small slits develops. Also see **slit tapestry.**

Stepping Stones. Quilts. Two different **block** designs for **pieced quilts** are known by this name. One is identical to **Jacob's Ladder** except for the color arrangement. The other Stepping Stones block is a **nine-patch** arrangement,

a. Stepping Stones

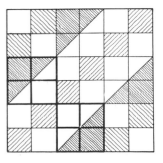

b. Variation

but the **patch**es vary in size. The four corner patches are made of nine-patches, and the four side patches incorporate triangles. The center is a solid square. The total effect is one of an eight-pointed star with a smaller eight-pointed star within it. See ill.

Steps to the Altar. Quilts. See **Baby Blocks.**

step up. Basketry. A particular stroke used at the end of each round of **waling** to literally step up to the row above, so that the waling continues horizontally, preventing a spiraled look. It is usually used on **stuff** of uniform size such as **whole cane** or **reed**, but not on **willow**, which is not generally uniform to begin with. Also see **Basketry: Woven Basket Construction.**

stereopticon. Toys. See **magic lantern.**

stereoscope. Toys. An **optical toy** that consists of double images printed side by side on a card viewed through a lens with a hood. When the head is placed against the hood and the card is set in the provided slot, the images on the card appear to be three-dimensional. Pictures for the stereoscope are taken from slightly different angles so that when the two images are superimposed, they appear rounded and solid.

sterling silver. Jewelry. See **silver.**

stick horse. Toys. See **hobby horse.**

sticking-up. Ceramics. See **luting.**

stick lighting. Stained Glass. The use of sharpened sticks to remove matted paint from glass. The technique can be used with either water or **oil-base paints.** The small dots, diamonds, stars, and other motifs produced by this method add an effect of sparkle and glitter. Also see **matting, painting on glass, stippling.**

stick loom. Weaving. See **backstrap loom, straw loom.**

stick puppet. Puppets. A beginner's **puppet**, simple to make, which consists of a **puppet head** of any kind stuck onto the end of a stick or dowel. A **papier-mâché** or rubber ball on a pencil, a Styrofoam ball on a **dowel** stick, or a turnip on the tines of a fork—all suffice, since the stick puppet can be improvised or sophisticated. Arms may be added by a crosspiece, and a cloth wrapped around the

whole thing for a garment. See ill. Also see **pencil puppet, rod puppet.**

stick reel. Spinning. See **reel.**

stick rider (stickreider). Toys. Any of a great variety of **articulated toys** that use figures such as clowns or cats attached to the ends of sticks in such a way that will move into various positions. The hands or front legs of the figure are attached to a **dowel** placed perpendicularly on the end of the stick. The dowel forms an **axle** over which the arms can move. The legs are **joint**ed and feet are attached by means of another dowel to the main stick. When the stick is jerked up and down, the figures move and change. It is derived from the German stickreiter toy and is variously known as cat-on-a-stick or man-on-a-stick.

sticks. Basketry. Very stout willow rods of 2–3 years growth. Because of their size they are usually used as the structural **spokes** on the bottom of a basket and as framing members for chairs, large hampers, and other heavy basketry work.

stick shuttle. Weaving. (Also called flat shuttle.) The simplest **shuttle**, a long, flat, narrow piece of wood with both ends notched to hold the yarn. It is sometimes called a poke shuttle since it is poked or pushed through the **shed.** It must be smooth so as not to catch on the **warp end**s. Yarn is usually wound lengthwise from end to end, but it can also be wound around the outside edges from arm to arm of the end notches. The stick shuttle can be used with all types of yarn, but the tendency is not to use it for fine yarns since they are handled quicker and more easily on a **boat shuttle.** A stick shuttle made of wood or fiberboard can be bought, but it can also be made at home out of strong cardboard. The most useful feature of a stick shuttle is its length: it can be passed from hand to hand as it goes through the shed. The most common long length is 24″, but they can also be bought in small sizes like 6″ for belt weaving. Stick shuttles are most suitable for weaving narrow fabrics and for use on looms with shallow sheds. Some of them have beveled edges, as opposed to rounded ones, in order to be used also as **beater**s. See ill.

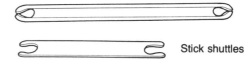

Stick shuttles

stick weaving. Weaving. See **Finnweave.**

stiffening. Puppets. Stitchery. Toys. Anything added to **fabric** to give it extra **body** or stiffness. An **iron-on interfacing** is sometimes used, which adheres the stiffener to the fabric. A **buckram** interlining will serve the purpose, or fabric can be sprayed with iron-on starch or dipped in liquid **starch** and ironed.

stiletto. Quilts. Stitchery. A tool used in **trapunto.** The stiletto, often made from bone, is smooth, fine, and pointed. Its point is used to separate the woven threads on the back side of the **coverlet.** The opening is spread with

Dowel construction   Dressed stick puppet

the stiletto, and then **stuffing** can be inserted. Also see **bodkin, English trapunto.**

stilt. Ceramics. See **kiln furniture.**

stilts. Toys. A pair of long wooden supports that raise the stiltwalker's feet high above the ground. A wood block or foot rest on which the walker stands is attached to each stilt. The top of each stick is held in the hand. It is an old game and the stilts are easily made at home.

stippler. Leather. A **stamping** tool used to embed decorative dotlike impressions in damp leather. See ill. Also see **stamp, tooling.**

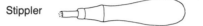
Stippler

stippling. China and Glass Painting. See **ground laying.**

stippling. Leather. A **tooling** technique in which background areas of the leather are given an all-over dotlike background with a **stippler,** stylus, ball-end **modeler,** a **Vibro tool,** or other fine-pointed **stamp.**

stippling. Stained Glass. A method of **painting on glass** that uses a small stick or the butt end of a paintbrush to let in small points of light through the paint. Also see **brushes, stick lighting.**

stippling. Stenciling. A term used for the technique of applying **paint** through a **stencil** with a **bob** or **stencil brush** with a vertical, dabbing motion. The bob or brush is dipped into paint, then held vertically over the cut-out area. The paint is applied with a light, dabbing movement, working from the edges toward the center of each opening. The end result depends on how much stippling is done. Light stippling may be used for **shading** areas with a spotted texture. By continuing the process the whole area can be filled in solidly. Also see **Stenciling: Painting.**

stippling. Weaving. A **tapestry** technique by which gradations of color are achieved by weaving spots or flecks of one color on a ground of another. It is essentially **pick-and-pick** weaving that would produce a vertical line except that in stippling, the pick-and-pick is kept to narrow bands. By changing the sequence of the two colors, the lines can be broken up and small squares or spots result. An optical illusion of intermediary shades can be obtained by increasing or decreasing the density of the spots in a given area. Stippling was employed in early **Navajo weaving.** It was called beading because it gave the effect of a string of small beads. It was used as a means of adding interest to a **filling** stripe. Prehistoric Pueblo weavers employed it and the technique was carried on by later Pueblos, who taught it to the Navajos and they then used it in their Moki blankets.

stirrup. Lacemaking. See **foundation loop, knotted lace.**

stitch. Crewel. Embroidery. Needlepoint. A term that can refer to the act of creating a fabric with a needle and thread, or, as in embroidery, refer to a threaded needle piercing a fabric and looping or knotting the thread over the fabric in a decorative manner.

stitch. Crochet. (Abbr. st.) The loop made with **yarn** and a **crochet hook.** Each complete, individual manipulation of the yarn is referred to as a stitch (whether it is **single crochet** stitch, **double crochet** stitch, or whatever), and it is the interworking of these individual stitches, according to a specific **pattern,** that forms a finished piece of crochet. Also see **Crochet: Basic Stitches.**

stitch. Rugmaking. An element in the making of an **embroidered** or **needleworked rug.** It involves a complete movement of the yarn through the **rug backing** by means of a needle, leaving behind a portion of the yarn on the backing. The stitches build up one by one, until the backing is completely covered or the decorative feature is finished. Any stitch that is short and compact can be used for an embroidered rug. Some of the more popular ones are **knitting** or **soumak** stitch, **tent stitch, cross stitch, tapestry stitch,** and **Hungarian stitch.** These are all flat stitches in that they do not stand up from the backing. There is also a **pile** stitch or the Ghiordes knot that is used in **needleworked rugs** to make either cut or loop **knotted pile.**

stitch. Stitchery. To sew or to draw thread through fabric whether by hand-sewing or by machine-sewing. A **stitch** may be used to **join** fabrics, as the **straight stitch** is used in a **seam.** It may also refer to any specific stitch of a certain repeated pattern arrangement, as a satin stitch, **blind stitch,** cross stitch, etc. Also see **blanket stitch** and **Stitchery: Stitches, Hand Appliqué, Machine Appliqué.**

"stitch down." Weaving. See **stitching.**

stitched-edge seam. Stitchery. A **seam finish** in which the **raw edges** of a **plain seam** are **press**ed open and sewn. Each of the raw edges is turned under and is stitched with a line of machine **straight stitch**es. It is sometimes called a clean-finished seam. See ill.

Stitched-edge seam

stitched joint. Puppets. Toys. A **joint** made in a fabric article by sewing lines of straight machine stitches where the bend or joint is to occur. A stuffed doll might be given jointed arms by first sliding or forcing most of the **stuffing** to either side of the **seam** line and then stitching through both layers of fabric. This can be done to make a joint separating the arm from the body and to give a stitched joint at the elbow.

This sewn joint is one of the simplest ways of making an **articulated** toy in fabric. The stitched joint is used in three-dimensional stitcheries and padded pieces and in fabric books to provide a binding. Also see **fabric joint, stuffed marionette.**

stitched tie-dye. Batik and Tie-dye. See **tritik.**

STITCHERY

Stitchery is a general term for work involving the use of a **needle,** thread or yarn, and fabric. It includes **appliqué** and **embroidery** and both hand and machine sewing. Stitchery is a free, interpretive craft that offers a means of personal artistic expression. Stitchery is distinct from needlework, which suggests a dependence upon stamped patterns, directions, and other limitations. It includes the use of appliqué and embroidery both by themselves or in combination with other techniques. It is **surface embellishment,** most commonly applied in **wall hanging**s, **soft sculpture, quilt**s, **banner**s, and clothing. There are few limits to the size possibilities for stitcheries; the primary limitation is that of the width of woven material available for use. To overcome this limitation, **mural**-size work is sometimes hung in separate panels.

"Stitchery" is a relatively new word, but there are wonderful examples of stitchery art from all over the world and from all ages. They find form in banners, costumes, flags, clothes, masks, tents, and umbrellas. Many are highly stylized and describe a way of living. Some are significant of a culture's values and others are strong, personal, vital statements. They all may inspire the contemporary stitcher. **Folk artist**s have always used this craft, often with striking and exciting results. Stitchery has survived through many other craft areas, such as dollmaking, the design of religious and ceremonial objects, toymaking, and quilting. The recent interest in the decorative use of stitchery on clothing reflects the interest in costume that has traditionally involved folk artists throughout the world.

Today stitchery is flourishing at home as a richly decorative embellishment for bags, clothing, curtains, **pillow**s, and quilts.

Perhaps the most significant aspect of stitchery is its approach to technique. When techniques override the concerns of concept, composition, or aesthetics, the work becomes a pedestrian example of needlework skills. When the creative aspect dominates, the work contains expressive or artistic merit. **Stitch**es and techniques must remain tools, not purposes or ends in themselves. The mere display of needleworking skills is not the makeup of stitchery.

There are no "right" and "wrong" ways of working in stitchery. Some approaches or procedures may be preferable for certain purposes, but no two projects and no two stitchers are alike. What is appropriate in one situation may be inappropriate in another. The techniques must serve the purpose of the work.

"Sewing" is a very general term for the **join**ing of one fabric to another with thread. It refers primarily to utilitarian aspects—**clothing construction** or **straight stitch**ing. For example, the face of a wall hanging might be done with stitchery, but the **backing** and **hem** are done with sewing. The creative element is the one distinguishing difference between stitchery and sewing.

Three-dimensional stitcheries, which have grown naturally out of stuffed quilts, **padded appliqué**s, and high relief work, offer sculptural possibilities that expand the potentials of stitchery still further. These stitchery forms are referred to as "soft sculptures." Their development was greatly stimulated by the work of sculptor Claes Oldenburg.

Stitchery can be the home art of homemakers, as it falls within the capabilities of nearly everyone. It provides an excellent medium for children and students because it requires few tools. Materials are familiar and readily available and space needs are flexible. But stitchery is not limited to a decorative use, to practical application, or to exploratory and experimental work. Its potential as a serious art form is expanded continuously by artists everywhere.

CLOTHING Sewn clothes involve traditional methods of **clothing construction,** whereas stitchery clothing suggests handmade or decorated **fabric**s, **nonsewn garment**s, recycled clothes, and embellished mass-produced clothes. A **caftan,** for example, offers great opportunity to use decorative fabric techniques while the garment itself requires a minimum of sewing, no fitting, and none of the usual clothing construction procedures; many primitive garments and ethnic costumes are adapted for use by craftspeople because they allow emphasis on the treatment of the **fiber** or fabric. In sewing clothes, then, the garment is the primary concern and the clothing construction involves skilled techniques. In stitchery clothing, it is the treatment of the fabric that has greater significance; the garment becomes a vehicle for personal artistic expression.

Blue jeans and other denim articles play a significant role in stitchery clothing; uniform workclothes are turned into unique personal designs. A **bleaching** process is sometimes used first, over which embroidery designs are added. Blue denims and work shirts are often the recipients of elaborate **appliqué** and embroidery designs, employing techniques from **iron-on appliqué** to **shisha** or **mirror embroidery.**

T-shirts and sweat shirts are equally popular as a basis for embellishment. It is notable that in all of these favorite body coverings, the original garment is particularly unpretentious and ordinary. The most common garments are given the most extraordinary treatment by stitches.

Masks are one of the new dimensions in **contemporary stitchery,** although, of course, masks have a long tradition in many other cultures. Many body coverings are costumes, allowing the wearer to play a role.

Breast plates and **bib**s provide stitchers with structures for **padded stitchery. Collage dress**es or garments allow fabrics of all kinds to be incorporated into the design and include everything from **mola**s to **antimacassar**s. Recycled clothes and **making do** are also a part of body coverings. Batik, quiltmaking, and tie-dye have all been significant in contributing traditional techniques for this work.

Among the techniques borrowed from quiltmaking for clothing, piecing or patchwork is undoubtedly the most frequently used. Unquilted pieced tops lend themselves beautifully to clothing design, as do individually designed appliqué or pieced blocks. The yo-yo construction common in coverlets of this century is as popular as the Cathedral Window design.

Patchwork denims are tremendously popular, as evidenced by the response to the Levi's Denim Art Show competition in 1974. The Museum of Contemporary Crafts in New York held one of the first shows to recognize the contemporary phenomenon of body coverings. This was followed by the Body Art Show at the Portland Museum and the Body Wear Show at the Oakland Museum. Numerous other museums and galleries have since given similar recognition to the many craftspeople, artists, and designers who have turned their talents to the design of clothing.

Crochet, needlepoint, knitting, and macramé all find their way into clothes. Simple embroidery and elaborate crewel stitches are all adaptable and appropriate.

Direct dye painting and **fabric painting** offer opportunities for painters and artists. **Felt appliqué, lace appliqué,** and **shadow stitching** have all quietly worked their way into clothes. **Marking pen**s and India ink drawing can be applied directly onto readymade garments, letting the design emerge according to the shape of the clothes. Batik and tie-dye offer another possible way of letting these two aspects of design merge.

BANNERS AND WALL HANGINGS One of the most popular forms of stitchery is the making of **banner**s and **wall hanging**s. The simplest approach to making any of these, and certainly the easiest for the beginner, is **felt appliqué.** It uses the most basic of all **hand appliqué** stitches, only the **running stitch** or **whip stitch.** It results in large areas of color and strong design impact with the least involvement in terms of time and skill. Felt appliqué is suitable for panels and banners of all sizes. It can be used in a **stacked felt** effect, in cut-through appliqué, or French knot appliqué.

Transparent appliqué can be accomplished in any of several ways, but all use a layer of **transparent fabric** as the top piece of fabric. The layers beneath may be embroidered or appliquéd, or one may use **felt** as a middle layer in a method called **shadow work.** Another transparent appliqué method is called **lace appliqué**; it uses antique laces, doilies, and needlework with **net, organdy, organza, tulle,** and similar fabrics. **Upholstery material**s or other fabrics that have good **body** provide suitable **background** material. The lacework is usually held in place by hand-sewn **tack** stitches. The transparencies may be sewn with a **blind stitch** or with a **machine appliqué** stitch. The **satin stitch** is most commonly used to give a smooth outline.

Burlap is a popular background material, but not a good one for detailed stitching. Closely woven fabrics work better; **hopsacking, homespun, kettle cloth,** lightweight **sailcloth,** sport **cotton**s, and **velveteen** are among the many materials which work well for either embroidery or appliqué. **Linen, silk,** and **wool** are more expensive than many **synthetic fabric**s but are especially nice for stitchery panels. Fabrics that have a **pile,** such as **velour** and **velvet,** are not easy to appliqué; the pile tends to move as it is compressed, shifting the position of the appliquéd fabric.

India ink drawing is sometimes incorporated into wall hangings. It can be utilized along with **direct dye painting** to add specific surface designs or drawings to be used with **stuffing,** stitching, or quilting.

Banners are usually larger in scale than wall hangings and vertical in proportion. When banners are hung on a wall, as they are sometimes installed in halls or churches, they need be only one-sided. That is, only the face needs to be finished, although even a one-sided banner or panel should be lined or **back**ed. If a banner is hung so that it comes out at right angles to the wall, it must be two-sided.

With careful planning, both faces can be sewn to the same single piece of background fabric. **Awning fabric, canvas, ticking,** sailcloth, or **acrylic canvas** works well for banners that must be durable, whether used inside or out. Acrylic canvas is the most permanent for outdoor use. Synthetic fabrics such as **nylon** or the materials used to make sails are filmy and light and will ruffle in a breeze. The material can be machine appliquéd, is durable, and comes in a range of semitransparent colors. Very rich textured fabrics are also adaptable for banners and are especially appropriate for a more ceremonious use. **Satin, Thai silk,** velvet, and **brocade** all add surfaces that enhance the banner's richness and visual appeal. Even **mylar, acetate,** and **mica mirror**s may be added for their decorative, reflective qualities.

Banners are often ornamented with **tassel**s, **pompon**s, **ball fringe,** or regular **fringe.** They are usually added at the lower edge of the fabric. Smaller **pennant**s and flags involve the same materials and techniques as banners but generally have less of an air of pageantry to them.

MURALS Large-scale **stitchery panel**s for permanent installation on walls are referred to as stitchery **mural**s. When they are installed in offices or public buildings some consideration must be given to the **mount**ing as well as to protective surfacing of the **fabric.**

Murals may be free-hung from a rod or bar at ceiling level, or they may be mounted on a frame of wood and the wood attached to a wall. Another excellent way to install a mural is to attach each fabric panel to a solid wood panel. For example, a series of stitchery panels, each 3' × 8', could be mounted individually on plywood and then hung as a single unit. Each wood panel would be cut 3' × 8' and would have a 2" × 2" or 1" × 2" board added on the back of each of the four edges, with **miter**ed or **butt** joint corners. These boards make the wood panel rigid and add stability. They also hold the fabric out so that it does not rest flat on a wall, thus giving it greater dimension and weight. The boards at the edge also make it possible to hang the panel flush against the wall. A hook or metal brace on the wood can be slipped over a corresponding brace on the wall so that all edges of the panel touch it. To mount a panel in this way, additional material must be allowed at each of the four edges so that the fabric can be stretched over the wood. The area of the finished panel is outlined in basting stitches on the front of the fabric. The basted fabric panel is then placed over the flat surface of the wood frame, being sure that the basting stitches line up exactly with the edges of the wood. The material is tacked in place.

Then the extra fabric is drawn around the 2″ × 2″ edge and stapled on the back. The corners are **fold**ed or clipped to make them smooth. If the panel is to be framed, the 2″ × 2″s offer a solid piece of wood to which the frame can be attached.

Some designers use an **adhesive** on the wood to help hold the fabric firmly in place. This must be carefully done to prevent the adhesive's soaking through. It should be used only with heavy fabrics such as **upholstery material**s, and a sample should always be tried first. There are various **fabric adhesive**s available in hobby shops, and a wood adhesive or **contact cement** may be tried. The use of an adhesive will probably prevent the removal of the fabric later for **dry cleaning;** however, many surface cleaners and **dry cleaning spray**s are available. Usually vacuuming will remove loose surface dust.

When a panel is to be installed in a public building, problems of safety and maintenance must be considered. Many fabrics are available with various **finish**es such as **Scotchgard** or moth proofing. These finishes can be applied to an already completed mural as well as to the fabric before use. Fire laws vary from state to state, and it is important to check on regulations that may cover any mural to be installed. Treatments are available to make yardage or finished work fire-resistant. Test samples are always recommended for the sprays and liquids available for home application. The nature of the installation and the local regulations covering fireproofing or fire resistance will have to be checked to learn which method is permissible or acceptable. Usually a certificate is given by a company who does the fireproofing or who sells you the material to do your own. This certificate is required by an inspector at the time of installation.

SOFT SCULPTURE Among the most recent innovations in the use of stitchery and fabric are three-dimensional soft **sculpture**s. They offer both a serious art form and one that lends itself especially well to humor and satire. The tremendous growth of interest in this field is due in part to the work of sculptor Claes Oldenburg. His gigantic and widely exhibited soft sculptures gave impetus to an entire new direction in work with fabric.

Closely related to soft sculpture are dollmaking and quiltmaking. Some craftspeople have taken the basic dollmaking techniques and turned them into an active and vital sculptural approach that emphasizes the human form. The **stuff**ed nylon stocking doll can be readily manipulated and shaped. The **single shape doll** and the **pillow doll** are similarly adaptable to **stuffed figure**s of almost any scale. Almost any **fabric doll** method can be adapted for use portraying people in soft sculpture.

Papier mâché also is considered a soft sculpture form. It is not "soft" in the way that fabric is, but in contrast to traditional sculpture materials such as stone or bronze, it is indeed soft. The papier-mâché method can also be used on figures of almost any scale. An **armature** may be required for larger pieces. Gauze or **cheesecloth** is sometimes substituted for part of the paper. Articles of real clothing may be employed to assist in depicting the figure's form.

Many quiltmakers who started working in a somewhat traditional way with quilts have been intrigued by the **stuffing** or **padding** process. Their quilts become more three-dimensional as they work, and may eventually depart from quilts entirely, working on stuffed or padded panels or fully dimensional **floor piece**s.

The processes of stuffing and padding are used in all kinds of three-dimensional stitchery. In its simplest form, soft sculpture is a surface padding offering a **bas-relief** surface. Pieces of fabric being **appliqué**d are partially sewn in place, then **filler** is slipped in through the open area and the remainder is sewn shut. Care must always be taken to assure that there is ample fullness in the appliqué piece to allow the stuffing to form a relief surface on the top. If the appliqué piece is stretched tightly over the **background** material, the fullness will make a bulge on the wrong side, losing the padded effect. Sometimes fabrics are **gather**ed, folded, or tucked to allow even more fullness on the surface.

The surface of the material itself may be gathered over another form. A wad of **cotton batting** or a ping-pong ball or similar form is placed under a fabric, then the fabric is drawn around it and sewed or tied, making a highly stuffed surface. Very high relief, or **alto-relief,** panels can be achieved by gathering in this way.

Most three-dimensional stitchery forms are shaped and sewn in such a way that the right sides of the material are placed together, the seams are sewn, and the material is turned right-side out. The stuffing or filler is then inserted in the pocket or opening thus formed. This is commonly used in sculptural forms and is similar to the approach used in making stuffed dolls or animals. When large rigid shapes are made, a wood or cardboard base may be used. Sometimes an armature of wire or wood is first built so that stuffed forms have a framework over which to rest.

Stitchery of stuffed fabrics may be accomplished using the **trapunto** methods commonly found in quilting. These offer a richly textured surface to wall hangings. Italian trapunto may be used for linear effects and **English trapunto** offers a method for stuffing large areas.

TOOLS AND MATERIALS Few crafts require so few tools as stitchery—and few can be so easily adapted to such limited work spaces. The two most essential tools are **needle**s and **scissors**.

Needles can be purchased in a wide range of sizes. They vary from the slender-shafted milliner's needles to heavy **carpet needle**s. The weight of thread or **yarn** being used and the firmness of the **fabric** being sewn help determine which needle is needed. The milliner's needle, because of the very thin shaft, pulls through fabric with ease. It is not a strong needle, however, and will break in heavier materials. Embroidery needles work well for flosses and threads of all kinds and are easily threaded. **Round-eye needle**s work well for **appliqué.** When yarns are used, a larger needle eye is required; either a darning needle or tapestry needle will do. The darning needle has a sharp point, whereas the latter has a blunt point for threading through the yarns of heavy **upholstery material.** Carpet or upholstery needles accommodate big yarns or cords; many are exceptionally long and some are curved.

Stitches can be taken on a large **wire mesh** or **hardware** cloth, or onto a screen of chicken wire. To make a substitute for a needle, in such cases, yarn can be wrapped with masking tape, making a rigid end that can easily be poked through the openings.

The most important single tool for the stitcher is a really fine pair of scissors. It is preferable to have one pair that is of the best quality than to have a variety of sizes of mediocre ones. A good all-purpose size has a 5″ blade. It is small enough for detailed trimming but large enough for cutting heavier fabrics. In selecting two pairs, embroidery or **trimming scissors** having a 2″ or 3″ blade could be coupled with cutting shears that have a 4″ or 5″ blade. The larger size will easily cut upholstery materials and heavy yarns or cords.

Scissors will have a great effect on a stitcher's ability to carefully cut fabric, as for appliqué. The best source for a really good pair is a cutlery shop that deals with good steel blades of all kinds. Many fabric shops offer adequate to good scissors. The slight difference in cost between a serviceable pair and a superb pair makes the investment worthwhile.

Other tools may be used from time to time for various projects. Many stitchers use **thimble**s, others do not. It is a matter of personal preference and of the weight of the material being sewn. On heavy fabrics a thimble is often a must to force the needle through. Embroidery hoops or frames are sometimes used when the fabric being worked must be under tension. Both **dressmaker's pin**s and large **T-pin**s are helpful.

The sewing machine should also be considered a tool. For machine sewing, most stitchers prefer any machine that will sew a satin stitch or **zigzag stitch. Straight stitch**es also have been used like drawn lines as well as to cover areas solidly with stitches. A straight-stitching machine will serve all normal sewing needs, but the zigzag capabilities will be an invaluable aid in appliqué. A commercial power machine will offer even greater possibilities. Machines can be rented by the month, making their use accessible to most stitchers.

It will be especially helpful in working on large-scale **machine appliqué** to have a table that fits next to the sewing machine to support fabric being worked on. Ideally the table should be both at the back and to the left of the machine.

For sewing clothes, a **dress form** will be a valuable aid. An iron and ironing board will be helpful on many projects, and a **needle board** is helpful when working on fabrics that have a **nap** or a **pile.** Good lighting is always essential. An engineer's or architect's lamp that has a flexible arm for adjustments vertically and horizontally is excellent. The light can be pinpointed on areas for close work.

Power tools or saws would be required only for the framing, **mount**ing, or **finishing** of completed works.

Almost any material through which a **needle** can be drawn is usable in stitchery.

Stuffed fabrics or **soft sculpture**s require tightly woven fabrics because **stuffing** puts an added strain on seams. A loosely woven material may separate if stuffing is tightly packed.

Synthetic fabrics have many advantages in all forms of stitchery, particularly for the color range, variety of weights, and fabric **finish**es used. A disadvantage of the synthetic is in the handling. In **hand appliqué,** for example, a synthetic fabric tends to be springy and return to its flat shape, whereas a cotton fabric can easily be turned under for **hemming.** Most stitchers prefer cotton or **cotton blend** fabrics for **appliqué** work.

The specific materials used depend upon the methods employed, the ultimate function of the piece, and personal preference for visual and **tactile** considerations. Some stitchers feel that the **natural fiber**s are preferable, whether they are **animal fiber** or **vegetable fiber.**

Textured fabrics offer a great tactile variety to stitchery. **Pile** weave fabrics, including plush or **velour, napped fabric**s, and smooth materials with a **sheen,** such as satin, add greatly to the palette from which the stitcher selects.

Specific kinds of stitchery do require specific materials. **Felt appliqué** and **French knot appliqué** invariably involve the use of felt. The thickness of the material is such that when several layers are used, as in **stacked felt,** a **relief** pattern is developed. **Shadow work, transparent appliqué,** and **lace appliqué** all utilize **transparent fabric**s such as **organdy, organza,** or **net.**

Stuffed fabric shapes may be formed from tightly woven materials or from jersey, **stretch fabric,** or **doubleknit fabric.** Denim art and blue jeans appliqué require their own fabrics. While materials as varied as **broadcloth** and **burlap** may both be used for appliqué, each has different potentials and limitations.

There are probably no materials that cannot be used in some way for stitchery. Even three-dimensional objects and found materials such as buttons, rope, shells, wood, and separately stuffed shapes are appropriate. Lace, leather, nylon, paper, transparent materials, photographs, and vinyl have all been successfully combined with stitchery.

Threads, flosses, **yarn**s, and cords of any weight are suitable for hand stitchery. The heavier ones may be **tack**ed in place or attached by **couching,** and lighter ones may be used for embroidery. Most stitchers select their **fiber**s in terms of color and texture.

In **machine appliqué** the **heavy-duty thread**s give better coverage than a regular sewing thread. Cotton **mercerized sewing thread**s are easier to sew with than **synthetic thread**s. Because cotton threads are becoming difficult to locate, it may be necessary to seek them directly from thread companies or mills. Some suppliers of commercial materials, **edging**s, or threads will supply them. The transparent synthetic threads offer an excellent means of appliqué with an almost invisible line, although most stitchers prefer the addition of the thread colors.

SETTING UP A WORKSHOP Stitchery requires no special studio and almost no equipment. A kitchen table or card table will do. Beyond the few essential tools, the necessary equipment is at an absolute minimum.

For the stitcher who is more involved, it is helpful to have a large table surface where work in progress can be left. In lieu of this, a large piece of ½″ or ⅝″ plywood covered with Naugahyde can be placed over a smaller table to provide ample elbow room and space to lay out materials.

Some stitchers store **fabric** in covered containers such as plastic bags or boxes or keep them in closed cupboards. Many others, however, feel that the problem of dust is a minimal one, and that it is far more important to have fabrics on open shelves where the colors and textures themselves are stimulating to the designer using them. Any accumulated dust is readily removed with a light shaking.

For small-scale work it is advisable to keep all the materials needed for a single project in one box or basket. That way the container can be picked up and work can proceed without any searching for equipment. When several projects are under way at one time, each should be kept ready in a basket or box.

Large-scale or three-dimensional pieces are best worked on when all materials can be left out. A studio is ideal. A room that can be used for this work where nothing needs to be put away is of great help. Even an area of room reserved just for this work will make it easier.

A bulletin board is especially valuable for stitchery work. Sheets of **Celotex** can be lightly nailed onto any existing wall to provide such a surface. The Celotex can be used as it is or it can be covered with **muslin, felt,** or any other fabric. A **white glue** can be painted onto the Celotex, then fabric layered over the top. This provides a surface to which things can be pinned or tacked so that they can be viewed from a distance.

When walls can't be covered, or when the surfaces are unsuitable for tacking, stapling, or taping, there is another simple possibility. Have a 1″ × 4″ board attached high on one wall or to the ceiling. This provides a surface onto which you can staple or nail so that work in progress can be temporarily hung for viewing.

When possible, having a sewing machine, ironing board, and workspace all available in one room is the best arrangement.

CUTTING AND GLUING   When **appliqué** is to be sewn in place, either by **hand appliqué** or **machine appliqué,** the cutting should be on the **grain** of the **fabric.** This is especially important on a symmetrical shape. A leaf shape, for example, should be placed so that the grain of the fabric runs **lengthwise** from one tip of the leaf to the other. That puts the **bias** or stretch of the material equally on the two sides. It is more likely that the two sides will remain identical after being sewn. A square or rectangular piece must be placed with the grain. If a circle or other curved shape is cut, the placement of the fabric will not matter.

To achieve sharp corners in hand appliqué, very simple shapes should be cut, avoiding any inside curves. For example, if a stem with several leaves is to be hand sewn, the places where the leaves and the stem join will be difficult to sew. If the leaves are cut separately and sewn on first, then the stem can overlap the leaves, touching the tips to make sharp corners.

Good cutting is the secret to good appliqué. Use the best pair of scissors you can buy. Always keep them clean, dry, and sharp. Cut slowly in smooth, complete strokes; do not "hack." Cut small shapes from a manageable size of fabric; the weight of surrounding fabric can prevent the accurate cutting of small shapes.

For some stitchery projects, **adhesives** may be used. There are various adhesives available, each with its limitations. The basic advantage to gluing is the speed of application. When projects are made for temporary use, as for a one-occasion party **banner** or a nonpermanent sign for a campaign, some of the **spray adhesives** will be adequate; sewing, which is more time-consuming, would not be necessary or especially appropriate. Fabric shops carry various **iron-on adhesives** that work very well for many **fabrics.** Some household or **white glues** will also work well, especially if heavy fabrics or **felts** are used. There are materials available by the yard that have adhesive that can be set on both surfaces. **Iron-on tapes** offer a quick way of applying fabric color in small areas. **Marking pens** can be used for additional detail.

Care must be taken to read directions and to be familiar with the fiber content of the materials being used. Some of the iron-on adhesives require a temperature above that which can be tolerated by **synthetic fabrics.**

HAND APPLIQUÉ   In **hand appliqué, appliqué** shapes are usually cut, allowing for ¼″ **seam allowance,** and pinned in place. Some stitchers **baste** pieces, although generally that is not the best procedure. When pieces are only pinned in place, the designer is free to shift or alter the positions of shapes as needed. The appliqué process of turning edges under means the pieces change in size as they are sewn; to accommodate for this change in size, the relative positions may need to be altered. Basting sometimes stretches **bias** edges. To first **hem** by pressing with an iron predetermines the shape. To have a complete control over the appliqué the shapes must take final form beneath the fingers as they are sewn.

Some stitchers find it very helpful to make a line of straight machine stitching exactly on the hem allowance of a piece to be appliquéd. Then the fold can be easily made on that stitched line. This is especially helpful on materials that are more difficult to handle, such as **silks,** synthetics, and heavier **velveteens,** or **wools.** It is important that the machine stitches be sewn with a color that matches the color of the material.

The color of the thread used in hand appliqué depends upon the **stitch** being used. If stitches are intended to show, then a contrast will take full advantage of the pattern of color added by those stitches. For a very strong contrast, such as black stitches on white, an extremely active pattern is developed and stitching must therefore be carefully done. Consideration must also be given to determine just how important the stitches are to be. If a hidden stitch, such as a **blind stitch** or **whip stitch,** is used, the **sewing thread** should match the fabric being appliquéd.

In the appliqué of woven fabrics, the most commonly used stitches are blind stitch, **running stitch,** and whip stitch. Sometimes an **overcast stitch** or **buttonhole stitch** is used, but less successfully; they tend to become more important than the shape being appliquéd because they are large stitch patterns that greatly emphasize the edge.

In **cut-through appliqué,** or **reverse appliqué,** the blind stitch or whip stitch is almost invariably used. As there are so many inside curves in this technique, a running stitch is neither appropriate nor easily sewn.

Another hand appliqué method involves the sewing of **felt.** The usual **felt appliqué** employs either a running stitch or a whip stitch. The significant difference in this work is that felt, a **nonwoven material,** need not be turned under. **French knot appliqué,** also utilizing the easily-sewn felt, is executed with French knots.

Some stitchers do a hand stitching appliqué in which fabric edges are not turned under. **Raw edges** may **fray** and **ravel** and this effect is elaborated upon by exaggerating and emphasizing it. The overall effect is one of spontaneity, vigor, and directness when it is well handled. Some silks and **rayons** fray in such a way as to add new **sheen** and color changes. The hand stitching in this very free approach to stitchery may cover raw edges, or the sewing may be placed inside the cut edges to deliberately allow for further fraying or pulling of threads.

The size and kind of **needle** used in hand appliqué is largely a matter of personal preference. A fine shafted needle is always easier to draw through fabric. The length of the needle is also an important factor, as a short needle will make it easier to take small, fine stitches.

In any stitches that show on the surface of appliqué, such as running stitch or buttonhole stitch, it is the consistency of stitch length that is most important. Stitches may be longer or shorter, according to the stitcher's needs or skills, but regularity of length and spacing add to the effect of the stitch pattern.

Most hand appliqué is sewn using a single strand of mercerized **thread.** Some stitchers prefer to use a double strand of thread on appliqué that is to be washed frequently or heavily used, as on children's clothes or **quilts.** The double threads may sometimes cross, however, so that the stitch does not appear to be perfectly smooth and straight. For most purposes, a single strand of thread will be adequate.

Embroidery floss may also be used for the sewing of hand appliqué. The six strands of floss should be cut to the desired length, usually about 18″, and then separated so that just one strand is used. Again, some sewers prefer to use a double strand, but twists of the threads will show. A single strand of floss is softer and slightly thicker than a mercerized thread, which has a smooth, harder finish. The added thickness of the floss gives more color to the stitches, which is significant when a contrasting color is used.

MACHINE APPLIQUÉ   When heavily textured **fabrics** or those of tight heavy weave are used, **machine appliqué** may be preferable to **hand appliqué.** It is sometimes essential, as some materials are too difficult to sew through by hand; in other instances the machine stitch may give the effect desired by the stitcher.

Machine appliqué may be accomplished in any of several ways. In one a **straight stitch** is used to simply outline the **appliqué,** either turning the edge under or not, according to preference. The sewing may be done back and forth over a cut or **raw edge,** or a shape may be encircled repeatedly by line after line of straight stitches. In either, the effect is one of pencil-like sketch lines used as a pattern to exaggerate or emphasize the cut fabric pieces.

Another method of machine appliqué involves the use of the closed zigzag or **machine satin stitch.** In this the raw edges are enclosed, adding a smooth solid line of color to the cut pieces of appliqué fabric. This **zigzag stitch** is especially appropriate for heavy fabrics such as **upholstery materials** because the size relationship between the size of line and weight of **yarns** is compatible.

While machine appliqué is not necessarily speedy, it is faster than hand sewing, especially on works that are large in scale. Whether or not to use the machine appliqué may depend upon several factors: weight of materials, the kind of wearability demanded from the finished piece, and the need for the wide line as another element in color and composition.

Because the satin stitch leaves a wide, smooth line of color at the edge of the appliqué fabric, the color of the thread becomes important. An area can be made very dominant or prominent through the use of a contrasting color. Areas can also be diminished in importance if the thread color tends to dissolve into the color of the fabric or disappear into the background color. Machine satin stitches offer another scale, that of the drawn line, to the designer.

FINISHING   The **finishing** of most stitchery pieces involves the **backing, edging,** or **hem**ming of the work and determining a means by which it may be hung. This applies especially to **banners** and **wall hangings.** The finishing in clothing is determined by the **garment;** in **soft sculpture** it is a matter of the individual form.

All panels should be **press**ed before the finishing begins. If the articles are soiled, wash only if you are certain all materials are washable and that they were **preshrunk** or **Sanforize**d; otherwise, dry clean. Many **dry-cleaning** solutions work very well, but should be tried on samples of your **fabric** before use.

To press **pile** fabrics, use a **needle board,** which allows you to press out wrinkles without flattening the textural weave. Other fabrics should be ironed according to their **fiber** content. Most **natural fibers,** which include the **cellulose fibers** (linen, cotton, etc.) and the **animal fibers** (wool, silk) iron easily and can withstand medium to high heat. **Synthetic fabrics,** made from **man-made fibers,** must be pressed according to individual instructions. Some are **blends** and can take medium-high heat; others will simply melt from excess heat.

When there are several layers of **appliqué** or heavy handwork, a **turkish towel,** a blanket, or similar **padding** should be laid down first, then covered with a smooth cloth or dish towel. The appliqué or embroidery can be placed face-down over the padded area and pressed. For most panels, merely turning them face-down on an ironing board will be adequate. While steam may be used on some fabrics, others will shrink or spot. Care must be taken in steaming, and you must know the fibers you are working with.

If a panel is to be **Scotchgard**ed, made **fire-resistant,** or treated with any other fabric **finish,** it can be done at this time, or it can be done after the panel is finished for hanging. It must be done at this time if the panel is to be **mount**ed.

The simplest means of finishing is probably by binding.

A precut binding, **bias tape,** or woven **edging** may be used. The **stitchery panel** is cut to finished size plus a ¼–½" extra at each of the four edges. The binding is often done using a strip of fabric cut on the **bias.** Because the binding is to be **fold**ed over the edge of the fabric, allowance must be made for the doubling. If a ½" binding is desired, the binding fabric must be cut 2" wide (1" wide plus ½" to be **hem**med on the front and ½" on the **back**). If the corners are rounded, the bias edge is an advantage because it can be stretched to fit around the curve of the corner. For most purposes, however, a straight cut is easier to work with, as it does not stretch or give as a bias edge does. For straight or **butt**-joints or for **mitered corner**s, use a piece of fabric cut with the **grain** of the fabric. It can be cut with either **lengthwise** grain or **crosswise** grain.

When a precut binding has been used to finish the edge of a panel, additional pieces of the same binding can be used to provide loops at the top to facilitate hanging (**a.**). A **rod** can be slipped through the loops and the rod is then set onto hooks that are attached at right angles to the wall. This binding method is most often used on **cut-through appliqué.**

Another method of finishing is the use of a **self binding.** The edge of the stitchery panel is turned and folded or hemmed at the two sides of the panel and stitched in place. The hems are turned to the back, leaving a smooth surface and edge on the face of the panel. The top and bottom edges are then turned and each is hemmed or folded back far enough to allow for a rod to be slipped through the open channel formed by the folding (**b.**). When all edges have been finished a backing fabric can be **slip stitch**ed on, if desired, to cover the reverse side of the stitches (**c.**).

A third finishing method requires that a backing fabric be cut to the same dimensions as the finished panel. The backing and the panel are placed with wrong sides facing and the edges of each are folded in, pinned, and **baste**d. The tops of the two fabrics are turned in the same way, on the **hemline,** then an extra row of stitching is added to make a channel for the rod or dowel that will hold it. An opening must be left at the ends of the top so that the rod can be slid through (**d.**). If a rod is used at the bottom edge, it is sewn the same way. A rod is sometimes used at both top and bottom of a panel to help stretch it and make it hang level and straight. See ill.

Each of these binding methods requires that some extra materials be available to make the channels for rods. Sometimes the method of binding is determined by the amount of material that is available at the edge of the finished stitchery panel.

If there is no extra material at all because the enthusiastic stitcher has worked right out to the edge, there are still some options in finishing. The stitchery piece may be **appliqué**d onto a larger piece of fabric to gain the extra allowance needed for hemming; the second fabric provides a mat around the stitchery. This is often a very effective way of hanging a panel and need not be kept in reserve for only those occasions when there is insufficient material with which to work. **Felt** projects are often appliquéd to another piece of fabric to be prepared for hanging. Even **cut-through appliqué** using felt is often done this way because the edges vary so greatly in thickness.

An alternate way of working with a stitchery that has been worked too close to the edges is to add strips of the same fabric or of a contrasting fabric onto the original piece. These strips may be narrow at the sides and bottom; at the top, the strip may be wide enough to slip a rod through.

Another finishing method is **mount**ing. To do this, first measure the finished size of the stitchery—that is, the area that is to show when the piece is finally hung. There must be a minimum of 2" extra fabric beyond the finished size at each of the four edges of the panel. For example, if a panel is to finish at 18" × 24", the fabric must be at least 22" × 28". A piece of plywood is then cut to the finished size, 18" × 24"; a ⅜" plywood is heavy enough to remain rigid, but thicker wood may be used. Thinner wood should be used only on smaller pieces or on those pieces where no wood frame will be added. The wood is placed on a flat surface, then the fabric is placed on top and folded over the wood to determine placement. It can be temporarily tacked in place, being sure that the **grain** of the fabric is aligned with the edge of the wood. Then the panel and wood are turned upside-down, with the face of the fabric down and the wood side up. Use a staple gun to attach the fabric to the back of the plywood. Fold corners. On the very heavy fabrics, folding too much bulky material will make a lumpy corner. Clip away the excess material. Lightly touch a bit of fabric glue to any **raw edge**s to keep them from **fray**ing. Always start stapling at the middle of each side, working out toward the corners. Check occasionally to be sure edges are even. When finished, the exposed area of wood on the back can be covered with an extra piece of fabric folded under and stapled to cover raw edges.

This mounting gives a thickness to the panel, moving the stitchery out from the wall by about ½". If a frame is desired, a simple strip framing can be nailed directly onto the edges of the plywood. Masonite and **Celotex** do not work well for mounting. Staples will not penetrate Masonite and will not hold in Celotex. A frame cannot be attached to the edges of either.

Finished panels should never be hung with a cord or string that is prominent, making a large inverted "V" above the panel. Various simple brass hanging devices are available for supporting rods. When panels are mounted, a simple hook on the back will be concealed. A sawtooth picture hanger is excellent. Usually the simpler rods and frames seem best, but they should always be selected according to the appropriateness for the piece of work.

A banner of medieval style may call for a large dowel rod with elaborate **finial**s. In most cases, mounting considerations are similar to those used in selecting a frame for a drawing or painting. For any piece of stitchery to be shown to full advantage, the binding and mounting should be done as carefully as the work.

CARE AND MAINTENANCE   Stitcheries are only as strong and permanent in color as the fabrics used. Care should be used to avoid leaving panels continuously in direct sunlight or in areas of strong light. Fabrics will fade in time. Some colors are more fugitive than others; blue dyes seem the most transient and the first to disappear or fade.

All fabrics will change slightly with age. They mellow

and soften and fade. Some may yellow. The chemical breakdown of some **natural fiber**s may cause yellow or brown spots, as is often observed in **linen.** Most stitchery works will show no appreciable difference for years.

When panels are stored they should be rolled if possible. Folds left for long periods of time may cause creases that will never come out. This is especially true of **appliqué,** as there is seldom a way of getting an iron to the fabrics that may be under two or three layers of material. If rolling the panels to be stored is not possible, refold them occasionally.

Mounted panels should be wrapped in cloth if they need protection from dust. Wrapping in plastic is not recommended for fabrics of any kind. An occasional shaking will remove surface dust, as will a light vacuuming with a brush attachment.

Stitchery panels (and all fabrics) thrive best in open air where they can be seen, enjoyed, and appreciated.

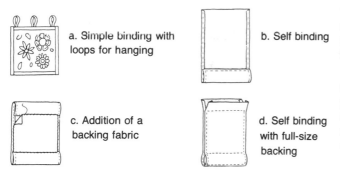

a. Simple binding with loops for hanging

b. Self binding

c. Addition of a backing fabric

d. Self binding with full-size backing

stitchery. Stitchery. A general, all-inclusive term for any art form or decorative **fabric** process which includes the application of threads and fabrics to a **background** with the use of a **needle.** Embroidery and **appliqué** are among most commonly used stitchery techniques. It most often refers to **wall hanging**s or **panel**s, though stitchery may also be used on any fabric articles, such as **body covering**s, **quilt**s, and **pillow**s. Many appliqué methods are included under the more general term of stitchery. Among these are **transparent appliqué, lace appliqué,** and **felt appliqué.** In contemporary use, **trapunto** and **couching** are stitchery methods. Also see **Stitchery.**

stitchery kit. Stitchery. A prepackaged, commercially prepared **kit** or collection, consisting of design or pattern, **background fabric,** and working materials for a **stitchery** project.

stitchery panel. Stitchery. A piece of **fabric** which has been treated decoratively with **appliqué,** embroidery, or **stuff**ed work. It is usually longer than it is wide, in contrast to a **wall hanging,** which may be of any proportion. The stitchery panel may be **free-hanging** or it may be **mount**ed over Celotex or a wood panel. Also see **Stitchery: Stitchery Forms.**

stitchery tapestry. Stitchery. A stitchery **wall hanging** or **panel** that is **free-hanging.** Technically, a stitchery piece is not a tapestry at all, though the term is sometimes used to designate any all-fiber panel.

stitches in waiting. Knitting. These are the stitches that are put on a **cable needle** when turning a **cable,** or the stitches on a **stitch holder** when turning the heel of a sock. While they are "stitches in waiting," they are being held in readiness for some special knitting procedure or pattern.

stitch holder. Knitting. A small plastic or metal tool (usually shaped something like a large safety pin) used to hold or transfer **stitches in waiting.** Also see **cable needle.**

stitching. Weaving. The process of weaving two or three layers of cloth and simultaneously joining them together. This is all done as part of the weave structure—not with needle and thread after weaving is finished.

A second meaning involves long **float**s in pattern weaves. To "stitch down" means having the **raiser**s or **sinker**s in such a position as to cut down the length of the float and yet not interfere with the pattern. Also see **stitching point.**

stitching groover. Leather. A tool used to cut a groove parallel to the edge of leather for recessed stitching. It is adjustable from $1/16''$ to $3/4''$ from the edge. The groover is replaceable. See ill. Also see **edge creaser** and **Leatherwork: Sewing Leather.**

Groover — Stitching groover

stitching horse. Leather. A viselike tool, similar to a **lacing pony,** mounted on a bench used to hold leather steady and to free both hands while lacing, punching, or stitching. The leather is inserted between the two upright wood pieces which are tightened with a wing nut or similar closing until the leather is held firm. The horse is straddled to work. See ill. Also see **double needle stitch.**

Stitching horse

stitching point. Weaving. The point where a back thread intersects and weaves with a face thread in **double** or **triple cloth** weaving. This joins the layers together so they are one cloth. The stitching pattern may be close, open, at random, or in a distinct pattern. **Quiltweave** is an example of stitching points in a distinct pattern. The purpose behind stitching the layers together is to make a heavy fabric, to reinforce a loose one by making it one with a heavier fabric (using the principle of having a backing), or to produce a faint pattern. Also see **double cloth, multiple-layered cloth, triple cloth.**

stitching punch. Leather. See **thonging chisel.**

stitch movement. Knitting. See **Knitting: Knit Movements.**

Stitch Witchery. Crewel. Embroidery. Needlepoint. A trade name for a gauzelike material that, when placed between two fabrics and heated, fuses the fabrics. It is useful for attaching linings or backings to needlework, and adds a slight stiffness to the piece.

Stitch-Witchery. Stitchery. See **iron-on adhesive.**

stock. Bookbinding. See **paper.**

stock. Metalworking. See **metal.**

stock character. Puppets. A standard or set character or player in a **puppet show,** as **Punch, Judy,** or any of the cast that usually accompanies them. They remain essentially the same in character from one performance to the next. The faces may be altered and the actions varied, but the viewer knows the character and may rely upon a consistency of response and action. Also see **popular theater, Pulcinella, Punch and Judy cast, Punch and Judy show.**

stock dyeing. Dyeing. Dyeing of natural or synthetic fibers before spinning them into yarn. The stock or bulk of fibers is well opened up so that the dye can be readily absorbed and is clean of foreign matter, dirt, grease, or clumpy or matted areas. The dyeing precedes **carding, combing,** and **blending.** This method of dyeing allows for good dye penetration, but the process is quite expensive when done commercially. It is used for heather or **tweed** yarns, which are made by spinning several colors of stock-dyed fibers together. Because of the blending possibilities, stock dyeing affords endless variations of colors in the yarn. Also see **dyed-in-the-wool.**

stockinet. Toys. A somewhat elastic knitted fabric that was manufactured for stockings and undergarments but popularly used for **fabric dolls** or **cloth body** dolls. Jersey has similar characteristics.

stockinette stitch. Knitting. See **stocking stitch.**

stocking doll. Toys. See **nylon stocking doll.**

stocking puppet. Puppets. See **nylon stocking puppet, sock puppet.**

stocking stitch. Knitting. (Also called the stockinette stitch.) The stocking stitch is most commonly used for socks. The front of the knit fabric has a smooth surface, with the look of tight, even, vertical chaining, emphasizing the vertical alignment of the stitches. The back of the fab-

ric, in contrast, has horizontal rows of loops. If you use the loopy side out, rather than the smooth side, the stitch is called reverse stocking stitch. The construction is: Knit 1 row, Purl 1 row. With circular needles, you simply knit every row. See ill. Also see **Knitting: Construction.**

Stocking stitch

stock millwork. Woodworking. See **millwork.**

stomper doll. Toys. See **dancing man.**

stone cement. Combine 25 parts water glass, 5 parts unslaked lime, 5 parts powdered white lead, and 1 part powdered chalk. Slowly add water, stirring constantly, until mixture is a thick paste. Use immediately.

stone pusher. Jewelry. See **bezel pusher.**

stone setter's cement. (Also called engraver's cement.) This cement is used in repoussé work. Melt and blend 2 parts burgundy pitch, 1.5 parts **rosin,** and 1.5 parts beeswax; add 1 part plaster of Paris. Stone setter's cement solidifies in cold water.

stone setting. Jewelry. See **bezel.**

stoneware clay. Ceramics. See **Ceramics: Clay.**

stoneware glaze. Ceramics. High-fire **glaze**s, containing **feldspar** or wood ash, that are compatible with the maturing of stoneware. Also see **celadon, feldspar glaze, raku glaze, salt glaze.**

stoning. Enameling. The process of scraping the cooled **enamel** with a carborundum stone to smooth and to level out the enamel by grinding it down. The work should be cleaned with water to improve both observation and abrasion. Sometimes stoning with an abrasive such as pumice is used as the final finishing process to achieve a **matte finish.** Also see **cloison, cloisonné, polishing.**

stop. Stained Glass. A strip of wood or metal trim nailed against a glass window to hold it in place once it has been set into its frame or sash. Also see **fitting.**

stop cut. Woodworking. When removing wood with a **chisel** or **gouge,** the process of making a cut with a saw or chisel on the outer perimeter of the area you wish to remove. This cut is made to terminate the forward movement of the chisel at the desired location. Also see **whittling.**

stop out. Enameling. See **resist.**

stopping knife. Stained Glass. A flat, blunt-edged knife, such as an oyster knife, usually with the end bent upward at a 30–40° angle, used for straightening **lead came.** It can be used as a hammer to tap glass into place and for driving in glazing nails when a blob of lead has been cast onto the end of the handle. See ill. Also see **farrier's nail, glazing, lathkin** and **Stained Glass: Glazing, Tools and Materials.**

Stopping knife

stopping out agent. Stained Glass. (Also called acid resist.) A mastic applied to areas of glass to prevent **etching** by an acid. Also see **aciding, flashed glass, rubber latex glue.**

stops. Leather. See **stamp.**

stored energy. Toys. Energy held in reserve to animate or move a toy. A compressed **spring** has potential power, as does a rubber band held under tension by twisting or stretching. Also see **Toys: Mechanical Toys and Moving Toys.**

storing. Lacemaking. See **Lacemaking: Cleaning and Care of Laces.**

storing quilts. Quilts. See **Quilts: Care of Quilts.**

stork scissors. Stitchery. Small special **embroidery scissors** or **trimming scissors** made to resemble a stork. They are made in several sizes, and in all of them the blades become the long beak of the bird and the feet rest on the round finger holes.

Storm at Sea. Quilts. Either of two old and popular **block** designs for **pieced quilts.** One is identical to **Kansas Troubles** and has a **sawtooth** edge incorporated into the **patch** pattern. The second quilt known by this name is made up of blocks using squares, **diamonds,** and triangles. They are arranged in various ways, but all suggest rippling waves. The **all-over** quilt effect is one of motion, thus the name.

storybook character. Toys. See **nursery character.**

storybook doll. Toys. See **nursery character.**

storytelling board. Toys. A **flannel board** and cutouts of **felt** that adhere to the board, used to illustrate a story as it is told.

storytelling quilt. Quilts. Any quilt that uses descriptive pictures of people or places to tell a story. These are almost always **appliqué quilts** and are highly individualized. Quilts made for children often include favorite characters from legends or from the Bible, or animals from fables or stories. Buffalo Bill, Red Riding Hood, Noah's Ark, and whales have all found their way into quilts. In some quilts, such as **Captain May in the Mexican War,** the storytelling aspect is secondary. In others, such as the **Harriet Powers Quilt,** the storytelling is the essence of the whole design. Storytelling quilts are usually one of a kind.

stove bolt. Metalworking. See **bolt.**

stove bolt. Woodworking. See **bolt.**

stove polish. Stained Glass. See **aciding.**

straight. Quilts. Stitchery. The length of the **fabric,** running with or parallel to the **warp.** The straight is the **lengthwise grain.**

straight- and round-end anvil stake. Metalworking. See **anvil.**

straight border. Knitting. See **border.**

straight chisel. Woodworking. See **chisel.**

straight-claw hammer. Woodworking. See **hammer.**

straight cross stitch. Needlepoint. See **upright cross stitch.**

straight cut. Woodworking. See **whittling.**

straight draw. Weaving. The simplest pattern of **drawing-in** the **warp end**s through the **heddles** on the **harness**es. It can be used with any number of harnesses from two on up, and forms the basis for all other **drawing-in drafts.** It proceeds in one direction only, and on **graph paper** it looks like a series of short diagonal and parallel lines. The number of threads in one repeat of a straight draw is equal to the number of harnesses being used. A four-harness, straight draw uses four harnesses only, and proceeds from harness #1 to #2, #3, #4, and then returns to #1 to repeat the sequence again. See ill.

Straight draw on...

a. 2 harnesses
b. 4 harnesses
c. 8 harnesses

A   B   C

straightedge. Stained Glass. See **Stained Glass: Tools and Materials.**

straightedge. Woodworking. Any perfectly straight edge can be used as a guide in drawing or scribing straight lines. It is usually a machined piece of steel that is not subject to **warp**age and that is likely to remain true. The edge of a try square or framing square is frequently used as a straightedge. Also see **Woodworking: Marking Out and Squaring.**

straight frame knitting. Knitting. The old knitting frames were the forerunners of the modern knitting machine and were either single or double bed. The frames measured 12–60″ in width with pegs made of wood, steel, or bone, ¼–½″ apart. Also see **rake knitting, spool knitting,** and **knitting.**

Straight Furrow. Quilts. A specific **set** for **blocks,** that produces diagonal bands of dark and light; also the name by which those quilts are sometimes called. A **Log Cabin** block sewn with one-half the block in dark patterns and one-half in light could be set so that the darks joined into long diagonal bands. Straight Furrow is an arrangement that can be used on the **Courthouse Steps** block or the **split nine-patch,** in which case the quilt might be known by either or both names.

straight Gobelin stitch. Needlepoint. See **Gobelin stitch.**

straight laid-in. Weaving. See **laid-in.**

straight life-eye needle. Leather. See **lacing needles.**

straight router bit. Woodworking. See **router bit.**

straight slit. Weaving. See **slit tapestry.**

straight snips. Metalworking. See **snips.**

straight stitch. Crewel. Embroidery. (Also called stroke stitch.) This is a single thread of any length worked in any direction at random. It is a very effective stitch when used for grass or scattered for highlights. It is often worked **detached** in combination with other stitches, or as a base stitch for other stitches. See ill.

Straight stitch

straight stitch. Stitchery. The single-line stitch made by all standard sewing machines. It uses two threads, one on top that comes from a spool, and one underneath that comes from a **bobbin.** It produces a line of evenly spaced stitches used for all general purposes, in **seam**s, and in **join**ing parts. The straight stitch is sometimes used in contemporary **appliqué** work to apply **fabric**s to a **background** using the sewn stitches like lines of drawing. In this way of working, the appliqué material need not have a **seam allowance** added at the outside edge. The **raw edge** is left showing and stitching occurs over it, sometimes incorporating **ravel**ings into the design.

In another method, the appliqué pieces are cut with an additional ¼″ seam allowance that is **baste**d under, then stitched permanently with the straight stitch.

Most **clothing construction** and regular sewing utilizes the straight stitch. Since the threads interlock, seams made this way are strong and firm. Also see **Stitchery: Machine Appliqué.**

straight tongs. Metalworking. See **tongs.**

stranding. Crochet. Knitting. A term used in multicolor work: stranding is the process of carrying the colors not in use along the back side of the crochet or knitting. These extra ″stranded″ colors lie in flat, horizontal rows against the work. See ill. Also see **back of stranding, color knitting, tapestry crochet.**

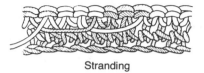
Stranding

strap. Lacemaking. See **bar.**

strap end punch. Leather. (Also called English punch, V-punch.) A tool used to punch out curved V-shape openings (up to 2″ long). Also used to shape ends of belts or straps. See ill. Also see **drive punch.**

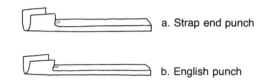
a. Strap end punch
b. English punch

strap lead. Stained Glass. Used in patching up cracks in the **lead came** of a glazed window once it has been secured in place. It is usually made by cutting a slice of a round-sectioned lead came the right width and length, placing it along the crack, fitting it in between the lead cames on either side, and then **solder**ing it into place. Also see **glazing, soldering iron** and **Stained Glass: Glazing.**

strap leather. Leather. Any leather, but generally cowhide of 5 to 8 oz weight, used for belts or saddlery straps.

strap loom. Weaving. See **backstrap loom.**

strapwork. Bookbinding. A geometrical pattern used in cover decoration, formed by interlaced double lines.

straw horn. Toys. A homemade, somewhat unmusical device that makes a loud sound when it is blown. It may be regarded as a **noisemaker** or **sound toy,** but hardly as a **musical toy.** A plastic drinking straw is flattened at one end and sliced off diagonally at each corner of that end. This makes a reedlike point that is placed in the mouth.

straw loom. Weaving. A **loom** made out of drinking straws in which the **warp** threads are drawn through the straws and secured. The **filling** is then woven around the straws and slipped from them onto the warp. The woven strips can be made as long as desired, but the width is usually limited to narrow pieces which are then sewn together if a wider fabric is wanted. On the same order is a stick loom, which is made out of long, wooden needles. These needles are threaded with the warp threads. The filling is woven in and out around the needles, as in the straw loom, and then slipped or pushed from the stick-needles to the warp.

streak. Gemcutting. The effect of scratching a **streak plate** with a specimen to aid in its identification. The resultant **color** left on the plate implies the composition of the stone. It is most effective with idiochromatic material, as allochromatic stones often leave a white streak; stones of 7 and over in **hardness** leave a scratch. Also see **cinnabar** and **Gemcutting: Identification of Gems.**

Streak of Lightning. Quilts. A specific **set** of **block**s and the name by which those **quilt**s are sometimes called. This particular set or arrangement combines dark and light areas in such a way as to suggest an **all-over** pattern that gives the effect of zigzagging bands. Streak of Lightning is an arrangement that can be used on various block designs such as **Log Cabin, Courthouse Steps, three-patch,** and **split nine-patch.** Such a quilt might be known by either or both names.

streak plate. Gemcutting. A flat piece of white, unglazed porcelain used to identify rough gem material. Also see **streak** and **Gemcutting: Tools and Materials.**

streaky glass. Stained Glass. These are transparent sheets of **antique glass** with colors streaked across the surface. They are made by mixing several pots of **glass** together. Because of its beautiful visual quality, it can be used by itself. Besides combining beautiful colors together in one sheet, many types also have a rippling surface. Most streaky glass is made in England. Germany makes a streaky glass called Danziger glass. Also see **English antique glass, reamy glass.**

stream retting. Spinning. See **flax.**

street artists. Those craftspeople and musicians who display their wares and talents on the sidewalks. Some are full-time itinerant craftspeople who move from one fair or street sale to another. Others join the street selling for supplemental income during holidays and festivals. Many of the musicians and craftspeople are highly talented and skilled, offering entertainment as well as good wares for reasonable prices.

street theater. Puppets. The **popular theater,** performed by vagrants or itinerant **puppeteer**s, of which almost no examples of either stage or puppets remain. Street entertainment was not regarded as a serious art form until recently, when interest in "pop" or **underground art** began to develop.

stress crazing. Plastics. See **crazing.**

stressed glass. Glasswork. See **tempered glass.**

stretched forming. Metalworking. See **raising techniques.**

stretched metal forming. Metalworking. See **raising techniques.**

stretcher. Quilts. (Also called end bar, end frame.) A board or bar that forms the end of the **quilting frame.** The stretchers are shorter than the **rail**s, and the quilt is attached crosswise in the frame. That is, the ends of the quilt are attached to the rails and those portions of the sides of the quilt exposed after **rolling** are attached to the stretchers. A part of the quilt is always rolled onto one or both of the rails, so the area exposed can be no greater than the length of the stretchers. Also see **Quilts: Quilting, Hand Quilting.**

stretcher. Weaving. An adjustable wooden or metal bar with sharp teeth at each end. It is used to maintain the fabric at full width during weaving by preventing the **selvage**s from drawing in. The teeth are stuck into the cloth just within the selvages at a point a little below the **fell.** The bar is open at this time. When the teeth are in place, it is closed flat and locked shut with a metal ring. As the weaving moves along, the stretcher is taken out and reinserted so that it is always positioned just below the fell. See ill. Also see **draw-in.**

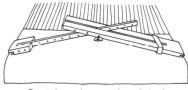
Stretcher about to be closed

stretcher strips. Crewel. Embroidery. Needlepoint. Wooden strips with mitered corners especially constructed for joining four pieces to form a square or rectangle over which **canvas** may be stretched. They are suitable for framing, blocking, or as a frame for working almost any kind of needlework. The strips, usually ½" thick by 2" wide, are available in most art-supply stores in almost any length at 1" intervals or may be cut to order. Also see **embroidery frame** and **Crewel: Finishing, Needlepoint: Finishing.**

stretch fabric. Stitchery. Any woven or knitted material which has structural "give" or elasticity. The stretch may result from the use of elastic yarns, fabric treatment, various special weaves, or treatment of the yarns. In the latter, yarns are twisted, coiled, or crimped in such a way that they can be stretched and will return to the original shape. In any **stuff**ed three-dimensional form, stretch fabrics are of special value.

stretching. Jewelry. A result of striking metals with a metal hammer. Blows at varying angles and different hammer faces will produce different directions of stretching. This stretching occurs in **forging,** sandbag shaping, blocking in a mold, and pressing. It is sometimes necessary to stretch a **bezel** or a ring that has been made too small.

To stretch a round or oval bezel, place it on a corresponding **bezel mandrel,** or use a smooth straight steel rod smaller than the bezel. Roll the bezel back and forth with medium pressure on a **steel block.** Bezels made of **fine silver** or high-**karat** gold should be checked frequently because they stretch quite readily. Other metals may require annealing if much stretching is necessary.

To stretch a **ring shank, file** the ring all the way around so that it has a flat upper surface; having the seam filed well is important. The shank should also be well rounded, having previously been rounded with a **rawhide mallet.**

Place the ring on a **ring mandrel.** Hammer the ring all the way around with a **raising hammer,** using slightly overlapping blows and keeping the hammer surface parallel to the surface of the ring shank. After you have gone around the ring once, remove it from the ring mandrel, so the mandrel is tapered, and replace it facing in the other direction. Continue hammering, reversing as many times as necessary until the correct size is obtained. Do not count on stretching a ring shank more than a quarter-size without **annealing.** Sometimes during stretching the **solder**ed **seam** will open no matter how well the joint is soldered or how careful you are with hammering, in which case it will have to be rebound with **iron binding wire** and resoldered.

stretching. Metalworking. See **raising techniques.**

stretching lead. Stained Glass. All **lead came,** even if it is straight, should be stretched before it is used. After straightening any twists, place one end of the lead came in a **lead vise.** The end may be folded back an inch or two before it is inserted in the vise. Grip the other end firmly with a pair of pliers and gently pull the lead out straight. Once it is straightened, put it aside carefully, as it can be easily twisted or bent. Also see **side-cutting pliers** and **Stained Glass: Glazing.**

stria stripe. Rugmaking. Weaving. See **stripe.**

striation. Stained Glass. This effect in a stained-glass sheet occurs only in **French antique glass** and **German antique glass.** It is created by the glass blower, who blows a glass bubble about the size of a volleyball and then turns the form in an iron bowl lined with small spikes. The bowl is called a hedgehog or porcupine. This process causes the glass to be streaked with a web of striations and gives the surface of the glass a brittle, crystalline appearance that glitters in sunshine.

strick. Spinning. See **flax.**

strié stripe. Rugmaking. Weaving. See **stripe.**

strike-off bar. Metalworking. See **sandcasting molding equipment.**

striking stick. Leather. A **mallet**like tool, covered with leather, used for striking **stamps** when **stamping** or **tool**ing. See ill.

Striking stick

striking the arc. Metalworking. The initial action in starting to **weld** with an **arc welder.** It is the specific act of touching or striking the electrode to the work to establish the spark connection that will produce the welding heat. Also see **Metalworking: Welding.**

string. Kites. A thin line of twisted fiber used with kites for the **guidelines, bridling,** lashing, and flying. For lashing joints or stick ends to be notched, a relatively fine grade of string or button thread can be used. The kite guideline can be constructed with a strong but not too heavy kite string. Also see **Kites: Kite Flying, Tools and Materials.**

string. Puppets. The lengths of thread or fiber that connect specific parts of a **marionette** to the **control bar.** The strings, or lines, are lifted or moved to **manipulate** the figure and suggest action. Usually **linen thread** or **carpet thread** is used. A string that is black tends to be less visible than a light one. Also see **arm string, control point, elbow string, hand string, head string, heel string, hip string, perch bar, shoulder string, skeleton** and **Puppets: Stringing the Marionette.**

string. Spinning. Weaving. A slender, sturdy group of spun fibers. String is thought of as being thinner than **cord** but thicker than **thread.** It has multiple uses for tying or lacing in weaving.

string. Toys. In many toys the string is the device by which the toy is set in motion. A **whip top,** for example, requires the use of a string to give the top momentum. Tug-starting toys, such as yo-yos, and **pull toy**s require a string or cord.

String is used in making **string doll**s and **string joint**s.

string control. Puppets. See **control bar.**

string doll. Toys. A simple doll made of cord, binding, or any thick, ropelike piece of fabric or string. The face or head and sometimes the body are **stuff**ed fabric, with lengths of the string forming arms and legs. A knot at the ends of the strings may suggest hands or feet.

stringed puppet. Puppets. See **string puppet.**

string heddle. Weaving. A **heddle** made of strong string or cord. These heddles come in three varieties: There are those that are part of colonial or Scandinavian **counterbalanced loom**s. They look like steel or wire heddles, have a **heddle eye** and are attached to the heddle bars or the **harness** itself. They are made on a **heddle jig** and are used to replace worn heddles. Looking exactly like string heddles, but having a different purpose, are the string heddles that are repair heddles and are used to correct mistakes in **threading.** They are made directly on the harness. A piece of string or cord is needed that is about 2½ times the length of the heddles already on the harness. The string is doubled in half and a half-hitch is made over the top heddle bar. The string is knotted around itself to form the top of the heddle eye. A space is left equal to the width of a heddle eye and another knot is formed that closes the bottom of the heddle eye. The two string ends are tied around the bottom heddle bar in a secure knot to hold the string heddle taut. Excess string at the knot should be trimmed. The string heddle can also be started at the bottom heddle bar and knotted over the top heddle bar. Where one starts the string heddle depends on what one feels is the easiest to do on one's particular loom. In any case, the heddle eye should be as closely aligned to the other heddle eyes as possible, or the **warp end** coming through it will not be in the correct position when the **shed** is opened. This type of string heddle is meant to be a temporary arrangement and the heddle is cut off when the warp is finished.

The third variety of string heddle is called a leash (or lisse), and is found on tapestry, inkle, backstrap, Navajo, and some **frame loom**s. Leash are simply loops of strong cord that go around every other warp end and are attached to a wooden heddle bar or stick. The loops may be a continuous string attached to the rod with half-hitches that also space the heddles, or they may be individual loops of cord attached to a continuous cord that has been previously half-hitched around the entire bar. In either case, the heddles must be replaced with every new warp. This is easier to do with the individual loops since the half-hitched heddle-spacer cord remains as is and only the loops are replaced. However, it is still tedious work, and weavers try to avoid it by carrying the new warp while winding it on the loom through the old string heddle, which is not too easy to do unless the heddles are very long and the warp is not too closely spaced. See ill. Also see **backstrap loom, doup, heddle cord, inkle loom, Navajo loom, tapestry loom.**

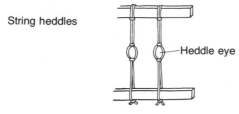

String heddles

Heddle eye

stringing. Puppets. Threading and tying the strings that connect the **marionette** to the **control bar**. Also see **carpet thread, florist's wire, linen thread, rag-doll puppet,** and **Puppets: Stringing the Marionette.**

stringing the marionette. Puppets. See **stringing** and **Puppets: Stringing the Marionette.**

string joint. Toys. Any **joint** used in **dollmaking** in which a string is the connecting device. A simple string joint for arms involves the use of a single string from one arm socket through the shoulders to the other arm socket, with an arm attached at each end of the string. A button can be used as a washer to allow easy movement, and the string is tightly knotted at each end. Sometimes the **pin joint** made with string is called a string joint. A loop of string can also be used to make a joint. For example, a string might run through the doll hand, into the wrist area of the lower arm, and back to the hand, making a complete circle or loop. Also see **cord joint.**

string puppet. Puppets. (Also called stringed puppet.) It is a **puppet** to which strings are attached so that the figure is **manipulate**d from a **control bar**. The string puppet is suspended so that it hangs from and is supported by the control bar. Also see **cloth marionette, dancing dollies, marionette, Punch and Judy show, puppeteer, rag-doll puppet, rocking, stuffed marionette,** and **Puppets: Definition, Making the Marionette Skeleton.**

string quilt. Quilts. A **pieced quilt** pattern that uses very narrow strips of fabric. It is in some ways similar to **Seminole patchwork,** although usually in a simpler arrangement. Also see **strip quilt.**

string top. Toys. Any **top** set in motion through the use of a string wrapped around the spindle and pulled quickly. The **whip top** is operated in this way.

strip. Papercrafts. See **paper strip.**

strip. Quilts. See **band.**

strip cutter. Rugmaking. A tool for cutting fabrics into strips for use in **braided** and **hooked rugs**. It clamps onto the edge of a table and the fabric is fed into it to be cut by turning the handle. The cutter comes with interchangeable blades for cutting different widths of strips. The widths on most models are from $^3/_{32}"$ to $2"$. When the blades become dulled, they can usually be sent back to the factory to be reground at a nominal cost. See ill.

Strip cutter for fabrics

stripe. Batik and Tie-dye. A pattern produced in **tie-dye** by **folding** and tying the **fabric**. It is one of the simplest tie-dye methods, although very versatile. The folded fabrics may be bound with **band tying, spiral binding,** or **crisscross binding** to give various effects. Lengthwise stripes are made when the **binding** runs the length of the material. Crosswise stripes require crosswise binding, going from selvage to selvage.

To produce a stripe, the fabric is **accordion pleat**ed or folded into a long strip (if tied or bound at this point, crosswise stripes can be produced); the accordion-pleated fabric is again accordion pleated, crosswise (**a.**); when all fabric is folded it is ready for binding; line binding will produce a narrow stripe (**b.**); band tying produces a wider stripe (**c.**). See ill.

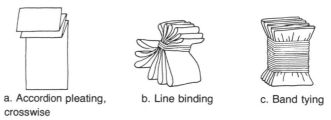

a. Accordion pleating, crosswise

b. Line binding

c. Band tying

stripe. Rugmaking. Weaving. A design in the **fabric** that produces parallel lines of color, texture, or open spaces running either vertically (**warp** stripe) or horizontally (**filling** stripe). Combined warp and filling stripes will give either a **plaid** or a **check** pattern. Stripes can be very simple, either two colors of equal amounts alternating with each other, or complex patterns of many colors and widths. Wide stripes create a bold pattern. Fine stripes tend to melt together to give interesting color and texture nuances. There are many types of stripes, some of which have definite names. A Roman stripe is a variation of the simple stripe where the areas of colors always remain the same, but these areas are usually broad and bold and use more than two colors. A pin or chalk stripe is a two-color stripe consisting of a fine line against a wide band of contrasting ground. Random stripes are mixed groupings of fine and bold lines. There may be many repeats or no repeat structure at all in the warp or filling. Strié stripes are very fine, random, warp stripes of many mixed colors that tend to give a striped textural effect. Mixtures of strié stripes with Roman ones give a composite stripe that alternates between bold areas and fine areas in a fairly regular repeat. Ombré stripes are stripes where colors graduate from one color to another; they demand much planning so that the **color blending** works out correctly.

To design warp stripes, take the various yarn colors and wind them around a piece of white mat or cardboard in the planned pattern in order to see how the proportions and colors react with one another. Working with colored crayons or marking pens helps with the proportions, but this is not a true indicator of the colors' effects on one another. The same sort of planning can also be done with regard to the filling stripes, but many weavers experiment directly on the loom.

Warp stripes are put into the warp during **warping** or they can be put in during **beaming** if the loom is being dressed from front to back. They are therefore in a fairly permanent position and much care should go into their planning beforehand. Filling stripes are put in during weaving and are much more spontaneous and can be changed at will.

In such weaving as tapestry and **flatweave rug**s, the warp is completely covered, yet it is possible to achieve warp stripes by alternating two filling colors in every other row of **plain weave**. For example, color A would be on the odd **end**s raised; color B would be on the even ends raised; this sequence would then be repeated. To change the placement of the two colors in the verticals, weave two **pick**s of the same color before returning to the alternation of colors. Horizontal stripes are made by the weaving of at least two picks of one color, and can be made by weaving as many picks as desired. Horizontals can be composed of more than two colors. Combinations of horizontals and verticals yield geometric patterns that, depending on the color placement, can give stylized flowers or figures. In **inkle weaving**, the design is all in the warp, since no filling is showing. Also see **pick-and-pick, sett, tapestry rug.**

strip heater. Plastics. An electrically heated hot strip used for bending sheet plastics. Its thermostat is generally set to a temperature of 325–350° F. See ill. Also see **Plastics: Thermoforming and Molding.**

Strip heater

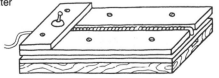

strip heating. Plastics. The process of heating plastic with a **strip heater** along a line or strip in preparation for bending it. Also see **Plastics: Thermoforming and Molding.**

strip method. Papercrafts. See **paper-strip method.**

strip papier mâché. Puppets. (Also called laminated papier mâché.) A **papier-mâché** process used in modeling. Paper that has been torn into narrow strips is wound or wrapped over a base of some kind. The finished papier mâché dries hard and is reasonably durable. Also see **Puppets: Making the Puppet Head.**

strippling. Stained Glass. See **whipping.**

strippling brush. Stained Glass. See **brush.**

strip quilt. Quilts. A **pieced quilt** that uses strips of **fabric,** all of the same width but varying in length. These are joined end-to-end to make strips as long as are needed for the width of the **quilt top.** The long strips are then joined to one another at the sides to produce a quilt top of horizontal bands. It is a quilt top easily sewn by a beginner and one in which straight lines of **quilting** are appropriate.

In a variation of the strip quilt, the pieces can be cut into identical lengths. They would make, in effect, bars similar to the outside bar of a **Log Cabin block,** or the bars of **Roman Squares.** Through the careful arrangement of these bars, patterns of zigzagging or waving lines can be produced.

strip repair. Bookbinding. The method used for repairing damaged back folds of **section**s and torn leaves using **paste** and commercially prepared mending tissue specifically intended for book repair or strips of lightweight 100% rag bond.

Cut the **paper** into strips ½″ wide and 1½″ longer than the length of the fold you are repairing. If you don't cut all the way through the paper on one end, so that the strips stay hinged by about ½″, you will find it easy to cut off the length you require and not have to deal with easily lost bits of paper. Brush paste onto a piece of glass, press a strip into the paste, lift it and pinch the ends together (with the paste inside, to prevent curling), and apply to the sheet.

Paste down the repair strip, centering it on the fold on the insides of the outside sheets and on the outsides of the inner sheets of the section. When the strip is wet it is liable to stretch, so handle it carefully: if stretched it will shrink again when dry and **cockle** the paper.

The procedure is the same for repairing the face of the page except that the strip is cut the same size as the tear. Also see **Bookbinding: Repair and Restoration.**

Stript-Ease. Leather. An inexpensive adjustable **draw gauge** with replaceable razor blades used to cut leather straps of even width. See ill. Also see **Leatherwork: Cutting and Edging Leather, Tools and Materials.**

Stript-Ease in use

stroke. Basketry. One complete movement of the **weaver** or binding element.

stroke stitch. Crewel. Embroidery. See **straight stitch.**

strong dents. Weaving. See **reed.**

stropping. Woodworking. See **sharpening.**

strotoscope. Toys. See **phenakistoscope.**

Stuart beadwork. Beadwork. A style of **bead embroidery** popular around 1630 when the Stuarts were the ruling family of Scotland and England. Traditional embroidery designs were used with the addition of small, bright beads to accent outlines.

stud. Leather. See **nailhead.**

stud. Woodworking. See **wood.**

stud bolt. Metalworking. See **bolt.**

studding. Leather. The decoration of leather with **nailhead**s, studs, spots, etc.

stuff. Basketry. The specific material used to make a basket. Also see **Basketry: Tools and Materials.**

stuff. Puppets. Quilts. Stitchery. Toys. To fill an area with **batting** or **filler** to give it a rounded or three-dimensional look. In the **quilt**making process, the filler is usually inserted as a complete layer between the **quilt top** and the **backing** before **quilting** is begun. In **English trapunto** or **Italian trapunto,** the **stuffing** is added after the sewing is completed. **Padded appliqué** involves a continuous kind of stuffing. To stuff forms in making **dolls** and **toys,** the parts or sections are sometimes completed (as arms, legs, ears, etc.), stuffed, and then joined. In other figures, such as a **single-shape doll** or the **arch-shape doll,** stuffing may be added as a final step before **slipstitch**ing the figure shut.

stuffed animal. Toys. Any **stuffed toy** made to resemble a real or imaginary animal. The **teddy bear** is among the best known of all stuffed animals, with the "**Gingham Dog** and the Calico Cat" being next in popularity. These toys are easily made at home, usually of original design. Also see **Toys: Fabric.**

stuffed fabric. Puppets. Stitchery. Toys. Three-dimensional forms constructed of woven materials that are filled with any of various kinds of **stuffing.** Some stuffed forms, such as **relief** soft art, use quilt stuffings, while other **soft sculpture**s can use any of a wide variety of materials. Also see **cloth marionette, puppet head, rag-doll puppet.**

stuffed figure. Stitchery. Toys. Three-dimensional forms, usually animals and human figures, filled with **batting** or **padding.** Some **soft sculpture**s consist of individual stuffed figures, others use figures in groups or combinations. Such figures have always been popular as **toy**s.

stuffed marionette. Puppets. (Also called soft marionette.) Any **string puppet** made from cloth. The parts of the figure are usually made separately and then **join**ted. Each part is **stuff**ed and completed before the figure is assembled. The parts are jointed by using tiny wire rings (jewelry findings) or a single stitch taken with cord. The parts are then attached to **string**s so that they can be **manipulate**d from above.

Very simple animals and figures need not be made up of separate parts. A horse or dog, for example, could be assembled in the way any stuffed animal would be made. The strings, attached to the head, front of body, and end of body, can be manipulated to make the animal gallop or run.

Sometimes figures can be made with the joints simply stitched. As the figure is stuffed, some places are left without **stuffing,** as at the knees, and a line of machine sewing at that place will make a movable **stitched joint.** Also see **cloth marionette** and **Puppets: Making the Marionette.**

stuffed quilting. Quilts. Stitchery. The process of using two layers of material in which areas are outlined with **quilting stitch**es, then **stuff**ed with a **batting** or **filler.** Stuffed quilting is very popular in contemporary wall hangings and soft sculpture because it allows for the completion of stitching, either by hand or machine, before the bulky **stuffing** is added. Some parts may be stuffed and others left flat. After the quilted lines are finished, a small slit is made in the bottom or back fabric. Stuffing is forced in through the opening and the slit is then **whip-stitch**ed shut. A highly sculptured surface can be achieved with this process. In contemporary work, it may be combined with a standard **quilting** technique to add emphasis to certain areas. Also see **English trapunto.**

stuffed-stocking puppet. Puppets. See **nylon-stocking puppet.**

stuffed toy. Toys. A child's plaything, usually an animal or figure, that is given three-dimensional form through **stuffing.** Any of various **stuffing material**s can be used. **Sawdust** and **wood wool** were the traditional **filler** materials, later replaced by wool or **cotton batting** and the synthetic or **Dacron polyester batting.**

The stuffed toy is popular among craftspeople and can easily be made at home. The outside or skin is made from any durable fabric, preferably one that is stain-resistant. It is sewn by hand or machine. Stuffed toys are among the favorites of all children, with **teddy bear**s and **rag doll**s the most prized of all. Also see **Toys: Fabric, Stuffed Toys.**

stuffer threads. Rugmaking. Weaving. Extra yarn that is used in either the **warp** or **filling** to add thickness, substance, weight, or padding to a woven structure. If used in the filling, they are known as stuffer **pick**s and give fullness and roundness to a **rib** effect. They lie under the face warp **end**s and never appear on the surface of the fabric or rug. Stuffer picks are heavier than the face ends and picks and must be followed by a hard **beat.** Stuffer warp runs between the face and the back of a fabric, never actually interlacing with the filling. It is found mainly in **rugweaving.** Although this type of rug is somewhat complex to weave (requiring two separate warps), the end result is a very thick and durable reversible rug. It can be woven as **double cloth** or **triple cloth** or as an imitation of double cloth. Stuffer threads are usually inexpensive bulky cotton yarns. Also see **piqué.**

stuffing. Leather. A technique of padding areas of **appliqué** leather to raise the motif on the background, giving it a three-dimensional look. The method is the same as for stuffing a pillow. Sew around the appliqué shape; push in padding as you start to close it, and finish sewing on the appliqué. Dampening the leather before sewing will make it more stretchy and pliable and allow the shape to build up with more stuffing.

stuffing. Quilts. Puppets. Stitchery. Toys. Any soft material used to add a three-dimensional character to fabric. In **padded stitchery** or in **quilt**s, a **Dacron polyester batting** or **cotton batting** is usually used, since both give smooth surfaces. In **soft sculpture,** stuffing may be any of a wide range of materials from paper or sand to synthetic foam or **fabric.** Any of these fillers, as well as **sawdust** or nylon stockings, can be used as the **stuffing material** for **doll**s and **toy**s.

stuffing material. Stitchery. Anything used to **stuff** or fill a **soft sculpture** or three-dimensional stitchery to give it form. The **stuffing** material selected for any sculpture depends in part upon the size and scale of the work and in part upon the surface material. While **Dacron polyester batting, cotton batting,** or **kapok** may be used for **padding,** a more rigid material is sometimes required for freestanding floor pieces. For fully three-dimensional work of small scale, **foam rubber** chunks, Styrofoam blocks, Styrofoam pellets, nylon stockings, straw, crumpled newspaper, shredded paper, rags, and packing materials all work well. Some of these will be suitable for larger sculptures, but those best suited for the large freestanding forms include old mattresses, pillows, foam rug padding, and builder's insulation materials used over **armature**s of wood or metal.

stumpwork. Embroidery. Embroidery that combines techniques such as **appliqué,** silk and gold embroidery, and/or **crewel** to achieve a raised effect. Shapes and motifs are worked in such a way that they are sometimes freestanding relief forms. The origin of the word is hazy, but it is thought that the French word *estamper,* meaning embossed, may have had direct influence upon it.

Magnificent examples of raised embroidery for church vestments have been passed down to us from the fourteenth and fifteenth centuries, notably from France. In a bishop's miter from the Sainte Chapelle, Paris, the figures of the Nativity are padded and stitched with silk, the surrounding architectural filigree is in raised gold threads, and the main details are outlined in seed pearls.

Sometimes, however, as in the fifteenth-century altar curtain of St. George and the Dragon (worked by a Flemish embroiderer living in Spain), the work is overornate.

In England, where at an early age young ladies of the eighteenth century were taught their stitches on a **sampler,** it was customary before they came of age for them to make a stumpwork box, picture, or mirror frame, to demonstrate their abilities with a needle even further. The designs were often Biblical themes, although the figures were dressed in contemporary costumes and were generally placed in an eighteenth-century formal garden—fountains, flowers, and manor house all worked in delicate raised stitchery. Jewels, metal threads, chenille, and brilliantly colored silks were used with such stitches as trellis, plaited braid, **bullion knot**s, and **French knot**s, on a background of white satin.

Sometimes the raised embroidery was combined with flat stitches, such as **laidwork,** to great effect. Later, designs were entirely raised by means of wire, so that whole freestanding gardens were worked to decorate the top of boxes.

During the Victorian era, raised work was done with wool on canvas using stitches such as **turkey work** clipped and modeled to imitate sculpture in relief. Animals and birds worked in this manner were often given glass eyes as a final touch of realism. Although similar, turkey work should not be confused with stumpwork as this type of raised work was done only in wool, while stumpwork uses a variety of thread and techniques.

Contemporary stumpwork may be collages including padded appliqué, and all kinds of raised textured stitching in wool (not exclusively turkey work). Artists are intrigued with the combinations of media, giving a great variety of experimental effects, combining embroidery with knotting, weaving, and appliqué, going all the way to soft sculpture. Also see **applying finished needlepoint to fabric, freestanding stumpwork with wire, looped stem stitch, raised cup stitch, seed stitch.**

S-twist. Rugmaking. Spinning. Weaving. See **plied fringe, twist.**

stylus. Ceramics. Glasswork. Metalworking . A pencil-like tool, the end of which is fitted with a very hard, sharp point (silicon carbide, diamond, etc.), that is used to incise metal, glass, or clay forms with writing or decoration.

styrene. Plastics. A **hydrocarbon** used in the manufacture of synthetic rubber. It is also a common dilutant for **polyester resin.** Because it is considered toxic, excellent ventilation is necessary when working with styrene. Also see **polystyrene.**

Styrofoam. Plastics. See **foam, polystyrene.**

Styrofoam. Puppets. Toys. See **polystyrene.**

Styrofoam. Stained Glass. See **lampshade construction.**

subconchoidal fracture. Gemcutting. See **fracture.**

substantive dye. Batik and Tie-dye. See **direct dye.**

substantive dye. Dyeing. See **direct dye.**

subtractive process. Stitchery. Toys. A way of working in which materials are cut away, removed, or subtracted, as opposed to the **additive process. Wood carving, cut-through appliqué,** and drawn-thread work are all subtractive processes.

suede. Leather. Any **hide** with a nap or brushed surface. The **finish** is produced on the inside, or flesh side, of the hide, skin, or **split** by buffing or grinding the fibers to a fine pile to raise the nap for a soft surface. It is widely used for garments, bags, linings, etc. Suede is available in a variety of colors. Lambskin suede, usually from New Zealand, is commonly used for garments. The skins are usually 5–8′. Also see **kidskin** and **Leatherwork: Care, Cleaning and Storage of Leather, Gluing and Bonding Leather, Tanning and Manufacture.**

Suffolk puff. Quilts. See **yo-yo quilt.**

sugar egg. Toys. A **hollow egg** shape made by pressing a special sugar mixture into a mold. It is usually about ¼″ thick and is rigid but breakable when hardened. The eggs may be handmade, although they are sometimes available through bakery or confectionary suppliers. The hollow eggs are used for **peep eggs** or decorated for Easter toys. When made for children the ingredients are all edible, so the egg becomes an **ephemeral toy** as well as an **edible toy.**

sugar maple. Woodworking. See **maple.**

sugar pine. Woodworking. See **pine.**

suint. Spinning. The dried perspiration of the sheep that lies encrusted on the fibers of its **fleece.** Also see **yolk, wool.**

sulfuric acid. Enameling. See **bright dip, cleaning metal, electrolyte.**

sulfuric acid. Glasswork. See **etching.**

sulfuric acid. Metalworking. See **scale** and **Metalworking: Finishing.**

sumakh. Also sumaq, summak. Rugmaking. Weaving. See **soumak.**

Summer and Winter weave. Rugmaking. Weaving. Patterns producing a reversible cloth with the **warp** predominant on one side and the **filling** on the other, and depending on color contrast for the best effect. The color contrast is achieved more through weave than color placement in the warp. It is a very geometric weave with a **drawing-in draft** composed in blocks which are made up of units of 4 threads—either 1-3-2-3 or 1-4-2-4. The width of the blocks and their placement gives the pattern. There are many variations possible here, as there are in the **treadling,** which commonly is **treadling-as-drawn-in** or in pairs, i.e., two **pick**s of filling instead of one for every **treadle** of the pattern. Since Summer and Winter weaves are woven with one pattern **weft** and one ground weft alternating, the pairs would always be split up by a **shot** of **tabby.**

Summer and Winter can be an interesting **texture** weave with experimental treadlings. It is also a weave very adaptable to **multiharness** weaving since the block unit can be expanded. The threading of Summer and Winter never allows a **float** over more than three threads. This makes for a tightly woven fabric strong enough for rugs, upholstery, drapery, pillow covers, and apparel. The exact origin of Summer and Winter weaves is unknown, but it is theorized that it came from Finland with settlers who emigrated to Pennsylvania. It was a popular weave for coverlets, which is where the name originates. They were woven with a light-colored side for the summer months and a dark side for the winter months. See ill.

Typical drawing-in draft for Summer and Winter weave

summer quilt. Quilts. Any lightweight, unpadded, unquilted bedcover; this is technically a **coverlet,** not a **quilt.** Sometimes the **Italian trapunto** technique was used for a summer quilt. A single thickness of fabric with an **appliqué** design sewn to it is also known as a summer quilt.

Sunbonnet Girl. Quilts. (Also called Sunbonnet Sue.) A popular **appliqué** design depicting a girl wearing a bonnet. In most versions, the skirt covers the feet and the bonnet supplies the head shape, making it an easily appliquéd **block.** The blocks are almost invariably separated by **band**s of color or solid blocks. The figures of the girl are sometimes accompanied by Overall Bill, the figure of a boy in blue overalls.

Sunbonnet Sue. Quilts. See **Sunbonnet Girl.**

Sunburst. Quilts. (Also called Mariner's Compass.) A **pieced** or **appliqué**d **quilt** design that may be worked in **block**s or enlarged to form a single design that covers the bed. The Sunburst usually starts from a six-pointed **diamond** star such as **Evening Star** or from an eight-pointed star such as **Star of Bethlehem.** The essential difference between the Sunburst and **star pattern**s is in the perimeter design. If the diamonds work out to suggest a circular shape, it is called Sunburst. If the diamonds are so arranged as to retain the star shape, it is identified as one of the star-pattern quilts.

The Sunburst may be of almost any size and usually

uses colors to form radiating circular **band**s. "Noonday" uses a variation of the Sunburst as its central motif. Also see **diamond patchwork**.

Sunday toy. Toys. A toy with religious overtones or connotations that could be played with on a Sunday. **Cutout**s of Biblical characters, **Noah's ark**s, and the **whirligig** figures were popular Sunday toys.

Picture **block**s or **jigsaw puzzle**s that depicted religious scenes were also acceptable as Sunday toys.

Sunflower. Quilts. See **Blazing Star**.

sungle. Spinning. Weaving. (Also called single.) The yarn resulting from the initial twisting or spinning of the fibers. Also called a single **ply**, it has a single direction of twist. Also see **spinning, twist**.

sunk. Weaving. See **shed**.

sun lace. Lacemaking. See **sol lace**.

Sunrise. Quilts. See **Rocky Mountain**.

Sunshine and Shadows. Quilts. See **Trip Around the World**.

sun spangle. Amber Carving. See **clarify**.

sunstone. Gemcutting. See **feldspar**.

super. Bookbinding. (Also called crash, mull.) Stiffened mesh or gauze that is glued to the back of a book as part of the **back lining** operation after the book has been backed to strengthen the **joint** and **spine**.

Super Tripoli. Jewelry. One of the best tripolis available. It is less **abrasive** than most tripolis, yet produces a high shine. It is available through Allcraft Tool & Supply Co., Inc., 215 Park Avenue, Hicksville, N.Y. 11801. Also see **buffing compound, lapping**.

supplementary yarns. Weaving. Those extra **warp** or **filling** yarns added to a **ground** set of warp and filling for color, pattern, texture, or weight. Supplementary warps or **weft**s are additions to the basic structure of a cloth and, theoretically, could be removed from the basic warp and weft interlacing and the fabric would still hold together. The Peruvians were, and are, great masters of supplementary warps, which they often **deflected** for additional decorative features. Also see **compound weaves**.

support. Mosaics. See **backing**.

support. Papercrafts. (Also called armature.) Any material that will hold up or provide a background for a papercraft design that is not self-supporting. Flat designs such as a **collage** or **relief** are generally mounted on heavy **paper** or cardboard. To prevent warping, glue a piece of paper on the wrong side of the cardboard backing. Three-dimensional sculptural forms, combining various paper-construction techniques, may be supported by doweling rods, wire, fine wire mesh, or **found objects** such as containers or boxes.

Sheets of newspaper can be crushed, then taped, into desired shapes for a base on which to apply **papier mâché**. Newspaper forms are often combined with **aluminum foil**, **chicken wire**, found objects, or other materials for sculptural forms. All pieces should be securely taped in position before applying papier mâché. Bowls, wastebaskets, and other simple forms can be used as a form for **molding** with the **paper-strip method** or for **weaving** with paper strips. Also see **clay**.

support bar. Stained Glass. See **saddle bar**.

surface embellishment. Stitchery. The addition of decorative work onto an already formed surface. **Appliqué**, **direct-dye painting**, embroidery, and tattooing are various kinds of embellishing treatments.

surface gauge. Metalworking. A marking tool used to even up the edges on a **raised** object. Insert a lead pencil or a scribing tool into the marker. Position the object against the **scriber** or pencil point and turn the form, or move the gauge around the securely positioned metal work to mark it. See ill.

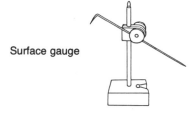

Surface gauge

surface plate. Jewelry. See **steel block**.

surface resin. Plastics. A **resin** designed specifically for good surface qualities, such as hardness and scratch resistance. It is painted on the finished surface after a **mold** has been removed and all surface irregularities sanded off. It also fills in any scratches and can eliminate polishing.

surface speeds of buffs. Jewelry. The following chart gives the relative surface speeds of the buffing wheel as determined by the diameter of the buff in relation to the spindle speed of the motor.

Surface Speeds of Buffs in Feet per Minute

Motor or Spindle Speed	Diameter or Buff			
rpm	2"	4"	6"	8"
1000	525	1050	1575	2100
1200	630	1260	1950	2550
1400	730	1470	2250	2950
1600	840	1680	2550	3400
1800	940	1890	2900	3800
2000	1050	2100	3200	4200
2200	1150	2300	3450	4550
2400	1260	2500	3750	5000

Surface Speeds of Buffs in Feet per Minute

Motor or Spindle Speed				Diameter or Buff
rpm	*2"*	*4"*	*6"*	*8"*
2600	1360	2700	4100	5450
2800	1470	2950	4400	5900
3000	1570	3140	4700	6250
3200	1680	3350	5000	6650
3400	1780	3560	5250	7000
3600	1880	3780	5600	7500

surfacing mat. Plastics. See **glass fiber.**

Surform tool. Metalworking. Plastics. Woodworking. An open-surface filing and planing tool used on plaster, plastics, wood, tile, aluminum, copper, and other metals up to the hardness of **mild steel.** It is especially useful for trimming **mold**s made of **casting plaster,** plastics, and other materials that tend to clog ordinary **file**s and **rasp**s.

The Surform tool is also used for rough planing and rasping wood surfaces. Because its blade is open and perforated, it is useful for working green or damp wood, which would clog a file. See ill.

Surform tool

suspended casting off. Knitting. See **Knitting: Casting Off.**

suspended head bar. Puppets. A special arrangement of the **horizontal control** used when a **marionette** has **joint**s between head and neck as well as between neck and torso. It is a much more difficult arrangement to control than when the head and neck are made in one piece. It allows for very subtle gestures of the head, but only in the hands of an extremely skillful **puppeteer** can it be regulated to avoid a wagging or bobbing motion. Also see **Puppets: Stringing the Marionette.**

swab. Metalworking. See **sandcasting molding equipment.**

swaddle. Candlemaking. See **rolled candle.**

swag. Quilts. A gently curving line that rises to peaks at intervals and then droops as though from its own weight. Swags are often **appliquéd** to quilts as **border** designs, usually in the form of ribbons or garlands.

swag and bow. Quilts. See **border.**

swage. Metalworking. See **blacksmithing tools, swage block.**

swage block. Metalworking. A rectangular cast-**iron** or **steel** block 2½–3" thick and approximately 6–18" long, with perforations and grooves, used for hammer-shaping forged objects. Place the swage block on the **anvil** or workbench and position the heated metal over the desired perforation. Hammer the metal into the perforation to make a cavity or depression. A swage block may also be used as a substitute for a lower swage. See ill.

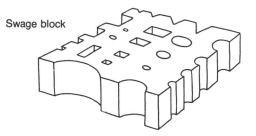

Swage block

swagging. Stained Glass. A decorative way of hanging stained-glass lamps; the chain is looped from one portion of the ceiling to another several times before the lampshade is hung from it. Each swag of chain is held by ceiling hooks. Also see **lampshade construction.**

swaging. Jewelry. See **edge thickening.**

swaging. Metalworking. See **blacksmithing techniques.**

Swastika. Quilts. (Also called Battle-ax of Thor, Catch-Me-If-You-Can, Fly Foot, Mound Builders, Wind Power of the Osages.) **Block**s made for **pieced quilt**s made up in any of various interpretations of the well-known Indian symbol. It was a motif used almost universally, and predates the American Indian designs with which most of us are familiar. The swastika is a variation of the cross. See ill.

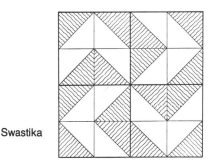

Swastika

swazzle. Puppets. A device used in **puppetry** consisting of two elliptical metal rings with a piece of silk or other material stretched between them. This is soaked in water, and the **puppeteer** then holds it in his mouth in a vertical position to alter his voice. It makes a shrill sound, and through the use of the swazzle a puppeteer can successfully vary his voice to fit different characters.

sweat soldering. Jewelry. A form of **soldering** generally applied to broad, flat surfaces to be joined together along their entire surfaces. One piece of metal has **solder** placed in position and allowed to flow. It is then placed on top of another piece of metal, and the solder is allowed to flow again, "sweating" the two pieces together. One of the beauties of sweat soldering is that it provides complete control and invisible, or nearly invisible, **joint**s.

The following is a step-by-step description of preparing a pieced, sawed-out design in 20-**gauge** metal for sweat soldering:

The **sawing** and **filing** of the inside edges of the design is completed. The outside contour is not filed at this time (**a.**). **Pickle** the piece of metal, rinse, and dry. **Flux** both sides. Position small **pallion**s of solder fairly closely together on the back of the metal and very close to the outside edge. If the pallions are somewhat rectangular, place the long side of the rectangle parallel with the edge of the metal. Placement is crucial, as eventually this piece of metal will be sweat-soldered to another piece of metal, and the outside **seam** must be perfect or there will be pits due to the lack of solder. Other areas have solder placed more sparsely throughout the metal so that during the sweating of the two pieces of metal these areas will be soldered down, but in more of a "tacked down" way. Any area of metal that has a small projection or a sharp point must have a small pallion of solder placed at its very tip, as it is this type of area that can be later caught, lifted up, and bent, or that may tear cloth while being worn (**b.**). After the solder is in position, warm the metal slowly to dry out the flux on the solder so that it will not pop or be blown out of position. Heat with a **torch** using a soft, brushing **flame,** until the solder just flows. Do not let it flow all the way down. If some of the mounds of solder seem too high, which might cause the sawed piece of metal to slide, they can be flattened with **carborundum paper** or a flat needle file after **pickling**. Pickle. Saw-cut another piece of metal, also in 20 gauge, at least 1 mm larger all of the way around than the sawed-out piece. This piece is the **baseplate,** and is made larger because the sawn-out piece that will be soldered on top of the baseplate tends to slide somewhat, and this will provide some leeway. Pickle, rinse, and flux both sides of both pieces. Lay the baseplate on a **heating frame** or **charcoal block.** Place the sawed-out piece on top of the baseplate, solder side down. Have a **soldering point** ready. Heat the work from underneath to get the baseplate hot. The top piece will get hot quite rapidly because it has less volume to heat. Heat the work until the solder flows, using the soldering point to cautiously press the two pieces of metal together. The solder flows in a bright line, especially around the outside edges. Pickle. The baseplate can have **liver of sulfur** applied to produce a contrast between it and the upper surface of metal. At this point, the excess metal of the baseplate and the unfiled rim of the top piece of metal can be filed away. This will even out the two levels of metal, making the piece appear twice as thick, and will smooth out the seam so it won't show (**c.**).

In this example 20-gauge metal has been used, but any other gauge, or pieces of differing gauges, can be used. Another way in which sweat soldering can effectively be used is when soldering small pieces of metal, such as wire, at an angle. The solder can be melted on the end of the wire in the manner described above, and then held in position with a **third hand** against the metal onto which it is going to be sweat-soldered. See ill. Also see **appliqué, lamination, needle file.**

sweat soldering. Metalworking. See **Metalworking: Soldering.**

swedge. Metalworking. See **blacksmithing tools.**

Swedish bobbin. Weaving. A **tapestry tool** that is similar to the **Gobelin bobbin** but is more slender and delicate and measures only about 5″ long.

Swedish braid. Rugmaking. Weaving. A very secure **finishing edge** with a plaited look that can be left as is, or can be turned back in **hemming.** The word "Swedish" has been added to the name of this edge even though the first evidence of its existence was in Denmark, where it appears on the edge of a woolen fabric dating from around 1000 B.C. The **warp end**s are finger woven or plaited with each other to form a solid band along the woven fabric. The width of this band is determined by how far each warp end interlaces with its neighboring warp ends. This can vary from as few as three ends to as many as sixteen or more, although within each piece, the amount is kept constant. The smaller amonts give a tight, narrow edge that looks braided and is often used as the finishing edge on rugs and tapestries, especially when a neat edge is wanted for hemming. The greater number of ends involved in this edge give a somewhat woven look and this wider band is the finished edge itself or it becomes the hem. The wider band is often called a woven edge.

To make the edge, turn the item face down and start at the left. Take in hand at least four single warp ends, or four groups of ends, depending on the **sett.** With the end at the furthest left, interlace under-over-under the three to the right. The working end surfaces and points toward the item. Take the end that is now at the left and repeat the under-over-under arrangement with its three right neighbors. This will continue until the ends are all braided and all ends point toward the item, with the exception of the four ends at the extreme right. These are made into a short, true braid and the end of the braid is either whipped or an **over-hand knot** is made. As the plaiting commences, push the interlaced strands toward the rug edge with the thumb. This will insure a tight edge. All the warp ends will be pointing toward the piece. They can be cut about ¾″ from the braid and stitched down to the back of the piece; darned into the edge of the piece as invisibly as possible and trimmed flush; or the warp ends can be threaded through a needle and drawn down through the braid to make a **fringe.** The short, true braid at the end can be left dangling as is, or folded back and sewn to the back of the piece. There is a shift of the warp ends to the left as one plaits, which is not noticeable unless a wide band is made. If this is objectionable, the plaiting can be started in the

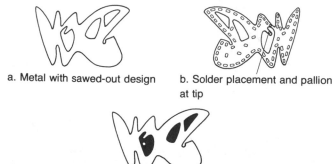

a. Metal with sawed-out design

b. Solder placement and pallion at tip

c. Trimmed finished work, baseplate oxidized with liver of sulfur

center of the piece and should proceed in two directions, toward each **selvage.** Another option is to start at each selvage and plait toward the center. In the case of a wide band, a triangular insert will have to be woven in the center when the plaiting is finished. This is done with an extra piece of warp yarn and is a compensating measure for the sideways shift in direction. There are many variations that can be achieved with the Swedish braid. These include color patterning in the edge when the warp ends are of different colors. See ill. Also see **finger weaving, whipping.**

Swedish braid

Swedish finish. Jewelry. (Also called brush finish.) A soft, lustrous, semimatte finish on sterling **silver** that brings out the bluish tones of the silver as opposed to the standard yellowish tones of sterling. Two methods are given below. The first is the rue Swedish finish, which requires more extensive equipment than the second method—a modified version that works extremely well.

Needed for the first method is a square gallon can with a ¼" rubber hose attached to the side near the bottom edge with a device to control the flow from a can of water mixed with a little household liquid detergent. The unit is attached to a motor-driven rotating brass brush, and the solution allowed to drip slowly onto the silver. The solution will drip off the silver into the pan in the **polishing hood,** which should be emptied frequently so that it does not overflow, or some other drainage system should be worked into the base of the **buffing** setup to carry the solution away from any electrical parts.

Place the work on a **heating frame** on a rotating **carborundum pan.** Do not use **flux.** Using a hot reducing **flame,** slowly rotate the work on the carborundum pan until the silver becomes completely oxidized (black in color). **Pickle.** The work will then become whitish in color. Rinse in clear water. Brush the entire surface with a fine brass brush saturated with the solution of water and detergent. Dry the work to prevent discoloration. Place the work on the heating frame and rotate on the carborundum pan, heating it with the reducing flame as before. This time, the work will remain white, except for any area that was missed during the first heating. Heat the work until it reaches the point where it would normally turn black. This is a tricky operation as the work must get hot enough, but not so hot as to cause any **solder seam**s to flow. Pickle. Brass-brush with solution again. Rinse, dry, and repeat at least three times. The copper in the sterling is oxidizing, forming **firescale** on the surface, while the pickle is removing the firescale and an upper surface of **fine silver** is being exposed. The fine silver surface is lightly textured by the brass brush. The more the technique is repeated, the deeper the layer of fine silver, and the longer the finish will last. This system is excellent for any work that will not get rubbed a great deal, such as a pin or necklace. A bracelet is not ideal as it generally receives harder use, but with repeated heatings and picklings it can work quite well.

For the modified second method, also called scratch brushing, the same technique is followed using the brass brush manually. The brass brush is rubbed back and forth so that the scratches are in one direction; this will add greatly to the beauty of the finish.

Do not use either method on pieces that contain gemstones, as the heat required for the finish will crack most gems. Also see **reticulation.**

Swedish fringe. Rugmaking. Weaving. See **Swedish braid.**

Swedish knot. Rugmaking. Weaving. A flat, knotted **tapestry weave** of uncertain origin. The Swedish knot is a form of weft **wrapping** belonging to the **soumak** family, rather than a knot. For this reason, many weavers classify it with the soumak techniques and call it one version or another of soumak. A new title is "single soumak," since the wrapping all takes place around a single **warp end** (this is not done in most other forms of soumak). It is used for rugmaking, but when used strictly as a tapestry technique, is sometimes called a French **Gobelin** knot, as it is often used in this type of tapestry.

In a tapestry, the Swedish knot is worked from the back of the weaving where it produces the flat knitted effect so common to soumak, while on the right side the fabric is **cord**ed or **rib**bed warpwise. The appearance of the right side somewhat resembles the **Egyptian knot** effect. **Plain weave** between each row is not needed in a tapestry, and the filling colors are worked in short stretches based on the **cartoon interlocking,** where the colors meet in a vertical line.

In a rug, the technique is usually worked right-side up and produces a knitted effect if the direction of the knotting is reversed in each row, and a **twill**-like look if it is not. It is often worked **selvage** to selvage with plain weave inbetween each row of knotting to stabilize the wrapping so that it will not slip around the warp ends. Whether in a tapestry or rug, the technique is done with a **butterfly** and with the **shed** closed.

To do the Swedish knot, begin (or end) by tying or looping the filling yarn around the first warp end. Working from left to right, take the filling yarn over the warp end and back under the same warp end while holding the filling thread down out of the way (**a.**). Pull the knot or warp tightly around the end and down next to the row previously done. All warp ends are continued in this same manner—wrapping over and back under each end. In the

Swedish knot

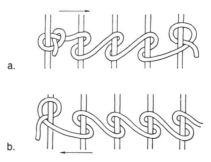

a.

b.

row running from right to left, the same procedure is once more followed—the filling goes over and under the end (**b.**). See ill. on previous page.

Swedish lace. Weaving. A category of weaves composed of a **plain-weave ground** with **float**s in spots, small areas, or large blocks, giving a lacy effect. It is **loom-controlled** and not true lace or **leno.** It has a very close textural and pattern similarity to lace Bronson, but the drafting plans are more similar to **huckaback.** A piece of linen lace found in a marsh dates the weave back to the Viking era. It has been an extremely popular weave in Scandinavia for centuries. The lacy or open effect is achieved by warp thread at the end of every group of floats. It interlaces firmly with the **filling** and causes the float threads to slide together, thereby creating the opening. The openings become much more apparent after washing the fabric. Although a lace weave, it can also be used on blankets and heavy linens. If it is **sleyed** sparsely in the **reed,** it can look very much like netting. Also see **Bronson weave.**

Swedish rölakan. Rugmaking. Weaving. See **rölakan.**

sweep cut. Woodworking. See **whittling.**

sweeps. Jewelry. **Precious metal**s that have been swept up from the floor or bench and saved for refining. Also see **lemel, scrap metal.**

sweet gumwood. Woodworking. See **gumwood.**

swell. Bookbinding. The increased thickness at the back of the book as a result of added bulk from the thread used to join the **section**s, or of guarded pages. Swell is used to advantage in forming the shape of a book that is pleasing to the eye by **rounding** and **backing** it. It is controlled by the choice of thread or number of stitches, and is reduced by **knocking down** and, to a lesser degree, rounding and backing.

swift. Spinning. Weaving. A turning device that serves to wind yarn into **skein**s or to unwind it from skeins. There are two types of swifts. One is an umbrella swift which clamps to a table and the yarn is held horizontally. When not in use, it folds up like an umbrella. It is ideal where floor space is limited (**a.**). The other is a squirrel-cage swift, which is a floor-standing, upright skein winder consisting of two cages or rollers around which the skein is held vertically (**b.**). Either swift is adjustable to the circumference of the skein. The entire "umbrella" turns when the swift is in use, while on the squirrel cage swift, just the cages rotate as the yarn is wound or unwound. Umbrella swifts developed from cross-frame floor swifts which date back to fifteenth-century Europe. The squirrel-cage swifts date from the early eighteenth century. As the umbrella swifts were changed into smaller, table models, some were made of scrimshaw or carved woods.

Spinners use swifts, but not as much as weavers or knitters, who unwind skeins in order to make **bobbin**s for weaving or balls of yarn for knitting. Umbrella swifts are the more common of the two swifts and can be found in most yarn and knitting shops. See ill. Also see **Spinning: Skeining.**

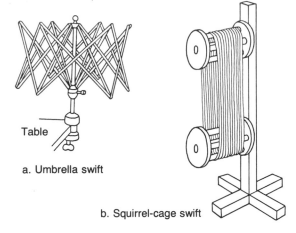

a. Umbrella swift

b. Squirrel-cage swift

swift roller. Spinning. See **carding machine.**

swing. Toys. A toy suspended from one or more ropes or chains for swinging back and forth. Probably Tarzan's grapevine or jungle vine with a knot in it is the simplest one ever devised. A heavy rope, knotted and hung from a tree, is a variation, known as a **rope swing.** Other popular kinds are the **bag swing, tire swing,** and **tub swing.** Also see **box swing** and **Toys: Rope and Swing Toys.**

swinging-weight toy. Toys. Any of a great variety of **animated toy**s in which a weight hung from two or more strings is used to transfer motion from one part of the toy to another. The **pecking chicken**s, the **carpenter**s, and the **churning scene** all use swinging weights. It is a toy of relatively late development, the first record of one being in 1869. It is probably Russian in origin. The **pendulum toy** is one kind of swinging-weight toy. See ill.

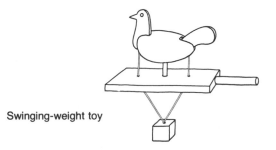

Swinging-weight toy

Swing-in-the-Center. Quilts. A **pieced** pattern design that uses a **nine-patch** set on end within a square. The corners of the nine-patch are made up of **four-patch**es. The **block,** made this way, is a combination of squares and triangles. However, the block can be joined in any of several ways and **diamond** shapes can be cut instead of the squares and triangles. See ill.

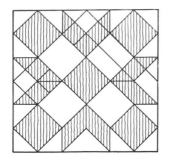

Swing-in-the-Center

swingle. Spinning. See **flax.**

swingling. Spinning. See **Spinning.**

swirl. Quilts. See **Quilts: Quilting.**

swish. Toys. See **bull-roarer.**

Swiss-cheese candle. Candlemaking. See **ice-cube candle.**

Swiss darning. Knitting. (Also called duplicate stitch.) A method of adding color to knit fabrics by embroidering over—tracing the actual shape of—the knit stitches selectively to form various design **motif**s. This is done on the knit fabric, using a tapestry needle and yarn of a different color. See ill. Also see **darning.**

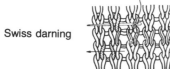

Swiss darning

Swiss patchwork. Quilts. See **raised patchwork.**

Swiss straw. Batik and Tie-dye. A **synthetic** material resembling **raffia** that can be used as a **binding.** It is made in long, fibrous, thin, flat strips. They have a sheen and are available in a bright array of colors at hobby or craft supply stores.

swivel. Weaving. See **swivel weave.**

swivel joint. Puppets. A connection or **joint** that swings and turns, as on a **marionette,** where two **screw eye**s are joined. Also see **free joint, movable joint** and **Puppets: Making the Marionette Skeleton.**

swivel knife. Leather. A tool with interchangeable blades used for cutting outlines of **tooling** designs on dampened leather. A regular, angle, double-line, filigree, or hair blade is used for cutting different types of decorative lines. The swivel knife is held in an almost vertical position, with the index finger in the bow of the tool and the main cylinder of the tool held with the thumb, middle, and fourth fingers. The knife is used to incise along the lines of the design, prior to **stamping** or **embossing.** Control of the swivel knife

takes practice but is essential to proper tooling. The little finger is usually used to guide the hand along the leather, keeping to the lines of the designs. Incisions must be made to the correct depth with one cut, pulling the knife up carefully at the end of each stroke. Be sure to keep the blade finely honed for best results. See ill. Also see **carving, flat modeling, outline tooling, pear shader, pro-gauge** and **Leatherwork: Care and Maintenance of Tools, Tools and Materials.**

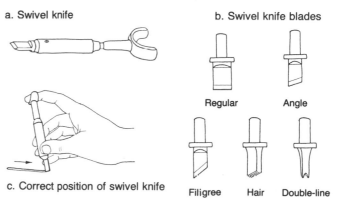

a. Swivel knife
b. Swivel knife blades
Regular Angle
Filigree Hair Double-line
c. Correct position of swivel knife

swivel weave. Weaving. Another name for a **laid-in** weave. The term is actually an industrial one that refers to small **filling** design areas resembling embroidery, woven against a **plain weave** background. The filling is carried by a number of small **shuttles** called swivels, which are lowered automatically to the correct positions above the **warp** and interlace with it when the warp threads in these positions are raised by a pattern mechanism. It is rarely used today, since it is more advantageous to have swivel effects done on a **Jacquard loom.** How the term came to be used with a laid-in effect is a mystery. But it is possible, since very fine and intricate laid-in patterns can look like swivel effects, that some handweavers with a knowledge of industrial weaving adopted the term to mean fine laid-in. Also see **laid-in.**

sword. Weaving. See **batten.**

symmetrical cutting. Papercrafts. (Also called monocut, one-fold, single-fold cutting.) A **cutout** made by folding a piece of paper in half, then cutting into the center fold. When unfolded, the resulting design will be symmetrical. This very basic, traditional method can be as simple as a valentine heart or as elaborate as a lacy doily. See ill.

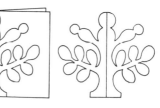

Symmetrical cutting

symmetry. See **asymmetry.**

synthetic batting. Quilts. Stitchery. See **Dacron polyester batting.**

synthetic dye. Batik and Tie-dye. See **aniline dye.**

synthetic dye. Dyeing. Dyes that are developed from a coal-tar base or other source through a chemical process. They can be produced more easily and cheaply than natural dyes and can also be depended upon to achieve the same color time after time. The color quality and fastness are not necessarily better than **natural dye,** but often synthetic dyes can be much brighter. Synthetic dyes came into being as a result of the discovery of a mauve **aniline dye** in England in 1856. Chemists all over Europe began to develop other synthetic colors. Germany was the leader in this development and it was not until World War I, when trade with Germany was cut off, that a dye industry began in the United States. It has grown to be a very large industry, producing many categories of synthetic dyes. In recent years the emphasis has been on formulating dyes for specific synthetic fibers. Some synthetic dyes are readily available for home dyeing. These would include the acid and **direct dye**s. Most synthetic dyes, however, are for commercial dyeing only. Also see **acid dye, aniline dye, direct dye, dye.**

synthetic fabric. Quilts. Stitchery. Any **fabric** made from **synthetic fiber**s. Because synthetics have some advantages in ease of care and washability, they are often combined with **natural fiber**s to make **blend**s. For example, a cotton blend may consist of 65% **cotton** and 35% **nylon.** The percentage of **fiber**s used in a blend is usually stated on the label.

Synthetic fibers are more resilient and springy and the **fabric**s made from synthetic fibers are more difficult to **appliqué** by hand than similar-weight **cotton**s.

synthetic fiber. Batik and Tie-dye. Any of those **fibers** produced chemically, as contrasted to **natural fibers.** Some common **man-made fiber**s are **acetate,** acrylic, **nylon, polyester, rayon,** and glass.

Synthetic fibers are not usually suitable for use in **batik** or **tie-dye** as they are resistant to **dye**s. However, some aniline and dispersed dyes are made specifically for use on synthetics.

synthetic fiber. Spinning. Weaving. See **fiber.**

synthetic resin. Mosaics. See **epoxy resin.**

synthetic thread. Stitchery. A **polyester thread** that has a coating of **nylon** or **cotton** over it. It is recommended for sewing on knits, **permanent press,** or **wash-and-wear fabric**s. Because it has a degree of elasticity, it is used on knits and **stretch fabric**s. While it is available in a wide range of colors, it comes in only one size. Many stitchers find it unsuitable for hand sewing because it tends to twist and therefore to knot.

synthetic varnish. Woodworking. See **varnish.**

synthetic yarn. Crewel. Embroidery. Needlepoint. Any of the man-made **yarn**s can be used in needlework. They are especially helpful to people who are allergic to wool, and often less expensive. Some of these yarns tend to swell after washing and can blur a fine design. Also see **acrylic yarn, cotton embroidery floss.**

taaniko twining, or **taaniko weaving.** Weaving. A **twining** technique by which the Maori people of New Zealand made cloaks with elaborately patterned borders. Taaniko weaving may also, in a sense, be regarded as **finger weaving,** but it is not weaving done on a **loom**—which was unknown to the Maoris. When they migrated to New Zealand, they were faced with a climate cooler than that to which they had been accustomed. Since twining was apparently known to them from basketry and mat making, they took the native New Zealand **flax** plant and, from its fiber, fashioned a type of yarn that they could twine into these warm cloaks. The cloak was the soft cream color of the unbleached flax while the borders were of strongly contrasting colors of **natural-dye**d black, yellow, and reddish-brown. These borders, the patterns of which were all determined by tradition and appropriately named, were the broad, decorative horizontal edges of the cloaks. Sometimes they also ran vertically up the edges as well. The design and proficiency of the technique made for a highly sophisticated variation of pattern twining that was in common use when Captain James Cook arrived in New Zealand in 1769. It is still known and done, but in a very limited way.

The Maoris used no frame for their twining, nor was the **warp** weighted. They simply held the strands in the lap and manipulated them with their fingers. However, when they had the band or part of it done, they often used two vertical pegs as supports to tie the twined area between, and then continued twining down the rest of the cloak. The method of taaniko twining puts one **weft** yarn on the surface and the other in a completely invisible position on the back side. This makes possible the strong color and pattern delineation. To do this twining, put one yarn in back of the warp. The second yarn, which appears on the surface, holds the first yarn in place by passing around it between every warp yarn. It never goes behind or around a warp yarn. The back yarn is always given a tight pull after every twist around it by the front yarn. This makes the back yarn lie straight and hidden on the back. The back and face are totally different looking, which is quite unlike the usual type of **weft twining.** The twisting of the front yarn over the back could take place also between pairs of warp yarns. The back and front can change position for the patterning, or several yarns can be carried on the back to be brought up to the front when needed. Multiple yarns, plus the close **sett** of the warp and weft, made for a very firm fabric. The Maoris had so perfected this technique that they were able to do shaped garments that had elliptical inserts and vertical wedges for rounding at the shoulders and extra room for comfortable sitting. They also used taaniko twining to make a short skirt consisting of just the decorative band at the top; the remainder was warp left as fringe. Their famous and beautiful feather cloaks were made by attaching feathers as they twined over the entire surface of the cloak. "Taaniko," also written "taniko," is the phonetic spelling of the twining technique. See ill. Also see **feather fastening.**

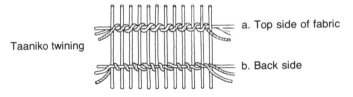

Taaniko twining
a. Top side of fabric
b. Back side

tabby. Weaving. A common handweaver's synonym for **plain weave.** It has been in wide use since about the beginning of this century. Very often it refers to the **ground weave** in a patterned fabric. As to the origin of the term, there are several nonvalidated explanations—the most popular being that it derives from "Tabbis," the Arab weavers' quarters in old Baghdad.

table. Gemcutting. See **facet.**

table. Spinning. See **wool wheel.**

table cut. Gemcutting. See **facet.**

table loom. Weaving. A small **harness loom** operated by hand power and placed on a table or desk during use. The **harness**es are usually lifted by front or side hand **lever**s, although there are other arrangements such as wheels, ropes, and knobs that can do the lifting. Table looms are **rising shed** looms in that the lever is pushed and the corresponding harness rises. They can have from 2 to 12 harnesses and, on rare occasions, 16. They come in widths from 8–32". There are no **treadle**s or **lams** and no **tie-up** as in a **floor loom,** so each harness acts independently. This has an advantage in that complex and long patterns with many different combinations of harnesses can be woven. Other advantages of table looms are that they are easily stored or transported (some models fold flat for storage) and are less expensive than floor looms. The disadvantage of table looms is the slowness of operation when only the hands are involved. Some wider table looms can be attached to a floor trestle or stand, but the harnesses are still lifted by a hand mechanism. Other types of table looms attached to a stand are capable of being converted to a true floor loom with the harness control changed from hand to foot power. See ill.

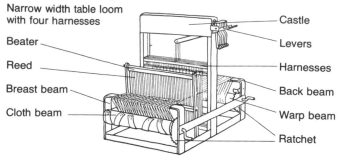

Narrow width table loom with four harnesses

Beater
Reed
Breast beam
Cloth beam

Castle
Levers
Harnesses
Back beam
Warp beam
Ratchet

table quilting. Quilts. Stitchery. A method of **quilting** without the use of **quilting frames** or a **quilting hoop.** In that sense it is similar to **lap quilting.** The **basted quilt** is spread out over a large table for quilting. The table surface can be used to catch the needle's point instead of using the left hand under the quilt.

table saw. Plastics. Woodworking. See **power saw.**

tablet. Weaving. See **card.**

tablet weaving. Weaving. See **Card weaving.**

tableware. Ceramics. See **Ceramics: Form.**

tabs. Papercrafts. See **fastening.**

tachyscope. Toys. See **zoetrope.**

tack. Basketry. A three-foot length of **willow** rod.

tack. Metalworking. See **tack weld.**

tack. Quilts. Stitchery. To take large **stitch**es to hold layers of material together temporarily. Similar to basting, though basting usually implies a long series of stitches. Tacking stitches may be used singly.

Sometimes tack means to take a single tiny stitch similar to the **catch stitch.** Used this way, the tacking stitch is not temporary. It may be the only and final stitch used to hold one piece of fabric onto another with tiny, almost invisible tack stitches. In **lace appliqué,** the laces and needlework are usually applied with a tack (or tacking) stitch. Also see **baste.**

tack cloth. Découpage. A lintless cloth that has been treated with resinous varnish so that it picks up dust. It is used to dust off the surface after sanding the découpage **finish.** Tack cloths are available at hardware stores.

tacking stitch. Crewel. Embroidery. Needlepoint. A small **straight stitch** used to hold down another longer stitch. A practical and decorative method for securing extremely long stitches. Also see **fishbone stitch.**

tacking stitch. Quilts. Stitchery. See **tack.**

tack weld. Metalworking. A small weld about ¼–½" long made first at the ends of, and at 6–8" intervals along, an unwelded seam to hold the metal in alignment before **running a bead** over the entire seam. As a verb, "to tack" means to make a tack weld.

tacky. Découpage. A term used to describe a partially dry surface. A test for the proper degree of tackiness can be made by touching the surface slightly with a clean fingertip. It should be somewhat sticky but not wet.

tacky. Plastics. A term used to describe a sticky surface of incompletely cured **resin.** Prevent or remedy this condition by **curing** the resin in a closed box, by covering the surface with an **air shield,** by using more **catalyst** in the surface pour, by heating the curing plastic with a **heat lamp,** or by coating the surface with a highly **catalyzed** resin or **surface resin.**

tac rag. Woodworking. A rag dampened with **varnish** and stored in an airtight jar. It is used to remove dirt and other loose particles from a surface that is being **finish**ed.

tactile. Stitchery. Having a surface that invites touch because of its appealing texture. The tactile nature of **fabric**s and wood greatly influences the effect and quality of the things crafted from them.

taffeta. Weaving. See **plain weave.**

tagua. Ivory and Bone Carving. See **vegetable ivory.**

tail. Bookbinding. The bottom edges of leaves and **board**s. Also see **leaf.**

tail. Kites. The kite tail is most often a line with several short lengths of cloth knotted around it that is fastened to the lower end of a kite. Its function is to stabilize the kite's flight by providing extended **drag** and proper directional orientation. With flat kites a tail is almost mandatory if uncontrollable looping and diving are to be avoided. When a kite is in flight the tail will sometimes dance and shimmy; the lighter tail is absorbing and counteracting the spinning action of the heavier kite, keeping the kite in a relatively calm state. The size of the tail is crucial, for a tail that is too long determines the motion of the kite; i.e., the tail will wag the kite. Too short a tail will be ineffectual. Trial and error are the best determinants of the proper tail for your design. You can start with a tail length roughly three to four times the width of your kite. Add or subtract until flight is stable. Multiple strips of crepe paper can be hung from the kite to serve as a tail. Also see **Kites: Construction.**

tail band. Bookbinding. See **head band.**

Tail of Benjamin's Kite, The. Quilts. See **Jacob's Ladder.**

tailor's chalk. Quilts. Stitchery. A hardened **chalk** used to mark **fabric.** Sometimes a soapstone or steatite is used, and it is then called French chalk. Any chalk or soapstone marker is usually ground into flat, bladelike shapes to facilitate making sharp lines. The **quilting pattern** is sometimes marked on the **quilt top** with either of these.

tailor's cushion. Stitchery. A ham-shaped or egg-shaped **stuff**ed form used under **fabric** to **press** curved lines stitching. It is helpful when making three-dimensional forms in stitchery or stuffed toys.

täkänä. Weaving. See **Finnweave.**

taken out. Quilts. Removed from the **quilting frame.** This is done when all the **quilting** is complete. When a quilter says she has "taken out" her **quilt,** it means the quilt is finished except for the **binding,** which is added after removal.

taker-in. Glasswork. See **gaffer.**

take-up. Weaving. The amount of yarn consumed in the **warp** as it bends over and under the **filling pick**s during weaving. Although no warp lies perfectly straight while interlacing with the filling, some warps bend more than others, depending on the following factors:
Composition of the yarn
Some **fiber**s, **twist**s, plies and **novelty yarn**s have more elasticity and therefore more interlacing capability than others.
Weave
The fewer interlacing points between warp and filling and the more **float**s, the less the take-up is. **Plain weave,** with the greatest number of interlacing points, has the most take-up of any weave; **satin weave** has relatively little take-up due to so few interlacing points.
Warp tension
A tight warp takes up less than a slack one.
Sett
A warp set at a low number of **end**s per inch takes up less than one with a high **sett.**
Beat
A heavy **beat** on a warp set high takes up more than a light beat or a heavy beat on a loosely set warp.
Take-up varies from, in some cases, almost zero up to 30%. For example, a **linen** warp for a tapestry or rug would have a minimal take-up as compared to a **worsted** used for a fine dress-fabric. The above factors would all have an influence on the amount of take-up.
Take-up should be allowed for when calculating the amount of yarn needed to weave a specific length of fabric, since a straight piece of yarn would be compressed into a shorter length due to take-up. The amount of compression of the filling, or width-wise in a fabric, is called **draw-in.** Also see **ply, warp calculations.**

take-up motion. Weaving. See **fly shuttle loom.**

talc. Ceramics. A compound in most whiteware bodies that is used as a source of **silica** and **flux.** Talc is slightly plastic and is used to lower the maturing temperature of stoneware clay and fire clay. Also see **maturity.**

talc. China and Glass Painting. See **French chalk.**

talc. Gemcutting. Hydrous magnesium silicate **crystal**lized in the monoclinic system. It has hardness of 1, **specific gravity** of 2.75, and a white **streak.** Soapstone (also called steatite) is a variety of talc. It occurs in various pale hues, is hand-carved, and is often dyed. Also see **Gemcutting: Hand Grinding and Polishing.**

talc. Plastics. See **filler.**

taleidoscope. Toys. An **optical toy** similar in form to the **kaleidoscope** but that reflects surrounding objects rather than objects within it. The taleidoscope has three mirror surfaces placed lengthwise within a tubular-shaped cardboard container. The mirrors form a triangle and the reflections create a six-sided pattern. Homemade taleidoscopes may be made from thin strips of **acrylic plastic sheet** in dark colors or clear strips painted opaque on one side. Also see **Toys: Optical Toys.**

talking beads. Beadwork. The Zulus of Natal, Africa, sent as messages or letters strung **trade beads** with bead colors selected for their symbolism. Each bead color had a meaning, such as white for love, pink for poor, black for darkness, blue for dove, and yellow for wealth. The beads were threaded on fiber made from the inner bark of the fig tree, and were sometimes woven on a simple **loom.** The messages were simple and often repeated several times. The letters were proudly kept and often several were worn around the neck. Also see **Beadwork.**

tallow. Candlemaking. Fat extracted from natural animal fat, usually of cattle or sheep, and rendered or purified for the making of candles. Because of its unpleasant odor and greasy surface quality it is considered inferior as a candle material.

tallow. Metalworking. Plastics. Lard or hard fat from animals, sold in stick or liquid form to be used as a **lubricant** or as a component in a recipe for modeling **wax.** In plastics, tallow is used as a lubricant on cutting blades. Also see **flux.**

tally. Lacemaking. See **leaf stitch.**

tambour frame. Crewel. Embroidery. Needlepoint. See **embroidery frame.**

tambour frame. Lacemaking. A polished wooden **hoop.** Mounted tambours, instead of smaller, hand-held hoops, are used by professional lacers. Tambours are either round or oval, the two hoops fitting one inside the other. The inside hoop is sometimes wrapped with velvet or ribbon to make a tighter fit. The net is placed between the hoops, which are then pushed together to hold the net taut for lacemaking. Some hoops are now sold that have a metal clamp on the outside hoop that tightens over the inside hoop when the net is in place.

tambour hook. Beadwork. Lacemaking. (Also called shepherd's hook, tambour needle.) A steel tool, usually the length of a sewing needle, used in lacemaking and for attaching **bead**s to fabric in **tambour work.** This small, sharp hook is made of steel and set in a handle of bone or plastic. Sometimes the handle is hollow and serves as a holder for other needles, which are interchangeable. See ill.

Tambour hook

tambour lace. Lacemaking. (Also called Irish tambour lace and Limerick Lace.) A lace, chiefly made around Limerick, Ireland, worked in a very fine **chain stitch** on net using **tambour hook** and thread. Tambour lace differs from **tambour work** only in the fabric upon which it is worked. Irish tambour lace has floral designs, with solid parts worked in the chain stitch and the large ornamented parts done in openwork **fillings.** The outside edge is strengthened by a woven braid with **picots,** held in place with a row of **buttonhole stitches.** The term "tambour" is derived from the French word meaning a "drum." Also see **Lacemaking: Needle laces.**

tambour needle. Beadwork. Lacemaking. See **tambour hook.**

tambour work. Beadwork. A style of **bead embroidery** in which **beads** are attached to fabric with a **tambour hook,** working the **thread** in embroidery stitches. Tambouring is worked on fabric that is stretched between two round frames similar to embroidery hoops to keep fabric taut while working. The name comes from a French word meaning "drum," because of the shape of the hoops.

The design is placed face down under the frame on the right side of the fabric. One hand operates the hook above the frame on the wrong side of the fabric, while the other hand, below the frame, threads the beads and presents the thread to the hook as it pierces through the fabric from above, pulling the thread up in a series of chain stitches and securing the beads along the outlines of the design.

Tambour work, which originated in the Orient, was extremely popular in England during the 1880s. Beads were applied to bags, belts, cushions, and upholstery. Prior to this time, tambour work had been done in England and on the Continent, primarily on gauzy fabrics such as muslin and fine cambric, so that the left hand could be seen through the hoop. This work was delicately done with white thread on white fabric. When the technique was perfected so that the hand below the frame could function underneath opaque fabrics, all types of rich fabrics, threads, and beads were introduced. Later developments of the technique replaced the tambour stitch with the chain stitch. Also, if the fabric was heavy, a hoop was not necessary so the work progressed more quickly.

tambour work. Lacemaking. **Tambour lace** and tambour work are both done in a **chain stitch** with a **tambour hook.** Tambour lace is done on a **net** fabric and tambour work is done on a fine **muslin** fabric. An example of tambour work is Swiss embroidery done on sheer muslin.

Tammann temperature. Ceramics. The **sintering** point in the firing cycle.

tamp. Metalworking. See **sandcasting molding equipment.**

tamping. Metalworking. (Also called ramming.) The process of packing down **molding sand** with a wooden rammer in a sandcasting flask. Also see **sandcasting molding equipment** and **Metalworking: Sandcasting.**

tang. Jewelry. Metalworking. The shank of a chisel **file, graver,** and **stake,** which fits into a handle or other holding device. Also see **bench hole.**

tang. Woodworking. See **rasp.**

tang chisel. Woodworking. See **chisel.**

Tangled Tares. Quilts. See **Kansas Troubles.**

tangram. Toys. An ancient Chinese **puzzle** consisting of seven parts.

taniko. Weaving. See **taaniko.**

tank furnace. Glasswork. The furnace used for melting **silica** and **flux**es in glassmaking, and from which the **gather** is made preparatory to **freeblowing** or glass can be ladled for molding.

A tank furnace can be made for the studio from high alumina refractory bricks, which form the tank; a castable refractory material, cast into a dome shape for the chamber above the melt; insulation bricks, which form the outer layer of the oven; and a gas burner, which mounts upside-down in the dome. See ill.

Tank furnace

tanner. Leather. A "manufacturer" of leather, i.e., one who takes **pelt**s from animals and transforms them through the process of tanning into **hides** or **skins** of durable, workable leather. Also see **Leatherwork: Tanning and Manufacture.**

Tanner's Council of America, Inc. Leather. An organization of leather manufacturers and distributors that has standardized the weight and thickness designations of leather; it disseminates information and publicity about leather to the general public.

tannin. Dyeing. A **mordanting** agent found in tannic acid, sumac leaves, and gallnuts (hard swellings on certain oak trees caused by infections from a gallfly). The gallnuts are a very rich source of tannin, which is available in drug stores as a pale brown powder. Also see **Dyeing: Natural Dyes.**

tannin. Leather. The traditional term for tannic acid, the astringent substance derived from oak bark, used in **tanning.** Also see **Leatherwork: Tanning and Manufacture.**

tanning. Leather. The process of preserving and turning hides and skins into flexible, workable, durable leather. Various tanning methods are used, such as **vegetable tanning, chrome tanning,** and others combining chrome and vegetable tanning. Also see **Leatherwork: Tanning and Manufacture.**

tantascope. Toys. See **phenakistoscope.**

tap. Metalworking. A tool with which to cut internal threads in a hole. The size of the tap is stamped on the neck, along with the diameter and the number of threads per inch. There are three main types of tap: The taper tap is for cutting threads completely through open-ended holes and to start threads in closed and partly closed holes. The plug tap is used after the taper tap to give more full threads in partly open holes. The bottoming tap is used after the taper and plug tap to cut a full thread into the bottom of a closed hole. See ill. Also see **die.**

Tap

tape. Bookbinding. Tape attached by sewing to reinforce the **back** of a book. It is available in unbleached linen and cotton, the former being the superior material, in widths of ⅜″, ⁷⁄₁₆″, ½″, and ⅝″. Starched bias tape may be substituted. Also see **sewing on tapes.**

tape loom. Weaving. See **bandloom.**

tape measure. Woodworking. See **measuring tools.**

tape needle. Rugmaking. Weaving. See **bodkin.**

taper. Candlemaking. A long, slender candle formed by the **dipping** or **pouring** process.

tapered drill bit. Plastics. An accessory tip for a **flexible-shaft machine** used for the internal **carving** of rigid plastics. See ill.

Tapered drill bit

tapered spindle. Jewelry. (Also called buffing spindle.) A threaded, tapered spindle that fits on the shaft of the **buffing machine** and on which the **buffs** are placed. It can be threaded for either the right or left side of the motor. See ill. Also see **buffing** and **Jewelry: Basic Operations.**

Tapered spindle

tapering wire. Jewelry. Reshaping the end of a wire or pin stem using a **bench pin** and a fine **hand file.** Wire is tapered before being drawn through a **drawplate** and re-

tapered every few **gauge**s. To taper wire or a pin stem, place the wire into the V-shaped notch of the bench pin, use a forward stroke with the hand file, and rotate the wire into the stroke of the file. If the wire cannot be hand-held, use a **pin vise** or a **ring clamp** for holding the pin stem. Smooth the pin stem with **carborundum cloth** or **emery cloth** and finish by **buffing.** Test a pin stem for sharpness by drawing it through a piece of fine cloth, such as silk. If it does not catch on the material it is sharp and smooth enough. A pin stem is tapered after being sawed to reshape the point. Also see **drawing wire, finding.**

taper tap. Metalworking. See **tap.**

tapestry. Crochet. A solid-looking crocheted fabric worked in designs using one or more colors and the **single crochet, half double crochet, double crochet,** and **Russian stitch.** Tapestry crochet can be either solid or open work; the solid is usually multicolor and the openwork only one color, with the design worked in open and solid mesh areas as for **filet crochet.** (In multicolor tapestry, the colors not being used can be **stranded** along the back of the work behind the stitches.)

Tapestry crochet is crocheted from one side only; the yarn is cut at the end of each **row** and rejoined at the opposite edge to begin the next row. Also see **stranding.**

tapestry. Needlepoint. This is the correct term for hand-woven designs. It has, however, been misused to designate needlepoint and, more specifically, **tent stitch.**

tapestry. Weaving. An ornamental textile used for covering walls and furniture and for curtains and hangings. It is derived from the Latin *tapete*, which means a carpet, a hanging, or a coverlet, and it originally referred to both woven and embroidered fabrics.

Tapestries are traditionally divided into two classes, depending on whether they are made on **high-warp** (haute-lisse) or **low-warp** (basse-lisse) looms. In both cases, a soft woolen **filling** is beaten down in place over hard **warp** threads so that the **weft** completely covers the warp. The design of the tapestry is produced entirely by the filling, with the warp playing its part only by serving as a vehicle to hold the weft threads together. The tapestry fabric has a characteristic **rib** effect running warp or lengthwise. Since the filling does not need to be carried **selvage** to selvage, but is worked only in sections according to the design or **cartoon,** many colors can be used across the width of the tapestry. This produces another characteristic of tapestry—either a small vertical slit or a joining at the point where two colors meet. Traditionally one thinks of tapestry as being pictorial, but modern ones are often abstract.

In more widely accepted usage, tapestry means a woven mural or **wall hanging.** However, in another context, it refers to any woven item—no matter how small—which has the **filling-faced** rib effect and color meeting characteristics mentioned above. It is a technical description as well as an artistic one.

There is no definite date for the beginning of tapestry weaving. However, it is known to have been on the scene early in the history of **weaving** and in countries as far removed from one another as China, Peru, and Egypt. In one form or another, on a sophisticated or a primitive level, it is still practiced in all corners of the world. One sees beautiful examples in South America, Guatemala, Poland, and the Middle East, and among the Navajos of the American southwest.

Perhaps the earliest evidence of tapestry weaving is in a tomb painting at Beni-Hassan, Egypt, dating from about 2000–3000 B.C., in which a low-warp tapestry loom is being used. There have also been found fragments of tapestry cloth in other ancient tombs (dating about 1500 B.C.) which show the Egyptians as master craftsmen. Both the back and front of their work are alike in their perfection and have no **float** threads or ends of threads sticking out. There was also great freedom in their technique and they thought nothing of deviating from the normal right-angle interlacing of warp and weft and curving the warp threads while weaving in the filling obliquely. Egyptian fabrics were woven of much finer warp and filling than the later Gothic masterpiece tapestries—undoubtedly because they were used as clothing and had to be pliable, whereas the Gothic works were mural hangings. The practice of using tapestry as clothing or decoration on clothing was carried on by the Copts, the Christian descendants of the ancient Egyptians. From around the second to eighth centuries A.D. we have many examples—all testifying to the high aesthetic and technical quality of Coptic tapestry weaving. They not only applied bands and panels of prewoven tapestry to a garment, but also specialized in incorporating the tapestry ornamentation directly into the looser-beaten **weave** of a fabric so that there was no separation between a gauzy cloth and the heavier tapestry decoration.

Tapestry weaving in Western Europe is thought to have come there from the Copts by way of the Arabs, who invaded Egypt, took over the existing weaving tradition, and eventually pushed on into Spain taking their craft skills with them. However, the Arabs already had conquered another great weaving culture—that of Persia, with its wealth of Sassanian tapestry weavers. It would be hard to say which tradition exerted the most influence on the Arabs and thereby on Europe. From Spain the techniques spread to southern France and later to Flanders. These early tapestries were known as "sarrasinois" after the Saracen followers of Mohammed, who were doing battle in France. There are, however, other expert sources that claim that Western European tapestry was sparked by the Byzantine silk **damask**s brought back by returning Crusaders or that the introduction of tapestry weaving goes back even earlier, to the time of the Roman occupation. The latter might be true in connection with the town of Arras in Flanders, where there were famous Coptic weavers living during the time when this area was the Roman Gaul. The invasion of the Huns put tapestry weaving into dormancy but later on, in the fourteenth century, high-warp tapestry weaving was flourishing so much in Arras that it became quite rich and prosperous and a tapestry became known as an "arras"—despite the fact that they were also being woven in Valenciennes, Tournai, and Brussels, other important tapestry centers.

However, the most famous medieval "tapestry" is not woven but embroidered—the Bayeux Tapestry, composed of 79 panels totaling 231 feet in length (but is only 20 inch wide). It chronicles the conquest of Saxon England by William the Conqueror of Normandy, ending in the Battle of Hastings in 1066. Worked in woolen thread of many colors on a **web** of white linen, it was made during the eleventh century for the Bishop of Bayeux, half-brother of William, and was used in the Bayeux Cathedral as a decorative hanging. The earliest surviving European true tapestries are also from the eleventh century. They are German-Romanesque and in a style called primitive—a term also given to Egyptian and Coptic and other early tapestry weaving, such as that from Peru. This stylistic term means that there is no attempt at modeling forms or shading colors through techniques such as **hatching** or hachure, but rather everything is woven in shapes of flat colors. The Arras tapestries of the fourteenth century used hatching, and by this time there was constant development in techniques for more realistic representation, while the inventive stylized design forms of the primitive works were forgotten. Size, technical considerations, and strength compelled these weavers to weave the tapestries sideways so that the warp ribs would run horizontally when the piece was hung. The fourteenth and fifteenth centuries brought forth the greatest number of magnificent European tapestries—no doubt due to the fact that these large and colorful woven murals ornamented the stone walls of medieval castles, at the same time softening their harshness and warming the interiors.

In addition to the previously mentioned cities, Paris was also known as a tapestry center as early as the thirteenth century and reached its zenith in the mid-fourteenth century. The Hundred Years' War had a devastating effect on the French tapestry industry and, although there was always an atelier operating, the industry as a whole never recovered its former scope. Tapestry itself changed during this time. The pinnacle that was reached during Gothic and early Renaissance times was lost in subsequent centuries when tapestries were created in imitation of paintings. The painters—including such well-known ones as Raphael and Rubens—were unfamiliar with tapestry techniques, and the paintings gained nothing by being translated into tapestries. However, tapestries remained in vogue, and in 1665 the Aubusson factory in southern France came under royal patronage while workshops in Paris were organized together in 1667 as the Royal Gobelins Factory. This began "the golden age of the **Gobelin tapestry**," but eventually—with the coming of the French Revolution and the Industrial Revolution—tapestry faded into the background and it wasn't until fairly recently that a comeback was made. Despite all this, these Gobelins and Aubusson managed to survive and are still active today.

One of the boosts given to contemporary tapestry weaving was in 1929 at the Barcelona International Art and Architecture competition, when Eva Anttila of Finland won a gold medal for one of her tapestries. Scandinavians had been practicing tapestry ("flamskvavnad" after the old tapestry centers of Flanders) since the time of the Vikings, but there had been no current recognition on an international scale. This encouragement allowed for the development of a Scandinavian tapestry theory that found its inspiration in the northern medieval tapestries and saw the artist as also being a weaver (if not the weaver who actually executed the final woven piece).

In 1939, Jean Lurçat of France, who had been experimenting with tapestries as purely decorative additions to a space, received a commission from the French government for cartoons for tapestries to be woven at Aubusson. Two other French painters were also given commissions and, in time, a government-supported French school of tapestry came into existence. The French school depends largely on the cartoons of painters and, in this way, keeps alive the traditions of Gobelins and Aubusson.

The techniques of both northern and French schools are essentially the same, but the artistic theory differs widely. In the French school, it is the artist-painter who creates the cartoon and is the most important element in the creation of a tapestry. The weaver copies the renderings faithfully and never changes, adds, or interprets a stroke. The end result is a flat, nontextured piece. The artist-weaver of the northern school refines and develops the texture of the tapestry and the color relationships as he goes along, so that the surface does not have the perfection of an Aubusson, but is rather a freer style.

The revival of tapestry has gained steady ground in recent years—partly because we once more have blank stone walls in architecture that need a textile to soften them. In the United States, a free approach has appealed more to weavers than the French traditional one. The American weaver has gone ever further away from this free base, developing an art form called **wall hangings.** When a tapestry becomes a wall hanging depends on the techniques used—sometimes all is woven in a tapestry manner; other times tapestry techniques form the base of the hanging, but texture or form are manipulated in a very free or sculptural way; or tapestry techniques are combined with those from the general weaving repertoire; or the techniques are totally foreign to tapestry weaving. Obviously, the further removed a woven piece is from tapestry, the more likely it is to be called a wall hanging. However, this does not necessarily happen, and pieces that have, at best, only a tenuous connection to true tapestry are sometimes called tapestries.

To weave tapestry, traditionally either a high-warp or low-warp loom would be used. In either case, the loom maintains the **ends** under strong **warp tension** and provides for two **shed** openings. Two are all that is needed for tapestry that is woven all in **plain weave,** with the various techniques coming into play as necessary when shapes, lines, or dots are being woven, as well as random **color blendings.** An **upright loom,** a **Navajo loom,** or a professional **tapestry loom** are examples of the high-warp loom, whereas a **harness loom** could substitute for a low-warp one. However, it is also possible to weave a tapestry on any one of the various types of **frame loom**s, a **backstrap loom** or a **warp-weighted loom.** On **cardboard** and **hoop looms,** the weaver would have to use a **needle** to go over and under the warp threads.

Warping the loom depends on the type of loom used.

Warps are either **continuous** when a frame is the basis of the loom, or they are put up as **warp chain**s when **warp peg**s, or a **warp beam,** and **cloth beam**s are used. With the exception of looms that have **treadles** and **harnesses,** the sheds are made by arrangements such as **shed sticks** and **heddle bar**s with **string heddle**s that are the modern equivalent of the "lisses" found on Gobelin and Aubusson looms.

Other **tapestry tools** take the place of **reed, beater,** and **shuttle** used in conventional weaving. These can be quite elaborate, but by reducing the tools to bare essentials, one could use a table fork as a **hand beater** and a **butterfly** as the yarn carrier.

The yarns used for warp in the past were determined by what was geographically available—**wool** in Western Europe, **linen** in Scandinavia, and **silk** in China. Today the weaver mainly uses cotton, wool, or a synthetic blend—the prime consideration being that the warp be strong and smooth enough to resist fraying and breakage during the constant **beating** down of the filling as well as give body to the tapestry. Another consideration is that the **sett** of the warp be sparse in order for the filling to cover it completely—therefore, strength must make up for a reduced number of threads per inch. The thickness of the warp yarn used determines the sett. In the tapestries of the great Gothic period, this thickness was from 8 to 14 threads per inch. Today the variance is much the same with more detailed designs calling for an even closer sett.

Wool was, and is, considered the favorite filling thread, with silk being used in the past as a highlight feature and sometimes with a touch of gold or silver. Today, wool often comes in blends with synthetics. Some weavers use wool-like synthetics as long as there is sufficient resilience so that the yarn beats down well. Although a contemporary weaver may use different thicknesses and **plies** of yarn, a beginner at tapestry would do well to use a soft yarn of the same type and **ply** for all colors throughout, in order to avoid different tensions and rate of packing down during beating.

In setting out to do a tapestry, the decision must be made as to whether the warp will run vertically or horizontally when hung, as this will affect the design and techniques used. It also will be a consideration in the choosing of the warp yarn, since the warp must bear the brunt of the weight if the piece is to hang warp-wise. One of the reasons for the endurance of the Gothic tapestries was that just about all were hung filling-wise, since this is where the strength lay, as there were so many more **picks per inch** than there were ends. Designs with many vertical lines would be easier to weave horizontally across the warp ends, as this would avoid overly long or too many slits or color joinings.

Another decision is whether to weave with the back of the tapestry facing the weaver, as traditionally done (with a mirror on the face side for the weaver to check his progress), or with the face side toward the weaver. Today, it has become quite popular to weave with the warp staying vertically when hung and the face up, since both allow the weaver more freedom in improvisation and interpretation of the cartoon. The cartoon today is also a much looser drawing than traditionally—every line and every color nuance used to be indicated either by paint or by a numbering system.

After the warp is on the loom, the weaver first puts in a row of **weft twining** or **weft chaining** to keep the warp spaced and stabilized and to give a firm starting edge for the weaving. A **heading,** which will serve as a hem, is woven at this point if desired. The sheds are opened by either treadles, shed stick, or heddle bar, or by pulling on the leashes (lisses), and the wefts are inserted only under the number of warp ends indicated on the cartoon for each specific color. The filling yarn is arced, so that there is enough yarn for good and easy coverage of the warp, and then is beaten down in place. Even though a filling strand may be required to go across the entire warp, it is inserted and beaten down only a few inches at a time so that the tension and coverage are the same throughout the tapestry. When the weft goes in through just one of the plain weave sheds, this is known as either a passage or a half-pass. When it completes both sheds of plain weave, it is then called a double passage or full-pass or course. The weaving proceeds in this manner all in plain weave and with **slit tapestry** being woven where there are vertical boundaries between two colors. If slits are not desired, techniques of **interlocking** and **dovetailing** are used instead. Other common techniques involved in tapestry are **hatching, stepping, teething, stippling, outlining,** and the working of **diagonals.** There are also many other methods that artist-weavers have developed to obtain greater shading, modeling, and texture variations.

The novice tapestry worker should take care that diminishing areas are woven first: i.e., if a design has a curve or slant, the color that is decreasing is woven first, and the color woven second that is advancing over the number of ends that the first one was decreased by. Should the beginner forget this, he will find unwoven areas of warp occurring that are not possible to fill in except with a needle—and even that is difficult. Another precaution that can be taken is in controlling the width of the tapestry. Often this begins to either narrow in as the weaver works upward, or the selvages curve in and out rather than being straight. As a remedy, the weaver can insert stout cords into both edges of the woven weft (to a depth of about 1–2″ from the selvages) and pull taut and tie around the side supports of the loom. Similar cords can be inserted every 1–4″ running up the selvages, depending on the severity of the narrowing or unevenness. This serves in lieu of a **stretcher.** However, it is up to the weaver to learn to control weft tension so that this does not occur repeatedly.

Upon completion of the tapestry, there are some **finishing** procedures that are done before the tapestry is ready for hanging. One of these is the **darning in** of the weft thread ends that cover the back of a tapestry. Traditionally these thread ends are left undarned, and the back appears as a maze of short thread tails. However, there may be a need to darn in those near the selvage for a short way in away from the edge, so that they do not stick out when the tapestry is hung. If the weaver has tucked the thread ends in around the warp ends or into succeeding sheds while weaving, they can be just clipped shorter or made flush with the fabric.

If the tapestry does not have **headings** to be used as hems, then **overcasting** or some other **finishing edge** must be used at the top and bottom raw edges. The slits are sewn up if desired and **blocking** is undertaken with tapestries that have buckled or have "bubbly" areas over the surface. As a final touch the tapestry can be **steam pressed.**

Although old tapestries often had hooks or rings with which to attach them to walls, today the most common way of hanging a tapestry is to mount it at the top edge onto a sturdy wood strip the length of the woven piece and then hang it by the wood strip at a slight distance away from the wall. A woven tape or band or **rug binding** can be used to attach the tapestry to the wood strip. Contemporary artists also have added weights or rods to the bottom of their tapestries or put them in frames or mounted them on a linen-covered piece of plywood or on a slab of decorative weathered wood. Also see **Aubusson tapestry, bubbling, crapaud, Egyptian knot, exposed warp tapestry, flat tapestry, flute, kilim, Navajo weaving, Peruvian weaving, rölakan, stripe, Swedish knot, tapestry rugs, tapestry weave, wrapping.**

tapestry beater. Rugmaking. Weaving. See **hand beater.**

tapestry fork. Weaving. See **hand beater, tapestry tools.**

tapestry loom. Weaving. A term reserved for either a traditional haute-lisse (**high-warp**) or basse-lisse (**low-warp**) two-**shed** loom, or a **frame loom,** or a **vertical** or **upright loom,** that is used primarily for **tapestry.** The low-warp loom is associated with the weaving coming from **Aubusson** and is sometimes called the Aubusson loom, while the high-warp loom is associated with **Gobelins** and is referred to as the Gobelin loom. Traditional tapestry looms have a device for holding the **warp** threads under tension (and usually a means of adjusting that tension), and a **shedding device** to open the warp into the two sheds of **plain weave** necessary for tapestry weaving. Within these requirements, there are many other looms that could be and have been used in place of either of the traditional looms. The ancient Peruvians did tapestry on a **backstrap loom,** while today the frame loom is perhaps most often used. The Navajos use a vertical frame loom for their tapestrylike rugs. When the frame loom is mounted on legs, it becomes an upright loom. A **rug loom,** rug **hooking frame,** or any loom on which two sheds are possible can be used as a tapestry loom. Tapestries can also be done on a **four-harness loom.** Since this type of loom has more capabilities than two sheds, it is never referred to as a tapestry loom. The harness loom is the only loom that is low-warp, other than the Aubusson loom. In essence, tapestries can be woven on practically every type of loom, but there are some looms on which it is easier or more practical (such as the upright or frame where the work is easy to view during progress), and some that have been built for this specific purpose and are thus called tapestry looms.

The quickly apparent difference between all the loom types mentioned above is size—an upright loom is larger than a frame loom, and the Gobelin and Aubusson looms are larger than the upright loom. However, there are also some differences in the manner in which the sheds are achieved—differences which are usually governed by size. With the small frame looms, a **shed stick** is used for one shed and the other is obtained by a **heddle bar** with **string heddle**s called leashes or lisse, or by picking up with the fingers. There are also frame and vertical models with specific shedding (as well as tensioning) devices particular to that model and patented by the maker. In upright looms, the shed stick and heddle bar arrangement can be used or the loom can have two **treadle**s attached to two **harness**es, which move horizontally back and forth. In this case, the entire shed is opened up each time one or the other treadle is pressed. This is considered by some professional tapestry weavers as putting undue stress on the entire warp with each shed opening, since generally only specific portions of the warp need to be activated. These portions are dictated by the tapestry design or **cartoon**. Tapestry weavers usually prefer professional looms, such as the Aubusson, which has a series of harnesses in pairs—with each pair controlling 16–24″ of warp. Each series of two harnesses has its own pair of foot treadles, which are pressed down as that specific part of the warp is needed. The Aubusson loom, unless it is built to order, is not available in the United States. The huge, in some cases almost room-size, Gobelin looms found in the factories in France use a shed stick and heddle bar arrangement.

A feature of many professional tapestry looms is the **warp peg**s, which are on the top side of the top frame of an upright loom. They are usually 2″ apart and the warp is tied to them in sections so that its tension can be adjusted where needed. Many of the upright looms have a **warp beam** rather than warp pegs, and in almost all models, there is a **cloth beam**. Some upright looms have a **beater** with a **reed**. The reed aids in keeping the warp constantly well spaced, but the beater really has no function in tapestry weaving since the beating is done in small sections with a **hand beater**. In some upright looms, there is provision made to attach a mirror on the back of the loom so that the person working a tapestry with the wrong side facing (the traditional manner) can view progress on the right side.

Upright tapestry loom with warp pegs

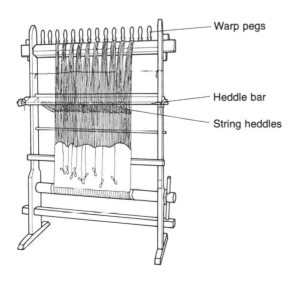

Warp pegs

Heddle bar

String heddles

The type of loom used dictates the type of warp that will be put on. A circular or **continuous warp** is possible on the frame and some upright looms. With the more professional looms, the warp is prepared beforehand and then put on the loom. See ill. Also see **chain warping, tapestry tools.**

tapestry needle. Basketry. (Also called raffia needle.) A big needle with a large eye commonly used for **coiled basketry.** It comes in a variety of lengths with pointed, blunt, or turned-up ends. See ill. Also see **Basketry: Coiled Basket Construction, Tools and Material.**

Tapestry needle

tapestry needle. Crewel. Embroidery. Needlepoint. (Also called blunt needle.) A blunt needle used to work needlepoint and embroidery stitches on the surface of a **background** fabric to avoid splitting the fabric's threads. Tapestry needles are available in sizes 13–26; the higher the number of the needle, the smaller the needle.

tapestry needle. Macramé. A blunt embroidery needle with a large eye used in **finishing** a piece of macramé work. Also see **Macramé: Tools and Materials.**

tapestry needle. Rugmaking. See **rug needle.**

tapestry rug. Rugmaking. Weaving. **Flatweave rug**s using traditional **tapestry** techniques and differing from wall tapestries only in subject matter and weight and durability of the yarn used. The most common tapestry rugs are **kilim**s that use a slit technique. However, they are also done with **interlocking** and **dovetailing** or a combination of these techniques. Sometimes **embroidered rug**s are erroneously called tapestry rugs if their **stitch** resembles a tapestry **plain weave.**

tapestry stitch. Needlepoint. See **Gobelin stitch.**

tapestry stitch. Rugmaking. (Also called Gobelin stitch.) A stitch having the ribbed effect produced by **tapestry** weaving. It is akin to the **tent stitch,** except that the stitches are taken parallel so that horizontal ribs result. Each stitch, which is taken over 2, 3, or more backing threads, travels its full length on both sides of the rug so that, in effect, it forms its own **padding** on the reverse side of the rug. There are several variations on the tapestry stitch, but at its simplest, when worked on **canvas mesh,** it goes as follows: Start bottom left and bring needle back to front; insert two holes above, emerging at the bottom of the previous stitch and one hole to the right. Insert two holes above and continue as for the previous stitch. The next row is begun at the left in the top hole of the previous row.

tapestry tools. Weaving. The implements needed in **tapestry** weaving to carry the filling yarns and to beat them down in place. To carry the **filling** tapestry, **bobbins** are used. This refers to either a **Gobelin bobbin** or a **Swedish bobbin** (both are also called pins because of their pointed tips) or the **flute** or Aubusson bobbin. On a horizontal (**low-warp**) loom, very small **boat shuttles** are sometimes used, but they are difficult to find and purchase. Finger bobbins or butterflies are perhaps the most popular type of yarn carrier since they require no special holder and are therefore economical. Very many of them can be used at the same time and, if made correctly, they do not come undone when dangling down during the course of weaving on a **high-warp** loom. They also are practical to use on the low-warp loom. Weavers are ingenious at using or inventing other types of carrier-tools that fit the requirement of carrying only small amounts of yarn and not coming undone during the weaving. In this category are knitting bobbins such as those that are used for the frequent color changes in making Argyle socks.

To beat the filling down in place, use either a pin-beater, such as the tip of the Gobelin or Swedish bobbin, or a tapestry fork or comb. Both types come in a variety of shapes and materials depending upon the culture and the era in which they originate. Some pin-beaters from Peru and those used by the early North American Indians were made of bone. Forks or combs are usually of a smooth, hard wood with the tines, or teeth, sometimes made of metal. Some have handles and others fit comfortably into the palm of the hand. One of the favorite beaters used by tapestry weavers is an ordinary metal household fork. Also see **butterfly, hand beater.**

tapestry weave. Weaving. **Plain weave** with the **filling** completely covering the **warp.** Many different colors can be worked at the same time because the filling does not weave **selvage** to selvage, but rather each color weaves back and forth as needed to complete a particular area of color. With many color changes, techniques have been developed to facilitate the changes and to further aid in representing the **cartoon** that is followed in weaving a **tapestry.** Some of these techniques are **slit tapestry, diagonal, outlining, dovetailing, teething, interlocking, hatching, stippling,** and **modeling.**

tapestry yarn. Crewel. Embroidery. Needlepoint. A four-ply twisted **yarn** that can be separated into two-ply strands for stitchery. Also see **Crewel: Materials** and **Needlepoint: Materials.**

tapete. Weaving. See **tapestry.**

tapper. Stained Glass. An instrument about 4—5" long, with a small brass ball at either end used for tapping **scores** to get a break started in the glass before the glass is actually parted. It is especially useful with **Norman slab glass.** Also see **parting.**

tapping. Jewelry. The making of screw threads with the use of taps and **dies** so that work can be screwed together where high heat or pressure is impractical for joining. The screw threads can also be used as a purely decorative device. Taps are used to cut thread in a hole drilled through metal or to thread a nut. Dies are used to cut the thread on the wire being made into the screw. Also see **drill press.**

tapping. Metalworking. The process of cutting threads in a hole with a **tap.**

Attach the **tap wrench** to the tap. Put the tap in the previously drilled hole. Push down and turn the wrench clockwise with one hand to start the thread. Check to see that the tap is aligned by using a **square.** After the thread is well started, turn the wrench with both hands a half to a full turn. To remove waste particles, reverse the tap direction for every half-turn forward. Use a lubricant, such as machine oil, to ease cutting, except with cast iron.

As an alternate method, a drill press may be used. It solves the problem of keeping the tap perpendicular to the work. The tap is put in the drill **chuck** and is turned—by hand power only!

tapping iron. Basketry. See **rapping iron.**

tap wrench. Metalworking. A special wrench used to hold a **tap.** Two types are the T and the 2-handle type. See ill.

Tap wrench, T-type

Tarascan lace. Weaving. See **Mexican lace.**

target. Beadwork. See **rosette.**

target. Toys. See **bull's eye.**

target toy. Toys. Any toy or **game** in which an object is hurled or projected by hand or by some contrivance at a target. The **bull's eye,** a series of concentric circles, is a common target. Most shooting toys are target toys. Included are the **peashooter, popgun, caddy, slingshot,** and **rubber-band gun. Bean bag** games may also employ a target.

tarkashi work. Jewelry. An **inlay** technique decorating wood with wire that has been highly developed in India and in Poland, where it is called **inkrustacja.** A well-dried hardwood is used. The pattern is drawn on the wood and then cut in at a right angle with a thin, sharp, knife blade. Thin metal cut into strips about 4 mm wide is then hammered edge-first into the cut grooves with a flat-faced hammer. The wire should be clipped off even with the ends of the cut groove before forcing it in. The metal can then be made flush with the wood by **filing** the entire surface. The filing should be done in the direction of the wood grain. Brass is the traditional metal used in this technique, but copper, silver, or gold can also be used.

tarnish. Jewelry. A surface discoloration of metals that is a thin film of sulfide or oxide formed when the metal is exposed to air. Also see **corrosion.**

tassel. Rugmaking. Weaving. Thick groups of yarn from 2½—10" and at least ½" in diameter at their folded and bound tops. The groups of yarn are of the same length, doubled at the center over a single yarn that acts as an attaching device, and kept in this position by another yarn, or **whipping,** that holds them together near the fold. They are used as attached ornamentation at rug corners or edges or on any fabric either at the edge or in the body of the weaving. The ancient Peruvians were very fond of tassels and put them on all types of fabrics, from **netting** to **tapestry.** At times they attached so many tassels that the whole fabric was covered with them.

To make a tassel, cut a piece of cardboard the length of the tassel desired and wind yarn around it. Insert a length of yarn through one end of the wound group and tie securely. This is the yarn that acts as an attaching device. Cut the group at the other end. Whip or tie the uncut end, starting about ½−2″ down from the tied yarn at the fold. The tassel can be inserted into a hem or woven edge and tied or very securely sewn in. Tassels are usually attached in lieu of a **fringe.** See ill. Also see **pompom.**

Tassels

tassel. Stitchery. A decorative dangling **finial** of **yarn,** cord, or thread, often used in bands or in corners of a finished piece or **pillow.** They are appropriately used on **banners,** on **flags,** or any place where the movement of these swinging yarns adds interest.

Tassels are made by first cutting cardboard the length desired for the finished tassel. Yarn, floss, or string is then wound around the cardboard from 25 to 50 times, depending on the weight of yarn and the plumpness required in the finished tassel. A yarn is then slipped between the cardboard and the yarn, so that all strands can be tied together at the top. The yarns are **clipped** at the bottom, and another strand of yarn or cord is tightly wound around all of the strands, about ½−1″ below the top tie and knotted. Ends are trimmed to make them even.

Tassels of commercial manufacture are available singly in a variety of sizes. Small ones are found added to a tape, similar to **ball fringe.** Readymade tassels come in **cotton, silk, wool,** or **synthetics.**

Tatting. Tatting is a single-**filament** knotted **lace** made in a design of **rings** and semicircles called arches, **chains,** or **scallops.** As is true in so many of the fiber arts, the origin of tatting is obscure. There was a type of heavy floor matting made in India called "tattie," which was used in doorways. It has been suggested that this was the origin of the word "tatting." The materials brought from Asia by the traders must certainly have played a large part in the introduction to Europe of this particular type of knotting. Another suggestion is that the English name was taken from the word "tatters," indicating the fragile nature of the work.

Records have been found of a type of knotting done with a shuttle in the fifteenth century in England. During the seventeenth and eighteenth centuries, ladies of the court in England, France, and Germany were making such knotted work. It consisted of a series of knots made in a continuous line on a cordlike filament, which was then applied to fabric with embroidery stitches.

Tatting is worked with **shuttle** and **thread,** using the fingers and hands to form the knots. These knots, or stitches, are the **double stitch** and **half hitch,** and decorative elements called **picots.** A tatter should have a tatting shuttle, a **crochet hook,** or a tatting **pin and ring,** and scissors.

To begin, lay out a design on paper, showing the placement of rings and chains with notations where picots will be placed for decoration or where you will attach the motifs together, and showing whether one or two shuttles will be used. If the design will be done in one color, and the **single thread** joining the rings or chains will be a part of the design, then use one shuttle. When two colors are used and the joinings between the rings and chains are covered with stitches, it is necessary to work with two shuttles. Indicate on the design where the two colors will occur. Tat a sample of one section of the design, **estimating the amount of thread needed.** In this sample try out any new combinations of motifs. Write out any **pattern** instructions to follow as you are tatting.

When the piece is completed, **tie off ends,** dampen the lace, if necessary, and pin out on the ironing board or some firm surface. Pin according to the original design, making sure all picots are lying in their proper position. Press with a pressing cloth between the lace and iron, steaming if necessary. Let dry on the board. For finishing an **insertion** or **edging,** steam press with a pressing cloth, making sure all picots are lying correctly.

The following are the abbreviations commonly used in tatting:

alt	**alternately**
att	**attach**
ch	**chain**
ch st	**chain stitch.** See **edging.**
cl	**close.** See **ring.**
ds	**double stitch**
k	**knot**
p	**picots**
r	**ring**
rw	**reverse work**
sep	separated
sp	**space**
tog	**together**
*	**asterisk,** repeat * to *

An asterisk indicates the repetition of all instructions from one * to the other *.

Instruction for a ring might read as follows: ring of 5 ds, 5 p, sep by 2 ds, and 5 ds, cl, rw. Translated, make a ring of 5 double stitches and 5 picots separated by 2 double stitches, close the ring, and reverse the work. Also see **making the double stitch, winding the shuttle.**

tatting. Weaving. See **nonloom.**

tatting bag. Tatting. A small bag that hangs over the wrist to hold the **loop thread** shuttle or the **ball thread** while tatting. It is about 4″ or 5″ square and has a band coming up from the sides that forms the wrist strap, or it may have a drawstring. The bag is also good for holding scissors, the tatting **pin and ring**, and extra shuttles and threads when you are not tatting.

tatting knot. Macramé. See **half hitch.**

T-bar. Stained Glass. A steel or aluminum T-sectioned bar used in the center of a very long window to support the weight in the center of the window. Also see **saddle bar.**

tea. Quilts. Stitchery. Tea is used for tinting or antiquing fabrics. In **lace appliqué**, to blend a series of various off-white and ecru laces, the entire collection may be dipped in liquid drinking tea, which gives a beige color of slightly greenish cast. The brewed tea also makes a good tint for antiquing fabrics used in repairing old **quilts**. The fabric or lace is dipped first in a weak tea, then left to dry. The color always looks stronger when it is wet. It may be dipped any number of times to give a continuously deeper color.

teacup. Quilts. See **Quilts: Quilting.**

teacup quilting. Quilts. A pattern of overlapping circles used as a **filling pattern** or as an **all-over quilting** design. The name was presumably derived from objects that served as templates. Also see **wineglass quilting.**

teak. Woodworking. A strong, durable **hardwood** from East India. Its beautifully grained, dark brown surface is slightly waxy and takes a high polish easily. Teak is commonly used for fine furniture and cabinets.

Tea Leaf. Quilts. A **geometric pieced block** pattern that resembles a sharply pointed leaf. A variation that combines four of these blocks is **Yankee Pride.** Other leaf patterns similar to this one are **Cactus Flower** and the **appliquéd** block **Oak Leaf.** See ill.

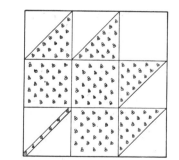

Tea Leaf

teapot. Ceramics. See **Ceramics: Form.**

teasel. Spinning. Weaving. The prickly seed pod of a wild thistle plant that was used as a primitive **carder** and later as a means of brushing up the nap of a woolen fabric after weaving. Teasels are about 2–4″ in length and 1½–2″ in diameter, measuring tip to tip the needlelike spines that

cover the entire surface of the pod. The teasel-growing center in the United States is Auburn, New York, and the Finger Lakes area south of it. To use as carders, a number of the dried seed pods were tied together to a holder with a handle. The arrangement resembled the shape of a hand carder. The use of the dried seed pods for **napping** goes back to the Roman era and continued down through the ages until modern times. The barbs on the pods are just strong enough to lift the fibers without tearing the cloth. Even though they are not as much used today, they still remain one of the best means of napping. A teasel is also a wire brush used instead of the teasel pod to nap fabrics. See ill. Also see **carding.**

Teasel pods attached to a holder for use as a carder

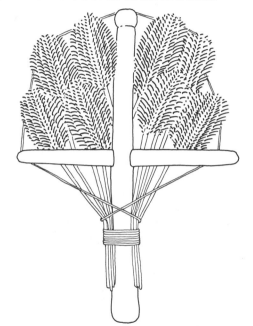

teasel. Stitchery. (Also called teazel.) The dried flower of a thistlelike plant called fuller's teasel. The short, curved, slightly flexible thistles are used to comb or brush **fabric** to raise a **nap** or fuzz on the surface. When teasels are so employed, the process is called gigging.

teasel brush. Knitting. A brush made of fine wires, or teasels, used for brushing a finished knit fabric made with **Angora** or **mohair** yarn to fluff up the wool and create a nap. A teasel brush is also used for the **felting** of other knit fabrics to give a smooth, feltlike finish.

teaseling. Weaving. See **napping.**

teasing. Spinning. Weaving. (Also called picking.) The process of preparing the fibers for **carding** by gently pulling them apart with the fingers. Teasing cleans the **wool** by releasing small stickers, pieces of grass, and dirt from the wool and by opening up the tight fibrous mass. The wool fluffs up as it is teased so that the amount of teased wool becomes greater in volume than it was unteased. Dirty wools may have to be picked several times. **Flax** is also teased, but usually just once to open up the fiber bundles. Teasing is done as a side-to-side motion with the hands pulling and spreading apart the fibers. See ill.

Also, the **napping** or fluffing up of a woolen fabric after weaving. This was originally done with a dried **teasel** seed pod.

Teasing

teazel. Stitchery. See **teasel.**

teddy bear. Toys. An all-time favorite **stuffed toy** in the form of a bear. The toy became immediately popular after President Theodore (Teddy) Roosevelt spared the life of a bear cub while on a hunting trip in 1902. A cartoon of the incident led to the creation of the toy, known first as Teddy's bear. Also see **Archie.**

teething. Weaving. A **tapestry** technique to avoid slits in color changes of adjacent areas. Instead of turning back each time at the same **warp end** as in **slit tapestry,** the turning back alternates between three adjacent warp ends. It is akin to **dovetailing** in that it gives an indistinct outline between two colors, but this blurry outline is much less distinctive than that produced by dovetailing. Teething also avoids the build-up of **filling** yarns that occur with dovetailing. It is sometimes used to strengthen a joining in a large traditional tapestry that will be hanging with the warp horizontal. The pull of the weight will then be dispersed among three warp ends instead of just weighing on one.

To do teething, the first **pick**s in the same **shed** of **plain weave** turn around adjacent warp ends and return. The next time the picks come to the same turn-around, they go to yet another adjacent warp end to the right or left of the original two warp ends, and there turn and return. The third set of picks turns around at the same spot as the first, the fourth set the same as the second. This alternating sequence is followed to the conclusion of the two-color area. Teething has many names—according to each weaver's whim. See ill.

Teething

teetotum. Toys. (Also called T-totum, totum.) A toy set in motion by twirling it in the fingers like a **top.** It was made in the late 1700s and had numbers painted on it. It was used in place of **dice** to avoid any contamination of children's minds by association with the wickedness of dice and gambling.

telescoping box. Toys. Either a box with a telescoping lid or a series of boxes that fit together. The telescoping lid

slides or fits completely over the box. If the box is a cube, open at the top, the lid is also a cube just slightly larger, open at the bottom. Boxes with telescoping lids are usually strong and can be used in various ways in toymaking.

Telescoping boxes in series are toys in themselves. Sometimes called pyramid boxes, or pyramid blocks, they can be stacked from large to small. As each box slides snugly over the one next to it in size, all the boxes fit into the largest box. These are sometimes decorated like **alphabet blocks** or building **blocks.** Most are paper-covered heavy cardboard.

telescoping lid. Toys. See **telescoping box.**

telsto. Jewelry. See **liner.**

temmoku. Ceramics. A Japanese technique that produces a dark glaze with pale, silverlike oil spots. Temmoku is applied to stoneware clay and fired in **reduction.**

temper. Jewelry. A quality produced in metals from exposure to heat or by being worked. For example, **annealed temper**ing is softening metal by heating; **spring temper**ing is working the metal until it becomes hard and springy; **hard temper**ing is working metal cold (at room temperature). Also see **annealing** and **Metalworking: Heat Treatment.**

tempera. Puppets. Toys. A **water-base paint** similar to **poster paint** but usually of a better quality. It is available in a dry powdered form to be mixed with water for painting, or as a ready-mixed paint of creamy consistency. Tempera paint is not waterproof and must be **finish**ed with **lacquer,** varnish, or other **fixative** to prevent smearing or smudging. Also see **baker's clay, casein.**

Temperance. Quilts. See **Pine Tree.**

tempera paint. Puppets. Toys. See **tempera.**

temperature. Candlemaking. Temperature is a critical factor in every element and every process of candlemaking. The **melting point,** or hardness, of the wax will determine how it will **mold** and how it will burn. The pouring temperature of the wax depends on the candlemaking method or **molding** technique used.

In the dipping process each successive layer must be poured at the right temperature to avoid melting away earlier layers. If the hot wax is to be poured over another layer of wax, as in the pouring of a layered candle or a **shell candle,** temperatures must be carefully regulated. Advice from suppliers of waxes and molds, experimentation, and a heat-resistant **thermometer** are all extremely valuable tools in determining the right temperature for the process.

temperature. Stained Glass. See **firing.**

temperature conversion chart. Jewelry. The chart on the next page gives Fahrenheit-to-Celsius and Celsius-to-Fahrenheit temperature conversions.

TEMPERATURE CONVERSION TABLES

Comparison of Thermometers
Freezing point = 32° Fahrenheit = 0° Celsius
Boiling point = 212° Fahrenheit = 100° Celsius

FAHRENHEIT TO CELSIUS

°f	°c	°f	°c	°f	°c	°f	°c
32	0	860	460	1360	738	1880	1026
212	100	880	471	1380	749	1900	1038
400	204	900	482	1400	760	1920	1049
420	216	920	493	1420	771	1940	1060
440	227	940	504	1440	782	1960	1071
460	238	960	516	1460	793	1980	1082
480	249	980	527	1480	804	2000	1093
500	260	1000	538	1500	816	2020	1105
520	271	1020	549	1520	827	2040	1116
540	282	1040	560	1540	838	2060	1127
560	293	1060	571	1560	849	2080	1138
580	304	1080	582	1580	860	2100	1149
600	316	1100	593	1600	871	2120	1160
620	327	1120	604	1620	882	2140	1171
640	338	1140	616	1640	893	2160	1182
660	349	1160	627	1660	904	2180	1193
680	360	1180	638	1680	916	2200	1204
700	371	1200	649	1700	927	2220	1216
720	382	1220	660	1740	949	2240	1227
740	393	1240	671	1760	960	2260	1238
760	404	1260	682	1780	971	2280	1249
780	416	1280	693	1800	982	2300	1260
800	427	1300	704	1820	993	2320	1271
820	438	1320	716	1840	1004	2340	1284
840	449	1340	727	1860	1015	2360	1293
						2380	1305
						2400	1316

CELSIUS TO FAHRENHEIT

°c	°f	°c	°f	°c	°f	°c	°f
0	32	430	806	680	1256	930	1706
100	212	440	824	690	1274	940	1724
200	392	450	842	700	1292	950	1742
210	410	460	860	710	1310	960	1760
220	428	470	878	720	1328	970	1778
230	446	480	896	730	1346	980	1796
240	464	490	914	740	1364	990	1814
250	482	500	932	750	1382	1000	1832
260	500	510	950	760	1400	1010	1850
270	518	520	968	770	1418	1020	1868
280	536	530	986	780	1436	1030	1886
290	545	540	1004	790	1454	1040	1904
300	572	550	1022	800	1472	1050	1922
310	590	560	1040	810	1490	1060	1940
320	608	570	1058	820	1508	1070	1958
330	626	580	1076	830	1526	1080	1976
340	644	590	1094	840	1544	1090	1994
350	662	600	1112	850	1562	1100	2012
360	680	610	1130	860	1580	1110	2030
370	698	620	1148	870	1598	1120	2048
380	716	630	1166	880	1616	1130	2066
390	734	640	1184	890	1634	1140	2084
400	752	650	1202	900	1652	1150	2102
410	770	660	1220	910	1670	1160	2120
420	788	670	1238	920	1688	1170	2138
						1180	2156
						1190	2174

tempered glass. Glasswork. A glass of exceptional tensile strength made by cooling molten glass quickly in air jets. The internal stresses developed produce a glass that can withstand greater stress than ordinary glass.

tempering. Metalworking. See **temper** and **Metalworking: Heat Treatment.**

tempering clay. Ceramics. The adding of water to clay. Also see **mixing.**

template. Ceramics. A card or sheet made of stiff material or metal cut to a desired profile of a pot, bowl, or plate. It is used as a guide to shape clay.

template. Gemcutting. A sheet of plastic, opaque or clear, with a graduated series of holes cut out, for marking a standard size and shape on gem rough; this insures that the finished gem can be mounted in a standard-size jewelry finding. Templates are available single, in double models for marking both sides of a slab, and in adjustable models for rectangles. See ill. Also see **cabochon** and **Gemcutting: Orientation.**

Standard template

template. Jewelry. A shape, simple or complex, made of **sheet metal**—usually brass or copper—used as a model for tracing with a **scribe** when a shape is to be sawed out in multiples.

template. Leather. A pattern cut from heavy cardboard or lightweight sheet metal meant for repeated use. Also see **Leatherwork: Cutting and Edging Leather.**

template. Metalworking. Plastics. Woodworking. A pattern of the same size and shape as the object to be made, used to test the accuracy of the form in the making. It may be a two-dimensional silhouette, or a three-dimensional pattern.

template. Stained Glass. (Also called pattern.) The shape cut out of a heavy paper or, occasionally, thin glass that corresponds to the size of the required piece of glass, as drawn in the **cartoon.** In making the templates, place a piece of 80–90-lb kraft paper or stencil paper on a drawing board. Cover it with carbon paper. Place a piece of lightweight drawing paper on top. Add another layer of carbon paper and place the cartoon on top of that. Use a hard (4-H) pencil to trace the drawing on the layers of paper. Numbering the design is important: each piece of designated glass in the design should be numbered in some consistent order on all copies. Before removing the layers of paper check to see that all the lines have transferred.

For a **panel** using **lead came,** the template is cut out with **pattern shears** or a **pattern knife.** For **copper foil,** the template is cut with regular scissors. If you cut out all the templates at one time, pin the cartoon to the workboard and fasten each piece lightly to the cartoon with double-faced masking tape so that it does not get lost. Also see **lamination, plating, pounce bag, squaring up.**

temple. Weaving. See **stretcher.**

templet. Weaving. See **stretcher.**

temporary basket. Basketry. A roughly made basket intended for disposal after brief use. Also see **Basketware.**

Tenerife lace. Lacemaking. See **sol lace.**

Tennessee Star. Quilts. See **star patterns.**

tenon. Woodworking. See **joint, mortise.**

tensile strength. Ceramics. The ability of a **clay body** and **glaze** to resist tension during **firing.** Also see **crawling, crazing.**

tensile strength. Jewelry. The ability of a metal to resist stress.

tensile strength. Leather. The stress to which leather can be subjected without tearing apart. Leather has very high tensile strength. Also see **chrome tanning, fat liquoring.**

tensile strength. Metalworking. The maximum force or stress a piece of metal can withstand under tension before it fractures. In the test used to measure tensile strength, the metal is pulled from both ends and the load it withstands is measured in pounds per square inch. A designer should consider the tensile strength when choosing a metal for constructions that must bear tension pressures. Certain metals, such as **aluminum,** lose their tensile strength when heated and must be supported when they are welded.

tensile strength. Spinning. Weaving. The maximum pressure or pull that can be applied to a fabric or yarn before it rips or breaks.

tension. In visual compositions, the state of strain or stress set up between two contrasting or divergent visual stimuli. A composition using only two **complementary colors** at full **saturation** and of approximately equal expanse can set up so much tension between the colors that they seem to vibrate. Other kinds of visual tension can be more subtle, such as the tension between the violent and powerful brush strokes in a van Gogh landscape and the customarily peaceful nature of landscape painting.

tension. Knitting. Tension is the pull on the yarn by the knitter; it differs from person to person and with each type of yarn. It is essential to maintain a constant, even tension in knitting to obtain smooth, professional results. To determine whether your tension is right for a particular knitting pattern, find the number of stitches per inch, specified at the beginning of the pattern. Using the correct size needles and the yarn you plan to use for the pattern, knit a test sample about four inches square, cover it with a damp cloth and press it with a hot iron, and then count the stitches per inch. If the number doesn't agree with the stitches per inch on the pattern, you may want to alter your needle size slightly (using one size larger needles if you have knit too many stitches per inch, or smaller needles if you have knit too few per inch).

tension box. Weaving. A device used for **sectional warping** that keeps the **warp** yarns at the same tension and in the right order in all of the sections as they are wound on from the **spool rack** to the **warp beam** of the **loom.** It is attached to the **back beam** directly over the section of the warp beam to be wound, and is moved along the back beam from section to section as needed. The yarn comes from the spool rack in the order that it is to appear on the warp beam and is threaded through a **reed** or comb located at one end of the tension box. Each warp thread is then guided individually over and under the wooden pegs in the tension box that act much as **lease sticks** do in regulating the tension. The reed acts as a **raddle** in spreading out each warp section. There is an optional attachment to the tension box, called a **counter,** that automatically counts the number of turns around the warp beam to insure that each section has the same number of turns. See ill.

Tension box

Counter

tension device. Spinning. See **tension screw.**

tensioner. Weaving. A device added to some manufactured models of **frame looms** that controls the tension of a **continuous warp.** The most common tensioning device is a board added on to the top of a frame loom. There are two screws at either end of this board. The warp goes around the board and, since tension problems arise when the warp gets too tight due to **take-up** in weaving, by screwing down on the screws, warp is released so that weaving can continue. Also see **tension box.**

tension screw. Spinning. (Also called tension device.) A device for controlling the tautness of the **driving band** of a **spinning wheel** so that proper spinning is possible. Slight variations in the tension of the driving band can cause differences in the **twist** of a **spun yarn.** On a **treadle wheel,** a tension variation affects the speed at which the yarn is drawn through the **orifice** and wound around the **bobbin.** The tension screw is loosened or tightened in order to move the **mother-of-all** with the **spinning head** or **flyer assembly** closer to the wheel or further away. This slackens, or tightens, the driving band which, in operation, should be just short of taut. At the correct tension, the wheel and pulleys turn easily and the band will not slip off. Also see **German wheel, wool wheel.**

tension stick. Weaving. A thin, flat stick inserted under the **warp end**s in a **frame loom** to permit later adjustment of **warp tension.** Usually there are two of them either taped or tied to the top and bottom of the loom so that they remain in place during the **warping** process. As weaving progresses and the **interlacing** process tightens up the warp, the sticks are removed and the warp is loosened. Depending on the elasticity of the fiber and how tight the tension of the initial warping is, the tension sticks can be put on in layers of two or three.

tentering. Weaving. The drying and stretching of finished fabrics after washing or dyeing. This is done on a frame to avoid **shrinkage** and to bring the cloth to the desired width at the same time the material is straightened or leveled. Moisture makes the fabric supple so that a uniform stretching is possible. The cloth is attached to the frame by tenterhooks going through the **selvage**s and holding it tight, while the wet material is jerked and pulled until the size is maintained. More modern machinery has produced variations on this basic method, which goes back to colonial times, when it was a standard procedure after dyeing. From those times, we get the expression "to be on tenterhooks." Also see **finishing.**

tent stitch. Needlepoint. A term used to include three stitches that look alike on the face of the **canvas** but are executed differently: **basketweave stitch, continental stitch,** and **half cross stitch.** The tent stitch is generally made with a small slanting stitch that crosses one intersection of the canvas. The size of the canvas determines whether the tent stitch is classified as **gros point** (5,7,8), **demi point** (10,12,14,16), or **petit point** (18 and up). Also see **flat stitch, rep stitch.**

tent stitch. Rugmaking. A diagonal stitch without the herringbone effect of the **knitting stitch.** It is also called half cross stitch, petit point and, in an enlarged version, gros point. It should be worked very closely together in order to give a flat surface effect. As one of its names implies, it is half of a **cross stitch.** To work the stitch on **canvas mesh,** insert the needle back to front and then front to back in the first hole above and to the right. Emerge to the front in the hole directly below. Continue on in this manner for the rest of the stitches. The right point of the stitches in this row is in the same hole as the left point of the stitches in the row above. See ill.

Tent stitch

ternary alloy. Jewelry. An **alloy** containing three metals.

terne plate. Metalworking. A sheet-metal product covered with **tin** and **lead** that is used mainly for roofing and tanks. Do not use this metal for crafting any food containers because the lead coat is poisonous.

terra cotta. Ceramics. An unglazed coarse-grained, low-firing, rapid-drying clay, often containing **grog,** that is used for large sculptures and architectural pieces.

terrycloth. Stitchery. A **cotton pile fabric** with uncut loops. It is similar to **turkish towel** material, but may have loops on just one side. It is lighter weight than turkish toweling and is often used in stuffed toys and animals for children, though the loops have a tendency to snag and pull loose.

tertiary color. See **primary color.**

terylene. Quilts. Stitchery. A lightweight, washable, quick-drying, synthetic **wadding** or **padding.**

tessera. Mosaics. Originally a small bit or tablet of wood or other material used as a ticket or token; later, any one of a variety of squarish materials used in the making of a **mosaic.** Tesserae were first imported from the Middle East by Western mosaicists around the middle of the fourth century B.C. Before that time, the mosaics were created from natural stone chips or pebbles. The square-cut tesserae greatly expanded the craftsman's capacity to refine his art inasmuch as the pieces could be much more formally set than could the natural shapes. Also see **Mosaics: Tools and Materials.**

tesserae. Mosaics. See **tessera.**

tesserae. Stained Glass. Small pieces of marble, glass, and shells, traditionally used in **mosaic** work. Also see **Tiffany, Louis Comfort.**

test kiln. Ceramics. A small **kiln** that can fire and cool quickly. Test kilns are useful for testing earthenware glazes.

tête de boeuf. Crewel. Embroidery. A French term meaning the "head of an ox," and descriptive of the stitch. This stitch is a combination of a **detached chain stitch** with two **straight stitch**es on either side.

Work a single detached chain stitch, coming up at A, going back at A again; loop thread under the needle and draw it through at B (**a.**). Go down at C outside the loop to hold it flat (**b.**). Make a pair of slanting stitches on either side of the detached chain, from E to F, and from G to H. The completed stitches may be scattered freely, or arranged in a checkerboard fashion (**c.**). See ill.

a.   b.   c. Tête de boeuf stitch

tetragonal system. Gemcutting. See **crystal.**

Texas. Quilts. See **Texas Lone Star.**

Texas Lone Star. Quilts. (Also called Aunt Eliza's Star, **Eight-Pointed Star,** Lone Star, Texas, **Variable Star.**) A **pieced star pattern** based on a **nine-patch** arrangement of squares and triangles. The pattern is identical for each name, but the arrangement of colors is different, giving the finished **quilt top**s distinctive patterns. See ill.

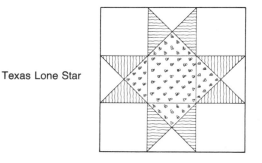

Texas Lone Star

Texas star. Quilts. See **star patterns.**

Texas Tears. Quilts. See **Job's Tears.**

Texas Yellow Rose. Quilts. See **Combination Rose.**

textile. Fabric Printing. See **fabric.**

textile. Stitchery. The **fabric** or material which is formed from **fibers** in any of a variety of methods including bonding, braiding, crocheting, knitting, knotting, **felting,** laminating, and weaving.

textile color. Fabric Printing. Colors for decorating fabrics are composed of either **pigment** or **dye.** Generally, the term refers to the pigment-base colors, or paints, such as the oil-base textile inks available from art-supply stores and craft shops for **block printing, stenciling,** or brushing directly on fabric. They are washable and dry-cleanable, and do not fade. An **extender** is also available to lighten the colors. A **thinner** may be needed, depending upon the printing technique to be used. A solvent is also available for cleaning. Water-base textile ink is also available.

Dye paste—a combination of dye, thickener, and chemicals—can be used for all fabric printing techniques. However, these colors must receive a **fixation** treatment for **fastness** of color.

Directions for use, as well as for any finishing required after printing, come with the colors.

textile ink. Fabric Printing. See **textile color.**

textile paint. Batik and Tie-dye. Stitchery. Toys. (Also called fabric paint.) A paint designed especially for use on **fabric.** Textile paints contain **pigment**s mixed with a vehicle or binder so they can be applied to the fabric. The pigments then coat the **fibers,** in contrast to **dye,** which penetrates the fibers. Most hobby and art supply stores carry several textile or fabric paints.

Silkscreen paints or acrylics both work well on fabric, although they may not leave the material as flexible or pliable as dyes. **Versatex** is a textile paint suitable for many fibers; it is used in **direct-dye painting, batik,** block printing, and airbrushing.

textile printing. Fabric Printing. See **Fabric Printing.**

texture. The structural surface quality of woven fabrics, paintings, or any object, especially insofar as surface effects contribute to the aesthetic appeal of a work. Contrasts of texture from rough to smooth, from **matte** to **gloss,** or from patterned to random are especially effective in sculpicelike work, where changing angles of light to the surfaces help define form.

texture. Ceramics. There are two types of textures that can be achieved in pottery. One is an actual roughness that can be created with the addition of **grog** to a **clay body.** The other texture is a visual one that can be accomplished with **pigment oxide**s added to the clay.

texture. Jewelry. A surface quality, usually one of feel as well as visual. "Smooth" and "rough" are textures. Also see **electric engraving tool, embossing, forging, fusing, liners, matting tools, repoussé, reticulation, stamping.**

texture. Rugmaking. Weaving. The surface quality of a **fabric** that adds a third dimension which can be felt as well as seen. The first meaning of texture is the actual number of **warp end**s and **filling pick**s per inch in a woven cloth. From here, the meaning went on to encompass the "hand" of a fabric, and now it has also come to stand for the appearance of a cloth. In the true sense, every fabric has texture, be it smooth and shiny or rough and dull. However, it is usually only when a surface is rough or irregular that it is alluded to as a fabric with texture. This sort of obvious texture can be achieved through color, **weave,** yarn, **sett,** or **beating. Tweed** fabrics are good examples of texture achieved through mottled coloring and a coarse yarn with a simple weave.

Color blending will aid in producing texture. A **texture weave** can produce an all-over, subtle, irregular surface, or the exaggerated texture of a **honeycomb weave.** A **textured yarn** can make a textured fabric or the texture can be obtained through a combination of yarns of different sizes, **twist**s, **fiber**s, and colors. In the sett and beating, **grouped thread**s in both warp and filling are a simple way to achieve a texture of ridges or **rib**s, while skip denting can give an open, lacy texture.

Texture spoken of in regard to rugs almost always indicates **pile** and especially the long, shaggy **rya**. However, it can also be applied to the rough and nubby surface of **flatweave rug**s woven with coarse **handspun** yarns. In tapestries and **wall hanging**s, texture can mean the addition of pile, knots, loops, **wrapping, soumak,** or unspun wool, to name a few of the inventive means contemporary artists have used to enliven the surface of their cloth. **Napping** the surface and color blending are two of the more usual means. Also see **tapestry, yarn count.**

textured yarns. Spinning. Weaving. Yarns that have an obvious variation in their thickness, i.e., thick and thin yarns. In truth, all yarns have texture, be it smooth or bumpy. However, when the term "textured" is used, it alludes to an irregular surface. Commercially, it is synonymous with **novelty yarns**, since to achieve a textured yarn, it is necessary to use elaborate equipment to obtain the curl, nub, or other surface variety. However, to most handspinners and handweavers, textured has come to mean the thick and thin yarn indicative of certain types of handspinning, and not the easily apparent feature of a novelty yarn. Textured yarns should not be confused with "texturized yarns," which alludes to the **filament** texturizing of synthetic yarns.

texture weave. Weaving. A **weave** having an all-over uneven or broken surface, yet not following any recognizable pattern even when repeated. **Crepe weave** is a good example of a texture weave. Experimental **threadings**, when used in combination with random **treadlings**, will often give interesting texture.

texturing. Candlemaking. Modifying the surface of a candle for decorative purposes either by adding **additives** to the wax before pouring or by working on the surface of the finished candle. Also see **decorating, mottling oil, pinching, sand candle.**

texturized yarns. Spinning. Weaving. See **textured yarns.**

Thai silk. Stitchery. Pure **silk** handwoven **fabric,** made originally for Siamese royalty. It is available in rich colors and **plain weave.**

Thames tunnel. Toys. One of a series of **viewing toy**s or **optical toy**s based on the principles of perspective. This one, made of paper, lets the viewer peer through an opening at one end, as with a **proscenium toy.** A series of papers, spaced apart at equal distances, shows a pair of arches, each cut out to allow the view to go beyond. Cut paper figures and similar additions are placed in the arches. The viewer sees through the series and the arrangement gives an illusion of looking a great distance. Also see **Toys: Optical Toys.**

thaumatrope. Toys. One of the first **optical toy**s, invented in 1925. It consists of a paper disk with different images on each of the two sides. When rotated rapidly the images flow together. The thaumatrope is twirled by means of **string**s attached to each side of the disk. When the strings are twisted, pulling on the string creates tension that makes the string untwist, thereby spinning the disk and visually binding the images. See ill. Also see **buzz button** and **Toys: Optical Toys.**

The two sides of a thaumatrope

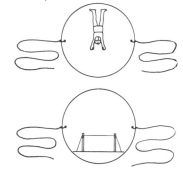

theorem work. Stenciling. (Also called Poona work.) Stenciled floral still-life pictures. Theorem work was a popular pastime in the nineteenth century. Dimension was added to the composition with **shading.** The outlines of the designs were traced on oil paper and a stencil was cut and then colored with ordinary water color. Then the design was fixed by brushing over it with a solution of gum arabic. These floral arrangements were often painted on velvet backgrounds and were also popular for making valentines. Also see **Stenciling: Designing and Cutting.**

thermal bonding. Plastics. See **heat bonding.**

thermal conductivity. Ceramics. The rate at which heat passes through a material. High thermal conductivity is desired in **kiln furniture** but not in the walls of the **kiln.**

thermal fastening. Plastics. See **heat bonding.**

thermal shock. Ceramics. The reaction that bodies, glazes, or **oxides** undergo during firing and that is reversed during cooling. Thermal shock is an important factor in **ovenware** because uncontrolled oven temperatures can cause damage. Too rapid cooling of a glaze can cause thermal shock and **crazing.** Also see **coefficient of expansion, spalling.**

thermal shock. Glasswork. The condition that glass is said to be in when the glass has been cooled too quickly from a heated or molten state. Usually thermal shock is sufficient to produce fractures in glass pieces. Thermal shock can also occur if glass pieces are heated too quickly. **Borosilicate glass** is especially resistant to thermal shock, as is **silica glass,** because of a tendency not to shrink in cooling. Also see **annealing.**

thermocouple. Ceramics. The activating part of a **pyrometer.** Two strips of dissimilar wire alloys are joined at one end. When the alloys get hot, a small electric current is set up in the circuit, which increases with the rise of temperature. This increase can be read on a pyrometer.

thermoforming. Plastics. (Also called heat forming.) A forming process of heating a **thermoplastic** in an oven or with a heating element until it softens, and then bending or shaping it while it is hot, either by hand or mechanically. Several shaping processes may be used. In oven forming, the plastic is softened in an oven and shaped; in **drape forming,** the heated sheet is draped over a form. In vacuum forming, the sheet is draped over a form and a vacuum machine under the **pattern** sucks the plastic down. **Blow molding** is a variation whereby the plastic sheet is blown onto the form. Also see **cold forming** and **Plastics: Thermoforming and Molding.**

thermohardening plastic. Plastics. See **thermosetting plastic.**

thermometer. Candlemaking. A heat-resistant thermometer, such as a candy thermometer, is a critical tool for candlemakers. It is suggested that it be placed in the melting pot before the **wax** begins to melt, in order to avoid damage by sudden exposure to the relatively high heat required to melt wax.

thermoplastic. Plastics. (Also called thermosoftening plastic.) Any plastic that will soften when heated and reharden when cooled. If heated beyond a certain point, however, it will decompose. Most thermoplastics can be dissolved by specific **solvents.** Examples of thermoplastics are **acrylic,** nylon, **vinyl, cellulose acetate, polyethylene, polypropylene,** and **polystyrene.**

thermosetting plastic. Plastics. Woodworking. (Also called thermohardening plastic.) Any plastic that will not soften when heated but will stay rigid until it reaches decomposition temperature. Examples are **epoxy, polyester, silicone plastic,** and **alkyd** plastics.

thermosoftening plastic. Plastics. See **thermoplastic.**

thickener. Batik and Tie-dye. A gel-like medium that can be added to **dyestuff.** It gives the **dye** a consistency that enables it to be painted onto the **fabric** for **direct-dye painting** or printing. Some companies produce thickeners for specific dyes. **Alginate thickeners,** for example, can be mixed by the dyer for use in **fiber-reactive dyes.**

thickener. Fabric Printing. A substance, such as a gum or starch, that is added to a **dye paste** to give it the consistency needed for applying to or printing on the fabric, and to keep the color contained within the design area. Gum arabic, gum tragacanth, and starch tragacanth are common thickeners.

thickening agent. Fabric Printing. See **thickener.**

thickening the edge. Metalworking. See **raising technique.**

thick oil. China and Glass Painting. See **fat oil of turpentine.**

thimble. Stitchery. (Also called thimmel.) A device used in sewing to aid in forcing a **needle** through **fabric.** It is a cap that fits over the end of the middle finger of the right hand (if the stitcher is right-handed). Commonly made of silver, brass, or steel, more unusual ones are of ivory, gold, leather, bone, iron, and china. Also see **Chinese thimble.**

thimmel. Stitchery. See **thimble.**

thinner. Fabric Printing. A liquid that is mixed with a **dye paste** or **textile color** to thin the consistency. Instructions for mixing and thinning are available from the manufacturer of the color. However, as a general rule, water-base colors are thinned with water and oil-base colors are thinned with turpentine.

thinner. Plastics. Woodworking. See **solvent.**

thinning prints. Découpage. A technique for making **prints** on heavy paper suitable for use in découpage by peeling away layers of paper from the back to reduce thickness. Dab white vinegar with a sponge on the back of the print. Separate the layers of paper at a corner or rub gently with fingers on the back to peel off layers of the thick backing. Allow the print to dry before applying **sealer.** Also see **razor thinning.**

third hand. Jewelry. (Also called mounted tweezers.) A device for holding metal pieces for **soldering** and **polishing** operations that frees the jeweler's hands. It consists of a heavy base onto which is usually mounted two ball-and-socket joints for maneuverability. Also on the base is mounted another unit with a slot and **thumbscrew** into which **cross-locking tweezers** and **clamps** can be affixed. Some units hold one pair of tweezers; others, two. In a complex soldering situation, because it is desirable to solder all pieces in one operation, as many as 15−20 third hands can be used at one time. See ill.

Third hand with cross-locking tweezers

thixotropic. Plastics. (Also called thixo.) An **additive** that causes **resin** to set. The resin becomes liquid when stirred, but reverts to its gelatin form when left standing. Thixotropic is added to **laminating resins** so that they won't run when applied to vertical surfaces. **Cabosil** is an example of a thixotropic agent. Also see **Plastics: Laminating.**

thong. Leather. A strip of leather, usually of **rawhide** or **latigo,** used for heavy-duty lacing or for binding or finishing work.

thong. Stitchery. Toys. A long, narrow strip of leather, sometimes used for lacing or fastening. For toys it is often used as a **pull string.**

thonging chisel. Leather. A tool for punching thong slits in leather as preparation for hand sewing or lacing. This tool is available with 1–8 evenly spaced thong slits, which make slits rather than holes for lacing. To use a one-prong thonging chisel, mark a line where you want the stitching on the leather. Hold the thonging chisel upright on the leather along the stitching line and strike it with a **mallet** or **striking stick.** Pierce the leather cleanly. If you are using a multiple prong chisel, place the first prong of the chisel in the last-punched slit as you advance the tool to achieve even spacing. The four-prong round hole punch is commonly used to accommodate round lacing. A diagonal thonging chisel is also available, with prongs placed to make diagonal slits rather than straight ones. A stitching punch is a tool similar to the thonging chisel and can be used the same way. See ill. Also see **drive punch** and **Leatherwork: Care and Maintenance of Tools, Sewing Leather, Tools and Materials.**

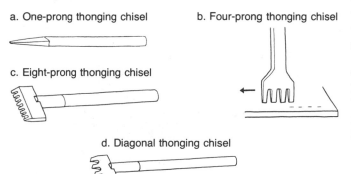

a. One-prong thonging chisel   b. Four-prong thonging chisel

c. Eight-prong thonging chisel

d. Diagonal thonging chisel

Thousand Pyramids. Quilts. (Also called Triangles.) A pieced **one-patch** design of equilateral triangles. When these one-patches are joined **hit-or-miss** they make an **all-over** quilt design. See ill.

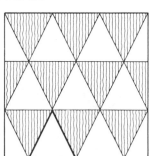

Thousand Pyramids

thread. Beadwork. Strong thread, such as nylon or strong linen, should be used. Special beading thread is available at hobby shops. Because manufacturers' size designations vary, experimentation may be necessary to find the correct thread for a particular use. For stringing beads, fish cord or dental floss may be used, but for **bead embroidery** or **bead weaving,** lightweight, strong thread is essential. For bead weaving, strong twisted nylon or buttonhole thread (waxed with **beeswax**) is used.

thread. Bookbinding. Thread drawn over **beeswax** is used to bind **sections** and **boards** together. Cones of #20 unbleached linen, and #25 bleached linen are available at bookbinders' supply houses. Heavy-duty button or carpet thread may be substituted.

thread. Leather. Many types of thread and **lacing** are used for stitching leather. Bookbinder's thread, saddler's thread, Dacron thread, or carpet thread is used for heavy-duty sewing and for items to receive stress. Fishing line is also useful for hand sewing. Linen thread is decorative and moderately strong. For machine sewing, nylon thread or cotton-covered polyester thread is available in all sewing shops. Dacron thread is used in the shoe industry.

Thread is often waxed by drawing it across a cake of beeswax before stitching, to strengthen and to prevent tangling. A sturdy, all-purpose prewaxed thread is available in several colors and thicknesses. To facilitate threading waxed thread through a needle with a small eye, unravel the ends of the thread and place them on the worktable. Lay the blade of a knife on top of the ends at a right angle to the table. Pull the ends of the thread under the knife to shave off excess. Then twist the thinned ends together and run them through a cake of beeswax. This thinned point will thread readily. Also see **harness needle** and **Leatherwork: Sewing Leather, Tools and Materials.**

thread. Spinning. Weaving. A **spun yarn** that is fine and hard, has considerable **twist,** and is **plied.** The term "thread" has sometimes come to refer to all sewing, basting, darning, or embroidery elements. It also is often used interchangeably with **yarn,** as when one speaks of "**warp** threads" and "**weft** threads." However, thread is a finer, more tightly and smoothly twisted and "finished" (in the sense of processing) strand of **fibers** than yarn. It is yarn that has been carefully drawn into a slender strand and then made into a fine **cord** by plying two or more of the strands.

thread. Stitchery. See **sewing thread.**

thread. Tatting. Thread for tatting should be tightly twisted and without knots or rough places, so the knots will slip easily when drawing up the **knot bearer** or closing the **ring.** Tatting thread or a good grade of crochet thread is suitable. Experienced tatters can use more of a variety of threads. The ombré thread, with its variegated shades of color, is very pretty for a dainty **edging.**

thread carrier. Weaving. See **back beam.**

thread count. Weaving. The number of threads or yarns in a square inch of fabric. Two numbers make up the thread count—one for the number of **warp ends** and the other for the number of **filling picks.** The amount of each per square inch is less when measured on the loom than when measured after the fabric is washed, shrunk, or otherwise finished.

threaded. Crewel. Embroidery. A threaded or interlaced stitch is worked over another stitch, such as **back stitch,**

chain stitch, or running stitch, by coming up through the background fabric at the beginning and weaving in and out of the original stitches. The interlacing does not pass through the fabric again until the end of the row, nor is it pulled tightly, as it acts as a decorative embellishment to the existing stitch. Another color may be used in the reverse direction to make the stitch even more decorative. Also see backstitch threaded, interlaced cable chain stitch, wave stitch.

threading. Weaving. Common name for drawing-in on a harness loom. It also refers to other looms as, for example, threading or pulling through the warp ends on a rigid heddle loom, or through the cards used for card weaving.

threading beads. Beadwork. Because most of the beadwork techniques are worked with threaded beads, an easy technique of transferring beads from the purchased string to the working thread or yarn is essential. The string on which the beads are strung can be joined to the working thread or yarn with a weaver's knot; beads are then passed easily onto the thread and are ready to be worked. If loose beads are used and the working yarn is too thick to go through a needle, thread a fine sewing needle with thread, with the ends knotted together. Pull the yarn through the thread loop thus formed. Pick up the beads on the needle and thread them onto the thread, then onto the yarn.

threading draft. Weaving. See drawing-in draft.

threading hook. Weaving. See reed hook.

threading the needle. Crewel. Embroidery. Needlepoint. Wrap the thread around the needle and pinch the thread tightly between the thumb and finger. Pull the needle out and continue to hold the now-folded thread firmly. Press the eye of the needle onto the thread; when the thread appears through the eye, pull it through. See ill.

Threading the needle

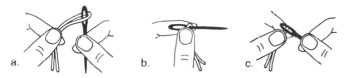

threading through the heddles. Weaving. See drawing-in.

Three Crosses. Quilts. (Also called Cross-upon-Cross, Golgotha.) A pieced block pattern showing a narrow cross overlapping a wider cross, with a square set between them. The cross goes diagonally across the square block.

three-dimensional puzzle. Toys. A simple jigsaw puzzle cut from thick wood and designed in such a way that the parts themselves become playthings or toys that can stand on edge individually.

three-dimensional weaving. Weaving. Woven pieces that are fully rounded forms in that the viewer can walk around them and observe them from all sides. Pieces of this type can be worked coming off a harness loom and then constructed into a three-dimensional form or can be made off-loom. Three-dimensional weaving on a harness loom uses mainly double cloth or multiple-layered cloth (3, 4, or more layers) that is stuffed to shape or held apart with armatures, frames, or wires in order to realize a form. When constructing the shape directly off loom, the basic weaving techniques and many other techniques such as plaiting, knotting, etc., are usually incorporated and the piece is more properly classified as fiber sculpture. Three-dimensional weaving primarily concerns itself with fiber sculpture; however, it should not be forgotten that a pillow or purse is also a three-dimensional object.

An older and more traditional meaning of three-dimensional weaving alludes to the use of texture weaves to make the surface of a fabric other than absolutely flat.

Three-in-One-Quilt. Quilts. A design for a pieced quilt that utilizes three different block designs into its all-over pattern: a nine-patch, a four-patch, and the eight-pointed star. They are joined in such a way that points of the stars touch, with the four-patch set diagonally between the rows of stars and the nine-patch set vertically between the diagonals of the stars.

three-layered fabric. Weaving. See triple cloth.

three-patch. Quilts. A block for a pieced quilt that consists of three equal rectangles of different colors joined in any of various ways. When sewn one above the other to form a larger rectangle, they can be outlined in black or some other solid color, as in Roman Squares. Some Victorian crazy quilts were made up from three-patch blocks.

Another three-patch is made up to form a square. One side of the square forms the base of a triangle with the point touching the center of the opposite side. This leaves two small triangles, one on each side. This block can be set in any of a variety of ways to form sawtooth, or zigzag, patterns or a Streak of Lightning arrangement.

threepenny. Basketry. A six-foot willow rod.

three-ply coil. Basketry. See waling.

three-quarter binding. Bookbinding. A binding similar to half-binding but with a greater proportion of leather on the sides.

three-rod plain border. Basketry. See Basketry: Woven Basket Construction.

three-rod wale. Basketry. See waling.

three-rod weave. Basketry. See waling.

three-row crossover. Beadwork. See continuous crossover loop.

three-square file. Metalworking. See **file.**

three-way dopping block. Gemcutting. See **dopping.**

throstle machine. Spinning. See **spinning.**

throw. Ceramics. To make pottery by hand using a **potter's wheel.** Also see **Ceramics: Throwing.**

throw. Quilts. See **slumber robes.**

throwing clay. Ceramics. See **Ceramics: Clay.**

throwing gauge. Ceramics. See **pot gauge.**

throwing off the mound. Ceramics. (Also called stack throwing.) An often used production technique that involves throwing many forms off one large lump of clay on the **potter's wheel.** A small bit of clay at the top of the mound is formed into a pot and removed with wire. The mound is then recentered, and the process is repeated until all the clay is used up. Also see **Ceramics: Centering.**

throwing process. Spinning. See **spun yarn.**

throwing stick. Ceramics. Interior **rib** used in throwing. It is commonly used in Japan and called "egote." See ill. Also see **Ceramics: Throwing.**

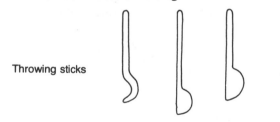

Throwing sticks

thrown out. Bookbinding. A page or map is said to be "thrown out" when it is guarded so that it may be pulled to lie outside of the **foredge** line of the text.

throw shuttle. Weaving. See **boat shuttle.**

thrummed rug. Rugmaking. An old sailor's method of making rope mats by poking short bits of raveled rope (and occasionally yarn) through a **canvas** backing so that a type of **pile** results. These "thrum" mats were put on a ship's rigging to keep the ropes from chafing in the wind. "Thrum" was used as a verb denoting the process of poking through the short pieces of rope. It is thought that the craft of rug hooking originated with thrumming, since a rug hook is similar to a marlinespike tool sailors used in ropework. Also see **hooked rug, pegged rug.**

thrumming. Jewelry. A technique of **hand polishing** used to reach difficult or nearly inaccessible areas. A length of string or cord—cotton, or nylon for longer wear—is held in a **vise** at one end or tied around anything stationary. The string is held taut and coated with a **buffing compound.** The work is then pulled back and forth across the taut string. The string also may be threaded through a pierced area in the work and used in the same fashion, or the work could be held stationary while the string is pulled back and forth. Also see **buffing.**

thrums. Needlepoint. Remnants of wool thread sold by the pound by carpet manufacturers and used by needleworkers for making needlepoint rugs. Also see **Needlepoint: Materials.**

thrums. Weaving. The lengths of **warp end**s that remain unwoven after the fabric has been finished and cut off the **loom.** This is calculated as part of **loom waste,** but in actuality it need not be waste, since thrums can be used as **filling** in **rag-rug** weaving, for **knotted pile** rug weaving, and to make **fringe** on all types of weaving. In the case of rag-rug weaving, where the thrums are used as a whole group of yarns, the groups are spliced where necessary. Thrums are the last end of the warp, and although there is waste yarn remaining at the beginning end of the warp, it is usually not long enough to be of any use. Thrums can be bought from certain yarn dealers or factory outlet stores at a much lower cost than regular yarn, which is sold in continuous yard lengths. Also see **splicing, yarn calculations.**

thumb pots. Ceramics. See **Ceramics: Hand-building.**

thumbscrew. Jewelry. A screw with an end specially designed so that it may be turned with the thumb and fingers. Also see **sawframe.**

thummel. Stitchery. A leather **thimble** in use during the Middle Ages and called, during the fourteenth century, a "themel." The leather piece was sewn up one side and had a stitch-on cap. Also see **sailor's palm.**

thunderbolt. Toys. See **bull-roarer.**

thunder-spell. Toys. See **bull-roarer.**

thunderstick. Toys. See **bull-roarer.**

ticking. Stitchery. (Also called pillow ticking.) Strong, durable, closely woven **fabric** in a plain or twill weave, commonly used to cover mattresses and cushions or **pillow**s. It has a characteristic stripe pattern woven into the material. There are various kinds of needlework and cross-stitching done on striped ticking that are known as **ticking work.**

ticking work. Stitchery. An embroidery made to resemble Oriental work. **Silk**s, braids, and **ribbon**s are used on striped **ticking** to make mats, **pillow**s, and screens.

ticktack. Toys. An **American folk toy** made from a notched wooden spool. It is a **noisemaker** or a **sound toy,** traditionally used as a Halloween toy. A spindle is run through the hole in the spool, which has sharp notches cut around each edge. A **string** is wrapped around the spool and one hand is used to hold the spindle so that the spool is against a windowpane. The other hand grasps and pulls the string, causing the spool to roll and create a loud clacking on the glass. Sometimes the spindle is attached to a handle. A large nail can be used as the spindle with the head of the nail serving to hold the spool in place. The toy is sometimes referred to as a ratchet spool or a window knocker.

Tic-Tac-Toe. Quilts. See **Shoo-fly.**

tidy pins. Macramé. See **upholsterer's pins.**

tie. Stenciling. See **stay.**

tied. Batik and Tie-dye. A **fabric** that has been bound with any of various **binding material**s to prepare it for the dyeing process in **tie-dye.** The fabric usually remains tied until the **rinsing** is completed, and sometimes until the fabric is dry and the **dye** has **set.**

tie-down. Weaving. A thread that is placed in a certain position in the **drawing-in draft** so that it will hold down long **filling floats.**

tied quilt. Quilts. Not a true **quilt,** as no **quilting stitch**es are used, but the tied quilt does consist of the usual three layers: **quilt top, filler,** and **backing.** The layers are tied and thus held securely together, giving a puffy effect to the bedcover. This type of quilt is often referred to as a **comforter.** The tying may be done with any strong cord—buttonhole twist, pearl **cotton,** or **linen** thread. Some quilters like to use a **wool** yarn so that when the quilt is washed the yarn will shrink and tighten.

To tie, yarn or cord is threaded and left without a knot. The needle is placed so that it goes straight down through all layers and then is brought straight back up, right next to the first stitch. The yarn is cut, allowing enough for tying. The two raw, or loose, ends are tied in a secure square knot. Some quilters prefer to take an additional tiny stitch over the knot for added strength. The ties should be placed within a few inches of each other if **batting** is used as a filler. A glazed batting will shift less in washing. A Dacron or other synthetic blanket or a bonded **Dacron polyester batting** used as a filler will not shift at all, so fewer ties are required. The knots can appear on the front or back (**a.**); a bead or button can be added with the tying, usually with the tie on the bottom and the bead on the front (**b.**). See ill.

Tied quilting

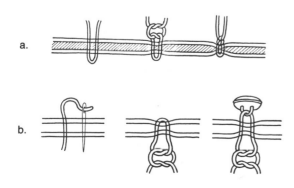

tie-dye. Batik and Tie-dye. Either the resist dyeing process of tie-dye or the fabric or the article produced by that method. An article of clothing, such as a shirt, treated by this process is sometimes referred to as a tie-dye. Also see **Batik and Tie-dye: Tie-dye.**

tie-dyeing. Dyeing. Weaving. See **ikat.**

tie in. Basketry. See **tying in.**

tie off ends. Tatting. (Also called splicing threads.) The term for the finishing process of severing the knotting and cutting off the ends of threads of a piece of tatting. When a unit or a row has been finished and a fine thread has been used, it is usually sufficient to tie a **reef knot** and cut off the ends. If heavier threads are used and knots would show too much, tie a small knot, lightly stitch the ends down to hold, and cut off.

When the thread on the shuttle is used up, wind another shuttle, tie the ends in a reef knot, continue to tat, and then go back and cut off the ends after they are worked into the tatting. It is best to join threads at a closing of a **ring** or at the end of a **chain;** in that way the knot made to join the threads will not hinder the pulling up of the thread to close the ring.

tie-on knot. Weaving. The knot used to attach the **warp ends** in groups to the front **apron bar** on the **cloth beam.** A group of warp ends goes over the apron bar and under the group, then is divided in half and tied in a single knot on top of the group. A second tying is not done until the **warp tension** has been adjusted on all the groups. At that time, a single bowknot can be tied, or a double knot. The first has the advantage of being easily untied to further adjust the tension or correct errors. The second retards the slippage of yarns that have no friction. See ill. Also see **tying-on.**

Tie-on knot

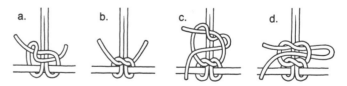

a.   b.   c.   d.

tie-up. Weaving. The process and order of attaching the **harness**es to the **treadle**s so that the harnesses can be raised or lowered. The order is shown in some manner on **graph paper** and, although the treadle can be attached directly to a harness, it is more likely that the treadle is attached to the **lam** of the harness. The term applies to a **floor loom** only and can be as simple as a direct tie-up which, in a four-harness loom, means that every treadle is attached to only one harness. This allows for a great diversity in the weaving since as many treadles as desired can be pushed down with each **pick** and the combination of treadles can also be changed with every pick. More complex is the indirect tie-up, which is the attaching of harnesses to treadles in the combinations needed for a specific weave. The advantage is that only one foot is used in the **treadling** for each **shed** opening so speed and rhythm are attained. But in a 4-harness loom there are only 6 treadles, so the limit is 6 combinations. The indirect tie-up is used in **multiharness** weaving where the feet cannot extend over all the needed treadles. There is also the standard tie-up, which includes a **twill tie-up** with 2 treadles attached for a **plain weave.** The order in which the treadles are pressed is called the **treadling sequence.** Also see **balanced tie-up, countermarch loom, drafts, lams, treadling sequence, twill tie-up.**

tie-up cords. Weaving. The cords that connect the **treadles** and **lams** in a **floor loom.** The simplest tie-up cords are two pieces of strong nylon or cotton cord that go through drilled holes, or screw eyes, found in both the lams and treadles. The two pieces attach together in a **snitch knot.** Refinements have been made by adding snap hooks like those found on dog leashes to one end of each cord so that they attach easily to the screw eyes. Another refinement is to add snap hooks to both ends of two loops of cord, so that the loops not only snap onto the lam and treadle, but are then snapped together, replacing a snitch knot. Chains can be used instead of cords with the snap hooks. Still other looms have metal rods that connect through a hole in both lam and treadle. These never need to be adjusted in length. Cords stretch when in use and need adjusting, but they are not as noisy as chains, nor do they slip out of holes as a metal connector might.

Tiffany, Louis Comfort. Stained Glass. Born February 18, 1848, in New York City, he lived there most of his life until his death in 1933. He was a painter, interior decorator, architect, and landscapist, and proficient in many other media as well. The eldest son of Charles Tiffany, who founded the well-known jewelry firm of Tiffany & Co., he is best remembered for his beautiful **opalescent glass,** or **Favrile glass,** first produced in 1893, and for his daring, inventive creations in stained glass. It was his determined intention to create glass that incorporated brilliant colors and varied textures.

During Tiffany's period hot glass was punched, pressed, squeezed with tools, and stamped with dies to produce wrinkled, bulging, and concave pieces of glass. One of the methods by which Tiffany himself produced jewellike glass was by scattering irregular bits of colored glass on a metal rolling table and then pouring either white or colored molten glass over the table and rolling it down, thus embedding the colored pieces in the glass sheet. He also used the technique of pressing molten glass into faceted molds to produce brilliant pieces of cut glass that, when set into a window, would change their shade of color according to the viewing angle.

Tiffany first used opalescent glass in combination with **antique glass** in a window produced for the Episcopal Church of Islip, Long Island. Tiffany windows were generally marked in the lower-right-hand corner. Most Tiffany windows made before 1892 are marked "Tiffany Glass Company." "Tiffany Glass and Decorating Company" was the inscription used between 1892 and 1900. "Tiffany Studios" or "Louis C. Tiffany" was used after 1900.

Another form developed by Tiffany was the glass **mosaic** designed for mounting on a wall. These mosaics embedded iridescent glass, mother-of-pearl, and transparent, gold-backed **tessera**e in the surface of a **cement** mortar slab with a white backing that reflected a soft luminous light through the glass.

Tiffany's lasting contribution was his demonstration that useful objects and necessities could also be designed and executed as art forms. He attempted to offer quality objects to the largest possible audience by training his designers and workers to work independently in producing as many beautiful objects as possible.

Tiffany foil method. Stained Glass. See **copper foiling** and **Stained Glass.**

Tiffany lamp construction method. Stained Glass. See **lampshade construction.**

TIG. Metalworking. See **welding.**

tiger cowrie. Shell Carving. (*Cypraea tigris.*) A shell with a mottled brown and white exterior layer, a white **middle color,** and a dark brown **ground color,** used for cameo carving. Also see **cowrie, helmet** and **Shell Carving: Shell, Tools and Preparation, Cameo Carving.**

Tiger Lily. Quilts. See **Lily.**

tiger's eye. Gemcutting. See **quartz.**

tight-backed. Bookbinding. A term indicating that the material that covers the **back edge** of the book is glued directly onto the **back.**

tight tie. Weaving. See **choke.**

tile. Ceramics. A flat or curved piece of tile clay. Handmade ceramic tiles can be cut from a large **slab** of clay.

tile. Mosaics. A thin, flat piece of fired clay, most often square or rectangular in shape, sold commercially as **ceramic tile, floor tile,** or **porcelain tile,** for flooring or bathroom walls. Glazed and unglazed varieties of tile can be purchased in most building-supply outlets. Although far inferior to **smalti** or **pressed glass,** tile is a relatively cheap **mosaic** material that can be creatively used by the skillful mosaicist. Also see **tessera** and **Mosaics: Tools and Materials.**

tile grout. Stained Glass. See **grout.**

timber. Woodworking. See **wood.**

tin. Dyeing. A **mordanting** agent of stannous chloride crystals in white powder form. It is a **mordant** used with others in dyeing as, for example, with **alum** in order to brighten colors—a process called **blooming.** In the past, it was used principally with **cochineal** in order to obtain a brilliant scarlet. Too much tin can, however, makes wool brittle and harsh.

tin. Metalworking. A soft, shiny-white, **malleable** metal that has little **tensile strength** and is mainly used as an **alloying** metal. It may also be used in sheet form when **raising**

forms by hammering. It does not **work-harden** when hammered cold, but softens. Restore the hardness by **annealing** at 437° F. Tin is resistant to organic acids and is therefore used for food containers. It may be soldered with a soft **solder** that melts at below 450° F, or with antimonial tin solder if the presence of **lead** is considered dangerous.

tin. Tincrafting. A soft, silvery white, crystalline metallic element that is malleable at room temperature and capable of taking a high polish. Tin oxide was mined as far back as 1500 B.C. for the production of bronze and pewter. It was discovered that tin was highly resistant to organic food acids, which in turn resulted in its use as a plating material for bronze and copper cooking and storage utensils. Thanks to its corrosion-resistant property, tin is still widely used as a coating, be it ever so thin, for steel sheet in the making of the modern **tin can.** Also see **Tincrafting.**

tin can. Tincrafting. A common container used for the storage of corrosive foodstuffs, until quite recently formed by dipping sheet steel in a hot tin bath. Today, as a result of the tremendous increase in the price of tin, many can manufacturers are either electrolytically plating the sheet metal with an extremely thin tracing of tin or substituting chemical coatings for the tin. Also see **Tincrafting: Tools and Materials.**

TINCRAFTING

Tincrafting, as the term indicates, is simply the craft of creating objects out of **tin plate.** Tin itself is known to have been mined in and around Cornwall by the Romans. The refined tin-oxide ore was used primarily in the making of bronze, but the Romans discovered that tin is particularly resistant to corrosion from organic acids, and they coated many of their copper and bronze cooking utensils with the metal.

Tin plate as we know it now was first manufactured in sixteenth-century Germany. The process, which involved coating a thin sheet of rolled iron plate with an even thinner layer of tin, produced a relatively crude but direct precursor of the tinplated material used today. Tinplating in England, and eventually mass tinsmithing activities in the American colonies, can be traced back to the development of superior iron rolling machines at Pontypool, England. A desire on the part of the iron rollers to produce a local tin plate led to the importation of the German tinplating process. In the eighteenth century, English production of tin plate had surpassed the German output on a quality basis.

The founding father of Yankee tinsmithing was Edward **Pattison,** a Scotsman by birth, who had been a pewter apprentice in England. Emigrating to the colonies, Pattison settled in Berlin, Connecticut, where he set up what appears to have been the first tincrafting shop in America. Prior to this, the colonists had either imported their **tinware,** or made do with items of pewter, iron, or wood. Pattison's business expanded to the point where almost all the people living in Berlin were involved in some aspect of tinsmithing.

Tincrafts, as a result, flourished during the latter half of the eighteenth century through the nineteenth century in this country. By the late 1800s, the United States was importing more tin than any other country in the world.

Tinware, produced in the Northeast, was carried to every part of the American continent by the fabled "Yankee peddler." The peddlers traveled everywhere in their own wagons (made for the trade) and they bartered their wares for wool, hides, hair, fur, flax, tallow, or even feathers. When the wares were gone, they headed home to sell the goods for real cash.

Today only the legend and a handful of full-time tinsmiths are left. Modern industry and modern metals and materials have replaced tin in the making of utilitarian objects, and the tincrafter is free to create objects that please the senses rather than serve the needs of the home. Modern tincrafts are much more likely to be decorative objects, such as those made by Mexican tinsmiths.

TOOLS AND MATERIALS   There was a time when tin sheet or **tin plate** was a relatively simple commodity to come by, but times have changed. If one is lucky, a retailer of tin sheet may be listed in your Yellow Pages. If not, the **tin can** that was about to be discarded will do just fine. Incidentally, today's tin can material is most likely sheet steel that may, or may not, have been quickly passed through an electrolytic bath of tin to produce a minute trace of tin on the surface. Tinned or not, the modern material works just about as well as old-time plate, and it sometimes comes with colored lacquer coatings inside (in place of the tin) that can be used for decorative effect.

Preparing the tin can for tincrafting is fairly easy, if the right kind of can opener is used. Not all can openers will remove the top and bottom can rims as efficiently as one would like; if a new can opener must be purchased, shop around and run a small test to see which type fits most easily over the rim of the can. A local hardware store should have a good supply of various can openers.

Once the can is opened, you will need cutting **snips,** shaping **pliers,** a **ball-peen hammer,** an **awl,** a small selection of concave shaping surfaces or bowls, a means for joining your material (riveting devices, or **soldering** equipment), some kind of drawing materials for creating and transferring your design to the tin, and your choice of materials for finishing the tin with decorative coatings.

The kinds of snips used in tin cutting can make all the difference. Basically, there are three types: Plain-edge snips make smooth cuts, like a big knife would make. Fine-toothed or fine-**serrated snips** leave behind a slightly crimped or finely beaded edge. Coarse-toothed snips produce a rougher but much more dramatic edge. Ideally the complete tinsmith shop would have one of each type mentioned. But for the beginner, the fine-toothed version is perhaps the best as a first tool. Theoretically you could work without pliers, but pliers do serve a distinct function; they are the shapers that twist, bend, crimp, and roll the cut tin into the final form. Two types of pliers are available: Needle-nose pliers are flat on the inside and are used for grabbing and **flattening** the tin; round-nose pliers are used for rolling the tin into cylindrical or conical shapes. Both are extremely handy for your shaping operations.

An awl or ice pick used for scribing, **scoring,** and **punching** holes is almost as mandatory as the ball-peen hammer. **Hammering** the tin to either flatten or round it is a basic part of the craft. While tin will naturally curve upward when hit with a hammer, the presence of a concave surface, such as a **dapping block,** or chopping bowl, will greatly simplify any rounding process.

Tracing paper for making patterns and transferring them to the tin should also be on hand. If the project involves joining several pieces of tin, some type of bonding material should be available. Epoxy glues will hold tin together, as will certain clear cements. However, the traditional technique for joining tin is soldering. **Solder, flux,** and either a **soldering iron** or a **propane torch** are all needed for this operation.

Finally, if the tin is to be covered by **japanning** with **varnish** or lacquer, or painted with a decorative effect, suitable materials must be in stock. This subject is covered more completely below.

SETTING UP A WORKSHOP   The setting up of a full-scale Edward Pattison-type tinsmith shop with a heavy-duty rolling machine, crimpers, and large-scale cutting devices is probably beyond the means of the average craftsperson. This, however, by no means rules out tincrafting on a slightly more realistic (and simplified) level. Using readily available tools, a wide range of objects can be made of tin, with discarded tin cans serving as the basic material. The only specific requirement for a workshop is a table sturdy enough to withstand the force of endless hammer blows struck during **hammering** or **punching** operations. In essence, a strong table (with the surface protected, if need be) and a good quality, wall-type can opener prove to be the foundation for the shop.

PREPARING THE TIN CAN   The **tin can** should be soaked in hot water until the label and any surface glue float free; then it is polished lightly with a fine grade of steel wool to remove all surface dirt. Polishing tin cans that have lacquered insides (if the lacquer color is to be used for its decorative effect) must be done very carefully with soft cloths and soap.

To shape a cleaned round can into a flat surface, the lids and both rims must be removed. Rims and lids should be saved, as they are quite useful in creating decorative objects. Remove the lids carefully with a can opener. To remove the rims, the can should be positioned on its side in the can opener so that the underside (or can side) of the rim fits completely under the cutting wheel. Most top-grade openers can handle this operation. With the rims removed, a seam cut should be made to open up the can. This can best be accomplished by cutting up the left side of the seam (if you are right-handed) so the more flexible nonseam side of the can may be manipulated with the left hand as the right one holds the snips. To avoid the possibility of mismatches in the cut, it is best to continue through with the cut from one end to the other rather than to cut part way from one end and part way from the other. Once the cylinder has been cut through, the entire seam can be cut away. **Flattening** the can is done with gentle bendings and then not-so-gentle stompings with the foot until it begins to lie flat, at which point the sheet should be hammered carefully—first on one side, then on the other—until you have a flat piece of **tin plate.**

Hammering is both an important and pleasurable part of tincrafting. Not only does it flatten and smooth the surfaces and the edges of the tin, but it also tends to make the tin more malleable for further shaping. Tin responds to hammering. It will bend, curve, or flatten with each stroke. Hammering the tin from one side only will cause the tin to curve slightly upward, toward the striking force. If a completely flat surface is desired, equal blows should be dealt on both sides of the can. To create raised or depressed surfaces, a curved bowl-like **dapping block** and the rounded end of the ball-peen hammer should be used. Many small blows will force the tin to your will. Be delicate and patient, and enjoy the hammering.

DESIGNING THE PROJECT   The types of projects one can create out of simple **tin can** plate are far too numerous to list, but they include everything from the simplest can-lid star ornament to the most elaborately cut, hammered, and raised Mexican-style mirror frame. Lanterns, sconces, candle holders, cut-tin flowers, jewelry, and the more traditional folded and soldered tinker's boxes can all be fabricated out of tin sheet.

Look around at samples of Early American **tinware;** examine the art of the Mexican tinsmiths; consider the tin material itself. These should suggest crafts projects in themselves.

In designing your project, it is best to construct a pattern on tracing paper, then transfer it to the tin sheet by **scoring** the tin through the pattern with a scribe or **awl.** If the flaps and overlays required to make your project seem complex, you might do well to first construct the entire piece out of stiff paper of light cardboard. It makes the mistakes and the cutting that much easier to bear.

CUTTING THE TIN   Only experience will teach you exactly how tin will react to your style of cutting. However, there are a few tips which should be passed along. For right-handed tinsmiths, when tin is snipped it curls down from the right side of the blades, and up from the left. This curling effect can be used to good advantage as a decorative effect. If, on the other hand, it is preferable to have the strips lie flat, they can be either manipulated with the fingers or hammered out, beginning at the base (or beginning of the cut) and working gradually to the far end or outer edge, **flattening** as you go. Not only does tin curl as it is cut, but the thinner you make the strips, the tighter it curls. With **fringing,** which involves making very narrow cuts into the tin, the curling effect is maximized. Once again, fingers or a hammer will eliminate the curl if it is unwanted.

In cutting out curved patterns on tin, the general rule is to cut counterclockwise, so that you are cutting away from the pattern rather than into it. In tight areas, where **notching,** vees, tight curves, and the like are required, it is best to bypass the tough cut until the mass of tin outside the pattern has been removed. In going back to the tough spots, it also helps to hammer the edges flat again prior to making an incision. Don't be afraid to hammer, cut, hammer again, then cut some more.

Cutting or **punching** holes in tin is a slightly different matter. A hole is a very simple thing, made by giving a good whack with a hammer to an awl or chisel that has been carefully positioned on a piece of tin plate placed on some kind of hardwood **hammering board.** The cutting implement itself will be chosen on the basis of the pattern involved; an **awl** makes a round hole; a **chisel** makes a narrow rectangular cut. Unless otherwise suggested, hit the tin with the implement from both sides, front and back. Once again, don't be afraid to rehammer the work to soften the edges of the holes cut with the awl. Hammer, hit with the awl or chisel, and hammer again.

FOLDING THE TIN Folding both strengthens tin strips by adding extra rigidity and provides a means for joining overlapping sections with either folded flaps or interlocking folds. With projects that require weight-bearing strips, such as wall candle sconces, the strips can be made much stronger if the tin edges are folded over and hammered flat. Boxes or sealed containers can also be assembled by constructing interlocking flaps on the joining edges of the tin sheet. These can be linked together and sealed by **soldering** or gluing. Professional tinsmiths have commercial machines that automatically mold their tin sheet into folds, but the same operation can be handled quite simply by scribing or **scoring** a folding line with an awl, then placing the tin along a table edge and hammering the flap into a right angle. Care should be taken to crease the line along the scribed mark as precisely as possible. For boxes, the table edge 90° bend is perfect as is. For strip strengthening, or interlocking flaps, the right-angled piece should be then laid out on the table and pounded flat so the tin bends back on itself as tightly as possible for rigidity, or with just enough room to hook onto another piece of tin if the fold is for locking or joining two pieces together.

JOINING THE TIN Tinplate can be bonded or joined in a variety of ways. The simplest technique involves **punching** holes along the outer edges of the two pieces to be connected and then inserting rivets, cotton pins, or thin wire lengths to secure the pieces together. Modern epoxy resin glues can also be used to hold tin together. Because they are packaged in two tubes—the epoxy in one and a catalyst in the other—they must be mixed; the process can be somewhat involved, but the bond itself is absolutely permanent. For the traditionalist, however, the only way to bond tin to tin is with a soft type of **solder.** For the beginner, **soldering** can seem terribly complex and extremely difficult; but once learned, it can be both the most effective and the most satisfactory way to work. Basically, soldering is the process of floating a hot liquid solder material between two pieces of tin and then allowing it to cool down to produce a solidified bond. The first step in soldering involves the cleaning of the metal surface to be joined with either a wire brush or a metal file. A clean joint is everything in soldering. The cleaned areas must then be coated with a chemical agent or **flux.** Commercial flux is available in most hardware stores as either a paste, liquid, or powder. If a **soldering iron** is used, the copper end of the iron must also be carefully scraped down to the bright copper surface, then coated with flux. Once cleaned, the iron should be heated (with a propane torch or gas stove flame, or if electric, by plugging it in) to the melting point of the solder; the most suitable solder for tin, soft solder, melts at somewhere between 390° F and 450° F. Then, carefully and evenly, coat the entire copper end with solder. Once the iron is tinned, the iron and the two pieces of tin to be joined should be heated to the melting point of the solder. The heat should be distributed equally between the two pieces of tin, as solder will flow to the hottest part of the metal. Take care not to overheat the tin plate; too much heat will result in discoloration. The heat of the tin at the seam must be equal to the melting point of the solder. Once everything is heated up, the solder can be picked up by the iron and carried to one end of the joint, held there until the tin sheet is warmed enough to draw the solder off the iron, then drawn along with the iron the length of the seam in one flowing motion from beginning to end. With practice you should be able to handle the action in one continuous move with no stops and starts during the soldering process. The seam, once coated, should be allowed to cool undisturbed. Only after the solder has set can the flux material be washed away with hot running water and a soft brush or cloth. All flux must be removed to avoid its permanently damaging the metal surface. One alternative to this method involves using a **propane torch** instead of an iron. With a torch, the metal area to be joined is cleaned and fluxed as in the soldering iron approach, but the solder itself is applied in a slightly different way. With the torch technique, small rice-sized pieces of solder, called **pallion**s, are coated with flux, then positioned or spaced out at equal distances along the length of the cleaned and fluxed tin joint. When the metal is heated with the torch to the melting point of the solder, the fluxed pallions melt and flow throughout the seam. As with the iron, the process should move continuously from one end of the joint to the other. Once again, all flux material should be washed away with hot water once the solder has set.

One advantage that solder has over epoxy is that a solder joint may be reheated and unstuck; an epoxy bond is a bond forever.

FINISHING THE TIN Tinware can be left to shine on its own or finished with paint and/or a clear protective finish, such as lacquer or **varnish.** In the United States, "tole" has come to mean any metalware that has been covered with a lacquered or enameled finish. It is a good deal fancier than just plain tin-plate.

The traditional decorative finish for tinware is lacquering or **japanning.** Lacquering was inspired by the opening of European trade with the Orient during the early 1700s. The enthusiasm for lacquered objects generated a Western commercial interest in finding a way for European craftsmen to duplicate the high-gloss japanned finish. Oriental lacquer was a byproduct of the *Rhus vernicifera* tree sap. It required years of experience to understand its complexities. However, after long series of experimentation, a variety of varnish products closely simulating the lacquered finish were invented. Japanning, or the production of high gloss finishes on metalware was soon to become a major industry in England.

To most of us, "tole work," "**toleware**," or "japanned tinware" most commonly brings to mind a tin object with delicate painting upon a dark brown or black background. In pure japanning, the dark background is the result of mixing the clear varnish with either lampblack (for an opaque black finish) or **asphaltum** (for the common dark brown finish). Vermilion added to the clear varnish produces a red japanning surface, while Prussian blue results in the colonial deep ultramarine finish. The density of the coloring depends on the amount of paint added to the varnish. Clear brown or asphaltum-tinted varnish became the basic japan finish during the late 1850s. Japanning, or a lacquered finish, however, was not the final touch.

On top of the high gloss finish, tinmakers also hand painted or stenciled flowers or patterned designs. The painting of flowers or "flowering" was a popular craft. Color pigments were mixed with varnish and turpentine and brushed onto the japanned surface with all the skill that the individual artist possessed. Gold leaf and **bronze powder** designs on tinware became popular as well. **Stenciling** had replaced handpainting as the decorative mode by the mid-nineteenth century. At first stenciling was dressed up with brush strokes to fool the eye, but eventually stenciled patterns became acceptable in and of themselves. Stenciled designs were fairly simple and often consisted of nothing more than a wicker basket filled with a selection of simple fruit and foliage.

For modern craftspeople who would like to reproduce traditional finishes, the process has been greatly simplified by the availability of commercial varnishes and oil paints. A mixture of one-third clear varnish and two-thirds asphaltum varnish brushed onto the finished tinware surface will recreate the familiar old-time dark brown painted undercoating. Prepackaged bronze metallic finishes with complete instructions attached allow for instant duplication of the old **bronzing** techniques. Stencils can be cut or, even more simply, purchased in a wide variety of colonial patterns. The common black lacquer finish is best simulated by mixing a tablespoon of clear varnish with a half pint of flat black enamel. Once completely dried for a full 24 hours, the surface can be sanded smooth, then covered again with a second coat, sanded, covered a third time, and sanded again. Stencils, either hand-cut or store bought, are best taped in place with masking tape and then brushed over and into all corners with a base coat of yellow ochre or raw sienna. Once allowed to dry completely, the oil paint can be highlighted within the stenciled pattern to create contrasting color accents. Gold or bronze powder can be applied according to the instructions on the commercial package. After stenciling, a clear coat of varnish should be used to seal the surface. The greater the need for protection (i.e., the heavier the use), the greater should be the number of protective coats. Sanding must occur between each coat. Commercial marking pens of felt-tip pens give to tin a colorful transparent surface, like that seen on much of the tinware from Mexico. A clear acrylic spray sold in most art-supply stores will, more or less, seal these colors against wear and tear. Hobby shops carry a wide range of spray-can colors that duplicate many of the colonial tole or tinware shades. Again, clear acrylic should be sprayed on to provide a more permanent surface.

tin glaze. Ceramics. A glaze that owes its opacity to tin.

Tinkertoy. Toys. The trade name of a **constructional toy** made of an assortment of carefully designed colored spools and **dowel** rods that fit together. Holes are drilled through the axes and radially into the disks. Also see **Toys: Constructional Toys.**

tin lap. Gemcutting. See **lap.**

tinner's rivet. Metalworking. See **rivet.**

tinning. Metalworking. The application of a thin film of **brazing filler metal** or **filler rod** to the area to be brazed. Tinning occurs as the **braze weld** is applied onto light-gauge metal, but on thick or heavy metal tinning must precede **braze welding.**

Tinning can also refer to the process of removing layers of **solder** and **oxide**s from the tip of a **soldering iron,** gun, pencil, or **soldering copper,** and then coating it with a film of **solder.**

To tin a soldering iron, file the tip until clean copper is exposed. Heat the iron until the copper turns yellow or light brown, then apply **flux** to the tip. Apply solder to the tip by holding the wire or rod against the hot iron and letting it spread over the tip. Remove any excess molten solder. The iron is then ready to solder with.

tinning. Stained Glass. The method by which the copper tip of a **soldering iron** is coated with **solder.** The tip is first shaped and smoothed with a file. It is allowed to heat up, then dipped into **rosin;** the solder is then melted on it. The act of tinning both cleans the tip and aids it in melting the solder. When it has been properly tinned, the tip of the soldering iron will look bright and smooth.

tinning. Tincrafting. The coating of a metal with molten tin by dipping in a hot tin bath or melting on tin **solder.**

tin overslip. Ceramics. A versatile technique used on **earthenware. Lead glaze** containing 10% **tin oxide** is used over a colored **slip.** The lead glaze dispenses the **oxide** evenly over the surface of a pot.

tin oxide. Amber Carving. Ivory and Bone Carving. Jet Carving. (Also called stannic oxide.) Pure white impalpable powder used for polishing. In part **putty powder,** it is the counterpart of the mineral cassiterite, made by calcining tin in an oxidizing atmosphere. For many years this has been an extremely important polishing agent, as it has the ability to polish almost all gemstones and organic materials, regardless of their individual characteristics.

tin oxide. Ceramics. An **opacifier** that is used in **stains** and **majolica** painting. Tin oxide changes the color qualities of most **pigment oxide**s. Substitutes for tin oxide are **zirconium oxide, titanium oxide,** and **zircopax** (a **frit**). Also see **white glaze.**

tin oxide. Gemcutting. See **abrasive.**

tin plate. Metalworking. A soft, low-carbon **steel** coated with a layer of **tin** to keep it from rusting. It is commonly used for tin cans and may be used for home tincrafts.

The two types of tin plate are charcoal and coke; they differ mainly in the thicknesses of their coatings: charcoal tin plate has a heavy coating of tin; coke tin plate has a lighter one. The thickness is commonly designated by a **gauge** number but may also be noted by weight, 55–275 lb (the weight of a standard box of 112 sheets 14″ × 20″) or by symbols 1C, 1X, 2X, 3X, etc., to signify weight.

tin plate. Tincrafting. Originally sheet iron dipped in **tin,** now most likely sheet steel electrolytically coated with an extremely thin coat of tin. In either case, many metals, such as iron, copper, and steel, can corrode under contact with organic acids, and are therefore coated with tin, which is highly resistant to corrosion. Tin plate is generally quite malleable and is the basic material used in tincrafting. Also see **Tincrafting.**

tinplate toy. Toys. A pressed toy made from a thin sheet of tin or pressed tin plate. Usually the parts were pressed, then assembled to form the three-dimensional toy. Most tinplate toys are richly hand-colored or glazed with a varnish and paint mixture to produce a translucent color. Boats, trains, carts, and sometimes animals were made of tinplate.

tinsel picture. Papercrafts. A style of picture popular during the early nineteenth century, in which prints of well-known persons, such as Shakespearean actors, were available with accompanying foil costume accessories that were cut out and glued in place on the figure.

tinsmith. Tincrafting. One who makes objects out of **tin plate.** Edward **Pattison** was in all likelihood the first American tinsmith. Also see **Tincrafting.**

tinsmithing. Metalworking. See **blacksmithing.**

tin snips. Metalworking. See **snips.**

tin soldier. Toys. See **toy soldier.**

tint. A variant of a **hue** made by adding white. Also see **monochromatic color triangle, value.**

tinted ground. China and Glass Painting. See **tinting.**

Tintex. Batik and Tie-dye. See **household dye.**

tinting. China and Glass Painting. A method of coloring backgrounds (**ground laying**) in which colors are painted on, then padded with a **silk pad** to blend. First rub the silk pad in a little **tinting oil** spread in the palm of the hand to help blend the colors evenly. Then pad over the surface with quick, light, circular strokes, occasionally wiping the pad with a clean rag, until the tint is even and has a dull, waxy texture. Set the piece aside to dry. If the color begins to lift off during padding, showing patches of white, it has been overpadded. If the surface is shiny and moist, too much tinting oil has been used and lint will settle on the surface. In such cases, clean off the tint and begin again. After **firing,** rub the tinted ground lightly with emery cloth or fine sandpaper to remove any grittiness.

tinting oil. China and Glass Painting. A **medium** for **tinting** made by mixing 5 parts copaiba balsam oil, 1 part oil of cloves, and just enough oil of tar to darken the mixture slightly.

tin-type metal lap. Gemcutting. See **lap.**

Tinuvin. Plastics. See **antioxidant.**

tin vanadium stain. Ceramics. See **vanadium.**

tinware. Tincrafting. Any one of a multitude of objects, usually of a practical nature, created out of **tin plate.** Tinware was the mainstay of the famed Yankee peddler, and the object of repair for the fabled American tinker. Also see **Tincrafting.**

tip. Basketry. (Also called top.) The narrow end of a **willow** rod.

tip. Metalworking. See **oxyacetylene welding equipment.**

tip cut. Woodworking. See **whittling.**

Tippecanoe and Tyler, Too. Quilts. See **Old Tippecanoe.**

tipping. Bookbinding. Pasting end sheet or insert to the signature of a book along the binding edge. In the case of endpapers, cover the folded sheet of endpaper with a **pasting guard,** leaving a ¼″ margin at the back fold exposed. Apply paste to this margin, line up the endpaper with the **head** and **back** fold, tip it into place, and rub it down. Place under a light weight until dry.

tippy. Toys. See **caddy.**

tire swing. Toys. Any **swing** made out of an old tire. Sometimes the tire is simply tied to a single rope and hung. It works, but is not very comfortable. In another variety a saber saw is used to cut the tire near the inside edge, leaving a section intact for the seat. The tire is then turned inside out so that the rider is seated on the smooth surface. A rope is tied to each ring, making it a double **rope swing.** See ill. on next page.

Tire swing

tissue paper. Papercrafts. Thin, crisp, semitransparent paper available in sheets in many brilliant colors. Tissue paper is used for decorative projects such as **paper flowers.** Tissue paper glued in overlapping layers makes an interesting **collage,** as the translucent layers of tissue build up vivid colors. **White glue,** diluted half-and-half with water, may be used with a brush for making such collages. Because it has a tendency to bleed slightly, care must be taken when working with glue-soaked tissue.

titania. Gemcutting. See **rutile.**

titanium oxide. Ceramics. A major **opacifier** when used either alone or in a **frit.** Titanium used in any quantity produces a semi-matte texture. Also see **rutile.**

tithing quilt. Quilts. A quilt on which members of a church wrote their names and the amount of money pledged to the church. The names were written in India ink at the edges of the **blocks.**

A variation of this quilt was also used to raise money for a church or other organization. Contributors paid a dime or a quarter to have their names inked onto a block. These were sometimes called signature quilts.

title. Bookbinding. The title of a book or chapter.

title page. Bookbinding. The second printed page of a book, always on the right, or **recto,** side of the page. It contains the names of the book and author and the date of publication. **Verso** of the title page is the **copyright notice.**

title piece. Bookbinding. A leather label stating the book's title, pasted to the back of a binding.

titling. Bookbinding. The application of the **title** to the cover of a book. For easy identification the title should appear on both the front cover and the **spine.** There are various means available for titling, such as **tooling** the letters directly onto the **cloth** or **leather** of the cover with heated dies, and blocking **foil.**

The simplest and most traditionally used method is to letter the label by hand on leather or **paper.** Cut a piece of cardboard the same size as the finished label; place it onto the cover while the glue used for covering the **boards** is still soft. Place the book between two pressing boards and

press for a few hours. Remove from the press and paste the already prepared label onto the depression created by the cardboard. The label will rest slightly below the surface of the rest of the cover, protecting it from wear and tear.

tjanting. Batik and Tie-dye. A tool used to apply molten **wax** to **fabric** in the **tulis** or **hand-painted batik** process. It consists of a cup or bowl to hold the wax, a spout through which the wax can flow onto the fabric, and a handle. The traditional tjanting, which has a beaten copper cup and a bamboo handle, has been commonly used in Java for centuries. Similar cones are now commercially manufactured and are available in most shops that carry **batik** supplies.

The tjanting is used as a drawing tool to make fine lines of wax that will **resist** the **dye.** The tool is dipped into a pan of hot wax to heat and fill the cup. Then, by tilting it, the wax is allowed to flow freely through the spout. This tool gives the batik artist far greater control over the design than is possible by using a **brush** and allows for the painting of a long, continuous line. See ill.

Tjantings

tjap. Batik and Tie-dye. A patterned block of wood used in the **tjap printing** or stamp printing **batik** process. The patterns of the batik tjaps are linear, made from thin strips of copper set on edge so that a fine line design results. The copper strips are soldered to a solid copper base that has an attached handle. Tjap printing is one of the traditional **Javanese batik** methods used in stamp batik.

tjap printing. Batik and Tie-dye. A traditional Javanese **stamp printing** method of **batik** in which the **tjap** is used. It is referred to as stamp batik or wood block batik.

The batik artist presses the stamp or tjap into a firm pad that has been saturated in molten **wax.** The copper of the tjap retains the heat and keeps the wax liquid until the stamp is pressed onto the fabric. The use of tjap printing greatly speeds up the time-consuming batik process. Another traditional batik method is the **tulis,** or hand-painting method, in which the **tjanting** is used. It is far more time consuming than the use of the tjap. Also see **printed batik.**

T-joint. Jewelry. A **joint** with at least two pieces of metal butting against each other at right angles.

toad-in-the-hole. Lacemaking. See **leaf stitch.**

Toad-in-the-Puddle. Quilts. (Also called Jack-in-the-Pulpit.) A design for a **pieced block** made up of triangles, squares, and rectangles. It is a square within a square within a square. The delightful name suggests that it might have been one of a series of designs made especially for children's trundle beds.

tobacco-bag quilt. Quilts. The small fabric bags in which tobaccos came packed were sometimes saved by thrifty homemakers and **pieced** for **quilt tops**. The material was usually white or off-white, and the printed design and lettering on the bag were used as the decorative motif for the **quilt**. These are true examples of **salvage art** and **making do.**

Another kind of tobacco-bag quilt was made from the polychrome labels of tobacco pouches. These depicted portraits of various famous people and public notables, such as kings, presidents, and generals, about the time of World War I.

Printed **felt** patches were given away with cigars during the first quarter of this century. The designs, printed on the rectangles of felt, included the flags of many countries or the blanket designs of various American Indian tribes and were used for quiltmaking. Part of the delight of these quilts is that they belong so specifically to a certain era. Also see **cigar-band quilt.**

tobacco cloth. Stitchery. See **cheesecloth.**

toenailing. Woodworking. See **nailing.**

together. Crochet. (Abbr. tog.) To work two or more stitches together as you would ordinarily work a single **stitch**, except the crochet hook is put through as many stitch **loops** as specified in the **pattern** to form one new stitch. Crocheting together not only decreases the total number of stitches per **row**, but also alters the shape of the crocheted object (as in the shoulder seam of a crocheted jacket). Also see **cluster, decrease.**

together. Tatting. (Abbr. tog.) To tie two threads together, as in the start of **working with two shuttles,** or to **attach** two **rings** or **chains** together. Also see **reef knot.**

toggle bolt. Woodworking. See **bolt.**

Tohiti. Basketry. See **cane.**

toile. Lacemaking. A French term signifying linen cloth. In lacework, the **motif** or floral areas could be said to have a toile, or flat linenlike, appearance in contrast to the background areas—toile referring to the motifed areas only.

toile de Jouy. Découpage. A design style in which vignettes of figures and landscapes are printed in shades of one color on a cream or white background. The style originated with the fabrics printed on cotton or linen from copper plates at Jouy, near Paris. The two-tone designs of rural scenes, ruins, bridges, and foliage were printed in red, blue, green, or brown.

toile de Jouy. Quilts. A material, named after its place of origin in France at the end of the eighteenth century, printed by means of engraved copperplate cylinders. The designs were pastoral, depicting mythological and historical scenes. The early copperplate printing was done in one-color prints of pink, brown, or blue on white. Earlier "fabrics from Jouy" were printed from hand-cut wood blocks, and these designs, made in several colors, found their way into early American quilts.

tole. Tincrafting. Correctly speaking, tole is the French word for **tin plate** or sheet iron. In terms of common usage, toleware is any tinware object that has been lacquered, varnished, painted, or in some other way decorated to cover the tin surface. "Japanned ware" is probably the most accurate description for what is most often called tole. Also see **Tincrafting: Finishing the Tin.**

toleware. Découpage. A term for tinware that has been painted and decorated. Tinware is frequently decorated with découpage. The tradition of decorating "tole" or tinware originated in France as an inexpensive and available substitute for porcelains. Freehand designs of flowers, garlands, and borders and **Creil** designs were used.

toleware. Tincrafting. See **tole.**

tombac. Enameling. See **metal.**

tombola. Toys. See **balance toy.**

tongs. Ceramics. A tool used to place **raku** into and to remove it from a red-hot **kiln**. See ill.

Tongs

tongs. Enameling. See **bright dip, cleaning metal, etching.**

tongs. Glasswork. See **jack.**

tongs. Jewelry. Metalworking. A tool for holding and lifting heated objects.

Forging tongs are used for holding heated metal when removing it from the **forge** and when hammering the metal over the **anvil** to shape it. It is common for **blacksmiths** to heat the tong jaws to red hot and hammer them over the stock metal to be used for a secure fit. This is necessary for safety and efficiency. The different types of jaws on each of the tongs are designed to fit around various shapes of metal stock. The flat-nose, open-mouth jaw (called straight tongs) (**a.**) grasps flat strips or sheets of metal. The square hollow bit (called box tongs) (**b.**) and the round hollow bit (called bow tongs) (**c.**) fit securely around square and round rods respectively. The semibox tongs (called forming bit) (**d.**) are used for shaping, and the bent-tip tongs (**e.**) are used to grasp metal in a parallel position to the tong. Forging tongs are generally 15–36″ long.

Foundry tongs (also called crucible tongs) are used to pick up **crucibles** of molten metal. The tongs with opening jaws are usually used to remove the hot crucible from the melting furnace and to set it into the circular pouring shank. Both the vertical lift and top lift pick-up tongs grasp the crucible from the top, while the casting, or pouring, tongs hold it from the sides. Although the latter can be used to pour the metal into the mold, it is much safer when pouring any crucible of medium size to use two persons to handle the two-man pouring shank, one person merely supporting the straight-ended handle while the other person on the double-pronged handle controls the pouring of the metal. See ill.

Forging tongs

a. Flat-nose, open mouth, or straight tongs

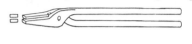

b. Square hollow bit, or box tongs

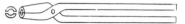

c. Round hollow bit, or bow tongs

d. Semibox, or forming bit tongs

e. Bent-tip tongs

f. Large hollow bit, or straight-lipped tongs

Foundry tongs

g. Vertical lift tongs

h. Casting or pouring tongs

j. Top lift pickup tongs

k. Single handle spade type pouring shank

m. Two man pouring shank

tongue. Puppets. Toys. A projecting tenon or strip by which something may be attached or fitted. A child's **wagon** may have a tongue or center piece that extends in front, to which a handle may be attached. **Toy train** cars may have connecting devices attached to tongues.

tongue-and-groove joint. Woodworking. See **joint.**

tongue depressor. Short, flat sticks with rounded ends, used by doctors in examining the throat. They have many

uses in the crafts studio, including paint mixing and construction of toys. They also provide good tools to work with clay.

tonking. Stained Glass. See **decalcomania.**

tool. Bookbinding. The name applied in a specific sense to the engraved metal bookbinder's tools with wooden handles used to impress designs by hand in a surface in the **finishing** of a binding. See ill. Also see **azured tool, blind tooling, fillet.**

Tool

tool-and-die steel. Metalworking. See **steel.**

tooling. Bookbinding. (Also called stamping.) The manual application of heated dies to the cover of a book for **titling** or decoration. Tooling may be done with metallic **foil,** colors, or blind (heated impressions without foil or color). **Handle letters,** decorative **tools,** or letters held in a **type pallet,** hand-vise **type holder,** or **type clamp** are used for tooling. Brass letters are usually used by binders, although regular lead printer's type may be substituted. A spatula-shaped tool called a lining **pallet** is used for striking straight lines across the spine. Also see **blind tooling, glaire.**

tooling. Leather. The process of decorating leather by incising designs with a **swivel knife** and pressing down damp leather with the use of **stamps** and **modelers** to create raised and depressed designs. **Stamping** is used for added patterning. Leather for tooling should be **top grain,** vegetable tanned. It is available as tooling cowhide or top-grade tooling **calfskin.** More economical tooling leathers may be used, such as tooling lamb, **pigskin,** and **cowhide** bellies. The leather should be at least 4 oz.

Before decorating begins, the leather project must be cut out and dampened. Heavy leather is dampened by **casing.** Lightweight leather is moistened with a sponge and cold water on the flesh side until the **grain** side darkens. Leave the grain side up on the work surface (marble slab or pounding board) until it begins to show signs of drying. It is then ready to be tooled. If the tooling is not completed after one session, the leather may be wrapped up and stored in the refrigerator. Care must be taken not to touch the damp leather with anything other than the tools, to avoid marring it.

The pattern is first drawn on paper and placed on the leather. Trace the lines with a ball end modeler stylus or pounce wheel so the pattern is impressed upon the leather. Don't press hard enough to penetrate it. A row of dots will suffice as a guide. These lines may then be traced with a lead pencil to make them more visible.

The **swivel knife** is the basic knife for cutting the outline of a design to be tooled and stamped. Hold the swivel knife at a vertical angle and incise the lines of the design, using the little finger as a guide. Lift the knife at the end of each line, using even pressure for cuts of uniform depth. Lines should be cut only once.

After the outlining is completed, indent all the ground

near the outline with a matte or stamp. If the outline disappears, the leather is too wet. It may be drawn again with a wheel or tracer. If the work dries out while working, moisten with a wet sponge. In addition to cutting the outline and stamping down the background, various tools are available for modeling the shapes into raised relief patterns and textures.

When the tooling is finished, let the leather dry for two days. If some detail is lost during drying, it may be touched up with a small additional moistening. Tooling is an old, traditional method of decorating leather; the scrolly flowers, leaves, and Western motifs of saddles, belts, wallets, etc., are familiar. Most tooling stamps are designed to work these patterns and have specific uses, but new and contemporary designs can also be made. Tooling requires practice with the swivel knife to gain control of the line and considerable experimentation with the various stamps available to see what possibilities and effects they offer. Also see **background tool, beveler, camouflage tool, carving, embossing, embossing wheel, flat modeling, ornamental cuts, outline tooling, seeder, shading, stippler, stippling, vibra-tool** and **Leatherwork: Setting Up a Workshop.**

tooling. Metalworking. (Also called metal tooling.) A process for creating relief designs in thin metal sheets by pressing hand tools against the backs. Tooling is used for surface enrichment on such objects as wall plaques, overlays, covers for boxes or books, and picture frames. Recommended for tooling are 32–36 **gauge copper** or **aluminum** sheets.

The tools needed for tooling are a hard instrument with a broad end and a finely pointed end, and a wooden molding tool with a flat, square end and a rounded end. Homemade tools can be improvised from ice picks, ball point pens, **dowels,** and wooden spoons.

Place a thick layer of padding (12 or more sheets of newspaper, or several blotters) under the metal. Begin by pressing your design in reverse with the tools, progressing from the outlines toward the center. Use long sweeping strokes. Increase your layers of padding underneath as you raise your design into higher relief. Flatten the background periodically by turning the metal face-up on a hard surface, and pressing it with the square end of a tool.

Because the metal is very thin, the relief must be filled with a hard substance when furnished, and then mounted securely on a background. Suggested materials for filling the relief sections are plaster of Paris, paraffin, Plastic Wood, plastic body putty, or plastic epoxy resin.

tool steel. Metalworking. See **steel.**

tool wax. Glasswork. The material used to coat the working surfaces of glassblowing tools, such as the points of **jacks,** so that the surface slides smoothly over the molten glass without binding or squeaking.

tooth. Ceramics. The rough or coarse grain in clay.

tooth burnisher. Bookbinding. A curved surface burnisher used for edge gilding and illumination.

tooth cutting. Papercrafts. Cutting along rolled or folded piece of paper on the diagonal to form regular V-shaped points along one side. See ill.

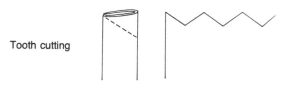

Tooth cutting

toothing. Weaving. See **dovetailing.**

top. Basketry. See **tip.**

top. Spinning. (Also called tops.) Combed **wool** ready for **spinning.** These are the long **staple** fibers for **worsted** spinning, prepared by **combing** out the short fibers. They should be parallel fibers of the same length, smooth, uniform, and with no foreign matter to speak of. Tops can be bought as a wheel of wool **roving** which has been commercially prepared for spinning.

top. Toys. A cone-shaped spinning toy of ancient origin. This **universal toy** is rounded and symmetrical with a pointed base. It is set in motion by spinning, which keeps it standing on the point at its base. There are many varieties of tops, but the three most common are the **spin top,** the **spring top,** and the **whip top.**

Tops are known to have existed in Egypt in the thirteenth century B.C., although various theories fix the origin of the top in New Guinea, China, or Japan. Tops have appeared in many different parts of the world at different times and may be regarded as **emergent toys.** Also see **peg top.**

topaz. Gemcutting. Aluminum fluorine silicate **crystallized** in the orthorhombic system with perfect **cleavage** parallel to the basal plane (i.e., perpendicular to the **C-axis).** Topaz has **hardness** of 8, **specific gravity** of 3.5–3.6, refractive indices of 1.61 and 1.635, vitreous **luster,** and occurs transparent to opaque colored yellow, pale blue, rose (may be heat-treated yellow topaz), and with some dichroism. It is usually **step cut** with the **facets** a few degrees off the cleavage faces to avoid sloughing off when **sanding** and **polishing.** Main crown facets are cut 43°; main pavillion facets are cut at 39°. Facets are polished on a tin **lap** with Linde A. Also see **faceting, polishing,** and **refraction.**

top basic wire. Beadwork. See **basic row.**

top-centered. Bookbinding. Placed above the center vertically and centered horizontally.

topdrop. Puppets. A short **curtain** or **drop** usually used in front of and in addition to the **backdrop** on the **puppet stage** or **marionette stage.** The topdrop may be used to indicate blue sky, rain clouds, sunlight, or moonlight, depending on the needs of the **puppet play.** It might also be painted with garlands, flags or chandeliers to suggest a particular setting. Also see **Puppets: Marionette Stage, Puppet Stage.**

top-dyeing. Dyeing. The process of dyeing a fiber or fabric twice in order to obtain a deeper or richer color, a new or third color, or **colorfast**ness. It starts with a first dyeing called bottom dyeing or bottoming and ends with a second dyeing called top-dyeing or topping. The two dyeings can be with the same color or different colors. Sometimes the first color is dulled in the two-step process and it is therefore recommended that a clear, bright color be used in the first **dyebath.** **Indigo** is often dyed with **woad** first to produce a more colorfast blue. A completely new color is obtained, for example, with a bottom dyeing in yellow and a top-dyeing in blue. The new color is green. A top-dyeing with the complement of the bottom color will result in a grayed bottom color. Top or overdyeing with gray or beige results in a soft new shade. Top-dyeing is often used to give already dyed yarns or fabrics of many different colors a related quality. This is done by dyeing them all in a weak dyebath of a desired hue or the complement most common to all. Overdyeing with black is often done when the first color has not turned out as desired. With natural dyes, getting a true black without top-dyeing is difficult.

top fuller. Metalworking. See **blacksmithing tools.**

top grain. Leather. (Also called full grain.) A term for the outer hair side, or **grain** side, of the leather, which is strong, smooth, and durable. The grain of leathers from different animals has distinct characteristics. Also see **chrome calf, lining leather, split, tooling** and **Leatherwork.**

to plaid off. Weaving. See **plaid.**

top-loading kiln. Ceramics. **Kilns** that are loaded from the top, usually electric kilns and kilns for **raku.**

tops. Spinning. See **top.**

topstitch. Stitchery. To sew on the top or right side of a **fabric** so that the stitches show on the **face** of the finished piece.

top-stitched seam. Stitchery. A **seam finish** for a **plain seam** in which the **raw edges** are first **press**ed to one side. A second line of stitching is then sewn on top, near the original line of stitching, going through all three layers of **fabric.** The **top-stitch** is a decorative addition and may be sewn in a contrasting color. Because it is exposed on the **face** of the fabric, care should be taken to keep the stitches evenly spaced and parallel to the **seam.** When both sides are stitched a **double top-stitched seam** is made. See ill.

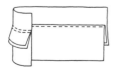

Top-stitched seam

topstitching. Leather. A seam finishing technique common in leather garments: The seam is stitched and seam allowances turned to one side, then stitching is sewn on the right side, topstitching the seam allowance in place. Also see **double topstitching, overlapped seam** and **Leatherwork: Sewing Leather.**

top swage. Metalworking. See **blacksmithing tool.**

topsy-turvy doll. Toys. (Also called reversible doll, two-headed doll, upside-down doll.) A **rag doll** with two heads, one at each end. A long skirt is attached at the middle so that it will cover the lower half, concealing the head not in use.

torch. Enameling. A tool that produces a flame for soldering, annealing, and melting **metals** and for **firing enamels.**

A mouth blowtorch or blowpipe uses city or bottled propane gas mixed with air supplied by the operator's breath for regulation of the heat intensity. This is the most practical and efficient apparatus for small pieces.

A propane torch consists of a nozzle and a regulatory valve screwed to the top of a cylindrical tank of gas under high pressure. The flame heats up to 2500° F, but its area is small and the flame must constantly be moved across the piece being heated. The work is heated slowly and evenly until the proper temperature, characterized by a reddish glow, is reached.

An oxyacetylene torch has a higher temperature range and is available in sizes ranging from that of a miniature transistor radio to units consisting of two tanks, valves, and a mixing nozzle.

The torch flame is used to blister and puncture **metal foil** and sheet metal.

Torch firing soft opaque white enamel produces a variety of color effects—shades of pink, blue, green, and purple-gold—caused by varying degrees of heat. Also see **cleaning metal, mercury gilding** and **Enameling: Tools and Materials.**

torch. Jewelry. A heating instrument used in soldering and annealing operations to heat metal. The propane torch (BernzOmatic) is most widely used. The gas (propane) mixes automatically with the air in the nozzle. Adjust the **flame** slowly until a bluish flame with a little yellow on the tip results. Always turn a propane torch off slowly (**a.**). The canister type of torch (propane torch) burns hot and clean; it is usually recommended as an inexpensive beginning torch. Small work up to 3″ can be soldered with a propane torch. On the **gas-air torch** there are individual hoses for gas and air that are regulated separately. To ignite a gas-air torch, turn on the gas and strike a flint lighter to create a spark. Slowly increase the air until the flame has a minimum of yellow. Several tips are available to produce a variety of flames from small needle flames to a large annealing flame. Turn off the air first, and then the gas after annealing. Gas-air torches have interchangeable tips of various sizes that regulate the size of the flame. An acetylene torch produces a very hot flame. Air combines with the gas at the torch tip (**b.**). The flame is controlled by changing the torch tips. Number 1 is used for jewelry-making and number 5 to anneal larger pieces (**c.**). See ill.

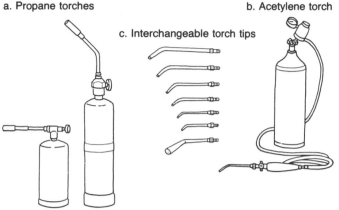

a. Propane torches

b. Acetylene torch

c. Interchangeable torch tips

torch. Metalworking. See **oxyacetylene welding equipment.**

torch firing. Enameling. Small enameled pieces may be fired with a **torch** instead of a **kiln.** The work should be supported so that the torch can work from below. A steel can with a hole cut for visibility can be set over the work to retain the heat. The direct flame of a torch can be applied to an **enamel** surface for **overfiring** effects. Also see **Enameling: Basic Operations.**

torsion. Jewelry. A strain caused by metal's being twisted.

tortoise shell. Jewelry. The mottled, horny substance of the shell of some turtles, used as an **inlay** material for color, texture, and pattern. Also see **piqué work.**

toscas. Beadwork. See **embroidery beads.**

toss-and-catch. Toys. See **spear-the-fish.**

toss game. Toys. Any **game** or toy in which an object is tossed or thrown at another. In **ring-toss game**s a hoop or ring is usually thrown over a projection or **peg.** In **bean bag** toss games, the bags are thrown through holes in a board. Toss games are often homemade. Also see **Toys: Games and Other Toys.**

totum. Toys. See **teetotum.**

tourmaline. Gemcutting. Transparent **crystals** of the hexagonal system with **hardness** of 7¼, **specific gravity** of 3–3.2, refractive indices of 1.61 and 1.65, granular to subconchoidal **fracture,** vitreous **luster,** and strong dichroism. It is oriented perpendicular to the **C-axis** for cutting. Some tourmaline exhibits a cat's eye when cut in **cabochon** form.

Clear tourmaline is called achroite. Red varieties are called rubellite. Indicolite is green or blue. Brown tourmaline is called dravite. One variety called watermelon tourmaline has a green outer layer and a pink interior.

Main crown **facets** are cut at 43°; main pavillion facets are cut at 39° to 40°. Facets are polished on a plastic **lap** with 14,000 grit diamond powder. Also see **faceting, polishing, refraction.**

tow. Spinning. Weaving. See **flax, linen.**

tow fork. Spinning. A **distaff** used in connection with the spinning of **flax** tow. It has forked prongs pointing upward around which the tow **roving** is interlaced. See ill. Also see **flax, linen.**

Tow fork

toy car. Toys. A popular **wheeled toy** made from any of a variety of materials. Among those most often handcrafted are those of natural wood; they are simple in form and durable. More elaborate versions may be stained or painted. Also see **Toys: Wheeled Toys.**

toy drum. Toys. A percussion **sound toy** that is a hollow cylinder with natural skins, plastic, or parchment stretched over the ends.

toy museum. Toys. See **Museum of Childhood, Pollack's Toy Museum.**

toy panorama. Toys. See **panorama toy.**

TOYS

Although toymaking is sometimes overlooked as a serious form of expression, few areas of the crafts offer a greater insight into the values held by a society. The toys made for, and given to, a child reflect those things considered important by the adult.

Toys are made basically to amuse and delight, but can serve to instruct as well. Toys allow for activity that imitates or is patterned after adult behavior and that aids in the development of a child's coordination and manipulative abilities. They also offer opportunities for fantasizing and role-playing.

Very often the toys or playthings that meet these needs are not manufactured or commercially produced. Almost all children will devise their own playthings from boxes, twigs, paper, or mud. But there is a distinction between a plaything and a toy. A plaything is any object with which a child plays and that offers a means of exploring some aspect of his world. The toy, by contrast, is designed and made specifically for the purpose of child's play.

Toys are often diminutive in size. This does not mean that they are **scale model**s or **miniature**s, but only that they are small. This makes it possible for the child to handle them, carry them, or operate them easily. Toys patterned on an actual object may exaggerate certain characteristics and eliminate others, so that the product is much altered from the original. A **toy car,** for example, might retain only a basic form with wheels, eliminating bumpers, tail lights, etc. A toy cat may be soft, cuddly, and small, with a long tail—gone are realistic proportions and claws.

Toys are made for the amusement and delight of adults as well as for children. **Adult toy**s may appeal to a more specific interest, but there is no denying that many are playthings. Miniatures or scale models, for example, are not really toys for children; such accurate reproduction of detail and scale is not usually of interest to a child. Very often, it is the design and production of toys that intrigues adults.

Toys are a reflection of the real world. This reflection can readily be seen in many examples. **Optical toy**s are based on principles of optics and visual stimuli, and it was through some of these toys that further interest in animation and cinematography developed. The paper **cutout**s of juvenile theater and the puppet theater are just a short step from the real stage. Mechanical toys, **balance toy**s, and **moving toy**s are based on the same laws of physics that apply to and govern the adult world and thus introduce the child to them. **Game**s that involve manipulative skills, such as **ring-and-pin, cup-and-ball,** and the **yo-yo,** are often as intriguing and challenging to adults as to children.

Almost every toy is to some extent a **learning toy,** but **educational toy**s or **scientific toy**s are specifically designed to teach. **Constructional toy**s and **building brick**s are made to allow a child to explore processes of building. **Alphabet blocks** combine both construction and specific learning skills.

Almost every country has some traditional **folk toy**s. These may be any of a variety of kinds of toys but are always those passed from one generation to another. The toys often represent, or are based on, some significant aspect of the culture that makes them.

Handmade, personally devised playthings have to a large degree been supplanted by mass-produced, colorful **plastic toy**s, few of which have any real intrinsic value. They are, however, plentiful and inexpensive, so that they are available to almost all children.

There are many different kinds of toys, and most seem to fall into some general classifications. For example, **wheeled toy**s compose a large part of all the toys made for children. **Doll**s and **stuffed animal**s are among the age-old favorites. "Construction toys" includes all **building toy**s from **blocks** to geodesic constructions. Many toys, however, refuse to be categorized, being unique and one-of-a-kind examples.

Toymaking has a history almost as old as man's. Archaeologists frequently unearth prehistoric examples of toys. However, any study of the history of toys reveals the difficulty of locating their specific origins. Many seem to be **universal toy**s, or **emergent toy**s—those that appear in various parts of the world at different times and that may seem to die out completely, only to emerge again in a different area. Some of these toys have an appeal so great and so broad that they do not relate to a specific culture or to a limited geographic area. Dolls, toy animals, and balls are among the toys of seemingly unlimited appeal.

The history of toys is often sketchy because in most cases little importance was attached to toys. **A princely toy** had a good chance of surviving, but the **slum toy** or **poor child's doll** was never considered worth noticing or keeping. What ancient toys have survived did so by being buried, by chance, with the remnants of a civilization. Toys of cast metal or ceramic were most likely to survive; those made from fibers or fabrics could not withstand the effects of time and weathering.

Excavations have been one of the best sources of the toys of antiquity. Drawings, illustrations, and paintings of children also provide good information. After about 1800, toymaking became an industry; catalogues, business records, and information are more plentiful from that time on.

Dolls have been dated as early as 2000 B.C. Some of these were of **clay,** wood, and bone, but the best were made of ivory, wax, fabric, and terra cotta. One excavated Egyptian doll had a wooden head, a body made of cloth, and movable arms. **Yo-yo**s have been excavated, indicating that they were known to children in Egypt as far back as 3000–2000 B.C. A variation of the **twirling yo-yo** was found in an Egyptian pyramid from the same period. This **momentum toy** was also known in ancient China, although the dates of its origins there are unknown. Many of the toys that originated in ancient Egypt and the Orient appeared again in societies that were chronologically later but that were at an earlier stage of development. That these toys emerged in different areas at different times suggests the phenomenon of the universal toy.

Glazed **composition top**s and balls dating from 1400–1200 B.C. and animal figures from 2000 B.C. are in existence. Wood balls and bladder-type balls are among the oldest known. Wheeled **push toy**s and **pull toy**s from Persia, 1100 B.C., and wheeled wooden horses and baked-clay horses of Egypt are among museum collections. A **wheeled toy** dated at 500 B.C. was found in Cyprus. In China, **kite**s date back to the third century B.C.

Dolls with movable arms and legs and changeable clothes were known to the Greeks and Romans. Some of their **carved wood** dolls had **mortise-and-tenon joint**s. Many of their other toys are known through paintings on vases and reliefs. Literary references show that toys were commonplace, and Socrates was known to have romped with his children on a **hobbyhorse;** Horace also mentions hobbyhorses. Animals were of special importance to the Greeks and Romans, and this was evidenced in their toys. They had terra cotta animals of all kinds, including the Trojan horse. Toys were made of bone, ivory, bronze, clay, leather, lead, and wood. Vase paintings also depict the use of masks, grotesque toys, **knucklebones,** and ball games of various kinds.

In medieval times dolls were made of clay, wood, wax, or **papier mâché.** Centers for toy and **dollmaking** had begun to develop; there are documents suggesting that by the fifteenth century dollmaking was an industry. Clay was the most commonly used material for animals and figures, including mounted riders, knights, and warriors. Windmills, hobbyhorses, and animals of tin, lead, or clay are the most frequently noted toys of medieval times.

In Europe toys were few and simple through the sixteenth century; **wind toy**s, balls, and toy weapons were among the most commonly available toys. Renaissance paintings show children holding and playing with dolls, and woodcuts depict toymakers at work. Dolls of this period were wooden, with **movable joint**s. In the seventeenth century, dolls were made not only of wood but also of wax, and some heads were made of glazed stoneware. Paper-pulp dolls and **gum tragacanth** dolls were being manufactured in Germany. By the eighteenth century, dollmaking was a large industry. The first crying wax **baby doll** was made about 1700, and walking dolls were being made by 1740. By 1780 dolls with turned wood bodies were produced, and later an **embossing dough** was added for further modeling and shaping. Germany, England, and France were all manufacturing dolls in large numbers.

The eighteenth and nineteenth centuries were years of tremendous growth in the toymaking industry, particularly in Germany. Along with the dolls, **doll house**s and wooden toys of all kinds were popular. **Toy soldier**s and "flats" of lead or tin were set on bases to stand upright. Variations of papier mâché were introduced from the East and used to make toys with remarkably fine details. Plaster, putty, and compounds of all kinds were developed and used with varying degrees of success. The 1700s also saw the development of **automatic toy**s; while mechanical devices had been in use for hundreds of years, it was during the eighteenth century that an attitude favoring elegance and frivolity allowed for the development of such toys. The designers of automata were well known, and the figures they created performed feats of incredible variety and complexity. Moving toys and **mechanical toy**s of all varieties were developed, including the famous **musical automata, clockwork toy**s, and key **windup toy**s. All of these were further improved and elaborated upon in the following century.

Tremendous changes occurred during the 1800s. First, changing attitudes toward children led to a widespread acceptance of toys. World trade routes opened and changes occurred in technology that made possible the production of many toys. Many, if not most, modern toys have their origins in toys produced during the 1800s. Among the toys that were produced during this time—but which had their origins in far earlier times—were **hoop**s, **swing**s, balls, yo-yos, **marble**s, and hobbyhorses.

In the 1800s, wood was still the most abundant and popular material for dolls and other toys. It was sometimes carefully **finish**ed, painted, and highly varnished. Other wooden toys were left natural. Papier mâché, pulp mâché, and composition were all frequently used, improved upon, and refined. Papier-mâché heads on **kid** bodies were used in dollmaking. There were also **earthenware doll**s, although few have survived.

In the second quarter of the 1800s, wax and wax over papier mâché became favored for dolls. In Germany papier-mâché heads were being produced along with china heads. Austria, Denmark, and France were also producing china heads.

In the 1850s dolls first appeared that made a distinction between baby dolls and those representing adults. Rubber was a new material, and elastic was introduced for string-ing. Rag was being used to reinforce the papier-mâché. **Frozen Charlotte**s came on the market about this time.

The 1860s saw the really fine development of **doll head**s, the "golden era" of dollmaking. Bisque heads, wigged and tinted, were made for bodies of wood or kid. Many new developments in toymaking were patented at this time. The **autoperipatetikos** came out in the 1860s, as did **ball-joint**ed dolls strung with metal or rubber—dolls were now able to sit down. Porcelain and wax were highly developed in French dolls, and in England, **rag doll**s were being manufactured.

In the 1880s the final big change was made from lady dolls to baby dolls. Babies had sleeping eyes, and wore gowns and long clothes. American Indian and black dolls were popular at this time, as were **character doll**s and **grotesque doll**s. The rag doll became even more popular.

The 1800s also brought lithography, and with it paper toys achieved new eminence. Juvenile theater and cutout sheets reached tremendous popularity. **Pollack's Toy Museum** in London attests to the ongoing interest in juvenile drama and the **"penny plain and tuppence colored"** sheets. Paper toys were abundant. Protean figures or **paper doll**s, **architectural plaything**s, and origami were all popular.

The use of rubber immediately influenced toy design. It was employed in making air-filled and solid rubber balls, **squeak toy**s, dolls, and toy animals. A little later, **celluloid** was introduced; the most outstanding of the **celluloid toy**s were produced in the early 1900s.

The development of optical toys in the 1800s was significant, as it paralleled the interest in animation and optics—the forerunners of photography and cinematography. Visual presentations of all kinds were developed, from panoramas to **peep show**s and **magic lantern**s. The Victorian preoccupation with intellectual pursuits made tremendous educational use of optical toys, particularly involving historical and geographical information in the visual presentations.

In the early 1900s printed cloth bodies and china heads were popular for dolls. Character dolls dominated the market. Celluloid dolls appeared, and dolls in military costume grew out of the Boer, Spanish-American, and Russo-Japanese wars. In 1913, Kewpies swept the doll world, followed by Happifats and whistling dolls. **Art Fabric doll**s were also popular.

The twentieth century has witnessed the manufacture of toys becoming a business of tremendous proportion throughout the world, with Germany and Japan among the best known for their toy exports. The toy industry throughout the 1900s has been well documented and many books are available for the collector to identify and date toys. **Military toy**s came to be made spectacularly realistic, although not without protest from many parents, pacifists, and educators. Toys in general became more and more mechanical, automated, and battery-run. Baby dolls were made to walk, talk, and cry. Big-sister dolls, such as the Barbie, created a whole new clothing industry devoted to costuming and outfitting the **mannequin**like dolls.

Model airplanes form a considerable portion of the twentieth-century toy market. Plastic parts have made possible the assembly of complex designs. The plastic can be cast with the finest of details, and the material is inexpensive enough to make the kit models accessible to almost all children. Cars, racers, planes, rockets, ships, and vehicles of all kinds have been produced in miniature, well formed and accurately designed. **Constructional** toys also expanded with the potentials of plastics enabling the manufacture of precisely fitted parts.

The study of child development also exerted an influence on toy production. The attitude of Friedrich Froebel, a German educator, was significant. While his own work was accomplished by the middle of the nineteenth century, his influence was most effective much later. He regarded toys as "occupations," and encouraged an approach that allowed children to discover through play, or to learn by doing. The organization of many kindergartens in terms of play activity has been based on his concepts.

Maria Montessori of Italy also influenced the design of toys for children through her work with their spontaneous interests. Simple, basic toys that had an educational function were favored—sanded building blocks and wood hammering toys. Susan Isaac's work at the Malting House School in Cambridge in the 1920s further influenced the present attitude toward play. She emphasized the importance of immediate experience, regarded toys as tools of learning, and particularly stressed that toys must be durable and sturdy.

Present-day craftspeople are continuing a tradition of folk toys that is in many cases influenced by the educational toys of this century. Most toymakers now respond in part to the material itself, using wood and cloth most frequently. The toys are often also personal and aesthetic statements.

Many fairs and craft markets today echo the fairs of the Renaissance, and the numbers and varieties of toys available are impressive. There is apparently a market eager for these handmade playthings, and many craftspeople support themselves in this way. The Dickens Fair, held annually in San Francisco, has a section devoted entirely to the work of present-day toymakers. The Renaissance Pleasure Faires in California and craft fairs all over the country provide a way of selling these wares to a public ready to buy them.

CONSTRUCTIONAL TOYS **Constructional toy**s, also referred to as **construction toys**, are essentially **building toy**s. That is, they consist of many parts that can be assembled in a variety of ways to produce structures—buildings, houses, bridges, etc. They are considered to be **learning toy**s because play with them involves the various principles of physics in construction and balance. These toys are also action or activity toys in the sense that they require the child to move or manipulate the parts. Some include simple machines—levers, inclined planes, pulleys, and parts of wheel-and-axle mechanisms. Constructions can be made from sticks, stones, bricks, sand, or mud, and as such they are **universal toy**s.

Among the most simple structural toys to make at home are wooden cubes. A 2″ × 2″ or 4″ × 4″ piece of wood, cut into lengths of the same dimensions, is a basic cube. Cubes can be sanded smooth and polished or stained, or they can be painted. Decorative papers can be glued to the surface of the **blocks** or the wood can be printed. Some picture-puzzle blocks have pictures on all 6 sides of each cube. When placed in a row in the proper sequence with the correct face up, the picture is revealed. When each block is turned one turn to the right, an entire new picture appears. Other building blocks are collections of cylinders, rectangular blocks, triangles, and arches that allow for a greater variety of structures. **Alphabet blocks** are a popular variation. Most traditional blocks depicted a letter or a number on one side with a picture on the other, and many contemporary ones follow this same format. While meant for building, the child is also exposed to the letters to become familiar with them and eventually to use them to form words. Later, the letters alone were cut from wood to make a popular educational toy well known in the Montessori schools. **Telescoping box**es provide pyramid blocks and are another old-time favorite that is still popular. Some are wood—others are made of illustration board or stiff **cardboard.**

Paper is also used in construction toys. Printed sheets, notched and sometimes perforated, allow for the assembling of elaborate structures, often of buildings of historical significance. **Cutout village**s have long been popular. The earliest cutout sheets were known as "découpage" in France and "bilderbage" in Germany. Similar toy sheets are available today in many countries throughout the world.

Among the all-time favorite construction devices are **Lincoln logs, Lego building brick**s, **Tinkertoy**s, and variations of these. Systems of connection are used, offering endless building possibilities. These **architectural plaything**s attract many adults as well as children. An assortment of constructional toys that utilize principles of geodesic construction are also available. Some have flexible plastic parts for connections, while others use cardboard or **rubber band**s.

DOLLS   Handmade **doll**s range from the simplest suggestion of a figure to the elaborately carved and **joint**ed wooden dolls. Some are made to be cuddled, loved, and handled by a child—others seem too fragile to be really used, and are perhaps dolls for adults, or dolls for display. Many dolls of antiquity were probably religious or votive figures or burial figures.

Clay became, and remained, a popular material for the making of dolls for centuries. A highly refined clay was used for the well-known **bisque doll head**s, and others of porcelain, china, and **Parian** also became popular. The doll head was often of one material, such as bisque, combined with a body of fabric or **kid**. Arms and legs were also often made of china. Some dolls were made entirely of china, with **string joint**s or **ball joint**s. Others were made as a single form, such as the **Frozen Charlotte**s, or all-in-one dolls. Today, clay is once again being used by a few craftspeople to produce dolls.

Wooden dolls have also been with us for centuries, though fewer have survived. The **penny wooden doll**s are known to collectors everywhere. They were **peg-jointed** and much more elaborate than the earlier **pestle doll**s. Few wood dolls are made today, except for the small wooden **clothespin doll**s.

Composition has changed considerably since it was first used. The earliest mixtures, such as **elastolin,** were susceptible to moisture. Other compositions using glues and resins developed, and **papier mâché** was also extensively used. The **bread-crumb doll** is another variation of a composition used for dolls. Wax is another material that for a period of years was a favorite in **dollmaking.** The **wax doll** was delicate, fragile, and subject to damage. It was not available to the average child because of its expense.

Dolls printed on paper, as in **cutout**s, have been popular for years. Protean figures were among the first **paper doll**s. Now, self-adhesive papers simplify their use.

The most popular dolls over all the years have been the **rag doll**s—those made of fabric. Simple **single-shape doll**s and **arch-shaped doll**s are easily made at home and much loved by small children. Some have simple **stitched joint**s or segmented bodies. These animated figures, or articulated dolls, are safe for small children. Similar easy-to-make dolls are the **sock doll** and **nylon stocking doll.** **Raggedy Ann** and **topsy-turvy doll**s are among the best-known rag dolls. Most are now **stuff**ed with **Dacron polyester batting,** although some are filled with cotton wadding or **cotton batting.** Kapok and **sawdust** are used very rarely now, and almost never in homemade dolls. **Wood wool,** once used commercially, has virtually disappeared.

Printing methods offer the possibility of silkscreen printing on fabric for producing multiples. The printing may be used on either fabric or **felt.** The photographic process expands this craft's potential greatly, allowing for the use of photographs in **portrait doll**s or **character doll**s.

Batik is a decorative form especially well suited to dollmaking, as is direct-dye painting. **Embroidery, appliqué, needlepoint, crewel** stitching, and fabric painting are all used on contemporary dolls. **Pillow doll**s, which utilize a pillow form as stuffing, may use any of those techniques on the pillow top. **Trapunto,** which is primarily a quilting technique, is sometimes used in dollmaking. Most of the methods and materials of **stuffed toy**s apply equally to dolls.

Various other materials are used in the construction of the **doll head** and **doll body.** Cornhusks were used for some, manipulated to produce charming figures. **Apple doll**s, figures with dried and carved **apple head**s, are popular folk toys in various countries. Corncobs, nuts, and materials of every variety have been used for the heads of toys and dolls. The doll is certainly a **universal toy** as well as an **emergent toy.** In a few cases, the replicas of human figures were ephemeral toys and even edible toys.

Many other toys developed out of playing with dolls and are related to dolls, such as **doll house**s, doll furniture, and **doll clothes.**

EPHEMERAL TOYS   Those **toys** that are perishable or edible are often referred to as ephemeral toys.

Among the materials used for these short-lived delights are flowers. Hollyhock dolls or fragile dolls of camellias are among the most popular. Toothpicks or similar small sticks usually aid in their construction. The life-span of a **flower doll** depends upon the temperature, humidity, etc., but they rarely last for more than an hour or so. Little sailing boats of inverted flowers are also a popular plaything. Daisy chains and crowns of leaves and blossoms are made from flowers of all kinds. Whether or not they are actually toys may be debatable; that children love making them, and that they are definitely ephemeral, is not.

Soap bubbles are another obvious example of ephemeral toys. Bubble blowers of all kinds have been devised to aid in soap-bubble blowing, and special solutions containing glycerin make the bubbles last a little longer. **Soap carving** is a related activity, used in making bath toys or water toys.

Most toys that fall into this ephemeral category are edible. Gingerbread made into the shapes of figures, letters, animals, and objects of all kinds have been popular for hundreds of years. Some gingerbread boys were gilded or frosted for added charm—currents and nuts supplied details. Few children have not devoured a gingerbread creature of some kind.

Baker's art has been popular the world over, and decorative breads and cookies are traditional in many countries. Some of the breads and cookies are edible and some are not. Among the edible products are those associated with specific countries. **Lebkuchen, springerle,** and honig-tirggel are among them. **Bread-dough sculpture**s from Mexico, Italy, Finland, and Switzerland are also edible. Beautifully painted figures from Ecuador and Peru may be eaten, although they are better described as perishable than edible; their delight is visual and the execution often exquisite.

Cookie art is a favorite of children everywhere. **Cookie-board** molds are used to impress designs on a stiff edible dough, or cookie cutters will divide rolled dough into animal shapes. There are **dark dough**s and light doughs, often used in combination.

Candies are well known as temporary toys. Many kinds are produced commercially, such as sugar babies or maple sugar candies, but others, such as **marzipan,** can be made at home. Chocolate rabbits and chickens are traditional Easter sweets, as are eggs of all kinds. **Sugar egg**s are often hollow with little scenes inside, viewed as though they were **peep egg**s or **peep show**s. Chocolate eggs are occasionally treated the same way, although more often they are decorated on the outside. Easter eggs, hardcooked before painting, are decorated by dyeing, painting, or even batik, as are the **pysanky egg**s of Eastern Europe. Some eggs are blown out to make **hollow egg**s and these are decorated and used ornamentally.

Among some of the perishable materials for dough sculpture that are not edible—but that may work better for modeling—are **bread clay, cornstarch dough, salt clay, salt dough,** and **baker's clay.** Many of these **inedible dough**s must be baked, but some can be dried at room temperature.

Ephemeral figures are among those that cannot really be said to be toys or playthings—and yet they cannot be disregarded here. Among these are jack-o'-lanterns, sand castles, snowmen, and scarecrows.

FOLK TOYS Out of the beliefs, traditions, and customs of people grouped together over a long period of time emerge those playthings classified as **folk toys**. Usually the groups of people are collected to form a cohesive unit, whether it is ethnic, racial, national, tribal, or geographic. Unity and continuity are essential for the perpetuation of folk toys, which must have some significance for the group to be made and handed down from generation to generation. Ordinarily the origins of such toys are lost; the design is altered slightly by each toymaker or by the availability of materials or tools. Folk toys are always handmade, and are often based on principles of physics utilized in ingenious and innovative ways.

The materials used in folk toys are almost always natural ones. Nails may be used, and tools are certainly employed if these are commonly available to the folk artist. Wood is undoubtedly the most common material. Other vegetable materials, such as cornhusks or corncobs, pine cones, cockleburs, nuts, and gourds, are frequently transformed into imaginative creatures, objects, or games. Metals are not commonly employed in making folk toys, although many Mexican ones are made from tin obtained by opening and flattening tin cans. This is a **making do** approach to design, and folk artists everywhere have adapted available materials to their own purposes.

Whittling, or wood carving, is most often accomplished with a jackknife or similar wood-carver. There are few folk toys that do not require the maker to whittle. **Clay** and fabric are also common materials of folk toys, including **earthenware dolls**, **penny wooden dolls**, and **rag dolls**. **Marbles**, or **mibs**, of clay have been known for centuries. Figures of animals and people have been made of all kinds of materials the world around. Eskimos may carve ivory or bone into the animals with which they are familiar, corncob animals come from Central America. The **twirling yo-yo** made with the shiny "cacoon" bean pods is made in the West Indies. The folk artist in each area adapts whatever native materials are available.

Folk tales, religion, and social mores are also interwoven with toys. Thus the **Haman knocker** is a toy associated with Israel, where it recalls an episode in Jewish history. The Daruma doll rocks placidly, resembling to the Japanese the sixth-century Indian Buddhist who founded Zen Buddhism. The **crib set** figures represent a Nativity scene to Christian people in various countries, and the **Kachina dolls** of the Hopi Indians represent religious figures. The **bull-roarer, slingshot,** and **diabolo** were all made originally for purposes other than play. Many examples of **baker's art,** or dough sculpture, serve the purposes of religion, superstition, or tradition, only to be consumed or played with later.

Among some of the traditional folk toys which have appeared in various parts of the world (under different names and often with slight changes) are **hoop rolls, tops, noisemakers, rattles, hobby horses, nested eggs,** and marbles. **Pecking chickens** and **climbing bears** occur most frequently in Eastern Europe. Among some of the best-known American folk toys are the **flipperdinger, whimmydiddle,**

and **peashooter.** Where they originated is not known. **Games** such as ball-and-cup or **ring-and-pin** are found in widely diverse cultures, making speculations on origin difficult. The most popular themes or subjects in folk toys seem to be birds and eggs, followed by horses and people. Animated figures and animals are most amusing and delightful to all, and are found everywhere.

GAMES AND OTHER TOYS Any contest, whether physical or mental in nature, that is played with a prescribed set of rules may be called a **game.** Games are not really toys, but make up an important part of play. They become suddenly popular and just as suddenly disappear—only to appear again later, or to be known by a new name.

Jigsaw puzzles, from the simplest to the most complex, challenge people of all ages to reassemble pictures, relying on visual clues. The most complex use repeated shapes in the **interlocking parts.** The **double-layer puzzle** is the simplest for small children. There are also **three-dimensional puzzles** and **geometric puzzles.** They are always kept in boxes or **puzzle bags,** as the loss of a single piece is a great frustration in puzzle assembly. Other kinds of **puzzles** are the **prisoner's lock** and **dissected pictures.**

Game boards are used in countless games, each one slightly different. Most craftspeople who make game boards produce the checkerboard-chessboard. The Game of India and backgammon use boards of a standard design, usually in wood with inlay. Some boards are painted, others may use a tissue paper collage or simple squares of colored paper or contact paper glued in place. Some are sewn on fabric, silkscreened on **felt,** or block-printed on paper or cloth.

Many games have parts that are moved or thrown. **Toss games** and **bean bag** games are included in this category, as are **knucklebones, jacks, dice, jackstraws, skittles,** and many others. Battledore and shuttlecock involve batting a feathered **ball,** whereas in **ring-and-pin** and **spear-the-fish** the parts are connected; these come closer to being toys.

MECHANICAL TOYS AND MOVING TOYS **Mechanical toys** include all of those that function on mechanical principles. They are motion toys, or systems in which the parts work or move together to some purpose. These toys "do" something. Some operate with strings, others with weights, counterweights, or levers. Some are set into motion by trickling streams of sand, others by water. While among the earliest of the water toys are those developed by Hero of Alexandria, and references to mechanical toys appear in the "Iliad," there were hundred of years following when the possibilities of mechanical operation of toys were ignored. During the Renaissance there was again great interest in mechanically operated toys and by the 1700s, automata, or **automatic toys,** were developed. They reached incredible complexity during the 1800s.

All **moving toys** deal in some way with motion. They may be simple examples of the phenomena of various forces on bodies, such as **tops** and **ladderwalkers.** Weighted toys rely on gravity to keep a round-bottomed toy, such as the **tumble doll,** upright. Other **balance toys,** made hollow and filled with shifting weights (such as ball bearings or mercury), are given erratic and repeated movements as gravity pulls the weight down, righting the toy. **Sand toys** are made to take advantage of the weight of falling sand to activate movable parts. The effect of added weight changes the balance, and in some of these toys the sand sets in motion the mechanical power of a lever, setting into motion some other aspect of the toy. Sand may fall onto a **paddle wheel,** giving continuous movement to the **axle** of the wheel, which in turn animates other parts of the toy.

Stored energy is another power source. A **spring,** when compressed, has stored power or energy. The **jack-in-the-box** operates on this kind of power. **Windup toys** and **clockwork toys** both store energy by winding springs of various kinds and controlling the release of the tension so that there is a more protracted period of animation. Key windup toys, so popular in the 1800s, are of this kind. Figures of all kinds were devised during that century to perform extraordinary tasks: orchestras played, acrobats performed, and monkeys wrote. In **rubber-band toys,** the twisting of the **rubber band** stores energy through tension created in the band. **Clothespin wrestlers, paddle wheel boats,** and **racing spools** operate this way. **Yo-yos, buzz buttons,** and **thaumatropes** all rely on the use of tension and relaxation in the control of strings to let inertia and kinetic energy keep the toy in motion.

Another method of moving or animating toys is through the use of air power. A tremendous variety of wind toys are set in motion through forced air. Among the simplest is the **blowpipe,** followed by the **peashooter** and **flipperdinger,** all of which are operated by blowing air through a pipe or tube that compresses it. The forced air then moves some other part of the toy. The **flying machine** and **alouette** both move or "fly" when air is forced past the propellers fast enough to give them lift. **Pinwheels** are spun or moved by running with the toy and holding the blades to face the wind. Even the simple **bubble blower** is a **wind toy.**

Toys may also be set into motion by any of several other means. Rockers are designed so that little resistance is offered to movement. When a toy set on rockers is tilted forward, gravity draws it back, and kinetic energy keeps it in motion. It takes little additional energy pouring in to continue the motion. The **rocking horse** and rocking shoo-fly operate in this way. Magnets may also be incorporated into a toy to animate parts. Many **magnetic toys** are used as bath toys, with the magnets being used to draw or lead objects by "remote control." Momentum and inertia are used in maintaining the action in other moving toys.

Many articulated or **animated toys** are set into action by the way in which they are handled. The **dancing man** is a good example. Other examples are the **monkey-on-a-stick,** the hand **puppet,** and the **do-nothing machine.** The toy itself does not move under power stored within it, but by energy applied directly to it. All such toys would thus be **action toys,** or **activity toys,** in the sense that a child playing with them does something. The **acrobat,** or flapjack, and the **cup-and-ball** are set in motion in this way.

Most automatic toys do not require activity on the part of a child. The **autoperipatetikos** doll was a complex **mechanical doll** that could walk unaided. It was followed by dolls and figures that made various movements and talked. Some early talking dolls contained small phono-graphs to produce sounds, others were operated by blowing into a tube to produce the sounds. Music boxes were installed with key windup mechanisms.

OPTICAL TOYS   **Optical toys,** or visual toys, have long fascinated both children and adults. Most of these are **viewing toys** based on various principles of optics and light.

The **panorama toy** was made in the 1700s, and the first public panorama was shown in 1785. The **historiscope** and **myriopticon** were variations. It was in the early 1800s that a concentrated interest in optics led to the development of new and significant toys. Among the first of these was the **thaumatrope,** invented in 1825, based on the optical principle of persistence of vision. The **kaleidoscope** and **debusscope** were invented at about the same time as the thaumatrope. A few years later the strotoscope and the **phenakistoscope** were invented. They had a completely different arrangement of parts but again relied on the persistence of vision. Similar toys were the magic disk, tantascope, phanascope, and **praxinoscope.**

The **zoetrope** and the **magic lantern** evidenced a continuing interest in movement and light. The **polyopticon** and **panoptique** were similar; all were based on devices described as early as the thirteenth century by Roger Bacon. The **lampascope** is another variation of the magic lantern.

In the middle 1800s a toy called **les métamorphoses** was invented, also known as polyoptic pictures. Various kinds of **proscenium toys** were also popular in the nineteenth century. The **kinora** was one of the early animated **peep shows.** Various kinds of viewing toys were made, including the **diorama** and the **zogroscope.** The **optical paradox** was another viewing toy. The **kittiscope,** invented in the early 1900s, was one of the first moving-picture machines.

Other, much simpler, optical toys which children can make are the **water lens** and the **water scope. Peep eggs** and the **Thames tunnel** toy are peep-show toys that can be made at home.

ROPE AND STRING TOYS   The string figure, or cat's cradle, is one of the simplest of all toys in that it involves no construction at all—simply a manipulation of the strings. In this sense, it is actually a game, and one in which the apparent simplicity belies the complexity of its many variations. **String** has been a part of numerous toys, but only in cat's cradle is the string itself the toy. A similar use is made of rope in the knotted rope swing or the jump rope.

Most toys use string to attach pieces or connect parts. The **ticktack, cup-and-ball, swinging-weight toys** such as the **pecking chickens,** and **string dolls** are examples. **Pull toys** use string as a handle. In other toys, tension may be applied to a string to animate the toy, as with the **monkey-on-a-stick,** the **apple mill, string top,** or yo-yo. The marionette, or string puppet, and the kite need string for manipulation.

Most string used in toys is of the ordinary household variety. It is usually white, inexpensive, and easily available. Nylon leader can sometimes be used, but not if the string must be wound; it is springy and resists winding. It also tends to stretch if weight is suspended from it, although it has far greater tensile strength than string. Synthetic cord is smooth and strong, and comes in a variety of weights. A twisted linen cord is satisfactory for stringing tops, yo-yos, and **jumping jack**s.

Swings are the most common rope toys. The old-fashioned **rope swing** has been popular for centuries, although it is now often supplanted by metal. There are double-rope swings such as board swings and box swings and single-rope swings such as **gunnysack swing**s, circle swings, and bag swings. A **tire swing** can use either a single or double rope. It is essential in planning a swing to consider some details carefully. First, a tree branch must be found that can support the weight easily; then, there must be adequate clear space to allow the rider to swing without danger of striking an object.

Manila rope is strong and commonly available. The rope will eventually rot, so care must be taken to check it periodically for fraying or wear. **Nylon rope** is smoother to handle, stronger, and more expensive. When using the nylon, care must be taken to tie it to the tree in such a way that the rope itself does not slide back and forth on the branch, as abrasion will wear it out. An improperly tied knot will also cause abrasion to the tree, wearing through the bark and possibly causing damage. Nylon or synthetic rope tends to fray when cut. After cutting a length for a swing, the ends can be melted over flame or heat, and the fraying will be checked. Be cautious in melting the ends because the nylon may drip if melted too much. It gets very hot and retains the heat for several minutes.

When swings are cut from wood, special attention must be given to **finish**ing the wood. Plywood must be well sealed and finished to prevent separation and warping of the layers. A board swing must be cut with the length of the grain going the length of the swing seat, from rope to rope. A thick, sturdy board is required. Holes should be drilled through the board for the ropes. The holes should be drilled far enough from the outside edge so that the strength of the wood between the hole and the outside edge is not lost. The seat must be wide enough for the comfort of the swinger.

The jump rope need be nothing more than a length of rope, unless the craftsperson decides to make handles. Wood is most commonly used for this, although fabric is also popular. Either material is smoother and easier to hold than the rope.

Pull strings for toys should be smooth, easily grasped, and durable. While nylon leader often seems appropriate on small, lightweight toys, it is difficult to knot. If used as a pull string, run the end of the leader through a **wood bead** and then tie it around the bead. Again, heat may help set the knot. Cotton string or cord is usable for a pull string but will not support much weight. It deteriorates if left outdoors or exposed to moisture. Manila rope is strong but has a scratchy surface that small children may find difficult to grasp. A heavy cotton cord or a smooth synthetic cord works well.

STUFFED TOYS   Among every child's favorite toys there is usually at least one well-worn **stuffed animal.** These soft creatures have found their way into stories, poems, and books. Pooh Bear, **Archie,** and the "**Gingham Dog** and the Calico Cat" are among the best known. **Raggedy Ann** and

Raggedy Andy grew from storybook characters, and Little Orphan Annie came from one of James Whitcomb Riley's poems. It is not unheard of for adults to still cherish such childhood companions.

Stuffed toys have the advantage of being soft and lightweight. They can be picked up, dropped on bare toes, or slept with. Many can be washed, some can accompany a child to the bathtub, and although they can be torn, they don't break.

Fabric balls are among the simplest stuffed toys. Made of wedge-shaped or hexagonal pieces of fabric, the balls are stuffed with **shredded foam rubber,** nylon stockings, or other **stuffing material. Fabric block**s, constructed of squares of fabric, are similarly made. **Seam** allowances are added so that the pieces can be machine-sewn, then turned and stuffed. One last seam must, of course, be left open to allow for turning and stuffing. If the balls or blocks are made of **felt** they can be whipstitched, or overcast from the top side. (Felt toys are not washable.) Some fabric blocks are made like **alphabet blocks,** with letters and numbers used to embellish the squares of fabric before they are **join**ed.

The stuffing material in any stuffed toy is determined by its eventual intended use. The advantage of **foam rubber** or shredded foam is that it is lightweight. It has the added advantage of being easily compressed, so it is often used in **bath toy**s.

The fabric from which a bath toy is made must also be washable; after removing it from the bath it can be squeezed to force most of the water out.

Nylon stockings also make good stuffing material. Nylon does not absorb water, so a toy stuffed with it can be wrung out and will dry quickly. Any toy stuffed with either foam rubber or nylon stockings can withstand the rigors of being left out in the rain—provided the fabric, embroidery, etc., can also withstand the water and weathering.

Other stuffing materials include beans, unpopped popcorn, or any similar hard, dry substance. Sand was used at one time, but tends to trickle out of even the tiniest openings. **Bean bag**s and **toss game**s may be filled with dried navy beans, loosely packed. **Sawdust, wood wool,** and wood shavings are all usable stuffing materials. The use of the toy is a factor in selecting the stuffing material. Kapok and cotton batting were formerly the most frequently used for stuffed toys, but have been largely replaced now by **Dacron polyester batting** or other synthetic batting. Kapok and cotton are not considered washable when used as stuffing because they absorb water, are slow to dry, and tend to mildew because of the moisture retained inside. The polyesters are more resilient, nonallergenic, and do not absorb moisture.

Animals are easily simplified in form so they are suitable as subject matter for stuffed toys. Sturdy fabrics are needed for durability—denim, **acrylic canvas,** duck, firmly woven cottons and synthetics. Other fabrics that offer good washability as well as inviting textures are corduroy, washable velveteen, terrycloth, and **fake fur.**

Some stuffed animals are made in sections. The finished parts, or limbs, are sewn on or are connected by rivets or **string joint**s to the body. Other animals are made all in one, and are animated with **stitched joint**s. Details of features are added in a variety of ways—embroidery, appliqué, direct-dye painting, etc., and the possibilities for variation are endless.

WHEELED TOYS **Wheeled toy**s are among the oldest and most popular of all toys. Many are devised so that the child can move or push the toy in play. Others are attached to **string**s or handles to make **pull toy**s. Almost all of these playthings with wheels are **activity toy**s, involving the child physically in the manipulation of the toy.

Some wheeled toys combine elements that go beyond simple movement. The attachment of sound devices, activated by the movement of wheel, makes **sound toy**s or **bell toy**s of them. **Friction toy**s are usually wheeled toys, and some automatic and key **windup toy**s are also on wheels. They are among the toys that craftspeople seem to most enjoy making.

Wheeled toys pulled by a cord have been popular for centuries. Animals on platforms, such as the sheep and horses on wheeled bases (with which most people are familiar), are also of ancient origin. Small carts, trains, cars, and **wagon**s are perennial favorites.

Wheeled toys can be made from a variety of materials—clay, wood, plastic, cast bronze, or sheet metal. Simple blocks of wood can be used to suggest cars, trucks, or even animals. Various shapes can be cut in the wood, making the rough outline with a bandsaw or saber saw. If the wood is no thicker than two inches, it can be cut on a small electric jigsaw. It is then sanded or smoothed with sandpaper, starting with a coarse grain and working up to medium and fine grains.

Wheels can be cut from any wood or plywood. However, many ready-cut disks are available. Spools, broom handles, large dowels, or wooden curtain rods can be sliced into sections for wheels. Checkers and round decorative wood pieces from lumber yards can also be used. Large wood beads make excellent wheels for small toys and have the advantage of being already drilled. Flat drawer pulls will also function as wheels.

It is important to drill **axle** holes in the body of the toy so that they are parallel to the bottom of the body. That will help keep all the wheels even. A drill press works best for this, but a power hand drill will do. It is almost impossible to drill holes exactly parallel when using a hand drill. There are other ways of attaching the wheels, however. A nail can be used as the axle for each wheel, with the nail going through a hole drilled in the wheel, and then driven part way into the body of the toy (**a.**).

Usually, in the assembly of such a toy, a dowel is used for the axle. A drill bit is selected with a corresponding-sized dowel, and the wheels and toy are drilled. Then the dowel is inserted through one wheel, the body of the toy, and out the other wheel. This is repeated for the second axle-and-wheels set. The wheel must remain free on the dowel, and the dowel must turn freely in the toy body. Something must be added at the ends of the dowels to keep the wheels from coming off; a thumbtack, a pin, or wooden drawpull can be set through the end of the dowel (**b.**).

A simple wheel-and-axle assembly is one in which tabs are cut as part of the side pieces of a wagon (**c.**). The axle is then run through the holes drilled in the tabs. If the base of

the wagon is cut from a thick board, it can be drilled through to make a hole for the axle (**d.**). In another method, the axle can be held secure to the bottom of a wagon by using staple nails (**e.**). See ill.

WOOD **Wood** has traditionally been the most commonly used material for **toy**s. It may now be supplanted to a large extent by plastic, but there is little doubt that wood is still the most popular.

The woods for toys are selected according to various considerations. **Hardwood**s, while they are beautiful and can be polished to a smooth, **glossy** surface, have certain disadvantages. They are harder to cut or saw, more difficult to find, and more expensive. However, they are more durable and can withstand more rough play than **softwood**s. The size of the toy is a factor in wood selection. A toy that must support weight needs to be stronger than one that will be pulled along by a **string.** Sometimes the woods are selected in terms of color. For example, **light wood**s and **dark wood**s might be specifically selected for a checkerboard. Contrasting wood colors might be selected for various parts of a **toy train** or animal.

The kinds of saws or cutting tools available would also have to be considered. If all cutting must be accomplished with a coping saw, then redwood, pine, or balsa wood is best. If power tools are available, then hardwoods and **plywood**s can be used. Seasoned wood, available from some lumber yards, is preferred, especially for large-scale projects. Wood that is unseasoned may warp if used in hand-carved projects, although clear pine boards, cut up for small toys, would pose no problem. Half-inch-thick clear pine is probably the wood most often used in toys.

Wood has its greatest strength on the lengthwise grain. Cutting should be done with this in mind. A toy horse, for example, should be cut so that the length of the **wood grain** runs the length of the legs. Cut across the grain, the legs would be more likely to break off.

Whittling requires few tools. It can, in fact, be accomplished with a **jackknife** or a carver and nothing else. The Barlow knife was the all-purpose whittling knife in early American times for wood carving. Another wood carving tool for larger projects is the drawknife. The chisel and mallet are also sometimes employed for large carved wood figures, as together they cut wood much faster than a handknife. A C-clamp is a helpful tool for whittling, although not essential. Care must always be taken to cut away from the hands, avoiding the danger of cuts. A pocketknife should have a good steel blade, and be kept sharp with an oilstone.

The coping saw, fretsaw, and scroll saw are all hand-powered saws. In using any of these a bench vise is helpful in holding wood secure. The electric jigsaw is a simply operated power saw, and some models are very efficient and safe to use. Band saws and table saws are high-powered machines that require knowledge and skill to operate. They are a tremendous help if toys are to be produced in any quantity.

Mitered corners or miter joints require very accurate cutting, so a miter box is usually necessary. The miter box is fitted with a hand-powered saw. A miter cut can be made accurately on a table saw, but it is very difficult with a hand saw or jigsaw. **Mortise-and-tenon** joints or tongue-and-groove joints are used in fine woodcrafting, but most toymaking can utilize butt joints secured with nails.

Wood parts and movable parts can be fitted and fastened with dowel or **peg-joint**s. Electric drills or hand drills can be fitted with drill bits to correspond to the sizes of the dowels.

Cut wood can be smoothed with sandpaper. Extremely rough edges can be cut down and much shaping can be done with a wood rasp. Files of various kinds aid in smoothing edges and corners, and some are made especially for curves and inside cuts. The half-round file and the rattail file make it possible to sand inside drilled holes and curves.

The use of the wood lathe requires expertise in woodworking. Most toymakers, producing a few toys for their own children or friends, will not need a lathe, but for the producing toymaker, it will greatly expand the possibilities. Lathe turning is essential for certain hollowed-out forms. The **nested egg**s, for example, are hollowed on a lathe. The **Noah's ark** animal ring makes ingenious use of a **lathe-turned** form. Turned wood is sometimes used to make the basic shapes, as in chess figures, which are then elaborated upon by cutting or carving.

Wood pieces can be joined by simpler means than the miter, mortise-and-tenon, or tongue-and-groove methods mentioned above. When the less difficult butt joint is used, the two pieces to be nailed together are often glued as well. **White glue** or wood glue is most often used, but any household glue or **airplane glue** will work.

The raw, sanded wood can be treated or **finish**ed in any of a great many ways. **Hardwood**s are often sanded smooth and left as they are, or oiled, but most toys are made of pine and similar woods, which require a wood finish. There are various simple ways of adding stain and color to wood. One of the most permanent is the use of oil-base paint. Any open spots, nail holes, dents, or spaces at joints should first be filled; wood putty or spackle can be used. Plywood almost always has openings on the edges and these should be filled. The filler should be sanded smooth, then the wood should be sealed with sealer, shellac, or varnish. When dry, it is sanded. Sometimes undercoat is used without a sealer. Either or both can be used, but the sealer is always applied first, then the undercoat. Sealer is used if a transparent finish is desired, and undercoat for an opaque finish.

After the undercoat or sealer is dry and sanded, the paint is added. Spray enamels, available in aerosol cans, are among the easiest to use. They are available in glossy, satin, or matte finish. Spray paint comes in a wide variety of colors and kinds, including **acrylic paint,** acrylic polymer emulsion paint, **acrylic spray, lacquer enamel,** and **high-gloss lacquer.** There are also clear spray varnishes and plastic coatings.

Any toy that may be mouthed or bitten on by a child must be painted with lead-free paint. Some paints still on the market may contain lead, and this will be noted on the label. All oil-base paints require **solvent**s for cleaning brushes and removing excess paint. Caution must always be used in handling the paint thinners, **mineral spirits,** acetone, or other solvents. The **water-base paint**s require only water for cleanup, and are excellent for children's use.

Latex paint is easier to use than oil-base paint, although it does not give a sheen or glossy surface. It can be coated with a **finish,** however. Raw wood without sealer or undercoat can be given a stain of thinned **tempera, food coloring,** or **watercolor paint;** it can then be given a coat of spar varnish or a similar finish.

Antiquing finishes can be used over painted or stained woods. Tissue papers can be collaged onto raw or sealed wood with varnish or clear plastic spray. Cutouts of colored paper can be glued on and sealed. **Contact paper**s, Mystik tape, or colored pressure-sensitive tapes can be used decoratively. None of these finishes is as permanent as enamels or oil-base paints and **lacquer**s.

There are many sources of wood other than lumber yards. Common household articles or containers made of wood can be put to a variety of uses. Wood spools are probably the most versatile of these **found materials.** They can be connected to round **wood bead**s to make **spool doll**s, or cut down to make spool tops. Spool racers, spool tractors, and spool rattles are all favorites, and **spool chain**s are made in brightly painted colors for babies. The **weaving spool** is also made from the wood on which sewing thread is wound. Many wooden spools are now being replaced with plastic, so perhaps the wooden ones will soon be a thing of the past.

Wooden boxes are a good source of thin wood. Some boxes can themselves be used as the toy—a cigar box, for example, with wheels added becomes a **wagon.** Drawers from old sewing machines or from small chests-of-drawers may provide the basic cart or wagon. Wood from boxes and fruit crates can be easily cut. Checkers make excellent wooden wheels, as do sliced wooden curtain rods. Moldings and **finial**s can be added to simple wooden blocks for the details of a train engine or a racing car. Drawer pulls can suggest the people in small cars, or might be used as wheels. Old furniture can be obtained at very little expense, and may yield a surprising amount of turned wood or wood doweling. Wooden clothespins also offer the figures for **clothespin wrestlers** and **clothespin doll**s. Scrap woods are often available from cabinetmakers and lumber yards in such variety that no sawing of the wood is required. A walk through the ten-cent store or thrift shop will turn up a surprising collection of wood—trays, boxes, lids, yardsticks, and kitchen tools. Broken rake handles or hammer handles can be sliced into sections for **ten pins,** sliced thin for wheels, or used for various parts in **constructional toy**s. A variety of wood is available to the toymakers, at almost no cost.

FABRIC   The fabric for rag dolls, stuffed toys, and cloth animals is selected for various reasons—strength, texture, pattern, availability, washability, or cost. Usually any of several fabrics will serve, so it is possible to find one that meets all or nearly all requirements.

If strength is a primary concern, canvas, duck, denim, and **acrylic canvas** are good. A swing seat, for example, would require one of these fabrics, or perhaps an awning material. Most synthetics are also very strong.

If texture is of special interest, as for a **teddy bear,** fake fur, velveteen, terrycloth, or other pile fabrics could be used. Velveteen is cotton and washable, velvet is not. Terrycloth is washable, but may snag. All are soft to the touch.

Sometimes pattern is of particular interest. A stuffed snake might invite the use of striped fabric. Tiny prints for **doll**s or **doll clothes** could be cottons or cotton blends. Stockinet, stretch fabrics, and nylon stockings can all be used for stuffed toys.

Washability is often a factor in children's toys. Broadcloth, blends, corduroy, kettle cloth, muslin, drill—all can be used appropriately. **Felt** has a soft texture in a wide range of colors, but it must be dry cleaned. **Scotchgard**ed fabrics that resist soiling, moisture, and stains are especially desirable for stuffed toys.

Jointed figures can be made in fabric by forming the parts separately. The completed parts are then assembled and stitched together. For example, arms that are first sewn, turned, and **stuff**ed can then be inserted in the side seam of the figure; **fabric joint**s can be made by stitching over the material where it is to bend.

To transfer designs from paper to fabric, any of several methods can be used. The large pieces can be cut as any dress pattern is cut, by pinning the pattern in place. If a drawing has been made it can be transferred to the fabric by using a transfer pencil. Dressmaker's carbon, embroidery carbon paper, or a tracing wheel and chalk may be employed to copy the design. When making a symmetrical shape, a **half-pattern** can be used. Graph paper will be of help in enlarging or reducing a drawing. The original drawing must be divided into a grid pattern so that it can serve as a guide in translating the drawing to graph paper. The graph paper can then be cut out and used as the pattern.

Among the many ways of adding detail and pattern to stuffed forms are batik, direct-dye painting, iron-on fabrics, hand appliqué, machine appliqué, and embroidery. Many batik artists have designed their work so that it can be cut and stuffed to make three-dimensional animals and toys. Direct-dye painting also allows for the design of single, unique pieces. Fabric painting can be accomplished with textile paints or with permanent dyes and aniline dyes, such as Procion, Versatex, and Inko dye—a few that are used. Silkscreen printing allows for production work, whereas the use of fabric crayon, iron-on appliqué, and permanent **marking pen** is limited to individually produced pieces. Iron-on tapes allow for a quick, direct, easy means of adding color and detail. Because they are heat-set, they can be used only on fabrics that can withstand the hot ironing. Most will last through several washings if they are properly applied. If they loosen, they can be ironed again, or new pieces can be used to replace them. Bonding tape, mending tape, and iron-on patches can all be used.

Hair can be made from yarn of any kind. Strips of **felt,** ribbon, or stitched fabric can be used. Real hair is sometimes added, taken from wigs, but is used less on dolls for children than on dolls for adults. Fringe, ball fringe, ribbon, rick-rack, laces, and stuffed cloth all make good hair or manes for fabric toys.

Mirror embroidery is sometimes used to add a decorative surface to stuffed forms. Various cloth birds and animals imported from the East are sometimes covered with the small mica mirrors outlined in buttonhole stitches.

The **stuffing material** used in fabric toys depends upon specific needs. If the toy is to be washed, a nonabsorbent filler must be used. **Dacron polyester batting** is commonly available; other polyester and synthetic battings can be used. If the stuffed toy is not washable, then the stuffing can be a nonwashable material, such as kapok or **cotton batting.** Most **sock doll**s, **rag doll**s, **baby doll**s, and stuffed animals will be washed at some time. If kapok is used as the filler, it can be removed before the toy is washed and then replaced. **Shredded foam rubber,** plastic foam, or foam pellets can be used as stuffing, but do not give the toy a really smooth surface. Shredded foam rubber can be squeezed to remove water, so it is a good choice in making **bath toy**s.

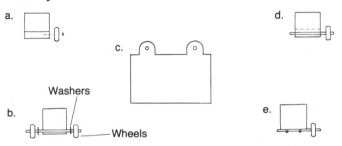

toy sheets. Puppets. Toys. The papers or sheets on which were engraved the characters for **Juvenile Drama.** These sheets were the "**penny plain and tuppence colored**" of the **toy theater.** Also see **Pollack's Toy Museum.**

toy soldier. Toys. Any small figure dressed in military uniform. Toy soldiers have traditionally been made of cardboard, clay, metal, plaster, and wood. **Flats** were made from metal or cardboard. Tin soldiers and lead soldiers, originally cast in molds of slate, were either solid or hollow. Toy soldiers have been so popular that in the 1840s there was an attempt to standardize size, making the toys from different companies and countries interchangeable. Those of wood or **papier mâché** were, by the nature of the materials, necessarily larger. Many toy soldiers are made less as toys for children than as **scale model**s for collectors.

Among the earliest remaining examples of toy soldiers are French tin figures of knights in armor and mounted knights of clay. Most toy soldiers today are made of a rubbery plastic. Also see **military toy.**

toy telephone. Toys. See **tube telephone.**

toy theater. Puppets. Stage productions in which the puppets are made from paper or similar flat material. The manipulators are at the stage sides, and a figure is moved by means of wires or sticks attached at the base of the figure. The "**penny plain and tuppence colored**" was the original paper figure, or **flat puppet,** of the toy theater. Any flat-figured puppet or paper-cutout puppet can be used on the toy-theater stage. Also see **Pollack's Toy Museum, toy sheets** and **Puppets: The Puppet Stage.**

toy train. Toys. A set of railway cars, usually including passenger cars, engine, and caboose. Simple ones for small children may be made of wood with interlocking connections between the cars and are often used as **pull toys**. Some of the earliest toy trains, of the middle 1800s, were operated by gravity on an inclined plane, and others of paper were on picture sheets or **cutouts**. More elaborate trains were cast or made of sheet metal. Mechanical locomotives were powered from steam, then **clockwork**, and, finally, electricity.

The manufacture of electric trains has become a business of great importance in the toy industry. Toy trains are made as **miniature**s or as **scale model**s, and many now are run in elaborately arranged sets that include landscaping, buildings, and remote-control operation. Also see **Hornby**.

T-pin. Macramé. A small steel pin with a crossbar at the top. This, or a similar type of **pin**, is an essential piece of macramé equipment and is used to anchor the macramé. No. 24 is a very good size. Also see **anchoring** and **Macramé: Tools and Materials**.

T-pin. Stitchery. A large, strong pin with a straight head, that makes the pin a T shape. Because the end can be easily handled, it is often used to hang **fabrics** or light **panels**. Too thick to be used to pin through most fabrics, it is generally regarded as a heavy-duty pin for temporary hanging.

T-pins. Jewelry. See **steel pins**.

trac. Basketry. See **border** and **Basketry: Woven Basket Construction, Border**.

trac-back. Basketry. See **border**.

tracer. Ceramics. See **slip trailer**.

tracer. Jewelry. Polished-steel tool used to produce lines of various widths according to the width of the tool. Also see **chasing, punch, repoussé, repoussé tools**.

tracer. Leather. See **modeler**.

tracery. Stained Glass. The arched shapes in the top of a Gothic window. In **glazing**, traceries start in the middle and work outward. Leads will have to be overlapped and cut together to get two angles joining neatly for curves. Use the **lathkin** on the inside of the **lead came**, gently rubbing it against the **heart** to stretch the leaf so that the came will bend smoothly. Also see **cusping, joints, mullion,** and **Stained Glass: Glazing**.

tracing. Stained Glass. A technique of **painting on glass** that originated when journeymen painters executed the painting from a **cartoon**.

Lay the stained glass over the cartoon on a table after the glass has been cleaned thoroughly with **acetone** (to remove any grease) and then dried. Mix paint as usual, but add a little more **gum arabic** and less water. Sugar or glycerine may also be added to make the paint flow more

easily. Use long, fine, round **brushes** to trace the lines of the cartoon onto the glass.

tracing cloth. Stenciling. See **architect's linen**.

tracing paper. Quilts. Stitchery. Thin, semitransparent paper used to trace designs. It comes in pads or in rolls. Also see **embroidery carbon paper**.

tracing pencil. Quilts. Stitchery. See **Quilts: Marking and Cutting**.

tracing wheel. Batik and Tie-dye. Quilts. Stitchery. A spiked disk or wheel attached to a handle so that the wheel rotates. Rolled over **embroidery carbon paper** the spikes leave tiny dots of carbon to mark pattern lines or designs. A tracing wheel is sometimes used to transfer designs from paper to fabric and to mark **quilting pattern**s. See ill.

Tracing wheel

track. Basketry. See **border**.

trackless train. Toys. Any **toy train** that runs without the use of a track or rails. Most handmade or homemade trains are trackless. Their wheels, made like those of a toy car or **wagon**, simply run over any flat surface.

trade beads. Beadwork. For centuries tons of beads reached the ports of Africa, and later North America, for use in transactions with the natives. **Glass beads** produced in Europe were used as currency in exchange for commodities such as animal skins and precious metals. Trade beads varied from a cheaply produced, coarse porcelain bead, usually white but sometimes brick red or bright yellow, that was used in East Africa, to the small **seed bead**, usually opaque white or medium blue, that was used by the American Indians.

Different trade beads had different values. The common beads, called conti, conterie, and **bugles**, were sold by weight and bartered in fathoms. More valuable beads, called perles, perli, and pearls, were sold by the number. The choice of beads was of utmost importance to the explorer or trader. Certain tribes preferred certain beads, but the preferences would change unpredictably from year to year. Arab traders who had traveled widely throughout Africa would advise the European merchants as to which beads were preferred in certain areas or along certain routes. An incorrect choice of beads could ruin a whole expedition.

Although trade beads were introduced into tribal cultures as a means of exchange, their color soon added another dimension to traditional ornamentation. Also see **pony bead** and **Beadmaking: Beadwork**.

traditional quilt. Quilts. See **Quilts: Definition**.

traditional quilt patterns. Quilts. See **quilt patterns**.

Traditional Roses and Rings. Weaving. See **overshot**.

trailing. Ceramics. Decorating by extruding **slip** or **glaze** through a nozzle onto a piece of **pottery** in a manner similar to icing a cake. See ill.

Trailing

trailing. Glasswork. The process in which blown-glass vessels can be decorated by allowing a thread of molten glass to be wound around the blown form. Typically, the **punty** makes a **gather** from the furnace, a portion of the gather is adhered to the vessel, and the vessel is rotated so that the thread, often colored, is drawn thin and wound onto the piece. Also see **drawing.**

Trail of the Covered Wagon, The. Quilts. See **Jacob's Ladder.**

tramé. Needlepoint. An old method of padding as a foundation for other stitches on penelope **canvas.** Strands of yarn are worked in long horizontal stitches on the surface of the canvas. The traméed stitches should always be of varying length to prevent ridges on the finished work. Many European needlework canvases are traméed in the design to be worked instead of painted. Between the double treads of the canvas, stitch long lines of thread in the colors required to form the pattern. Use split stitches if you need to cover a space of longer than an inch with a particular color. Join new colors in the same way, bringing the needle up through the end of the previous stitch, splitting the thread. When the tramé lines have been laid in, work **half cross stitch** on top in matching color, completely covering the traméed threads. When finished, the two layers of threads and stitches will give the design a slightly raised effect. See ill. Also see **Needlepoint: Preparation and Layout.**

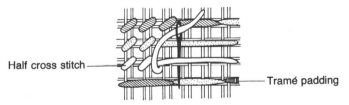

Half cross stitch —
— Tramé padding

tramp iron. Ceramics. Small particles of iron found in clay after mining and processing. Also see **magnetic filters.**

transcribing weaves. Weaving. Changing the **drawing-in draft** and the **chain draft** (**tie-up** and **treadling sequence**) in order to convert a weave from one group of **harness**es to another group. The simplest example would be to convert a 4-harness weave into an 8-harness structure.

transfer. Stitchery. Commercial iron-on design made for embroidery. While many are somewhat trite in design,

when **pad**ded and **stitch**ed they have design potential for both **appliqué** and **quilting.**

transfer jig. Gemcutting. See **dopping.**

transferring design. Rugmaking. Weaving. Marking the design or outline of shapes and patterns on the **rug backing.** The rug design usually is seen first in a small size—either a sketch that the rugmaker has drawn or a pattern obtained from some other source. This small drawing can be kept as is, or traced and then redrawn on **graph paper.** On the graph paper, each square represents a space, threads, part of an inch, a knot, or a stitch—whatever is necessary according to the type of rug backing and technique used. The graph paper becomes a chart that the rugmaker will follow, changing each color according to what the chart says. It is in effect a small model or scale drawing of the large rug. If this method of transferring designs is used, no drawing is made on the rug backing; instead, it is a method of counting threads or spaces as the work proceeds.

If a full-sized drawing is desired, draw a grid over the working sketch and divide it into halves and quarters. On the rug backing do the same—draw lines dividing the rug shape into halves and quarters. The design is redrawn on the rug backing following its lines from grid to grid. A full-sized drawing can also be done free-hand on wrapping paper. This is best done on the floor, so that the rugmaker can stand back and see the design as it will look lying on the floor. The yarn to be used can also be placed in the proper areas to help visualize the color effect. After the design is complete, it is transferred to the rug backing using dressmaker's carbon, which is placed between the design and the backing. If the design is to be worked with a **punch needle** or **speed hook,** it must be reversed and traced on the back of the rug backing, since work proceeds from back to front. In all techniques worked from the front, the design is traced on the top or right side of the backing. To reverse a design, the easiest way is to tape it against a window and redraw the lines of the design on the back of the paper as they show through the paper.

Simple or repetitive designs can be cut out of paper, placed on the rug backing until an appealing arrangement is found, and then traced around directly onto the backing. If a design is to be reduced or enlarged, use the gridwork method mentioned above. Working on **canvas mesh** for a **latch-hooked rug** would necessitate putting the full-sized drawing under the mesh and following the lines of the design through the holes and tracing them with a marking pen. Some rugmakers also like to paint their design directly on the rug backing in colors related to those that they will use in the yarn. Care must be taken that only those paints that will not run in washing or dry cleaning are used. In whatever method of transferring is used, it is important to remember that the rug shape and size are determined first and drawn on the rug backing with allowance for the hem. If the backing is not rigid enough, it is wise to tape it, tack it, pin it, or weight it with heavy objects, so that it will not shift around while tracing or drawing. A drawing should first be done with soft pencils, chalk, or charcoal sticks and then finalized with a felt-tipped marking pen.

The method for transferring a design in weaving is that of a scale drawing on graph paper with each square of the graph paper representing a specific number of **end**s and/or **pick**s. This is done for such woven techniques as **laid-in** or **knotted pile.** See ill. Also see **cartoon, round rug, shaped rug.**

Tracing a full-sized drawing

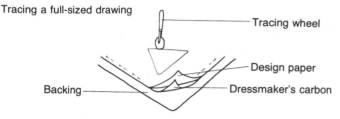

transferring designs to metal. Jewelry. There are numerous methods for transferring designs to metal. It is advisable to draw as skillfully as possible to the exact scale of the finished piece, as a rough sketch may be difficult to translate to the correct scale. Also, a scale drawing enables you to see exactly what you have; changing scale can completely alter relationships within the design.

If the metal is greasy or tarnished, **pickle** it so that you will have a clean surface. Coat the metal with a thin, smooth application of **yellow ochre casein** or **Chinese white.** With a #2 pencil, coat the entire back of your drawing with graphite, holding the drawing up to the light to make sure all areas are covered. You can use carbon paper if you prefer. Place the drawing on top of the dry ochre or Chinese white and hold the metal and drawing up to the light to center them. Lay them down, trace around the metal, and cut the form out with scissors. Using masking or cellophane tape, tape the drawing to the metal, carbon side against the ochre or Chinese white. Carefully trace your drawing with a sharpened pencil. Lift the tape from all edges except one. Keeping one finger on the drawing as well, carefully lift up the edges of the drawing to make sure that you have traced every area. If you have missed an area you can put the tape back in place and complete the tracing. Remove the drawing. Coat the transferred design with about three light coats of clear acrylic spray. Do not apply a thick coat as it will run and possibly take the drawing along with it. The purpose of the acrylic is to keep the drawing from rubbing off while you are working; it will, however, still rub off if you handle it too much. As soon as areas are sawed out you can place your fingers in those places for support. When the acrylic is completely dry, you can saw or drill. After your design is completely sawed out, the acrylic and casein or Chinese white can be removed by holding the metal under hot running water for a while and rubbing with your thumb. Save the original drawing.

Alternatively, you can coat the back of the drawing with a smooth, thin coat of rubber cement after taping the drawing carbon-side down to the ochre or Chinese white. Also, coat the metal with a thin covering of rubber cement and allow it to dry completely. If you do not let the rubber cement dry completely on the paper and the metal before

you press them together, it will take a long time for the glue to dry. Place the rubber-cemented drawing against the rubber-cemented metal and smooth down, using light pressure. Begin sawing or drilling. After you have finished sawing out your design, peel off the remaining paper and rub off with your thumb the rubber cement that is left on the drawing. With this method you lose your drawing unless you first make a tracing of it. If you are going to make two of something, say a pair of earrings or a pair of cuff links, you must make a tracing, as you will need two drawings.

If you want to make a transfer for engraving purposes, use the first method with Chinese white and no acrylic spray. You can go over the transferred design very lightly with a scriber and then rinse off the Chinese white. Also see **engraving.**

transferring prints. Découpage. A technique of lifting the printed image from a paper **print** and transferring it to another surface, making it thinner and thus more suitable for découpage. Eight to ten coatings of clear **acrylic,** such as **polymer medium,** are brushed on the front of a print, each one allowed to dry before applying the next. The print is then soaked in water until paper can be peeled from the back by rubbing gently with the fingers, leaving the printing inks of the picture attached to the clear acrylic film. Then one can proceed as usual with cutting and gluing to the surface to be decorated.

transformation puppet. Puppets. A **puppet,** usually a **marionette,** designed in such a way that the figure can be transformed during a performance. For example, a puppet of a woman might turn into the figure of a dragon by employing **trick-puppet** techniques. What appear to be loose sleeves on the figure's costume could become wings when **string**s are pulled to lift and unfurl them. A toad might be transformed into a prince by the raising or lowering of strings that are attached to a pullaway costume.

transite board. Jewelry. A hard compressed asbestos composition board used to cover working areas to protect them from the flame and heat of soldering **torches.** It comes in several thicknesses and is made in sheets as large as 4' × 8'. It is available through jewelry supply houses and lumber yards. Do not **solder** directly on its surface, as transite board has a tendency to crack from the high temperature required. A **soldering pan** can be placed on top of the transite to hold the work during soldering. An **asbestos pad** can be placed on the transite and soldering done directly on its surface. Also see **carbon ring stick, charcoal block, heating frame, magnesium block.**

translucent cookie. Toys. (Also called stained-glass cookie.) Decorative toy cookies made with areas of translucent color. They are an example of **cookie art** made from **edible dough.** Rings (or other shapes with open areas) rolled of cookie dough are made on waxed paper. Clear hard candy, such as Life-Savers or lollipops, is crushed and placed in the open areas. When baked at 325° for just a few minutes, the candy melts and fuses with the cookie. The melting time varies according to the candy, and the longer it cooks, the less intense the color of the candy glass will be.

transom. Stained Glass. The small window over a door or fixed window. They usually open to provide ventilation. Transoms are often executed in stained glass.

transparency. See **opacity**.

transparent appliqué. Stitchery. Any of several approaches to **hand appliqué** or **machine appliqué** that utilizes **transparent fabric, sheer fabric,** or see-through materials.

In one, the semitransparent or **transparent material** is **appliqué**d to a **background** material. For machine sewing, an upholstery-weight fabric or any material with weight and **body** will work most easily. The transparent fabrics may be white or colored **organdy, organza, net,** or any similar material. A satin or **zigzag stitch** is used to catch all the **fray**ing cut edges of the appliqué pieces. This type of transparent appliqué is often used in combination with **lace appliqué.** If this approach to transparent appliqué is to be hand sewn, edges are turned under or else they are sewn flat and lines of cord or **yarn** are sewn over the **raw edges** with a **couching** stitch.

In a second kind of transparent appliqué, colored materials are placed between two layers of fabric and stitched into place. The bottom layer is an opaque, usually white, fabric. Pieces of **felt, wool, cotton,** etc., are laid in place on top, then the transparent fabric goes over that, sandwiching the colors between. Tiny **running stitch**es are used to outline the areas of color which show through the transparent material. These stitches hold the color fabrics in place and serve to accent the colors. If felt is used for the middle layer of color, any stitches used over the top give a **quilt**ed look. The total effect is one of soft pastel colors and a smooth surface. Organdy is more satisfactory for this work than organza, since it has more "give" or life to it and will adjust to the layers beneath it better than a **synthetic fabric** will.

A third method of transparent appliqué makes use of a light coming from behind a panel, as in a window. Delicate laces or doilies may be sandwiched between layers of organdy or similar semitransparent material. Stitching can outline those areas to hold the needlework in place, and some additional embroidery may be added.

transparent contact paper. Stitchery. An adhesive-backed clear plastic sheet designed to be used as a shelf cover. It can be applied to photographs, prints, and reproductions to protect and strengthen the paper so that they can be incorporated into **stitchery panel**s or **banner**s. The contact paper can be used to protect any decorative surface.

transparent enamel. Enameling. See **enamel, metal foil.**

transparent fabric. Quilts. Stitchery. Any woven material through which color can be seen. Most are actually semitransparent, but when color will show through well enough to retain a definite hue, the material may be said to be transparent. In some **fabric**s the weave may be very open, as in a gauze, mesh, or **net.** Or the material may be so gossamer or fine that it can be seen through. **Organdy, organza,** marquisette, and voile are among the latter, along with various **chiffon**s and thin window-curtain materials, called glass curtains.

Transparent fabrics are used in **lace appliqué, shadow work, transparent appliqué** and **shadow quilting.**

transparent finishes. Papercrafts. See **protective finishes.**

transparent glaze. Ceramics. A **glaze** that permits light to pass without diffusion so that the clay body can be seen. **Opacifiers** destroy a transparent glaze so the decoration under it cannot be seen.

transparent material. Quilts. Stitchery. Any clear substance through which light passes. **Acetate,** glass, **Mylar,** Plexiglas, **transparent fabric,** transparent **contact paper,** and other clear plastics are all transparent materials which may be incorporated into various craft projects to offer see-through or window effects.

transparent tapestry. Weaving. A hanging that can be seen through and usually viewed from both sides. Most of these tapestries are not completely see-through, but semitransparent. They are not woven in a **tapestry** technique, but are done mainly in a **laid-in** technique with a fine thread used as a **plain weave binder** between the shots of pattern which occur only in designated areas. The **warp** is of equally fine yarn. Also see **HV technique.**

transposed warp. Weaving. A term given to weaves or techniques in which the **warp** does not all lie in a straight line arrangement, but portions of it travel diagonally to interlace with other warp **end**s and/or the **filling.** This is done for the sake of zigzag, diamond, or other similar shape, color, or pattern development in the **cloth.** These transposed ends are sometimes called **crossed warp**s.

Transvaal jade. Gemcutting. See **garnet.**

trapeze cut. Gemcutting. See **facet.**

trapunto. Quilts. Stitchery. A technique of **stuffing** or **padding.** The designs are sewn in double rows through two layers of material, the back layer is snipped between the rows or the threads are stretched apart, and the padding or stuffing material is slipped inside. This stuffing may be accomplished with **cotton** cord as in **Italian trapunto,** or it may be done with **batting** as in **English trapunto.** This technique is used in clothing, quilts, wall hangings, and small fabric articles.

The trapunto quilts are often referred to as whitework quilts or **white-on-white quilt**s because they use no **piecing** or **patch**ing of materials. Not all trapunto quilts were white; some were worked on a solid-color material. Others used colored **quilting threads** to give a delicate line of color at the edge of the trapunto area. See ill., next page.

English trapunto, showing the back side of the work

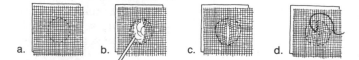

a.   b.   c.   d.

trapunto doll. Toys. A figure made by using fabric decorated with **trapunto.** The doll figure is worked flat on a layer of sheer material placed over another layer of fabric. Stitched lines are sewn through both layers by hand or machine. **Stuffing** is used to fill the areas of the face and body between the lines of stitching. The back and front of the doll are made separately, then these parts are sewn together and more stuffing is inserted between them.

Travel Star. Quilts. See **Arkansas Traveler.**

travertine. Gemcutting. See **calcite.**

trays. Stained Glass. See **kiln tray.**

treadle. Spinning. A flat piece of wood underneath the **driving wheel** of a **spinning wheel.** The treadle or foot pedal is attached by means of the **footman** to the driving wheel. "Treadling" is pushing on this foot pedal, thereby turning the driving wheel. This revolves the **flyer** and **bobbin** at great speeds, and the thread is simultaneously twisted and wound on the bobbin. The treadle is an addition that frees both hands for drawing out the wool and feeding the yarn into the **orifice.** Also see **treadle wheel.**

treadle. Weaving. A foot pedal that is the mechanism by which **harness**es are raised or lowered in **floor loom**s. Treadles are located at the bottom of the loom; their number corresponds to the number of harnesses in the loom, or to two more than the number of harnesses. In some looms, primarily older ones or primitive harness looms, the treadle is attached directly to the harness. Otherwise, the treadle attaches to a **lam** by way of **tie-up cord**s and the lam, in turn, is attached to the harness. The treadles are hinged usually to the front floor support beam of the loom, but in older looms, some are hinged at the back. A treadle can be attached to many harnesses or just one—depending on the **tie-up.**

The word "treadle" can also be a verb meaning to depress the foot pedal in order to raise the harnesses and form the **shed.** A **treadling sequence** is followed so that the correct weave structure is obtained. Also see **counterbalanced loom, countermarch loom, jack type loom.**

treadle cord. Weaving. The cord attached to the **treadle** when making a **snitch knot** used in the **tie-up.** Often the entire **tie-up cord** is called the treadle cord.

treadle loom. Weaving. See **foot-power loom.**

treadle wheel. Spinning. (Also called Brunswick wheel, flax wheel, foot wheel, Irish wheel, low wheel, saddle wheel, Saxony wheel.) A **spinning wheel** equipped with a foot pedal (treadle) to turn the wheel, thereby freeing the spinner's hands for **drafting** the fibers. In addition, it has a mechanism that winds on the yarn as it is twisted or spun. Invented in the sixteenth century by a German woodcarver named Jürgen, it is known as the **flyer assembly.** The treadle wheel operates when the spinner steps on the treadle, which activates the large wheel through a connecting flat stick called a **footman.** As the wheel rotates, the **driving band** which runs from it to the pulleys in the flyer assembly rotates the **flyer.** This twists the fibers that are being fed by the spinner, who regulates the twist by letting them slip either more slowly or faster through the fingers. The spun yarn passes through the **orifice** of the spindle and around the **guide hook**s of the flyer to the **bobbin** on which it is wound. The spinner moves the yarn from hook to hook as the bobbin fills up. The flyer assembly is mounted between the **maiden**s on the **spindle** shaft which revolves in two leather bearings. The maidens are supported by the **mother-of-all** which rests in a flat stand called the bench or table. The **upright**s holding the wheel are also mounted in the table. In addition, there is a **tension screw** which regulates the tension of the driving band, and a **distaff** for holding the fibers that are needed for spinning. Wool can be spun without the distaff, but not flax. The original treadle wheel was called either a Brunswick wheel or Saxony wheel after the town and state in Germany from which Jürgen came. Only the slant of the table varies between the two wheels. Since that time, there have been many different models of the treadle wheel, with as many different names. See ill. Also see **chair wheel, double spinning wheel, German wheel.**

Treadle wheel

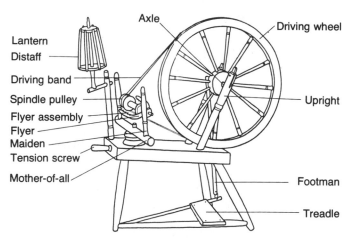

Lantern
Distaff
Driving band
Spindle pulley
Flyer assembly
Flyer
Maiden
Tension screw
Mother-of-all
Axle
Driving wheel
Upright
Footman
Treadle

treadling. Weaving. See **treadling order.**

treadling-as-drawn-in. Weaving. (Also called **tromp-as-writ,** woven-as-drawn-in.) The process of converting the **drawing-in draft** to a **treadling draft** and following this in the weaving of the fabric. This is a traditional way of weaving **overshot** where the conversion is by threading units. **Harness** unit 1-2 in the threading would mean 1-2 treadled—for as many times as this unit appears in a block of the pattern. The result is a squared pattern with **twill** blocks running diagonally through the center of the square. To make sure that the square is achieved, compensation is made in the filling by reducing the number of shots in each block.

treadling order. Weaving. The sequence or pattern in which the **treadles** are pressed down during weaving so that a specific weave is attained. Commonly referred to as the treadling, it is for **floor loom** weaving only, but it has its counterpart in the **chain draft** used for **table looms.** The treadling varies with what the weave is to be. However, there are some treadling sequences that have come down from colonial times, such as **treadling-as-drawn-in** and **opposites.** Also see **draft, overshot.**

treble crochet. Crochet. See **double crochet.**

Tree Everlasting. Quilts. (Also called Arrowhead, Herringbone, Path of Thorns, Prickly Path.) A popular **pieced quilt** design made from the **two-patch.** It is **pieced** in such a way that the tree shape runs the length of the quilt.

Tree of Life. Quilts. An **overall appliqué quilt** design showing a large curvilinear spreading tree. The design was derived from the Indian **palampores** of the 1700s. Also see **Pine Tree.**

Trenck's lock. Toys. See **prisoner's lock.**

Triangles. Quilts. See **Thousand Pyramids.**

triangle stitch. Needlepoint. A popular nineteenth-century geometric pattern was a square made up of four triangles. The base of each triangle forms a side of the square, and all apexes meet in the center. Work a horizontal stitch over four mesh, decreasing to over one mesh, to form the apex of the triangle. Work the second triangle, increasing from two to four mesh.

trick puppet. Puppets. A **puppet** or **marionette** designed to produce startling or surprising effects on stage. Sometimes a head is knocked off a puppet, revealing another smaller head beneath it. Trick puppets are often designed to combine two or more figures or characters into the body of one. Also see **transformation puppet, two-faced puppet.**

triclinic system. Gemcutting. See **crystal.**

tricot. Stitchery. See **nylon tricot.**

trim. Découpage. See **gold-paper trim.**

trimming. Bookbinding. Although the terms "trimming" and "cutting" are often used interchangeably, they are not in fact synonymous. A book is "trimmed" when the blade cuts only the longest leaves; "cutting" indicates that the blade pares each **leaf.** The trimming operation is performed with a **plow,** or with a straightedge and mat knife in the case of thin books.

To trim, mark a trim line across the head of the book. Lay a straight-edged cutting board of plywood or heavy cardboard against the trim line. On the back place a piece of cardboard and another cutting board and insert them into the **lying press.** Be certain the trim line is even with the front member of the press and the **back** of the book is on your left. The blade of the plow must be adjusted perfectly square with the press (lying flat on the cheek of the press) and should be freshly sharpened; a white Washita stone is recommended. A slightly rounded cutting point will cut best. The blade can be adjusted with shims to make it ride square.

Tighten the press on the book, checking that it remains square as you tighten it. Remove and begin again if it is not square. Feed the blade only on the forward stroke and cut only a few leaves with each stroke. Advance the cutting edge by turning the screw only a little each time. The attempt to cut more than two or three leaves at a time will cause the sheets to tear, and will also dull the plow blade. Repeat the process for the **tail.** The procedure for trimming the foredge is the same, except the cut is in the direction of the **grain,** allowing the blade to be fed on the forward and backward stroke.

trimming. Ceramics. See **turning.**

trimming plane. Woodworking. See **plane.**

trimming scissors. Stitchery. (Also called trimming shears.) Small **scissors** that have one pointed blade and one blade with a rounded tip. They are smaller than **cutting scissors** but larger than **embroidery scissors.** Their primary use is for detailed cutting and careful close work.

trimming shears. Stitchery. See **trimming scissors.**

trim saw. Gemcutting. See **slabbing saw.**

Trip Around the World. Quilts. (Also called Around the World, Grandma's Dream, Sunshine and Shadows.) A name given to an **all-over set** and to a specific **block.** The **all-over pattern** is made up of equal **pieced** squares. It is a **checkerboard** arrangement with blocks placed on edge, giving a **diamond** pattern to the total. It usually starts with one square at the center, which is encircled by blocks of another color. The next row of squares is a third color, etc., so that the rows vary from dark to light or deep to pale colors. This is a popular design among the **Amish quilt**ers, who made stunning use of color. They usually add a wide **border** to finish the quilt. Trip Around the World was a popular pattern in the late 1800s and again in the 1930s. Many variations of it are found in contemporary quilts.

The pieced **block** pattern uses quarter-circles sewn into a block. The blocks are then joined so that the quarter-circles are reassembled to form a new circle. Each circle is surrounded by radiating quarter-circle rays. The design was supposed to have been named by the waiting wives of sea captains. It is also called Around the World and is a variation of **Drunkard's Path.**

triphane. Gemcutting. See **spodumene.**

triple-beam balance scale. Plastics. See **balance scale.**

triple cloth. Weaving. A fabric made of three distinct **warp**s, each interlaced with its own **filling**. These three warps and three fillings make three layers of cloth that are woven one above the other and are held together by a pattern of **stitching point**s. These stitching points hold the fabric together from front layer to center layer to back layer. If the layers are woven in **plain weave**, they demand at least six **harness**es—two harnesses for each layer. Triple cloth can be a heavy fabric that is suitable for coats or capes, or a fabric three times the loom width, or a **3-dimensional hanging**. The hangings need not be heavy cloth; often they are gauze-like constructions with the layers spread out to give the three-dimensional shape. Triple cloth also broadens the color-effect possibilities by enlarging the number of different solid color **block patterns** that can be achieved. Anni Albers has used this concept of expanded color block patterns in many of her wall hangings. Triple cloth was also done by the early Indian weavers of Peru on simple **backstrap loom**s. See ill. Also see **double cloth, stitching point**.

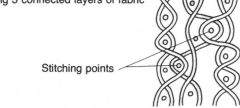

Triple cloth showing 3 connected layers of fabric

Stitching points

triple crochet. Crochet. (Abbr. tr, tr c.) To make triple crochet: yo 2, insert hook in 5th ch from hook, * yo, work 2 loops off *, rep * to * 2. Also see **Crochet: Basic Stitches, Decreasing**.

triple dovetailing. Weaving. See **dovetailing**.

triple foundation chain. Crochet. See **Crochet: Basic Stitches**.

Triple Irish Chain. Quilts. See **Irish Chain**.

triplet. Gemcutting. A gem made of three units cemented together, such as an **opal cabochon** backed with black gem material to simulate black opal and covered with a clear **quartz** cap to protect it from scratches.

The term also applies to an eye **loupe** with three lenses.

triple triple crochet. Crochet. (Abbr. tr. tr. Also called triple treble crochet.) The triple triple crochet is an elongation of all the loops involved in making the **triple crochet** stitch.

To work stitch: yarn over 4 times. Insert hook in 7th ch from hook, pull loop through (5 loops on hook), yo, *yo, work 2 loops off *, repeat * to * 5 times, stitch is complete. Chain 6 before turning.

triple twist. Basketry. See **waling**.

tripod. Jewelry. A flat ring of metal supported by three long legs used with a **heating frame** so that flame may be directed from underneath. See ill. Also see **soldering**.

Tripod

tripoli. Gemcutting. See **abrasive**.

tripoli. Jewelry. Metalworking. Plastics. An abrasive cutting compound that removes fine scratches and smooths the surface of metal, preparing it for further polishing if desired. Tripoli can be used on all metals. Also see **buffing, buffing compound, Super Tripoli**.

Tristom-and-twist stitch. Needlepoint. See **long-armed cross stitch**.

tritik. Batik and Tie-dye. (Also called stitched tie-dye.) A sewing technique or method used to **resist dye** in the **tie-dye** process. In this method, fine to medium-weave fabrics work best, as the heavier-weight materials will not compress tightly enough to give satisfactory results. The success of tritik, or sewn tie-dye, depends upon the small running stitches that are drawn up very tightly to produce **gather**s. These stitches must be pulled so close that dye cannot penetrate the fabric. A strong thread such as linen **carpet thread** is used for sewing. The thread is always knotted before sewing, and tightly knotted again at the end of the stitching. If a large area is to be stitched, the thread may have to be doubled for added strength. A crewel needle has an eye large enough for the carpet thread, but not so large as to leave holes in the fabric. The **fastening-off** must be carefully done for tritik, as the stitched work must remain tightly packed on the taut thread. Tritik may be used for various kinds of designs. The simplest are straight sewn shapes, straight lines, curved lines, or **zigzag** bands. Shapes can also be sewn or drawn with lines or running stitches. For example, a flower or fruit or any other specific shape can be done this way. Variations may be achieved by sewing through double layers to form lines or bands, or by **pleat**ing and sewing. **Oval**s and **diamond**s may be formed in tritik, as well as any other geometric variation. Oversewing is another way of forming stitch patterns.

The tritik method always demands a very strong **dyebath**; the material cannot be immersed for a long time, or the dye will penetrate the stitched lines.

A sewing machine can be employed for tritik also. Loose stitches must be taken, then drawn tight and tied. Sewing machine tritik can produce complex designs of great detail. A heavy-duty thread should be used for the machine-stitched tritik, sometimes referred to as "sewing machine tie-dye." Also see **circle, join, sewn spiral, sewn tuck**.

trivet. Enameling. A support for an enameled piece when it is fired. Ideally it should hold the work at its edges, where contact with the heated **enamel** is minimal. It should allow even heat flow, and it should be easy to move in and out of the **kiln**. The firing rack may be wire mesh or an asbestos or marinite board into which pins can be inserted. Use a firing rack and fireproof fibreboard for flat shapes with one enameled side and for **plique-à-jour** work (**a.**). A grooved trivet is used to hold several small samples for color-testing enamels with the pieces touching the trivet only at their edges (**b.**). Ceramic or metal star trivet (**c., d.**) are used to support round-bottomed shapes. Ceramic or metal slits may be used on a stand. Use an adjustable winged trivet to support pieces with contact only at the edges (**e.**). See ill. Freeform trivets can be fashioned out of stainless steel strips for special purposes, such as suspending a ring. Also see **firing, firing fork, plique-à-jour,** and **Enameling: Basic Operations, Tools and Materials.**

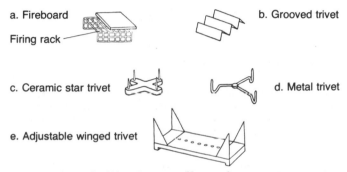

a. Fireboard
Firing rack
b. Grooved trivet
c. Ceramic star trivet
d. Metal trivet
e. Adjustable winged trivet

tromp-as-writ. Weaving. A colloquial expression coming from colonial times and meaning **to-treadle-as-drawn-in.**

trompe l'oeil. Découpage. A term from the French words "tromper," to deceive, and "oeil," eye. It is a fool-the-eye technique of decorating a surface with paintings or **cutouts**, in actual scale, of objects that are so lifelike and so skillfully applied to the surface that they look real. This technique of visual deception has traditionally been used in depicting window, doors, furniture, and other architectural details on walls to give the illusion of reality. Trompe l'oeil has also been widely used for still-life representations of actual-size fruit, foliage, insects, and so on. The technique is easily adapted for use in découpage.

trompe l'oeil. Embroidery. Needlepoint. A type of realistic representation sometimes used in needlepoint or embroidery. By artful shading and coloring, the design is made to look three-dimensional.

Tropical American mahogany. Woodworking. See **mahogany.**

troughs. Stained Glass. See **lead bins.**

trowel. Mosaics. A tool designed for spreading plaster or a bond or adhesive such as cement or mortar. Mason's trowels with pointed end and plasterer's trowels with square ends are available through most hardware stores in a variety of shapes and sizes. Also see **Mosaics: Tools and Materials, Setting the Material.**

trowel. Stained Glass. A stiff, spatulalike tool used for applying and moving **cement** around **slab glass** in **dalle-de-verre.**

trowel and lifter. Metalworking. See **sandcasting molding equipment.**

true bias. Stitchery. A cut in **fabric** which follows neither the **lengthwise** nor **crosswise** threads, but goes exactly between at a 45° angle. The true bias has the maximum amount of give and stretch.

true check. Weaving. See **checks.**

true loom. Weaving. See **Indian weaving.**

true plaid. Weaving. See **plaid.**

true reel. Spinning. See **spinning.**

truing. Metalworking. The process of checking the alignment of forms and the accuracy of curves in a symmetrically raised object. Use **measuring tools** such as **calipers** and a **surface gauge** to mark the top trimming line. Another method is to use a **template** in the form of a cutout silhouette to check fit around or over the sides of the form.

Tryon toy. Toys. The hand-crafted toys produced in Tryon, North Carolina. Two school teachers, Eleanor P. Vance and Charlotte L. Yale, established a center for toymaking there in 1915 to train men and women in high-quality hand craftsmanship of toys using native materials.

try square. Bookbinding. The try square is used to make lines that must be square across the **back** of a book to indicate where sawcuts will be made for stitching.

try square. Metalworking. Woodworking. See **squaring tools.**

try square. Woodworking. See **squaring tools.**

T-stake. Metalworking. See **anvil.**

T-totum. Toys. See **teetotum.**

tub. Bookbinding. The structure that supports the **lying press.** It is made from wood and is about 30″ high.

tube. Papercrafts. See **cylinder.**

tube. Weaving. See **spool.**

tube drawing. Jewelry. See **drawing tubing.**

tube drill. Gemcutting. A tube drill is a boring device made from a hollow cylinder of copper, brass, or mild steel. The tube drill is inserted into a drill press and used with **abrasive** contained in a dam of putty built up on the stone around the place where the hole will be. Water is used as a coolant. The drill is moved up and down while it is running to allow the grits and water to flow into the tube and grind through. Some gemcutters bend the end of the tube slightly to impart a wobble, but most tube drills have a flare at the tip (called a set) that provides clearance for the drill. Some tube drills are charged with diamond powder (embedded in the leading edge); they can be secured in a basin of water, but should be handled very lightly when breaking through the material. Proper speed for drilling holes ⅛−½" in diameter is 3,000−4,000 rpm; for ½−1", use 2,000−3,000 rpm; and for 1−3", use 1,200−2,000 rpm. Tube drills may be used to cut out blanks for **cabochon** cuts. Also see **carving point, charging, drilling jig** and **Gemcutting: Tools and Materials.**

tube-holding jig. Jewelry. A hand-held **vise,** adapted to hold **tubing** steady, with a surface or slot as a guide for **sawing** tubing and keeping the cut at an exact right angle. It is also used for holding **wire.** Some tube-holding jigs have an extension that regulates length when several pieces of tubing or wire of the same length are required. See ill. Also see **hinge.**

Tube-holding jig with extension regulator

tube telephone. Toys. A toy telephone made from a garden hose or similar tubing. A funnel is placed at each end to serve as earpiece and mouthpiece. The tube carries the sound, and the two children playing with the device alternate speaking and listening, moving the funnel from ear to mouth as needed.

tubing. Jewelry. Round and square tubes of various sizes that are made commercially by extruding. See ill. Also see **drawing tubing, tube-holding jig.**

Commercially available silver tubing

tubing. Weaving. See **tubular weave.**

tub machine. Gemcutting. See **machinery.**

tubular weaving. Weaving. A **double cloth** structure where both **selvage** sides are joined and a tube is woven. The top and bottom layers are woven alternately with the **filling** yarn going from top to bottom layer and, during this process, joining the sides. To give the tube a seamless look, the edges should be threaded in the **reed** as single threads for the first, and last, three **dent**s. Tubular weav-

ing can be done on four **harness**es, since all that is required is two harnesses for the top layer and two for the bottom. This is for a **plain weave** in both layers. The warp colors of the top and bottom layers never interchange, but it is possible to get variety through introducing filling stripes that go around the entire tube. Tubular weaving can be used for garments, pillow covers, bags, and wall hangings. The tube can be connected at the top and bottom and stuffed to form sculptural free-standing units.

tucks. Weaving. See **double cloth.**

Tudor embroidery. Crewel. Embroidery. See **Elizabethan embroidery.**

tuft. Quilts. The small puff of **cotton** cord that identifies **tufting,** or **candlewicking.**

tufted fabric. Stitchery. **Fabric** ornamented with soft, fluffy, brushlike buttons of **cotton** yarn that are sewn and cut at intervals. **Tuft**s are most often used on bedspreads; when placed with spaces between them, the material is known as "candlewick." When the tufts are in close rows, the fabric is called chenille.

tufted quilt. Quilts. A bedcover embellished with **cotton** tufts. The handmade ones were traditionally worked on a single layer of material, such as **sheeting** or light **cotton.** When the **tufting** process was complete, the cover was washed, and the shrinking helped to hold the tufts snugly in the fabric. **Candlewicking** or **roving** is used to make the tufts. A single fabric wide enough for the entire **coverlet** is preferable, so that no seam will show.

A more accurate designation for this type of bedcover would be "tufted coverlet" or "tufted bedcover," because it does not involve **quilting.**

tufted rug. Rugmaking. See **hooked rug.**

tufted stitch. Crewel. Embroidery. Needlepoint. See **Turkey work.**

tufting. Quilts. (Also called **candlewicking.**) The art of decorating material through the addition of puffed ends of **cotton** yarn. When hand sewn, these fabrics, often used as **bedspread**s, have carefully and skillfully placed tufts. When machine sewn, the tufts are usually in continuous lines and are familiarly known as chenille. A short darning needle or notched tufting needle (hard to find) is used. Candlewicking or other cotton cord is used for the tufts.

tufting. Rugmaking. Weaving. See **candlewick, looping.**

Tulip. Quilts. Any of a variety of **block** designs using both **piecing** and **appliqué** in which there are (usually three) full-face flowers. The overlapping of names and patterns between quilts featuring peonies, lilies, and tulips makes it very complicated. Generally, the lily quilts show two flowers in profile, and the peony or tulip designs show full-face views. Tulip and peony patterns may also refer to specific single-flower block designs.

Among the tulip patterns are those that feature eight-pointed flowers based on the diamond shapes of the **LeMoyne Star,** such as the Cleveland Tulip or Cottage Tulip. Old tulip patterns include Conventional Tulip, Mrs. Ewer's Tulip, Colonial Tulip, and Tulip Tree.

In appliqué the tulip is one of the most popular of all block designs. Used in an unending variety of arrangements and colors, it is also referred to as **Peony.** Also see **Lily.**

Tulip Lady Fingers. Quilts. A **block** for a **pieced quilt** composed of a **nine-patch** variation that has darts or arrowheads pointing in from each corner to touch a center square. See ill.

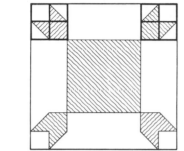

Tulip Lady Fingers

Tulip Tree. Quilts. See **Tulip.**

tulis. Batik and Tie-dye. A traditional **Javanese batik** method in which the designs are drawn freehand using hot **wax** on **fabric.** These **batik**s are among the most exquisite examples produced anywhere in the world. The **tjanting** is employed in this work to hold and dispense the wax. The tulis batik requires much more time to produce than the **tjap** batik, which is also a traditional Javanese technique.

tulle. Stitchery. (Also called illusion.) A fine-mesh **net,** usually of **silk** or **nylon.**

tulle embroidery. Embroidery. See **darning on net.**

tulle stitch. Lacemaking. See **buttonhole stitch.**

tumbaga. Jewelry. An alloy of 82 parts **gold** and 18 parts **copper.**

tumble. Gemcutting. See **baroque.**

tumble doll. Toys. (Also called rocking doll.) A self-righting doll made in a manner similar to the **Daruma doll** but not necessarily with a cone-shaped top. It is sometimes lead-weighted at the base so that it will remain upright.

tumbler. Gemcutting. See **tumbling.**

Tumbler. Quilts. A **pieced one-patch** quilt using the trapezoid for an **all-over pattern.** The name was derived from the household drinking glass, parallel at top and bottom, with the sides flaring out toward the top. The **patch**es alternate, one upright and one upside-down, in long strips. The strips are then joined in such a way that the narrow or wide ends of the tumblers meet. It was most popular as a **dark quilt.** See ill.

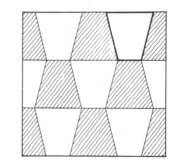

Tumbler

tumbler. Toys. See **jumping jack.**

tumbling. Gemcutting. A grinding and **polishing** process in which gem rough, **abrasive,** and water are rotated in a barrel called a tumbler (**a., b.**). Gems formed by this method are called **baroque**s; they have smooth, rounded irregular shapes. Opaque varieties of **quartz, garnet,** and amethyst are best recommended for tumbling.

Sort the gem rough according to **hardness** and size. Stones of the same hardness and approximately the same size and shape should be used in each batch. Wash the stones thoroughly with a bristle brush, detergent, and water, or tumble them with water and detergent for two hours.

Mark a line about halfway up the inside of the barrel; fill the barrel with stones up to the mark; take the stones out and weigh them. One pound of silicon carbide abrasive is added for each eight to ten pounds of stones. Refill the barrel with the stones. Add the appropriate amount of abrasive, a small amount of soda, and enough water to cover the stones. Too much water will overload the barrel; too little will prevent the stones from cutting freely. Set the machine in a cool place. Select the proper speed and start the machine. Keep a log, noting the weights and types of stones and abrasive and the time when each step of the operation is started. Tumbling proceeds from coarse grinding to medium and fine grinding to polishing. In each step progressively finer grits are used.

The diameter of the barrel determines the most efficient operating speed. In the following example, the diameter is measured in inches and the speed in revolutions per minute:

Diameter (in inches)	6	8	10	12	14	18	24
Speed for round barrel (in rpm)	54	48	42	38	35	31	27
Speed for hexagonal barrel (in rpm)	32	29	25	23	21	19	16

The proper speed can be recognized by the swishing, rather than clicking, sound of the tumbling material. If the speed of the barrel is too high, the stones and abrasive mud will be carried above Point A and will fall to the bottom with jarring contact and little grinding against each other. If the barrel speed is too low, the contents will not be carried higher than Point B and will slip backward around the barrel sluggishly with little abrasive effect. Remember that fragile stones require low speeds (**c.**). See ill. on next page.

Depending on the roughness of the surface of the stones, start tumbling with an abrasive of 80, 60, or 46 grit. If the stones are smooth, start with 220 grit. Tumble for four to six days. Shut off the machine, open the barrel, and remove the stones, being careful not to drip abrasive on the moving parts of the machinery. Wash the stones and barrel thoroughly. Do not wash waste down the drain because it will harden; bury it or put it in the garbage. Use a plastic colander to rinse the stones because an aluminum one will mark them.

Put the stones back in the barrel; if they do not come up to the halfway mark, add filler of old, nonusable tumbled stones. Cover with water, adding soda, and $1/8-1/10$ of the original measure of the abrasive. Start the machine. If most of the stones are rough after the fifth day, recharge with abrasive. When stones are sufficiently smooth, proceed to a finer grit (500) after washing stones and barrel thoroughly. Do not add more abrasive at this stage; let it wear out. Tumble for three to five days. Remove stones and wash them.

Examine stones closely and discard any that are chipped or fractured. Fill the barrel halfway, adding fillers, such as sawdust, cornmeal, and nutshells, up to 10% of the barrel volume. Add water, a tiny amount of detergent powder, and tin or cerium oxide weighing $1/20$ the weight of the stones. (Do not go by the weight of the stones before the tumbling operation began; there's usually a 15–20% weight loss in coarse grinding.) Start the machine using a lower speed than before to avoid damage to the stones. After two or three days, examine the stones daily. There should be no noticeable difference in the stones' appearance when wet or dry.

Wash the stones and barrel thoroughly. Put the stones back in the barrel; add water and enough nonfoaming soap powder to make a thick solution. Tumble for six to twelve hours. Rinse the stones off. Also see **Gemcutting: Tools and Materials.**

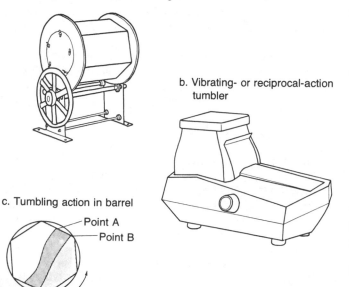

a. Rotating barrel or drum tumbling machine

b. Vibrating- or reciprocal-action tumbler

c. Tumbling action in barrel

Point A
Point B

Tumbling Blocks. Quilts. See **Baby Blocks.**

tumbling man. Toys. A **balance toy** that probably originated in China. The original toy was a figure of wood or **papier mâché** and had mercury inside the head to weight it. The Austrian version of this toy was later made using a ball bearing as the weight. The arms and legs of the toy are outspread so that when placed on steps the figure tumbles down, moving as the weight shifts inside the head.

tumpline. Weaving. see **belt loom.**

tungsten. Metalworking. See **steel.**

tungsten arc welding. Metalworking. See **welding.**

tungsten carbide. Metalworking. See **carbide, steel.**

tungsten inert gas welding. Metalworking. See **welding.**

tungsten wheel. Stained Glass. A **glass-cutter** with a very hard cutting **wheel.** Though the tungsten may never wear out, it makes a coarse cut that mars the glass.

Tunisian crochet. Crochet. See **afghan stitch.**

Tunisian knitting. Knitting. A centuries-old method of knitting that originated in Tunisia and is based on **slip stitches** (done a row at a time) and knitting into the back of the fabric (also done a row at a time). Tunisian knitting can take the form of **Tunisian stitch, horizontal** or the **Tunisian stitch, oblique,** depending on the order in which **over**s are knit into the pattern. Tunisian knitting stitches were often used in the past to divide the elaborate multicolor patterns of **Albanian knitting.**

Tunisian stitch, horizontal. Knitting. This Eastern stitch follows the principles of Eastern knitting and begins on the **back of knitting** side of the work. This stitch is slightly different from Western stitches and requires some practice to master, but produces a warm, sturdy pattern that makes it ideal for outdoor garments.

To knot the horizontal Tunisian stitch:
Cast on any number of stitches.
Row 1: * Sl 1 k-w, yo* Rep * to * across the **row.** Take care not to lose the **over** when turning.
Row 2: * K 2 tog-b*, rep * to * across the row.
See ill. Also see **Tunisian knitting.**

Tunisian stitch, horizontal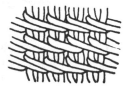

Tunisian stitch, oblique. Knitting. This is a traditional Eastern stitch that knits into a thick-textured, sturdy fabric.

Begin with any number of stitches on the **back of knitting** side of the work.
Row 1: *yo, s 1 kw*, rep * to * across row.
Row 2: *K 2 tog b*, rep * to * across row.
See ill. Also see **Tunisian knitting.**

Tunisian knitting, oblique

tunnel kiln. Ceramics. See **continuous-firing kiln.**

Turkey. Rugmaking. Weaving. See **knotted pile.**

turkey call. Toys. A **sound toy** or **noisemaker** originally made to attract wild turkeys while hunting. It is often played with because of the sounds produced, and is considered to be a traditional **American folk toy.** It consists of a small lidless box to which a paddle-shaped cover with a handle is loosely hinged. The cover is coated with chalk and is moved by means of the handle to produce a gobbling sound, giving it the name "gobbler box." Also see **crow call.**

Turkey knot stitch. Crewel. Embroidery. Needlepoint. See **Turkey work.**

Turkey red. Dyeing. See **madder.**

Turkey Tracks. Quilts. See **Wandering Foot.**

turkey work. Crewel. Embroidery. Needlepoint. (Also called Ghiordes knot stitch, plush stitch, tufted stitch, turkey knot stitch, velvet stitch.) A series of loops anchored by straight stitches that give a tufted effect if cut. The stitch can be worked over knitting needles to insure even loops. The closer the stitches, the denser the pile. Keep the needle horizontal when making stitches (**a.**). The thread passes below the needle when making the straight stitch (**b.**) and above the needle when making a loop (**c.**). Continue across the row coming up in the same hole as the previous stitch (**d.**). The loops can be left uncut (**e.**) or cut for a pile effect (**f.**). Turkey work is a dramatic highlight on any background fabric or canvas. See ill.

Turkey work

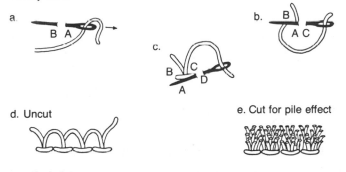

Turkish knot. Rugmaking. Weaving. See **knotted pile.**

turkish towel. Stitchery. A thick material from which bath towels are made. It has a **pile** of uncut **cotton** loops. The material makes an excellent padding for **pressing appliqué** or **napped fabrics.** It is also a favorite **fabric** for

making children's stuffed toys, since it is textured, soft, and washable.

Toweling, since it is usually cotton, is also used in some tie-dye projects.

turnabout-Johnny. Toys. See **pinwheel.**

turned weave. Weaving. A weave with the **treadling** reversed, so that what was weaving on the back side is now weaving on the front side, and vice versa. This is done when turning a **sinking shed tie-up** into a **rising shed tie-up.** Turned weave can also be a weave composed of two blocks which are weaving in direct opposition to each other in terms of **risers** and **sinkers,** i.e., what is down in one block is exactly what is up in the next. Another version of a turned weave is to take a weft pattern weave where the design is formed by **filling floats** and transform it into a **warp** pattern weave with the floats of the warp now giving the pattern. See ill.

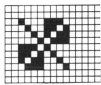

Two block turned weave

turned-wood animal. Toys. (Also called animal ring, ring horse.) A **toy** animal made by a unique process developed in Germany in the 1800s. A section of wood, usually a disk-shaped piece sliced crosswise from a tree trunk, was shaped or turned on the wood lathe in the profile of an animal. The ring was then cut into slices, yielding a number of individual ring animals. Some final shaping, carving, or sanding finished the toy; horns or tails, when needed, were carved separately and glued on. Many were carefully finished, modeled, and painted. These animals were called "reifentiere" in Germany and are also known as Noah's ark animal rings or ring animals. They are usually characterized by having the animals' hind quarters slightly larger than the front, as the animals were wedge-shaped pieces of a ring. A similar system was sometimes employed in making soldiers or other figures and toys. See ill.

Turned-wood animal

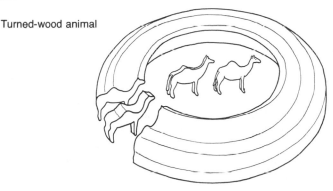

turn in. Weaving. The act of tucking into the **selvage** the beginning and ending tails of the **filling** yarn. This is done in the next **shed** that follows the tail. With heavy yarn, the tail can be tapered and tucked in, or darned into the selvage when weaving is completed.

turning. Ceramics. The trimming of a thrown **pot** on the **potter's wheel.** Bottles, jugs, and most pots can be trimmed at the final step in throwing or when **leather hard.** In a case where a **foot ring** is required, the piece must be inverted and recentered (**a.**). For tall pots, a **chuck** is used to support the pot during trimming; for bottles requiring foot rings, a cylinder chuck, flared out at the top, is attached to the wheel, and the bottle rests in it (**b.**). To recenter a pot for trimming, place it in the center of the wheel "by eye." To aid in correctly recentering, a wooden tool or pencil, held down firmly on the wheel, is slowly pushed toward the piece as the wheel rotates, until the implement juggles it into place so that the tool just touches the pot all the way around as the wheel spins. When the pot is properly recentered, hold it in place by adhering it to the wheel with wet **clay.** The excess clay is removed with the wire turning tool to form the foot ring (**c.**). See ill. Also see **chatter.**

Turning

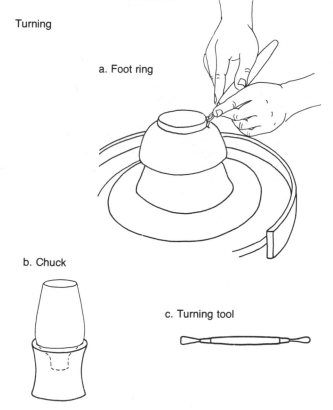

a. Foot ring

b. Chuck

c. Turning tool

turning. Crochet. When a **row** of crochet is completed, the work is turned to the other side, or reversed, to begin the next row. It is important that one or more **chain** stitches be made before actually beginning the row. This raises the **yarn** to the level of the row to be worked, and prevents puckering. Specific turning instructions are always listed with a **pattern.** Also see **Crochet.**

turning. Knitting. The method of creating a diagonal line without **casting off** a set number of stitches every **row,** thereby creating "steps" in the knitting. **Knit** to the last three stitches, and bring the yarn forward as if to make a

purl stitch. **Slip** the next stitch knitwise and pass the yarn around the **slip stitch** to the back of the work. Return the slipped stitch to the other needle without knitting it. Turn the work and purl back. Continue this turning process every other row for as long as necessary.

turning. Plastics. See **lathe turning.**

turning. Woodworking. See **wood turning.**

turning large panels. Stained Glass. Large **panels,** especially when they have been soldered on only one side, have to be carefully turned to prevent the glass from cracking. The solution is to slide the panel off the working surface, letting it tip by itself, and turn it around so that the unsoldered side faces you. Then slide it back the same way onto the working surface.

turning tool. Ceramics. See **turning** and **Ceramics: Tools and Materials.**

turnip top. Toys. A small **whip top** in the shape of a turnip.

turn pins. Lacemaking. See **picot.**

turns-per-inch. Spinning. Weaving. See **twist.**

turntable. China and Glass Painting. See **banding wheel.**

turpentine. A colorless aromatic liquid distillate of the wood and sap of pine trees. It is used as a solvent and cleaner for gums, waxes, **rosin,** oil, and paint.

turpentine. Stained Glass. See **aciding.**

turpentine. Woodworking. See **solvent.**

turpentine asphaltum. China and Glass Painting. A thick brown liquid available from the hardware or paint store, used for masking background areas during **acid etching.** If the liquid becomes stiff, thin it with turpentine.

turquoise. Beadwork. (Also called malkat.) Turquoise, generally found in the arid regions of the world, is a semiprecious stone composed of hydrous aluminum phosphate colored by copper salts. It is deposited by water action and found in the veins of rocks. This mother rock, or matrix, is responsible for its markings. Sometimes there are thin black lines, or brown or black blotches. The coloring of turquoise varies from pale chalky blue to dark greenish blue.

Turquoise has been used in jewelry and **beadmaking** since ancient times. Egyptian **faience** resembled turquoise so closely that it would seem to have been made in imitation of it. In fact, some ancient inscriptions refer to faience as "false malkat." Turquoise was highly regarded in Tibet, where it was used for currency, and in China, where it was used mainly for decoration and inlaying.

In the Americas, turquoise was used in South America by the Incas in Bolivia and Chile, and used extensively in the Southwest United States, where it is mined. The Pueblo Indians made discoidal and cylindrical turquoise beads. They revered turquoise as the stone that stole its color from the sky. The Southwest Indians still use turquoise as a vital ingredient in their jewelry crafts.

turquoise. Gemcutting. Hydrated aluminum iron and copper phosphate with **hardness** of 6 and **specific gravity** of 2.6–2.8. Turquoise is opaque, crypto-**crystal**line, decomposed by hydrochloric and nitric acids, and has a granular **fracture** and a waxy **luster.** It occurs colored green or blue. Turquoise is cut with sandpaper and polished with tin oxide on leather without **machinery** as it tends to overcut. Oils should not be used for slitting, as they will darken the blue temporarily; the stone will fade to green afterward. Overheating will cause white spots. Ammonia or detergents will also cause bleaching. Sunlight can cause the color to fade, but human contact restores and preserves it. The **matrix** is often included in the finished gem. In the case of spiderweb turquoise, it enhances the design. Synthetic turquoise is made with copper phosphate, styrene, and coloring agents. Also see **Gemcutting: Handgrinding and Polishing.**

tusche stencil. Silkscreen. The silkscreen printing **stencil** commonly associated with **serigraphy.** The technique invites experimentation in achieving tonal effects.

Designs are worked up directly on the screen, using **tusche** crayon or paint (**a.**). As the printmaker draws or paints, areas of the mesh are visibly filled with tusche, so the design is easy to alter or improvise as the work proceeds. Light pressure with a crayon, or dilute tusche lightly brushed on, will fill areas of the screen incompletely and the print will show tone or shading in those areas.

When the design is complete, the entire screen is covered with a solution of water and glue. The glue must be of a kind that remains soluble in water, even after it dries. Apply the glue by scraping it smoothly over the top surface of the screen with a small piece of cardboard or the equivalent (**b.**). When the glue dries, the tusche remains trapped beneath the layer of glue. Next, application of a solvent like kerosene to both sides of the screen, but especially to the bottom, dissolves the tusche away, and the glue layer laid over the tusche, having no anchor to hold it, floats away, leaving the screen open in those areas (**c.**). The open areas of the screen are thus the areas that were previously painted or drawn in on the screen. The screen is ready for printing right away and can last for several hundred impressions before pin holes begin to develop in the hardened glue stencil.

One drawback of the tusche-glue stencil is that the edges of the glue stencil are somewhat rough and fragile. Some improvement can be made by sizing the screen beforehand with a starch-and-water solution. This sizing gives the tusche a smooth surface to lie on, with the result that edges of the finished stencil are sharper.

Reclaiming the stencil merely requires redissolving the glue with warm water; if there is a possibility of a rerun, the screen stencil can be held.

Another type of tusche stencil technique uses lacquer instead of water-base glue, and it will produce stencils suitable for use with water-base colors. See ill.

Tusche stencil preparation

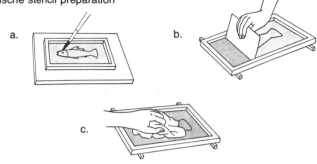

tussah silk. Spinning. Weaving. See **silk.**

tweed. Weaving. Originally the Scottish word for **twill,** today it means a heavy woolen fabric woven in a **plain** or twill **weave,** having a mottled effect due to the color mixing between **warp** and **filling** or in the **yarn** itself. The original Scottish fabric came from the area around the Tweed River on the border between Scotland and England. A tweed yarn has a varicolored or mottled effect due to the different colored **fiber**s put into the yarn during **spinning.** A "tweed effect" is spoken of in reference to mottled coloring. Also see **color blending, piece dyeing, stock dyeing.**

tweed yarn. Knitting. A yarn of one main color that has flecks of other colors spun into it. When this yarn is knit into the fabric, it produces an overall tweed effect.

tweezers. Découpage. Although cosmetic tweezers can be used, pointed tweezers from craft or stamp stores or dental tweezers are more flexible for handling delicate **cutouts.** Tweezers are useful for positioning delicate parts when gluing the cutout to the découpage surface. Also see **Découpage: Setting Up a Workshop.**

tweezers. Enameling. See **Enameling: Tools and Materials.**

tweezers. Gemcutting. See **dopping.**

tweezers. Jewelry. A tool consisting of two prongs joined at one end. There are hundreds of shapes of tweezers, and many variations on the basic form. There are two main types, those that close when they are squeezed, and those that open when squeezed (**cross-locking tweezers**), such as the type used with a **third hand.** Some tweezers are straight, others have curved ends. Tweezers are primarily used to pick up small work and can be used to place solder **pallion**s into position. The cross-locking tweezers that have a type of asbestos riveted to the handle, so that the handles remain cool while the tweezers hold work during soldering, are excellent.

T-weld. Metalworking. See **weld.**

twice-woven rug. Rugmaking. Weaving. A rug that is woven with either chenille yarn or cut strips of old rugs as **filling**. Also see **chenille fabric, novelty yarn**.

twill. Crewel. Embroidery. Twill is the best **background fabric** on which to work crewel. Originally it was made of a combination of linen (for strength) and cotton (for softness). Now it is generally made of linen, but is also available in cotton and silk, and comes in a natural beige and off-white, or oyster, color. Also see **linen fabric**.

twilled plaiting. Basketry. (Also called diagonal plaiting.) A basic type of **plaiting** in which the **active element**s are parallel, come from two directions perpendicular to each other, and weave or **float** over and under more than one element at a time, forming a diagonal pattern similar to twill fabrics. See ill. Also see **herringbone** and **Basketry: Plaited Basket Construction**.

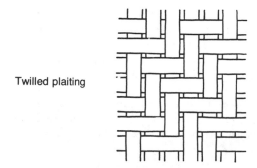

Twilled plaiting

twilled weaving. Basketry. A type of **weave** in **woven basketry** in which the structural **element**s (**stakes**) are parallel and run in one direction, and the **weaver** (or **active element**) interlaces over and under more than one **stake** at a time. It is similar to **twilled plaiting**.

twill tape. Stitchery. A **ribbon**like strip of strong and fairly heavy **cotton fabric** woven so that there is a diagonal pattern of parallel lines. Because of its durable structure, twill tape may be attached at the edge of a **banner, flag,** or **panel** so that **grommet**s may be set into it.

twill threading. Weaving. Another name for the straight drawing-in draft. The name probably comes through association, since only on a **straight draw** can a **twill** be woven.

twill tie-up. Weaving. A common **tie-up** that will produce the **twill weave** if the **harness**es are threaded in a **straight draw**. The **treadles** are tied up 1 and 2, 2 and 3, 3 and 4, 1 and 4. This is also the twill **treadling** if a direct **tie-up** is used. Weaves other than twill diagonals can be woven using the twill tie-up.

twill twining. Weaving. **Weft twining** using **paired warps** in such a manner as to achieve a compact twill or diagonal line. In each line of the twining, the weft goes around successive pairs of **warp**, always moving over to the left or to the right by one warp **end** so that the diagonal is formed.

Zigzag twining results when the diagonal goes to the left for a time and then to the right.

The term is also used in compact **warp twining** when two warp ends enclose two weft threads at a time, and each time alternate the weft threads by enclosing one of the former pair and one of a new pair. A steep warp diagonal is thus formed. See ill. Also see **Ojibwa weaving**.

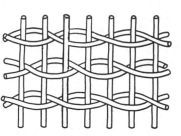

Twill twining

twill weave. Weaving. The second of the three basic weaves. It is formed by doubling the **plain weave** structure and staggering it so that a diagonal line is formed. The term "twill" meant "to double," and it originated in Scotland as a name for a diagonal or bias effect in fabrics. Plain weave's symbol is $\frac{1}{1}$. Doubled, this would be $\frac{2}{2}$, and it is read as "two up, two down." This means that in the first **pick** of weaving, two **warp end**s are raised and two are lowered in order to form the **shed** for the **filling** thread to go through. In the second pick, the two threads raised are not the opposite ones as in plain weave. Instead, one thread that was previously raised, and its neighboring thread that was not raised before, are the "two up" in the second pick. With every successive pick, the **float** of each filling thread is set one warp end to the right or left of the float of the preceding filling thread. If the move is made to the left, the diagonal line runs from right to left and a left-hand twill is formed. If the move is made to the right, the diagonal line runs from left to right and a right-hand twill is formed. The right-hand twill is the more commonly woven of the two. If the right-hand twill and the left-hand twill are combined into one weave, the result is known as a reversed twill, pointed twill, or zigzag twill. The twill line travels in both directions. Where the change of direction occurs, there is a point. If the point is not there or the diagonal direction not clearly evident, the weave is called a broken twill. The twill line can be reversed in either the warp or the filling. Usually, when the reversal occurs in the warp, the weave is called **herringbone** or chevron.

There are **warp-faced** twills ($\frac{2}{1}$) showing more warp than filling, and **filling-faced** twills ($\frac{1}{3}$) that show more filling than warp. These are called uneven twills. Balanced twills are those in which the warp and filling are equally exposed. If the number of ends per inch and **picks per inch** are equal to each other, the diagonal line will be at an inclination of 45°. Steep twills are designed to rise at a sharper angle than this. The opposite is true of reclining twills or flat twills, which are formed to be less than 45° and are, therefore, closer to the horizontal. The steep twill is the more popular of the two.

There are also **undulating twill**s, which are not straight diagonal lines, but curved ones that become wider or thinner at various spots, and fancy twills, which have more than one twill line in the repeat and are often part of another weave effect.

A twill is a softer, more lustrous, and more pliable weave than plain weave. It is strong, durable, and with good draping qualities, which makes it a natural for apparel fabrics. This, plus the fact that the weave lends itself to countless variations, makes twill very popular. The popularity has resulted in as many names for twill weaves as there are variations. Often the same name will mean two different kinds of twill patterns. However, in methods of construction, all agree: The numerical symbol is the telling factor. It not only tells what warp ends have to be raised and what have to be lowered in order to get the design, but also, by the sum of the numbers in the symbol, it tells the number of harnesses it takes to weave a certain twill. A $\frac{4}{2}$ symbol would mean that this is a twill woven on 6 harnesses with 4 ends raised and 2 lowered in each pick. The smallest number of harnesses necessary for a twill is three for a $\frac{1}{2}$ twill. This repeats on three ends and three picks. The number of possible combinations is almost limitless, as long as there are enough harnesses on the loom to weave it with. See ill. Also see **bird's eye pattern, diamond twill, rose path.**

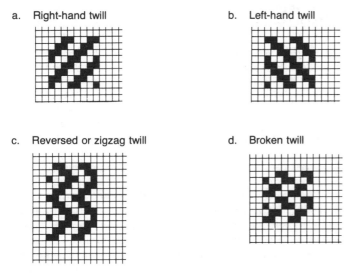

a. Right-hand twill   b. Left-hand twill

c. Reversed or zigzag twill   d. Broken twill

twine. Spinning. Weaving. A rough-textured **ply** yarn that is made of medium **twist** single yarns with the ply twist going in the opposite direction of the single yarns twist. Twine is made of **sisal** and other **bast fibers.**

twined edge. Rugmaking. Weaving. A **finishing edge** in which the **warp end**s are twined around each other in successive rows. The **twining** can proceed left to right, right to left, or from the center out in both directions. Starting at the left, a **half turn** is given to the two end strands of **fringe** (a.). They then continue twining with half turns between each warp strand, until an inch or so of the starting two ends remains untwined (**b.**). These tips point toward the body of the fabric as the twining is pushed up close to it. The next two warp ends that are sticking out of the twining are then twined in a similar manner for the same number of ends as the first twining, so that they emerge pointing toward the body in a position to the right of the

first two tips (**c.**). This procedure is continued across the entire fabric. No fringe exists, for the ends pointing upward are trimmed short or darned into the fabric. Twined edges give a strong edge because of the natural lock formed by the twining. See ill.

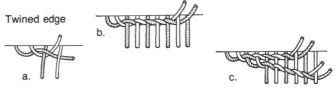

Twined edge

twined plaiting. Weaving. See **sprang.**

twined weaving. Basketry. (Also called twining.) A type of **weave** in **woven basketry**: The **active element** or **weaver** twists around and ties the structural elements or **stake**s in place. One example of twined weaving is fitching. See ill. Also see **Basketry: Woven Basket Construction.**

Twined weaving

twining. Basketry. See **twined weaving.**

twining. Weaving. The twisting or turning around each other of two or more threads belonging to the same position or group to enclose threads of the opposite position or group and thereby construct **cloth.** The two positions can be called **warp** and **weft.** If the warp twists around and encloses the **filling,** it is called **warp twining.** If the filling twists around and encloses the warp, it is called **weft twining.** Sometimes the word "cording" is used when speaking of dense warp twining, because the thick fabric resembles a heavily **rib**bed or **cord**ed cloth. Pairing is sometimes used for simple weft twining. When most craftspeople say "twining," it is weft twining they are speaking of; they tend to disregard warp twining or include it all under "**card weaving,**" since weft twining is the more popular and common of the two. For example, weft twining is often used as a spacing device for warps on **frame loom**s, **Navajo loom**s, and the like. It is never referred to as "weft twining," but simply as "twining." "Openwork twining" refers to a gauze effect that can be achieved by having the weft and warp openly spaced or randomly spaced—some close together, and some far apart.

Twining, whether weft or warp, must have at least two elements, or threads, twisting together. So-called one-strand weft twining is really **chaining** derived from a crochet chain stitch. Twining is an enclosing technique rather than an **interlacing** one, such as **weaving.** However, twining is composed of a warp and weft—as is weaving—and sometimes the phrase "twined weave" is used erroneously in reference to twining. It frequently falls under a weaving technique, whereas it is not weaving but rather an aboriginal link between basketry and shelter-building and, later, true weaving on a **loom** of some sort. The earliest extant cloth twining was discovered in Anatolia and dates back to about 6500 B.C. This was still rather naïve twining. Far more developed was the twining practiced by the pre-Inca Indians of Peru. Such fabrics have been found dating from 2500 B.C. Twining was apparently their fabric-making method until a concept of **heddle**s and a **shedding device** developed, and then it gave way to weaving, although some twining was always done for specific effects.

Twining was, and to some extent still is, a technique at home on all continents. In North America, the early Southwestern cliff dwellers used twining, as did the Chilkat tribes of the Northwest and the Indians of the prairies, the Great Lakes, and the Northeast. Also see **Chilkat blanket, Navajo selvage, Ojibwa weaving, Salish weaving, taaniko twining, twined edge.**

Twinkling Star. Quilts. See **Feather Star.**

twirling yo-yo. Toys. (Also called cacoon yo-yo, twirling toy.) A **folk toy** of the West Indies similar to a **yo-yo**, being a **momentum toy.** It is made of cacoon bean pods and is identical to the **moulinet** except for the kind of seeds used. This one uses dried bean pods instead of nuts. In principle, the toy operates the same way as the **apple mill.** One version of twirling yo-yo has been dated at about 2000 B.C., making it one of the oldest known toys.

twist. Lacemaking. (Abbr. T.) A basic movement in **bobbin lace,** done by placing the right **bobbin** of a pair of bobbins over the left **bobbin** of the same pair and laying it on the **pillow.** A twist is always from right to left within the pair. Bobbins #1 and #2 of the pair are interchanged, and, after the movement is completed, assume their regular numerical order of bobbins. See ill.

Twist

twist. Spinning. Weaving. The direction in which a yarn is twisted in **spinning** or **plying.** This direction can be clockwise (running from right to left) and produce a left-hand or S-twist yarn, or it can be counterclockwise (from left to right) and produce a right-hand or Z-twist yarn. When two S-twist singles are plied, they usually combine to form a Z-twist yarn, and when two Z-twists are plied, they form an S-twist. The difference in direction between the original singles and the plied yarn is necessary to keep the two strands interlocked.

The degree of twist a yarn has is called turns per inch. This is determined by the nature and length of the fiber and the end use of the yarn. It can have a few twists, or turns per inch, and be called a soft-twist yarn, or have many turns per inch and be called a hard-twist yarn. Soft-

or low-twist yarns are good for **filling** or in any work where they will not undergo much stress. A **warp** yarn should be a hard twist, since the warp undergoes tension and beating.

The direction of the twist is controlled during hand-spinning; however, there sometimes occurs an overtwist of a yarn which causes it to look kinky and makes it impractical and unattractive for use. The cure is to place the **skein** around a **reel** and leave it under tension for a while. This will stretch out the kinks. A commercial tightly twisted yarn is known as a crepe spun yarn and its crinkly feature is considered desirable. It gives a rough, pebbly texture to the finished cloth. See ill. Also see **doubling.**

a. S-twist yarn   b. Z-twist yarn

twist bit. Woodworking. See **drill bits.**

twist drill. Jewelry. See **hand drill, twist drill gauge.**

twist drill bit. Metalworking. Plastics. Woodworking. See **drill bit.**

twist drill gauge. Jewelry. A steel plate perforated with holes that are used to measure the diameter of twist drills. They are marked in sizes #1, the largest, through #80, the smallest. The plate is also usually marked with decimal equivalents. Also see **hand drill.**

twisted fringe. Rugmaking. Weaving. See **plied fringe.**

twisted knot. Crewel. Embroidery. See **French knot.**

twisted stitches. Knitting. Twisted stitches can occur by inserting the needle into the **stitch** incorrectly. When **unraveling** back after making a mistake, care must be taken to return the stitches to the needle in the proper direction. If it is more difficult than usual to insert the needle into the stitch, chances are good that it is being twisted. A complete understanding of stitch movement will help the knitter take a stitch off the needle without twisting the stitch, regardless of how it sits on the needle. Also see **Knitting: Knit Movements.**

twisted warp. Weaving. See **gauze weave.**

twisted wefts. Weaving. A color technique in which contrasting colors of **filling** yarns are placed in the open **shed** and twisted before being beaten down. Two or more colors can be used. A flamepoint or arrowhead design can be achieved by twisting in alternate directions in each shed. If the twist is the same in each shed, a diagonal pattern will result. Controlled twisting as to number of twists in a shed and their placement can give a spotty or tweedy effect mixed in with a stripe.

two-chambered kiln. Ceramics. See **chambered kiln.**

two-faced puppet. Puppets. A figure that has a face on both the front and back. The **puppet** can be turned around on stage to show the other side of the **puppet head** and to reveal a change of expression or character. Also see **trick puppet.**

two-headed doll. Toys. See **topsy-turvy doll.**

two-layered fabric. Weaving. See **double cloth.**

two-man pouring shank. Metalworking. See **tongs.**

two-patch. Quilts. A right-triangle **patch** that, when sewn together with another, forms a **block.** The triangles are made by cutting either a square or a rectangle diagonally in half. **Birds in Flight,** along with all its variations, and **Tree Everlasting** are two-patch designs. See ill.

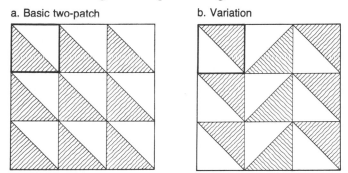

a. Basic two-patch   b. Variation

two-piece throwing. Ceramics. Large pots are often thrown in two or more sections and joined when **leather hard.** The early amphora forms were done in this way.

two-ply yarn. Crewel. Embroidery. Needlepoint. See **Crewel: Yarn.**

two-prong lacing needle. Leather. See **lacing needles.**

two short stitches. Crewel. Embroidery. See **Roumanian stitch.**

two-sided Montenegrin stitch. Needlepoint. See **Montenegrin cross stitch.**

2/2 dovetailing. Weaving. See **dovetailing.**

"two up, two down." Weaving. See **twill weave.**

tying in. Basketry. (Also tie in.) Securing the **slath** or bottom **sticks** that will form the **foundation** of the basket. Also see **Basketry: Woven Basket Construction.**

tying-in. Weaving. Attaching new **warp ends** to a **warp** on the **loom** in order to change the color of sections of the warp. The warp is in the process of being woven and the color changes are made to gain a special effect, to obtain two or more different warp color patterns in one warp, or to change the color pattern every few inches, as might be the case in a sample warp. First, the new color pattern of the warp is planned and some of the color of the original warp is included. The ends of new color to be introduced

are counted, and a warp is made of just the new colors. The length is equal to the amount of warp left on the loom or the amount that will be woven in the new color pattern. The **chain**ed warp is attached to **lease stick**s in front of the **beater.** The warp on the loom is cut an inch above the **fell** in those sections where the new colors are to be introduced. The end loop of the **warp chain** is cut in small groups. Both the cut ends of the warp on the loom and the cut ends of the chained warp are tied together in a **weaver's knot,** or any small, tight knot, following the planned color pattern. After all the ends are tied, small groups of knots are pulled through the **reed** and **heddle**s. When all the knots are at the back of the loom, the new warp is pulled completely to the back until 3–4″ of it remains down from the fell line. In the back of the loom, the weaver's knots are cut and the procedure follows similar to that of mending a **broken end.** Small groups of bow knots are tied, attaching the new warp to the old warp. In the front, the new warp ends are wound in a figure 8 around horizontally placed pins. As the warp advances during weaving, the bow knots are untied and retied further away from the **harness**es. In place of pins, fine knots can be made to secure each new and old warp end individually.

tying-on. Weaving. Attaching the **warp ends** in equal groups to the front **apron bar** after **threading** and **sleying** are completed. This is the last step in **dressing the loom** and one of the most vital since the **warp tension** is controlled by the care taken in tying-on. Each group or bundle (called a **bout** or bight) must be tied to the apron bar in the same tension as its neighbor. To do so, take a group of ends equal to the thickness of the forefinger (the smaller the group, the easier the tension can be controlled; in very widely spaced or thick groups, the ends in the center of the group are often difficult to control). Tie this group around the center of the apron bar in order to stabilize the bar so that it won't be pulled to one side and out of the **apron cord**s. Then tie successive groups going from either right to left, or left to right, along the width of the warp. A **tie-on knot** is used. In the initial tying-on, it is just tied as a single knot. The tension is then adjusted by pulling up on the ends of the tie-on knot going from group to group, right to left (or the reverse direction). Pass your hand lightly over the warp in back of the **harness**es and, if any loose spots are felt, pull up on these warp ends at the knot. Uniformly adjust the tension a third time at the knots, at the same time either double-knotting or making a half or full bow knot to prevent the ends from slipping out of tension during weaving. An alternate method to tying-on is **lacing on.**

Also, attaching a new warp to a warp already on the loom. Time is saved in that threading and sleying are omitted. However, the new warp yarn must be close to the same weight of the old warp yarn, since the **sett** will be the same for both. The weave patterns possible with the threading remain the same. The usual method of tying-on is by knotting the new warp to the already existing warp with a **weaver's knot** or a similar small, tight knot. The woven cloth of the old warp is cut off and the warp is tied in front of the beater, or the ends are taped in front of the **beater** to a long strip of masking tape. The new warp is placed on **lease stick**s that are tied and suspended in front of the beater or attached to the **breast beam.** The last loop of the **warp chain** faces the beater. The **lease cord** is cut, the warp is spread, the ends are cut section by section and tied end by end to the old warp ends. After completion of the tying-on process, the knots are gently maneuvered through the **dents** and **heddle eyes,** and the warp is beamed and tied to the front apron bar in the usual manner. Tying-on is used when a weaver wants to weave another warp in the same threading and yarn weight as the one just finished, or by production weavers who weave large amounts of **yardage**—usually in the same pattern and type of yarn, but only changing the colors or the **warp arrangement.** With production weavers, a short or "dummy" warp usually remains permanently on the loom for constant new warps to be tied to it. Also see **beaming, tying-in.**

tying out. Lacemaking. In **bobbin lace,** a tying out is necessary when a lacer is finishing a section of **lace** and has no further use for the **bobbin**s from that section, but will be continuing on in the lacework.

Tie each **pair of bobbins** together in two **reef knot**s to prevent them from slipping, and bring the **worker**s around them, one above and one under; then tie the workers together in a sufficient number of reef knots to hold, and cut the workers off.

Tyndall effect. Gemcutting. See **luster.**

type clamp. Bookbinding. An instrument designed to hold single pieces of type for the application of the **title** to a binding. The lower screw adjusts the width of the jaws and the upper screw tightens the jaws around the letter.

type holder. Bookbinding. An instrument that holds lines of type for **tooling** titles on bindings.

Tyrian purple. Dyeing. See **natural dyes.**

Tyrolean knitting. Knitting. A style of knitting originally practiced in the Austrian Tyrol. The yarn used is usually white and is worked in **cable** and **bobble** patterns that are afterward embellished with colored embroidery in leaf and flower designs.

u

Überfang. Stained Glass. See **flashed glass.**

U-came. Stained Glass. See **lead came.**

Ulano swivel knife. Silkscreen. See **stencil-cutting tools.**

ultimates. Spinning. Bundles of short lengths of flax fiber. They usually are available to spinners who do not grow or process their own flax. Also see **flax, linen.**

Ultra-Cal. Plastics. See **casting plaster.**

ultraviolet. See **color.**

ultraviolet stabilizer. Plastics. See **antioxidant.**

umber. Ceramics. A **pigment oxide** darker than **ocher** and **sienna** that is used as a stain, **glaze,** or **slip** colorant. When calcined, it is called burnt umber.

umbrella swift. Spinning. Weaving. See **swift.**

unakite. Gemcutting. A variety of granite with **hardness** of 6½ and **specific gravity** of 3.25–3.5. It contains red **feldspar,** white **quartz,** and green **epidote** grains. Unakite is polished with tin oxide for ornamental purposes. Also see **polishing.**

unbalanced weave. Weaving. See **balanced weave.**

unbleached muslin. Quilts. Stitchery. See **muslin.**

uncut pile. Rugmaking. Weaving. See **pile.**

undercut. Metalworking. Plastics. The sloping sides of molds that lock the cast object into the mold and prevent its easy removal. In **sandcasting** metal, the undercuts must be eliminated in the design of the **pattern** in order to be able to remove the pattern from the **molding sand** prior to pouring in the metal. Also see **mold.**

underfiring. Ceramics. The failure of the kiln to reach the required firing temperature, resulting in a bisque that is very porous and breakable. Underfired **glaze** is opaque and liable to crawl. Also see **crawling.**

underglaze. Enameling. A liquid black painting medium which is fired in a transparent **enamel.** A design is drawn onto a clean **metal** or pre-enameled surface with a pen or sable brush. This will turn matte when it dries. A dry, transparent enamel such as **flux** is dusted on—wet enamel would blur the drawing—and fired. Reverse designs may be made by covering the surface with underglaze, then scratching out the design. Also see **color testing, firing, matte finish, overglaze, sgraffito.**

underglaze color. China and Glass Painting. (Also called inglaze color.) The decoration painted on unglazed china using **onglaze color.** It is dusted with fluxed **glaze** before each **firing.**

underglaze pigment. Ceramics. Pigment applied to **bisque** or raw clay and covered with a glaze. Underglaze colors are limited to the oxides that will withstand the firing temperature of the glaze. Also see **binder.**

underground art. Counterculture art, or the use of art forms and themes which are not generally accepted as "art." Extremely creative, full of humor and audacity, highly inventive, it often boldly ignores the standard or accepted approaches, flouting normal procedures. Also see **blue jeans funk, pop.**

Underground Railroad, The. Quilts. See **Jacob's Ladder.**

underlay. Weaving. See **laid-in.**

undulating twill. Weaving. A **twill weave** that is composed of curved or waved diagonal lines instead of the usual straight diagonals. It can be formed by designing a twill weave in which the **floats** of the diagonal move in an irregular pattern, instead of moving over by one **end** with every **pick,** as they do in a regular twill. However, this type of undulating twill takes upward from 8 **harnesses** in a loom to weave it. The same wavy effect on four harnesses can be achieved by one of two other ways. The **threading**

Undulating twill on four harnesses

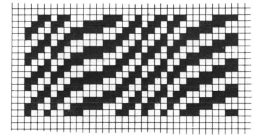

can be changed so that the warp threads are grouped on the same harness in twos and threes and other harnesses are skipped in a manner planned to achieve the wavy line. A second way this line can be achieved is by combining groups of threads in an irregular **sleying** so that some **dent**s may have three or four ends crammed into them and other dents may go empty. See ill. Also see **grouped threads.**

uneven dyeing. Batik and Tie-dye. Failure to achieve **level dyeing,** or even penetration of the **dye** into the fibers. **Wetting out** will help avoid the uneven coloring in the **tie-dye.** It may occur if fabrics are too crowded in the **dyebath** or if the fabric **finish**es are not carefully removed. To cover the uneven saturation of the dye, another dye process can be used. Re**wax** or retie the material, then immerse in a darker dyebath.

uneven fracture. Gemcutting. See **fracture.**

uneven twill. Weaving. See **twill weave.**

unfluxed color. China and Glass Painting. Color that does not contain **flux** and therefore will not adhere to the surface of the china during **firing.** Unfluxed color can be mixed with **fluxed color,** or a flux **glaze** must be applied over the unfluxed color before firing. Also see **China and Glass Painting: Preparing China and Paint.**

unglazed china doll. Toys. See **bisque doll.**

unglazed doll head. Toys. See **bisque, Parian.**

UNIMA. Puppets. The Union Internationale des Marionettes, an organization founded in Prague in 1929 to unite the **puppeteer**s of the world. The union regards **puppetry** as an art that addresses itself to both children and adults, and has dedicated the art to the service of peace. It serves to link puppeteers from all over the world and to organize conferences and festivals.

union dye. Batik and Tie-dye. See **household dye** and **Batik and Tie-dye: Dyes.**

Union Square. Quilts. A **block** for a **pieced quilt** that is identical to the **Delectable Mountains** with the exception of the center. In this version a square is substituted for the star. See ill.

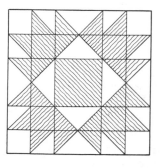

Union Square

Union Star. Quilts. A **geometric pieced pattern** with a five-pointed star. See ill. Also see **star patterns.**

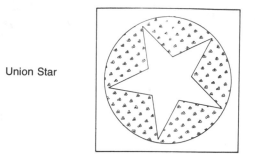

Union Star

United States Stamping Law. Jewelry. In the United States, the marking of articles made of precious metals is controlled by the Federal Stamping Law (U.S. Code, Title 15, Chapter 8, Sections 294–300). Violations of the Federal Stamping Law are punishable by a $500.00 fine, three months' imprisonment, or both.

In the stamping of gold, the **karat** declared on the stamp must not be more than ½ karat lower than the stated stamp if tested (assayed) with the **solder.** The entire article cannot be less than one karat different from the stamped mark. Gold that is 10K can be stamped as such, but an **alloy** that is less than 10K cannot be stamped, as the percent of gold is so low that the amount of the alloy metal is greater than the gold content.

The National Bureau of Standards, in conjunction with the Department of Commerce, publishes several pamphlets called "Commercial Standards" that state regulations for stamping precious metals. Such pamphlets are available for ten cents each from the Superintendent of Documents, United States Government Printing Office, Washington, D.C. 20025. Also see **gold filled.**

United States Standard Gauge. Jewelry. See **gauge.**

unit of repeat. Weaving. Refers to the number of **warp end**s and **filling picks** a **weave** pattern needs to duplicate or repeat itself in its entirety. This would appear warp or widthwise in the **drawing-in draft,** and filling or lengthwise in the **treadling order** or **chain draft.**

universal shears. Jewelry. **Shears** constructed to cut **sheet metal** in straight or curved lines. Also see **aviation snips, snips.**

universal toy. Toys. A toy common to children the world over. Universal toys are usually fundamental or basic in nature and, as do folk myths and religious traditions, spring up in different times and places with no apparent connection. Because of the way they reappear in various cultures, they are sometimes referred to as **emergent toy**s. A few universal toys are **ball**s, **top**s, **doll**s, **hoop**s, and toy animals of various kinds. Also see **bird toy, pecking chickens** and **Toys: Construction Toys, Dolls.**

unkind. Basketry. Describes basketry material that is hard on the hands, or rough to handle, as opposed to pliable, easy-to-work **stuff,** which is "kind."

unraveling. Knitting. Unraveling is most commonly done when a mistake has been noticed in a completed **row** of knitting. It is the process of gently and evenly pulling stitches off the needle and "unraveling" them a stitch, and then a row, at a time. Unraveling is also done when too many stitches (or rows) have been knit, causing the fabric to be either too long or too wide. Care should be taken to maintain the correct position of the stitch on the needle when working the **knit stitch uncrossed** and the **purl stitch uncrossed.** See ill. Also see **Knitting: Knit Movements.**

a. Knit stitches

b. Purl stitches

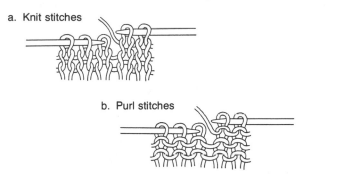

c. Correct position of stitch on needle when working knit stitch uncrossed and purl stitch uncrossed

unsoldering. Jewelry. Removing a previously **solder**ed area. If many joints have been soldered and one unit must be removed, unsoldering is very difficult. Coat all **seams** that are not to be unsoldered with **yellow ochre** or **yellow ochre casein;** coat all other surfaces with **flux.** Secure the work into an **asbestos pad** with **T-pins** or with several **third hand**s to facilitate removing the piece being unsoldered. Heat until the solder flows, and at once lift or push the piece off. Lift whenever possible, as pushing will leave a track of messy solder that is difficult and time consuming to remove. The tool used to lift or push the piece must also be heated, or the solder will **freeze** upon contact. If the piece to be removed is too hot or is unevenly heated, it will fracture when lifted.

untying. Batik and Tie-dye. Removing the **tie-dye** cord or untying the fabric itself, depending upon the tie-dye method used.

As knots become tight when they are wet, various methods may be used to assist in untying knots. One method is to place some object on the fabric before the knot is tied. A smooth stick of wood or small roll of tag board will do. After dyeing, the stick is slid out, leaving a little slack or looseness under the knot. In another method, loops or rings of cord are slipped over the fabric before it is knotted. It is then tied in such a way that one loop extends from each of the two tight sections of the knot. After dyeing, pulling these loops in opposite directions helps loosen the knots.

To remove the cords themselves with which the tie-dye fabric is bound, cutting may be necessary. Because knots are so tight that it will be difficult to untie them, try to clip off any knots that protrude rather than to cut a string and risk clipping the material itself. In cutting the knot, grasp it and pull it out away from the fabric, slipping a scissors blade into the opening and cutting away from the fabric.

updraft kiln. Ceramics. The simplest form of a **kiln.** Fire beneath the floor rises through the **ware** in the kiln to a chimney at the top. Heat is wasted and the ware at the base of the kiln fires better. The kiln is nonetheless very popular because of its simplicity. See ill.

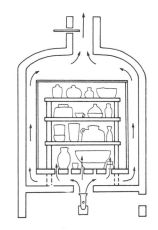

Updraft kiln

upholsterer's pins. Macramé. (Also called tidy pins.) Upholsterer's pins are long, bracket-shaped pins used in macramé to anchor knots or rows of knotting to the knotting surface to help keep the work even. Also see **anchoring.**

upholstery material. Stitchery. Heavy-textured **fabric**s woven from a great variety of **fibers,** most commonly of **synthetic** and **wool,** used primarily in upholstering furniture. Because of the good range of textures, fibers, and colors available, it is often used as a **background** material for either **hand appliqué** or **machine appliqué.** Since it is sometimes a **backed material,** the density of the fabric should be checked for the amount of resistance it offers to the **needle.** Most upholstery fabric is woven to 54″ or 60″ wide, which is of special value in large-scale stitchery. Fabric shops and department stores offer a limited range and variety of these materials; the greatest range of choices is available through an interior design or interior decorating firm.

upholstery needle. Stitchery. See **needle.**

upper fuller. Metalworking. See **blacksmithing tools.**

upper swage. Metalworking. See **blacksmithing tools.**

upright. Spinning. The stationary post supporting the wheel in a **wool wheel.** There are two uprights in a **treadle wheel.**

upright control. Puppets. See **vertical control.**

upright cross stitch. Crewel. Embroidery. Needlepoint. A **cross stitch** variation worked on vertical and horizontal lines rather than diagonals. This stitch can be worked on any **background fabric.**

In needlepoint, "straight cross stitch" refers to a series of upright cross stitches done over any even number of mesh.

upright Gobelin stitch. Needlepoint. See **Gobelin stitch.**

upright loom. Weaving. A loom standing on two legs or supports and having the **warp** in a vertical position. It can be quite large and is most often used for rugs, tapestries, and wall hangings. In its simplest version, the upright is a large frame with a **shed stick** and **heddle rod** for opening the **shed**s. The warp is usually wound as a **continuous** one by going around the top and bottom horizontal beams of the frame. In more elaborate models, there are foot **treadle**s connected to **harness**es to open the shed, **cloth** and **warp beam**s in order to have longer warps, and a **beater** with **reed.** Other uprights fall in between these two versions and differ chiefly in the manner of opening their shed. One of the great advantages of an upright loom, no matter what the model, is that the weaver can see the larger part of what he is weaving—in full view, hanging before him. Also see **Navajo rug loom, tapestry loom.**

upsetting. Basketry. One of the most important steps in making a basket. It consists of properly turning up the bottom **spokes** or **stakes** of the basket into the proper angle to form the sides. Usually a **round** or two of **waling** is used both to provide a **foot**ing for the basket and a strong weave from which the basket shape will **spring.** Also see **Basketry: Coiled Basket Construction, Plaited Basket Construction, Woven Basket Construction.**

upsetting. Jewelry. See **edge thickening.**

upsetting. Metalworking. A hammering technique for thickening a piece of metal. It may be done during **forging** when the metal is hot; or when the metal is cold, during **raising,** for example, when **thickening the edge** of an object. Also see **blacksmithing techniques, raising techniques** and **Metalworking: Blacksmithing, Raising.**

upside-down doll. Toys. See **topsy-turvy doll.**

uranium oxide. Ceramics. A **pigment oxide** used in low-fire **lead glaze**s to produce yellow. Tin-**vanadium,** zirconium-vanadium, and praseodymium yellow stains have greater flexibility and present no radiation hazard.

urea. Batik and Tie-dye. A solid crystalline compound used in the thickening formulas for **dyestuff**s. It is also an ingredient of the **chemical water** solution used in preparing **fiber-reactive dye**s for various direct-dye methods. Urea is available at chemical suppliers and sometimes at shops which carry **batik** or dye materials.

urethane. Metalworking. Plastics. See **polyurethane.**

urethane. Woodworking. See **polyurethane, varnish.**

urethane liquid plastic. Toys. A fast-drying, glossy-plastic coating for wood, used similarly to **enamel paint.** This plastic paint is extremely flammable and must be used with adequate ventilation. It is available as a spray and is sometimes called urethane plastic varnish.

urn. Quilts. See **vase and urn patterns.**

utilitarian pottery. Ceramics. Functional pottery for everyday use.

utility knife. Leather. (Also called mat knife.) An all-purpose cutting knife (X-acto is a common brand name) with replaceable blades used for general lightweight leather projects except cutting **suede,** which is cut with **scissors.** See ill. Also see **square.**

Utility knife

uvarovite. Gemcutting. See **garnet.**

Uvinul. Plastics. See **antioxidant.**

V

vacuum casting. Jewelry. A form of **casting** that removes any bubbles from the **investment** mixture while it is still in its liquid state, prior to and just after pouring the investment over the **wax model.** This is done by placing the mixed but as yet unhardened investment on a table that has a hole in it. This hole is connected to a vacuum pump. A bell jar covers the investment. When the vacuum pump is turned on, it causes the investment to froth, releasing any air trapped in it by pulling the air out through the hole in the table. Vacuum equipment is also used during actual casting, but without the bell jar. After the **burnout,** the metal that will be used for the casting is melted in a **crucible.** The hot investment and surrounding **flask** are removed from the kiln and placed over the hole in the vacuum table. Some form of asbestos or silicone rubber that can withstand temperatures of over 1000° F should be used to separate the hot investment and flask from the table so that the table will not burn. If a 4″ flask is used, the size of the hole in the material that separates it from the table should be at least 3″. The vacuum pump is turned on and the molten metal is poured from the crucible into the investment. The metal is sucked into the cavity of the burned-out investment, completing the casting process. Also see **centrifugal casting.**

vacuum former. Plastics. (Also called vacuum-forming machine.) A machine for **thermoforming plastic** that sucks the plastic sheet down onto a **pattern** with holes in it by creating a vacuum. The machine consists of a temperature-controlled electrical heating element, a holding frame on which the plastic is fastened, an air compressor, and a platform for the pattern (also with holes in it). The vacuum former may range in size from a few inches across to many feet in diameter for molding furniture and sports equipment. See ill. Also see **Plastics: Thermoforming and Molding.**

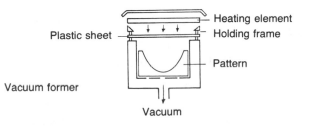

vacuum forming. Plastics. See **pattern, thermoforming,** and **Plastics: Thermoforming and Molding.**

vacuum-forming machine. Plastics. See **vacuum former.**

valentine. Papercrafts. A traditional papercraft design, the valentine greeting card has been interpreted in many ways. **Pin-pricking** has been used for elaborate, lacy patterns. **Cutouts** have been done on folded paper for repeated hearts, flowers, and other traditional designs. These intricate paper cuttings were often combined with ribbons, locks of hair, dried flowers, and so on, and mounted on contrasting paper with handwritten messages. See ill.

Valentine

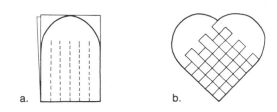

a.   b.

valley stake. Metalworking. See **anvil.**

value. One of the three qualities of **color,** it is also known as brightness level, lightness or darkness, **tint,** or **shade.**

A pure **pigment** of any **hue** to which white has been added will be lighter than the pure pigment and is said to have a higher value. A pure pigment of any hue to which black pigment has been added will be darker, and is said to have a lower value. Pigment hues that have been raised in value by the addition of white are called tints. Pigment hues that have been darkened by the addition of black are called shades. The addition of either white or black or of both reduces **saturation.** The value of green in the natural **spectrum** is low. The value of yellow in the natural spectrum is high. It is possible to add white to a sea-green hue to the point where its value is higher than a natural lemon yellow. It is possible to add black pigment to a lemon yellow so that it will have the same value as a sea green.

The concept of value is extremely important to **color harmony.** Colors of equal value and equal saturation are likely to harmonize almost regardless of hue. Also see **broken color, color clash, discord, monochromatic color triangle.**

vanadium. Ceramics. A **pigment oxide** that produces a weak yellow when used alone. **Frit** with **tin oxide** to produce a stronger color is available commercially as tin vanadium stain. Also see **stain.**

vanadium. Metalworking. See **steel**.

Vandyke stitch. Crewel. Embroidery. A **cross stitch** with a braid down the center. To make the Vandyke stitch, work a cross stitch and slide the needle under the top of the previous stitch (**a.**). The stitches overlap in the center (**b.**). The needle pierces the **background fabric** at the sides of the stitch (**c.**). See ill.

Vandyke stitch

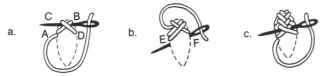

a.   b.   c.

vanishing point. See **perspective**.

Variable Star. Quilts. A design for a **pieced block** that forms an eight-pointed star. It is a **split nine-patch**, and well named, as it provides the basis for numerous variations. **Dolley Madison Star** and **Old Tippecanoe** are similar, although the **patch**es are split into a different arrangement of triangles and squares. See ill. Also see **Texas Lone Star**.

Variable Star

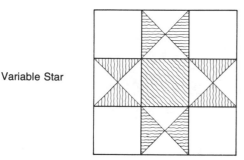

variegated yarn. Crewel. Embroidery. Needlepoint. A yarn made up of repeated sequences of consecutive colors, useful for random color changes. Also see **ombré yarn**.

varnish. Découpage. Papercrafts. A liquid coating that dries to a hard, clear finish. Varnish, available at hardware stores and craft shops, comes in high-gloss or matte finish.

varnish. Tincrafting. See **Tincrafting: Finishing the Tin**.

varnish. Woodworking. A traditional wood **finish** that has been in use since ancient times. It dries hard and nearly transparent, and when rubbed will produce a high gloss. It is resistant to moisture and many corrosive substances. There are two main types of varnishes: traditional oil varnishes and modern synthetic varnishes.

Oil varnishes consist of fossilized gums, or resins, from tree sap and use tung or **linseed oil** as a vehicle and **turpentine** as a thinner and drying agent. Oil varnish formulas vary mainly according to the ratio of oil to resin; generally, those with a high oil content (long-oil varnishes) are better able to withstand weathering and rough wear, while short-oil varnishes are faster-drying and are conducive to **rubbing** to a high polish.

Cabinet varnish is an all-around varnish used on interior work. Easy to apply, it can be rubbed with **pumice** stone and oil or water to produce a high gloss. Rubbing varnish is a short-oil cabinet varnish intended for hard, high-gloss interior finishes. Flat varnish dries dull or semigloss and is usually applied as a final varnish over cabinet varnish. It does not require rubbing. Interior spar varnish is recommended for desks, bar tops, and other highly used interior wood surfaces. It dries very hard, and may be rubbed to a satin gloss. Exterior spar varnish is a long-oil varnish recommended for all types of exterior use. It is relatively slow-drying, cannot be applied over another finish, and will not take a high gloss.

Synthetic varnishes are composed of synthetic resins like bakelite, alkyds, or polyurethane, with china wood oil as the vehicle and varnalene or xylol as a thinner. Because of chemical processes, they are faster-drying than oil varnishes.

Polyurethane (or urethane) varnish is the most common synthetic varnish; it produces a very tough, flexible surface for both interior and exterior surfaces. It is highly resistant to acids, alkalis, grease, hot and cold water, and alcohol.

Because varnish tends to dry slowly, apply it only in a dust-free environment that is well ventilated but with as little draft as possible. Temperatures of 70–80° F are ideal for proper application and drying.

Remove all dust with a **tac rag** and clean the surface by wiping it down with benzene. A perfectly clean brush is essential. Remove dust, old paint, and loose hairs. Stir the varnish gently to avoid bubbles. Fill the brush and flow the varnish on, but across the grain. Refill the brush and continue flowing in long, full strokes, starting beyond the last point covered and working toward it, then away from it, to prevent overlap.

Squeeze the brush dry and begin brushing the varnish—with the grain. As the brush fills with varnish, dry it again thoroughly. The final brushing is also done dry, but this time hold the brush almost vertical, and use just the tip of the dry brush.

When the varnish has dried hard, if a second coat is desired, sandpaper lightly with a 3/0 garnet or 500A wet-or-dry sandpaper soaked in water or benzene to aid the cutting action of the abrasive. Clean with a tac rag and apply the second coat the same way as the first.

Varnish is best rubbed with pumice and a lubricant such as oil or water to produce a high-gloss finish. Also see **Woodworking: Finishing**.

varnishes. See **vehicle**.

varnish stain. Woodworking. See **wood stain**.

vase. Ceramics. See **Ceramics: Form**.

vase and urn patterns. Quilts. Any of the scores of surprisingly diverse **appliqué block** designs based on a container with flowers; two such patterns are Kentucky Flowerpot and Flowers in a Pot. Some exhibit an attempt at a formal arrangement, but most fill the available space with stems, leaves, and flowers in a full pattern. The urn or flowerpot sometimes remains the same from one quilt to the next, but the quiltmaker's penchant for a certain color or a preference for some other flower leads to changes that individualize the quilts.

vase caps. Stained Glass. Two cone-shaped brass cover plates that fit onto round necks of finished stained-glass lampshades. One is located on the inside and one on the outside; they sandwich the glass between them.

Vaseline. Leather. See **Leatherwork: Finishing Leather, Tools and Materials.**

vat. Batik and Tie-dye. A **dye liquor** containing a **dyestuff** in a soluble form but which cannot, in that form, **dye** fabric. Only after the fabric has been steeped in the liquor and then exposed to air does the dye affect the fabric. Exposure to air, or oxidation, precipitates a change in the dye, allowing it to combine with fibers and assume its final color. All **vat dye**s perform in this way. Any substances that must be **vatted**, such as **indigo** or **potassium permanganate** crystals, are also called vat dyes.

Also, a large vessel, tub, or container used to hold the dye liquor.

vat dye. Batik and Tie-dye. A class of **dyes** characterized by the unique development of color on fabric only after the dyed fabric is exposed to light and heat. The **dyebath** does not indicate what color will be produced. These dyes are used on cotton, linen, silk, and have good **colorfast**ness. They may be used at room temperature and they dye within a few seconds. They are expensive and are quite complicated to prepare. Once prepared, they require constant attention and have a short life, losing their potency with age. The chemicals used in the dyes (**caustic soda,** or sodium hydrosulfite) can burn, so these dyes must be handled with care and kept out of the reach of small children. They work only on **natural fiber**s.

Most vat dyes contain pigments to which **lye** and caustic soda must be added to form a **leuco** base, although some come already prepared. In leuco state, the colors are able to combine with fibers as dyes, being absorbed by the fibers rather than coating the fibers as pigments ordinarily do. When the dyes are developed by heat the final colors appear. The heat may be applied in any of several ways. Ironing will develop and set the color by using a medium heat on the damp material. If the fabric is placed in an oven at 200° F for 20–60 minutes, the full color will develop. A flat piece of fabric, laid out in a single layer on a cookie sheet, will develop rapidly, whereas a thickly wrapped piece of tie-dye will require a much longer time for the heat to penetrate. Exposure to direct sunlight offers adequate heat. The **batik**ed fabrics should not be over-baked because of the hazard of fire, and care must be taken in heating any **wax.** A **steamer** or pressure cooker may be used, but dry steaming is necessary to prevent the running of colors. Dry steaming is not hazardous for wax.

After dyes are set the fabric is rinsed in warm water, washed in soapy water, and rinsed again.

Inkodye is the most commonly used vat dye. It can be thinned for **dip-dyeing** or painted directly onto the fabric.

The soda and lye are premixed, making any additions unnecessary.

Caledon dyes must be vatted by the dyer, and extreme caution must be used. The directions and precautions which accompany the dye must be carefully observed. Also see **Batik and Tie-dye: Dyes.**

vat dye. Dyeing. Dyes having the greatest **colorfast**ness in regard to both light and washing. **Synthetic** vat **dye**s are also resistant to acids, alkalis, and **piece dyeing.** Vat dyes are produced on the material by oxidation (or exposure to air) and are insoluble in water; they can be converted into soluble compounds by the use of a chemical reducing agent which increases the affinity of the dye to the fiber. Also see **indigo.**

V-board and clamp. Jewelry. A hardwood board with a V-shaped notch at the end. It is fastened to the **bench** with a **C-clamp** and used for support during **sawing** and **filing.** See ill. Also see **bench pin.**

V-board and clamp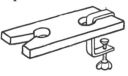

vegetable dye. Batik and Tie-dye. A **natural dye** made from plants. Roots, bark, and lichens are common sources of vegetable dyes. Most require the use of a **mordant** on **fabric** to make fibers receptive to the **dye.**

vegetable dye. Dyeing. See **natural dye.**

vegetable fiber. Batik and Tie-dye. Stitchery. Any **cellulose fiber** found in nature, the most common of which are cotton and linen. Coir (from coconut), **hemp, jute, kapok, ramie,** sisal, and straw are other vegetable fibers. All are **natural fibers,** which means that they will be receptive to most **dyes.** Also see **alkali test, burn test, oil test** and **Batik and Tie-dye: Identifying Fibers.**

vegetable fiber. Spinning. Weaving. See **fiber.**

vegetable glue. Stitchery. Toys. A good **adhesive** for **fabrics.** Unlike **white glue** or **household cement,** it does not soak into the fabric and stain it. It should be applied in a smooth, thin layer. It is not very fluid, dries fast, and is soluble in water.

vegetable ivory. Ivory and Bone Carving. Vegetable ivory is obtained from the albumen lining of the seeds of the fruit of the South American dwarf palm (*Phytelephas macrocarpa*). The tree yields six or seven fruits of about 25 pounds each, and each fruit contains 6–9 seeds. The seed cases are removed, revealing a liquid white inner lining that eventually hardens. Vegetable ivory is also known by the names of "tagua," "anta," "pulli punta," and "homero" in various localities in South America, and is imported to England under the name of "corozo nut." It is naturally a colder white than dentine ivory.

Western use of vegetable ivory has been largely confined to buttons, but in Japan it has been used artfully in **netsuke,** carefully stained to age and disguise it to imitate ivory. Also see **synthetic ivory.**

vegetable printing. Block Printing. See **potato block printing.**

vegetable tanning. Leather. (Also called bark tanning, oak tanning.) A **tanning** process in which pelts are soaked in tanks of water and oak bark or other vegetable extracts in a succession of increasingly strong solutions. Then they are removed from the tanks and stacked with tanning material in between and left to age for about six months. Finally they are given a washing process. This is an old technique, largely replaced today by faster methods such as **chrome tanning.** However, leather for **tooling** and **stamping** must be vegetable tanned. Also see **combination tanning** and **Leatherwork: Tanning and Manufacture.**

vehicle. The liquid in which pigments are suspended before being applied to a surface. Oil-base paints frequently use linseed oil as a vehicle. In water colors, water is the vehicle. Vehicles are also called mediums. Artist's paints often use vehicles that include, besides the basic oil, varnishes to produce a **gloss** when the paint dries, and chemical driers to hasten the drying or setting time.

veiner. Leather. A **stamp** which imprints curved, veinlike patterns.

veining. Batik and Tie-dye. See **crackle, fracturing.**

vellum. Bookbinding. Calfskin treated with lime and not tanned like leather.

velocipede. Toys. Originally any of a variety of early bicycles or tricycles. Later the term was used to refer specifically to a child's tricycle. Toy velocipedes were popular in the last quarter of the nineteenth century, including those that were mechanically run and usually depicted a rider on the vehicle. One museum toy shows "Uncle Sam Going to the World's Fair" on a three-wheeled velocipede.

velour. Quilts. Stitchery. (Also called plush.) A soft, heavy material with a short, thick **pile.** The word is often used interchangeably with **velvet,** which it closely resembles. Velour may be made of **cotton, wool, silk,** or **rayon,** although cotton is the most common. Cotton velour is slightly heavier than cotton **velveteen.**

velvet. Quilts. Stitchery. Any of a great variety of **fabrics** that have a thick **pile,** either cut or uncut, made of **silk, rayon, acetate,** or **nylon.** The back is usually shiny or slippery, in contrast to the back of **velour,** which is not.

velveteen. Quilts. Stitchery. (Also called cotton velveteen.) A **cotton velvet** with a cut pile that is brushed to give it a nap. The pile is shorter than that on velvet. Velveteen is washable. Because of its lustrous texture it is a favorite in

appliqué, stitchery, and toys. It is suitable for various quilts, especially those of more contemporary design with large pieces. The velveteen would be too bulky if it were to be cut into tiny **blocks** for a **Mosaic quilt** or for **Irish Chain.**

velveteen plush. Quilts. Stitchery. Similar to **velveteen,** but it has a longer and higher **pile** than ordinary velveteen or **velvet.**

velvet stitch. Crewel. Embroidery. Needlepoint. See **Turkey work.**

veneer. Woodworking. A thin piece of wood. **Softwood** veneers may be **laminated** in layers to make **plywood** sheets or curved molds for structural shapes. A single layer of an expensive or rare **hardwood** may be used to cover an inferior one, giving the appearance of a solid piece at a fraction of the cost. Differently colored veneers may also be cut in tiny pieces and used to make decorative patterns in **inlaying** and **marquetry.**

veneer core. Woodworking. See **plywood.**

Venetian glass. Glasswork. The glass historically made in **Murano.** It was a variety of **soda-lime glass,** the lime obtained by burning seaweed and plants. The use of manganese oxide as a decolorizer to obtain clarity was a closely guarded secret that kept Venetian glass in a class by itself. Venetian glass was sometimes textured by plunging a molten form into water and then immediately reheating it. Also see **crizzling, Worshipful Company of Glass Sellers.**

Venetian glass. Mosaics. See **pressed glass.**

Venetian lace. Leather. See **Florentine lace.**

Venetian point. Lacemaking. See **point de Venise.**

Venetian tube bead. Stained Glass. See **millefiore.**

vent. Jewelry. Metalworking. A channel or small hole in a closed **mold** to allow trapped gases to escape while **casting** molten metal. Vents are attached to the piece only and must not come in contact with the spine cones. Also see **flask, gate, sprue** and **Metalworking: Sandcasting.**

venting. Jewelry. Metalworking. The process of making **vents** in a **mold** prior to **casting.** Also see **Metalworking: Sandcasting.**

venting. Kites. The principle of **aerodynamics** that calls for providing an opening or vent on the kite surface through which some of the high air pressure on the underside of the kite may be released. Venting greatly reduces resistance and increases flight stability. In the **box kite,** the vent is the middle section of the kite between the two covered cells.

Venus' hair stone. Gemcutting. See **quartz.**

verd-antique. Gemcutting. See **serpentine.**

vernacular arts. Those arts belonging to or growing out of a particular place, village, region, or country. They include both the **folk arts** and the **popular arts.** While the folk arts consist essentially of the hand arts, those things made to be used, or handicrafts, the popular arts may be machine-made or produced elsewhere, and used commercially. The decoration of foods and clothes may fall somewhere between popular and folk arts.

Vernacular arts have a generally impulsive quality, full of self-assured gusto that more than compensates for any lack of aesthetics or taste.

vernis Martin. Découpage. A French term used in the eighteenth century for **lacquer ware.** The name originated with the development and manufacture of **varnish** by five brothers named Martin.

Versatex. Batik and Tie-dye. Trade name of a water-soluble, **colorfast,** washable fabric paint. It can be applied by **brush** or airbrush and is **heat set** by **ironing.** Originally designed for use in silk screening, it is also usable for **tie-dye, batik, stencil**ing, blockprinting, and sponge printing. While Versatex is nontoxic, it should be used with good ventilation.

verso. Bookbinding. The left-hand page of facing pages, or the back side of a **leaf.**

verso. Découpage. The term used to describe the back side of a print. Also see **bleeding ink** and **Découpage: Selecting Prints.**

vertical bar. Puppets. See **vertical rod.**

vertical clove hitch. Macramé. See **vertical double half hitch.**

vertical continental stitch. Needlepoint. See **continental stitch.**

vertical control. Puppets. (Also called perch control, upright control.) The special arrangement of **control bar** and **cross bars** to which the **strings** of a **marionette** are attached and which is held vertically to **manipulate** the marionette. Also see **arm bar, arm string, back string, hand string, hip string, rod, vertical rod** and **Puppets: Stringing the Marionette, Manipulating the Marionette.**

vertical double half hitch. Macramé. (Also called vertical clove hitch.) Double half **hitch**es worked on a vertical **holding cord.** Vertical double half hitches are an integral part of **Cavandoli work** (forming figures and patterns against a background of horizontal double hitches) and the **angling** technique. See ill.

Vertical double half hitches

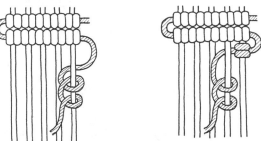

vertical dovetailing. Weaving. See **dovetailing.**

vertical lattice. Basketry. A type of **twined weaving** in which the majority of **elements** (or rods) are tied vertically. An example of vertical lattice design would be a picket-type fence consisting of a series of vertical rods or stakes that are backed and tied to a few horizontal ones by a **lattice wrapped weave.**

vertical loom. Weaving. A loom in which the **warp** is in a vertical position when weaving. This includes most **tapestry loom**s, certain rug looms, **frame loom**s, and **warp-weighted loom**s. If the loom is on legs or supports, it is also known as an **upright loom.** Also see **high-warp, Navajo rug loom, tapestry loom.**

vertical rod. Puppets. (Also called vertical bar.) The **control bar** of the **vertical control** for a **marionette.** The **rod** is grasped while the figure is being **manipulated.** Also see **armbar.**

vertical soumak. Rugmaking. Weaving. See **soumak.**

vertical stripes. Weaving. See **pick-and-pick, stippling.**

V-gouge. Leather. See **adjustable V-gouge, rampart gouger.**

Vibra-tool. Leather. A Vibra-tool or any flexible shaft machine can be used for such **tooling** operations as **outline tooling** and **stippling.** This is, of course, much faster than the traditional method of using the swivel knife and appropriate stamps. Several Vibra-tool attachments lend themselves well to tooling operations.

vibrator. Jewelry. An electric machine used in **casting.** It has a flat, round surface plate connected to a motor which vibrates that surface. It usually has a range of vibrating speeds. It is used when the **investment** has been mixed and is still in the **rubber bowl,** which is placed on the vibrator and held down firmly. The vibrations bring the air bubbles trapped from the mixing of the investment to the surface where they break. If a vibrator is not available, the same effect can be achieved by holding the rubber bowl firmly and striking it up and down on a table or the floor.

A vibrator is also used after the investment has been poured to cover the **wax model** and to fill the **flask.** The flask and invested metal are placed on the vibrator to remove air bubbles that have been trapped during the pouring of the investment. However, the vibrations do tend to break the **sprue** from the **sprue cone**, or the sprue from the model. Also see **investing**.

vibrator. Stained Glass. A device attached to the bottom of the table on which **concrete** is being cast; it helps to settle casting concrete around **dalle-de-verre**.

Victorian crazy quilt. Quilts. Whereas the **crazy quilt** was an assemblage of every scrap available, the Victorian crazy quilt was more selective. **Velvet**s, plush, brocade, and **silk**s were used. Embroidery was more elaborate, with gold threads and silk floss being added. The quilt was often kept in the parlor as a lap robe or "throw" for the sofa or piano, and it was sometimes referred to as a **slumber robe**. Some carefully planned crazy quilts used fan-shaped forms. The fans ranged from a quarter-circle to a full circle. Also see **fan quilt**.

Victorian crochet. Crochet. See **afghan stitch**.

vicuña. Knitting. The rarest and finest knitting fiber known to man. Vicuña fleece is golden in color, soft, silky, strong, and resilient. It is used primarily in high quality coats, dresses, and jackets.

vicuña. Spinning. Weaving. The smallest relative of the **llama** and **alpaca,** its wool is known as the "aristocrat of fibers." Its **fiber** has the finest diameter of all known **animal fibers**, being less than one-half the diameter of the finest sheep's wool. The fiber, which varies from shades of golden-chestnut to deep fawn to white, is strong, resilient, very soft, and silklike. This undomesticated animal lives in the highest regions of the Andes Mountains in Peru and Bolivia. For its prize wool, the ancient Incas would round-up the vicuña, **shear** it, and set it free. Today, uncontrolled hunting has so diminished the herds that the vicuña is on the borderline of extinction.

Viennese lace. Knitting. A knit "cobweb" lace of great intricacy, with floral and leaf shapes developed within a filigree background. The traditional materials used to knit it are fine cotton or silk. The finished lace is often mounted on fine net, and is sometimes lightly starched.

viewing toy. Toys. Any toy that amuses through the sense of sight. Most **optical toys, peep shows, diorama**s, **magic lanterns, proscenium toys,** and the **Thames** tunnel are viewing toys. Also see **Toys: Optical Toys.**

vine border. Quilts. See **border.**

vinegar trace paint. Stained Glass. A dark-colored glass paint that can be used only for specific dark outlines and for shadows.

It is mixed with water, vinegar, and **gum arabic** to a rather thick solution. The proportion of gum is left to the painter's discretion. Too much will not allow the paint to flow smoothly; with too little, the paint flows well but does not adhere to the glass.

The paint is applied with a long, thin brush called a tracer or tracing brush. The brush is kept wet, as is the glass, so that the paint is applied wet on wet. Once a brush stroke has dried, more paint cannot be applied over it; rather, the paint must be removed from the glass and reapplied.

The vinegar medium allows the paint to flow and burns out quickly.

The trace paint is fired at 1100° F. The kiln should be turned off when the paint looks shiny. Also see **tracing.**

Vine of Friendship. Quilts. See **Drunkard's Path.**

vinyl. Plastics. A **thermoplastic** manufactured in many forms, such as sheets (for **thermoforming** and constructing), **foam,** solid blocks, paints, and sealants. Plastisol (or fusing vinyl) is a vinyl compound used for **dip coating.** It looks like cornstarch in water and remains a suspension of discrete particles until heated. The vinyl and **plasticizer** fuse to form a solid at temperatures above 250° F.

vinyl chloride. Plastics. See **polyvinyl chloride.**

Vinylite VMCH. Plastics. See **polyvinyl chloride.**

Virginia Lily. Quilts. See **Lily.**

Virginia Reel. Quilts. See **Indiana Puzzle.**

Virginia Star. Quilts. See **star patterns.**

virgin wool. Spinning. Weaving. A term that can mean either the first clipping from a yearling sheep (a sheep that has never been sheared before), or **wool** that has never been processed in any way before being spun into the finished yarn. In the latter case, it is also known as "new wool."

One kind of wool that has never been used comes from such places as mill ends and cutting table scraps. The fibers are broken up and completely reprocessed before a new yarn is made. Reused wool is made from rags or old clothing which are cleaned and shredded into fiber and then chemically processed. Reused wool is nearly always blended with some stronger new wool.

viscose rayon. Batik and Tie-dye. Stitchery. See **rayon.**

viscosity. Ceramics. The nonrunning quality of a **glaze,** caused by **alumina** which retards the flow of glaze **flux** while firing.

vise. Jewelry. Metalworking. A stationary tool for holding work in place while hammering, filing, etc. Because the jaws are usually grooved for tight grip, protect soft, hot, or finished metalwork by covering the vise jaws with a soft sheet metal such as copper, or with strips of scrap wood.

POST VISE This vise has a post that rests on the floor to steady the work and which forms the back jaw of the vise on the upper end. Adjust the height of the post vise so the tops of the jaws are even with your elbow to facilitate even filing and comfortable hammering (**a.**).

BENCH (OR MACHINIST'S) VISE   This usually has a swivel base which is fastened to the top of a workbench, and lightly grooved hardened metal jaws. The **bench vise** can be used to secure jewelry in position for working (**b.**). See ill. Also see **C-clamp, clamping tools, clamp-on vise, engraver's block, hand vise, pin vise, ring clamp.**

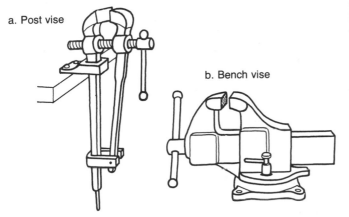

a. Post vise

b. Bench vise

vise. Stained Glass. See **lead vise.**

vise. Woodworking. See **clamping tools.**

visible increase. Knitting. See **Knitting: Increasing.**

visiting wheel. Spinning. See **German wheel.**

vitreous. Ceramics. Pertaining to the glassy, nonabsorbent quality of a **clay body** or **glaze.**

vitreous luster. Gemcutting. See **luster.**

vitreous tessera. Mosaics. See **pressed glass.**

vitrifiable color. China and Glass Painting. See **onglaze color.**

vitrified silicone stone. Stained Glass. One of the tools needed for working with laminated glass. It is used for the final **dulling** and smoothing of the glass pieces before they are set into the clear polyester **epoxy** or **resin.** Also see **lamination, polyester resin technique.**

V-notch. Leather. See **Leatherwork: Sewing Leather.**

voided line. Embroidery. The division between two rows of blocks of stitching only by a narrow and even spacing between them. The **background fabric** is allowed to show through.

voile. Stitchery. See **transparent fabric.**

volatility. Jewelry. The vaporization of a substance at a specific temperature.

volatilization. Ceramics. The point at which materials pass into a vapor at high temperatures.

volcanic ash. Ceramics. A volcanic lava that is roughly equivalent to 70 parts **feldspar** and 30 parts **flint.** It is used for making **glaze**s.

volcanic glass. Gemcutting. See **obsidian.**

V-punch. Leather. See **strap end punch.**

V-stitch. Stitchery. A loop of thread held down at its base by another stitch. The finished stitch looks like the letter V. The stitch construction is actually the same as a lazy daisy, the first step of a feather stitch, or a **Y-stitch.**

vue d'optique. Découpage. (Also called peep show.) A three-dimensional arrangement of folded and cut paper **prints** mounted in a box with a peephole. It was popular in Europe during the eighteenth and nineteenth centuries. Several prints were cut up and placed in the shallow space in such a way that the perspective was accentuated to give the illusion of greater depth. Also see **shadow box.**

W

wadded quilting. Quilts. Any **quilting** that consists of three layers and has a **filler** of some kind of **wadding** or **batting.** The wadding can be of any thickness, depending on the degree of warmth or protection required.

wadding. Quilts. Soft material for **stuffing** or filling quilts. It is a nonwoven **filler,** or **batting.**

waffle-weave. Stitchery. A texture woven into a **fabric** with alternating tensions on the threads. The pattern has raised lines which form a **grid pattern** design resembling a waffle. It is a weave commonly found in the **cotton fabric** called waffle-weave **piqué.** Some fabrics are now made which imitate the weave by imprinting or embossing the design.

waffle-weave. Weaving. See **honeycomb weave.**

wagon. Toys. A four-wheeled cart or vehicle with a handle by which it can be pulled. Most wagons are boxlike and open so that they can be used to haul or carry a cargo. Wagons are usually included with other **farm toys** and are also made as **pull toys** or **push toys.** Larger wagons, or coaster wagons, are made so that a child can ride in them, usually with one child pulling another. They are often manufactured of metal or of metal and wood. Also see **Toys: Wheeled Toys.**

Wagon Tracks. Quilts. See **Jacob's Ladder.**

waist. Weaving. A term given to a distortion of the fabric due to pulling in the **filling** too tightly at the **selvages.** The weaver usually attempts to remedy this by not pulling so much; the fabric resumes its true width, but an indentation remains at the selvages that resembles a woman's waist.

waist loom. Weaving. See **backstrap loom.**

wale. Basketry. See **waling.**

waling. Basketry. In **woven basketry,** a **weave** in which three or more **rods** are worked in sequence in front of two, three, or more **stakes,** and then behind one or more stakes and out to the front again.

Waling is employed where strength is required. It is often used at the **upsetting** of a basket to create a ridge of thicker weaving (a **foot**) and to hold the shape of the **siding.** Waling is also used to correct a basket that gets out of shape in the process of working.

Three-rod weave, three-ply coil, and triple twist are alternate names for three-rod wale, the most common form of waling. Four-rod wale, sometimes called four-ply coil weave, is made exactly as three-rod wale, but with four rods.

To begin a three-rod wale, mark the first stakes and insert three **weavers** in the spaces between the first four consecutive stakes. Taking the furthest left-hand weaver, pass it in front of two stakes and behind one and out to the front (**a.**). Continue this weave around the basket with each weaver until you reach your first stake, which you have marked (**b.**).

To **step up,** reverse the order. Take the furthest right-hand weaver in front of two stakes, behind one, and out to the front (**c.**). Do the same for the middle weaver and then the furthest-left one (**d.**). With the step-up completed (**e.**), continue around the basket as before, again starting with the furthest left-hand weaver. See ill.

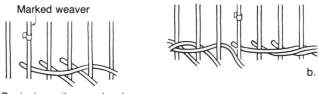

a. Beginning a three-rod wale

b.

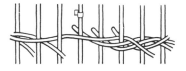

c. Begin step-up

d.

e. Step-up completed

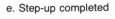

walking wheel. Spinning. See **wool wheel.**

wallboard. Woodworking. See **gypsum board.**

wall hanging. Stitchery. **Panel**s of **fabric,** usually decorative in structural detail or through the use of **appliqué** or embroidery, hung from a **rod** or support. The term is sometimes used to mean any **stitchery panel,** though it indicates one that is not **mount**ed with a rigid frame. Woven tapestries, macramé, pieced **quilt**s, or appliqué can all be used as wall hangings. Also see **Stitchery: Stitchery Forms.**

wall hanging. Weaving. A term coined within the last twenty years to mean a nonfunctional fiber piece constructed on the loom or off the loom as an art form which is related to painting and sculpture. It is an outgrowth of **tapestry,** but it is unlike a tapestry in that it does not strictly adhere to a **cartoon,** and is more concerned with aspects of fiber and weaving or other fiber techniques. Wall hangings have a visible texture and thickness, whereas a tapestry is flat-surfaced. Often the material used is a determining factor in the aesthetics of a piece, rather than an abstract or representational design. The material can be fiber or fiber supplemented with fur, feathers, metal, stones, leather, shells, ceramics, plastics, or beads. In some instances, no fiber is used at all.

A wall hanging can be totally **loom controlled** or it can be a **free weaving** or **finger weaving.** It can incorporate weaving with **knotting, wrapping,** knitting, crochet, and stitchery, or not be woven at all, but constructed of fiber in any one of a number of techniques. Wall hangings may be shaped, whereas tapestry is either in a rectangular or square format. There is also considerable range in terms of size and method of support. Some wall hangings are the size of small miniatures, whereas others are huge woven walls. It would be supposed that the term "wall hanging" would mean that the finished piece was meant to be hung on a supporting wall. But included under the category of wall hangings are some pieces that are suspended from the ceiling and others that stand by themselves on the floor. The even more recent term "fiber sculpture" has now come to denote these three-dimensional objects that are self-supporting.

Although the term was not in use in the 1920s, wall hangings were first produced at the Bauhaus in Germany by the weavers Gunta Stölzl and Anni Albers. Albers later went on to be a motivating force in the work of many American weaver-artists. Wall hangings have become an international concept, surfacing in the United States in the late 1950s and early 1960s. Among American wall-hanging artists, Lenore Tawney is one of the earlier ones; and she has been an inspiration to later weavers and other fiber artists. She, along with many American wall-hanging artists, acknowledges the influence of pre-conquest **Peruvian weaving.**

wallpaper paste. Découpage. Papercrafts. A wheat paste, sometimes called fox paste, that is mixed with water and used for gluing wallpaper. Wallpaper paste is used in découpage to cover large background surfaces, such as screens, with **decorative paper.** It does not adhere to surfaces painted with oil-base paint.

Wallpaper paste is often used in **papier mâché** for the paper-strip method or for laminating.

wallpaper paste. Puppets. Toys. See **wheat paste.**

walnut. Woodworking. (Also called black walnut.) A fine grained, durable **hardwood** excellent for delicate **whittling, woodcarving, marquetry,** cabinet work, and furniture. Its color ranges from yellow sapwood to dark violet and chocolate-brown heartwood. It is strong, heavy, easily worked, and takes a fine finish. It has good shock resistance and has therefore been used for gunstocks and airplane propellers. Because walnut has become relatively scarce, it is now used mostly as a **veneer.** European walnut is named according to the country of its origin (French, English, and Italian).

walrus ivory. Ivory and Bone Carving. (Also called morse ivory.) Walrus ivory is known to have been used before the eleventh century. It is oval in section, less dense than other ivories, and the internal hollow extends quite far. It is nevertheless a material of good quality. It can weigh up to eight pounds and varies in length from 18″ to 36″. Also see **Ivory and Bone Carving: Preparation, Carving, Finishing.**

walrus skin. Leather. Skin from a walrus—or occasionally from seal, embossed to look like walrus. Both of these are endangered species, and there are many less expensive leathers easily substituted.

wampum. Beadwork. The word "wampum" is derived from the Algonquian word "wampumpeag," meaning string of "white shell beads." The North American Indians made the inside of a hard clam shell, the quahog, into long purple or white beads. The purple came from the edge or lip of the clam, the white from the center of the shell. The white had half the value of the purple, which was more scarce. The columellae of the conch shell was also used for white beads. The shells were shaped into small cylinders by grinding them on stones. The holes were bored from both ends with a small stone drill or with a reed or split stick and sand. The wampum bead was polished with fine sand and buckskin, then strung on cords of vegetable fiber or sinew. The strung beads were used as currency and woven into belts of geometric pattern for personal adornment or prestige. The wampum belt was the symbol of authority, and the most important belts were preserved as official records of treaties and land transactions. Wampum belts were exchanged or surrendered upon ratification of treaties or defeat in battle.

Later, steel tools were used to manufacture wampum commercially (by the Campbell Company). The commercial beads were longer and more uniform in shape than the handmade beads. Also see **bead weaving** and **Beadwork.**

Wandering Foot. Quilts. The original name of an **appliqué block** that later was called Turkey Tracks. It depicts three-toed tracks that point to the four corners of the blocks.

Superstition in colonial times was such that no child

was permitted to sleep under a **quilt** of this design. It was believed that a malign influence would invoke a propensity for an unstable, roving life, or a "wandering foot." No bride would ever risk sewing such a quilt for her **dower chest.** A search for adventure, or wanderlust, had led thousands of young men west, looking for gold and land. Many were never heard from again and were mourned as dead. It was fear of this "wandering foot" that made quilters attempt to exorcise the fatal spell or evil genius of this quilt by changing its name to Turkey Track. It was also called **Iris Leaf** in later versions. See ill.

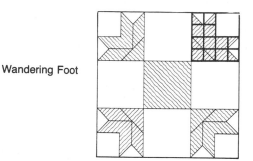

Wandering Foot

Wandering Vine. Weaving. See **overshot.**

wane. Woodworking. See **wood.**

war bonnet. Featherwork. See **Featherwork.**

ware. Ceramics. A general term used for all **pottery** or procelain clay objects, whether fired or not.

warm color. See **cool color.**

warm colors. Red, orange, and yellow are the basic warm colors. They tend to advance or move forward and are generally considered stimulating, cheerful, and active.

warp. Basketry. The name given to the structural or **passive element** around which the **active element** or **weft** is woven. These **elements** may be used singly or in pairs, parallel or latticed, and generally determine the shape of the basket. They are referred to as **spokes** or **sticks** when they are used for the **base** of a basket, and as **stakes** when they are used for the sides.

warp. Quilts. Stitchery. The lengthwise threads in a woven **fabric** that are threaded onto the loom. When pieces of fabric are cut **"on the grain"** or "with the grain," they are placed lengthwise, following the warp thread. They run parallel to the **selvage** of the material.

warp. Weaving. The threads running lengthwise on a **loom** or in a piece of fabric. The **filling** passes through the warp to interlace, or weave, and form **cloth.** The warp threads are placed parallel to each other on the loom and are stretched to have tension; without **warp tension,** the interlacing process cannot be achieved. A warp is characterized by its length and width and what the **sett** or number of threads per inch is. For weaving on a **harness loom,** the length and number of total ends is measured out and

counted during **warping** on a **warping board** or reel prior to putting the warp on the loom. On most **primitive loom**s, a **continuous warp** that is warped directly onto the loom is used. On a harness loom, the warp can be very long (the maximum for most handweavers does not exceed 20–25 yards), whereas on a primitive loom the length and height of the loom determines the length of the warp possible. Only on some **frame loom**s is it possible to get a length longer than the loom length, and then the maximum would be twice the length of the loom. The individual threads in a warp are called **end**s. A warp can be made up of a very few ends, as for narrow belt weaving or weaving with coarse, heavy yarns in the warp, or thousands of ends—where the warp is for weaving very wide fabrics and using fine yarns. Warp yarns can be coarse or fine, but they must be strong enough to withstand the warp tension, not fray apart during the beating down of the filling, and not cling together so that a **shed** is difficult to obtain. Also see **warp reel, warp specifications, yarn calculations.**

warp. Woodworking. See **wood.**

warp and buckle. Stained Glass. A condition that can develop in leaded glass **panel**s when vertical and horizontal leads are improperly balanced, causing the panel to lose shape. In order to prevent this condition, vertical leads, whenever possible, should run their full lengths with horizontal leads joined to them. Also see **Stained Glass: Glazing.**

warp arrangement. Weaving. One repeat of the pattern of the **warp.** This is a layout of how the threads are aligned as to color, type of yarn, and fiber content.

warp beam. Weaving. The rotating lower beam at the back of a **floor** or **table loom;** it is where the unwoven **warp** is wound and stored ready for weaving. The warp is not attached directly to the warp beam, since its diameter is too large to do this. There are, however, cords fastened to the warp beam which hold the much thinner back **apron bar.** The warp goes around this bar and is pulled by it around the beam. Every warp beam has a **friction brake,** a **ratchet,** or some similar device to keep it from revolving while weaving. Some looms can be equipped with a second warp beam, located below the usual warp beam. Double warp beams are used to independently adjust tension on different sections or yarns in a warp, or for special double warp-beam effects. Also available are sectional warp beams, which have spaced pegs in them and call for a special kind of beaming. Combination beams are an improvement on this; they can be constructed so that they turn inside out and allow for either **sectional warping** or standard **chain warping.** Also see **jack-type loom, table loom.**

warp beam rod. Weaving. An alternate term for the back apron bar. See **apron, apron bar.**

warp brocade. Weaving. See **brocade.**

warp calculation. Weaving. See **yarn calculations.**

warp chain. Weaving. The **warp** as a series of continuous loops similar to a crochet chain stitch. The chain is made after the **end**s have been counted and measured; it is in preparation for putting on a **harness loom**. It is a temporary arrangement used to shorten the warp's length so that it facilitates handling in removing the warp from the **warping board** or **reel** and transferring it to the **loom**. The chain also prevents the warp from tangling. See ill. Also see **chaining**.

Warp chain being removed from a warping reel

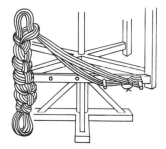

warp counting cord. Weaving. See **counter**.

warp dyeing. Dyeing. Dyeing the warp by one of two methods: If the whole is to be dyed, then a **warp chain** is made and dyed. If the warp is to be dyed in spots or areas to produce a random coloring, the warp can be made either into a chain or left in a stretched position on a warping reel or board, a frame or table or after the warp is on the loom. The control of the areas to be dyed is in proportion to how much of the warp is exposed and how tautly it is stretched. The greatest control would be on a frame or loom where every warp end is exposed and stretched individually. The least would be with the warp in chain form, where the spotting can only have a random effect since the ends are not under tension and are together as a group.

In dyeing the total warp, care should be taken in making the warp chain so that all lease cords and chokes are tied loosely and the chain itself is made very loosely. This will insure complete dye penetration. In addition to the usual ties made on a chain, the last loop of the chain next to the cross is tied loosely to the first loop made when passing the warp ends around the first peg. The chain should be presoaked in warm water before washing with soap flakes. The soaking may take several hours or overnight for all threads to be thoroughly soaked. The rest of the dyeing would proceed as for **skein dyeing**. Also see **ikat, spot dyeing**.

warp end. Weaving. See **end**.

warp end bar. Weaving. An optional device found on a **frame loom** that enables the weaver to weave a warp twice the length of the frame length. The warp end bar is a dowel rod placed on the back of the loom and having the warp ends going around it. The bar is pushed to rotate the warp around the loom as the weaving proceeds. In the **warping** process, the beginning of the warp is tied to the bar and then goes around the loom. When the warp reaches the warp end bar, it goes around it and returns in the direction from which it came. If this method is not followed, the warp will be immobile. At the end of warping, the warp is tied to the bar. Also see **frame loom, Salish weaving**.

warp-face. Weaving. (Also called warp-faced.) A term indicating that the **warp** predominates on the face or top side of a cloth. There are weaves that have so many **raiser**s that a warp-face fabric results with a few **filling sinkers**' being seen. Other fabrics are composed of the warp entirely covering the filling; the usual occurrence is that the fabric is warp-face on both sides. **Inkle weaving** would be an example of the latter. The **sett** must be very close, which sometimes causes a sticky **shed** as warp yarns cling together. Warp-face fabrics are usually very strong and have warp stripes as their predominant pattern. In **rep weave**s, a horizontal rib is the result of packing in the filling into a very closely set warp. Also see **satin weave**.

warp-faced. Weaving. See **warp-face**.

warp hook. Weaving. See **reed hook**.

warp ikat. Dyeing. Weaving. See **ikat**.

warping. Ceramics. A malformation that can occur at any stage in the making of a **pot**. It can be due to thin **rim**s on pots, uneven bases or **foot ring**s, too fast drying, or firing on a bent **kiln** shelf. Also see **pyroplastic deformation**.

warping. Plastics. See **distortion**.

warping. Weaving. The making or winding of the **warp**—prior to putting it on the **harness loom**—so that the calculated number of warp **end**s is obtained in the right sequence and in the correct length, with all ends having the same tension. To wind the warp, a weaver uses either a **warping board** or a **warping reel**—both of which facilitate getting the correct length and winding warps of many yards in a relatively small space. For very long warps and speed, the warping reel is preferred. Before beginning the winding, a guide or **measuring cord** can be put onto the board or reel.

To make the warp on a reel, start at the bottom of the reel by tying the warp yarn to a peg projecting from the bottom horizontal bar. Go around the reel the correct number of times to make the length that is desired. At the end of this length, the warp thread goes around projecting pegs on the upper horizontal bar. One winding of the warp thread from the bottom peg to the top peg is equal to the length of one warp end. When the warp thread goes around the top peg and begins its return journey to the bottom peg, this is the beginning of the second warp end. When this thread reaches the bottom peg and turns around to go back up to the top peg, this is then end #3. The projecting pegs are the beginning and terminus of each warp end. A **cross** is made between the pegs at the upper horizontal bar. This is the **portee cross**. Another cross, known as the **porrey cross,** can be made around the pegs at the bottom horizontal bar, but it is not necessary to have this cross (the portee cross is necessary to maintain order). The tension is maintained by the yarn's always being held taut during warping. If a large number of ends are to be warped, a **counter** or counting cord is used. When the warping is finished, the cross is tied with a contrasting color **lease cord,** and **choke**s are tied along the length of the warp. The warp is then ready for **chaining** and transferring to the loom.

To make the warp on a board, the warp yarn is tied to a peg projecting from the frame. The peg that is chosen for the tie determines the beginning of the warp. The weaver then goes back and forth across the board until the desired length is obtained and a cross is made between the pegs, signifying the end of the warp. From the beginning peg to the ending peg, the length is equal to one warp end. When the warp thread is taken around the ending peg to return to the beginning peg, this is end #2. When this thread reaches the beginning peg and turns around it, this is the start of end #3. As in the warping reel, the beginning and terminus pegs on the warping board signify the beginning and ending of every single warp end. Two crosses can also be made, if desired, as in the reel. A counter can be used; the lease cord and chokes are tied before chaining off the board.

As an alternate to using either a warping board or reel, you can use **warping post**s or any device that will remain stable while the warp is being made under tension and that will allow for the cross and the desired length to be made. Common household items that are sometimes used are door knobs, chairs upended and weighted so that they will not shift, and tables upended. In the countryside, sticks can be driven into the ground at the proper distance for the desired length. Three sticks are used in the same manner as warping posts. But the length can be much longer than with warping posts since, with sticks, there is no need to have something stable to clamp onto (as there is with the posts). The use of sticks for warping is a time-honored method in the weaving cultures of Asia, Turkey, Greece, and Central America, as well as other places.

The above manner of warping is sometimes referred to as **chain warping** (as opposed to **sectional warping**). The term "cutting" the warp is also used (rather than "winding the warp" or "warping"). **Paddle warping** is warping with a **warping paddle** when many different colors are used in the warp in small repeats.

On most **primitive loom**s, the warp is made directly on

the loom. No board or reel is required, nor is a cross. However, the **warp tension** is maintained as the loom is being warped. See ill. Also see **continuous warp, warp arrangement, yarn calculations.**

warping board. Weaving. A strong wooden frame with spaced pegs around which the **warp** is measured and wound. It is usually rectangular with the long sides measuring 1 yard and the short sides one-half yard, and it allows for the making of a warp of up to 10 yards in length. However, smaller and larger warping boards are also available. The boards can be hung on the wall at a height convenient for winding, or laid flat on the table. See ill. Also see **cross, lease peg, warping.**

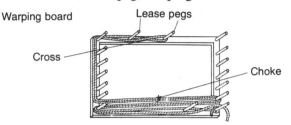

Warping board — Lease pegs — Cross — Choke

warping creel. Weaving. See **warping reel.**

warping drum. Weaving. See **warping reel.**

warping frame. Weaving. See **warping board.**

warping mill. Weaving. See **warping reel.**

warping paddle. Weaving. A flat, oblong piece of wood with a handle that is used to facilitate making a **warp** of many different yarns or colors that are repeated in a consecutive order. The paddle has two rows of holes, numbering from 8 to 20 per paddle. As many different yarns as there are holes in a repeat can be accommodated. There are some paddles with alternating slits and holes that are somewhat similar to a **rigid heddle.** The purpose of the paddle is to assure an individual **cross** for each yarn, even though the yarns are carried as a group when making the warp. See ill. Also see **paddle warping.**

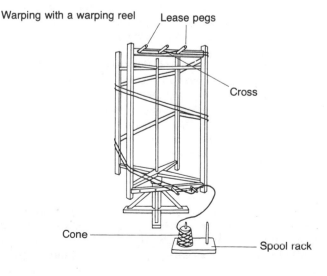

Warping paddle

warping paper. Bookbinding. A paper pasted to a **board** or other surface for the purpose of counterwarping it.

warping post. Weaving. Wooden peg or rod used in making a **warp.** Each post is in a square wooden base that is clamped onto a table or counter with a C-clamp. There are three posts needed. The first and last posts are clamped at the distance apart that will give the desired warp length. The middle post is clamped nearer to the last post and is used for the making of the **cross.** Warping posts are usually homemade, but they can be also bought in handweaving-supply stores in some areas. They are inexpensive tools for warp making, but their drawback is that the length of the warp is somewhat limited. See ill. Also see **warping.**

Warping with a warping reel — Lease pegs — Cross — Cone — Spool rack

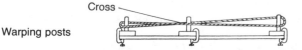

Cross

Warping posts

warping reel. Weaving. (Also called warp winder, warping creel, warping mill, warping tree, warping drum.) A large revolving wheel with rectangular sides, around which the **warp** is measured and wound. The four sides are open and have wooden supports at each long edge. This structure is attached to a central rod around which it revolves. In turn, the rod is positioned either vertically or horizontally to a base, with the vertical position being the most common. There are wooden supports with pegs for the short sides of the rectangle. There are two of these short supports—one with three pegs for the **portee cross,** and one with two pegs for the **porrey cross.** Both supports are movable and can be set in between whichever long edges are desired. Although it is possible to get warping reels in a few different sizes, the most popular is a vertical warping reel that measures one-half yard between the long sides and which makes a complete trip around the reel that is equal to two yards in length. In order to attain the needed length, the weaver can make several trips around the reel and also move the short pegged supports to wherever he wants the beginning and end of the warp to be. They can also be adjusted up and down, for ease in **warping** and as another means of controlling the length. If both supports are totally removed, the rectangular sides can be folded together and the reel stored in a more limited space than it occupies when fully opened. Some reels can be totally dismantled to store in a box. The advantages of using a reel as opposed to a **warping board** are its flexibility with regard to the length of the warp, and its speed. The length can be rather short or can go up to more than twenty yards. The speed comes from the revolving feature of the reel; some weavers maintain that the horizontal one can be revolved even faster than the vertical reel.

warping tree. Weaving. See **warping reel.**

warp interlock. Weaving. See **scaffold wefts.**

warp painting. Weaving. The painting of a design directly on the **warp** and then weaving the **filling** through. The painted design is seen—but not as sharply as it was painted, because the filling going through subdues the colors and makes the outlines hazy. This has the same effect as **warp printing,** except that in warp painting, the weaver can be freer in the design and number of colors used. Although warp painting can be done with textile paints, some weavers prefer **acid** or **direct dyes** and use them as paints. The painting is done with the warp stretched on the **harness loom.** The design is painted in short sections from in front of the **beater** to the **fell.** An alternate method is to tape a complete warp to a covered table, paint it, and then transfer it to the loom. There is a great chance of the threads shifting or twisting around, and some retouching may be necessary when the warp is ready for weaving. The warp should be closely **sett,** so that the painted design will stand out. On a **frame** or **tapestry loom,** the entire design

can usually be painted when the warp is on the loom. However, because warp threads have a tendency to twist around while weaving on these looms, there will be retouching of spots during the course of the weaving. Obviously, in whichever way warp painting is undertaken, the paint must be dry before weaving is begun.

warp peg. Weaving. Sturdy, handlelike pegs set into the top of some **tapestry looms,** around which the warp has to be tied. It is possible to adjust the **warp tension** by loosening or tightening the ends of the warp around these pegs. The warp is first made on a **warping board** or reel, chained, and then put on the tapestry loom. The **warp chain** is partially undone in order to tie the warp around the pegs and then it is rechained with its long length left to dangle from the pegs down the back of the loom. As the weaving progresses, the warp is released from the pegs and the woven part is wound around the roller at the bottom of the loom. Also see **chaining, warping reel.**

warp pile. Rugmaking. Weaving. A **pile weave** with an extra **warp** forming the **pile.** This warp is wound on a separate **beam** from the basic warp which weaves with a **filling** to form a **ground** fabric. The pile warp is much longer than the ground warp and is placed on **harnesses** other than those threaded with the ground warp. Every time the **shed** for the pile is opened, a wooden or metal rod is inserted instead of the filling. The rod's diameter determines the length of the pile. However, the rod can be pulled forward to make the pile extra long. After every **pick** of pile, the ground weave is beaten in to hold the pile in with the fabric. The rods are inserted according to the desired spacing of the pile. Usually the fabric is woven using four or five rods, so that each one is not removed from the pile until subsequent rows of ground weave and pile have been put in. Often when a second **warp beam** is not available, the second warp can be weighted with the weights hanging over the back of the loom. Terry cloth is an example of a warp pile fabric which has pile loops on both sides of the fabrics. The loops can be cut or left uncut.

warp plan. Weaving. See **drawing-in draft.**

warp printing. Weaving. The printing of a design on a **warp,** using silk-screen or block printing or some other printing technique. The entire warp is printed in advance of the weaving on a printing table and is then transferred to the **loom** to be woven. The effect is similar to **warp painting.**

warp protector. Rugmaking. Weaving. See **finishing edge, fringe.**

warp specifications. Weaving. The information required in order to be able to dress a **loom** prior to weaving. This includes the type, **weight,** and color of yarn or yarns to be used in the **warp;** their **warp arrangement;** the **cut length** of the warp; the **sett** and width of the warp; and the **drawing-in draft.** Also see **dressing the loom, warping.**

warp stick. Weaving. The flat sticks inserted when winding the **warp** onto the **warp beam**. They are used in place of heavy or corrugated paper and are inserted once in every revolution of the beam. Sometimes "warp stick" is used when referring to the back **apron bar**. Also see **beaming**.

warp tension. Weaving. The even tautness of the **warp ends** that makes **weaving** possible. It can be a very tight tension or a somewhat looser tension, but it must be the same for each warp end in order for the **filling** to interlace in a straight line and not in a wavy one. Tension is also necessary to obtain straight **selvages**. Even tension of the warp is strived for on whatever **loom** the weaver is using, and should be arrived at before weaving begins. On a **harness loom,** even tension is obtained by the care taken during **beaming** and **tying-on**. It is loosened or tightened by adjusting the front and back **ratchets**. Adjustments to individual or groups of warp ends that are too loose can be made after weaving begins, but they are a nuisance to keep track of. These adjustments consist of inserting folded pieces of paper, small pieces of cardboard, or little sticks or wooden matches under the loose warp threads until they are as tight as the rest of the warp. They must be reinserted each time the warp is advanced. Some **tapestry looms** have **warp pegs** that are used to adjust the tension. **Frame looms** using **continuous warps** have **tension sticks** added on beforehand. These are removed as weaving progresses in order to loosen the warp, which is taken up during the **interlacing** process. Unique ways of maintaining tension are through the pull of the weaver's body when using a **backstrap loom** and through the use of heavy weights attached to the bottom of the warp ends in a **warp-weighted loom**. Also see **Navajo loom, shaped weaving, take-up**.

warp tensioner. Weaving. See **tension box**.

warp twining. Weaving. To twist **warp** yarns around each other in order to form a **fabric**. A **filling** yarn secures the twist in place. The **twining** of the **warp ends** is usually done in pairs, but it can also involve three or four ends in a twist, rather than just two. When warp twining is done as **counter twining**, two warp ends twist in one direction (an S-**twist**), while the neighboring two twist in the opposite direction (a Z-twist), and this order is repeated across the entire warp for a specific effect. Another variation that can occur in warp twining is in the placement of the filling. In some twists, one filling yarn can be inserted; in others, two or more. Each twisting group of warp yarns need not twist to close around each row of filling. A pair or group of ends can twist around a filling strand, but the neighboring pair or group need not twist at that time, but can wait until another row of filling is inserted and then twist enclosing two filling strands in its loop. Hand warp twining is rarely done, but with the aid of **cards,** it has become popular as the craft "**card weaving**." In card weaving, the warp is the primary focus and the fabric is compact and sturdy. However, warp twining is also related to **gauze weaves**—open, airy structures in which the twist is manipulated with a **pick-up stick** or **doupes**. Visually there is also a tendency to link warp twining and **sprang**, but in the latter, the twist characteristics are not those of warp twining. Also see **Navajo selvage, twill twining**.

warp-weighted loom. Weaving. A **loom** in which weights are attached to a vertically hanging **warp** in order to provide the necessary **warp tension** which enables the weaver to make a **shed** or opening through which the **filling** threads are passed. It is one of the most ancient looms known and is thought to have developed as an outgrowth of the **twining** process that long preceded weaving. (Twining on a weighted warp is easier to manipulate than on a free-hanging one.) It can be assumed that Stone and Bronze Age fabrics in Europe were woven on this type of loom, since loom weights have been found in sites of the Swiss lake dwellers. Warp-weighted looms appeared in pre-Dynastic Egypt around 2000 B.C., where they were used for fine weaving—coarser cloth or rugs probably being woven on a **ground loom**. The **warp ends** were tied in bunches to a **whorl** of clay to keep the warp threads taut. In Scandinavia, Iceland, and Greece, stones were used as weights to keep the warp threads taut. Warp-weighted looms are pictured in Greek vase paintings of the fifth century B.C.

Traces of a warp-weighted loom have been found in southwest Asia, in the Pacific islands, and among the North and South American Indians. These were mainly used for twining, as they still are (although only on rare occasions) by the Chilkat Indians. Lapp tribes in Scandinavia also still use warp-weighted looms in making **flatwoven rugs**.

In the simplest version, the loom consisted of a horizontal wooden beam supported at each end by two vertical posts. Around this top **warp beam** the warp ends were tied, then weighted down—either in groups or individually. Most often the weights were stone, although sometimes clay whorls were used, as were pieces of metal. **Shed sticks** and **heddle bars** were used to open up the sheds. Either both were used, or just one or the other. Shed sticks were inserted either across the entire width of the loom or in small sections, and/or the heddle bar was put in place after the warp was on. Projecting pegs supported the shed stick and heddle bar, or they were tied in place with cords. For those warp-weighted looms intended for twining, there was no need for any shed arrangements. Some of the early Greek looms had an elaborate top beam that was for ornamentation, though sometimes it had projecting pegs that held loose hanks of yarn and **bobbins**. On occasion there was a bracing beam at the bottom between the two upright poles. The weaving proceeded from the top down, so that the filling was beaten up as it was put in. The cloth was rolled around the warp beam as it was finished. In this manner, very beautiful and ornately patterned textiles were woven—particularly among the Greek weavers.

Although warp-weighted looms are usually associated with vertical warps, there are several past and present instances where the warps were made on **horizontal looms**. These have been in use for centuries in the Middle East, Greece, and North Africa. The weights can either be elaborate overhead constructions, or attached to and hanging from the back of the loom. In the former case, the horizontal loom could be a pit loom (thought to have evolved from the ground loom). The weights are large stones or bags of sand. Whether a pit loom or one above ground, this type of warp-weighted loom is a relative of the **harness loom** and the weaving proceeds as it would on a harness loom. The weights serve as a modern **ratchet** would. Before inventions such as the ratchet or some sort of device to hold the tension, the use of added weights was found on many types of looms. See ill. Also see **Chilkat blanket, finger weaving.**

Schematic drawing of warp-weighted loom

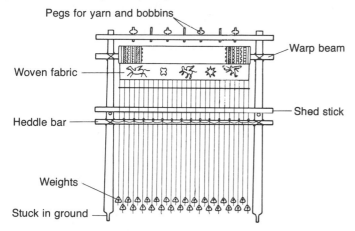

warp winder. Weaving. See **warping reel.**

wash-and-wear. Batik and Tie-dye. Stitchery. A **finish** for **cotton** or **linen** fabric that makes it **wrinkle resistant** whether wet or dry and reduces **shrink**age. While this finish limits the ability of fabrics to absorb **dye** and is therefore a disadvantage to the **tie-dye** or **batik** artist, it is often preferred for **appliqué** work, as little ironing is required after washing. Permanent **pleat**s and **crease**s eventually do wash out, even after the wash-and-wear treatment. This process has now, to a large extent, been replaced by **durable press.**

A chemical recipe to remove wash-and-wear fabric finish so that fibers will be receptive to dye can be made. The fabric may be simmered for 30 minutes at 190° F in a chemically treated solution of ½ ounce hydrochloric acid to 2 gallons 190° F water. This solution should not be used on permanent press, so it is important to carefully read any labels describing the finish. Removing wash-and-wear finishes is important for batik and tie-dye or for any fabric that is to be dye-heated. Also see **Batik and Tie-dye: Fabrics for Dyeing.**

washer. Metalworking. Woodworking. See **bolt.**

washfast. Batik and Tie-dye. Color that is fast or permanent to washing. A major factor in a color's being washfast is water temperature.

washing. Knitting. Knit fabrics must be washed carefully and handled with care. Knitting should be washed by hand in cold water and mild soap. It should be rinsed thoroughly; a fabric softener may be added to reduce the static electricity that is created by washing so many fibers.

Do not fabric-soften linen fibers, which may be sized with starch.

After washing, the knitting should be blocked on a flat surface and left to dry away from direct heat and sunlight. Also see **blocking.**

washing enamel. Enameling. A process of removing impurities and fine particles from powdered **enamel** prior to use to improve its color and brilliance. Enamel is washed by adding two parts clean water to one part ground enamel, stirring, then allowing the enamel to settle. The water and floating residue are poured off. The process is repeated until the water remains clean. A drop of nitric acid will dissolve impurities.

To dry the enamel for dusting, place it on a paper towel or on aluminum foil on top of the **kiln.**

washing soda. Batik and Tie-dye. (Also called sal soda, soda ash, sodium carbonate.) The **fixing** agent for **fiber-reactive dyes.** Its addition creates an alkaline solution necessary to produce the molecular reaction which unites the **dye** with the fiber. It is available in most grocery stores. It can also be used in an **alkali test** to identify fiber content in fabrics.

Washington Sidewalk. Quilts. A complex design for a **pieced quilt** in which each **block** consists of over 30 pieces. It is one of several quilt designs named for President Washington. See ill. Also see **presidents' quilts.**

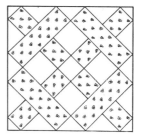

Washington Sidewalk

Washington's Puzzle. Quilts. A design for a **pieced quilt** consisting of **blocks** of offset, or tilted, pattern. It was named for George Washington. See ill. Also see **presidents' quilts.**

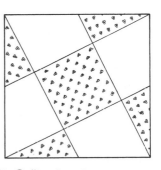

Washington's Puzzle

Washington's Quilt. Quilts. See **Coronation.**

Washita oilstone. Woodworking. See **sharpening stone.**

wash-off batik. Batik and Tie-dye. A variation of **paste-resist batik.** In this technique **dye** covers both the fabric and the resist but penetrates only the fabric. The same method can be used on paper in the **paper-batik** process. When the waterproof dye has **set,** the water-soluble resist is washed off. Wash-off **paste batik** can be accomplished using a variety of pastes, including library paste, **wheat paste, flour paste,** or cornstarch. Unthinned poster paint or undiluted tempera paint work well as resists, or gum arabic (about the consistency of cream) can be applied for a different kind of surface effect. Whatever is used, it should be thoroughly dry before **waterproof ink**s are brushed on. The ink will penetrate the fabric, dry, and set. After it is set, the resist can be washed away.

wastage. Weaving. See **loom waste, yarn calculations.**

waste leaf. Bookbinding. See **cloth-jointed endpaper, endpapers.**

waste mold. Metalworking. Plastics. See **mold.**

water-base paint. Stained Glass. See **oil-base paint, sticklighting.**

water-base paint. Toys. Any paint that is soluble in water while it is still in liquid form. Brushes used for water-base paint can be cleaned in water. The paint may be waterproof when it is completely dry. **Latex paint, acrylic paint, tempera, poster paint,** and **watercolor paint** are all water-base. Also see **acrylic spray, baker's clay.**

water bath. Candlemaking. See **Candlemaking: Cooling the Mold.**

waterbreak. Jewelry. A test to make sure metal is grease-free before coloring. After using abrasives, **steel wool,** or **pickle,** hold the metal under slowly running water. If the water does not separate or "break," the metal is grease-free.

water buffalo skin. Leather. (Also called buffalo skin.) Skin from the flat horned buffalo of the tropics. A thick, tough skin, often used for moccasins and sandals.

watercolor paint. Toys. Water-soluble pigments usually made in small hard cakes, as in the tin schoolbox sets of colors. Watercolor paints are also available in tubes. They are not waterproof when dry and need a spray coating of shellac, varnish, or spray-on fixative as a **finish.**

water cutter. Toys. A **momentum toy** that consists of a circular serrated disk with two holes drilled through it. **String**s or cords are run through the holes. The disk is twisted on the strings, then pulled from both ends to straighten them out. This movement causes the disk to spin, twisting and untwisting the strings as force is applied at the ends. The strings are pulled in an alternating action to cause tension and relaxation. When set so that the disk touches water as it spins, it merits its name as a "water cutter." Also see **buzz button, whizzgig.**

water displacement. Jewelry. A method for determining the amount of metal required for **centrifugal casting.** Take a transparent glass vessel with an opening large enough to be able to insert the **wax model** and add water. Mark the water level on the outside of the vessel. Insert the wax model below the surface of the water. If it floats, push it beneath the surface of the water with a piece of small wire. If the wire nicks the wax model, repair it or the mark will be in the casting. Pushing the wax under water will raise the level of the water. Mark it again at this new level. Remove the wax model; the water will drop back to the original level. Place metal or **casting grains** into the vessel until the water reaches the second mark. Add a little more metal to this amount to account for the **sprue**s and a portion of the **sprue button,** for the same purposes as in **weighing metals for centrifugal casting.**

water flower. Toys. A small capsulelike toy of rolled or folded papers from Japan. The roll of paper is dropped into a tumbler of water and the paper opens and unfolds to magically reveal a flower. One end of the flower is weighted, as with a small shell, to keep it sunk in the water. As the rest unfolds it floats toward the top. It is a **paper folding** process similar to that used in **origami.**

water gilding. Découpage. See **gilding.**

water gilding. Jewelry. Gilding **brass** and **copper** by immersion. Mix 1½ parts gold chloride, 60 parts hydrogen potassium carbonate, and 200 parts water. Boil in a **Pyrex glass** container for 2 hours. The solution will first turn yellow, and then green when it is ready for use. Dip brass and copper work in the hot solution for ½ minute. Also see **fire gilding** and **Jewelry: Safety Precautions and First Aid.**

water glass. Glasswork. A kind of glass made by adding soda ash (Na_2CO_3) to silica sand (SiO_2). Soda ash is an excellent **flux;** the addition of 25% soda ash will reduce the fusing temperature of silica from 1700° C to 800° C, but the resultant glass is soluble in water. To overcome this problem, **stabilizer**s, such as limestone ($CaCO_3$), are added.

water lens. Toys. A simple homemade magnifier that consists of a piece of transparent flexible plastic (such as a plastic bag) tied or taped firmly over the open end of a plastic or cardboard bucket. Several large holes cut into the sides of the bucket allow for light to enter and make room for the hand to reach in and place objects. When water is placed on the plastic top, the top will stretch or sag slightly, forming a concave "lens." It will then serve to magnify any object set under it. A variation of this toy is the waterscope. Also see **bath toy** and **Toys: Optical Toys.**

watermark. Bookbinding. A design made during the manufacture of a sheet of **paper.** It is the trademark of the maker.

watermelon tourmaline. Gemcutting. See **tourmaline.**

Watermill. Quilts. See **Windmill.**

Water-of-Ayr stone. Metalworking. See **abrasives.**

waterproof cement. Toys. See **acetate glue.**

waterproofing. Stained Glass. See **cementing** and **Stained Glass: Glazing.**

waterproof ink. Batik and Tie-dye. A permanent ink that can be painted over **wax**ed areas in the **batik** process. These inks are often used to add details of finely drawn lines to finished **tie-dye** or batik fabrics. Accents can also be added with permanent felt-tip pens containing waterproof inks. The inks may be diluted and also mixed. They are water soluble while they are being used, and waterproof when **set.** As they are not guaranteed to be washable, it is best to have them dry cleaned.

waterproof sandpaper. Plastics. See **abrasives.**

water putty. Woodworking. See **wood filler.**

water repellant. Stitchery. See **Scotchgard.**

water resistant. Leather. See **Leatherwork: Finishing Leather.**

waterscope. Toys. A simple magnifying toy or device made from a small plastic bucket. It allows the viewer to see under the surface of water in a creek, pond, lake, or bathtub. The bucket has a viewing circle cut out of the bottom. The top is covered with a transparent flexible plastic food wrap or bag that is tied or held in place with an elastic or rubber band. When the bucket is tipped upside down so that the plastic-covered top is pushed into the water, the viewing circle allows a view into the water. As the plastic is pushed up from the water pressure, a magnifying lens is produced. It is similar in principle to the **water lens.**

water stain. Woodworking. See **wood stain.**

water toy. Toys. A toy in which the energy for movement is provided by water. A **paddle wheel,** for instance, turned by dripping water, could operate cranes and pulleys to set other parts in motion. **Hero of Alexandria** made many ingenious toys powered by water.

Water Wheel. Quilts. A **split four-patch** design for a **pieced block.** It is similar to **Churn Dash** and is sometimes

Water Wheel

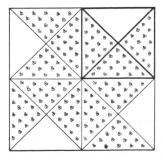

referred to as "**Windmill,**" although this name also refers to another design. See ill.

wattling. Basketry. Twisting or intertwining rough materials such as sticks, branches, or twigs to form game fencing, traps, fish weirs, and the like. It is a crude form of **wickerwork.**

Watts Towers. Mosaics. See **Rodia, Simon.**

wave stitch. Crewel. Embroidery. A series of small stitches that create a wave effect. Make small vertical straight stitches at even intervals across the top of the shape to be filled. Position the needle below and to the right of the first small stitch and work threading across the row (**a.**). The needle pierces the background fabric at the ends of the longer stitches. In all subsequent rows the threading is worked through the bottom of the longer stitches (**b.**). This stitch can be worked open or closed. See ill. Also see **open filling stitch, threaded.**

Wave stitch

a.　　　b.

waving. Rugmaking. Weaving. See **bubbling.**

wax. Batik and Tie-dye. Toys. A hard, brittle, fatty substance obtained from a variety of sources. Most waxes are blends of animal, mineral, and vegetable waxes and usually include **beeswax,** palm wax, and **paraffin.**

Liquid wax made for use in polishing wood usually contains all three in a turpentine medium. After application the turpentine evaporates, leaving a wax coating on the wood. Paste waxes also use a vehicle that will evaporate and leave a wax coating.

The wax used in **batik** is not mixed with a vehicle but is made liquid by melting. Most **batiking wax** is a combination of beeswax and paraffin.

Also, to apply wax in any of various ways to fabric. The batik artist can wax with a **tjanting,** a **brush,** or a **tjap.**

wax. Candlemaking. Any of various natural, unctuous, viscous, or solid heat-sensitive substances, consisting essentially of high-molecular weight hydrocarbons or esters of fatty acids. Wax is the main substance in candles. Several kinds of wax, such as **bayberry** wax, **beeswax, tallow,** and **spermaceti,** are used in candlemaking, but most candles today are made from **paraffin,** a petroleum by-product.

wax. Découpage. Any fine furniture paste wax can be used as the final polish for completed découpage designs. The wax is applied to the thoroughly dry **finish** with a damp cloth and then polished with a soft, dry cloth.

wax. Gemcutting. See **dop.**

wax. Jewelry. A soft, impressionable, readily molded substance. There are hundreds of kinds of wax available—pure natural waxes, synthetics, and combinations of natural and synthetic waxes. Many of the waxes used for making the model in preparation for **lost wax casting** are dental waxes, usually available through a jewelry or dental supply house. Dental waxes are quite refined, and therefore excellent for **centrifugal casting**; they **burn out** completely, leaving behind no residue that would result in an incomplete **casting**. They are available in various forms, including sheets, strips, rods, half-round wire, and solid forms. Sheet and wire dental waxes are available in the same Brown and Sharpe **gauge**s as metal. Dental waxes come in different colors; the colors are an indication of how the wax handles. For example, pink wax, available in sheet form, is a relatively soft wax that becomes workable at body temperature, and green wax, available in round and half-round wire forms, becomes soft and workable but does not lose its form at body temperature.

There are numerous other waxes besides dental wax. These can be soft, pliable, brittle, dry, sticky, or any of numerous other characteristics. There are waxes, such as **file wax,** which can be sawed and filed, and a number of waxes available from a sculpture-supply house that usually must be purchased in large amounts. Experiment with different types of wax to learn their capabilities. Also see **alcohol, centrifugal casting machine, dental tools, Karvex, lamps.**

wax. Leather. **Beeswax** and finishing wax, available in cakes, are used for sealing and polishing edges of leather. Wax is also used for waxing **thread** to facilitate hand stitching. Also see **Leatherwork: Finishing Leather, Tools and Materials.**

wax. Metalworking. Wax is used in metalworking as a temporary protective finish to prevent tarnishing and corrosion and for making models of objects for **lost wax process** casting. Ordinary nonyellowing commercial floor paste or automotive waxes may be used for surface protection. Wax for modeling and casting may be purchased ready-made from many of the large petroleum companies (e.g., Mobil) and sculpture and dental supply houses, or you can prepare a wax mixture yourself from ingredients purchased separately.

Dozens of recipes have been formulated by various craftspersons through the years. Some of the recipes are just as personal as those devised for **patina**tion or the coloring of metals. An example is the Alfred Lenz modeling wax formula (*The Alfred Lenz System of Lost Wax Casting*, National Sculpture Society, New York, 1933, p. 10):

Substance	Parts	
white beeswax	100	
paraffin	100	
druggist's lead plaster	50	(Formula: lead monoxide 1000 grams, olive oil 1000 grams, lard 1000 grams, boiling water in sufficient quantity)
petroleum jelly	50	
cocoa butter	25	(added in cold weather if needed)
lanolin	100	

Melt the ingredients together in a double boiler.

Other formulas add rosin, **tallow, turpentine,** and other varieties of wax. Use wood or metal tools to model and shape the wax. Metal tools may be heated to smooth and cut through the wax. Wood tools should be coated with oil or dipped into melted paraffin to keep them from picking up and sticking to the modeling wax as they are used.

wax. Plastic. A natural or synthetic substance made from esters, fatty acids, alcohol, and hydrocarbons. It is used as a **polishing compound, mold release agent, sealant,** and **air shield.**

wax. Woodworking. A final **finish** applied to wood that is to be polished. Waxes may be natural or synthetic and come in liquid, paste, or spray form.

Carnauba wax, from a species of Brazilian palm tree, is the most commonly used natural wax in woodworking. Because it is the hardest of natural waxes, it is always mixed with other waxes to make it easier to apply. Beeswax is a natural wax product of the honeybee. It is fairly hard and is available in white or brown. Paraffin is a soft wax made from petroleum and is often incorporated into other waxes to ease application. Silicones are mixed with other waxes to help produce a very hard surface and to make application easier.

In addition to these waxes, wax **stains** have been developed that permit staining and waxing a piece of wood in one operation. Their only disadvantage is that they do not fill in or stain all the wood pores.

To apply a paste wax, thoroughly clean and dry the wood surface. With a soft cloth, apply the paste in small circular motions over a small area. Allow the wax to dry, then briskly rub the area with another soft cloth. Continue polishing until the desired luster is obtained. Also see **Woodworking: Finishing.**

wax bath. Candlemaking. A container of melted wax heated to 200–210° F. It is used to provide a thin overlay on candles with minor surface defects, or to give a uniform binding surface to complex candles built of several different molded sections. Wax baths can also be used to coat **carved candles** with a second color of wax.

The simplest technique for wax bathing is to dip the candle in the melting pot while holding the candle by the wick with pliers. Once adequately bathed, the candle can be dipped in cold water to provide a glossier surface.

wax carton container mold. Candlemaking. See **cardboard container candle.**

wax doll. Toys. A doll of which either the entire body or just the head is made of wax; they were made from ancient times up to the twentieth century. Pure beeswax was sometimes used, although usually resins, turpentine, or other materials were added to make the wax more solid. Some wax **doll head**s were solid, but more often they were molded and reinforced from the inside with a **composition.**

Waxed doll heads were formed first of another material, such as **papier mâché,** and were then coated with a layer of wax. All wax dolls were fragile and subject to temperature changes, scratches, and abrasion.

waxed end. Stitchery. A thread or string which has been waxed or stiffened on one end. Sometimes a **white glue, beeswax,** or similar stiffener is used. The stiff end makes it easier to thread **bead**s, **spool**s, buttons, and sequins.

waxed thread. Featherwork. Common thread strengthened by drawing it over a cake of beeswax. A thick thread can be thinned by separating the strands and cutting several strands shorter. The end is rubbed with beeswax and easily threads the needle. Prewaxed thread is available commercially in several colors from craft shops.

waxed thread. Leather. See **thread.**

waxer. Stitchery. (Also called wax leaf.) **Beeswax** wrapped in **cheesecloth** and attached to a small wood handle, so that it resembles a candy lollipop. This is used on a hot iron to make the surface glide smoothly over **fabric**s during ironing.

wax frame. Batik and Tie-dye. See **batiking frame.**

waxing up. Stained Glass. One technique for attaching precut pieces of stained glass for a leaded **panel** to a clear sheet of glass so that the glass can be seen in a total composition in front of a window. The pieces are secured in their correct position by dripping molten beeswax at the corners of the pieces and between their joints. Even margins representing the **heart** of the **lead came** are left around each piece of glass. See ill.

Spooning wax between glass pieces

wax lap. Gemcutting. See **lap.**

wax leaf. Stitchery. See **waxer.**

wax model. Jewelry. The shape of a proposed piece of jewelry made in wax in preparation for **lost-wax casting.** See ill. Also see **centrifugal casting, flask.**

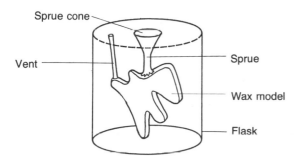

wax pencil. Batik and Tie-dye. A pencillike drawing tool that has a colored wax through the center in place of lead. The **wax** makes a wider line than lead, but not so thick as crayon. Wax pencils are made to mark on glass, ceramicware, or other similar materials on which lead pencils will

not take. They can be used in **wax-resist drawing**s in the **batik** process.

wax removal. Batik and Tie-dye. See **boiling, removing wax.**

wax resist. Batik and Tie-dye. The **batik** process of impregnating areas or portions of a material with **wax** and then **dyeing** it. Waxed areas **resist** the **dye** so that when the wax is removed the original design appears. The wax-resist process is the basis of fabric batik, **paper batik, tjap printing,** and **tulis** batik.

wax resist. Ceramics. See **resist method.**

wax shrinking. Candlemaking. See **cave-in** and **Candlemaking: Refilling the Mold.**

wax stain. Woodworking. See **wood stain.**

waxy luster. Gemcutting. See **luster.**

weathering. Ceramics. The process of exposing clay over a period of time to rain, sun, and frost, to improve its **workability.**

Weathervane. Quilts. A **nine-patch pieced block** design that shows a square set into a square along with a diamond pattern. This name is sometimes used to refer to the **Kansas Troubles** design. See ill.

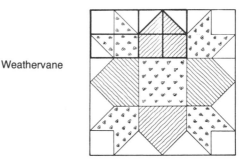

Weathervane

weave. Basketry. The process of interlacing the material of a basket. It usually refers to a specific type of pattern or a way of building up the siding, **border,** or **base** of the basket. Usually, a flexible active element is woven around a structural **passive element.** Also see **Basketry: Woven, Plaited,** and **Coiled Basket Construction.**

weave. Weaving. The pattern in which the **warp** interlaces with the **filling** in order to produce a fabric. The weave decides the structure of the cloth, whether it is simple or complex. There are three acknowledged basic weaves: **plain weave, twill weave,** and **satin weave.** All other weaves are said to be **derivative weaves, combination weaves,** or **compound weaves.** Weaves can be pictured before weaving by **drafting** on **graph paper.** This representation is called a **weave draft.**

weave analysis. Weaving. (Also called pick-out.) The taking apart of a swatch of woven fabric in order to discover what the **weave** is and how it was obtained as regards the **drawing-in draft, tie-up,** and **treadling order.** The swatch should be of a size that has two or three repeats of the weave. Some weaves using heavy yarns can be analyzed at a glance, but usually the analysis is done with a **pick glass** that magnifies the weave so that the weaver can either "read" it through the glass, or take it slowly apart strand by strand, and in so doing see the over and under interlacing of each **end** and **pick.** It is also necessary to have on hand **graph paper,** straight pins, pencil, and a tapestry **needle** or hat pin to facilitate separating the threads in the swatch in the picking-out process. It is usually the **filling** that is withdrawn pick by pick. It is necessary to reproduce one whole **repeat** of both **warp** and filling on the graph paper as the **weave draft.** In the swatch, the repeat can usually be spotted by eye and is then marked off by straight pins. If the repeat is in doubt, it is always wiser to go one end or one pick beyond the indicated repeat to see if this is indeed the beginning of the next repeat. Before the pick-out process is begun, the number of ends and picks in the repeat are counted and this amount is marked off on the graph paper. As the fabric is analyzed pick by pick (or end by end), each pick is noted on the graph paper, with the filled-in squares signifying the warp going over the filling, and the empty squares indicating the filling over the warp. When the weave repeat is satisfactorily noted on the paper, the vertical columns are examined to see which ends are interlaced in the same manner (i.e., which have the same **riser**s and **sinker**s in the same sequence), and those ends that weave identically are given the same harness number. The highest number is the total of harnesses required to weave the swatch. In order to see what the tie-up and treadling order would be, the **chain draft** is written down first. The number of harnesses is copied down one side of the weave draft in straight numerical sequence. The vertical columns belonging to each number are also copied. This gives a simple chain draft, which is all that is needed for reproducing the weave on a **table loom** or with a direct tie-up on a **floor loom.** The horizontal lines of the chain draft are checked to see which are identical to each other. Those that are identical are assigned the same number. The highest number is the total number of **treadle**s needed. The numbers that read up the column indicate the treadling order. The tie-up is read

horizontally for each treadle, and a filled-in square on the graph paper (or riser) would indicate a tie-up on a **rising shed** loom. On a **sinking shed** loom, the empty squares would indicate the tie-up. There are variations in the method of establishing the tie-up and treadling order, but the manner of finding the weave draft and drawing-in draft remain essentially the same for all weavers. To make the weave analysis complete, the warp and **filling arrangement**s should be indicated to the side and above the weave draft. See ill. Also see **warp arrangement.**

weave draft. Weaving. A representation on **graph paper** of the weave structure as it looks in the woven cloth. On paper, every horizontal row of squares is one **filling pick;** every vertical row, one **warp end.** The filled-in (or "x"ed in) squares are warp ends that the **harness**es have raised over the filling. The empty squares are filling picks that are covering the part of the warp not raised. A weave draft indicates pattern or weave structure. It does not indicate **sett, beat,** color changes, or yarn textures. Weave drafts are based on the interaction between the **drawing-in draft** and the **chain draft,** or the **treadling order** with the **tie-up.** Where certain harnesses are shown as being lifted and placed above where they occur in the drawing-in draft, a square is filled in there to show a warp end rising. A weave draft, however, can be designed or derived from other sources, and then the other drafts are devised to achieve the weave draft structure. It is only in the second instance that weave drafts are necessary. For the actual weaving of a cloth, only the information as to the threading and the lifting of harnesses is needed. A weave draft is plotted to see what the weave looks like, to see if there are unusually long **float**s, and to determine how the next **repeat** joins the basic repeat. Also see **corduroy, draft, M's and O's.**

weaver. Basketry. The **active element** or **weft** in **woven basketry.** It is usually a flexible **rod** of **willow** or **cane,** used to secure or **bind** together the structural **element** or **warp** in the construction of a basket. Also see **Basketry: Woven Basket Construction.**

weaver's knot. Beadwork. Lacemaking. A strong, slender knot used to repair broken threads. In beadwork, also used when transferring beads from a purchased strand onto heavier thread. In lacemaking, also used when adding a new thread to a **bobbin.** See ill. Also see **slip knot.**

Slip knot

a.   b.

Weaver's knot

c.   d.

weaver's knot. Weaving. A knot thought to be unique to weavers, but in some quarters it is known as a sailor's knot. It is used in **tying-on** new warps and in some cases, which involve using very fine yarns, mending broken warp ends. It is a flat, permanent knot that cannot slip or untie. See ill.

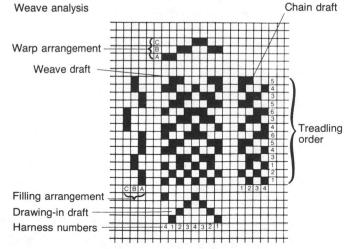

Weave analysis   Chain draft

Warp arrangement

Weave draft

Treadling order

Filling arrangement
Drawing-in draft
Harness numbers

Weaver's knot

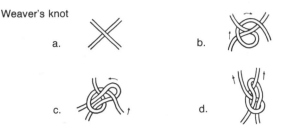

a.

b.

c.

d.

weaver's records. Weaving. The information and notations that a weaver keeps about a sample or finished piece of weaving that enable him or her to reproduce it again. It is used as a basis for another experiment or idea, or as a warning to avoid certain errors. The basic information that is usually kept in these records includes: **warp specifications, filling** information (**tie-up, treadling order, filling arrangement, picks per inch**), equipment used (**reed size,** etc.), yarn samples, swatch or sketch of what was woven, **weave draft,** and **finishing** information that would include length and width before and after finishing, how the piece was finished, and the results. It is also a good idea to include in the records information about the yarn, where it was purchased and the cost. **Dyeing** information can be noted here if the yarn or fabric was dyed at home. Finally, it should be noted to whom the fabric or piece was sold, or where it was shown, and the purchase price. Any method of keeping the records in order can be followed. Either file folders or a loose-leaf notebook with a binder that has wide capacity rings is recommended.

weave symbol. Weaving. The numbers above and below a line that indicate the **interlacing** points of the first **pick** of a **weave.** Two common weave symbols are **plain weave:** $\frac{1}{1}$; and **twill weave:** $\frac{2}{2}$. $\frac{4}{1}\frac{2}{4}\frac{1}{2}$ is an example of a fancy twill. The numbers above the line indicate the **risers;** those below, the **sinkers.** The numbers added together total the number of **ends** and picks needed for one **repeat** of the weave. The total also indicates the number of **harnesses** needed to weave the pattern.

WEAVING

Weaving is the art of **interlacing** vertical and horizontal components into a **web** or **cloth.** The vertical component is called the **warp** and its individual elements, the **warp ends.** These are held parallel and rigid on a **loom,** which in its simplest form is merely a frame. The rigidity gives **warp tension** so that it is easier to form an opening or **shed** through which the horizontal component, called the **filling, weft,** or woof, passes during the interlacing process. In the most common type of web, the interlacing between warp and filling is done at right angles.

Weaving is a diverse craft. One person can approach it as a practical means of obtaining an end object; to another, it is an art form or a technical tour-de-force; yet another finds it a form of therapy, with the motions of the body rhythmically complementing the motions of the loom.

Weaving, done as a practical craft, produces **yardage, loom-shaped** clothing, items for the home, and countless other small and large accessories for everyday living. It is also an art form, having a centuries-old tradition under the heading of **tapestry,** and also a new and freer concept of artistic expression in the form of **wall hanging**s or **fiber sculpture.** How the practical or the aesthetic is achieved depends on whether the weaver chooses to be involved with **loom-controlled** weaving or a type of **free weaving** in which **finger-manipulated** techniques play the most important role.

Often, there are overlaps between these two types of weaving. However, there are certain things distinctly associated with each type. Loom-controlled weaving is done on a **harness loom,** involves **drafting,** and can range into complex weave structures or **pattern weave**s that ultimately might employ as many as 16 or 24 **harness**es. Finger-manipulated techniques have evolved from so-called primitive weaving and tapestry, and are usually done on the simplest type of loom possible. Its emphasis is on manual workings with yarn which are impossible to reproduce with mechanical equipment. In either case the raw material used to fashion a practical or art object is **thread, yarn, rope,** or any type of natural or synthetic **fiber.** The range of thickness and texture is almost endless. Nonfiber elements such as plastic, paper, metal, or wood can also be interlaced to form a woven web.

Peripheral to weaving, but much used by contemporary artist-weavers as well as by early fiber workers, are **non-loom** and **finger weaving** techniques such as knotting, **looping, netting, plaiting, braiding, wrapping, weft chaining, twining** and **card weaving.** Weaving, as well as the above techniques, is a structural art in which the object or cloth is created out of strands of yarn and the color, design, and pattern are formed by the interaction of the warp and filling. However, it is also possible to apply color and design through techniques such as **ikat, warp painting,** and **warp printing.**

Exactly when weaving first surfaced is lost in the past. When archaeologists bring a culture to light, they can not always depend on the actual cloth or its structure to tell them about the weaving and fiber life of that culture. Only in a few places in the world were the climatic conditions such that textiles were preserved well enough to serve as clues to that culture's fiber development. Instead, researchers have had to depend on impressions in clay, remnants of weaving tools and equipment, drawings and paintings in tombs, and, when available, written records, in order to determine when and how man began to interlace two separate elements in weaving.

It is logical to assume that weaving resulted as an outgrowth of other textile crafts such as plaiting, netting, looping, and twining—crafts that could be done with the fingers and needed little or no other equipment. **Matting** and **felting** are also thought to have preceded weaving.

The first weaving fibers were probably branches, grasses, and rushes. These materials were fairly rigid and, as such, the interlacing process could be done without a loom. It was not until the first flexible fibers were used that the need arose for some arrangement to make the interlacing easier; this need resulted in the development of the loom.

From the time of the first loom, the history of weaving

begins to parallel the history of the loom, and presupposes that there was a concurrent development in both spinning and dyeing. Although the manner of interlacing and finger techniques were perfected in early times, it was the incentive of saving time and labor that prompted weavers to develop their looms. A simple supporting stake that held a number of free-hanging warp threads progressed to a warp-weighted loom that, in turn, evolved into a two-bar loom that could be either a ground loom or a vertical loom; this continued development finally resulted in the harness loom.

The first appearance of weaving on a loom varies; surviving from the late Stone Age are the remains of the Swiss lake dwellers of 3000 B.C. These remains are associated with the warp-weighted loom. Such too was the case with remaining woven textiles of the Egyptians of 5000 B.C. These were **linen** fragments preserved in a tomb. (It should be noted that, up to recent times, the warp-weighted loom was also in use on the North Pacific coast by the Indian weavers of the **Chilkat blanket**s.)

The Egyptians were noted for the fine, gauzelike quality of their weaving. One piece of cloth, found at Thebes, had 152 warp ends to an inch; another was so delicate in texture that the whole length could be easily pulled through a finger ring. This fine cloth, used for garments as well as mummy wrappings, was woven on warp-weighted looms. Eventually the Egyptians developed a horizontal **frame loom** or ground loom that was used to weave rugs and tapestries. Both looms were used simultaneously for many centuries.

The Egyptians did not do much with color, pattern, or other fibers. They preferred the crisp, semitransparent whiteness of the natural linen. **Wool** was considered unclean, and color was not introduced until the XI Dynasty (c. 2000 B.C.), when simple weft stripes of color were woven in or patterned inserts were put in by **needleweaving** in areas of warp left exposed for this purpose.

Quite different were the fabrics of the ancient Assyrians, Babylonians, and Chaldeans. Paintings and bas-relief sculptures have established that these peoples had a great love for bright colors and elaborate design, and interwove much gold thread along with the basic wool fiber. Although dating the first appearance of weaving in Mesopotamia is difficult, we have clay tablets dating from 2200 B.C. that served as account books for what appears to have been a weaving industry.

Palestine and Phoenicia were other important textile centers of the ancient world. Fragments of wool and linen weaving have been found that date back to about 3000 B.C.

In ancient Greece, fabrics for clothing and tapestries were woven on warp-weighted looms. The Greeks had a great love of beautiful fabrics, and a rich vocabulary concerning weaving developed. Also, the goddess Athena became the patron of weaving.

The weavers of these ancient cultures were established into what we might call weaving "factories," where they were segregated by the type of cloth they wove.

The craft spread rapidly in the ancient world. Greece exported her fabrics to Rome; Romans did little weaving, considering it to be demeaning. Rather, they preferred to import woven textiles, or depended on the weaving of slaves from weaving countries. Eventually there were free tradesmen who organized weaving factories and had shops selling to those Romans unable to afford weaving slaves. In time, guilds were formed and different types of weaving were produced throughout the Roman Empire.

There is also evidence that weaving was being done in other parts of the world. In India, it is surmised that there was a long history of cotton cultivation and weaving, although the written records do not show evidence of such until the seventh century A.D. In China, legend has it that about 2700 B.C. silk was discovered. The first tangible evidence of silk cloth comes from the Chou Dynasty (771–256 B.C.), but the textile's extreme fineness indicates a long period of prior development. This production of silk was a carefully guarded secret and did not become known in other areas for many centuries. About A.D. 300, Chinese weavers settled in Japan, bringing with them their knowledge of silk. And it was not until two centuries later that the secret of silk was smuggled to the West by two monks who had lived in China. Constantinople, under Justinian, quickly established itself as the silk-weaving center for the West.

Up to this point, loom development had mainly to do with fiber yarns such as linen, wool, and cotton. Silk, being a **filament** yarn, had to have much more special attention and care, and it is thought that the Chinese worked out harness weaving in the form of a **draw loom**— an attempt to effect control and smoothness in their weaving. This type of loom became quite prevalent after the third century A.D. in the East, and eventually found its way into the West.

The early Coptic weavers of Egypt produced lively and excellent work in their textiles. Their weaving was often a combination of plain cloth and elaborate tapestry and **pile** weaving achieved on either the warp-weighted or ground loom.

With the coming of Islam, the Coptic weavers became the weavers for their conquerors. The Arabs had their own craftsmen, but the weavings of the Copts (and Sassanians of Persia) were by far superior. The Arabs carried the craft of weaving with them on their conquests, establishing workshops in new lands. Such a case was the fine silk workrooms in Spain. They also exported their **knotted pile** techniques and design flair.

Aside from these Arab-established workshops in Europe, other weaving centers had developed as a result of the Roman Empire. These workshops continued to produce long after the Romans had left, and became the basis for the cloth-producing areas of the Middle Ages. However, the bulk of the weaving was done in the homes by the women in order to supply the needs of their households. The medieval loom was the harness loom, which had come up through Spain and Italy, the loom in use today. Any excess weaving not needed in the home was given to the lord of their area as feudal taxes. Cloth was then sold, bartered, and used in lieu of currency. The wool and linen fabrics that were woven were coarse, simple, sturdy, and unadorned lengths of cloth, usually brown in color. Serge, a woolen **twill** fabric originating in Roman Gaul, was an important medieval cloth, as was **linsey-wool.** Sumptuous and exotic fabrics, however, were obtained by the nobles through trade with the Middle East. As towns began to develop, weaving workshops took on more importance, and many new ones were established. A textile industry developed that was controlled by guilds which would, in time, become important political and economic entities.

Although most cloth was still of a rather plain variety, the art of tapestry weaving began to flourish in such areas as France and Belgium. In time, some new fabrics began to appear that were more than just plain and durable. These included napped fabrics, **brocade**s with gold thread, and silk cloth.

The products of weaving enjoyed a tremendous upgrading during the time of the Renaissance in both quality and visual aesthetics. It was a period when art and beauty were celebrated, and wealthy patrons satisfied themselves by ordering garments made of fabrics which were beautiful in themselves and would also enhance the wearer. Wall coverings and upholstery followed this same trend.

Quantity also increased in European production. The newly developed bourgeoisie also demanded the finest in textiles. This trend was to continue in the ensuing centuries.

While Europeans were weaving on harness and draw looms to obtain the elaborate textiles they desired, equally sophisticated weaving was being done on simple two-bar looms in North, Central, and South America. From before A.D. 1200 until the Spanish conquest, weavers of the Western Hemisphere were producing fine-quality and beautiful textiles. The apex was perhaps achieved in **Peruvian weaving**, which is recognized as surpassing all others in inventiveness of weave structure and pattern and color development. The Indian weavers, who banded into workshops to produce elaborate and exquisite textiles for the glory of the Inca ruler and his court, knew just about all current weaving and other textile techniques. Some of their techniques, such as **scaffold weft**s, were discontinued and lost. However, the arid climate of the Inca Empire has kept many examples of their fabrics intact, and a complete textile record of their culture can be followed.

The **backstrap loom** was used by the Indians of Central and South America, whereas the **Navajo loom** was an **upright loom.** All Indians in North America constructed cloth in some fashion or other, but it is Navajo weaving that has come down to us as the best and only true North American **Indian weaving.**

When the colonists came to America, the main emphasis in their textile needs was on durability and thrift. Some colonists arrived with looms and patterns from the homeland. All were self-sufficient in terms of textiles, weaving everything from sheets to clothing—and then finding a way of reusing the items when they were reduced to rags. Self-sufficiency was necessary, but it was not encouraged by mother England since this took trade away from her own industry. Much cloth was imported into the colonies from England and in the coastal cities purchased by the residents. But inland all was dependent on the (female) weavers of the household. With time and in certain locales there arose weavers who supplied other families with their cloth needs. Colonial weaving soon had patterns that were typical of America and specific regions and events. Small textile factories with handlooms were set up in many of the

colonies—the first one established as early as 1638 in Massachusetts. Textiles from Europe became more and more a commodity that only the rich could afford.

By the eighteenth century, weaving techniques in Europe had reached their peak and all weaves used by today's weavers had been devised and formulated. Many of them actually go back to the time of the Renaissance. Some of the more technically advanced were velvet, **corduroy, damask,** and **gauze weaving.** The only thing lacking in all of the techniques was speed to fulfill the demands of the people. The eighteenth century brought the **fly shuttle loom**—invented by John Kay in 1733. His son improved it in 1760 by inventing the use of multiple shuttle boxes on each side of the loom. Slowly the speed was being increased. However, the big turn in events did not come until the invention that automated spinning and in its wake brought the mechanization of looms and the Industrial Revolution.

In the 1780s the "iron man" appeared—a loom that changed the shed and threw the shuttle automatically. It did in one day what it took a handweaver a week to do. Handweavers rebelled by smashing and burning equipment, but to no avail—once discovered there was no turning back, and a fast way of spinning and weaving was here to stay.

Edmund Cartwright's power loom (patented 1785) did simple fabrics. The intricate patterns achieved by the draw loom were accomplished by the **Jacquard loom** (first exhibited in 1801). Even in the weaving of the most complex patterns the weaver sitting in front of the loom and in control of all operations was totally eliminated. **Handweaving** survived only in those countries where labor was cheap enough to compete with power. So it has happened that where there were poor peasants, handweaving was still being done as a necessary occupation in the twentieth century and, in many cases, using time-consuming meticulous techniques on primitive equipment.

The new machines produced large quantities of fabric quickly, but in time it was seen that unique fabrics wanted in just small amounts had no place in this production. More and more, standard types of fabrics were being woven that could appeal to the greatest number of people who had no desire for anything beyond a serviceable fabric. As this trend has continued, it has, ironically, brought back the handweaving wiped out by the power looms. The desire for something individual, and for the character of handwoven fabrics, along with the desire to work again with the hands, has led to the current weaving revival. This in turn has been made possible by the larger amount of leisure time available due to industrialization.

Although the Industrial Revolution had such impact on the United States that one would believe handweaving was completely swept away, this is not entirely the case. It has continued right on up to the mid-twentieth century in isolated hills and valleys of Appalachia and in other such pockets where people were too poor to participate in the benefits of the Industrial Revolution. Their simple life was to some extent still based on self-sufficiency and barter. There were attempts in the early part of this century to establish cottage industries among weavers located in certain areas. For the most part it was too early for this kind of venture, since the rest of the populace was not ready to embrace handmade textiles. However, it served to keep alive patterns and traditional methods.

The traditional aspects of weaving were carried on by many independent weavers in various parts of the country. One of the most noted was Mary Meigs Atwater (1878–1956), who took up weaving to keep her days busy after she moved with her husband to a remote Montana mining community. She did considerable research into traditional techniques and patterns, recorded them, and published them in "The Shuttle-Craft Guild Bulletin," her own newsletter-magazine for the members of a weavers' guild she organized. It was the first such guild in the United States.

Although this type of handweaving was a throwback to the era before industrialization, weaving had survived as an art form through the industrial revolution in the guise of tapestry. These were all woven in the old European tapestry ateliers. However, there had been an attempt to establish the first tapestry workshop in the United States in New York City under the guidance of William Baumgarten, who, in 1893, persuaded a Frenchman, M. Foussadier, to leave his master craftsman position at the Royal Windsor tapestry works in England and emigrate to the United States. He was to superintend a group of French tapestry weavers from Aubusson, who likewise had been induced by Baumgarten to emigrate. Although commissions and prizes were received by the group, it was not a venture that survived up to present times.

Aside from the traditionalists and an isolated tapestry weaver here and there, there were few others who were involved with handweaving. One of these few was Dorothy Liebes, who was at the opposite pole from traditional weaving. A California artist turned weaver, she exalted in color, unique yarns and other materials, and texture. As early as 1930 she began weaving the textiles that made her name a hallmark in both handweaving circles and the weaving industry. She served as an impetus for other creative minds to participate in a type of weaving that explored materials, color, texture, and design rather than following patterns laid out in colonial times.

By mid-century there was a decided increase in the number of handweavers. This is not to say that it was the landslide movement that it became in the 1970s, but after World War II there was a small growth rate every year, and the weavers could be divided into three categories: There were the traditionalists, mainly interested in established patterns and very involved with technique. For the most part these weavers approached weaving as a leisure activity or second occupation. Then there were the designer-weavers who had opened up professional studios to weave yardage or specific items for architects, decorators, and other clients. In time they also wove samples that were later reproduced on power looms. Dorothy Liebes was the first to make her mark as a designer-weaver in the early thirties, and Jack Lenor Larsen became the noted name in the fifties. There was also the third category, a small one, comprising tapestry weavers, most of whom had learned their craft in Europe and were involved in weaving flat art textiles primarily in the style of the Aubusson tapestries. The first

influence that touched all three of these categories came from Scandinavia in the 1950s.

Handweaving in the Scandinavian countries had continued to be done by the rural or farm class even though these countries were quite industrialized. Their tradition of weaving was very much intact, whereas the American weaving tradition had a decided break from the time of the industrial revolution. Many of our weave patterns and techniques stem from this tradition, which had developed and improved upon itself and recorded the progress through the years. The Scandinavian handicraft traditions had also transmitted themselves to the art and design fields. This produced a large body of work in fiber, as well as in ceramics, metal, and glass. Handcrafts were viewed as an art form rather than as strictly utilitarian.

This influence spanned the ocean and was the stimulus for many young weavers, opening up avenues to self-expression. However, this still involved fabric, or perhaps rugs or tapestries. It was not until 1963 that a new art form appeared in a weaving exhibition at the Museum of Contemporary Crafts in New York City. Called at first the "new tapestry" or "woven forms," the name "wall hangings" finally evolved—especially after another show devoted to this medium was displayed in 1969 at the Museum of Modern Art in New York City.

Prior to 1963, wall hangings had been woven. Early ones by Dorothy Liebes could have been confused with yardage, and Gunta Stölzl and Anni Albers from the Bauhaus Design School in Germany made hangings that were self-contained works of art in touch with tapestry but going beyond it. Later, such artists as Lenore Tawney and Alice Adams broke even more from the tapestry base. These were all isolated instances as wall hangings evolved as an outgrowth of both tapestry and fabric weaving. The weavers were trained as artists and felt their expression lay in fiber.

The isolated instances were enough of a movement by 1963 that the Museum of Contemporary Crafts put together the show to celebrate this new fiber art form. There were woven pieces here that were involved with free-forms and texture and included many hand techniques that could not be reproduced even on a handloom. Other objects were constructed into the pieces, and in many cases a bas-relief structure was the end result. There was no confusion possible between this art form and yardage.

Since that time, experimentation has been such that from wall hangings the next step was to fiber sculpture, where the end product was either a three-dimensional object or an environment built of woven or otherwise constructed fiber items. By 1972, "fiber sculpture" had entered the weaver's vocabulary.

The situation today finds weaving still in the upswing and involvement on all levels—from deep artistic commitment to casual hobby. There are still the three categories mentioned earlier. But in addition, there are now the wall-hanging and fiber-sculpture artists, who produce work for exhibitions and public and private commissions. Some work alone in their studios, but the tendency is to have apprentices or paid workers, since the fiber pieces involved are usually of such a large size that many hands are needed to complete the work within a reasonable amount of time.

Another newcomer is the production weaver, although in some ways he goes back both to colonial times and to the designer-weaver. The production weaver usually lives in the country (as opposed to the artist-weaver, who seeks the proximity of the big-city art market) and makes yardage and clothing or small items for sale to individuals or craft shops. The hobby weaver has not remained the traditionalist he was before; but, in partaking of the craft for the pure pleasure of weaving, is experimenting with many techniques and new materials and has expanded his range to include everything from placemats to wall hangings.

DEFINITIONS   There are many different kinds of weaving. To those who work on harness looms, or even more complex looms, their weaving is called by a variety of names, such as "true weaving," "general weaving," "mechanical weaving," or "fabric weaving" (even though items other than fabric can be woven on harness looms). These names and others stem from different points of view. To a person manipulating the harnesses to get weave patterns, this may appear to be the only "true" weaving, while **primitive loom** weaving may almost be regarded as play. A devotee of primitive loom weaving—where finger-manipulation plays such an important role in obtaining the final result—would regard harness loom weaving as next-of-kin to power loom weaving, and would thus consider it mechanical weaving. Hence, one breakdown in defining weaving is according to the equipment used. Harness-manipulated versus finger-manipulated is how we have come to regard these two categories. However, in reality, harness-manipulated weaves can be done with time and patience on primitive looms, and finger-manipulated techniques can be worked on harness looms. The connection between harness-manipulated and harness looms with finger-manipulated and primitive looms is not one of what is actually possible, but the fact that finger-manipulated work usually turns out a freer piece of finished weaving, and so is not connected with a piece of machinery—i.e., the harness loom. The reverse thinking is true of harness-manipulated weaves.

A second breakdown is according to what is being produced: whether the weaver makes utilitarian objects, fabrics and fabric samples, wall hangings, art weavings, or tapestries. It is usually implied that different equipment is used for each type of production. But this is not necessarily so, since art pieces can be done on harness looms, and utilitarian pieces on **frame looms** (or others without an automatic **shedding device**).

Another division is between the traditionalists and the contemporary weaver. Although "traditionalist" usually means the weaver involved with traditional pattern weaving on a harness loom, it could also mean a traditional tapestry artist. The contemporary weaver is usually considered to be an avant-garde wall-hanging or fiber-sculpture artist; but "contemporary" also applies to a weaver who approaches fabric weaving with contemporary concepts of texture, yarn, and color, and whose vocabulary is, in many ways, quite different from the traditional weaver's—even though they may be using the same type of equipment.

The vocabulary in weaving is such that the same item or concept could have a number of different names, depending on which type of weaving is being done. There are also certain words that just pertain to specific kinds of weaving, while other words, such as "shed" or "**heddle**," are known in all categories. This has caused an overabundance of names and, in some cases, confusion. There have been attempts to simplify, codify, and standardize weaving terms. In some cases this has worked out, but complete standardization has yet to be achieved. An example is the words "filling," "weft," and "woof"—all meaning "that which is interlaced with the warp." Which word is used depends on the type of weaving done, the region, teacher, or weaver's age. In many cases, none of the existing terms seemed specific or descriptive enough, so new terms were coined that added to an already existing barrelful of names.

The sources for these various names include the early workshop factories and the subsequent power loom industry. The terms are generally English in origin; Scandinavia, with its strong, unbroken handweaving tradition, patterns, and effects has added others; French terms, mainly associated with tapestry, and Arab words referring to rug-making abound. From our own colonial past come other names that are usually very descriptive and "folksy" sounding.

"Techniques" in weaving are not weave structures that can be diagramed on **graph paper,** achieved by having the harnesses open the sheds and then throwing the **shuttle** selvage to **selvage.** Rather, techniques are finger-manipulated effects usually classified as free weaving, meaning that the filling is worked into or around the warp ends by hand either in a random placement or selvage to selvage. A random placement could result in what is known as a **discontinuous weft.** Often this weft is worked along with a **ground weave** that serves to hold the whole structure together. If the technique is such that the filling is no longer at right angles to the warp, it is called an **eccentric weft.** If the position of the warp is altered from its normal parallel thread position, then this is called **crossed warp**s, **distorted warp, diverted warp,** or **transposed warp.** Such hand manipulations of the warp and filling can be done on any kind of a loom. For the ground weave, usually woven as **plain weave** or **tabby,** there is the need of one shed and a **countershed.** This can also be picked up by hand at the most basic level or, for greater ease, by a **shed stick** for one shed, and **heddle bar** with **string heddle**s or a **heddle cord** for the other. The manipulated filling yarn is carried through or around the warp ends in either **butterfly** form, by hand, or using some simple shuttle. It is beaten down into position by a batten, **hand beater**s, or the regular **beater** on a harness loom.

Finger-manipulated techniques can be roughly classified as pattern, close or rug, and **openwork techniques**—with many types of techniques being interchangeable. For example, a rug technique could also serve as a pattern technique. Some common pattern techniques are **dukagang, HV technique,** and **laid-in.** Close or rug techniques would be wrapped ones like **soumak, Swedish knot,** and **Egyptian knot,** the knotted pile ones including both **flossa** and **rya** and **flatweave rug**s (which would be **kilim**s, **rölakan,** and **tapestry rugs**). There is also a type of low loop pile that is not knotted, but achieved by **looping.** It is also called **boutoné** and **candlewick.**

Openwork techniques are known also as gauze weaves and **lace weaves.** They include **leno, Mexican lace, Spanish lace, Brooks Bouquet, Danish Medallion,** and **Peruvian lattice.** Some of them are done using a **pick-up stick** and are known as **pick-up weave**s.

Closely related to and overlapping the finger-manipulated techniques are the tapestry techniques. These are **slit tapestry, interlocking, dovetailing, diagonal**s, **hatching, teething, stippling, mottling, crapaud,** and limning or **outlining.** Tapestry weaving is done using a **tapestry weave,** which is plain weave beaten down so that the warp is completely covered. This results in a **flat tapestry** traditionally referred to as either a basse-lisse or **low-warp** tapestry or a haute-lisse or **high-warp** tapestry. This refers to the type of **tapestry loom** used in the weaving process. A **cartoon** is used in both types, as are various **tapestry tool**s, such as the Aubusson bobbin or **flute, Swedish bobbin,** and **Gobelin bobbin.** Contemporary offspring of traditional tapestry are transparent tapestries and exposed warp tapestries, as well as all types of wall hangings.

The forming of weave structures, although quite possible on a primitive loom, is a time-consuming and laborious process, and most weavers prefer to use harness looms which are either **table** or **floor loom**s, hand-operated or **foot-power loom**s. The parts of the loom are all the same on these looms and only differ in that the **treadle**s attached to the **lam**s, which in turn are attached to the harnesses, open the shed on a foot-power loom, while **lever**s or some other attachment opens the shed when the harnesses are operated by hand. The warp is usually much longer on a harness loom than on a primitive loom and is rolled and stored in the rear of the loom around the **warp beam.** It is attached to this **beam** via an **apron bar** that in turn is attached to the warp beam by an **apron** or **apron cord**s. The warp travels in parallel strands of yarn (or ends) from the warp beam up and over the **back beam** to the **castle,** the central structure in the harness loom and its main difference from the primitive loom. In the castle are located the harnesses, and the warp is attached to them by being threaded through the **heddle eye**s of the heddles.

After passing through the heddles, the warp is threaded through the dents of the **reed** located in the beater. Finally, it is tied to the front apron bar, which attaches it to the **cloth beam** down in the front. As weaving progresses, shuttles are used to throw the filling through the open shed. The beater pushes the filling down in place, and the cloth grows. As it does so, the cloth beam is cranked at the front **ratchet** and the warp beam released at the back ratchet or **friction brake** so that the woven cloth can be pulled forward over the **breast beam** and wound and stored around the cloth beam.

It is possible to get to this point without some knowledge of drafting or reading **draft**s, but in order to proceed beyond a beginner's comprehension it is necessary to obtain this knowledge. **Drawing-in draft**s tell the pattern of threading through the heddles. **Chain draft**s tell the order of raising the harnesses. For a foot-power loom, the chain draft is broken down into **tie-up** and **treadling order,** or plan. A picture on graph paper of the finished weave structure is known as the **weave draft** or draw-down and consists of **raiser**s and **sinker**s (which correlate to the warp ends being raised or pulled down by the harnesses). The **straight draw** (or **twill threading**) and **point draw** are examples of simple drawing-in drafts, while direct and **twill tie-up**s are two common ways of connecting treadles to lams on a **four-harness** foot-power **loom.**

The **basic weave**s are plain, **twill,** and satin. From them it is possible to get all sorts of variations and **derivative weave**s, **combination weave**s, and **pattern weave**s. **Overshot** is a popular pattern weave based on a twill with a tabby **binder thread.** Other pattern weaves go by such interesting names as **crackle weave**s, **M's and O's,** and **Summer and Winter weave**s. These are all considered the **simple weave**s, since just one layer of warp and filling is used. There are also the **compound weave**s, which result in **double cloth** (which includes **tubular weaving**), **triple cloth,** and other multiple-layered cloths.

Rugweaving, although mentioned earlier as having finger-manipulated techniques that produce the designs, texture, or pile, is often done by many people as a harness-manipulated craft. It can range from the weaving of simple **rag rug**s on two-harness **rug loom**s to corduroy weaves, whose **float**s give an automatic pile, to **warp pile** constructions requiring special equipment on the loom in order to produce the effect.

Aside from pattern, weave, and technique development, all cloth—whether harness- or finger-manipulated—attains part of its character by the **density** of its **sett** and the heaviness of the weaver's **beat.** Known as ends and **picks per inch,** the weaving comes out as a **balanced cloth** if both are equal to each other. If the warp prevails, a **warp-face**d fabric results and, if the filling is more or totally in evidence, then the fabric is weft- or **filling-faced.**

Two examples of warp-faced weaving are **inkle weaving** and **card weaving.** Both result in long, narrow strips or belts. Belt or bandweaving can be done on any type of equipment with any kind of technique that suits the weaver. However, inkle weaving has its own particular loom, called an **inkle loom,** and card or tablet weaving is done with hole-punched **card**s. The latter is really **warp twining,** not weaving.

Names like **Ojibwa weaving** and **Salish weaving** also refer to a type of twining, although this Indian weaving also included real weaving. "Finger weaving" was the name given to their weaving, but, to most of today's weavers, this term means plaiting. All of these nonweaving techniques are in some way related to weaving and are thought to be the predecessors of weaving, along with braiding, looping, netting, and knotting. Many contemporary artist-weavers incorporate these techniques along with their other finger-manipulated work. See **off-loom weaving.**

New names are constantly being coined. Sometimes there are new aspects, but often it is just a variation of either a harness or finger-manipulated concept. Needleweaving, **shaped weaving,** and **three-dimensional weaving** are three new names in current vogue.

In order to achieve the interlacing process, there are basic steps that are performed. The first is to open the shed, then to pass the filling through the open shed, and, lastly, to beat or press the filling in place. In formal terms this can be alluded to as **shedding motion, picking,** and **beating.** The warp is stretched taut on a loom to make all the actions proceed easily and smoothly. Depending on the complexity of the loom and the length of the warp, there are also two additional steps that are taken, called the let-off motion and the take-up motion. The first releases unwoven warp and the second winds the woven cloth.

EQUIPMENT   The loom is the one essential piece of equipment needed for weaving. It can range from the simplest type to the most complex. Other tools are needed, but substitutes can usually be improvised.

Simple looms, lending themselves best to finger-manipulated techniques and simple weave patterns, are: **cardboard loom**s, **box loom**s, frame looms, **belt loom**s, backstrap looms, Navajo looms, and Salish looms. All of these looms are used today and have in common a continuous warp and a shedding device comprised of the shed stick and heddle bar, or something equally basic. Warp-weighted looms are seldom used today; this is also true of the **bow loom** and the **bandloom. Straw loom**s, **branch loom**s, and **hoop loom**s are evidence that almost anything can be pressed into service to use as the vehicle to hold the warp. There are various tapestry looms and rug looms used for these specific kinds of weaving.

Sophisticated looms, on which it is easiest to weave harness-manipulated constructions, are the **jack type loom,** the **countermarch loom,** and the **counterbalanced loom. Draw loom**s and **dobby loom**s are even more mechanical in their operation, although still activated by the weaver. For most floor looms it is more comfortable for the weaver to sit on a **loom bench** rather than on a chair or stool.

The warp has to be put on the loom, and the more sophisticated the loom, the more complex is the process of making the warp and putting it on. The warp for the harness looms, as well as for some upright looms, is made independently of the loom on a piece of equipment called the **warping board** or **warping reel.** Here it is measured out, under tension, in length and number of warp ends. **Warping post**s, as well as homemade inventions, can be used instead. For warps of many colors, a **warping paddle** is sometimes used. **Spool rack**s can be used to hold the **cones** and **spools** of yarn. For yarn that comes in **skein** form, a skein winder, or **swift,** is used. A **ball winder** makes the yarn into balls to use for **warping.**

To get the warp on the loom, **lease sticks** (and sometimes a **raddle** or spreader) are used. For threading the loom, a sley or **reed hook** is used.

Once the warp is on and the weaving commences, the harness loom weaver uses a **boat shuttle,** with a **bobbin** or **quill** of filling thread in it, to weave with. The bobbin is wound on either an electric or hand **bobbin winder.** A **stick shuttle** or a **rug shuttle** may also be used if the need arises. To compensate for the **draw-in** at the selvages, a **stretcher** or templet can be used.

There is a type of floor loom in which the warping is called **sectional warping** and is done directly onto the loom.

This loom has a **sectional warp beam** and, to facilitate the warping, a **tension box** with a **counter** is used.

By comparison, a simple or primitive loom needs little or nothing, because the warping is done directly on the loom. Some looms come equipped with **tensioner**s or **tension stick**s which are used to control and adjust **warp tension.** The only additional tools needed are a batten and comb or hand beater.

For special techniques there are certain tools used no matter what type of loom is in question. For some lace techniques a pick-up stick is used. For pile a **flossa rod** or a pile **gauge** is used. All of these tools can be homemade or a substitute found that will do the job just as well.

YARNS AND FIBERS   The raw material that a weaver uses for his craft is fiber made into **yarn** or **thread.** Within this field is a tremendous range. The fiber itself could be either natural or man-made. It could be from an animal, plant, or mineral source if natural, and could go in scope from strands of gold to **grass fiber** to **horsehair.** Every year there are more sources and shops opening to offer the weaver an ever-lengthening list of possibilities with which to weave.

Not only is the fiber source vast, but how that fiber has been treated in terms of **spinning** and **plying** can extend the weaver's raw-material range even further. After the first few warps, every weaver will begin to gather a few basic facts about thread and yarn, such as **twist,** size, thickness (called **yarn count**) and **ply.** Direction, tightness or angle of twist, and diameter all matter when a fiber is first being spun into a yarn called singles. Two or more singles yarns can be combined to form a **plied yarn.** If plied yarns have been combined with each other to form a very heavy yarn, this is then in the **cable** or **cord** category.

If the twist is barely there, it is called roving and is best left for filling use and not for warp. If, during twisting and plying, certain things have been done to the yarn so that it has bumps, knobs, or loops, one gets a **textured yarn,** more commonly known as **novelty yarn.** Cotton yarn can be **mercerized** to enhance it. A good quality of wool yarn has a fine **loft** to it, but synthetic yarns obtain a degree of loft only after they have been texturized and become **bulked yarn**s. Today there are many yarns made of mixed fibers—synthetics with natural as well as various natural fibers blended together. If the fiber content is unknown or doubtful, there are a number of **burning test**s the weaver can undertake to determine what the fiber is made of.

Yarn comes in skein, spool, or cone form, and even as a large **cheese.** Weavers have long known wool, linen, cotton, and silk, but today they have opportunities to buy yarn made of **alpaca, Angora** goat (called **mohair**), **camel hair, cashmere, cowhair, llama,** and **ramie.** The desire to weave larger and rougher-textured pieces, and to make fiber sculpture, has expanded weavers' horizons into trying **sisal, jute, hemp,** and **raffia. Twine** and **string,** as common as they may seem, are often used. Many weavers have improved on the thickness of bought yarn by **doubling** their yarns on a **doubling stand.** Other weavers have taken up spinning in order to get the yarn texture they want, and many do home **dyeing** in order to get their desired colors.

Still other weavers have wanted to go beyond the interlacing of fiber and have chosen to weave with rushes and reeds, plastics, leather, fur, paper, metal, and a whole variety of other natural and man-made items. Many weavers mix fibers with non-yarn materials such as shells, feather, bones, and beads.

WARPING   Warping is part of the process known as **dressing the loom.** This process is reserved mainly for the harness looms and is the preparation of the warp and loom for weaving. A similar procedure, much simplified, is needed for the primitive loom.

In the case of harness-loom warping, the correct number of warp ends must be measured and wound out in the correct length under even tension. A system of **yarn calculations** gives the needed number and length. With this information a warp can then be wound on the necessary equipment. Various methods are used according to which piece of equipment is at hand, but in all cases a **cross** is made to maintain the warp threads in consecutive order. This is later tied with a **lease cord. Choke**s are other ties made at spaced intervals down the length of the warp to facilitate removal and transfer of the warp to the loom. As optional aids, a **counter** and **measuring cord** can be used to assure the correct amount and length of warp threads. **Paddle** warping is often practiced by weavers who work with many colors.

The procedure on a warping reel, board, or equivalent equipment is known as **chain warping** since the next step is the **chaining** of the warp to shorten its length and make it easier to transfer to the loom. Some types of tapestry looms use a chained warp, but the method of putting this on the upright loom differs from that of putting it on a harness loom and depends on whether or not the tapestry loom is equipped with **warp peg**s.

On almost all primitive looms the warping is done directly on the loom or sticks that will become the loom. A **continuous warp** is made of either a figure-8 or a circular type. These warps go around the length (height) of the loom. An even simpler continuous warp can be made that is just on one side of a loom, going around nails or notches that space it and hold it in position.

Once the simple winding of the continuous warp is done the weaver is ready for the remaining few steps necessary to get the warp ready for weaving. This includes insertion of the shed stick and preparing the heddle cords and heddle bar. There can be more than one heddle bar—depending on the type of pattern weaving being done. The string heddles or heddle cord take more time to prepare if the warp is very dense. Although there are traditional methods for this preparation, weavers have developed various alternative methods as time-saving devices. Last (or on some looms, after the winding) comes the **chain spacer** or twining, to spread and secure the warp in a spaced position. Some primitive looms, such as the Navajo and backstrap, have unique features of warping and transferring to the final loom position. Although these looms may require a step or two more, neither works with a **warp chain** system (as does a harness loom).

BEAMING AND THREADING   Once the above tasks are finished, the primitive loom weaver is ready to begin weaving. On the harness loom the warping is just the first step in dressing the loom, and the weaver now takes the warp chain to the loom for **beaming**—an operation reserved almost exclusively for this kind of loom. **Spreading the warp** to its correct width is one of the first actions, no matter which method of beaming is followed. There are two basic methods with many variations on each method. The **Beriau method** is one example of a variation that was quite popular a number of years ago.

The ultimate object in beaming is to get the warp wound around the warp beam with all layers of warp under equal tension and all warp threads running straight in each layer. To aid in this, layering or **padding** is followed so that each layer of warp is controlled as much as possible as it goes around the warp beam. **Warp stick**s can be used for the same purpose.

Whether **threading** the loom comes before or after beaming depends on the method of beaming chosen. Prior to threading, the heddles are checked to see that each harness has at least the needed amount and that the necessary ones are centered in each harness. Threading through the heddles is known as **drawing-in,** and threading through the reed is known as **sleying.**

When beaming and threading are completed, the next step is the **tying-on** (using a special **tie-on knot**) or **lacing on** of the warp to the front apron bar. During this process any inadequacies in the tension are adjusted. The treadles are then tied-up on a floor loom according to the desired pattern.

The loom and warp are checked out for any apparent errors in threading and sleying, for alignment of heddles and reed, and for equal length of all **treadle cords** so that the open shed is clear and wide. These checkup procedures go under the name of **gating.** On a counterbalanced loom they also involve adjusting the **roller**s and **pulley**s so that the harnesses are suspended evenly.

HARNESS LOOM WEAVING   If the warping, beaming, and threading of a harness loom seem to take a long time, it is all compensated for by the speed, ease, and **rhythm** with which weaving proceeds. On a floor loom a treadle is stepped upon and the shed opens up. The weaver throws or places the shuttle through the shed in front of the beater and brings the beater forward to push the filling in place. The beater is returned to its original position back against the harnesses, and another treadle is stepped on for a different shed opening. The shuttle returns back through the shed and the beater is brought forward once again to push this weft thread up against the preceding one. The weaver continues on in this way, alternately pushing the shuttle from right to left and from left to right with the hand on the center of the beater, bringing it forward with every **pick** or **shot** of filling. The cloth grows and finally the **fell** or beat-up point is too close to the beater. The warp must be advanced forward. The back ratchet is released and the cloth is wound frontward around the cloth beam.

More empty warp glides into position to be woven. The ratchets are tightened so that good warp tension is achieved again. The process of weaving continues—the harnesses move up and down to give the sheds and the beater, backward and forward to beat the filling down. The weaver strives for an even beat and well-managed selvages.

The process is interspersed with the bringing forward of more warp as needed, until the project is finished or the warp woven off. It is never all woven off, for some remains behind the beater and in the heddles as **loom waste.** However, it is not really wasted yarn. Weavers call it **thrums** and use the short lengths in other weaving projects.

Usually the first piece of weaving on a new warp is the **heading** that straightens out the **bout**s of tied warp and is used to check for any errors in threading not caught before. **Bobbin winding** takes place either before weaving or as the bobbins run out of filling yarn. In the actual weaving, the yarn from the new bobbin is attached to the yarn that has run out by **piecing** or overlapping. Should any of the warp threads break during weaving, there are ways of mending the **broken end**s and **darning in** the tips when the weaving is finished.

For a table harness loom the process is the same except the sheds are opened by the hand pressing a lever or rotating a wheel or some other such device. Since it is not a combined motion between feet and hands as on the floor loom, some weavers feel that the rhythmical movement, so much a part of harness weaving, is lost.

DRAFTING   The knowledge of drafting is essential to the weaver who wishes to understand how the harness loom functions and how to create for it. Drafting is the shorthand symbolic language written on graph paper that explains the ways the warp is threaded through the heddles and what harnesses are raised or lowered in order to achieve a certain design. As mentioned earlier, the drawing-in draft and chain draft, or treadle tie-up and treadling order, give this information. If there is no treadling plan, a knowledgeable weaver might experiment with various treadlings or try **treadling-as-drawn-in** or weaving on **opposites**.

A weave draft shows the pattern of actual interlacing between warp and weft. The three basic weaves are plain, twill, and satin. From this basic level the weaver can go on to explore all sorts of **fancy weave**s. For **texture weaves** there are **crepe weave**s, **honeycomb weave**s, and **huck weave**s. If the **warp arrangement** and **filling arrangement** colors are placed in specific positions a **log cabin pattern** can be obtained or a **hound's tooth check**, as well as all types of other **check**s and **plaid**s. **Block weave**s give a weaver opportunity to design and try different kinds and sizes of pattern weaves.

When a weaver gets more adept at drafting, he or she can try a hand at **transcribing weaves** from four-harnesses to **multiharnesses**, or in designing **profile draft**s that are even a more condensed method of indicating a large pattern effect than ordinary drafting.

Weave analysis is the opposite of drafting and then weaving a cloth. Here a finished fabric is shredded apart in a specific way so that the weaver can establish how it was threaded and in what order the harnesses were raised.

In addition to the expanded ranges that a weaver can explore through drafting, it must be remembered that design and weaving life is not limited to just loom-controlled patterns. One can also try the finger-manipulated techniques on the harness loom—either in conjunction with loom-controlled effects or by themselves as the entire fabric.

PRIMITIVE LOOM WEAVING   On primitive looms the warping and other prior-to-weaving arrangements go quickly, but the actual weaving moves much more slowly than on a harness loom. There are certain finger-manipulated techniques that do not require a shed. These can be done with equal ease on either a harness or primitive loom. Once a shed is needed for any interlaced structure, the pace slows down considerably. Under the classification of primitive loom are such types as the warp-weighted and Salish that have no shedding devices at all; and the ground, Navajo, backstrap, and frame looms, that do have shedding devices.

Undoubtedly, when man first started weaving on a loom, he passed the weft over and under the warp threads by hand. In the next row he returned the filling by keeping the over-and-under arrangement, but now going over the warp end he had previously gone under, and under the one he had gone over. This simple weaving came to be known as plain weave and is the basis for the two sheds normally provided for on a primitive loom by the shed stick and heddle bar. All extra sticks or bars are for special patterns.

When the shed stick is inserted, it goes under every other thread—be the odd-numbered threads, for example. The heddle cord or string heddles that are attached to the heddle bar are then run under every even-numbered thread. These will form the countershed. In recent years the addition of a **rigid heddle** to some backstrap and frame looms has served to take the place of both shed stick and heddle bar and give both the first shed and the countershed.

To get plain weave, the shed stick is turned on its side pushing up the odd threads and the first shed is opened. The filling is inserted across the shed on a small stick or **bobbin** shuttle, a butterfly, one of the small tapestry bobbins or any other small, lightweight filling carrier. The filling is beaten down in place using a batten or hand beater. The different types of primitive looms have beating arrangements of either batten or hand beater or the use of both—depending on the loom used and how heavy the beat needs to be. Whenever a hand beater, comb, or fork is used, the beating down starts at the point the filling entered the shed and goes on with short, sharp taps to the side where it exits from the shed. This method allows for as much laxity in the filling yarn as possible, so that it interlaces fully with the warp.

There are two ways to make the second shed that has the warp threads attached through the heddle cord or string heddles. The basic action is that the string has to be pulled down or up to lift the warp ends. Whether down or up depends on the position of the loom—whether it is a **horizontal loom** or a vertical one.

The heddle bar can be lifted so that all warp ends attached are lifted at one time. An extra shed stick or the batten is placed inside the shed and turned on its side to prop open these warp ends. The filling is then inserted and the rest proceeds as for the first shed. The shed stick or batten is removed and then reinserted every time this shed is made by the heddle bar. This would also be true for all pattern heddle bars.

The cord or heddles can also be pulled down or up in groups in whatever amount the weaver's hand can grasp comfortably. The filling is inserted through the warp in small sections until it reaches the other selvage. This is a much slower method than lifting the heddle bar; however, when the weaving is not going selvage to selvage, it works just as well. One hand grasps the heddles and pulls, while the other hand inserts the filling. The filling is pushed from one open section to the next. The beating down is done after the filling is all the way through. It starts at the point of insertion if a hand beater is used. Many contemporary artist-weavers who work on both small and wall-sized frame looms prefer to pick up both sheds by hand—without the use of heddle bar or shed stick—feeling that in this way there is more intimacy and rapport with the work.

Weaving on a primitive loom can proceed from the bottom stick or edge to the top stick or edge. The amount that can be woven is limited to the space between the top and bottom. However, there are also circular warps that rotate around a frame loom, thereby giving twice the amount of warp or weaving space. Normally the warp is attached to a **warp end bar** to facilitate pushing the warp around the loom. If this type of circular warp is used, then the weaver works from the bottom up until the fell is too close to the heddle rod to open a good shed. Then the bar is pushed so that the weaving moves downward and more empty warp is exposed below the heddle rod. Tension devices may be relaxed before the warp is moved and then adjusted for tightness after the warp is in its new position. The Navajo loom has a unique feature for both controlling the tension and bringing the fell down to where it is always comfortable for the weaver. However, this feature does not extend the length of the warp beyond the top and bottom bars. The same is true of the backstrap loom, where the weavers roll up the fabric around a bottom or first stick to bring them closer to the fell, which is constantly moving away from them. It is a feature for comfort, but not one that gives any additional warp length.

Weaving on primitive looms, in most cases, moves upward from the bottom toward the top. However, on warp-weighted looms it must move down from the top; and on other looms, such as simple frame looms where there is no heddle bar, it can also move from the top down if the weaver so desires.

When the weaving is completed, the weaver cuts the project off at the warp end bar or at the top and bottom stick or edge. There is much less waste than on a harness loom—in some cases no waste at all, since the empty warp left protruding from the cloth can be made into a fringe. It is also possible to make a four-selvaged piece on a primitive loom by weaving from one end of the warp completely to the other—from the point where the warp goes around a stick, cord, or nail at the bottom to where it does so at the top. The weaving at the finish is done with **bodkin**s, or wooden or metal **needle**s, since the fell is too close to the end of the warp for a shed to open, and the weaving has to be done with a needle going over and under to make the interlacing.

FINISHING   Whether the weaving has been done on a harness or primitive loom, most woven items have to have some type of **finishing** done to them. This could range from the simplest tying of a **fringe** to more involved procedures like **sponging** or **napping.** Exactly what should be done depends on the fiber, yarn, dye, and technique or weave used, and what the end purpose of the woven piece is.

Usually the first finishing step for all pieces is the darning in of broken ends and of the beginning and ending tails of filling yarn. In some cases there is a different first finishing step that involves **overcasting** or **hemstitching** the first and last picks before the item is taken off the loom. This is done to secure these picks and prevent the fabric from unraveling. Machine stitching is another way of doing this after the piece has left the loom.

Many times the weaver feels the need for a more decorative way of securing these picks and makes a **finishing edge** or a fringe. Some techniques that could be used include making a **braided fringe, Damascus edge, looped edge, overhand knot**s on groups of fringe ends, **Philippine edge, plied fringe, Swedish braid, twined edge,** or **wrapped edge.** Groups of fringe ends can also have wrapping or **whipping** around them, and more fringe or **pompon**s or **tassel**s can be added. If there has been a **weft fringe** left or added, then this also must be taken care of in some way to assure it stays intact and the selvage ends do not shift out.

Darning the warp ends back into the edge of the fabric gives a neat, straight edge and is often used in conjunction with **hemming.** As an alternative to a fringe, decorative edge, or hemming there is sewing on a **binding** and hemming that to the back of the cloth. Finishing details can often be planned as the warp is being made. Other times it is not until the piece is finished on the loom that it becomes apparent what type of edge would best complete it.

It is quite common and often necessary to wash finished items in order to get yarn **blooming** and proper fabric **shrinkage,** as well as rid the item of surface dirt in the yarn picked up during weaving. Many items do not get the desired **hand** until they are washed. This washing is usually done in lukewarm to hot water with a mild detergent. The exact temperature and type of soap depend on the yarn used.

Steam pressing is one way of getting shrinkage without washing, although this could be only the most minimal type of shrinkage. Again, this would depend on the fiber used and also on how extreme the steam pressing is. When done in conjunction with **blocking** it can be quite a severe process. Controlled, partial shrinkage can be obtained by a sponging procedure, such as **London shrinkage. Fulling** is possibly the most extreme method of shrinkage, whereas **tentering** is done to avoid shrinkage.

If the weaver wants a soft, furry surface to the fabric, then this is done after other finishing has been completed by **teasing** or napping the fabric with a **teasel** or brush. Sometimes narrow-loom pieces are woven in sections meant to be joined together after all sections are done. This **joining** of pieces is done with a **lacing stitch** of one variety or another, a decorative stitch, or a technique like crochet if it suits the woven item.

Just as the weaver expands the use of materials, so too does the weaver go beyond simple projects to expand the use of color and **texture** through experiments with **color blending, grouped thread**s, and **mixed warp**s. Exploring new weave structures, patterns, techniques, and shapes can be an endless process of discovery. To help in the experimentation, there are **sampler blanket**s or **gamp**s for fabric research, **maquette**s for wall hangings, and **reeling**s of proposed warp colors and yarns. The experiments and finished projects should be documented by the **weaver's record**s so that they can be duplicated, improved upon, or used for reference.

Although the hand techniques, such as braiding, plaiting, and twining, were the predecessors of weaving today, the path has now taken a different twist. Weavers are going to and rediscovering these techniques after having become involved with fiber through weaving. They incorporate these techniques into their weaving or use them alone for their own beauty. Some of this rediscovery has been due to a renewed interest in all aspects of Indian weaving and the weaving of other cultures not involved with looms as today's weavers know them.

Looking at items such as the **Assumption sash** and the **Hopi Indian wedding sash** has led people to try first simple plaiting, and from there go into more complex methods, such as **chevron plaiting, double plaiting, multiple band plaiting, frame plaiting,** and **sprang.** Ojibwa weaving, Salish weaving, and **taaniko twining** have led to a renewed interest in **weft twining** with its **half turns, full turns, counter twining,** and **twill twining. Weft chaining** and **meshwork,** produced by looping and netting, are just two more of the rediscovered techniques weavers now use in their working of **fiber fabricated** two- and three-dimensional objects.

weaving. Basketry. A term used to describe the cumulative **stroke**s, or stitches, used to make up the fabric of a **basket.**

weaving. Macramé. Macramé cords can be woven together to form open, loosely meshed areas, often within a diamond-shaped space formed by rows of diagonal **half hitch**es. Cords are worked in a basic under/over weaving fashion to form an all-over grid. See ill.

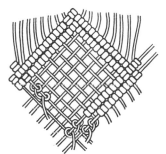

Weaving

weaving. Papercrafts. The traditional concept of interweaving to form a meshwork is adapted to papercrafts by using paper strips. The strips can be cut individually, then combined in various designs. Or slits can be cut within a sheet of paper, making a frame for inserting varicolored strips in and out of the background slits.

In **papier mâché,** weaving can be used for **molding** meshwork forms over a **support,** such as a bowl or wastebasket. Apply a light coating of petroleum jelly to the support to prevent sticking. Tear long newspaper strips about 3" wide, soak with **papier mâché paste,** then smooth away excess paste with the fingers. Roll each strip until it is about 1" wide or less, depending on the size of the final design, with the torn, ragged edges turned under. Place an uneven number of strips over the form in one direction, then weave the strips in and out in the other direction. Turn under all raw ends. It may be helpful to add a dab of **white glue** where strips cross to ensure proper adhesion. Allow the woven form to dry completely before removing it from the support. See ill.

Weaving paper strips

weaving spool. Toys. (Also called spool loom.) A simple weaving toy used to make cords or "horse reins." A wooden spool is used. Four brads or small nails are pounded into it at one end to form a circle. Yarn, drawn through the spool opening, is looped around the brads. Each loop is, in turn, drawn over the yarn line and the end of the brad, making a new loop.

web. Weaving. A handweaving term for the finished product of the interlacing of **warp** and **filling.** It pertains to the structural part of the cloth as opposed to any pattern effect in it. Handweavers also use the term "web" when referring to the woven fabric between **breast beam** and **fell.**

web stitch. Needlepoint. This stitch gives the appearance of diagonal weaving. It works up quickly, gives a secure backing, and works well on a large mesh **canvas,** making it a practical stitch for rugs.

Long diagonal stitches are taken first, then small **tent stitch**es are worked over them. Each row of tent stitches alternates in position with those of the previous row.

Come up at A and go down at B, making a tent stitch over one mesh of the canvas. Come up at C one mesh above and one mesh to the left of B. Go in at D, one mesh below and one mesh to the right of B, making a long slanting stitch. Come up at E one mesh immediately above B (**a.**).

Go in at F, making a small stitch across the long slanting one, and come up at G on the other side of the stitch, one mesh below and one to the right of E (**b.**).

Go in at H, over the stitch, one mesh to the left and one below G. Come up at J (**c.**). Now make another long slanting stitch, close to the previous one (**d.**).

Web stitch

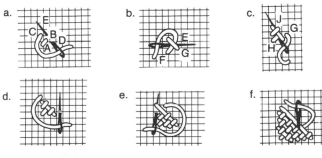

Work all the way back, placing slanting stitches across the line alternately with those of the previous row (**e.**). The finished effect has the appearance of diagonal weaving (**f.**). See ill.

wedding pillow. Stitchery. A **pincushion** traditionally made as a gift for a bride. Usually names or monograms were included with a date, and often a heart. Sometimes new pins were stuck in it, arranged to form a shiny heart or spell a name.

Wedding Ring. Quilts. A **pieced block** pattern that shows a square within an octagon, suggesting a ring or **wreath** shape. This block is sometimes incorporated into larger, more complex blocks. **Crown of Thorns** is one design that uses the Wedding Ring as its central motif.

wedge. Stained Glass. See **cutting anvil.**

wedge weave. Weaving. A variation on the **tapestry weave,** used by the Navajo Indians as a means of creating a zigzag color pattern in their blankets. It is a diagonal build-up created by the **filling,** which begins gradually on only a few **warp end**s, but then includes more and more ends as the work grows obliquely until the desired angle is achieved. The build-ups are wedge shapes which produce tension on the warp threads because of their angle and because of the unequal amount of filling that is placed between them. This pushes or bulges out the warp ends at the **selvage**s. At regular intervals, the Navajo weavers reversed the direction of the build-up, or zigzag, and the selvage bulge was scalloped in a large curve. This distortion gave rise to the second name for this technique—"pulled warp." See ill. Also see **Navajo weaving.**

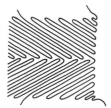

Schematic drawing of the angle of weaving in wedge weave and introduction of new colors at an angle

wedging. Ceramics. A method of removing air from clay. Wedging increases **plasticity,** density, and consistency in a **clay body.** Also see **deairing, kneading.**

wedging board. Ceramics. A surface for **wedging** or **kneading** clay; it is usually made of plaster or a slightly porous material. This allows the clay to come away cleanly. The surface should not be so porous as to dry out the clay too rapidly.

weed vase. Ceramics. See **Ceramics: Form.**

weeping willow. Quilts. See **Quilts: Quilting.**

weft. Basketry. (Also called binder and woof.) The name given to the **active element** in a basket. It is the binding element in all basketry and is used to tie together or secure the structural **element** or **warp.** Also see **weaver.**

weft. Quilts. Stitchery. (Also called filling thread, woof.) The **crosswise** thread in a woven **fabric,** going from **selvage** to selvage. In cutting, this may be referred to as "**cross-grain**" or "across the grain."

weft. Weaving. Another word for **filling.** It is just as popular and common to use "weft" as "filling"; which term is used is sometimes just a matter of locale or teaching. "Weft" is an English term and is older, while "filling" is new and American. "Woof" is older than either, and comes from early Anglo-Saxon usage and was the true word for **warp**; through the years it somehow became interchangeable with weft and has remained so, although it is rarely used today.

weft chaining. Rugmaking. Weaving. A technique in which loops of **weft** or **filling** enclose the **warp end**s and form the surface of the **cloth** or are made to be a decorative addition on the surface. The loops look like a chain and are made in the same manner as a chain stitch in crochet. Usually, though, fingers are used instead of a crochet hook. Chaining can be worked across the warp ends going either from right to left or left to right. If the starting direction is reversed with each row, the loops slant in opposite direction and a type of herringbone effect is achieved. The chaining does not have to go in a straight line, but can be curved or slanted as desired. Chaining can make up the entire surface of a fabric and the loops can be loose, tight, raised, or pulled in. Chaining can also be used in certain areas of a woven piece for design emphasis or texture, or it can be interspersed with rows of weaving or **finger-manipulated** techniques. Weft chaining is akin to weft **twining** in that it encloses the warp ends. It can be used in combination with weft twining.

To do chaining, the warp is in a closed **shed** position. The filling yarn can pull off from a spool or ball of yarn. Going from right to left, tie the filling yarn to the first outside right warp end. Place the yarn under the warp. Pull enough of the yarn up before the first end to form a small loop. Lay this loop over the first end and with the thumb and forefinger go through this loop to pick up more yarn from underneath to form another loop to the left of the first one and between ends 1 and 2. Pick up yet another loop between the second and third ends, and pull through the previous loop. This is continued until all the warp ends are enclosed in loops. Either continue now with a second row moving from left to right, or cut the yarn from the spool or ball. If the chaining is continued, a loop or two should be made of the filling yarn before beginning the second row in order to prevent drawing-in at the **selvage**s. If the yarn is cut, pull it through the last loop made and this will lock the chain and prevent it from undoing. If the last loop is not locked, then one tug of the filling yarn will undo the chain.

Another way to start chaining is to tie a loop in the filling yarn that will act as the first chained loop. This is laid on top of the first right warp end and the yarn is placed underneath and drawn up from below as explained above.

If **cord** is used in place of yarn, and the loops are pulled up tightly so that no slack is left in the chain, it acts to space the warp and hold it in place on a **tapestry** or **frame loom.** The chain goes at the very beginning of the weaving in this case, or it can be placed at the very end. It is usually removed after the weaving is finished and taken off the loom, but it can remain in and form a firm finished edge for the piece. When chaining is thus used as a **chain spacer,** the filling cord is tied to the sides of the frame, which helps to spread and stabilize the warp.

Variations on the basic chaining technique are possible in terms of color and texture changes. One such texture variation that produces knobs on the cloth surface is made by chaining a series of loops in the filling yarn above the surface of the fabric in between the enclosing of warp ends in the usual chaining technique. Another type of effect can be achieved by not enclosing every warp end separately, but rather skipping over several warp ends and then enclosing them in a single loop. Chaining in an open shed gives yet another effect. Feathers, beads, and other items can be caught and held in the chained loops. Weft chaining alternating with a **plain weave** ground makes a sturdy, heavy rug with an effect similar to **soumak.** If the yarn used for the chaining is heavier and softer than the **ground weave** yarn, the ground weave will be hidden and only the chaining will show on the surface. In a **flatweave rug,** chaining can be spotted in areas for design or texture interest. See ill.

Weft chaining being used as a chain spacer

weft-face. Weaving. See **filling-face.**

weft fringe. Weaving. A **fringe** produced by **filling** yarns either on the **selvage**s or inside the weaving. In the latter case, the filling ends are pulled up outside the **shed** and left on the surface of the weaving as texture and decoration and are either left loose or braided, wrapped, or otherwise finished. This type of weft fringe is found mainly on **wall hangings.** Another type of weft fringe produced at the selvage can be done on wall hangings as well as on pillows, garments, place mats, and napkins. The filling yarn can be either left out at the selvages indiscriminately or in measured lengths, going around extra guide threads at each selvage. These guide threads are put into the **reed** at a specific distance from the weaving **warp end**s. They control the width of the fringe, since the filling yarn goes around the guide threads during weaving. The guide threads are removed when the weaving comes off the **loom** and the filling loops are cut to make the fringe. **Hemstitching** is usually added to hold weft fringe in place, but the fringe can also be braided, knotted, or whipped. A measured selvage weft fringe, when used in conjunction with a warp fringe, is called a four-sided fringe.

weft looping. Rugmaking. Weaving. See **looping.**

weft protector. Rugmaking. Weaving. See **Damascus Edge, finishing edge, looped edges, Philippine Edge, twined edges.**

weft streaks. Weaving. Undesirable darker or lighter horizontal streaks in a fabric, usually due to uneven beating. A heavy **beat** will compress the **filling,** while a light beat will space it sparsely, and the color of the cloth will be affected according to how much of the filling is covering the **warp.** The weft streaks appear as darker or lighter shadows—sometimes just a few **picks** wide, other times perhaps extending for a half inch. Weft streaks are common among beginning weavers, and occur at the point where the weaver stops weaving to advance the warp and then begins to resume the **rhythm** in weaving again. Short streaks across the cloth are sometimes caused by imperfect dyeing of the filling yarn. Large darker and lighter areas of filling indicate that yarn was taken from different dye lots and the color match was not perfect.

weft twining. Rugmaking. Weaving. A method of **twining** in which pairs of **weft** threads twist or turn around each other while enclosing the warp threads. A standing frame of some sort is often used so that the warp threads are suspended from the top bar of the frame and are either free-hanging or weighted at the bottom to keep them taut and in position. Twining can also be done on a **frame loom.** It can proceed from top to bottom or bottom to top. In twining, each weft is a double strand—one strand going in front of the warp and the other in back of it. Then the strands are twisted or twined together before continuing on to the next warp thread or set of warp threads. The warp can be completely covered by the weft or left open in spaces.

Simple twining is done with **half-turn**s of the weft (**a.**). There is also twining with **full turn**s and **paired warp**s and **countered twining,** to mention a few of the possible variations on the technique. If each of the two strands are a different color, there are various patterns that can be obtained according to which of the above variations are used and the direction of the twist in each row. It is also possible to twine with three or four strands; besides the added color interest, a different textural look results in the twining (**b.**). If, for example, each of three strands goes under one warp and over two, and this order is followed in staggered progression, an effect of a twisted cord is obtained. Braiding the three strands as they go through their under one, over two order gives a braided effect. Another variation is to make loops out of one of the strands during simple twining. This can give a **pile** effect if the loops are closely spaced. Instead of each strand lying flat against the warp, one strand is always pulled up by hand or with the aid of some gauge, such as a knitting needle. All of the above is for **selvage** to selvage twining. Twining can also be used for tapestry by twining each color only in the area of the design it belongs to. It is a very effective means of making a rug, since a compactly twined fabric is firm and durable.

One of the most common ways most weavers employ twining is by using it to space the warp on a **frame loom.** Simple, or half-turn, twining is usually done just at the bottom of the warp, but it can be done at the top, as in **Navajo weaving.** By using attractive colors, it becomes a decorative device as well as a functional one. Its other functions are to hold in place the woven areas around a section of **exposed warp** in a tapestry or **wall hanging** and to outline a pattern area.

For any kind of selvage to selvage twining, the weft yarn should be about four times the warp width. If the weft yarn is being used as a spacer, it can be tied to the left-hand side of the frame loom, or it can be doubled and attached with a **lark's head knot** to the right side. If it is being used as the weft, it can be tied around the first warp end on the left or simply doubled in half with one strand lying over the warp and the other under. The twining is then started. The above directions are for left-to-right twining, but twining can just as well go from right to left. When using the twining as a spacer, the weft yarn ends can be tied to the right-hand side of the frame after the row of twining is completed. This keeps the warp stretched out and taut. See ill. Also see **Chilkat blanket, Ojibwa weaving, Salish weaving, taaniko twining, twill twining.**

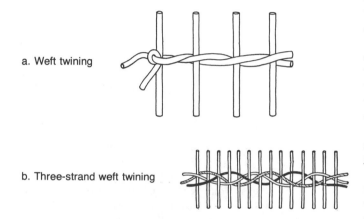

a. Weft twining

b. Three-strand weft twining

weft wrapping. Rugmaking. Weaving. See **Egyptian knot, soumak, Swedish knot, wrapping.**

weighing metals for centrifugal casting. Jewelry. A method for determining the amount of metal needed for a specific **wax model.** The wax model plus the equivalent of the weight of the sprue or sprues required for the model are weighed. This can be done simply by cutting lengths of wax the same as the sprues.

If sterling silver is used, the weight of the wax is multiplied by 10. To this amount add ¼ oz extra for small work, such as a ring, or ½ oz extra for larger work, such as a pin. This extra metal acts as a small reservoir of metal—in case it is needed during the slight **shrinkage** of the metal upon cooling. If 14k gold is used, multiply by 12 plus the extra ounces as above. If 18k gold, multiply by 18 plus the extra ounces as above. Also see **water displacement.**

weight. Leather. See **Leatherwork: Weight Designations and Grading.**

weighted toy. Toys. See **balance toy.**

weld. Dyeing. An ancient yellow **dyestuff** made from the leaves, stalk, flowers, and seeds of the weld herb or dyer's mignonette. A tall annual plant, it grows wild throughout the Mediterranean and was cultivated in England and Scotland. It was found in Swiss neolithic settlements, which perhaps could make it the most ancient of dyes. It was in use up until the advent of **synthetic dyes.** Weld is used on wool and silk. It gives a soft texture to wool. The color range is from a clear, bright yellow, using **alum** as a **mordant,** to lemon yellow and yellow olive, which occur with other mordants.

weld. Metalworking. A joint made by using two pieces of metal. The joint is formed by first **tack-welding** the ends of the pieces together, with the beginning ends of the seam edges about ¹/₁₆" apart and the ends of the seam edges about ⅛" apart (for a short weld). The separation is to compensate for the contraction of the molten metal, which will draw the seam opening together as the **welding** progresses. With a neutral **flame** on the welding **torch,** make a molten **puddle** with the tip of the flame on both pieces. Having achieved a deep puddle, introduce a **filler rod** into it and **run a bead** along the seam to complete the weld. There are five basic types of welds.

Butt weld

Two pieces of metal are placed so they butt up against each other edge to edge. Bevel only one edge of the joint if the metal pieces are ¼–⅜" thick, and both edges if over ⅜" thick. Butt welding is not a dependable weld for **forge welding.**

Fillet weld (also called T-weld)

Use this to join the edge of one piece of metal at right angles to the face of another.

Lap weld

Use this joint where extra strength is needed. Overlap the two pieces of metal and run a bead over both edges of the seam. When forge welding, overlap one part over the scarfed end of the other piece.

Corner weld

This joint is used to attach pieces of metal at right angles to each other at their edges.

Edge weld

Use this weld to join pieces of metal together flush at one edge.

welding. Metalworking. (Also called fusion welding.) The process of joining pieces of metal together by heating them to molten temperatures so that they flow together and fuse.

Forge welding is the oldest welding process known. It is commonly used in **blacksmithing** for joining wrought **iron** or mild **steel.** The metal is heated to a molten stage on the **forge,** then the parts to be joined are put together one on top of the other and hammered together quickly to fuse them.

Oxyacetylene welding (also called gas welding or oxacetylene fusion welding) uses a **flame** fueled by a mixture of **acetylene** and pure oxygen. It may be accomplished with or without **welding rods,** although a welding rod is usually heated to melting along with the **base metal** pieces to be joined to flow extra metal into the welded joint.

Braze welding (also called brazing and formerly called bronze welding) is a **soldering** rather than a true fusion welding. The **base metals** to be joined are not melted, but are joined by melting a **brazing rod** on the joint between them, which forms a surface alloy that adheres to the metal. Braze welding is used to join or repair cast iron, malleable iron, aluminum, copper, and brass, and to join dissimilar metals together. An **air-acetylene** flame instead of an oxyacetylene flame may be used because this process requires lower temperatures than oxyacetylene welding.

Arc welding (also called shielded-metal-arc welding, SMA, and electric arc welding) fuses the metals by the heat of an electric current or arc (generated by an **arc welder**) passing between an **electrode** rod and the metal. The metal core from the weld **puddles,** as in oxyacetylene welding. The burning electrode coating makes a shield of gas around the weld, preventing oxygen and nitrogen from combining with the metal and creating impurities. A **flux** is contained in the electrode that floats **slag** to the top of the molten metal, forming a protective crust over the weld. Arc welding is used more than oxyacetylene welding for welding metals over $^3/_{16}''$ thick.

Heliarc welding (also called TIG, tungsten insert-gas welding, tungsten arc welding, gas-tungsten-arc welding, GTA, and heliweld) fuses metals by the heat of an electric current or arc passing between a tungsten electrode mounted inside a gas shielding cup and the metal surfaces. The cup directs a blanket of inert gas (argon, helium, or a mixture of both) over the weld area. This gas shield prevents oxides (which prevent a good bond) from forming on the weld and overheating or burning of the electrode and weld puddle area. No flux is used. The electrode is not consumed as in ordinary arc welding, and the arc is very steady. This process is used on aluminum, **stainless steel,** copper-nickel **alloys,** and **bronze,** with or without **filler metal.** It is particularly useful for welding thin sheets and metals where the heat dissipates rapidly, for deep penetration of the welds on thick pieces, and for greater ease of temperature control when welding. Although this was predominantly an industrial process, it is now increasingly used in sculpture.

Metal-inert-gas welding (also called MIG, gas-metal-arc welding, and GMA) is another gas-shielded-electric welding process, very similar to heliarc welding. The major difference between them is that MIG has a consumable wire electrode that is continuously fed to the welding tip. A spool of filler metal is controlled by a trigger on the handle of the welding gun. The gun may also have a water-cooling system. The advantage of this method is high speed, which is good for production work. It is now primarily an industrial process, but may gain greater craft use in producing multiple editions of art objects. Also see **blacksmithing techniques, oxyacetylene welding equipment** and **Metalworking: Blacksmithing, Welding.**

welding flux. Metalworking. See **flux.**

welding goggles. Metalworking. See **eye protector, oxyacetylene welding equipment.**

welding rod. Metalworking. (Also called filler rod.) A wire or rod composed of **filler metal,** used to join seams in gas fusion **welding** and braze welding. There are many different types and sizes of welding rods; the choice depends on what metals are being joined and how thick they are. In general, the rod should be as thick as the metal being welded; with very thick metals, however, simply use the largest-diameter rod available and make several welding passes over the joint, or use arc-welding methods instead.

Some metals, such as **aluminum,** stainless **steel, brass,** and **bronze,** require the use of **flux** with the rod, and some rods have the flux already in them. Flux is also used to aid in welding dissimilar metals together (e.g., **copper,** brass, **nickel,** and nickel **alloys** can be welded to low-carbon steel and cast **iron** or one to another).

Welding rods of cast iron and steel are available for welding those metals. GA 60 welding rod is an alloy-steel rod used on low-carbon and low-alloy steels. Brazing (or brass filler) rod made of a type of brass called Muntz metal (60% copper, 40% **zinc,** and small quantities of other elements) can be used for braze-welding brass, bronze, nickel, and iron.

welding torch. Metalworking. See **oxyacetylene welding equipment.**

welt. Knitting. A pattern of horizontal ridges made by a combination of knit and purl rows. Also see **Knitting: Construction.**

welting. Stitchery. A decorative bound **edging** made by covering **cotton** cording with **bias fabric** strips. Welting is often inserted in a **seam** or used as edge trim.

welt patterns. Knitting. See **Knitting: Construction.**

West German glass. Stained Glass. See **German antique glass.**

West Indian mahogany. Woodworking. See **mahogany.**

wet charging. Enameling. See **wet inlay.**

wet firing. Ceramics. A type of **raku** in which clay is dried during the firing process. The newly thrown pot is placed into a preheated red-hot kiln.

wet inlay. Enameling. (Also called wet charging, wet packing.) A technique of applying **enamel** moistened with **binder** to the consistency of cream. The excess moisture should be absorbed with a paper tissue or eye dropper so that the enamel is just wet enough to flow. Sections of enamel are deposited with a **spatula** and packed into place with a **spreader.** Enamels can be juxtaposed or blended into each other. The colors will remain independent particles after firing. The edge of the piece may then be tapped or vibrated with a ripple-handed tool to set the enamel and draw up moisture. Limoges is a similar technique that uses moist enamel applied with a **sable brush,** often in multiple firings because layering colors offers a wider range of tints. Also see **cloison, cloisonné.**

wet-or-dry sandpaper. Jewelry. Metalworking. Plastics. Woodworking. See **abrasives.**

wet packing. Enameling. See **wet inlay.**

wet pan mixer. Ceramics. (Also known as a Simpson-type mixer.) A machine used for blending and grinding clay. Heavy wheels or rollers revolve in a circular iron pan, turning and mixing the clay. Also see **ball mill, pug mill.**

wet salting. Leather. See **Leatherwork: Tanning and Manufacture.**

wet spinning. Spinning. Commercially, the passing of **flax roving** through hot water immediately before **drafting** in order to soften the gummy binding matters. This permits the fibers to slip past one another easily. **Linen** line fibers are always wet-spun, as are a few other bast **fibers.** Tow fibers cannot be spun this way.

In handspinning, both line and tow are wet-spun to make the fibers adhere to each other and facilitate **spinning.**

wetting agent. Jewelry. See **debubblizer.**

wetting out. Batik and Tie-dye. Dyeing. Wetting a piece of fabric prior to immersion in the **dyebath,** to ensure thorough dye penetration. The fabric is soaked in lukewarm water (for **tie-dye**) or cool water (for **batik**) for 3–5 minutes; allow the excess water to drip off the fabric before immersing in the dyebath. Fabrics for tie-dye are wet-out after **binding.** Wet-out fabric will give a sharper **resist,** although this step is not essential for batik or tie-dye.

Fabrics for **dyeing** are wet-out in a solution of warm water and powdered soap for 10 minutes or until saturated. Wetting out promotes dye penetration and is necessary for natural and synthetic dyes. Also see **level dyeing, mordant** and **Dyeing: Synthetic Dyes, Natural Dyes.**

whale teeth. Ivory and Bone Carving. Whale teeth are considered inferior to most other varieties of ivory, partially because of their small size. The sperm whale is the only large whale with teeth, usually 40–50 of a strong constitution. It was upon these teeth that the Yankee whaler practiced his art of **scrimshaw.**

Fresh tooth is softer and easier to work than older teeth that have dried and hardened. The tip is softest and takes the highest polish. The outer enamel is softer than the inner enamel; power tools are recommended when cutting recesses for inlay. The long, curved, outer side of the tooth provides the greatest carving area. The internal hollow of a whale tooth may extend ¼–⅔ the length of the tooth. Also see **Ivory and Bone Carving: Preparation, Carving, Finishing.**

wheat ears. Lacemaking. See **leaf stitch.**

wheat paste. Batik and Tie-dye. Puppets. Toys. A powdered mix that is stirred into water to make a mixture that is about the consistency of heavy cream. It is used as the adhesive in **papier mâché** or **pulp mâché** work. Wheat paste is available at hardware, wallpaper, and department stores and at hobby shops. It is inexpensive and can be purchased in small quantities. If wheat paste is unavail-

able, a mixture of flour and water may be substituted. Also see **glove-type hand, paste batik, sawdust mâché.**

wheat paste. Papercrafts. See **wallpaper paste.**

wheel. Jewelry. See **buff, grinding wheel.**

wheel. Lacemaking. Tatting. A basic **motif** in **needle lace** and tatting that may be used as part of the **design** theme or as a **filling.**

With needle and thread, work an even number of long stitches from the center outward. These foundation threads, called **bars,** resemble the spokes of a wheel. In the **darning stitch,** work the thread around and around, over and under the bars, to about half the radius of the wheel. Never fill the wheel entirely with stitches. By working the stitches over an even number of bars, a different effect will be achieved in the wheel than by working over and under an uneven number of bars. See ill.

Wheels

a. Even number of bars   b. Uneven number of bars

wheel. Spinning. A term that can mean the **driving wheel** on a **spinning wheel,** or can be used as an everyday reference to the spinning wheel itself. Also see **treadle wheel, wool wheel.**

wheel. Stained Glass. Another name for a **glass-cutter** with a hardened-steel-wheel cutting edge.

wheel. Toys. See **Toys: Wheeled Toys.**

wheel boy. Spinning. See **wheel finger.**

wheel dolly. Spinning. See **wheel finger.**

wheel dresser. Gemcutting. A tool used to true the edge of a **grinding wheel.** Through use, the edge of the grinding wheel may become deformed and bumpy, a condition which can **fracture** delicate stones. Various wheel dressers are used to flatten the working surface of the wheel. A diamond-point wheel dresser gives a fast rough. The seven-diamond point renders a very smooth resurfacing.

These tools are held on a tool rest just barely touching the high spots on the wheel; they are moved back and forth from side to side across the wheel until a new true surface is achieved. This process is called dressing the wheel. See ill.

a. Rotary wheel dresser with steel teeth

b. Diamond point

c. Seven-diamond point

d. Diamond bar dresser

wheeled boat. Toys. A toy **boat** made as a **floor toy** and never meant to be used on water. **Noah's ark**s are usually either wheeled or flat-bottomed, for use as **pull toys** or **push toys**.

wheeled toy. Toys. Any of countless toys that use one or more wheels and one or more **axle**s. The toys can be pushed or pulled, and include barrows, cars, carts, **wagon**s, coasters, and trains.

Wheeled toys include small windup or mechanical toys with wheels partially hidden from view by the outer shell of the toy. Often made as mice, bugs, or other small animals, when wound up and released they appear to run erratically around on any smooth surface. Also see **Toys: Wheeled Toys**.

wheel finger. Spinning. (Also known as wheel boy, wheel dolly.) A wooden stick measuring about 7–9″ long that a spinner used to keep the **wool wheel** turning while backing away from the wheel during the spinning of the yarn. A knob at the end of the wheel finger caught at the spokes of the wheel and turned it.

wheel head. Ceramics. A flat, circular slab mounted to revolve on the vertical axis of a flywheel. It is the place where clay is thrown on a **potter's wheel**.

Wheel of Chance. Quilts. A **pieced four-patch block** design that forms a circle in a square; the circle is formed from **fan**s. See ill. Also see **Harvest Sun**.

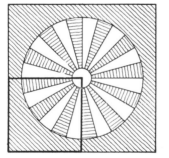

Wheel of Chance

Wheel of Fortune. Quilts. A name given to any of several **pieced quilt** patterns. One uses radiating strips of color surrounded by another circle of radiating strips of color. Another version is identical to **Burgoyne Surrounded**, and a third uses Wheel of Fortune interchangeably with **Hearts and Gizzards**. See ill. Also see **Quilts: Quilting**.

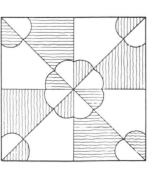

Wheel of Fortune

wheel of life. Toys. See **zoetrope**.

Wheel of Mystery. Quilts. See **Winding Ways**.

wheel rake. Jewelry. Metalworking. A flat, two-handled piece of wood with several rows of broad metal teeth, used to clean **buffs** (except felt buffs) when they have been overcharged or need cleaning. Each compound should have its own buff. A wheel rake can also be used to restore the original surface of a buff or to reshape it for special uses. A hacksaw blade can also be used if a wheel rake is not available. A piece of metal or wood, if the **wheel** is allowed to run against its edge, will remove compound from an overcharged wheel. Also see **buffing**.

whetstone. Leather. See **Leatherwork: Care and Maintenance of Tools**.

whetstone. Woodworking. See **sharpening stone**.

whetting. Woodworking. (Also called honing.) The general operation of **sharpening** a chisel, blade, or other tool on its cutting edge. It is performed after all the rough **grinding** is done and before the final stropping of the **bevel**. Keeping cutting tools sharp is one of the most basic operations in woodworking, as well as being a safety measure; a dull blade requires more pressure to cut with and is thus more dangerous to use. Also see **sharpening** and **Woodworking: Sharpening**.

Whig Rose. Quilts. Any of a great variety of **appliqué** designs depicting roses with leaves. They are usually **set in** an **all-over pattern**. Both the Whigs and the Democrats claimed this quilt design, inspired by the presidential campaign of 1840, so it is known as both Whig Rose and Democrat Rose. Slight variations in the design produce Whig Rose with Buds and Mexican Rose patterns. Whig Rose and many of its variations are called **Harrison Rose**, after William Henry Harrison.

whimmydiddle. Toys. (Also called gee-haw whimmydiddle, hooey stick, propeller stick.) An **American folk toy** carved from three pieces of green **hardwood**. The toy was originally made by the American Indians and is still made by them in some parts of the Southwest and in Appalachia. A small propeller is attached by a nail to the end of the basic notched wood stick. Another smaller stick is rubbed over the notches and the propellers are magically set in motion. The "gee-haw" refers to the left or right turns of the propeller and comes from the directions given by a driver to a team of horses to make them turn right or left. The direction of turn for the propellers is controlled by the

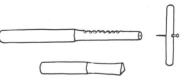
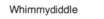

Whimmydiddle

way the fingers are placed when the rubbing stick is used. No two whimmydiddles perform exactly the same, and the twirling of the propeller varies greatly according to the way the operator uses the rubbing stick. Some whimmydiddles have extra branches, so that several propellers may be twirling at one time. See ill. Also see **action toy.**

whiplash. Toys. An **American folk toy** that consists of a flat, fish-shaped form, usually long and narrow, notched at one edge. This piece, sometimes called the dart, is sent flying through the air through the use of a stick to which a **thong** is securely attached. A loop at the end of the thong is slipped into the notch of the dart. (The dart angles back, away from the head of the fish shape.) The handle is held with one hand and the tail of the dart is held by the other. A whipping motion of the stick sends the dart or arrow on a speedy, spiraling flight of some distance. This toy should be used carefully and in a large open area.

whipped chain stitch. Crewel. Embroidery. A decorative **chain stitch** used for straight lines or borders.

First work a row of chain stitch. Then change to a blunt tapestry needle, come up at A, and slide needle through from B to C. Pick up the chain stitches only; do not go through the material. Continue, sliding the needle lightly under each chain, without pulling the thread too tightly. The finished effect should be like a raised cord. See ill. Also see **border stitch, whipping.**

Whipped chain stitch

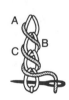

whipped fly stitch. Crewel. See **fly stitch, whipping.**

whipped wax. Candlemaking. A decorative technique used to embellish the outside of finished candles. Melt **paraffin** that has a low **melting point** to 190° F, allow it to cool until a slight film forms on the surface, then beat with a rotary beater until fluffy. A tablespoon of cornstarch can be added to increase the tackiness. The whipped wax, which resembles a frothy meringue, is spooned onto the candle.

whipping. Crewel. Embroidery. A means of decorating an already worked stitch. The whipping thread, often of a contrasting color, goes through only the **background fabric** at the beginning and at the end of a row of stitches. The action is over and around the ground stitch. The whipping stitch can be used effectively around a single row of stitches or to join several rows together for a border. It is important to maintain an even tension while working this technique. Whipping can be used on such stitches as the **chain stitch,** the **fly stitch,** the **running stitch,** and the **stem stitch.** Also see **interlaced cable chain stitch, whipped chain stitch.**

whipping. Rugmaking. Weaving. **Wrapping** the ends of a braided or loose **fringe** or **tassel** to prevent it from coming open. Whipping differs from other forms of wrapping in that the area wrapped is small; it is used primarily as a holding device and the manner of securing the wrapping yarn is unique to whipping. It is used in reference to fringe or tassel endings and not to wrapping as in **wall hangings** or **fiber sculpture.** The term "whipping" is common as a scout finishing technique of braiding items such as key or whistle chains.

To whip, take a strand of yarn about 10″–12″ long and lay 2″ of it in a loop along the area to be whipped. The loop should be pointing toward the bottom of the area. Wrap the yarn tightly around the area enclosing the loop, but leaving about ½″ of it exposed below the whipped area. Through this exposed loop goes the tail end of the whipping yarn. The other end of the loop is then pulled, drawing the loop with the tail end underneath the whipping. The exposed tips of the ends are trimmed and the closure is completely hidden. See ill.

Expanded view of whipping which proceeds downward and is then pulled to hide closing

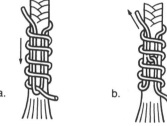

whipping. Stained Glass. (Also called strippling.) A technique for **painting on glass** in which the almost-dry paint is fanned by a badger brush to create wide varieties of shading. After the paint has been applied to the glass and it is still wet, the badger—held between the thumb and forefinger and barely touching the drying paint—is fanned vigorously, creating a random pattern of clear glass and dense black. Also see **brush, matting, staining.**

whiproll. Weaving. See **back beam.**

whipstitch. Bookbinding. See **oversewing single sheets.**

whipstitch. Leather. A simple loop stitch used to join and decoratively finish the edges of leather. Leather is prepared for stitching with evenly spaced thong slits or round holes. Cut lace 2½ times the length of stitching area. Cut a point at one end and insert the opposite end between layers to be joined. Put the end of the lace through the first hole and pull taut. Bring the end around to the front of the leather again, looping it over the edge, and insert it into the second hole. Be sure the lace doesn't twist; the **grain** side or curved side should be out. Continue in the same way, keeping all the stitches at the same angle (**a.**). At the end, cut the lace and tuck the end between the layers being sewn (**b.**). Insert a dab of glue at the beginning and the end of the lace, between the layers. Tap glued ends with a **mallet.** See ill. Also see **edge stitch, Florentine lacing, lacing** and **Leatherwork: Sewing Leather.**

a. Starting the whipstitch

b. Tying the end

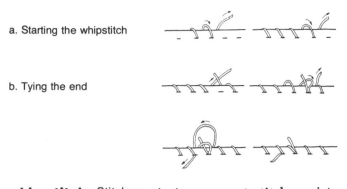

whip stitch. Stitchery. A tiny **overcast stitch** used in **appliqué** in which the **needle** moves in diagonal lines from the appliqué **fabric** to the **backing** fabric. It is a tight stitch and can be made very fine. See ill. Also see **hidden whip stitch.**

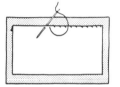

Whip stitch

whip top. Toys. A **top** or spinning toy believed to have originated in China. It is whipped, or set in motion, through the use of a **string** wound onto a **peg** or stick.

whirler. Ceramics. See **banding wheel.**

whirligig. Toys. Either of two distinct **American folk toys.** Both have blades or propellers that are activated by moving air.

In one, the air is blown through a **blow pipe.** It is like a **flipperdinger,** but instead of raising a **pith ball,** the air streams in this toy turns a **paddle wheel.**

The other toy consists of a wooden figure, usually a man, with blade or propeller arms. When moving air strikes the propellers, they spin or turn rapidly so that the arms swing in great circles next to the body. It can be set into action by holding the figure up high by means of a stick attached at the bottom and running with it.

Other whirligig figures are attached to a base and are set in motion by a breeze. By whatever means the arms are turned, the whirligig is a **wind toy.** See ill.

Whirligigs

whirly top. Toys. See **finger top.**

whistle. Toys. (Also called bamboo whistle.) A small toy or device used to make a clear, shrill sound by blowing or forcing air into a hollow tube or cavity or against a thin edge. Whistles are among the most popular of playthings throughout the world, and must be considered **eternal toys.**

A simple whistle consists of a narrow-necked bottle partially filled with water. When air is forced across the top of the opening by blowing on it, a sound is produced. The height of the water in the bottle affects the pitch. A collection of these bottles makes an amusing **sound toy.** When a group of people "play" these bottle whistles together, alternating turns to produce melodies, it is referred to as a bottle band.

Whistles can be made from reeds, bamboo, or any similar hollow stick. They are often carved from wood or formed in clay in the shape of birds, known then as bird whistles, or in animal forms. Metal whistles are more often manufactured than handmade, although simple ones can be devised from rolled tin.

To make a whistle, cut a section of bamboo (**a.**), notch, and fit with a plug (**b.**). The plug is cut flat on one edge (**c.**), then inserted and fixed in the bamboo so that the flat portion goes under the notched opening (**d.**). See ill. Also see **crow call.**

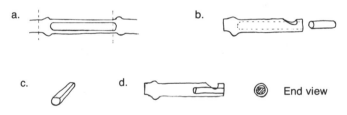

a.   b.

c.   d.   End view

white. Basketry. Peeled, dried, commercial willow used for light-colored basketry.

White Cross. Quilts. See **Chimney Sweep.**

white diamond polish. Jewelry. Metalworking. See **buffing compound, polishing compound.**

white glaze. Ceramics. A **stoneware** glaze that is often naturally white and opaque. **Kaolin** and flint clay are used to make white clay bodies. **Tin oxide** produces the purest and best quality white **opacifier.** Also see **magnetic filter.**

white glue. Mosaics. A polyvinyl acetate **adhesive** available through most hardware stores and hobby shops. White glue is an excellent adhesive that dries clear. It is not waterproof, and therefore should be used only on **mosaics** that will be completely protected from the elements. Casein glue, a type of white glue, also available in most hardware stores, is even less resistant to water than the polyvinyl acetate adhesive.

white glue. Puppets. Stitchery. Toys. Any of a wide variety of fast-drying trademarked **glue**s. All are standard household glues or all-purpose **adhesives** that are opaque white in liquid form but milky, semi-clear, or clear when dry.

They are effective on cardboard, paper, cord, string, tissue, fabric, and wood. While some are recommended for use on smooth surfaces such as metal and glass, there are other adhesives made especially for those materials. White glue can be thinned with water. Although weather-resistant, white glue is not waterproof and may soften on exposure to moisture or water. It is nontoxic, has no harmful fumes, and the hands can be cleansed of excess glue by washing in water. It is available at hobby shops and hardware or variety stores. Some common ones are Elmer's, Glu-bird, Glu-All, Wilhold, Ad-A-Grip, and Sobo. Also see **animal glue.**

white glue. Woodworking. See **adhesives.**

white gold. China and Glass Painting. A mixture of **gold** and **silver** that produces silver with a yellow cast. It doesn't tarnish as easily as silver. About six parts liquid bright silver are mixed with seven parts gold. After **firing,** apply a second time, using matte silver in the mixture instead of liquid bright silver, and refire.

white lead. Ceramics. A major low-fire **flux** that produces a glossy **glaze** with relatively few faults. The use of lead as a flux has a different effect on the **pigment oxides** used than do the alkaline compounds. The addition of calcium, **silica,** or **alumina** to a **lead glaze** will increase hardness and resistance to wear. Lead fumes are poisonous. Lead glazed jars should not be used to hold concentrated citric juices or vinegar. A nontoxic **lead silicate** can be produced by **frit**ting the lead with silica. Also see **boric acid.**

whitening. Stained Glass. (Also called whiting.) Powdered calcium carbonate or chalk, used finely ground. A ⅛" topping is placed on the **kiln tray** and dried out in the **kiln.** Glass is then placed on the tray. The layer of whitening helps prevent the glass from sliding around. It also protects the tray from direct heat and lengthens its life. The layer of whitening should be made level by slowly drawing a strip of **plate glass** the inside width of the tray over the whole length of the tray. Also see **pounce bag** and **Stained Glass: Glazing, Tools and Materials.**

white oak. Woodworking. See **oak.**

white-on-white quilt. Quilts. (Also called whitework quilt.) An **all-white quilt** made in a style that is sometimes referred to as English quilting or **English trapunto.**

white pine. Woodworking. See **pine.**

white rouge. Jewelry. See **buffing compounds.**

whitesmithing. Metalworking. See **blacksmithing.**

white work. Embroidery. White-on-white embroidery has been done all over the world, throughout history. Because it is monochromatic, the effect is gained by drawing out threads, cutting the background linen, or working with close stitching on a sheer or transparent background to obtain a shadow effect.

Hedebo is a Danish form of cutwork in which ovals and shapes of varying sizes are cut out of the **background fabric.** These are then bound closely around the edges in a monochromatic thread, and filled with lacy loops and wheels. Flat geometric stitches are worked between the cut-out shapes, also in monochromatic thread, to link them in an all-over design.

Broderie Anglaise is an English form of cut-work in which overcast round or oval eyelet holes form the design. Eyelet embroidery is often used as an edging, with scallops of buttonhole stitch as a finish to the border.

Richelieu is cutwork that is finished by working buttonhole stitches around the edges; it is bolder in effect than Broderie Anglaise. Using the **herringbone stitch** or the double **back stitch,** Richelieu is worked on the reverse side of a sheer fabric, such as organdy or **batiste,** to form a broad band of opaque stitching. It is occasionally combined with pulled work.

Pulled work is a form of openwork, traditionally associated with the Scandinavian countries, that became popular in England in the eighteenth century and was combined with quilting. Open-weave linen is drawn together with small geometric stitching, using a fine self-colored linen thread and a blunt **tapestry needle** (to avoid splitting the threads of the background). All kinds of lacy patterns—some very bold, some with more delicate open effects—can be made with this stitching, which has an effect similar to drawn-thread work.

Drawn-thread work is narrow or broad bands of thread drawn out of the background linen (which must have a clear-cut weave, whether it is fine, coarse, or even homespun in effect). The open bands are then secured on either side by **hemstitching,** and then woven or knotted in different patterns. Whole areas of linen may be worked with drawn threads by first outlining the area with trailing or **buttonhole stitch**es and then drawing out evenly spaced threads in either direction. The resulting grid may be whipped together to form a firm mesh to use as a basis for woven or interlaced patterns. Drawn-thread work is often combined with flat stitches.

Flat stitches are the counted **satin stitch** patterns that can be so effective in white-on-white embroidery. They became an integral part of the background, being worked out to cover an area with repeat designs to give the appearance of a brocaded weave.

Mountmellick work is an Irish embroidery in which the raised **Mountmellick stitch** gives an embossed effect to the design. Also see **self-color.**

whitework quilt. Quilts. See **all-white quilt, trapunto.**

whiting. Amber Carving. Beadwork. Ivory and Bone Carving. Whiting is **chalk** that has been ground and then purified by removing silica particles. It is used as a mild polishing agent for soft organic materials and metal. Also see **beadmaking.**

whiting. Ceramics. Whiting is the major high-fire **flux** that produces a harder surface than lead or alkaline compounds. For this reason, small amounts are added to low fire **glaze**s. Like the other fluxes, whiting has an effect on certain **pigment oxide**s, especially chrome green. Whiting has a limited use in the **clay body,** where a small amount reduces porosity and lower vitrification temperatures. Also see **vitrify, wollastonite.**

whiting. China and Glass Painting. A calcium carbonate powder mixed with water to form a paste that is painted on the **kiln** shelf to prevent glass from sticking to the shelf during **firing.**

whiting. Jewelry. Metalworking. See **abrasives.**

whiting. Plastics. See **filler.**

whiting. Stained Glass. See **whitening.**

whittling. Puppets. Toys. A simple **wood carving** process, most often used on small projects, accomplished with a jackknife or carver. Sometimes "whittling" refers to aimless carving having no purpose, but it is usually done to make small toys, **whistle**s, decoys, or ornamental pieces. Whittling requires no tools other than the pocketknife. **Soap carving** is a simplified form of whittling.

whittling. Woodworking. Whittling is **woodcarving** on a small scale. Shapes are carved from wood by hand with a knife. Whittling is employed to make small woodware and general wood pieces too small for machines.

Whittling tools are used in a combination of strokes and grips. In the full-hand, straight away whittling grip, the knife is held as you hold a hammer (**a.**). It uses the entire hand, wrist, and arm, and is therefore difficult to control. The cut is made away from oneself. In the thumb grip, the knife is gripped and used as in the straight away grip, but the thumb is held across the back of the blade for more control (**b.**). The full-hand, pulling cut grip is also the same, except that the knife is drawn toward oneself (**c.**). It is a strong grip but offers little control. In the forefinger grip the index finger is held over the back of the blade for making cuts or incising lines (**d.**).

For a straight cut, use a full-hand grip. Push the blade through the wood at right angles. It is good for removing waste wood quickly.

For a sweep cut, use either a thumb or a full-hand grip. Draw the blade through the wood diagonally in a sweeping motion. A sweep cut is generally used to produce long, rounded cuts.

For a stop cut, make an incision by drawing the blade along a line, using a forefinger grip. A stop cut is made to prevent further cuts from splitting past this cut.

A tip cut uses the tip of the blade with either a full-hand or forefinger grip. It is used to drill holes or for putting in details.

A chisel cut is a short stroke used to round off a shape by removing small pieces. The blade is slightly twisted in the cut, using wrist action.

A scraping cut is used to remove rough edges and small shavings by scraping the blade perpendicularly over the wood. Scraping cuts are generally very hard on the knife edge.

A saw cut employs a forefinger grip and is used to saw through a piece of soft wood (such as balsa) without crushing the fibers.

A rocking cut uses a full-hand grip. This cut is used to cut off or make a strong, deep incision by rocking the blade back and forth in the cut. See ill. Also see **Woodworking: Whittling and Woodcarving.**

Whittling grips

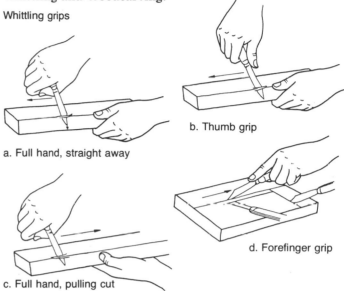

a. Full hand, straight away

b. Thumb grip

c. Full hand, pulling cut

d. Forefinger grip

whittling tools. Woodworking. The most basic tool used for **whittling** is the clasp knife, in which the blade closes into the handle. The two most common types of clasp knives are the penknife, a lightweight knife with two thin blades measuring up to 3″ long when closed, and the jackknife, a heavier knife often with only one blade, 3–5″ long. These knives use the following type of blades common to whittling:

Pen blade

The most common all-around whittling blade. It is generally small, about 1½–2″ long. The blade has relatively straight sides with both edges slightly rounding to a point (**a.**).

Cut-off pen blade

This blade is about the same size and general shape as the pen blade, but it has a sharp, strong point due to the cut off angle of the tip. It is good for corners, **chip carving,** and deep, straight outline or tip cuts (**b.**).

Clip blade

This generally longer blade provides a rounded cutting edge together with a long, sharp point. It is good for general cutting and smoothing, and for deep cutting of hard-to-reach places (**c.**).

Spey blade

A short blade with a very strong, convex tip. It is good for tip cutting and smoothing of background work and for cutting round grooves (**d.**).

Spear blade

A strong, larger version of the pen blade, used for heavy cutting and roughing out a shape (**e.**).

Punch blade

A medium-light blade used to ream or drill holes. It is tapered with a sharp edged groove that's the length of the blade (**f.**). See ill. on next page.

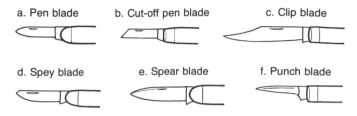

a. Pen blade   b. Cut-off pen blade   c. Clip blade

d. Spey blade   e. Spear blade   f. Punch blade

whizzgig. Toys. An old **momentum toy,** similar in principle to the **moulinet,** and in design to the **water cutter.**

whole binding. Bookbinding. See **full binding.**

whole cane. Basketry. See **cane.**

whole cloth quilt. Quilts. **Coverlets** or **quilts** made from full pieces of yardage. No **piecing** was utilized and the fabric was not cut into **blocks.** Traditionally, printed fabrics were used for these bedcovers. Today, "whole cloth" quilts are made from printed sheets, and baby quilts are made from printed **flannel.** Usually **quilting** outlines the designs in the fabric, although some are simply **tied quilt**s.

whole stitch. Lacemaking. A basic movement in making **bobbin lace.** To form the whole stitch, two pairs of **bobbins** are used. The pairs cross, twist, **cross,** and **twist.** This constitutes the whole stitch, and therefore it is composed of two **half stitch**es. Also see **cloth stitch.**

whorl. Spinning. The weight placed at the end of a hand **spindle** to maintain the revolving motion necessary for **spinning.** It comes in various shapes and sizes but most commonly is a small disk-shaped object of clay, stone, wood, metal, ivory, or bone. Some whorls are beautifully carved and ornamented—particularly those coming from ancient times. The location of the whorl on the spindle depends on the manner of spinning. It could be near the lower end of the spindle, near the center or near the upper end. The whorl evolved into the pulley on a **spinning wheel.** The **driving band** connects it to the wheel, so when the wheel is revolved, this acts upon the pulley and it in turn revolves the spindle. Also see **bobbin pulley, spindle pulley.**

wick. Candlemaking. The device that draws up the melted wax by capillary action to the flame, which melts more wax to further feed itself. The development of the wick must be considered one of man's major breakthroughs. The earliest wicks were most likely hollow reeds or stalks. These gave way to crudely manufactured, twisted plant wicks, which were gradually replaced by loose-spun strands of cotton—until around 1825, when the **braided wick** was invented. This allowed the wick tip to drop outside the flame area, thereby greatly reducing the problem of **smoking.** The modern candlewick is a complex length of tightly braided or plaited threads, usually bleached and treated with a **mordant.** Wicks are sized according to the number of ply, or threads. Care should be taken in selecting the right size wick for each candle project. Too thick a wick for the diameter of the candle can cause smoking; too small a wick can cause **dripping.** Also see **Candlemaking: Selecting the Wick.**

wicker. Basketry. See **willow.**

wicker-weave. Basketry. The name given any of the variety of **strokes** or **weaves** used in wickerwork. Also see **Basketry: Woven Basket-Construction.**

wickerwork. Basketry. Wickerwork is a form of **woven basketry** that uses **willow rod**s as the primary material. It consists of a system of rigid willow **stakes,** the **warp,** held together by flexible willow **weaver**s, the **weft.** The most common **stroke** is a simple over one, under one pattern. See ill.

Wickerwork is also the name given specifically to **willow** basketry. Also see **Basketry: Woven Basket Construction.**

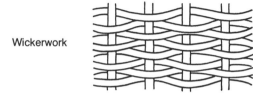

Wickerwork

wick holder. Candlemaking. A small square metal piece with prongs to hold the wick in place at the bottom of the candle. The wick holder is often used with **container candle**s where the **wick** cannot be inserted through a hole in the bottom of the receptacle.

wick hole. Candlemaking. With molds where it is impossible to insert the wick before pouring the wax, a hole must be bored in the wax after it has hardened in the **mold.** This can best be done with a heated **ice pick** or skewer. Also see **Candlemaking: Wicking the Mold.**

widening circles. Quilts. See **Quilts: Quilting.**

wig. Jewelry. See **mop.**

Wild Geese Flying. Quilts. See **Birds in Flight.**

Wild Goose Chase. Quilts. A **geometric pieced block** design made from either two or three patches. See ill. Also see **Birds in Flight, two-patch.**

Wild Goose Chase

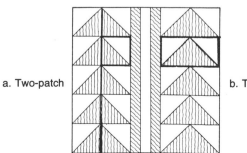

a. Two-patch   b. Three-patch

willemite. Gemcutting. Zinc silicate **crystal**lized in the or-thorhombic system with **hardness** of 5½, **specific gravity** of 4, and yellow-green **color**.

William and Mary stitch. Needlepoint. See **rice stitch**.

Williams facet head. Gemcutting. See **faceting unit**.

williamsite. Gemcutting. See **serpentine**.

willow. Basketry. (Also called hedgerow, osier, wicker, withe, withy; the Latin name is *salix*.) The traditional basketry material grown in cultivated beds or picked wild from hedgerows. Because it is not machined to a specific diameter (as **cane** or reed is), each shoot or **rod** must be carefully graded before making it into a basket. By nature it tends to be stiffer than cane and tends to kink rather than **flow;** for this reason it is usually not recommended for beginners.

Willow rods are cultivated in three species. The **sticks** of *Salix vinimalis* are often called osier. They are noted for their large size, coarse outer texture, and large **pith** centers. They are used for making large baskets and chair frames. The rods of *Salix triandia* have been cultivated for length and workability. They have less pith, a tight, close texture, and taper to fine **tips**. "Black Maul" is a commercial name for this variety, which is noted for its length (up to 6'). It is of excellent quality and well suited to **skein-work**. A similar but smaller willow rod is the Pomeranian, which has been specifically developed for its slenderness and is used primarily for fine work. *Salix purpinea* produces the smallest of willow rods—for example, the **dicky meadow** grade. The rods are 1'3" to 3'6" long, thin, very pliable, and extra **kind**.

Parts of the willow include the **tip**, the narrowest end, and the butt, which is the larger and thicker end. The **belly** is the concave surface, and the **back** the convex surface, of the rod. "Skein" is thin strips cut from the outer part of a willow rod with a shave or **cleave;** it is used for **wrapping**.

Willow may be purchased in buff, brown, or **white** condition, except for "Salix purpinea," which does not come in white because of its small size. White is commercially finished and is peeled and dried. Buff is first boiled with its bark on and then stripped and dried. Brown has been dried with the bark and peel left on. "Ragged" is the term for the roughest of willow rods, and is used primarily for coarse work baskets or bottom structures.

Willow is sold commercially in **bolts** or bundles. The following grading terms refer to the length of the willow rod:

dicky meadow or red bud: 2' or less
tack: 3'
short-small or luke: 4'
hullings: 4' lengths of green willow
long-small: 4'
threepenny: 6'
middlesboro: 7' to 8'
great: 8'6" to 10'

See ill.

a. Cane

b. Willow

willow. Spinning. See **spinning**.

win. Ceramics. To dig or mine clay.

wind chimes. Stained Glass. See **mobile**.

winding. Knitting. Yarn from **skein**s must be wound into balls prior to knitting. When winding yarn, the tension of the winding must be kept loose by winding the yarn over at least two fingers. If tension is tight, the elasticity of the yarn will be "wound out of it." Also see **ball winding**.

winding reed. Basketry. See **cane** and **Basketry: Woven Basket Construction**.

winding the shuttle. Tatting. If you are using a metal **shuttle** with a removable reel, remove the reel from the shuttle, tie one end of the **thread** through the hole in the reel, and wind the thread to fill the reel; do not overfill, as this extra thread is likely to be soiled by the fingers while working. Holding the shuttle in the right hand, with the hook toward the left, place the reel back into the shuttle with the thread hanging downward and on the right side of the reel.

If you are using the type of shuttle with the bridge joining the blades of the shuttle, tie the end of the thread through the hole in the bridge and wind the thread snugly around the bridge, but do not overwind the shuttle; that is, extend the thread beyond the blades of the shuttle. In winding the shuttle, hold it in the right hand between thumb and index finger with the hook or the extending tip to the left, and wind the thread clockwise. This winding will finish with the end hanging downward on the right side of the reel or bridge.

As you gain experience in tatting, it may not be necessary to tie the thread to the shuttle to begin winding.

winding the warp. Weaving. See **warping**.

winding toy. Toys. See **yo-yo**.

Winding Walk. Quilts. See **Kansas Troubles**.

Winding Ways. Quilts. (Also called Wheel of Mystery.) A **block** pattern that may be either **appliqué**d or **pieced**. Each block consists of four petal-shapes with concave curves on the end of each petal. When blocks are **set** in an **all-over pattern,** the curved lines join to form unending overlapping circles, as in **Robbing Peter to Pay Paul**. This pattern is usually done in just two contrasting colors, alternating the **background**. See ill. on next page.

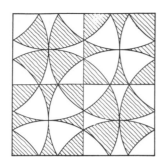

Winding Ways

Windmill. Quilts. (Also called Broken Dishes.) A **block** for a **pieced quilt** in which the main design element consists of triangles of various sizes. The triangles are **pieced** into **four-patch** designs. The possibilities for variety in the arrangement of the **patch**es and in the **set** of the quilt are limitless. Corn and Peas, **Dutchman's Puzzle,** Follow-the-Leader, **Hourglass,** Mill Wheel, **Pinwheel,** Watermill, and Water Wheel are just a few of the variations on this block. See ill.

Windmill

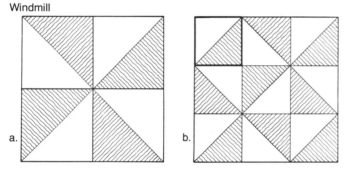

a.   b.

windmill. Toys. See **pinwheel.**

Windmill Blades. Quilts. An arrangement of **Log Cabin blocks** that combines dark and light patterns in such a way as to produce new **all-over pattern**s. When the Log Cabin block is made as a hexagon or an octagon, Windmill Blades and many other combinations are possible.

window cut. Papercrafts. A **symmetrical** cutting with interior areas cut out. It resembles a stained-glass window.

window knocker. Toys. See **ticktack.**

Windowpanes. Quilts. A pattern for a **pieced quilt** that results from an unusual **set** of the **Shoo-fly** block. The **blocks** are used as an **all-over pattern** set on the diagonal.

window screen. Needlepoint. Commercial window screening can be used as a **background fabric** for modern needlepoint designs.

Wind Power of the Osages. Quilts. See **Swastika.**

wind toy. Toys. Any toy in which parts are moved or propelled by moving air. Sometimes the wind animates the toy; in others, the toy is swung through the air or air is blown in through a tube or pipe. The **whirligig, airplane, kite,** and **pinwheel** are common wind toys.

windup toy. Toys. Any mechanical or **clockwork toy** in which a key or some similar device is used to wind up, or tighten, springs that, when released, relax and animate the toy. Sometimes a pull **string** is used in place of the key to wind up the toy. It may be referred to as a "key windup toy" when a key is used. In toys such as the **racing spool**s or **clothespin wrestlers,** the parts are wound up to put tension on a rubber band that animates the toy when it is released.

wineglass quilting. Quilts. An **all-over pattern,** sometimes used for a **filling pattern,** that takes its name from the wineglass used as a **template.** The design consists of a series of overlapping circles. Also see **Quilts: Quilting, Hand Quilting.**

wing. Puppets. A sidepiece of scenery, or part of the stage **set.** It is usually a vertical panel placed to angle toward the stage back. It screens the **backstage** area from view and is usually decorated as part of the set. Also see **Puppets: The Marionette Stage.**

wing dividers. Leather. A compasslike tool used in leather for etching circles, dividing areas equally, and spacing stitching. See ill.

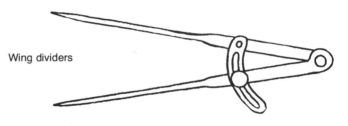

Wing dividers

wing dividers. Woodworking. See **marking tools.**

Winged Square. Quilts. A **pieced nine-patch** with a **sawtooth** pattern.

Winnie-the-Pooh. Toys. A book character created by A. A. Milne. The stories describe the adventures of Christopher Robin and his **stuffed animal** friends, including Winnie-the-Pooh, or Pooh Bear. Pooh is a favorite of many children, and **teddy bear**s are often named in his honor. Piglet, Eeyore, Rabbit, Owl, and Kanga and Baby Roo are among the other **nursery character**s from this book that are frequently made by craftspeople.

wire. Beadwork. Wire for **beadwork** is available in various gauges that have been standardized by the metal industry. The higher the gauge number, the finer the wire. The following types of wire are commonly used for beading: brass, stainless steel, galvanized, annealed steel, and enameled wire in various colors. Brass wire is sometimes referred to as gold wire.

For use in **bead flowermaking,** fine, pliable **spool wire** or beading wire is used. General assembly and binding is usually done with galvanized, annealed steel wire (#32), called silver wire. For **stem wire,** heavier wire is available. Also see **Bead Flower Making: Tools and Materials.**

wire. Jewelry. Metal in the form of a flexible thread. Wire is readily available in gold, silver, copper, brass, and many other metals. It ranges in gauge from extremely fine to as thick as it can be while still remaining flexible, after which it is considered rod. It is available in many shapes, the most common being round, half-round, square, rectangular, and triangular. By **wrapping** with wire, it is possible to make entire pieces of jewelry without the use of **solder**. Wire is employed both in functional and decorative techniques in jewelrymaking. Also see **drawing wire, drill and wire gauge, iron binding wire, piqué work.**

wire. Metalworking. See **metal.**

wire brush. Jewelry. Fine brushes made of brass, steel, and nickel, available in a large range of shapes, sizes, and densities for use on the **buffing machine.** They are made of straight or crimped wire. The crimped wire wheels tend to work better because the crimp in the wire provides support for each individual wire, making it rigid while in motion. They last longer if they are occasionally reversed on the buffing machine. They are used for a number of purposes, including **matte finish**es and preparing surfaces for electroplating. The brush can be used dry, which will produce one quality on the metal, or the metal can be dipped into a detergent and water solution to produce a soft, extremely lustrous finish. Brass brushes tend to give silver the color of stainless steel. Nickel and steel brushes provide a coarser texture; brass, a finer one. Pressure applied against the rotating brush should be very light both for the best results on the metal and for the longevity of the brush. Wire brushes leave a slight deposit on the metal's surface; this can be washed off with fresh detergent and an old toothbrush. Protective eye shields should be worn when using a wire brush, as the wires occasionally fly out. Also see **bristle brush, Swedish finish.**

wire brush. Leather. See **crocking** and **Leatherwork: Care, Cleaning, and Storage of Leather.**

wire brush. Stained Glass. See **Stained Glass: Glazing.**

wire cutters. Beadwork. For use in **bead flowermaking**, a small, sharp pair of jeweler's pliers, or needle-nose **pliers** with a serrated cutting edge are recommended.

wire hand. Puppets. See **hand.**

wire hangers. Stained Glass. The wire hangers used for hanging clothes can be reshaped and used as skeletal supports such as **armature**s, or for stained glass **free-form** sculpture.

wire mesh. Stitchery. Any screen or cloth made up of crisscrossing lines of wire. A wire mesh which has large spaces, such as **hardware** cloth, is suitable for use in various **stitchery** projects. Small-gauge meshes are sometimes used in **soft sculpture**s to make three-dimensional forms, or as a base for **papier mâché** or **pulp mâché.**

wire nail. Woodworking. See **nail.**

wires. Knitting. Very fine, thin knitting needles used by the knitters in the Shetland Islands. Also see **Shetland knitting.**

wire solder. Jewelry. See **silver solder.**

wire wick. Candlemaking. Under certain circumstances, particularly with **container candle**s, where it is difficult to position the **wick** in place, a wire or metal-core wick can be used. This core of manganese or fine lead keeps the wick rigid, yet burns as the outer wick burns. Wire wicks are available at most hobby shops in a variety of thicknesses to accommodate different **mold** size requirements.

wiring. Stained Glass. See **banding.**

wishbone doll. Toys. A very simple doll made in colonial America from a chicken wishbone. A ball of wax or similar material was added for a head, and cloth was wrapped around the bone to suggest the clothes of the doll. This is an example of a **making do** approach to toymaking. The wishbone doll is similar to some **poor child's doll**s.

wisteria line. Enameling. A technique of **overfiring** a soft, opaque **enamel** until it becomes transparent and sinks into the layers of transparent enamels below. Most often used are a soft, opaque gray, turquoise, or chartreuse enamel, fired high and fast to achieve a pale brownish purple veil.

Another effect can be achieved by scratching through the thin opaque enamel before overfiring, as in **sgraffito**, leaving fine, soft lines.

witch stitch. Crewel. Embroidery. See **herringbone stitch.**

withe. Basketry. See **willow.**

withy. Basketry. See **willow.**

withy. Metalworking. See **blacksmithing tools.**

woad. Dyeing. An ancient blue **dyestuff** made from an Old World herb of the mustard family. The blue dyestuff was obtained from the leaves of the plant. It was called dyer's weed, or woad, and was used primarily for woolens. The first known mention of woad in Europe is by Julius Caesar in his descriptions of his campaign in Britain; the ancient Britons painted their bodies with woad before going into battle.

Along with **madder**, Charlemagne promoted the cultivation of woad in the eighth century. When **indigo** was imported to Europe in the seventeenth century, woad was no longer the principal blue dye. However, it was still used as a bottom dye for indigo in order to achieve extra **colorfast**ness. It is interesting to note that both woad and indigo contain the same dyestuff; it is, however, more potent in indigo. Woad leaves are fermented with ammonia or lime to draw out the dyestuff. Upon contact with air, the woad dye will oxidize from yellow to blue. No **mordant** is necessary. Also see **bottoming.**

wolf. Toys. See **bull-roarer.**

wollastonite. Ceramics. A mineral used as a replacement for **whiting** and flint, it reduces firing **shrinkage** and improves **heat shock.** It can be used in both the **clay body** and the **glaze.** Wollastonite is also used for very strong bodies of electrical **porcelain** clay and as a source of calcium in **glaze**s.

woman's work. An old expression for any work which is tedious, never done, or which must be redone constantly. **Patchwork** and mending were "woman's work." Also, those chores and services traditionally performed by women.

wonder camera. Toys. See **polyopticon.**

Wonder of the World. Quilts. A variation of **Drunkard's Path** that uses the **Robbing Peter to Pay Paul** design motif. See ill.

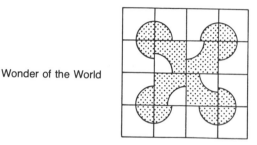

Wonder of the World

wood. Beadwork. A readily available material for making **beads** of various sizes and shapes. After cutting or sawing and drilling, wood beads can be colored by immersing them in dye, then coated when dry with varnish. Also see **Beadmaking: Basic Operations.**

wood. Ceramics. See **kiln fuel.**

wood. Kites. The basic material used in the kite **framework.** Most kites are constructed of **bamboo, spruce,** or commercially available doweling rods. **Balsa,** a lightweight, easy-to-work material, is used only for small, lightweight kites. Also see **Kites: Framing Materials.**

wood. Woodworking. Wood is a fibrous cellular structure that makes up the bulk of a tree. Wood is one of man's most important natural resources, abundant and accessible in most parts of the world. It is used for fuel, paper, shelter, and craft and artistic uses. It is relatively inexpensive and easy to work or shape with either hand tools or with power equipment. It is light in weight compared to other materials, warm to the touch, and, when properly finished, visually gratifying.

A cross-section of any tree trunk will reveal the major parts of the tree's structure (**a.**). The outermost layer, the bark, protects the cambium, the liquid layer from which new wood and bark grow. Beneath this is the sapwood, which surrounds the heartwood. The sapwood carries the water and other nutritive elements up the tree, is lighter in color and generally softer, and is most prone to disease. The heartwood, which is dead sapwood, is darker than the sapwood and forms the structural core of a tree. The center of the tree is called the pith; it is the soft tissue where the

growth began. It sometimes deteriorates and leaves a hollow center. The concentric lines are the annual rings, marking the seasonal growth of the tree; they are responsible, along with the knots and other irregularities, for the figure, or surface designs, on a board. The radiating darker lines coming from the center are called medullary rays; they store and conduct food horizontally through the tree.

There are two main methods of sawing logs into lumber: plainsawing and quartersawing (**b.**). See ill. In plainsawing, the entire log is sliced in parallel boards; in quartersawing, the log is first quartered, then boards are cut from each of the segments. In plainsawed wood, much of the grain is at an angle of less than 45° to the face of the board; as the wood dries, the annual rings tend to straighten, resulting in a curved warp, or cupping, of the board. In quartersawed (or log-cut) boards, the grain is more nearly at right angles to the face, so seasoning produces less warpage and checking, and the boards last longer. Because quartersawing is more time-consuming and wastes more of the log, it is reserved for fine hardwoods, in which warpage must be kept to a minimum and a closer-grain figure is desired.

Lumber is called green when it is first cut and its moisture content is high. In order to cut and work lumber easily, as well as to make it stronger, more resistant to decay, and stable for use, much of the moisture is removed. This is achieved by seasoning or air drying or kiln drying. Air-dried lumber is left, covered, to dry in the open air, and slowly loses its moisture over a period of years. Kiln drying is more common and faster; the lumber is placed in an oven and heated for a number of days. Seasoned lumber is relatively immune to decay when its moisture content is below 20%; most kiln-dried lumber has a 12% moisture content.

The word "grain" refers to the fibrous and cellular structure of wood; in the phrase "with the grain" it refers to the overall direction of the fibers, which run the length of a tree and lengthwise in most boards. Grain also refers to the patterns of light and dark (the figure) on the surface of a board (the face grain) formed by cutting lengthwise through the annual rings. The end grain is the relatively rough and porous fiber structure that is exposed when a piece of wood is crosscut perpendicular to its grain.

A wood is described as close-grained when the annual growth rings are close together (generally true in **hardwood**s, which grow more slowly than **softwood**s); coarse-grained wood has the lines far apart. "Open grain" is a term used confusingly, sometimes to mean coarse grain, sometimes to refer to the relatively large pores of woods like oak or ash. ("Close texture" and "coarse texture" are less confusing terms to refer to the porosity of wood, but they are not commonly used.)

Wood tends to split along the grain (which is why logs are easy to split); it takes much more effort to cut across the grain than with it. The ability to identify and respond appropriately to the demands of the grain direction is one of the signs of a skilled woodworker.

Lumber must be graded or evaluated according to its quality and size in order to be sold. Two grading codes exist, one for softwoods and the other for hardwoods.

Softwoods, which come from conifers, are graded according to the size and quality of the entire board. If it is relatively free from knots, defects, and blemishes, it is called select and subdivided into A (best), B, C, and D. The better select grades may be used in visible construction—for example, furniture and other finished areas. If the softwood has a number of defects and blemishes and is nṛ suitable for a finished surface, it is graded "common." Common softwood is subdivided further into numbers 1 (best), 2, 3, 4, and 5 (poorest).

Hardwoods, from deciduous trees, are graded by the amount of blemish-free lumber on a given board. If one side is flawless and the other side is relatively free of knots, it is graded either "firsts" or "seconds." The next grade is select, and lesser grades are numbers 1, 2, and 3 common.

Lumber is the large category of wood or timber that has been cut into specific sizes and shapes and is ready for use by carpenters and woodworkers. The widths are usually cut in even-numbered inches; lengths range from 8' to 20' at 2' intervals. Thicknesses vary, usually in ¼" intervals up to 1¼", then in multiples of 1". Hardwood is usually purchased in random lengths and widths in ¼" designations.

Lumber is rough-sawn to nominal sizes, usually given in full-inch increments (e.g., 1" × 10", 2" × 4", etc.). Hardwood is commonly sold rough-sawn, but for most uses, wood must be **planed** (or **dressed**) on one or more sides, which, with shrinkage, reduces its size. In softwood, the actual or dressed size of a nominal two-by-four is 1⁹⁄₁₆" × 3⁹⁄₁₆", and a nominal one-by-six is ¾" × 5½". Keep this information in mind when planning your wood constructions.

Virtually all lumber is sold and priced by the board foot, a unit of 144 cubic inches (e.g., 12" × 12" × 1"; or a 2" × 6" board, 1' long). A price may also be quoted for a running or **linear foot** (one foot of length regardless of width and thickness); **molding**s and other millwork are always sold that way.

There are names for certain classes of lumber dimensions. Timber is lumber 5" or more in its smallest dimension, used in heavy construction. Post is square lumber, 4" × 4" or larger. Stud is lumber 2" × 3" or 2" × 4", commonly used for framing-members in house walls. Plank is lumber 2–5" thick, commonly used with the wide surface set horizontally, as on a floor. Board is lumber less than 2" thick, and lattice is lumber less than 2" × 3".

Fabricated woods (plywood, hardboard, particle board) are laminated or pressed wood or waste wood products made for special qualities such as strength and resistance to warping and moisture. Thicknesses range from ⅛" to 1¼"; fabricated woods are most commonly sold in standard 4' × 8' panels, although larger sizes are available.

Most wood defects (except knots) are a result of decay, improper drying and seasoning, or improper storage of lumber. The following defects are blemishes or imperfections in wood that affect its marketability:

Check

A shallow lengthwise crack or surface separation in the wood.

Split

A crack that goes fairly deep into the wood. Both checks and splits are the result of improper drying.

Knot

Hard and generally dark circular spot where branches grew. Knots may become loose enough to fall out, leaving knotholes.

Peck

Area of rotten wood commonly caused by localized decay in a living tree. Pecks will not become larger in lumber that has been seasoned.

Shake

Separation between and parallel to annual rings that occurs lengthwise in the wood.

Wane

Bark or an area void of wood at the edge or corner of a piece of lumber.

Warp

Any distortion of a true or plane surface. This includes both cupping and bowing. Cupping results when a board curls across its width for the entire length. A bow is primarily a bend in a board along its entire surface.

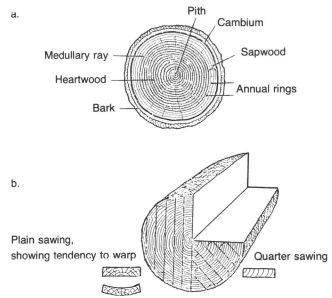

a.

Pith
Cambium
Medullary ray
Sapwood
Heartwood
Annual rings
Bark

b.

Plain sawing, showing tendency to warp

Quarter sawing

wood adhesive. Stitchery. Toys. Any of various waterproof **glue**s or cements made especially for use with wood. Some are two-part **epoxy glue**s that are permanent outdoors; other glues, such as **white glue** or **contact cement,** are good only for indoor use.

wood alcohol. Toys. See **alcohol.**

wood appliqué. Toys. A way of detailing or decorating wood; patterns or designs are cut from thin wood and adhered to a larger wood background. The method gives a rich relief surface and is used on wood objects of all kinds, from toys to wall panels and signs. In its use of pattern and flat areas of color it is similar to fabric **appliqué.** Wood pieces are usually painted before being adhered.

wood bead. Stitchery. Toys. A **turned wood** shape with a hole for threading. Wood beads are often used on children's toys, to add decorative details. They have many uses in toymaking and can be combined with yarns or threads in stitchery.

wood block. Block Printing. A section of wood from the trunk of a tree with the grain running along the surface ("plank grain"). A design used for block printing is cut into it. Wood blocks have been the traditional material for printing in many cultures. The Japanese preferred cherry, apple, or pear, but occasionally used sycamore. Today, although almost any type of wood can be used, pine is most common because it is easily obtainable and cut, and has an attractive grain. It may have knots, but these can be worked into the design. Plywood is also used; it should be at least ⅜″ thick to prevent warping. Rough wood, such as used for packing crates, is suitable for only simple shapes in which the wood grain texture is emphasized. For subtle designs, a finer wood must be used. Also see **Wood-block printing.**

wood block. Fabric Printing. A rectangular piece made of solid wood with a pattern cut into one surface for inking and printing on fabric with textile color. The grain of the wood is an important characteristic that must be considered in designing and cutting. In general, the wood block is more suitable for cutting bold areas than for fine details. Also see **wood block printing.**

wood-block printing. Block Printing. Fabric Printing. A traditional printing technique in which a **wood block** is cut in **relief,** inked, and the design is printed on fabric or paper. Wood, because of its natural grain, often produces a characteristic texture on the print.

Traditional block-printing methods are used for designing, cutting, and printing wood blocks. **Cutting tools** with blades permanently mounted in the handles are best for use on wood. The same basic shapes are used as for **linoleum-block** cutting. A **bench hook** on the worktable will facilitate cutting the block. A **mallet** is sometimes used to drive a chisel or gouge when clearing spaces. When cutting away spaces with the U-shaped gouge, be sure that all boundaries or outer edges of areas are first deeply cut with a knife, especially those across the grain, to prevent the gouge from running along the grain and accidentally splitting off a larger piece beyond the borders of the design.

For fabric printing, textile color should be used and printing should be done on a padded table. A system of **registration** should be planned before printing repeated patterns. The size of the **repeat** is determined by the manageability of the block; wood blocks larger than 12″ square are difficult to print evenly. A small repeat motif can be cut several times on the same wood block, thus reducing the number of times the block must be stamped. Also see **Block Printing: Tools and Materials, Designing and Transferring, Cutting, Printing Techniques** and **Fabric Printing: Designing.**

wood-block tie-dye. Batik and Tie-dye. Any **tie-dye** method in which wood sticks, blocks, boards, or chunks are used in the **binding** of the fabric. The fabric may be sandwiched between two boards and secured with C-clamps or **tied,** or the wood may be wrapped as in **bundle tie-dye.** Sometimes the fabric is tied over dowels.

woodcarving. Woodworking. The process of artfully removing areas from wood by a variety of techniques to create forms and designs. As a craft it has been used since ancient times to enhance and decorate boats, furniture, and architecture. It is similar to **whittling** but is executed on a larger scale with a different set of tools and slightly different methods.

In relief carving, the design is carved on the surface of a panel or two-dimensional plane. The wood is removed from around the design, which stands out against the background. How high a form projects from the background determines whether the relief is called high relief or low (or bas) relief. To relief carve, draw the design on the wood surface or panel. Isolate the form by carving the background down with a straight or bent **gouge.** Articulate or carve the edges of the raised form so that they make a rounded transition to the background; a straight **chisel** or gouge may be used.

Incised carving is similar to relief carving in that a wood panel or surface is used, but instead of the design being raised by carving down the background, it is hollowed out. Incised carving may be made by cutting out an outline or actually carving out the material inside the outlines to create the image. To incise carve, draw the design on the surface of the wood. With a sharp knife or **chisel,** stop-cut along the outline of the form you wish to delineate by incising down and to the inside of the form's edge. Remove the remaining material by working from within out to the **stop cut,** leaving the background higher.

Chip carving uses the techniques of both relief and incised carving. The forms, which are mostly geometric patterns, involve carving straight planes into the surface of the wood in such a way as to chip out certain sections to reveal the design with alternating relief and incised forms. To chip carve, draw the design on the surface of the board or panel. Because most chip carving is done in flat planes, select the appropriate size of straight or **skew chisel,** and stop-cut down on the perimeters of the areas you wish to remove. With the chisel held at the appropriate angle, make slanting cuts from the upper edges to the depth of the stop cuts. This will release the appropriate chips. By selectively making these chips in a given area, one can reveal a form through raised and hollowed areas.

Pierced carving (also called fretwork) is relief carving separated by space from the background. The wood or panel is pierced or cut entirely through in background areas. The remaining form must attach to the surrounding areas in enough places to support it. It is used in furniture decoration, perforated screens and railings, and fancy scrollwork. To pierce carve, draw the outline of your design on the surface of the wood panel. Next, drill holes in the areas to be pierced. Make them large enough to accept the blade of a jigsaw or keyhole. Cut and remove these areas. Continue carving. Round and articulate the forms as in relief carving—but more so, as there is no background. If pierced areas are large, carve the design first so you don't have to worry about supporting it. Dimensional carving is freestanding, without a background. All wood is removed from outside the design. Dimensional carving usually utilizes aspects of pierced, incised, relief, and chip carving. Most freestanding wood sculpture is dimensionally carved. Also see **Woodworking: Whittling and Woodcarving.**

woodcarving tools. Woodworking. The tools necessary for **woodcarving** duplicate those of woodworking, with a few exceptions.

Roughing-out tools remove the wood quickly and easily. Besides **saws** and **drilling tools,** the **adz** is used, plus wood **chisels** and **gouges** of a variety of shapes and sizes. The most commonly used gouge is straight; in cases where a deep cavity is being carved, a bent or spoon gouge is used. Straight and skew chisels are used for flat cuts; a V or parting gouge is used to separate a form or to incise a line. Woodcarving mallets are necessary when wood is tough or when you want to remove large amounts quickly without injury to your hands. Mallets come in weights from 7 to 30 ounces; the hardest and best are made of **lignum vitae.**

After the form is roughed out, abrading tools are used for further smoothing or refining. These tools are wood **files, Surform tools, rasps,** and **rifflers;** they differ from ordinary woodworking tools only in that they are more varied in size and shape.

For finishing, regular woodworking tools may be used—**scrapers, planes, whittling tools,** and even the edge of a piece of broken glass may help to get the final finish. Further refining may be done with **sandpaper, steel wool,** and other **abrasives.** Also see **Woodworking: Whittling and Woodcarving.**

wood cement. Toys. See **wood glue.**

wood chisel. Woodworking. See **chisel.**

woodcut. A relief image or design cut with knives into the surface of a block of wood. The wood remaining at the original level becomes a surface to print from. The raised area is inked with a **brayer** and then pressed against the surface to be printed. The image made with this process is also called a woodcut. Also see **letterpress.**

woodcut. Block Printing. See **wood block.**

wood cutout. Toys. A simple wood toy sawed in a single shape. If wood of ½″ thickness is used, the toys will stand on edge. Wood cutouts are not **joint**ed or articulated. Some wood animals that appear to be single wood cutouts with additional carving or shaping are actually cut from **lathe-turned** rings. They are called **turned-wood animals.**

wood doll. Toys. See **dollmaking.**

wood engraving. Block Printing. A printing technique using the end grain of close-grained hardwood for the **printing block.** The wood is cut in slices across the trunk of the tree, producing a slice with end grain—rather than with the grain (called plank grain), as for **wood-block printing.** Holly, pear, and boxwood are commonly used for wood engraving blocks. The wood is seasoned for several years before it is suitable for use. Because the trees are rather small, and only the hardest parts of the wood can be used, the blocks are generally very small, usually less than 8″. Larger blocks are made by fitting and gluing small blocks together. The surface of the block is planed to a glassy smoothness.

Wood engravings are cut with engraving tools, which produce a fluid line with a single stroke. In "white-line engraving" the design is drawn spontaneously in white lines on the background. The graver, or **burin,** is the oldest and simplest engraving tool, similar to the metal-engraver's burin. It engraves lines of varying width. The deeper the graver is driven into the wood, the wider the line. Various other tools are available for engraving lines of varied width, for lines of even width, and for clearing spaces. The engraved line is incised, and therefore is white in the print. The cutting is usually done on a block darkened with ordinary writing ink so the pale cut lines show clearly. Many variations of linear shading and texturing can be achieved. Wood engravings are printed with a press, or by hand rubbing with a **burnisher.**

wooden needle. Weaving. See **bodkin, needle.**

wooden-spoon doll. Toys. A doll made from a wooden mixing spoon, similar to a **pestle doll.** It is sometimes considered to be a Yugoslavian **folk toy,** but is probably an **emergent toy.** A face is painted or drawn on the bowl of a spoon, either front or back. The spoon handle serves as the doll body and is often clothed. It is an example of a **making do** approach to toymaking.

wood file. Woodworking. See **file.**

wood filler. Woodworking. Any of a variety of materials used to fill holes or dents in wood to produce a smooth surface.

Water putty is cream-colored plastic powder that is mixed with ⅓ part water. It sets quickly, dries hard, and can be stained with powdered pigment. Plastic Wood is fast-drying paste filler that comes in various wood colors and requires no mixing. Plastic Wood tends to shrink when hardening; cracks and holes must be overfilled to start with, and sanded to finish. Oil putty is slow-drying glazing-type putty with a **linseed oil** binder. For best results it is used on primed and painted surfaces. Another filler can be made by mixing a small amount of animal or vinyl-resin glue with the fine, powdered sawdust of the wood to be filled. After it dries in the cracks it takes stain and other finishing processes very well.

To apply wood filler, clean the hole or crack of all loose or foreign matter, particularly grease or chemical residue. Press the filler with a **putty knife** down into the hole firmly. Take the edge of the putty knife and lightly run it over the hole to remove any excess from the surface.

wood firing. Ceramics. One of the early methods used to fire **kilns;** it requires the continuous stoking of wood both in preparation and during firing. It gives a quality to both **earthenware** clay and **stoneware** clay that is unmatched by other fuels. Also see **gas kiln, oil-fired kiln.**

Wood Lily. Quilts. See **Lily.**

wood mask. Toys. A covering for the face or head, made of **carved wood.** Wood masks have been used by various cultures throughout the world, usually for religious or ceremonial purposes or in drama. Among the best-known wood masks are those made by Northwest American Indians, Africans, and Central and South Americans.

wood screw. Woodworking. See **screw.**

wood stain. Woodworking. A transparent coloring agent, used to enhance or change the color of woods or to unify a blemished wood surface. Stains are colors or dyes added to a medium or vehicle to ease application and absorption. The following is a sample of different types of stains:

There are two types of oil stain: Penetrating oil stain is the most common, and is ready to use and to apply. It is made from coal-tar dyes dissolved in a **thinner,** and comes in a limited variety of colors. This stain is easily **bleached** out if necessary. It may tend to bleed, so sealing with **shellac** is recommended before the wood is finished with **varnish** or **lacquer.** It dries in about 24 hours. Pigment oil stain is a tube oil color that must be mixed with **linseed oil,** turpentine, and a dryer (such as **Japan dryer**). Although difficult to prepare, it is easy to apply by simply brushing it on and wiping off the excess with a rag. It takes at least 24 hours to dry and, as with the other oil stain, must be sealed before other finishes can be applied over it. Pigment oil stains are not deep-penetrating and tend to fade in time.

Water stain is an aniline or vegetable dye dissolved in water. Water stains are fast-drying, come in the greatest range of colors, and are deep-penetrating. The stain must be prepared by adding the dye powder to boiling water. In addition, the wood must be presoaked and allowed to dry again before application so the stain will saturate the wood evenly and will not raise the grain of the wood. Water stains cannot be used on previously stained wood.

Alcohol spirit stain is aniline-dye powder mixed with denatured alcohol. It comes in a limited range of colors and dries very rapidly. Quick drying is good for small objects, but is a disadvantage when attempting to apply an even coat to a large surface. Alcohol stains do not penetrate very deeply and tend to fade in time. They may be applied easily over previously stained areas and are therefore good touch-up stains.

Chemicals such as potash, lye, soda, acetic acid, and ammonia react chemically with most woods and generally act more as tinting agents than as coloring agents. Chemical stains must be applied carefully with rubber gloves and noncorrodible equipment because they are often caustic. Apply them as you would a water stain.

Wax stains contain penetrating oil, wax, and a drying agent, and are intended to stain, seal, and wax-finish in one operation. They are easy to apply, will not **bleed,** and can be **bleached** out or finished over if necessary. Wax stains are not deep-penetrating and tend to not stain all the pores completely.

Varnish stain is basically a **varnish** with a penetrating-oil stain in it. It is intended to both stain and give a protective finish in one operation, but does neither well. It is acceptable for interiors of cabinets, and other inconspicuous places.

Before applying stain make sure the wood surface is thoroughly clean, dry, and free of all particles. Try to work on horizontal surfaces to prevent the stain from running. Test the stain on an undersurface or scrap piece of the same wood to check its color and penetrating qualities. Seal the end grain beforehand with **shellac** and lightly sand it before applying the stain (the end grain absorbs stain faster and becomes darker than the face surfaces). With a full brush, apply the stain quickly and evenly—with the grain. Work in from the edge; try to avoid overlapping by starting with a full brush back from where you left off. Wipe off excess stain with a clean cloth in the direction of the grain. Let it dry. Apply additional coats if a darker color is desired. Clean up with the appropriate **solvent,** and dispose of oily rags in a closed metal container.

wood stone. Gemcutting. See **quartz.**

wood turning. Woodworking. (Also called lathe turning, spin turning, turning.) The process of shaping rounded forms (like bowls, trays, dowels, lamp bases, and legs) on a **wood lathe. Wood-turning tools** work by cutting away wood on the spinning form. It is one of the few forms of woodworking in which one can turn out a finished product, including the polishing, in one operation. It was used as early as 3000 B.C. by the Egyptians, and predated almost all other woodworking machines. There is record of its use from the time of the Roman Empire through the Renaissance. In 1500 Leonardo da Vinci invented a device for the wood lathe to keep the spindle continuously turning. Wood turning as a craft was highly respected, and the first guild devoted to it was formed in Germany in 1587. There have always been close connections between woodturners and cabinetmakers, for turning was used for the legs and other supports for tables and chairs. Today lathe techniques have advanced so that nonsymmetrical shapes, such as rifle butts and ax handles, are also turned.

There are two basic types of wood turning: spindle turning and faceplate turning. In spindle turning the work is mounted between the headstock and tailstock on a lathe and dowel-type forms are cut. In faceplate turning the work is mounted to a faceplate on the headstock; forms such as bowls are turned by this method. Also see **Woodworking: Wood Turning.**

wood-turning lathe. Woodworking. The lathe, one of the oldest tools used to machine wood, is used to produce rounded forms. The modern wood lathe consists of a headstock assembly, which turns the wood; a tailstock assembly, which holds the wood; a lathe bed, which aligns the two centers; and a tool rest, on which the lathe tools are supported while cutting.

The headstock assembly is essentially the driving spindle to which is attached a live center, or spur center, which centers the wood. The spindle is driven by a motor sometimes connected with variable-speed pulleys. To turn bowls or plates a faceplate attachment is used in place of the live center.

The tailstock assembly holds and centers the turning to the headstock. The tailstock spindle contains the cupped or dead center which is adjusted by the tailstock feed and tightened by a spindle clamp. The entire tailstock slides in the lathe bed and is locked by a tailstock clamp.

The lathe bed is the supporting bridge that keeps the centers aligned and in which both the tailstock assembly and tool rest slide.

The tool rest is the horizontal guide on which the lathe tools are supported while cutting. It is adjusted and clamped to the lathe bed by the tool-rest clamp.

The size of a wood lathe is determined by the maximum turning diameter the lathe can accept, measured from the live center to the lathe bed, and the maximum length between centers. The standard size is a 12″ lathe with a 36″ bed. The speed range for a good wood lathe is 350–3,600 rpm. See ill.

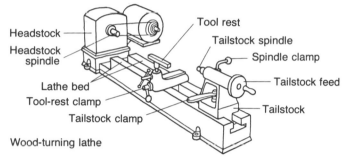

Wood-turning lathe

wood-turning tools. Woodworking. **Wood-turning** tools consist of a variety of **chisels**, gouges, and **measuring tools**. The lathe chisels and gouges have shorter, sturdier blades and longer handles than ordinary gouges and chisels. Wood-turning chisels are of five basic shapes.

Gouge

The **gouge** is the most frequently used lathe tool, used for **roughing out** and cutting **coves**. It is round-nosed and hollow on one side, like regular gouges, and comes in ¼″, ½″, and ¾″ sizes (**a.**).

Skew chisel

Frequently used to smooth cylinders and to cut beads, V-grooves, shoulders, etc. It is a double-ground flat chisel whose tip is cut on an angle to its sides. Skew chisels come in ½″ and 1″ sizes (**b.**).

Diamond- or spear-point chisel

A ½″ scraping tool used when the desired contour matches the diamond-shaped tool tip (**c.**).

Roundnose chisel

A ½″ scraping tool with a rounded nose used for rounded **grooves**, coves, and corners (**d.**).

Parting tool

A double-ground ½″ chisel used to scrape, cut off ends, and make cuts to required diameters (**e.**).

Measuring tools used in wood turning include dividers, used to locate centers and to mark and step off measurements of a spindle turning; inside calipers, used to measure the inside diameter of bowls and cups; and outside calipers, used to measure the outside diameters of rounded forms. See ill. Also see **Woodworking: Wood Turning.**

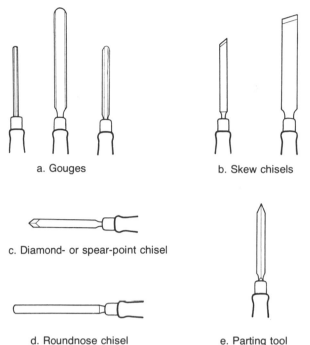

a. Gouges

b. Skew chisels

c. Diamond- or spear-point chisel

d. Roundnose chisel

e. Parting tool

wood vise wedge. Amber Carving. Ivory and Bone Carving. Shell Carving. A small wedge of wood can be of immeasurable help in holding irregularly shaped objects in the vise. See ill. Also see **beeswax, carpet underlay.**

Use of wood vise wedge

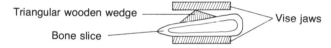

Triangular wooden wedge

Bone slice

Vise jaws

woodware. Woodworking. The products of the woodworking processes. Woodware may be furniture and cabinets. But the term has come to refer more specifically to household utensils such as wooden bowls, forks, spoons, and the like.

wood wool. Toys. Fine pine shavings, or strands and fibers of other woods, similar to wool in their springiness or resilience, and similar to **sawdust.** It was used as the **stuffing material** in stuffed **dolls** and animals in the 1800s, and was still in common use as late as 1920. Better toys were stuffed with kapok, but sawdust or wood wool was the common **filler.**

woodworker's vise. Woodworking. See **clamping tools.**

WOODWORKING

Woodworking is the craft of shaping or joining **wood** or wood products into finished articles. Its basic operations include **measuring, sawing, drilling, planing, sharpening** of tools, **jointing, gluing, turning, carving,** and **finishing.** The products of woodworking include architecture, sculpture, boats, cabinets and furniture, tools, and **woodware** such as bowls and household utensils.

The making of these products has developed into specific commercial occupations and crafts. The **carpenter** has been responsible for the working and joining of timber for structural use in architecture. The **cabinetmaker** and wood turner are responsible for the finishing of the architectural interior. The design and decoration of wood has resulted in the crafts of **whittling** and **woodcarving**, wood **inlay**, and **marquetry**, while the **woodcut** and **wood engraving** serve the printer's craft.

Because wood is easy to work, abundant, and widely distributed, woodworking is one of the oldest and most universal crafts. The shaping of a club or spear or the scraping out of a partially decayed log for a boat were its primitive beginnings. The subsequent history is closely allied with the development of the tools used to carve and work wood, such as the ax, adz, saws, blades, and drills. As early as 3000 B.C., the Egyptians were already producing some of the finest figure carving, furniture, and shapes in wood ever seen. They are also credited with the invention of the first wood-turning lathe. The ancient Greeks carved large wooden statues over which bronze sheets were hammered and riveted together. The Roman Empire saw the rise of larger sailing ships of wood. In Japan we see the development of entire temples and their woodcarvings of religious figures. The medieval West produced fine woodworking in churches, furniture, and tools.

The popularity of decorative woodworking came to a peak in the beginning of the eighteenth century. Examples of contemporary craftsmen include Grinling Gibbons, who did architectural woodcarving, and Thomas Chippendale, whose furniture is prized and imitated as classic of that period. During that time, power tools were just beginning to become available. The **circular saw** was invented in Holland as early as 1777, and the planing machine was patented in England. Soon afterward, other power saws, sanders, lathes, and other tools, were developed.

Contemporary woodworking has not only seen the development of better machines and tools, but also the broadening of the traditional uses of wood with fabricated wood products and the introduction of **plastics** into them. Woodworking remains an important industry as well as a challenging craft.

Because of the importance of personal instruction necessary for the safe use and operation of power-shop woodworking equipment, this craft section will only deal with descriptions of and instructions for hand tools and their basic operations (with the exception of wood turning). A few basic power tools are described, but it is not recommended that they be operated without skilled supervision and instruction.

SETTING UP A WORKSHOP   The ideal shop is well lighted, dry, well ventilated, and large enough to permit easy movement while working. It should have an area to store both new and scrap lumber easily. It should contain a sturdy workbench about 33–35″ high (depending on your height), equipped with a **woodworker's vise,** and there should be adequate grounded electrical wiring for all power equipment. All frequently used tools should be kept visible and within easy reach.

A safe shop has nonslippery flooring (particularly around power tools); a fire extinguisher; a metal cabinet for storing paints, solvents, and other finishing materials; a broom and dustpan (or a vacuum cleaner) for cleaning floors and work areas; and both a regular trash can and a sealed metal trash can for combustible finishing rags. There should be no open flames in the shop, because sawdust and solvent fumes are highly flammable.

Basic tools for a woodshop

Handsaws: crosscut and rip; **plane**s: a jackplane and a block plane; **chisel**s: a set of firmer chisels; **hammer**s: a claw hammer and a wooden mallet; screwdrivers: assorted; **measuring tool**s: a steel tape or folding rule; **drilling tool**s and **bit**s: a hand drill with twist bits, a brace with auger bits, a **countersink**; squaring tools: a tri-square or framing square, and a bevel gauge; **clamping tool**s: a woodworker's vise and other clamps of sizes appropriate to the work to be done; **pliers;** knife; **awl; nailset;** center punch; **sharpening stone**s; first aid kit; expendable materials: pencils, **glue,** sandpaper, **nail**s, **bolt**s, **screw**s, paintbrushes, **paint**s, stains, **solvent**s, and other finishing materials.

CARE AND MAINTENANCE OF TOOLS   Because of the large scope of maintenance of all woodworking tools, the following are general suggestions for tool care. Specific instructions may be obtained in the individual tool entries.

The proper care and maintenance of all wood tools, both hand and power, is essential to the safety of the operator and to the life of the tool. All tools and blades should be kept sharp. Large saw blades are best sharpened by a professional. Small blades for **jigsaw**s, **coping saw**s, etc., are inexpensive enough to be replaced when dull. **Screwdriver** blades should be kept squared. Heads of **hammer**s and similar tools should be kept secure to their handles. **Drill bit**s should be kept sharp to avoid burning the bit or splitting the wood. Awls and **bradawl**s should receive occasional sharpening. Place a drop of oil on all movable connections to prevent rust and reduce friction in joints. On all power equipment, a periodic overhaul is necessary, including checking brushes, cleaning, and lubrication. Most power tools come with suggested timetables and directions. Because woodcarving or woodcutting blades dull easily when they contact metal, they should be used carefully and be properly covered or sheathed when not in use.

GRINDING AND SHARPENING   Perhaps the most frequent maintenance job in a woodshop is grinding and sharpening cutting tools, including knife blades, **chisel**s, **plane iron**s, **drawknive**s, **adz**es, **spokeshave**s, and scrapers. The sharpening operation includes grinding, whetting, and stropping.

Grinding

Grinding is necessary only when a blade is chipped or very dull. Check the **grinding wheel** for cracks and to see that it is properly dressed. Secure the tool rest about 1″ away from the wheel. With the eyes well protected, turn on the grinding wheel, being sure it is revolving toward you. Place the tool firmly on the tool rest and lower the blade slowly to the wheel so that the **bevel** lies flat on the stone (**a.**). Maintaining this angle (30°), move the **chisel** or **blade** back and forth across the stone to avoid grooving the stone in one spot. Avoid prolonged contact of the tool with the grinding wheel, because excess friction will change the **temper** of the tool. Cool the ground edge in water after every few passes on the wheel. If an edge has been broken, first grind the tool at right angles to the wheel and then restore the bevel. When a rough **burr** develops and a consistent angle is attained, the tool is ready for **whetting.**

Gouges, because they are rounded, must be rolled on the tool rest and moved across the stone at the same time to render a sharpened edge.

Skew chisels have a bevel on both sides and a cutting edge which is at an angle to the sides. To both grind and sharpen a skew chisel, it must be rested on the tool rest to one side of the centerline of the grinding wheel; it must be held firmly, since the force of the wheel will tend to twist the tool away.

Whetting or honing

Secure a medium-grift **sharpening stone** on a workbench and lubricate it with either oil or water. Place the beveled edge of the ground tool on the surface of the stone and gently push it forward against the stone, being careful to maintain the beveled angle. Continue these forward strokes until the rough grinding marks have been removed from the cutting edge (**b.**).

To remove the **burr** that developed during grinding, turn the blade over and place it flat to the stone, and with the same forward strokes, push the tool against the stone for a few strokes. Do not remove the burr on scraping tools.

When a finer edge is desired, use **slipstone** in the same way as the oilstone.

Because gouges are rounded, they must be whetted on a curved oilstone and slipstone to remove the burr.

Stropping

Place the blade on a flat piece of wood or on cowhide that has been glued to a flat board and rubbed with jeweler's rouge. Next draw the tool across this strop away from the cutting edge for a few strokes on each side of the

Grinding and sharpening

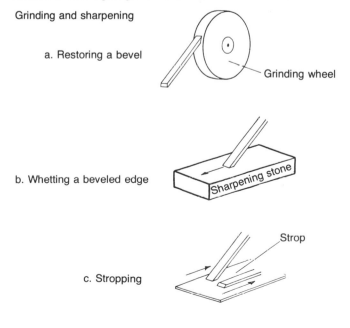

a. Restoring a bevel

Grinding wheel

b. Whetting a beveled edge

Sharpening stone

c. Stropping

Strop

blade (**c.**). See ill. Strop carving tools frequently while working to keep edges sharp for a longer time without using a sharpening stone.

SAFETY AND FIRST AID   Safety rules for a shop: Never smoke in a woodshop. Dress safely, with hair and clothes tucked in or rolled up, and all jewelry removed. Do not use power tools you are unsure of. Keep all blades and tools clean and sharp. Keep all handles firmly fastened. Always direct cutting action away from the body. Use or wear safety glasses when cutting or grinding with power equipment. Secure all work firmly before starting to cut, plane, or hammer. Before cutting or drilling, make sure the wood is clear of hidden nails or other obstructions—on both sides of the wood! Get a good footing and plant yourself firmly and comfortably before working. Work and walk in a shop with measured steps and deliberate actions. Return all tools to their proper places. Clean up all work areas and surfaces when finished. Keep the shop well ventilated, particularly when working with toxic or flammable fumes.

First Aid. The most common injury in a woodshop is a cut or nick by a knife or blade. If the cut is small, wash it out, apply an antiseptic, and cover with a bandage. If the injury is large, apply direct pressure to stop the bleeding and see a doctor. The injured person should always remain calm. Always keep a first-aid kit in the workshop, and know how to use it.

MARKING OUT AND SQUARING   Marking out and squaring lumber is one of the most important steps of woodworking. Much of the success of accurate **jointing** depends on accurate and orderly measuring and marking of the wood. Rough marking may be done with a pencil, but for greater precision, cut a line with a **knife.** All marking is done with the aid of **measuring tools;** the most commonly used are the flexible retractable steel tape and the folding rule. Squaring is accomplished with the aid of **squaring tools** such as the framing square and tri-square. Most squaring tools also have measuring calibrations.

To square, mark, and measure a board: Select a board which does not have obvious wood defects. Check the board for **warping, cupping,** etc., by holding a straightedge to it in various directions over the face. If, while holding it up to a light, you can see light under the straightedge, it is low or uneven in that spot. Plane until level. Plane an edge parallel to the **grain,** or select one already planed. Check it to see that the edge is even and square to the face with a tri-square (**a.**). This edge will be your reference edge, which all other markings will have to relate to. To square the end, place the square on the board so that the blade is flush to the reference edge and the tongue is pressed flat close to the end of the board (**b.**). Holding the square securely, take a sharpened pencil or knife and draw a line across the board, using the tongue of the tri-square as your guide. This line will be perpendicular to the reference edge. This is the basis of all squaring operations. To measure, it is important to make sure the end of the measuring tool is hooked over the edge of the board or that the end of the rule is flush to the edge. Most retractable tapes have a hook on the end riveted in such a way that it can slide to compensate for the thickness of the hook, whether hooked over the end of a board or pushed in for measuring an inside dimension. With a rigid rule, use your finger to match edges (**c.**). See ill.

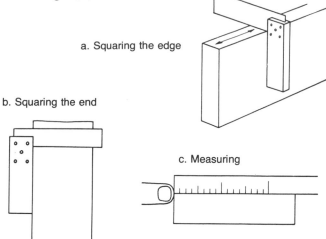

a. Squaring the edge

b. Squaring the end

c. Measuring

CUTTING AND SAWING   The accurate cutting and sawing of wood is essential to proper fitting and jointing. Before beginning any saw cut, it is important that the wood be properly supported and securely held. This is usually done over a **sawhorse** or strong box for larger pieces, at a height where the right knee and left hand can hold the wood comfortably (**a.**). If the wood is very long, it should be supported on the end to prevent too much vibration. For smaller pieces, secure the wood with a clamp. Also check to see that the line of cut is clear of **nails, screws,** etc., and that you are not cutting away your support.

Crosscutting. With the proposed saw cut properly marked perpendicular to the grain, hold the crosscut saw by grasping the handle and extending the index finger toward the cut to aid in keeping the blade vertical (**b.**). See ill.

Start the cut by placing the blade section nearest the handle to the waste side of your line of cut. With the free hand, grasp the board and use the thumb and index finger as a **fence** or guide for the side of the saw blade.

Slowly draw the saw backward one or two strokes or until a small **kerf** is made, deep enough to freely begin to

Sawing

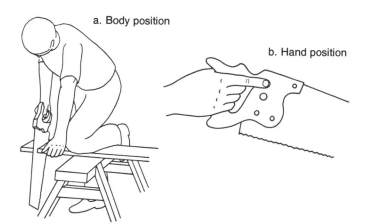

a. Body position

b. Hand position

saw. Regrip the board at a comfortable distance away from the saw blade.

Begin cutting by holding the saw at a 45° angle, pushing the saw blade forward (the cutting stroke) smoothly and without too much pressure, in a long, even stroke. At the end of the cut, draw the blade back. Continue this back-and-forth motion, remembering that you are cutting only on the forward stroke. If the blade is sharp, little effort will be necessary.

Toward the end of the cut, reach over with your free hand to support the waste piece to prevent it from falling and splitting the good end.

If the board is thick, you may want to hold a **tri-square** to the blade to ensure a square cut.

Ripping. Using a **rip saw,** ripping is done in exactly the same manner as crosscutting, except that the cut is with the **grain** and the blade is held at a 60° angle.

Contour cutting. Using a **coping saw** or **keyhole saw,** make sure the wood is properly supported and that the blade angle is kept constant and visible. Usually you will want to hold the blade perpendicular to the surface of the wood. For interior contour cutting, first **drill** or **bore** a hole large enough to insert the saw blade. A coping saw is generally held with one hand and a keyhole saw held much like a crosscut saw. Contour cutting is basically a combination of crosscutting and ripping, except it is done lightly because the blades are thin and generally not **temper**ed.

Backsaw cutting. Clamp or hold the wood securely in a **miter box.** Place the **backsaw** in the desired groove for the miter and begin cutting on the backstroke. Keeping the saw blade level, saw until the cut is completed. The cut must be made carefully so as not to ruin the miter box.

BORING AND DRILLING   To bore a hole mark the center of the hole to be bored with an **awl** or center punch and choose the type and size of **auger bit** needed. Insert the bit into a **hand brace** and tighten it by revolving the **chuck.** Clamp the

Boring

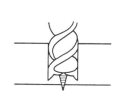

a. Starting

b. Finishing the hole

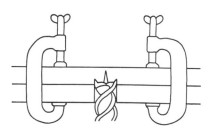

c. Boring with scrap wood

wood in a **vise** and position the bit perpendicular to the surface of the wood. Bore until the spur of the bit starts to come through the other side, then stop. Do not go all the way through, or the wood will splinter (**a.**). Withdraw the bit and finish boring the hole from the other side (**b.**). Another way to keep the wood from splitting is to back it with a piece of scrap wood (**c.**). See ill.

To drill a hole or countersink a hole, see **Woodworking: Screwing,** below.

To stop-bore a hole, attach the **bit stop** to the auger bit or twist-drill bit at the proper height. Bore into the wood until the bit stop prevents further progress.

NAILING Start the **nail** by tapping it into the wood lightly. When driving large nails, strike a full blow, gripping the hammer near the end; for small nails and **brad**s, merely use wrist action. Although nails embedded at a slight angle to the surface have more holding power than those driven in at a right angle, drive the first nail in straight to avoid pushing the wood out of its proper position.

When the nail head is driven nearly level with the wood use only light blows to prevent damaging the surface. If you bend the nail while striking it, draw it out and start another. The new nail should be started in another place so that the first hole doesn't lead it off course.

When nailing near the end of a board, tap the sharp end of the nail with the hammer face to blunt it slightly. This helps prevent the nail from splitting the wood.

Setting. After driving in **finishing nails**, place the **nail set** squarely on the head of the nail and tap it with the hammer to recess the nail about $1/16''$ under the surface. If you are driving nails close to the ends or edges of **hardwood**, first **drill** small holes where the nails will go with a **drill bit** slightly smaller than the nail to be used.

Pulling nails. Wedge the nail head in the V of the claw and rock the hammer backward until the handle of the hammer is nearly vertical. A piece of thin wood between the hammer head and wood surface will protect a fine finish. When drawing out a long nail, use a block of scrap wood under the hammer head for extra leverage.

SCREWING When a **screw** is used to fasten two pieces of wood together, it is always necessary to provide some sort of **pilot hole** for it. For very small screws and **softwood**, it may be enough to punch a small hole with a **bradawl** or **gimlet;** for medium screws in softwood, a simple drilled hole may be adequate; but with larger screws in **hardwood**s, and at the end of any board, more care must be used. With most screws it is necessary to provide a **countersink** for the head; with all screws, drill an anchor hole for the shank and a lead hole for much of the length of the thread. See ill.

Selecting the right screw for the job depends—among other things—on the size and finish of the boards and the amount of strain the screws must bear. The screw must be at least $1/8''$ shorter than the thickness of the boards being joined. Most of the thread must be in the second board; if you will be using the screw to tighten the joint, the head should seat firmly in the top board and the shank fit quite freely in it, so the threads, gripping in the second board, can pull the top one down. The top board will always be **face grain**; if the screw is going into **end grain** (which holds the threads less securely than face grain) in the second board, use a larger and longer screw for better holding power.

Select the right **drill bit**s; hardwoods will need slightly larger holes than softwood. Use this chart as a guide:

screw number	4	5	6	7	8	10
diameter (in inches):						
shank of screw	.112	.125	.138	.151	.164	.190
drill bit for anchor hole	$7/64$	$1/8$	$9/64$	$5/32$	$11/64$	$3/16$
for pilot hole, softwood	$3/64$	$1/16$	$1/16$	$1/16$	$5/64$	$3/32$
for pilot hole, hardwood	$1/16$	$5/64$	$5/64$	$3/32$	$3/32$	$7/64$

If you are countersinking the screw deep below the surface, use an auger bit of an appropriate size; most **countersink bits** come in only one size. A **pilot bit** consolidates all three steps.

Mark the position of the hole with a bradawl or center punch to keep the drill bit from drifting as you start to drill.

Secure the boards together before drilling; clamp them, use a thin nail in the position of one of the holes while you drill another, or simply hold them firmly.

Select the right **screwdriver** for your screw; the blade should fit snugly into the slot—too small a screwdriver will chew up the head and slot; too large will mar the wood. (Use a Phillips-head screwdriver for Phillips-head screws.)

Insert the screw into the hole; if you are using hardwood, soap or tallow on the threads will ease turning the screw in. As you start to drive the screw in, hold the screw and the screwdriver shank in one hand and press and turn the handle with the other. Use firm, even pressure to turn the screw clockwise; as the screw begins gripping, you will need to press down less and can use more of your energy in twisting. If the screw is too tight in the hole, remove the screw and enlarge the lead hole; twisting too hard on a screw can break it between the thread and shank.

If the screw is countersunk below the surface, you may wish to cover it with a **wood filler** or a **plug** to hide and protect the head.

Pilot hole for wood screw

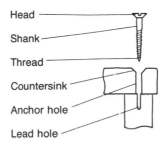

Head
Shank
Thread
Countersink
Anchor hole
Lead hole

PLANING Correct planing procedures are essential to the quality and finish of all woodworking. There are three basic types of planing: face surface planing, edge planing, and **end grain** planing. All three demand that the plane iron or blade be clean, sharp, and devoid of nicks. It is also important that the board be firmly secured in a **woodworker's vise** or clamped to the workbench.

Adjusting the plane. If the plane has a cap iron, adjust it so that the cap is squared to the plane iron and 1/16" back from the edge of the blade for regular wood—closer to the edge for more difficult woods.

Square the blade to the opening in the bottom of the plane by pushing the lateral adjustment lever in the desired direction.

Adjust the depth of the blade by turning the knurled adjustment knob.

Check the adjustments by holding the plane up to a light, upside down, and sighting down the sole of the plane. Two or three shallow cuts are easier and produce a cleaner edge than one big cut (**a.**).

Planing. Since most planes require two hands to operate, proper hand pressure is required to produce a straight surface or edge. As you start planing, pressure should be transferred from the front of the plane to the entire plane by the middle of the cut and to the heel or rear of the plane at the end of the cut (**b.**).

Face surface planing. Because the face surface is usually wider than most planes, use a **fore plane** or **jack plane** because their blades are generally slightly rounded and will prevent the corners of the blade from scoring the wood.

Secure the wood with a clamp or vise, making sure that the holding jaws do not project above the planing surface.

On each pass with the plane, stand well over the board with your feet firmly planted, because you are taking off a full blade's width of wood.

Systematically push the plane in long, even, adjacent strokes over the entire surface of the wood.

Test the surface for flatness in all directions by holding a straightedge to the surface.

Edge planing. With the edge of the board firmly clamped in a horizontal position, hold the front of the plane on the starting edge with the palm of the forward hand, letting a finger or two slide along the wood to act as a guide to keep the plane from wandering.

Next, push the plane over the edge in long even strokes while keeping the plane square to the sides of the board.

Check for accuracy with a straightedge or **square.**

End grain planing. The most difficult surface to plane is the **end grain,** because the wood tends to split at the end of the cut. Any of these three methods of planing may be successfully used:

Chamfer the far corner opposite the direction you are planing. Slowly plane down the surface until the corner is square (**c.**).

Plane the end grain by starting at either end and working in toward the center (**d.**).

Clamp a piece of waste stock to the far end of the board you are planing so that it is level with the surface being planed. Then plane the end grain without fear of splitting the end corner.

Order of planing surfaces. There is a specific order to planing surfaces when squaring a board (**e.**). See ill.

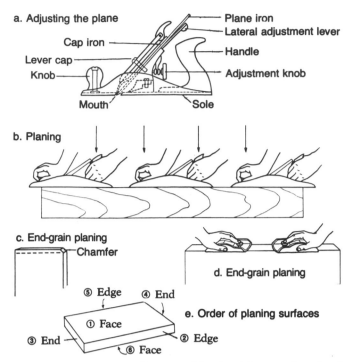

a. Adjusting the plane — Plane iron — Lateral adjustment lever — Cap iron — Handle — Lever cap — Adjustment knob — Knob — Mouth — Sole

b. Planing

c. End-grain planing — Chamfer

d. End-grain planing

e. Order of planing surfaces
⑤ Edge ④ End
① Face
③ End ② Edge
⑥ Face

GLUING AND CLAMPING Preassemble the joints to be glued before putting the **adhesive** on.

Select the proper **clamp**s and adjust them to the correct openings; clamp up the entire work, still without glue. Prevent the clamps from marring finished surfaces by cushioning the jaws with scrap strips of wood between the jaws and the work. This is especially necessary with metal clamps, which will exert considerable pressure.

Disassemble the pieces in an orderly fashion, remembering the order and location of the clamps. Apply the glue and reassemble the work.

Test the clamped assembly for squareness with a **square;** the parts may have shifted while the clamps were put on. Adjust clamp positions to correct. Tighten the entire assembly securely, being careful not to make the clamps so tight as to squeeze the glue out of the joints.

JOINTING For descriptions and uses of these joints, see "**joint.**"

Butt joint. To make a good butt joint, the end of the butting member must be cut or planed as **square** as possible. After gluing it, secure the joint with nails, screws, or other fasteners (**a.**).

Blocked joint. Reinforce the butt joint by cutting a squared or triangular block of wood the length of the butt joint; the grain should cross the grain of the other members.

Glue the block into the angle of the joint and secure it with nails or screws. Since the fasteners can be inserted through the block and into the main boards, the blocked joint is often used when it is desirable not to have nails or screws visible on the outside of the joint (**b.**).

Dado joint. Carefully mark out the proposed **dado** with the aid of a **square** and a sharp knife. It should be the width of the board to be inserted, perpendicular to the sides, and the depth should be about 1/3 the thickness of the board to be dadoed (**c.**).

Cut to the waste side of the lines on the face of the board, down to the depth of the finished dado, with a **backsaw.**

Using a **chisel** about the width of the dado, remove the waste stock between the two **kerf**s. Smooth with the chisel or a **rasp.** Test the joint for fit by assembling it dry. Square the end of the second board if necessary (**d.**).

Glue and assemble the joint; secure with nails or screws (**e.**).

Rabbet joint. A rabbet is like a dado at the end of a board.

The rabbet is marked with the aid of a **marking gauge.** On the end of one board, mark the thickness of the second board and ⅓–½ the depth of the wood to be rabbeted (**f.**).

Use a backsaw to cut the rabbet (**g.**).

Glue, assemble, clamp, and secure with screws or nails (**h.**).

Half-lap joint. This joint may be used at the end or middle of either board being joined.

Cross half-lap joint is constructed with boards of equal width and thickness.

After determining the point on each board where the two are to cross, carefully line them up side by side. Using a square, mark the common width of both boards across each face and down to ½ the depth on each side (**j.**). Check the alignment (**k.**).

Cut halfway down each board with a backsaw, sawing inside the marks. Additional kerfs cut between the marks will make the chiseling easier (**m.**).

Remove the waste with a chisel. Assemble dry to check fit. It is obviously better to make the original cut too shallow or narrow and enlarge it than to go too far in the first place. Adjust cut if necessary to assure flush fit. Glue, assemble, and secure (**n.**).

Miter joint. The most common miter joint is the right-angle or 90° **miter.**

Carefully mark out with the aid of a **combination square** or **sliding-T bevel** a 45° line across the ends of both boards to be mitered. The angle of the miter is always one-half the overall angle of the joint.

Place each piece in a **miter box** and carefully cut off the ends with a **backsaw.** A miter box should be attached to the work surface so as to remain stationary while sawing.

Assemble dry and with a **tri** or **framing square** check that the combined angles total 90°.

Reinforce the joint by nailing, screwing, or **doweling.** Glue and assemble.

Blind mortise-and-tenon joint. The pieces to be joined must be squared as for a butt joint.

Lay out the tenon on the end of the tenon member and mark it carefully with a knife. The tenon is usually about ⅓ the thickness and width of the board; the length depends on the available depth for the mortise (**p.**).

With a backsaw, carefully cut the tenon on the waste side of the tenon lines and the shoulder lines (**q.**).

Trim the tenon carefully with a chisel until it is perfectly square. Mark out the size of the mortise on the mortise member (**r.**).

With a **brace** and **auger bit** whose diameter is slightly less than the width of the mortise, bore a series of adjacent or slightly overlapping holes to the desired depth. A bit gauge will be helpful to gauge the depth (**s.**).

With a **mortise chisel** of the appropriate size, clean out the mortise until the tenon fits well (**t.**). Glue and assemble. If the joint is well made, no additional reinforcing is necessary.

Doweled joint. Square and plane both pieces to be joined. Clamp the two pieces of wood together and accurately mark the centers where the **dowels** will go, using a **tri-square.** Some carpenters mark and drill one hole first, and use a **centering pin** to locate the second hole. It is very important to have the dowel holes accurately lined up (**u.**).

Using dowels about ⅓ the thickness of the wood, select

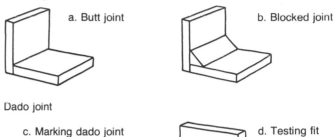

a. Butt joint   b. Blocked joint

Dado joint

c. Marking dado joint   d. Testing fit

e. Assembling dado joint

Rabbet joint

f. Marking rabbet

g. Cutting rabbet

h. Assembling rabbet

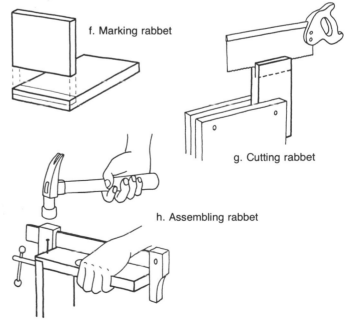

Cross half-lap joint

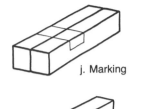

j. Marking

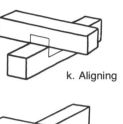

k. Aligning

m. Cutting

n. Assembling

Blind mortise-and-tenon joint

p. Laying out tenon

q. Cutting tenon

r. Laying out mortise

s. Boring out mortise

t. Chiseling out mortise

Doweled joint

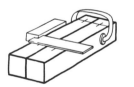

u. Laying out dowel location

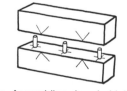

v. Assembling doweled joint

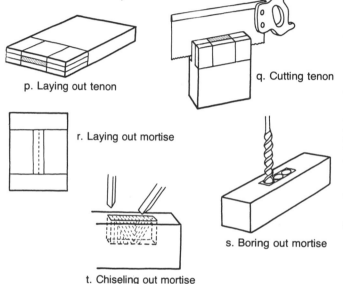

the corresponding auger bit. Start the holes with a brad-awl; then bore down to the desired depth with the brace and bit—usually four or five times the diameter of the dowel. To keep the hole absolutely perpendicular to the surface, a **doweling jig** is helpful. Drill the corresponding hole in the second piece.

Cut the dowels a little shorter than the total depth of the two holes. Round the tips and groove the dowels so the glue is not forced out of the joint.

Check alignment, glue, assemble, and clamp (**v.**). See ill.

WHITTLING AND WOODCARVING   Select a **wood** that is suitable to your needs. If you are a beginner, use a **softwood.** Check its size, **defects,** and soundness from decay; know what to expect before you begin.

Check and know the direction of the **grain.** This is most important.

Draw your design on the wood so that the majority of your work will be in the direction of the grain. Draw on one side if it is **relief carving** and on all sides if it is **dimensional carving.**

Roughing out. Visualize in large planes where and how much wood you will have to remove and select the best tool to quickly remove it. The tool you select will be determined by the size of the wood you are working on and the shape you will form. Use a **saw, gouge,** and **mallet;** an **adz** on larger carvings; and a **spear blade** with a **straight cut** or **saw cut** if whittling.

After the basic shapes are blocked out, round off the forms with a gouge and mallet for carving, or a **sweep cut** with a **chip** or **pen blade** for whittling.

Always rough out the largest forms first and leave the smaller forms and details until last.

If the forms are to be left large and rounded on large carvings, abrading tools like **rasps** or **wood files** are used to smooth down the gouge marks, unless a rough surface is desired.

If details are desired, select smaller chisels or gouges for woodcarving, and finer blades for whittling. It is usually here that flat chisels, V gouges, or **cut-off pen blade**s are used to delineate or incise lines. Small holes are drilled or bored with a **punch blade.**

Tighten up the forms with a wood **scraper** or other sharp edge, and then **sandpaper** to the desired smoothness.

Finish the wood with a protective coating of **wax, linseed oil,** or other wood **finish.**

WOOD TURNING   Spindle turning. To center the wood on the lathe requires the following steps:

Cut the stock desired for turning as square as possible and a bit longer than the finished form.

Locate the centers by drawing diagonal lines through the corners of both ends (**a.**).

Cut saw **kerf**s on these lines; where they intersect will be the centers. For accuracy, punch these points with an **awl** or **center punch.**

Remove the live center from the lathe and tap it into one end of the wood with a **mallet** so that the spurs fit into the saw kerfs.

Place both back together on the lathe.

To support the tail end, move the tailstock up to the work so that the dead center is almost engaged into the tail center of the wood. Lock tailstock clamp.

Turn the tailstock feed until the dead center bites firmly into the centering hole and surrounding wood. A drop of oil here will lubricate the wood. Fasten the tailstock spindle clamp.

Before beginning to turn, be sure that all the adjustments are secure and that the wood revolves without hitting the tool rest. The eyes should be protected with a face shield during all turning operations.

If the wood stock is over 2½" square, round off the corners in an octagonal shape before putting it on the lathe. This will lessen vibration.

As a general rule, the larger the wood turning, the

slower the starting speed should be. Slowly increase the speeds as you approach finishing operations.

Good lathe position is important. Stand sideways facing the lathe with most of your weight on your forward foot. One hand should slide along the tool rest while gripping the tool a few inches back of the cutting edge. The other hand should hold the handle overhand and against the hipbone. In this way, the entire body is used to control the cutting tools.

Roughing the wood. Adjust the tool rest about ⅛" away from the wood and ⅛" above the center line (**b.**). Tighten.

Turn the spindle stock by hand to see that it clears the tool rest.

Adjust the lathe to a low speed and turn it on. Be sure to wear eye protection.

Start to turn about 3" from the tailstock end by placing a ¾" **gouge** on the tool rest, slightly tilted so as to throw the shavings away from the operator (**c.**).

To avoid splitting, never start at the end of a piece of wood. Move the gouge into the revolving wood to make the first cut. Start the second cut about 3" to the left and move it toward the first cut until they meet. Continue making a series of cuts until you reach the live center, then reverse your direction. Keep cutting like this until the spindle stock is roughly round and slightly larger than the desired diameter.

Smoothing. Set the outside **caliper**s to the desired diameter and slightly increase the speed of the lathe. With the large **skew chisel** on the tool rest, make a shearing cut with the middle of the cutting edge—not the point. Move the skew slowly, maintaining this angle with the handle slightly lower than the tip (**d.**).

Hold the skew overhand for heavy smoothing, and with the fingers underhand for lighter smoothing. Continue smoothing until the spindle is the desired diameter. Check with the calipers.

Parting. With the lathe running slightly faster than for roughing or smoothing, place the **parting tool** on its edge and high on the tool rest. Gradually lower it into the wood and down toward the center as the cut is being made.

Place the calipers in the parting groove opposite the side you are cutting on.

With the groove made slightly larger than the parting tool so as not to burn the tool, continue cutting until the calipers fall into place when the desired diameter is reached (**e.**). See ill.

Sanding. Complete all cutting and scraping before beginning to sand on a lathe; this prevents dulling tools with abrasive particles in the wood. As with all sanding, start with the coarsest **grit** and work toward the finest.

With the sandpaper in the palm of the hand, lightly but firmly lay it on the top of the turning to permit you a better viewpoint to watch the progress. It may be necessary to support the work with one hand from below if the turning is long and thin.

Keep the sandpaper moving to avoid cutting rings or grooves in one spot.

Finishing on a wood lathe is similar to all wood finishing, with a few exceptions.

Apply **stain, shellac,** or **lacquer** by rotating the turning by hand or at a very low speed.

After staining, let the article sit and dry thoroughly before returning it to the lathe. This will prevent centrifugal action from forcing the stain out prematurely.

Rubbing and polishing may be accomplished by bringing the rubbing felt and **pumice powder** or **wax** into contact with the turning as it revolves.

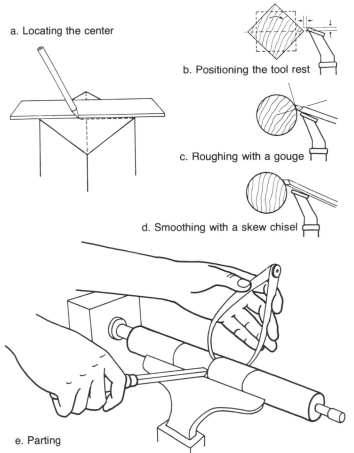

a. Locating the center

b. Positioning the tool rest

c. Roughing with a gouge

d. Smoothing with a skew chisel

e. Parting

Scraping, filling, and sanding. Remove all mill marks from the visible parts of the wood with a **plane** or **cabinet scraper.**

Remove all traces of **glue** around **joint**s, as **stain**s will not penetrate glue.

Remove dents by applying a cotton pad soaked with hot water or by moistening the dent and applying a medium-hot iron. Avoid burning the wood. Repeat this until the blemish or dent is raised.

Fill all holes and cracks with **wood filler.** Let dry.

Starting with the coarsest **sandpaper,** cover a **sanding block** and sand all flat surfaces with the direction of the **grain.** Progress to the finer **grit**s. Use the sandpaper around your finger or a **dowel** to get at curved or contoured edges.

Sand all edges lightly, and dust clean with a **tac rag.**

Stained wood finish. After the surface has been prepared, select the appropriate **wood stain** or **bleach.** Apply and let dry. If necessary, apply the appropriate type of **grain filler** and let dry.

Seal with at least two coats of **shellac** to prevent the grain filler and stain from **bleeding** through. Lightly sand between coats.

Shellac may be left as a final surface, but for a higher gloss, apply either **varnish** or **lacquer.** In all three cases it is usually necessary to smooth down between successive coats by **rubbing** with a **rubbing compound** or other fine **abrasive** to get a high gloss. See each specific finish for instructions.

For added surface protection, clean the surface and apply a good paste **wax** or furniture oil. Let dry, then buff to the desired gloss.

Painted wood surfaces. After the surfaces have been prepared, apply a coat of shellac to the **knots** to prevent the resins from later bleeding through the paint.

Select and apply the appropriate **paint.** Let dry.

woof. Basketry. See **weft.**

woof. Quilts. Stitchery. See **filling, weft.**

woof. Weaving. See **filling, weft.**

wool. Batik and Tie-dye. Quilts. Stitchery. A **natural fiber** from sheep's fleece. Wool also refers to the **fabric**s woven from the woolen **fiber**s. It must be dry-cleaned or washed with care to avoid any extreme temperatures or changes in temperature that cause **shrink**age. If moisture, heat, and agitation are used, **felting** may occur. Wool fabrics are resilient, soft, and have good insulating qualities.

Wool fabrics were traditionally used in **quilt**making, especially because of their warmth. At one time natural, or unspun, wool was also used as a **filler** for quilts.

Because of the affinity of wool for many dyes, it is often used in **tie-dye** and **batik.** The soft, textured surface of wool makes it very inviting and popular for all kinds of **stitchery** and sewing. It is often used in a **blend** (part wool, part synthetic) for large **panel**s or stitchery **mural**s.

wool. Spinning. Weaving. The term applied to the soft, wavy hair which covers the bodies of sheep and certain other animals such as **alpaca, vicuña** and various goats. The hair, when seen under a microscope, is covered with tiny, overlapping scales which catch each other when the wool is pulled and spun into yarn. This quality makes wool the easiest natural **fiber** to spin into yarn. Wool's origin as a textile fiber goes back to the Second Stone Age, although most likely it was used before that. We know that by 3000 B.C. the Babylonians were already experts in spinning and weaving fine wool.

The coat of wool on a sheep is known as the **fleece.** The fleece of sheep raised for wool is usually cut off, or shorn, once a year—in the spring or early summer. The fleece is cut close to the skin of a live sheep with electric clippers and removed in one piece. Wool taken from a dead sheep is known as dead wool or pulled wool, and is less valuable than fleece wool. The average weight of the fleece is 7−8 lbs. Shearing is usually done in dry weather and fleeces are stored in a dry place, since moisture favors the growth of wool-disintegrating molds. A handspinner can buy a whole fleece or part of one from some suppliers of weaving and spinning equipment, or directly from someone who raises sheep.

After shearing, wool goes through **skirting,** or the removal of torn and dirty parts that can be sold for cheap wool, and **sorting,** or grading the wool from the various parts of the fleece. The quality of the wool depends not only on the part of the body from which it comes, but also on the type and breed of the sheep. Wool from **Merino sheep** is classified as among the very best, because it has a medium-long **staple** and is very fine. The properties which determine the value of wool are the fineness of the diameter of the fiber, length of staple, strength, elasticity, amount of **crimp,** softness, pliability, uniformity, color, and **felting** and spinning properties. Any one fleece contains a mixture of fine, medium, and coarse fibers. The predominant diameter of the fiber determines the fineness of the fleece. A uniform length of staple is of great importance because of the difficulty of spinning fibers of unequal lengths. Wool staples vary in length from ¾" to 15", depending on whether the wool is from a sheep or a specialty animal. The color of wool ranges from white to gray, brown, and black.

Shorn wool contains a large amount of natural grease called **lanolin.** The lanolin and the **suint** (perspiration) together are called the **yolk.** Wool from which these substances have not been removed is known as "wool in the grease." If the wool is not to remain in the grease, it must next be washed or scoured. Scouring in warm water with a mild soap or a commercial wool scouring solution removes the grease and dirt without injuring the staple. With the natural grease removed, the wool fibers are now dry and brittle, so before spinning they must be sprayed with vegetable or mineral oil in order to make them be pliable and adhere to each other. This is done after **teasing** or picking the wool apart to remove any remaining foreign matter and to pull apart the fiber mass. At this point, before oiling, the wool can be dyed. This is known as fleece or **stock dyeing.** If the wool is not dyed now, it can be dyed after it has been spun into yarn.

On the basis of staple length, it is decided whether the wool should go through just **carding,** or both carding and **combing.** The shorter staples only will be carded; they are spun into woolen yarn directly after carding. Combed wool is of long enough staple to be combed into a ropelike strand or **top,** used in the spinning of **worsted.** Because of the shorter fibers that woolen yarn is made of, it has a soft, fuzzy texture, while worsted is smooth and silky. Due to the natural crimp, all wool is noted for being a resilient fiber. The elasticity makes for wrinkle resistance, but also causes a high percentage of shrinkage. Wool is partially water repellent, but once wet it is very absorbent and takes a long time to dry. It is an excellent insulator because of its scalelike structure that allows a lot of air space around the fiber or yarn. In addition, it is a very flexible fiber, lightweight, and long-wearing. Wool burns very slowly so it creates no fire hazard. In fact, wool blankets are used to smother flames. Also see **lamb's wool, spinning, yarn count.**

wool cording. Quilts. See **roving.**

wool dyeing. Batik and Tie-dye. Special consideration must be given to the dyeing of **wool,** as it will shrink from sudden temperature changes. It should never be taken from a hot **dyebath** to the cold-water rinse. Machine agitation may also damage wool, so gentle hand washing is better. Before dyeing wool, it should be washed in warm water (about 100° F) regardless of the **dye** to be used. Because wool is a **natural fiber,** it has an affinity for many dyes. Check directions and labels on dyes for special problems in wool dyeing.

To dye wool with **fiber-reactive dye**s the dyebath must be hot; therefore, fiber-reactive dyes cannot be used in the **batik** process on wool, as the heat would melt the **wax.** It is suitable for use in **tie-dye,** however.

The process for dyeing wool with fiber-reactive dye varies slightly from the usual procedure. Mix dye and **salt** according to directions. Add fabric, then heat the dyebath and simmer it for 10 minutes. Next, add white vinegar, about ¼ cup per gallon of water. Simmer an additional 10 minutes and remove from heat. Do not add **washing soda** or other fixer. Rinse in hot water, avoiding temperature change, then rinse in sudsy water. Rinse again and dry.

woolen count. Spinning. Weaving. See **yarn count.**

woolen yarn. Knitting. Soft, thick yarn made from loosely spun wool, used most often in sweaters, blankets, and afghans. When knit, the wool fabric can be brushed to produce a napped, feltlike fabric. Also see **felting, teasel brush.**

woolen yarn. Spinning. Weaving. See **spinning, wool.**

wool in the grease. Spinning. Weaving. See **wool.**

woolly toy. Toys. Any stuffed doll or **stuffed animal** made from worsted or a similar woven wool fabric. It is called woolly only to distinguish it from those toys made of cotton or cotton flannel.

wool-on-wool coverlet. Quilts. A bedcover of **wool** blanketing, heavily covered with large-scale decorative patterns worked in heavy wool yarns. Both hooking and needlework are employed. Because the yarns made the coverlets heavy, they were sometimes called **bed rug**s.

wool roving. Quilts. See **roving.**

woolskin. Leather. See **shearling.**

wool wheel. Spinning. (Also called great wheel, high wheel, Jersey wheel, muckle wheel, walking wheel.) A large-size wheel for the spinning of yarn. It took the place of the **spindle** in Europe in the fourteenth century by offering a faster way to spin yarn. It is a hand-operated wheel. As the wheel rotates, a **driving band** running from the wheel to the spindle turns the spindle, which is now held by the **maiden**s and **mother-of-all** in a horizontal position perpendicular to the wooden support (called a bench or table). As the spindle turns, the spinner takes a few steps backward to draw out the fibers. The fibers are twisted into spun yarn and, when there is a length of this yarn, it must be wound onto the spindle. The wheel is then turned part of the way in the opposite direction to bring the yarn

to the center of the spindle, and it is turned again in the original (clockwise), direction as it is wound onto the spindle. The spinner steps forward in this operation and, then backward again as the spinning is resumed. (It was said that a spinner could walk twenty miles during a day spent spinning.) The yarn is wound around the spindle in a cone shape, building up gradually from the inside out. In addition to the mother-of-all and the large wheel attached to the bench by a rigid **upright,** there is also a **tension screw** at the bottom of the mother-of-all support that is used to control the tension for proper spinning. The device for holding the spindle in place is called a **spinning head** and ranges from a very simple loop to a complex structure. See ill. Also see **spinning wheel.**

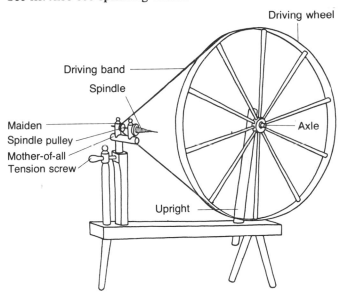

workboard. Stained Glass. See **Stained Glass: Glazing, Tools and Materials.**

worked. Quilts. See **Quilts: Quilting, Hand Quilting.**

worker. Lacemaking. (Also called leader, runner.) A pair of **bobbin**s that move from side to side in some of the **bobbin lace** stitches. They go through the bobbins (called **passives**) that are lying on the **pillow.**

work-harden. Jewelry. Metalworking. To progressively become hard while being hammered or worked cold. As the metal hardens, it sometimes becomes brittle. Anneal the metal frequently as you work to resoften it. **Gold, lead,** and **pewter** do not work-harden.

work-hardening. Jewelry. The molecular structure of **nonferrous** metals changes formation when the metal is worked in processes such as **bending, forging, repoussé, rolling** and **drawing wire.** This work-hardened quality can be used when it is necessary for metals to be stiff. For example, a bracelet may be too soft to maintain its shape, but working the metal makes it work-hardened, producing more structural strength. A forged necklace can be formed with an integral clasp, which is kept closed because of work-hardening that produces **spring tension.**

On the other hand, work that becomes too work-hardened before the processes are completed must be annealed to relieve this quality, or the metal will **fracture**. Also see **annealing, forging**.

working. Leather. Decorating leather moistened with water by various **tooling, embossing,** or **carving** techniques. Also see **modeler**.

working drawing. Stained Glass. See **cartoon**.

working life. Plastics. See **pot life**.

working with two shuttles. Tatting. It is necessary to work with two **shuttles** when two colors are used, when a **single thread** joining a series of **rings** or **chains** is to be covered, and when making **Josephine picots**.

Wind two shuttles, each with a different-color thread, and tie the ends of the two threads together. Hold this tie between thumb and index finger; pass one thread over the top of the fingers, and wrap twice around the little finger. Let the shuttle connected to this thread hang down. Sometimes this thread is called the **ball thread**. This corresponds to the **loop thread** when using one shuttle, and serves the same purpose.

The other shuttle, held in the other hand, makes the same movements as when one shuttle is used. By alternating the shuttles at the **close** of a ring or completion of a chain, various color patterns may be achieved. See ill.

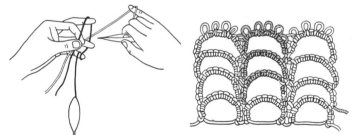

a. Correct position of thread   b. A tatted lace edging with picots

work-shirt embroidery. Stitchery. A popular form of needlework which utilizes a great variety of embroidery and **stitch**ing on blue **cotton** work shirts. Mirror embroidery is often used along with needle weaving and **chain stitch**, feather stitch, **French knots**, and other common embroidery stitches.

World Without End. Quilts. (Also called Four Star, Priscilla.) A **pieced** four-pointed star having a square in the center. It is an **all-over pattern** in which dark and light colors are usually alternated from one **block** to the next.

worm stitch. Crewel. Embroidery. See **bullion knot**.

worry beads. Beadwork. See **Beadwork**.

Worshipful Company of Glass Sellers. Glasswork. The seventeenth-century group of glassworkers who dominated the glass industry in England at the time. They commissioned George Ravencroft to develop a new variety of glass using native materials to compete with the **soda-lime glass** then imported from Venice. In three years Ravencroft produced **lead-crystal glass,** a spectacular success and still an important glass today. Also see **Murano**.

Worshipful Company of Goldsmiths. Jewelry. A guild established in 1300, from which the word "hallmark" originated (it literally means "the mark of the Goldsmiths' Hall"). Objects made of precious metal are sent to either Goldsmiths' Hall or another branch of the guild. They are assayed, then stamped and returned to the maker. Objects that do not meet the standards are refused the stamp. If this offense is repeated by the maker, the article is destroyed. For information write Worshipful Company of Goldsmiths, Goldsmiths' Hall, London, England. Also see **United States Stamping Law**.

worsted. Knitting. A smooth, hard, twisted yarn made from long, parallel-combed, staple wool. Knitting worsteds are probably the most commonly available sport yarns and are used in socks, sweaters, afghans, etc.

worsted. Spinning. A yarn of high quality made of long-staple **wool fibers**, evenly combed, and tightly twisted in **spinning**. Worsted yarn is smooth-surfaced and lustrous. The worsted system, or method of spinning, is reserved for the longest and finest **staples**. In hand-spinning, after **combing** and the removal of the **noils**, the fiber is given a looser twist, since the fiber's length does not need more than this. Also see **yarn count**.

worsted yarn. Crewel. Embroidery. Needlepoint. A firmly twisted **yarn** or thread spun from combed fibers of the same length. It is used for weaving, knitting, or needlework. Worsted can also refer to the cloth woven from these yarns that has a hard, smooth surface with no nap and is useful as a **background fabric**.

woven-as-drawn-in. Weaving. See **treadling-as-drawn-in**.

woven base. Basketry. See **Basketry: Woven Basket Construction**.

woven basketry. Basketry. One of the 3 basic types of basket structures or processes. It consists of intertwining or weaving a flexible **active element** or **weft** around a structural **passive element** or **warp**. The variations in the weaves result in the **checked weave, twilled weaving, wicker weave, wrapped weave,** and **twined weaving**. Also see **Basketry: Woven Basket Construction**.

woven binding. Quilts. See **Quilts: Binding**.

woven binding. Stitchery. (Also called woven tape.) A tape used to finish a **raw edge** of fabric. It is similar to a **bias tape,** but it may be either **bias** or on the **grain**. When it is bias, a **fold**ed edge must be turned under, as with bias tape. When it is on the **straight** or "**on the grain,**" the **binding** has **selvages** at both edges so that no **hem** allowance is needed.

woven edge. Rugmaking. Weaving. See **Swedish braid.**

woven plait. Lacemaking. See **leaf stitch.**

woven rug. Rugmaking. Weaving. See **rug weaving.**

woven tape. Stitchery. See **woven binding.**

wrapped edge. Rugmaking. Weaving. A **finishing edge** technique where **warp end**s are wrapped around each other to form a compact, tightly locked edge. The **wrapping** is done horizontally rather than vertically as in normal wrapping. It proceeds across the warp ends in the same manner as **Swedish braid**, but instead of just interlacing, each warp end wraps around every warp end it travels under and over. A variation is to combine wrapping with **finger weaving**. The wrapping is done only at the beginning and end of each working warp strand. The rest is interlaced as in Swedish braid. "Wrapped edges" is also used as a term when referring to the **whipping** or wrapping of groups of warp ends to make a **fringe**. See ill.

Wrapped edge

wrapped weave. Basketry. A basic **weave** in **woven basketry**: The **weft** or **active element** is **coil**ed about or wrapped around the **warp** or structural member. Also see **Basketry: Woven Basket Construction.**

wrapped weave. Weaving. See **Brooks Bouquet.**

wrap petals. Beadwork. See **continuous wraparound loop.**

wrapping. Basketry. (Also called lapping.) The process of binding or wrapping a handle **bow** or other **rod** with **willow skein** or flat **glossy wrapping cane.** Decorative effects or **listing** patterns may be obtained by weaving in a **leader** or two. See ill.

Wrapping · Leaders · Rods

wrapping. Jewelry. The wrapping of **wire** around another wire or around another form of metal, such as **sheet metal** or rods, either to hold different units of metal together or to form entire pieces of jewelry. The wire should be well annealed if it has been drawn through a **drawplate.** It is usually soft enough as it is purchased to use for wrapping. The wire used can be of different **gauge**s; for example, to wrap 20-gauge wire around a core of 18-gauge wire, begin with the wires parallel and the ends even. Start wrapping about 1″ from the end to provide leverage during wrapping. The two pieces of wire can be held tightly together with a **ring clamp** during the wrapping. Wrap one piece of wire around the center core of the other, keeping the

wrapping as tight, smooth, and uniform as possible. Do not allow the wire to develop a kink while working with it. As at the beginning of the wrapping, leave extra wire at the end so that the last turns can be made more easily by using the leverage provided by the extra wire. See ill.

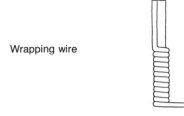

Wrapping wire

wrapping. Rugmaking. Weaving. A hand technique involving the spiral winding of one yarn or group of yarns around another yarn or group of yarns that acts as a center core for the winding to go around. This type of wrapping done around vertical elements is often referred to as **warp** wrapping. It can be in the body of the piece or as a **fringe** at either end of it. Wrapping and pulling **warp end**s together creates a type of **openwork weave.** Up until a few years ago, wrapping was relatively rare. Now it has become a popular technique, tried by most weavers and used frequently in contemporary wall hangings. The winding concept is simple, but it is the multitude of design uses it can be put to and its sinuous coiled look that make it so popular. This popularity has been helped along by numerous internationally known wall-hanging artists, each of whom uses wrapping in different ways. Olga de Amaral of Colombia has had a long involvement with spiral wrapping, first in actually wrapping the warp, and then in producing wrapped coils that interweave with prewoven strips. In effect, she is using the wrapped coil in place of yarns as either warp or **filling.** In certain pieces, the coils compose the entire piece, with perhaps a minimum of another technique to space or hold them together. Sheila Hicks, an American living and working in France, wraps masses of vertical linen or cotton threads with silk to form long chains that are later structured into walls or **fiber sculpture.** Jagoda Buic, a Yugoslavian artist, uses spiral-wrapped elements horizontally attached to a background. It gives a high relief of pattern against a flatter **tapestry** background and also adds texture.

Care must be taken to do wrapping tightly, maintaining an even tension during the winding process. The winding proceeds as a spiral, but it is done in a horizontal position. That is, the tip of the yarn to be wrapped is laid against the core and then it is held there as the yarn is taken around and around the core horizontally. Pulling up on the yarn every so often tightens it up around the core and gives a compact coil. When the amount desired is wrapped, or the yarn runs out, the remainder of the yarn is darned into the coil with a needle. The needle is pulled out of the coil at a convenient spot and brings with it the last tip of the yarn, which is then trimmed off. This provides a secure closing for the coil and also an invisible one. When a small amount of wrapping is done as a **finishing edge** to bind a fringe, a **whipping** method of securing the yarn is used.

There is another type of warp wrapping, done on a **loom,**

which uses a continuous filling, i.e., the wrappings are not separate coils, but have a connecting element in the thread that wraps around a warp end (making it into a short coil) and then goes to the base of the neighboring warp end to wrap that. Each coiled element is done in a closed **shed** and is linked with a diagonal thread. Wrapping can also be used as a means of **outlining** in a **tapestry**, in which case the wrapping thread wanders from warp end to warp end according to the contours of the shape it is outlining.

The ancient Peruvians used wrapping in yet another way; they wrapped warp yarns in certain areas as required by the design. This very fine wrapping was then interwoven with a filling, so that instead of a mass of wrapped ends, it created a diffused effect in both pattern and texture and is somewhat similar to the concept behind **warp painting** or **ikat**. The Peruvians also made slit tapestries of wrapping. They wrapped groups of warp yarns and then regrouped them in the next rows to make more wrapping for a final effect that often was a lacy openwork tapestry. Certain American Indians of the Northwest used wrapping of the weft before **twining** it into carrying straps. The Hopi Indians use a type of supplementary weft wrapping in their so-called brocaded sashes. "Weft wrapping" is the term given to wrapping that proceeds in right angles to the warp, whereas the wrapping previously discussed here covers the warp by going spirally around it. In weft wrapping, the wrapping yarn can also cover the warp by successive, tightly packed rows—or it can be simply a decorative addition to a **ground weave**. The wrapping yarn (one strand or more) goes from one warp yarn to another, crossing it and going around a warp yarn (but not necessarily every one) as it attaches it into a fabric. The best known examples of weft wrapping are **soumak** and the **Egyptian knot**. See ill.

Wrapping worked downward to enclose beginning tip

wrap reel. Spinning. See **reel**.

wreath. Quilts. A design frequently used in **appliqué quilts** that consists of a garland of leaves in a circular form. The leaves are often combined with stems, tendrils, flowers, or fruits. Also see **wreath patterns**.

Wreath of Pansies. Quilts. One of the many **appliqué wreath** designs incorporating flowers, stems, and leaves in a circular arrangement.

wreath patterns. Quilts. The most intricately patterned of all designs for **appliqué blocks**. These circular garlands consist of leaves and stems of all shapes and sizes,

punctuated with flowers, fruits, and buds. There is tremendous vitality in the patterns and colors and much originality in the combinations. **Wreath**s combine foliage with roses, tulips, or cherries, and many are named for states. Every appliquéd wreath has some distinctive element that makes it unique.

Most appliqué wreath designs are sewn onto **background** blocks that are then **set** to make the quilt. In some stunning variations, however, the wreath is enlarged to make a huge circular garland that covers the top of the bed. Sometimes one wreath is encircled by another, and garlands of the same pattern festoon the **border**. Some patterns of the wreath motif are **Bridal Wreath**, Cherry Wreath, Dahlia Wreath, Garden Wreath, **Martha Washington's Wreath**, **Memory Wreath**, Rose Wreath, and **Wreath of Pansies**.

wrench. Metalworking. Woodworking. A tool to provide leverage for holding and turning **nut**s and **bolt**s.

An allen wrench is the simplest and most specialized wrench, used for tightening socket-ended set **screw**s. Each wrench is L-shaped, made of a single piece of bent wire with a hexagonal cross section (**a.**). Allen wrenches come in sets up to ½" in diameter.

An open-end (or crescent) wrench is used for the rapid turning of nuts. Because the end often slips off the nut, the wrench has earned the knickname "knuckle-buster." It is commonly sold in sets for standard nuts from 13/64" to 1⅝".

A box wrench has a closed end and grips the bolt head or nut on all corners; it therefore grips better but is slower to use than the open-end wrench. Box wrenches are sold in sets with sizes similar to open-end wrenches.

An open-end box wrench is a combination of the previous two; both ends fit the same size nut or bolt (**b.**).

An adjustable wrench is a crescent wrench with an adjustable jaw, available in a range of sizes from 6" to 12" (**c.**).

A monkey wrench is an F-shaped adjustable wrench with smooth jaws, best for large square bolts and nuts. See ill.

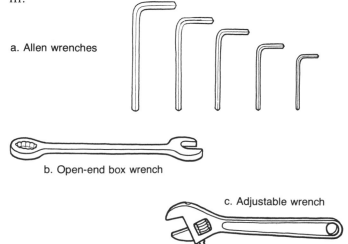

a. Allen wrenches

b. Open-end box wrench

c. Adjustable wrench

Wrench Quilt. Quilts. See **Shoo-fly**.

Wrenshall slip clay. Ceramics. See **slip glaze**.

wrestlers. Toys. See **dancers.**

wrinkle resistant. Batik and Tie-dye. Stitchery. A **fabric finish** in which the material is treated so that it will resist crushing, wrinkling, or creasing. The term does not mean that the fabric will not wrinkle—it means that the wrinkles can be ironed out or will disappear if the material is shaken or hung. **Wash-and-wear** and **durable press** are both finishes which have wrinkle-resistant properties.

Synthetic resins are used to treat the materials and give them resilience, though some wrinkle-resistant processes use oxidized starches. These finishes affect the fabric's affinity for **dye** and may make them unsuitable for **batik** or **tie-dye.** For those uses where **crease** or wrinkle resistant finishes are desirable, the durable press is superior since it locks in shape and locks out wrinkles, leaving **seam**s flat.

A formula which may be used to remove a wrinkle-resistant finish is given under "**removing fabric finish.**" This treatment would make the **fiber**s more **receptive to dye**s.

wrought bronze. Metalworking. A **bronze** casting whose surface has been developed by means of hammering and punching instead of by the usual **filling,** chiseling or **grinding.** This is not done by most commercial art foundries today. A sculptor must ask for the rough, unfinished casting and clean and work it himself.

wrought iron. Metalworking. See **iron.**

X

X-acto knife. Leather. See **utility knife.**

X-acto knife. Plastics. A hand knife with interchangeable blades used for scoring and **cutting** thin sheets of **plastic.** Also see **Plastics: Cutting.**

X-stitch. Leather. See **cross stitch.**

y

yag. Gemcutting. See **garnet.**

Yankee Pride. Quilts. (Also called Autumn Leaf.) An intricate pattern for a **pieced block,** ingeniously arranged to suggest one form growing out of another. Basically, four **diamond** stars surround a central star. If just one corner or one star of this design is used, it is identical to **Tea Leaf.**

Yankee Puzzle. Quilts. A **block** for a **pieced quilt** that consists of four squares, each of which is divided diagonally into four triangles. It is a **split four-patch** design. See ill.

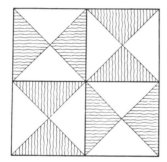

Yankee Puzzle

yardage. Weaving. Fabric woven by the yard and later either cut up and sewn into clothing, upholstery, pillows, drapery, or various small items, or left in one piece to be used as wall covering. Yardage usually implies a small color and weave **repeat.**

yardage counter. Weaving. See **counter.**

yarn. Crewel. Embroidery. Needlepoint. A thread of twisted fibers of cotton, wool, or synthetic filaments (such as rayon and nylon). The synthetic yarns are less expensive than the wool yarns, and are nonallergenic. The synthetics, however, do not wear as well as the natural threads, and are liable to swell after washing and blur a fine design. Also see **acrylic yarn, Appleton crewel wool, Berlin wool, Broder Medici wool, bullion thread, cashmere, cotton embroidery floss, cotton tapestry yarn, crochet cotton, Filo floss, Filoselle, gold purl, Japanese gold and silver, knitting yarn, linen thread, Lurex thread, Maltese silk, mohair, ombré yarn, Persian yarn, rug wool, silk yarn, synthetic yarn, tapestry yarn, variegated yarn, worsted yarn** and **Crewel: Materials, Needlepoint: Materials.**

yarn. Quilts. Stitchery. Spun strands of **fiber** used in a variety of ways for various kinds of embroidery. The fibers may be **wool, silk,** flax, **cotton,** or **synthetic.** The yarns are used to tie **quilts,** to embroider on various **stitchery** forms, and in **couching** for toys and dolls.

yarn. Spinning. Weaving. A general term for any continuous, twisted strand of natural or man-made **fibers** or **filaments** suitable for weaving, knitting, braiding, and other fabric constructions. It is considered heavier than **thread** and is characterized by its fiber composition, thickness, number of strands or plies, direction and degree of twist, and texture. The yarns that are **plied** need not have the same characteristics—the difference can produce a **novelty yarn** which has a very distinct surface texture, such as a loop or bump. A yarn such as **chenille** is a woven yarn. Yarns can be composed of one, two, or more colors. Also see **novelty yarn, ply, spinning, twist, yarn count.**

yarn calculations. Rugmaking. Weaving. The formulas or necessary procedures used to deduce the amount of yarn needed for weaving. The warp calculation has to be figured out first. After the width of a piece has been decided upon, and its density (**sett**), these two factors are multiplied together; set × width = total number of **warp end**s. Added to the width before the multiplication is the **draw-in,** based on the resiliency of fibers being used. This is only added on when the full weaving width of the **loom** is not being used and there is room to add on an inch or two. Otherwise, the weaver must realize that there will be some amount lost in the width due to this draw-in. If the **selvage**s are of the same yarn as the rest of the warp, they are added on after multiplication.

The next calculation is that of the length of the warp ends that will be put on the loom so that the finished piece will be the length desired. The **finished length, take-up,** and **loom waste** are added together to arrive at the total or **cut length.** Generally, about ½ yard is added on to a table loom for the loom waste and 1 yard for a floor loom. The take-up depends on the fiber content, with wool being the most resilient and linen the least (as far as the natural fibers are concerned). Once the total number of ends and the total length are arrived at, these two figures are multiplied together and the total number of yards of warp yarn needed is obtained. This number is for a solid colored warp. If the warp is multicolored and there is a **repeat,** divide the number of ends in a repeat into the total number of warp ends to obtain the number of repeats across the warp. Then count the number of threads of each color in a repeat and multiply each color number by the number of repeats. This will give the total number of ends of each color. Multiply each color total by the total length of the warp and the result will be the total yardage needed of each color.

If the number of threads in a repeat is limited to about 3 or 4 threads, a quick way to get the total yardage of each color is to divide the total yardage of warp yarn by ⅓ or ¼. If the warp is in a large multicolored stripe that is not repeated, then each color of the stripe is calculated as an individual warp.

To find the amount of **filling** yarn needed, the **picks per inch** have to be determined first—either by making a sample or through past experience. The number of picks per inch and the total width desired are multiplied together and the number of inches of filling yarn per inch are arrived at. This number is converted to yards of filling per yard and then multiplied by the total number of yards to be woven. The new number is the total number of yards of filling needed. If the filling is multicolored, count how many times each color appears in an inch. Multiply each color number by the width of the fabric. The result is the number of inches of each color of yarn used in one inch, or yards in one yard. Multiply each color by the total number of yards to be woven.

After the total number of yards for each color of the warp and filling is obtained, the yarn can be ordered according to the poundage that comes closest to having the necessary yardage. This can be done for all types of weaving except for **pile rugs**, for which there has to be an extra calculation. The amount of yarn for the **pile** has to be arrived at; this can be done as outlined under "**rug sampler**" or in a more precise manner based on the knots per inch and strands of yarn per knot. These two figures are multiplied together and then this new figure is multiplied by 2½ times the **pile height**. For example, if the pile is **rya**, this could be about 2″ in pile height, and 2½ times that would be 5″. If there are 4 knots per inch, and each is composed of 3 strands of yarn (which equals 12″), then the formula would be 12″ × 5″ = 60″ of yarn for one inch of a rya rug. Then multiply the width of the warp times 60″ and this new figure with the number of rows planned for the entire rug. This is all in inches, so the final amount has to be divided by 36 for the total yardage needed for the pile.

yarn count. Spinning. Weaving. A number system designating the size or thickness of **single** yarns. There are actually two systems. One—for cotton, wool, linen, and spun silk—is based on the amount of yarn it takes to make up one pound. A fine yarn has more lengths per pound and therefore carries a higher number than a heavy, coarse yarn. A #1 yarn of cotton has 840 yards to a pound. A #6 would be 6 times this amount, or 5,040 yards per pound. It is 6 times finer than the #1, so it would take more of it to make up the pound. A #½ would be half of 840 yards, or 420 yards.

When a yarn is plied, two numbers are used—for example, 2/10s. This indicates that the yarn is composed of two #10 single yarns twisted or plied together. The smaller number indicates the number of strands plied together while the larger number indicates the thickness of a single strand. The **ply** number is divided into the yards per

pound of the #10 singles. This would mean that a 2/10s has 4,200 yards per pound. It is twice as thick as a #10 singles, which has 8,400 yards per pound.

Spun silk is measured using the cotton count, but when a plied yarn is involved, the ply and count are multiplied; a 2/10s spun silk yarn would be 16,800 yards or 20 times 840 yards.

Linen is measured in **lea**s, with one lea equaling 300 yards. Four leas would be 1,200 yards, and a four leas 3 ply would be 400 yards. Other **bast fiber**s are measured in leas also.

Worsted or **combed wool** is 560 yards per pound, and the plied yarns are calculated as for cotton. Woolen or **carded wool** has two separate systems. The cut system uses a base of 300 yards to one pound of #1 cut wool. There is also the American run system, which is the one in more general use. Run wool has 1,600 yards in a pound of #1s. A 4-run wool would be 6,400 yards per pound.

The other system for designating yarn thickness is called the denier system. It is for filament silk and most synthetics. It is based on weights per length: the coarser the yarn, the higher the number; the finer the yarn, the lower the number. The denier system dates from the sixteenth century, when the king of France revived the use of an old Roman coin and used it as the standard weight for measuring silk. A #1 denier is equal to 4,464,528 yards in one pound. All numbers larger than #1 are divided into 4,464,528. The same denier count is used for synthetic **filament** yarns.

yarn cutter. Rugmaking. See **gauge.**

yarn doll. Toys. A small, simple doll made entirely from yarn. The hank of yarn is tied at one end and then inverted so that the yarn strands fall down over the knot. The tasslelike shape is then tied in any of various ways to suggest a head, body, arms, and legs. It is a **folk toy** found in various parts of the world.

yarn-dyed. Stitchery. **Dyed** before being woven, as opposed to **piece-dyed.** When yarns are dyed there is a more thorough saturation of color into the **fibers.**

yarn dyeing. Dyeing. See **skein dyeing.**

yarn gauge. Rugmaking. Weaving. See **gauge.**

yarn holder. Weaving. See **spool rack, swift.**

yarn organizer. Crewel. Embroidery. Needlepoint. There are various tools and methods of separating and holding yarns neatly so one can work with them more easily, such as snap tape, **braid**ing, or a yarn palette.

yarn over. Crochet. (Also called **over.**) A crochet movement in the formation of a **stitch.** Before inserting the crochet hook into the loop of a stitch, the yarn is wound over the hook back-to-front in such a way that the yarn can be caught by the hook and pulled back through a previous stitch. See ill.

Yarn over

yarn-over stitches. Crochet. A term referring to **half double crochet, double crochet** and all other stitches that use the **yarn-over** process to lengthen a stitch.

yarn package. Spinning. Weaving. A general term indicating any wound arrangement of yarn whether on a **spindle, spool,** or **cone.**

yarns. Crochet. Yarns for crochet can be of natural or man-made fibers. The size, weight, or ply of yarn is selected according to the work being done. Smooth yarns will work into a clean, even piece of crochet; textured yarns will give a fuzzy or uneven appearance. Some crochet yarns, such as jute, linen ramie, and twine, are thick and sturdy—perfect for mats, room dividers, and wall hangings. Others, like the novelty metallic yarns and thin, soft, animal fibers, are perfect for evening wear. Still others, such as the delicate crochet cottons, can be worked into fine, lacelike fabrics. Also see **Crochet: Tools and Materials.**

yarn-sewn rug. Rugmaking. A term applied to a type of **needleworked rug** made in the United States and Eastern Canada during the eighteenth century and the first quarter of the nineteenth. Using yarn spun at home out of wool and flax and dyed with natural dyes, the women of this period sewed the yarn through a **ground cloth** of homespun linen or tow grain bags. The yarn was sewn through this backing with a continuous running stitch that was left in loops on the surface of the rug and that formed a pattern of short, flat dashes on the back. Usually the loops were cut in order to have a soft **pile** surface. The loops were sewn following the shape of the design with each color of yarn. The design was often of a nautical or patriotic motif, which has brought up the possibility that the rugs were designed and sewn by sailors and their wives.

In the eighteenth century these yarn-sewn pieces were used more for covering tables, chests, and chairs than as rugs. Some small hearth rugs were made, and there was a category called "bed ruggs," made to be used solely as bed coverings. In this case the backing was made of wool.

The rugs made by French settlers in Quebec and Nova Scotia were called "Acadian" rugs and had a bas-relief effect produced by clipping down the pile of the background so that the design motifs were raised against it.

The yarn-sewn rugs are said to have led to **hooked rugs,** which have the same kind of face pile and back stitch but are produced with a hooked implement rather than a needle. There is some speculation that the switch from needle to hook may have come about at the beginning of the nineteenth century with the rise of fabric mills throughout New England and the easy and cheap availability of cloth that could be cut into strips. These strips could be easily pushed through a backing, but not sewn through it.

yarn size. Spinning. Weaving. See **yarn count.**

yawning boards. Bookbinding. Cover **boards** that curl away from the text of a book.

yellow brass. Metalworking. See **brass.**

yellow colorant. Ceramics. See **pigment oxide.**

yellow ochre. Jewelry. Metalworking. (Also called limonite.) A powdered pigment used to inhibit the flow of **solder. Seam**s or **joint**s that have been previously soldered can flow again when new components are added to the work. Yellow ochre mixed with water to the consistency of sour cream is painted over previously soldered joints, and left to dry. **Flux** all exposed surfaces of the metal as usual. Begin heating with a low flame; the ochre must be dried thoroughly or it may turn brown-black and pop off. Do not allow any yellow ochre to mix with the flux, as the ochre may then be pulled along to the new joint and prevent it from soldering. It can also contaminate the **flux brush** and the flux if not used carefully. Yellow ochre does not prevent previously soldered joints from flowing. It does prevent the solder from flowing out of the joint. Yellow ochre can also be used to inhibit solder from flowing up into a **catch.** Yellow ochre must be removed before putting work into a pickle or it will contaminate the solution. Also see **Chinese white, reticulation, transferring designs to metal, yellow ochre casein.**

yellow ochre casein. Jewelry. It can be used in all the ways that **yellow ochre** can, but with more ease—especially during heating, because it will not pop off. It need not be mixed from a powder, as it is already in a liquid base, making it generally easier to use. It is usually not available in jewelry-supply houses, but can be found at art-supply stores.

yellow pine. Woodworking. See **pine.**

yellow rouge. Jewelry. See **buffing compound.**

yolk. Spinning. The fatty grease secreted by the sheep through its pores and deposited on the **wool** fibers. Yolk gives lubrication and nutrition to the skin and **fleece** and aids **fiber** growth. A sheep with a weak yolk would also have weak fleece. **Suint** is secreted with the yolk, but it is readily separated from it in the **scouring** process. Yolk has very good healing qualities and in a purified state appears as **lanolin** (used in pharmaceuticals and cosmetics).

Young Man's Fancy. Quilts. See **Goose-in-the-Pond.**

yo-yo. Quilts. (Also called Suffolk puff.) One of the many small circular pieces of **fabric** sewn in a unique way to make up the novel **yo-yo quilt.** It is unusual, although not especially utilitarian. Circles about 3″ in diameter are cut from printed or plain **cotton fabric**s. Each circle is turned under about ¼″ at the perimeter, right-side down over the wrong side. With the right side of the material held toward the worker, a short **running stitch** is taken about ⅛" from the folded hem. (A **backstitch** will not do, as these stitches are to be gathered and pulled tight, drawing the outside edge into the center.) This makes a small circle, about 1½" in diameter. If the stitches are sewn evenly, there will be a smooth row of gathers. The thread is then knotted and the circle is pressed flat. These finished circles, or "yo-yos," are then sewn together to make the **yo-yo quilt.**

yo-yo. Toys. A **string** toy made of two disks joined by a short piece of **dowel.** String is attached by means of a loop over the dowel, then wound tightly, and a loop at the other end is slipped over the finger. The yo-yo is made to move up and down on the string.

The yo-yo is a **momentum toy,** popular in Greece and the Far East in ancient times. It remained quietly present as a toy until 1790, when it suddenly became wildly popular. A yo-yo had been brought to the French Minister of State, who enjoyed Chinese curiosities, by missionaries from Peking. It was introduced by the French émigrés and was thus called the émigrette. Over 100 years later, in the 1920s, it again swept England and America. This winding toy was known as the quiz, Prince of Wales toy, and bandoleer or bandilure, and not until after 1932 was it called yo-yo (which was originally a trademark). Also see **emergent toy.**

yo-yo doll. Toys. A fabric doll made by stringing a series of **yo-yo**s together in such a way that one is stacked flat on top of another. One series of these strung yo-yos forms each of the arms and legs, and another series is used for the body. The head is **stuff**ed fabric or a stuffed stocking made roughly into the shape of a ball.

yo-yo quilt. Quilts. An **all-over pattern** consisting of small gathered circles called **yo-yo**s. Technically, because there are no **quilting stitches** joining several layers, it is a **coverlet** or **bedspread.**

The finished yo-yos are sewn together at the edges, using a **whip stitch** or overcast stitch. This leaves an opening between each group of four. The yo-yo quilt may be left so that smooth circles form one side and gathered circles the other, with a lacelike effect from the open spaces, or the **quilt top** of connected yo-yos can be sewn to a piece of **backing** material. If the second method is used, the stitched and gathered side of the yo-yos is left exposed, as it is more decorative than the smooth side.

Y-stitch. Stitchery. A looped **stitch** made the same way as the **V-stitch,** but with a longer line at the base. It resembles the letter "Y."

yttrium aluminum garnet. Gemcutting. See **garnet.**

Z

zanni. Puppets. The buffoons, mimics, and jugglers who performed in the late-fifteenth-century Italian traveling troupes. "Zanni," or later "zany," meant buffoon and harlequin, and made up the beginning of the **commedia dell'arte.** The character of **Pulcinella** developed through this itinerant **popular theater.**

zany. Puppets. See **zanni.**

zebrawood. Woodworking. An exotic **hardwood** from West Africa whose **figure** and coloring resembles a zebra's markings, with parallel brown or black stripes on a lighter, yellow-brown background. It is used for furniture, cabinets, and **marquetry.**

zigzag. Quilts. See **sawtooth.**

zigzag chain stitch. Crewel. Embroidery. This stitch is exactly like **chain stitch,** except that every stitch is worked at an angle to the previous one, as shown. The angle may be increased or decreased, according to the effect required. Like interlaced running stitch, this stitch needs length to show it to its best advantage. See ill.

Zigzag chain stitch

zigzag fold. Papercrafts. See **accordion pleating.**

zigzag pattern. Batik and Tie-dye. A **chevron** pattern produced in **tie-dye** by a **folding** process. It is ideally used on narrow strips of fabric or for producing background patterns.

To fold for the zigzag pattern, the fabric is first folded in half lengthwise. One chevron occurs with each fold. A second fold leaves the fabric divided into fourths, yielding two chevrons, or zigzags. When the lengthwise folds have been made, the whole fabric is **accordion pleat**ed on the diagonal, **tied,** and then **dyed.**

zigzag seam. Stitchery. A **plain seam** which is similar to the **stitched-edge seam,** except a machine **zigzag stitch** replaces the machine **straight stitch.** The **raw edge** need not be turned under when a zigzag stitch is used.

zigzag stitch. Quilts. Stitchery. The back and forth **stitch** which can be made on any sewing machine that has a zigzag capability. The needle moves from side to side, with space between the stitches, so that a pattern of zigzags emerges. It is used as an **appliqué** stitch, especially on nonwoven fabrics. When woven fabrics are used, **frayed** edges may show through an open zigzag, so a tight or closed zigzag called the **machine satin stitch** is used. This stitch is adjustable in width and in closeness of stitches.

zigzag stripe. Batik and Tie-dye. See **rope-tying.**

zigzag twill. Weaving. See **twill weave.**

zigzag twining. Weaving. See **twill twining.**

zimba. Toys. See **spear-the-fish.**

zinc. Metalworking. A bluish-white **base metal** that is brittle at both high and low temperatures, but **malleable** and **ductile** between 250° F and 300° F. Zinc is chiefly used for **galvanizing ion** and **steel,** and as an **alloy** of **silver solder, brass,** and **bronze.** Sulphuric acid is a by-product of the purifying process of zinc. Fumes from melting or welding zinc (zinc oxide) are toxic, but not cumulative as with **lead.** Zinc poisoning (also called metal-fume fever or zinc shakes) can be caused by eating acid foods stored in the zinc containers. Symptoms of poisoning are fever, coughing, an increase in the white blood-cell count, and chill.

zinc came. Stained Glass. A lead substitute made of zinc. It has little flexibility and cannot be used in windows with curved glass. Its rigidity is good for outer borders, for reinforcing long windows, and for making **sample racks.** It is usually made in **II-section** came with extra-wide channels good for extra-thick glass. Also see **lead came.**

zinc chloride. Metalworking. See **flux.**

zinc chloride flux. Stained Glass. See **flux.**

zincite. Gemcutting. A zinc ore with **hardness** of 4¼, **specific gravity** of 5.64, and red or orange-yellow **color.**

zinc oxide. Ceramics. At high temperatures, zinc oxide is a **flux.** It will produce a crystalline surface when used to excess in a **glaze** low in **alumina. Opacity** will develop if zinc is used in a high alumina, low calcium glaze with no borosilicate fluxes. Zinc oxide increases the maturing range of a glaze, promotes a higher gloss and brighter colors, and reduces expansion.

zinc poisoning. Jewelry. (Also called metal fume fever.) Zinc poisoning is caused by breathing zinc fumes produced in the smelting of metals that contain high percentages of zinc, such as some brasses and bronzes; by casting with zinc, which produces fumes during heating; and by heating metal coated with zinc, such as galvanized iron. If it is necessary to perform any of these operations, ventilation should be excellent and a respirator-type face mask that is approved by the U.S. Bureau of Mines should be worn. The poisoning is not cumulative, but the fumes can cause fever and coughing followed by chills, and also an increase in the white blood-cell count. After the fever is gone there is a slight immunity, but not enough to prevent another immediate attack.

zircon. Gemcutting. Silicon and zirconium oxides **crystallized** in the tetragonal system with **hardness** of 7½, **specific gravity** of 3.95−4.71, refractive indices of 1.79 and 1.995, adamantine to vitreous **luster,** and conchoidal **fracture.** Zircon is transparent and occurs in, cloudy red, yellow, brown, violet, and colorless varieties. When radioactive it displays a halo. It is cut on an iron **lap** with 400 grit silicon carbide **abrasive** with main crown **facets** at 43° and main pavillion facets at 40°. It is polished on a tin lap with Linde A. Also see **faceting, polishing, refraction.**

zirconium oxide. Ceramics. An **opacifier** that is seldom used alone but is combined with other oxides or **fritted** into a more stable silicate. Zircopax, a **frit,** replaces **tin oxide** as a **glaze** opacifier.

zircopax. Ceramics. See **zirconium oxide.**

zoetrope. Toys. An **optical toy** first patented in France in 1860 and later marketed as the zoetrope in England in 1867. It was another version of the daedelum or wheel of life, which was invented in 1832, and is based on the same principle of persistence of vision. The toy consists of a metal drum that has thin vertical slots or perforations. The drum is set on a rod and the rod is attached to a heavy base in such a way that the drum can be rotated on its axis. Paper strips are placed within the drum that depict figures in a progressive series of movements. The drum is twirled on its axis and animates the figures. The zoetrope was significant in the development of the camera and motion pictures. Eadweard Muybridge, whose experiments in 1878 contributed greatly to the development of cinematography, used a zoetrope to analyze some of the movements of figures in his own work. The tachyscope was a variation of the zoetrope, utilizing photographs taken with a still camera instead of hand-drawn pictures. Also see **kittiscope** and **Toys: Optical Toys.**

zogroscope. Toys. An early-eighteenth-century **viewing toy** that employed mirrors set into a long box to give perspective views when seen through a peep hole. **Protean views** were later added, involving the use of two pictures pasted together. The view of such pictures could be altered by changing the light source. Thus a scenic view might be shown on one slide or picture, and by changing the light source a rainbow might appear in the sky from the lighting of the second picture. This is the principle used by Daguerre, the photographer, in his famous **diorama**s in the 1820s. Also see **Toys: Optical Toys.**

Z-twist. Rugmaking. Spinning. Weaving. See **plied fringe, twist.**